DISCARD

Eyewitness to Watergate:
A Documentary History for Students

Edited by
David Hosansky

CQ PRESS

A Division of Congressional Quarterly Inc.
Washington, D.C.

CQ Press
1255 22nd Street, NW, Suite 400
Washington, DC 20037

Phone: 202-729-1900; toll-free, 1-866-4CQ-PRESS (1-866-427-7737)

Web: www.cqpress.com

Interior design: Judy Myers
Cover design: Kimberly Glyder

Cover photos: President Richard M. Nixon, National Archives and Records Administration; news of Nixon's resignation, Bettmann/CORBIS.

CQ Press gratefully acknowledges permission to reprint the following surveys from Harris Interactive Inc.: page 45, survey by Louis Harris & Associates, conducted April 18–23, 1973; page 98, survey by Louis Harris & Associates, conducted July 18–22, 1973; page 167, survey by Louis Harris & Associates, conducted November 12–15, 1973; page 206, survey by Louis Harris & Associates, conducted March 24–29, 1974. All rights reserved.

♾ The paper used in this publication exceeds the requirements of the American National Standard for Information Sciences—Permanence of Paper for Printed Library Materials, ANSI Z39.48-1992.

Printed and bound in the United States of America

10 09 08 07 06   1 2 3 4 5

Library of Congress Cataloging-in-Publication Data

Eyewitness to Watergate : a documentary history for students / edited by David Hosansky.
  p. cm.
 Chronological collection of articles from Congressional quarterly weekly reports pertaining to Watergate originally published in 1973 and 1974.
 Includes bibliographical references and index.
 ISBN-13: 978-0-87289-416-7 (alk. paper)
 ISBN-10: 0-87289-416-9 (alk. paper)
 1. Watergate Affair, 1972-1974. 2. United States—Politics and government—1969-1974. 3. Nixon, Richard M. (Richard Milhous), 1913-1994—Resignation from office. 4. Watergate Affair, 1972-1974—Sources. 5. United States—Politics and government—1969-1974—Sources. I. Hosansky, David. II. Congressional quarterly weekly reports. III. Title.

E860.E98 2007
973.924—dc22

                                    2006038527

CONTENTS

LIST OF FEATURES

Many chapters conclude with "Points to Ponder," discussion questions that encourage students to reflect on the legal and political issues addressed in this volume. These appear on pages 25, 41, 49, 59, 80, 87, 103, 115, 143, 158, 186, 200, 218, 252, 271, 283, and 299.

Guide to *Eyewitness to Watergate: A Documentary History for Students*

The various elements of *Eyewitness to Watergate* can be identified by their appearance. Introductory text, commentary, and other contributions by editor David Hosansky appear in a font different from the material originally published in the *Congressional Quarterly Weekly Report* (CQWR). For examples please see below.

CQ CONGRESSIONAL QUARTERLY WEEKLY REPORT, NOVEMBER 24, 1973

With a feature from December 1, 1973

WATERGATE:
Vital Work Ahead for Senate Committee

Editor's introduction

The Senate Watergate Committee continued its work during the fall amid mounting concerns in Congress and among the public about the Watergate scandal. The committee's witnesses late in the year were little-known political contributors and people who used unscrupulous methods to try to undermine competing campaigns.

On Nov. 21 came the shocking news that one of the Watergate tapes contained an 18-minute inaudible portion. The gap, discovered by President Nixon's personal secretary while transcribing the tape, spurred speculation that the administration was suppressing evidence related to Watergate.

Amid sinking poll numbers, Nixon faced questions not only about Watergate but about other potential scandals as well. In particular, he was battered by allegations that he had underpaid his taxes.

Original CQWR article

The contrast between Senator Baker's two observations was understandable. Ten weeks is a relatively short time, but Watergate disclosures came so quickly in the fall of 1973 that politicians and pundits alike found themselves eating their words.

In September, the Senate Watergate Committee was in recess after hearing from key witnesses: John W. Dean III, John N. Mitchell, John D. Ehrlichman and H. R. Haldeman. So what more could be expected of a dramatic nature?

Editor's comment

Original CQWR feature

■ IMPEACHMENT

Editor's feature

One of the common misconceptions about American government is that impeaching a president removes him from office.

The Constitution, however, lays out a two-step process for removing a president or other high public official. Impeachment is merely the first step. The House of Representatives has the power to impeach a president with a majority vote. Such an act may be thought of as a formal criminal charge against the president, much as a citizen may be formally charged, or indicted, by a grand jury. The Constitution says that a president may be impeached for "treason, bribery, or other high crimes and misdemeanors."

But Watergate had a life of its own. Like a snowball rolling downhill, it continued to grow until it created one constitutional and cabinet crisis after another—and ultimately the presidency itself was endangered. First there

WATERGATE ANNOUNCEMENT TEXT

The president said he had reached an agreement with the Senate Watergate Committee to allow his staffers to testify in front of the committee.

Following is the text of President Nixon's announcement on the Watergate scandal April 17.

I have two announcements to make. Because of their technical nature, I shall read both of the announcements to the members of the press corps.

The first announcement relates to the appearance of White House people before the Senate select committee, better known as the Ervin committee.

was the court battle over the President's refusal to hand over the tapes. Then came the firing of Cox and the resignations of Attorney General Elliot L. Richardson and his deputy, William D. Ruckelshaus. Then the President reversed himself and agreed to release the tapes. Then it was learned that two of the nine tapes never existed, and it developed that the seven remaining tapes were not distinct. And from it all emerged the threat of presidential impeachment.

IMPEACHABLE OFFENSE: OPINION OF NIXON ATTORNEYS

Reprinted from *Congressional Quarterly Weekly Report,* March 23, 1974

Following are excerpts from a Feb. 28 analysis prepared by James D. St. Clair, John J. Chester, Michael A. Sterlacci, Jerome J. Murphy and Loren A. Smith, attorneys for President Nixon:

ENGLISH BACKGROUND OF CONSTITUTIONAL IMPEACHMENT PROVISIONS

"The Framers felt that the English system permitted men. . .to make arbitrary decisions, and one of their primary purposes in creating a Constitution was to replace this arbitrariness with a system based on the rule of law. . . . They felt impeachment was a necessary check on a President who might commit a crime, but they did not want to see the vague standards of the English system that made impeachment a weapon to achieve parliamentary supremacy. . . . "

Legislative Recommendations

In addition to investigating the White House, members of Congress wanted to make sure that nothing like Watergate would happen again. Many lawmakers focused on the need to regulate campaign contributions, which were at the heart of the Watergate scandal.

Editor's comment

While a wide variety of remedies were suggested, almost all those interviewed agreed that some controls would have to be put on the use of cash in future campaigns. Free-flowing cash—hundreds of thousands of dollars of it—was at the heart of the Watergate scandal, it was believed. Cash in large, untraceable quantities bought the Watergate burglars and paid for the coverup.

There was a secret $350,000 cash fund in the White House that helped get things going and, according to testimony by Frederick C. LaRue, a Nixon re-election committee official, and Anthony T. Ulasewicz, a money courier, $449,000 was raised on quick order to maintain the burglars and pay their lawyers' fees. Herbert W. Kalmbach, a Nixon lawyer and fund-raiser, told the committee of getting $75,000 in $100 bills from a California businessman by telling him it was for a "special assignment."

Original CQWR feature

Submerged in all the mind-boggling events were the hearings of the seven-member Senate Select Committee on Presidential Campaign Activities—the Watergate committee. Its witnesses since September were relatively unknown dirty tricksters and political contributors. They lacked the glamour and impact of their predecessors, so for many Americans the hearings became only a small part of the Watergate story.

CQWR text omitted

Points to Ponder

- If a congressional committee wanted to obtain all the president's documents dealing with an important threat to national security, should the president turn them over? What about documents touching on a sensitive political issue, such as policies about abortion? Under what situations should a president be required to turn over documents?

- If a president is elected by the people and answerable to the people, why should he or she have the right to refuse to share information with them or with Congress?

- If Congress wants documents that might show wrongdoing by one of the president's top aides, should it have the power to force the president to turn them over?

Discussion questions

INTRODUCTION

On Nov. 7, 1972, President Richard M. Nixon won re-election in a historic landslide. The most successful political leader of his generation, he had already put his stamp on the nation's foreign and domestic policies. Now he appeared within reach of establishing a new, long-term Republican majority. Although deeply disliked by many on the left, he won over most voters by combining tough, law-and-order conservatism with moderate policies such as arms control agreements with the Soviet Union.

But just as he seemed at the pinnacle of his power, Nixon met with disaster. He would resign his office in disgrace less than two years after his re-election. The reason: a scandal known as Watergate.

Watergate is the most notorious case of political corruption in U.S. history. The scandal began with the arrest of five burglars in Washington, D.C.'s Watergate building in June 1972—less than four months before the election. By the time it ended, Nixon and many of his top White House and campaign aides were implicated in engineering the burglary or attempting to cover it up. Several previous presidential administrations had been engulfed in significant scandals, sometimes even resulting in cabinet officials facing criminal charges. But never before had major criminal activity been traced directly to the president himself. And never before had a president been forced out of office.

Watergate created shock waves that reverberated through the political system. It sparked a serious constitutional crisis that embroiled all three branches of government. It also jeopardized the independence of federal agencies, such as the Central Intelligence Agency (CIA), because the White House tried to use them to serve its political goals. But our system of government survived. It may even have emerged stronger than before because Congress, the courts, and other institutions made sure that Nixon could not get away with abusing his power. "A president has been deposed," wrote Clifton Daniel of *The New York Times*, "but the republic endures."

Watergate remains a significant moment in political history primarily for two reasons.

First, it shows the extent to which a president can become dangerously corrupted. Nixon's crimes could have landed him in prison for 30 years or more. He sought to use government agencies, such as the CIA and the Internal Rev-

enue Service, to protect his political career and punish his critics. He also faced accusations of tax fraud and of using his power to help companies and organizations in exchange for campaign contributions. His campaign staffers broke a variety of laws to discredit his Democratic opponents. They even engaged in burglaries and wiretapping.

Second, and perhaps even more important, Watergate illustrates the enduring power of the U.S. Constitution. Nixon, the most powerful man in the country, attempted to cover up his administration's crimes. He said he did not have to cooperate with congressional investigations, a special Justice Department prosecutor, or even court orders. He went so far as to fire the prosecutor who was investigating him. But congressional leaders and judges refused to yield. They forced the president to turn over crucial evidence that clearly linked him to serious felonies. The press also reported aggressively on the scandal and revealed corrupt activities throughout the Nixon administration. By the summer of 1974, investigators had amassed so much evidence of the president's misdeeds that Congress appeared certain to exercise its constitutional power to impeach him and remove him from office. On Aug. 9, realizing that he had no chance of salvaging his presidency, Nixon stepped down.

Before Nixon, only one president in history—Andrew Johnson in 1868—had faced impeachment. But Johnson came under fire for his political disagreements with Congress rather than for an abuse of power. He survived in office after the Senate acquitted him. Before Nixon, Congress and the courts had never confronted a president who took advantage of his office to engage in criminal activities. Watergate took the country into uncharted political territory. It raised a fundamental question: can the most powerful man in the nation be held accountable for his actions?

In many countries, the head of state could suppress an investigation or even drive his enemies out of office. But under the U.S. Constitution, the legislative and judicial branches of government have authority to hold the president accountable for his actions. One of the important legacies of Watergate was establishing that no person—not even the president—is above the law. As Gerald R. Ford said upon being sworn in as Nixon's successor: "Our Constitution works. Our great republic is a government of laws and not of men. Here, the people rule."

PURPOSE OF THIS BOOK

This book is designed to explain both the Watergate scandal and the safeguards in the Constitution that guarantee the democratic form of government in the United States. It brings together primary materials in the form of *Congressional Quarterly Weekly Report* articles written during 1973 and 1974. These articles, selected from the complete record of Congressional Quarterly coverage of Watergate, provide students with a front-row seat to the most significant moments in the unfolding scandal. To help explain the context of Watergate, this book also includes summaries and interpretations of major events.

The Watergate scandal illustrates how the Constitution guides the daily functioning of the U.S. government. The founders divided the government into three branches to dilute political power. They designed a system of checks and balances to prevent one political leader, or branch of government, from abusing power. Watergate emerged as a supreme test of that system. When Nixon in 1974 had to defer to the authority of the Supreme Court and Congress, he was actually deferring to our constitutional form of government.

Although the Watergate scandal is unique in American history, the Constitution is continually being tested. Political leaders in all three branches of government regularly try to assert as much power as they can. This book illustrates how Watergate relates to numerous instances of tension among the branches of government, including cases in which presidents appeared to exceed their authority. It illuminates the role of external organizations, including political parties and the news media, in our constitutional system of government. And it demonstrates that political officials, to this day, stretch the limits of the Constitution.

THE WATERGATE STORY

"A third-rate burglary attempt"

Early on the morning of June 17, 1972, five burglars were arrested in Washington, D.C.'s Watergate office building. The men were found in the national headquarters of the Democratic Party. Questions arose immediately about the possible involvement of Nixon's re-election team in the break-in. One of the burglars, James W. McCord Jr., was the director of security for the Nixon re-election committee. The White House moved immediately to distance itself from the break-in, which Nixon's press secretary, Ronald L. Ziegler, termed "a third-rate burglary attempt."

Although unknown at the time, the break-in was tied to illegal actions undertaken by Nixon's re-election campaign and the White House. The campaign raised an unprecedented amount of money—more than $60 million. Much of the money was illegally donated by corporations. Investiga-

tors would eventually determine that secret contributions were used to pay for illegal tactics, such as spying on or smearing Democratic presidential hopefuls. The money also financed the Watergate break-in, and it was used later to pay the burglars to remain silent about their activities.

Lawrence F. O'Brien, the Democratic national chairman, filed a $1 million lawsuit against Nixon's re-election committee on June 20. He called the break-in "an incredible act of political espionage." But John N. Mitchell, Nixon's campaign manager and the former attorney general, insisted that the Nixon campaign had nothing to do with the burglars. Nixon himself also indicated that the White House had no connection to the break-in. At a June 22 news conference, he said he could not comment further because District of Columbia police and the Federal Bureau of Investigation (FBI) were investigating.

In truth, Nixon did not want the FBI to investigate. Instead of being removed from the situation, the president was deeply involved in an illegal attempt to force the FBI off the case and to cover up the criminal conspiracy that led to the burglary. The plan was to persuade the CIA to tell the FBI that an investigation would interfere with sensitive CIA operations in Mexico. But the CIA refused to go along with the ruse.

While Nixon was running for re-election, the White House successfully kept a distance from the burglars. The House Banking and Currency Committee in the summer and fall of 1972 looked into reports that certain funds contributed to the Nixon re-election campaign had been used to finance political espionage activities. But committee members friendly to the White House voted down an attempt by the chairman to investigate. The chairman, Democrat Wright Patman of Texas, also asked four administration officials to testify before the committee. But the White House declined, claiming executive privilege. (Executive privilege refers to the right of a president to keep certain matters secret if their disclosure could hurt the nation.) A frustrated Patman said Nixon had "pulled down an iron curtain of secrecy to keep the American people from knowing the facts."

After Nixon won re-election easily in 1972, it looked as though interest in the Watergate burglary might fade away. But a criminal investigation was raising new questions. The investigation, by a federal prosecution team in Washington, uncovered papers that pointed toward Florida, Mexico, and the mishandling of money. It had also led to the arrests of two additional suspects in the Watergate break-in, who had ties to the Nixon White House and the re-election campaign.

Unfortunately for the White House, the trial of the Watergate burglars took place in the Washington, D.C., courtroom of U.S. District Court judge John J. Sirica. He was known as "Maximum John" because of the severity of his sentences. Sirica had many questions about the Watergate break-in. "This jury," he said before the trial opened in January 1973, "is going to want to know what did these men go into that headquarters for? Was their sole purpose political espionage? Were they paid? Was there financial gain? Who hired them? Who started this?"

Sirica started to get some answers on March 23, the date on which the defendants were scheduled to be sentenced. On that day, McCord, who was one of the Watergate defendants, wrote the judge a letter. McCord said additional people were involved in the break-in. He also said that pressure had been applied to try to force the defendants to remain silent, and that incorrect testimony had been given in court. It was a vital break in the case. The coverup had started to crack.

Congress Weighs In

Meanwhile, the Senate in February created a special Watergate committee to investigate the scandal. The committee, chaired by Democrat Sam J. Ervin Jr. of North Carolina, opened a series of sensational hearings in May that were carried live on nationwide television. It heard stunning testimony from John W. Dean III, the former White House counsel. Dean made comprehensive allegations against Nixon's closest aides. He disclosed a March 1973 meeting in which he told Nixon that the seven Watergate defendants were demanding about $1 million in exchange for remaining silent. Such payments would violate the law. Nevertheless, the president, according to Dean, "told me that [paying the money] was no problem." Dean's testimony also revealed that the administration audited the tax returns of its political enemies in order to harass them.

Other witnesses blamed some of Nixon's most trusted aides. They implicated officials such as Mitchell and White House chief of staff H. R. Haldeman. Called to testify were several top White House officials who had already resigned because of the burgeoning scandal. Nixon, however, denied any wrongdoing. It appeared uncertain whether investigators could determine whether he or his top aides had broken the law.

But in late July, the Senate Watergate Committee's hearings took a dramatic turn. A former White House aide, Alexander P. Butterfield, revealed that the White House had taped Nixon's private conversations. Investigators quickly realized that the tapes could show conclusively whether Nixon was involved in the Watergate coverup. But Nixon, knowing the importance of the tapes, did not want to turn them over.

For the following year, the Watergate investigation was dominated by legal battles over the tapes. A grand jury investigating Watergate issued a subpoena, or legal order, for the turning over of nine of the tapes just days after Butterfield's disclosure. The grand jury was working with a special Watergate prosecutor, Archibald Cox, a Justice Depart-

ment employee who was aggressively trying to uncover the scandal. Nixon refused to comply with the subpoena, arguing that the tapes were protected by executive privilege. Cox went to court to force Nixon to hand over the tapes. Both Sirica and an appeals court sided largely with Cox. The court rulings would force Nixon to turn over the tapes to Sirica, who would review them. If Sirica determined their disclosure would not harm the national interest, he would pass them along to Cox and the grand jury.

What happened next was remarkable. Nixon and his lawyers tried to strike a deal with Cox in which they would prepare summaries of the tapes, which would be verified independently for accuracy. In return, Cox would have to agree not to seek any more tapes. Cox rejected the offer. On Saturday, Oct. 20, 1973, Nixon ordered his attorney general to fire Cox. Both the attorney general and his deputy resigned rather than carry out the order, which they felt undermined the independence of the Watergate investigation. The number-three man in the Justice Department, Solicitor General Robert H. Bork, finally fired Cox. The episode quickly became known as the Saturday Night Massacre. Congressional leaders expressed outrage. They began floating the possibility of impeaching Nixon. Administration critics worried that the president was placing himself above the law.

Moving toward Impeachment

Getting rid of Cox did Nixon little good. Under pressure from Congress, Nixon appointed a new Watergate special prosecutor, Leon Jaworski. The new prosecutor proved just as aggressive as Cox. Nixon also tried to calm his critics by turning over the tapes that had been subpoenaed. But some of the tapes contained vital gaps. Experts who reviewed them said they were deliberately erased. Both Jaworski and the Senate Watergate Committee demanded additional tapes. Nixon again resisted, continuing to claim executive privilege. He also faced new problems, such as charges that he underpaid his income taxes and provided political favors for major campaign contributors.

Congress took a historic step toward impeachment in February 1974. It gave the House Judiciary Committee broad powers to investigate the White House and recommend whether Nixon should be impeached. The committee subpoenaed additional tapes, but Nixon refused to turn them over. Instead, he offered to meet with committee leaders and answer their questions. But the committee would not accept that compromise. Nixon then agreed to provide them with transcripts of the subpoenaed tapes. That temporarily mollified some, although not all, members of the Judiciary Committee. But the transcripts were inconsistent, and committee members realized they would need the tapes to determine what had actually been said in the conversations. At this point, Nixon said he would not

President Richard Nixon delivers his farewell to the White House staff Aug. 9, 1974, with his family looking on.

provide any more material. Even his fellow Republicans warned him that he was making a mistake. In another ominous sign for the president, a frustrated Jaworski went to the Supreme Court to force Nixon to comply with his own subpoenas for tapes.

At the end of July, the Judiciary Committee approved, by wide margins, two articles of impeachment against the president: obstruction of justice and abuse of presidential powers. The committee also narrowly approved a third article: contempt of Congress. All the committee's Democrats, and several of its Republicans, supported impeachment. Just before the committee votes, the Supreme Court issued a unanimous decision directing Nixon to turn over the tapes that Jaworski needed. The Court's ruling was particularly noteworthy because four of the justices had been nominated by Nixon. The president, who had earlier hinted that he might not comply with a Supreme Court order, said he would cooperate.

Nixon's situation appeared desperate. The full House was set to debate impeachment in late August. A majority of members were likely to vote to impeach the president.

Under the Constitution, the Senate would then hold a trial. If two-thirds of the senators voted guilty, Nixon would be forced out of office.

On Aug. 5, 1974, Nixon's fate was sealed with the release of three previously undisclosed transcripts. They revealed the plot to thwart the FBI investigation of Watergate. Congress and the public learned especially incriminating details from a taped conversation between Nixon and his chief of staff, H. R. Haldeman, that took place on June 23, 1973, in the Oval Office of the White House. In the conversation, Nixon told Haldeman that the FBI should receive an order: "Don't go any farther into this case." This revelation was particularly damaging after Nixon's repeated denials of involvement in the coverup.

In Congress, even many of Nixon's defenders now said it was time for him to go. Three days later, on national television, Nixon announced that he would resign. He did not admit his guilt. But he conceded that he could no longer count on a base of support in Congress.

"As long as there was a base, I felt strongly that it was necessary to see the constitutional process through to its conclusion," he said. "But with the disappearance of that base, I now believe that the constitutional process has been served, and there is no longer a need for the process to be prolonged."

If Nixon had come forward with the facts during the early stages of the scandal, he might have saved his presidency. It was the continuing coverup that dragged him down, not the earlier break-in. But Nixon tended toward secrecy. He had always been a loner with few intimate friends. In his administration and re-election campaign, he relied on the advice of a few people who shared his passion for secrecy. The tapes of private White House conversations would reveal suspicion and hostility at the highest level of government. Out of this atmosphere emerged Nixon's basic response to the scandal. First he denied any involvement. Then he pledged to cooperate with investigators even though he resisted their inquiries. Then he tried to shift the blame elsewhere, especially to the press. He also used such defenses as arguing that other presidents had engaged in similar acts. He tried to justify his actions on the grounds of national security. Only when his last legal maneuvers were exhausted did he leave office—although still without admitting guilt.

For all his misdeeds and secrecy, Nixon might have survived in office if not for the incriminating tapes. Without them, investigators may never have gathered clear evidence of Nixon's involvement in the coverup. Nixon also had the misfortune of facing an aggressive Congress run by the opposing party. If his own party, rather than the Democrats, had run Congress, the investigation on Capitol Hill might have been less thorough.

Vice President Gerald R. Ford was sworn in as the new president on Aug. 9, just minutes after Nixon's resignation took effect. One month later, Ford issued a controversial pardon to Nixon to prevent him from being prosecuted. But many of Nixon's former top aides were sentenced to prison.

THE AFTERMATH

In the years following Watergate, Congress passed a number of laws intended to prevent such an abuse of power from happening again. Lawmakers sought to reform the system of campaign contributions, make it easier for the press and public to obtain government documents, and limit the ability of the executive branch to eavesdrop on citizens. Despite all these reforms, a basic question remains: can our system again prevent a president from abusing his power?

Some experts think presidents can get away with exceeding their authority because it is extremely difficult to investigate them. There has also been speculation that other presidents misused their power and escaped punishment only because they were not investigated as thor-

oughly. Even when an administration is thoroughly scrutinized, it could be hard to distinguish between genuine corruption and the use of power to protect the nation from its enemies. "History will deal more kindly with Richard Nixon than did his contemporaries," predicted Edward Hutchinson, the leading Republican on the House Judiciary Committee. "The abuses of power charged against the president were probably no greater than have occurred in some other administrations. What to one man seems an abuse of power appears to another to be strong executive discretion."

Although no scandal after Nixon has risen to the level of Watergate, several administrations faced serious charges of corruption. The administration of President Ronald Reagan was rocked by charges in 1986 that it helped sell arms to Iran, an enemy of the United States. It used the proceeds to fund an anti-communist guerilla organization in Nicaragua known as the contras. But Reagan, unlike Nixon, was never directly tied to illegal activities. His presidency survived, although some of his aides faced criminal charges.

In 1998 President Clinton was impeached after lying under oath about an affair with a White House intern. But Clinton, unlike Nixon, was charged primarily with wrongdoing in his personal life rather than abusing his office. He was acquitted by the Senate.

Finally, President George W. Bush has faced allegations of violating the Constitution. Critics have denounced his administration for eavesdropping on Americans without obtaining warrants and for detaining suspected terrorists without granting them rights. Bush has argued that his actions were necessary for national security. In the first few years after the Sept. 11, 2001, attacks, Congress was reluctant to challenge Bush's aggressive use of executive power.

Despite these controversies, most analysts believe Watergate showed that corruption, even at the highest levels of government, will be punished. Two days after Nixon's resignation, historian Henry Steele Commager concluded that Watergate had tested the Constitution in an unprecedented way. The nation, he believed, emerged stronger than ever. "The long-drawn-out process of inquiry by committee, by the courts, by the Congress is a stunning vindication of our constitutional system," he wrote. "[W]e have demonstrated to the world and, let us hope, to future generations that the Constitution is alive and well, that it can be adapted to the exigencies of governance, and that in an emergency an enlightened and determined democracy can protect and defend its principles, its honor, and its heritage."

Watergate and other major events also have had substantial consequences for the news media. The press, sometimes referred to as the fourth branch of government (or the Fourth Estate), plays a major role in exposing government corruption. The stunning Watergate revelations by reporters, especially Carl Bernstein and Bob Woodward of *The Washington Post*, helped drive Congress to investigate the Nixon administration. But Nixon and his allies tried to deflect attention from the scandal by attacking the credibility of witnesses, journalists, and news organizations. Such tactics have become commonplace since Watergate. Over time, this has undermined public confidence in the news media. It is uncertain whether news organizations would be able to perform the same kind of watchdog function today, especially as they struggle to be heard in an era of increasingly diverse news sources on the Internet.

Another important consideration is the role of the political parties. During Watergate, moderate lawmakers in both parties played a vital role to ensure fairness. They pressed for Congress to investigate the scandal thoroughly and impartially, preventing both Nixon's liberal critics and his conservative allies from using the scandal to pursue their political goals. Since Watergate, however, elected leaders have become increasingly partisan. In Nixon's time, conservative southern Democrats and northeastern liberal Republicans moderated the views of their parties. Now, however, almost all of the conservatives in Congress are Republican and almost all of the liberals are Democrats. As a result, it is uncertain today whether lawmakers could overcome their partisan feelings and judge a president fairly. This increasing partisanship could be seen in the 1998 impeachment of President Clinton, a Democrat. Congressional Democrats overwhelmingly defended him; congressional Republicans overwhelmingly criticized him.

As for Nixon, his days as a political officeholder ended in 1974. He suffered from a severe depression after leaving office and almost died after surgery for phlebitis. But after his health rebounded, he battled to rehabilitate his reputation. He wrote a number of books on foreign policy and became an informal advisor to his successors in the White House. When he died in 1994, each of the five living presidents attended his funeral.

"President Nixon's journey across the American landscape mirrored that of his entire nation in this remarkable century. His life was bound up with the striving of our whole people, with our crises and our triumphs," President Clinton said at the funeral. "May the day of judging President Nixon on anything less than his entire life and career come to a close."

Clinton's words were part of a laudable impulse to heal old wounds. But as this book demonstrates, the lessons of Watergate go far beyond concern over the tarnished reputation of a statesman. The political crisis dramatized the danger of the rising power of the presidency, at the expense of Congress and the courts, in an era of heightened concern about national security. The president, as chief executive of the government and commander-in-chief of the military, inevitably amasses more power when the nation is facing a major threat. But Nixon's misuse of the investigatory powers of the FBI, CIA, and Internal Revenue Service—often in the name of safeguarding the nation—show the dangers of unchecked presidential power.

Watergate, clearly, is an important event with many lessons for today. The news stories, speeches, transcripts, and records of private conversations that follow present a record of this dramatic moment in the U.S. political system. As the story of Watergate unfolds in the pages of this book, it is worthwhile to observe the conflicting roles of elected officials, top White House aides, investigators, judges, and journalists. These conflicts are echoed, sometimes in more subtle forms, throughout American history and even to the present day. They are an inevitable, if sometimes unpleasant, byproduct of government by the people. The conflicts serve as haunting reminders of why our founders foresaw the need to prevent the concentration of all power into a single government entity. Even as Watergate illustrates the dangers of government corruption, it also illuminates the enduring strength of the American government.

PART I: BREAK-IN AND SENATE INQUIRY

INTRODUCTION:
Senate Hearings Bring Watergate before a Nationwide Audience

Never before did a congressional investigation receive so much attention. From mid-May until early August 1973, American television screens were filled with politicians and former government officials testifying before the seven-member Senate Watergate Committee.

The committee's investigation would continue for more than a year, with a final report issued in July 1974. But its greatest impact was felt during this first phase. This was the period when the committee publicly questioned many of the most important men of the Nixon administration to learn all it could about White House—and presidential—involvement in the Watergate break-in and coverup.

And it was during these hearings that information emerged that eventually brought the Nixon presidency down in ruins.

BUILD-UP TO THE HEARINGS

In mid-March, investigators into the Watergate break-in got their first big break. One of the Watergate burglars, James W. McCord Jr., wrote a letter to U.S. District Court judge John J. Sirica, leveling charges that eventually implicated the Nixon administration. He said defendants were pressured to remain silent about the burglary and to commit perjury, or lie under oath.

"There was political pressure applied to the defendants to plead guilty and remain silent," McCord wrote. "Perjury occurred during the trial in matters highly material to the very structure, orientation and impact of the government's case and to the motivation and intent of the defendants."

McCord's letter was the break that investigators had been waiting for. In its aftermath, pressure on the White House built as press reports implicated more and more past and present administration officials. Heading this list was John N. Mitchell, Nixon's former attorney general and former campaign manager.

The growing political pressure forced Nixon to pledge cooperation with the Senate Watergate Committee. He had initially refused to let members of his administration testify before the Senate Watergate Committee. Instead, he claimed executive privilege—the right of the executive branch to withhold some (but not all) information about its activities.

But in mid-April, the White House reversed its position in the face of growing evidence of administration complicity. Nixon said that members of his staff would appear voluntarily when requested to do so. Although the White House had repeatedly denied involvement in Watergate, Nixon reported that he had started "intensive new inquiries" into the affair on March 21 "as a result of serious charges which came to my attention."

As the scandal worsened, Nixon went on nationwide television on April 30 to announce the resignations of four top White House officials: Nixon's two chief aides, H. R. Haldeman and John D. Ehrlichman; the president's counsel, John W. Dean III; and Attorney General Richard G. Kleindienst. The president appointed Elliot L. Richardson as the new attorney general.

BUTTERFIELD AND THE TAPES

Witnesses before the Watergate committee—including present and former Nixon aides—would provide revealing, and sometimes shocking, information about the Watergate scandal. The committee's most important finding was that tape recordings had been made of many presidential conversations in the White House during the period when the break-in occurred and the coverup began. The tapes contained evidence that ultimately led to Nixon's resignation.

The disclosure of the tapes' existence came from a surprise witness, Alexander P. Butterfield. He had been an assistant to H. R. Haldeman, former White House chief of staff, before becoming head of the Federal Aviation Administration in March 1973.

In a private session with Senate committee investigators on Friday, July 13, 1973, Butterfield revealed the installation of the tape recording system. He said it was requested by the president for historical purposes and maintained by the Secret Service.

Jolted by the significance of Butterfield's statements, the committee put him in the witness chair when public hearings resumed. On Monday, July 16, the American people heard the news.

Immediately, a struggle for the tapes began. The legal battle would last almost exactly a year, from July 23, 1973, when the Senate committee and the Watergate grand jury subpoenaed the first group of tapes, to July 24, 1974, when the Supreme Court ruled that Nixon had to turn over the tapes to the grand jury.

DEAN'S POINTING FINGER

An earlier clue to the taping system had come from John W. Dean III, when he appeared before the committee in June. Dean was the first administration official to implicate Nixon directly in the coverup. He told the committee about one conversation with the president on April 15, 1973, when Nixon had spoken "in a barely audible tone" while discussing executive clemency for one of the Watergate defendants. (Executive clemency refers to the president's power to reduce a prison sentence or pardon a convicted criminal.) At one point in the conversation, said Dean, Nixon had asked him "leading questions, which made me think that the conversation was being taped."

Altogether, Dean spent five days in the witness chair in June 1973. By the time Dean walked out of the hearing room, he had raised serious questions about the role Nixon had played in the Watergate scandal. Besides Nixon's discussion of clemency, Dean charged that Nixon knew of the coverup as early as September 1972, six months earlier than Nixon had acknowledged.

The young lawyer, an admitted conspirator in the developing scandal, began his testimony by reading a 245-page statement. He described Watergate as "an inevitable outgrowth of a climate of excessive concern over the political impact of demonstrations, excessive concern over leaks, an insatiable appetite for political intelligence, all coupled with a do-it-yourself White House staff, regardless of the law."

He contributed one of the memorable phrases of the whole affair in his account of a March 21, 1973, meeting with Nixon. He said he had warned his leader of "a cancer growing on the presidency."

Further evidence of the peculiar atmosphere within the Nixon White House was found among some fifty documents submitted by Dean to the committee. One was a memorandum containing a list of twenty persons to be given White House treatment as "political enemies." The full list of enemies contained the names of more than 200 individuals and of 21 organizations. In his memo, Dean wrote about "how we can use the available federal machinery to screw our political enemies."

OTHER ADMINISTRATION WITNESSES

The first phase of the Senate Watergate Committee hearings in the spring and summer of 1973 featured a parade of past and present officials of the administration, the Committee for the Re-election of the President, and men involved in the burglary. Many of the witnesses were later convicted of conspiracy and perjury in criminal trials—or pleaded guilty to charges that grew out of the scandal.

One of these witnesses, Jeb Stuart Magruder, former deputy director of the Nixon re-election committee, accused Mitchell of helping plan and cover up the 1972 break-in. Mitchell, a tight-lipped witness, denied Magruder's accusations.

Ehrlichman, who was convicted in January 1975 with Mitchell and Haldeman for participating in the coverup conspiracy, denied any wrongdoing. He defended as legal and justified on national security grounds the 1971 burglary of Pentagon Papers defendant Daniel Ellsberg's psychiatrist (see box on Pentagon Papers, p. 44).

Haldeman startled the committee by testifying that he had taken home and listened to some of the taped presidential conversations that had been withheld from the investigators. He too denied any involvement in the coverup.

Some of the most important testimony came from McCord. He told of offers of executive clemency in return for a guilty plea. He said he met secretly during the trial of the Watergate burglars with John J. Caulfield, a former White House aide who did undercover work for Dean. McCord was told that the clemency offers came "from the very highest levels of the White House," McCord testified.

LATER HEARINGS

The Watergate committee resumed its public hearings in the fall of 1973 to examine two other aspects of the scandal, campaign "dirty tricks" and financing.

Nixon's re-election, the most richly financed in history up to that time, had received money contributed in violation of the law. Much testimony was heard during the first phase of the Senate hearings concerning hundreds of thousands of dollars that were managed secretly and sometimes put to illegal use. Some of the money helped pay for an imaginative and widespread campaign of espionage and sabotage directed at the Democrats. The Watergate break-in was part of this campaign.

But congressional and public interest in the Senate inquiry waned by the fall of 1973. Headlines had already told of unscrupulous tactics and illegal corporate campaign contributions, some made by men who later testified before the committee.

The center of the Watergate stage had shifted from the Senate hearing room to the presidential tapes and the investigation being conducted by the special Watergate prosecutor. In addition, attention was turning to the House, which had the constitutional authority to impeach the president. The television cameras were packed up, and the Senate committee concluded its hearings and started working on its final report.

WATERGATE SCANDAL:
A Senate Search for the Truth

The Senate created a special committee to investigate the Watergate scandal in February 1973. It took this action in response to growing concerns about the scope of the Watergate break-in and coverup.

The Watergate scandal began as a seemingly isolated criminal event. Police arrested five burglars who had broken into the Democratic national headquarters in the Watergate office complex early in the morning of June 17, 1972. President Nixon, untarnished by the news about Watergate, easily won re-election a few months later. But by the spring of 1973, the break-in had developed into one of the biggest political scandals in American history. As one disclosure followed another, Watergate was recognized as one piece of a much larger operation involving political spying and sabotage. Reports emerged of large amounts of secret campaign cash that were used to finance illegal operations. The scandal threatened to implicate a number of White House officials.

In the months following the break-in, the five burglars and two accomplices had either pleaded guilty to serious criminal charges or been convicted. But many important elements of the scandal remained unsolved. One of the biggest mysteries was the role of the White House, and even of President Nixon himself. A federal grand jury was investigating the matter. But with the public losing confidence in the president, many believed that a congressional investigation was needed to dig out all the facts.

INCREASING QUESTIONS

The Watergate break-in quickly spawned charges of serious political wrongdoing. A top Democratic campaign official charged that Republicans had been wiretapping Democratic headquarters before the June 17 arrests. News stories linked the wiretapping with officials in the White House and Nixon's re-election campaign. The press also reported on large sums of campaign contributions that were used to fund the Republicans' espionage operations. The General Accounting Office, an investigative arm of Congress, concluded that Nixon's re-election committee had violated several election laws.

Republicans were also accused of sabotaging Democratic campaigns. Their actions included forging letters, leaking false items to the press, investigating Democratic campaign workers, and seizing confidential campaign files. They worked to undermine the presidential campaign of Sen. Edmund S. Muskie of Maine, who was considered a serious threat to Nixon's re-election prospects. Many of the alleged acts of sabotage were illegal.

Republicans denied many of the charges. As early as August 1972, Nixon claimed that no one currently in his administration had been involved in the bugging. He said that "technical violations" of federal campaign laws had been made by both Democrats and Republicans. He added that such violations may occur because overzealous people sometimes do things during campaigns that are wrong. But such violations, he said, should not be covered up.

Democrats worried that the Watergate scandal was not being investigated thoroughly. Both the White House and the FBI were looking into the matter, as well as the federal grand jury. Officials in the Nixon administration who oversaw the FBI pledged that the agency would launch a comprehensive investigation. But reports circulated that the FBI's investigation was being hindered by White House officials.

Congress, which was controlled by Democrats, first tried to examine the scandal in the summer of 1972. House Banking and Commerce Committee chairman Wright Patman, a Texas Democrat, wanted to investigate campaign contributions to Nixon's re-election campaign that were associated with the Watergate break-in. But Nixon allies on his committee voted down the proposed investigation. Patman next tried to get four administration officials to testify before his committee. But he again ran into a dead end. Nixon claimed executive privilege—the right of a president to prevent at least some private information from being shared with another branch of government. (For more about executive privilege, see p. 39.)

But while Congress was temporarily stymied, the judicial process moved forward. In January, the seven men charged with the break-in at the Watergate office complex were brought to trial. It was the White House's bad luck that the presiding judge, John J. Sirica, was a no-nonsense man who had been nicknamed "Maximum John" because of the severe sentences he handed down. Sirica was impatient that the trial focused mostly on the actual break-in. He believed it should examine why the burglars went into the Democratic headquarters, where their money came from, and who hired them.

The seven Watergate defendants were scheduled to be sentenced by Sirica on March 23. One of the defendants—James W. McCord, the former director of security for the Nixon re-election committee—wrote the judge a letter. He claimed that additional people had been involved in the break-in and that the defendants had been pressured to remain silent about the others who were involved. He said that perjury—a serious crime that involves lying under oath—had been committed at the trial. McCord's letter represented one of the first big breaks in the case.

SENATE WATERGATE COMMITTEE

Meanwhile, the Senate on February 7 had voted 77–0 to create a special committee to investigate the scandal. The formal name of the committee was the Select Committee on Presidential Campaign Activities. But most people referred to it as the Senate Watergate Committee. The seven-member committee had broad powers, including the authority to issue subpoenas, or legal orders, to obtain evidence. It was chaired by Senator Sam J. Ervin Jr., a North

Carolina Democrat. Ervin had a folksy manner, but he was well-versed in constitutional issues.

The committee almost immediately clashed with the White House. Ervin vowed to get White House staff members to testify before the committee, even if that meant arresting them. He dismissed a suggestion by the White House that administration officials testify informally, and not under oath Nixon, despite his reluctance, was under considerable pressure to cooperate with the committee. A poll showed that many Americans believed some Nixon aides had known in advance of the bugging. Some voters said the scandal would make them less inclined to vote Republican in 1974. Many Republican leaders worried about the impact of the scandal.

The scandal appeared to grow more serious in February and March when the Senate Judiciary Committee held hearings to confirm Nixon's nomination of L. Patrick Gray III to become FBI director. During the hearings, senators heard new disclosures about espionage and Watergate. For example, it appeared that Nixon's personal attorney told the FBI that he helped arrange the payment of $30,000 to $40,000 to an alleged saboteur. The committee also learned that Nixon's re-election campaign had tried to impede an FBI investigation of Watergate. Gray's nomination was withdrawn in April.

A break-in at an office building in Washington, D. C., early in the morning of June 17, 1972, has developed into one of the best-publicized pieces of political skullduggery in American history. The name of the building in which five men were arrested at 2:30 a.m. that day has become the word commonly used to describe not only the break-in itself but the widening circle of events surrounding it. The name is Watergate.

The five men were arrested in Democratic national headquarters, offices occupying a suite on the sixth floor of the Watergate office-apartment-hotel-shopping complex, one of the swankest in Washington. The men were carrying electronic surveillance equipment. They were wearing surgical gloves to prevent leaving fingerprints.

Incredibly, sometimes accompanied by cynical laughter, typified the initial public reaction to the bungled break-in. But, as one disclosure followed another, the laughter faded and the Watergate incident was recognized for what it was: one segment of a much larger political spy puzzle involving espionage and sabotage, implicating White House officials and financed with hundreds of thousands of dollars in secret campaign funds.

Often in a major scandal, a number of investigations will take place simultaneously. In the case of Watergate, a federal prosecutor was working with a grand jury to conduct a criminal investigation into the Watergate break-in. (For more about grand juries, see p. 53.) In addition, the former Democratic Party chairman filed a civil lawsuit against the Republican Party over the break-in. A civil lawsuit does not result in somebody being sent to prison but instead seeks money for various types of misbehavior. Eventually the various investigations and lawsuits, plus revelations printed in the press, spurred Congress to mount its own investigation.

In a little more than seven months, the five burglars and two of their accomplices had either pleaded guilty to or been convicted of felonies. But most of the puzzle remained unsolved by early spring of 1973. A federal grand jury was continuing its investigation. Three civil suits awaited trial in U.S. District Court in Washington. A constitutional dispute over the President's right to refuse to permit his staff to testify before congressional committees cost a nominee the prestigious job of FBI director.

The Watergate complex in Washington, D.C.

All the unanswered questions had created a growing uneasiness among Republican officials who feared damage to their party. An increasing number of Republicans were speaking out publicly against administration handling of the charges and were demanding candor and cooperation with investigators.

Senate Investigation

All the still-undisclosed facts, it was hoped, would be brought to light by public hearings to be conducted by a bipartisan, seven-member select committee of the Senate. The committee, chaired by Sen. Sam. J. Ervin (D. N. C.), was expected to begin hearings in late April or early May. *(See the committee members and staff, p. 26.)*

The committee was established by a unanimous vote of the Senate Feb. 7. The resolution establishing the committee (S Res 60) provided subpoena powers and authorized $500,000 for completion of the investigation and writing of a report by Feb. 28, 1974.

Samuel Dash, a Georgetown University law professor who is chief counsel for the investigative committee, discussed a few of the committee's ground rules with Congressional Quarterly. Without committing himself to a timetable, Dash said that public hearings would begin "as quickly as possible." Private investigation by him and minority counsel Fred Thompson was under way, he added, and "This is going to be, as far as I'm concerned, a very careful, a very thorough investigation."

Dash said he and Thompson were assembling a staff, starting with a "core team of specialists," that might number "in the 30s or 40s" when the investigation reaches its peak. Although he expects the committee to complete its work within the allotted time, he mentioned the possibility that, if necessary, the investigators might have to exercise their option for an extension of time and money to finish their job.

Arrangements must be made for a hearing room large enough to accommodate the large crowds expected to attend the hearings. One ground rule, Dash said, is that the hearings will be open to press and public. A one-day closed hearing on March 28 produced so many leaks to the press from unidentified sources that further closed hearings were canceled.

"The success of the investigation will depend on the staff," Dash said. He expects the initial public hearings to last about a month, followed by continued investigation by the staff through the summer and more extensive hearings in the fall, he said. The investigation is expected to be broad in scope, exploring not only the details of the Watergate but other charges of political wrongdoing by both the Republican and Democratic Parties.

The ultimate goal of the committee, said Dash, was to discover "what impact (all this) has on the election process in a Democratic country." The final report, he said, might contain recommendations to reform existing election laws.

The Bugging and Break-in

Federal investigators initially focused on the Watergate burglars. Not until months after Nixon's re-election in November did attention turn to the role of top White House officials in engineering the burglary and then attempting to cover it up.

After the initial reports on the June 17 break-in, the Watergate incident dropped temporarily from the headlines. Not until late summer did the story of the broader scandal start to unfold. But, even during its absence from the news, a federal grand jury was conducting a secret investigation that led to the indictment of seven men. Many of the revelations that gradually came to light were the result of diligent digging by and occasional leaks to the press.

The Conspirators. These were the five men arrested by Washington police in the Democratic offices:

- Bernard L. Barker, a Miami, Fla., realtor and a former Central Intelligence Agency (CIA) employee who reportedly had a role in the Bay of Pigs invasion of Cuba in 1962.
- Virgilio R. Gonzalez of Miami, a locksmith who emigrated from Cuba during Fidel Castro's rise to power.
- Eugenio R. Martinez, a member of Barker's real estate firm and an anti-Castro Cuban exile with CIA associations.

- James W. McCord Jr. of Washington, security coordinator for the Republican National Committee and the Committee for the Re-election of the President, a former FBI agent and CIA employee. He was fired the day after the break-in.
- Frank A. Sturgis of Miami, an associate of Barker who had connections with the CIA and had participated in anti-Castro activities.

The five were charged with attempted burglary and attempted interception of telephone and other communications. On Sept. 15, the grand jury indicted them and two other men for conspiracy, burglary and violation of federal wiretapping laws. The two others, involved in the break-in but not arrested until later, were:

- E. Howard Hunt Jr. of Washington, a former White House consultant, writer of spy novels and former CIA employee. Hunt's consulting work included declassification of the Pentagon Papers.
- G. Gordon Liddy of Washington, counsel to the Finance Committee to Re-elect the President, former FBI agent, former Treasury Department official and former member of the White House staff. Liddy was fired for refusing to answer the FBI's questions during an investigation of the Watergate incident.

At a trial in January 1973, Hunt, Barker, Sturgis, Gonzalez and Martinez pleaded guilty. Liddy and McCord were convicted.

Partisan Reaction. Lawrence F. O'Brien, Democratic national chairman at the time of the break-in, called it "an incredible act of political espionage." John N. Mitchell, former attorney general and, until July 1, President Nixon's re-election campaign manager, said the five men arrested at the Watergate "were not operating either in our behalf or with our consent."

These allegations suggest that Nixon's aides used wiretaps to listen in on private conversations of Democratic officials. The aides did so during the president's re-election campaign, which raised concerns that advisors to Nixon violated the law in order to hurt Democratic prospects for winning the election.

More Bugging. On Sept. 7, O'Brien, then the campaign manager for Democratic presidential nominee George McGovern, charged that Republican-sponsored surveillance of Democratic headquarters had been going on before the June 17 arrests. He said that his phone and that of R. Spencer Oliver, executive director of the state chairmen's association of the Democratic National Committee, had been tapped for several weeks. Information from the taps had, he claimed, been monitored and transcribed in a motel across the street from the Watergate.

O'Brien said the five men arrested on June 17 had come to repair a faulty tap on his phone and to install a bugging device nearby. On May 27, he said, the presence of campaign workers had prevented some men from setting up eavesdropping equipment in McGovern campaign headquarters on Capitol Hill.

News stories on Sept. 16 identified Alfred C. Baldwin III, a former FBI agent and an alleged participant in the Watergate bugging, as the source of O'Brien's information. In a copyrighted interview published in *The Los Angeles Times* Oct. 4, Baldwin said he had delivered eavesdropping logs to the President's re-election committee less than two weeks before June 17. He said the material was sent to someone besides the seven men indicted, but he did not name that person.

The Washington Post reported on Oct. 6 that Baldwin, who was granted immunity from prosecution in return for his cooperation with investigators, told the FBI that memos describing wiretapped and bugged conversations in Democratic headquarters had been sent to three persons: William E. Timmons, Nixon's assistant for congressional relations; Robert C. Odle Jr., director of administration for the re-election committee, and J. Glenn Sedam Jr., the committee's general counsel. The charges were denied.

The Money Morass

Money would emerge as a central theme of the Watergate scandal. Nixon's aides used large sums of campaign funds to pay for illegal activities such as wiretapping and the Watergate break-in. Much of the money was donated illegally, sometimes in cash, from wealthy individuals and corporations. The Nixon campaign committee did not always follow federal law requiring the donations to be disclosed. Some of the early Watergate investigations, detailed in this article, looked into whether Nixon campaign officials violated campaign spending laws. But both federal investigators and reporters would ultimately dig deeper into the scandal, tracking campaign money to determine the illegal activities that it funded. A government source famously told Washington Post *investigative reporter Bob Woodward to "follow the money" if he wanted to get to the bottom of Watergate.*

As the grand jury was hearing witnesses throughout the summer of 1972 in connection with the Watergate bugging, reports began to appear about enormous sums of money, obtained under unusual circumstances, for use in the Republicans' intelligence operations.

GAO Investigation. An investigation by the FBI and the General Accounting Office's (GAO) Office of Federal Elections began Aug. 1 into the finances of the President's re-election committee. The investigation was started after *The Washington Post* reported that a $25,000 check intended for Nixon's campaign had been deposited to the Miami bank account of Bernard Barker, one of the men arrested at the Watergate.

Kenneth H. Dahlberg, midwestern finance chairman for the Nixon campaign, said he had given a cashier's check for $25,000 to Maurice H. Stans, the former secretary of commerce who was Nixon's finance chairman in 1972, as he had been in 1968.

The Washington Star-News reported on Aug. 10 that additional contributions of $89,000 had been deposited in installments in Barker's account, bringing the total to $114,000. The article quoted investigators as saying the Republicans had a "security fund" for their national convention.

A GAO report released Aug. 26 cited five "apparent" and four "possible" violations of the Federal Election Campaign Act of 1971 by the re-election finance committee. The report was turned over to the Justice Department for further action. These were among its disclosures:

- The committee failed to keep a detailed account of the $25,000 contribution. It was given anonymously, but the donor was revealed to be Dwayne Andreas, a Minneapolis, Minn., grain executive. Andreas and Dahlberg, it was later revealed, were both directors of a bank that was granted a federal charter on Aug. 22. Both denied any connection between the contribution and the charter.
- The committee did not disclose details of the $25,000 contribution in accordance with the 1971 campaign law.
- The committee failed to keep a detailed account of the money spent from the $25,000 Dahlberg check or from the four checks totaling $89,000, drawn on a Mexico City bank and eventually deposited to Barker's account. Stans told the GAO that the four checks were from donors in Texas who wished to remain anonymous by contributing before April 7—the deadline for anonymous contributions before new reporting requirements took effect under the 1971 law.

- The committee kept inadequate records, not only on the $114,000 in anonymous contributions, but on the balance of $350,000 deposited on May 25 to the credit of the Media Committee to Re-elect the President. Hugh W. Sloan, former treasurer of the finance committee, said the $350,000 had been kept in a safe in Stans' secretary's office. Only Stans and Sloan had access to the safe. Stans told the GAO that the funds had been collected before the April 7 deadline and that any records pertaining to them had been destroyed after April 7.

Indictment, Settlement. The GAO investigation led to the indictment of the re-election finance committee on eight counts of campaign spending violations. The committee was fined $8,000 on Jan. 26, 1973, in U.S. District Court in Washington after pleading nolo contendere—no contest—to the charges.

Barker Trial. Another trial that resulted from one of the Republican financial transactions was that of Barker, the Miamian in whose bank account the secretly contributed money had been deposited. Barker was indicted in Dade County (Florida) Criminal Court on a charge of fraudulently using his notary public seal to indicate that the $25,000 check from Dahlberg—the Dwayne Andreas contribution—had been endorsed in his presence.

Barker pleaded guilty on Sept. 15. He was found guilty on Nov. 1 and given a 60-day suspended sentence on the condition that he surrender his notary license.

Banking Committee Probe. But the Barker trial and conviction were only subsidiary elements in the movement of much larger amounts of money through his firm's account.

The House Banking and Currency Committee staff distributed to committee members on Sept. 12 a report claiming that finance chairman Stans knew of the transfer of $100,000 in contributions from Texas donors through a Mexican bank and into the campaign treasury. The report was leaked to the press.

According to the report, the money was delivered, along with an additional $600,000 in contributions, to the re-election committee on April 5, two days before the deadline for identifying donors. Included in the $100,000, said the report, was the $89,000 deposited to Barker's account on April 20.

The report said that Stans had denied knowledge of the Mexican bank transfer at first but later had admitted knowing about the transaction when he was confronted with conflicting testimony from a Texas fund-raiser. Stans issued a statement denying any knowledge of the Mexican transactions and calling the committee report "rubbish" and "transparently political."

By a 20–15 vote on Oct. 3, the Banking and Currency Committee rejected a probe of Nixon campaign finances. The rejection was bipartisan; six Democrats joined 14 Republicans in preventing the investigation. It was opposed by the Justice Department on grounds that it would interfere with the criminal trial of the seven Watergate defendants.

A report by Democratic members of the House committee was released Oct. 31, making additional charges of campaign fund mishandling by the Nixon re-election committee. A re-election committee spokesman said the report was a "dishonest collection of innuendo and fourth-hand hearsay." Among the allegations in the report:

- The re-election committee had developed the capability of monitoring the bank accounts of Democratic senators and representatives. The charge was attributed to a friend of Hugh Sloan, the former campaign treasurer. Sloan's attorney called it an "absolute lie."
- Alfred Baldwin, the Watergate bugger who had been granted immunity, was hired for $18,000 a year to record not only political discussions but personal conversations.
- At least $30,000 had been channeled to the Nixon committee through a Luxembourg bank before the new campaign spending law took effect.
- The campaign finance committee had committed massive bookkeeping errors and omissions, including one $800,000 discrepancy between committee records and bank records of cash on hand in April 1972.

Funds Returned. The contributor of the mysterious $100,000 identified himself early in 1973. He was a Texas oilman, Robert H. Allen. He acknowledged that $89,000 of his donation had been deposited to the Barker account. In a letter to Stans, he asked that the $100,000 be returned for personal reasons.

The return of Allen's $100,000 was announced on March 9 by the re-election finance committee. Also returned to its donors, the re-election committee said, was another $555,000. Of this amount, $305,000 was given back to Walter T. Duncan, a Texas land speculator, and $250,000 to Robert L. Vesco, a New Jersey financier. Duncan needed the money to pay off debts. Vesco had been accused by the Securities and Exchange Commission of a $224-million stock fraud. His contribution of $200,000 to the Nixon campaign was the object of another GAO investigation. The other $50,000 was not involved in the investigation.

Vesco's Role. The interaction of Vesco with the President's finance committee was brought to light in a court deposition made public in New York City on Feb. 27. His $200,000 contribution was delivered to the committee in cash on April 10, 1972, three days after the new reporting law took effect. But it was never reported to the GAO.

Vesco is accused of swindling investors in IOS Ltd., an overseas mutual fund corporation. Although the $200,000 contribution and another $50,000 contribution—given after April 7 and reported as required—were returned to Vesco on Jan. 31, the finance committee claimed the law had not been violated, because Vesco had intended to contribute the money before the deadline and it was "constructively in the hands" of the committee before April 7.

The court deposition, made by an attorney who was an associate of Vesco and was Nixon's campaign manager in New Jersey in 1972, linked John Mitchell, Maurice Stans and the President's younger brother, Edward Nixon of Edmonds, Wash., to the Vesco contribution. The deposition stated that:

- Late in 1971, then attorney general Mitchell phoned the U.S. embassy in Geneva, Switzerland, expressing interest in the jailing of Vesco on the complaint of a former IOS customer. Vesco was freed on bond within a day. Mitchell later denied any wrongdoing; he said he made the call at the request of the attorney who gave the deposition, Harry L. Sears.
- Vesco said that Stans had asked for the contribution in cash. This request was later confirmed by Edward Nixon. A re-election committee spokesman denied these statements; Stans and Edward Nixon were unavailable for comment.

More 'Apparent Violations.' A GAO report charging the President's re-election finance committee with four new "apparent violations" was referred to the Justice Department on March 12 for possible prosecution. The chief subject of the report was the $200,000 Vesco contribution. It was "undisputed," said the GAO, that the contribution was not delivered to the finance committee until after the April 7, 1972, deadline.

The committee labeled the GAO report "irresponsible" and said the committee's handling of the Vesco contribution had a "conclusive precedent." That precedent was the $25,000 Andreas contribution of April 10, 1972, which, according to the committee, had been ruled within the law in a Justice Department report on Jan. 11, 1973.

The Secret Fund. Recurrent references have been made since the fall of 1972 to a secret fund, kept in a safe in Maurice Stans' office, that allegedly was used to finance the Watergate bugging and broader espionage and sabotage operations. Press reports have said that high Republican officials in the re-election campaign and on the White House staff have had knowledge of the fund. Many of these reports have been denied, but full details on the fund and its uses have yet to be revealed.

In September 1972, *The Washington Post* quoted sources involved in the Watergate investigation as saying that John Mitchell, while attorney general, personally controlled a secret fund used to finance intelligence-gathering operations against the Democrats. Mitchell denied the charge.

Quoting federal investigators and grand jury testimony, the Post reported on Oct. 25 that H. R. Haldeman, the White House chief of staff, was one of five men authorized to approve payments from the fund. The cash fund, according to the story, fluctuated between $350,000 and $700,000. The White House said the reference to Haldeman was untrue and the report was "based on misinformation."

The first acknowledgment by a campaign official that the fund existed was made in a Washington television interview on Oct. 26 by Clark MacGregor, who had replaced Mitchell as Nixon's campaign manager on July 1. MacGregor said no money from the fund had been used for illegal purposes. And he repeated the denial of Haldeman's authority for making disbursements from the fund.

In its August report, the GAO asked the Justice Department to investigate the fund. The department took no action. In its March 12 report, the GAO repeated its request for a Justice Department investigation of the fund, which included Vesco's $200,000 contribution.

Espionage and Sabotage

Several Nixon campaign aides would eventually be accused of spying on and sabotaging Democratic candidates. Hardball tactics are commonplace in political campaigns, and it is not unusual for officials on a campaign to try to collect unsavory information about the opposition. But the Nixon campaign proved to be unusually dirty. Some of the tactics, such as forging letters and seizing confidential campaign files, violated the law.

Reports of an alleged widespread Republican network of espionage and sabotage against the Democrats, paid for out of the secret cash fund, began to appear in the fall of 1972. The first article, published in the Oct. 10 *Washington Post,* was dismissed as a "collection of absurdities" by a re-election committee spokesman. Information in the article was attributed to FBI and Justice Department files. Among the activities described in the Post article were:

- Following members of Democratic candidates' families and assembling dossiers on their personal lives.
- Forging letters and distributing them under Democratic candidates' letterheads.
- Leaking false and manufactured items to the press.
- Throwing campaign schedules into disarray.
- Investigating Democratic campaign workers.
- Planting provocateurs at the national political conventions.
- Seizing confidential campaign files.
- Investigating potential contributors to the Nixon campaign.

Muskie Campaign. According to the Post story, one of the targets of Republican sabotage was Sen. Edmund S. Muskie of Maine, a candidate for the Democratic presidential nomination. One of the incidents most damaging, and perhaps fatal, to his campaign was a well-publicized letter alleging his use of the pejorative word "Canuck" to describe Americans of French-Canadian descent. That incident made headlines in February 1972, before the New Hampshire primary.

The Post account said that one of its reporters had been told by Ken W. Clawson, deputy director of White House communications, that he had written the letter, which had been attributed to a man in Florida. Clawson denied the charge.

An interview with Muskie (conducted before the Oct. 10 report) was published in the Oct. 13 Post, quoting him as saying that he had been victimized by a "systematic campaign of sabotage," including:

- Theft of documents from his files.
- Middle-of-the-night telephone calls to voters from impostors claiming to be Muskie canvassers.
- False items planted in newspapers.
- Facsimiles of his envelopes used to mail embarrassing material under his name—including one assertion that two of his opponents for the nomination had engaged in illicit sexual acts.

A Tampa, Fla., secretary said that she had participated in a scheme to disrupt Muskie's primary campaign in Florida, *The New York Times* reported on Oct. 25.

Enter Segretti. The alleged recruiter of the provocateurs for the Nixon campaign was a young California lawyer and former Treasury Department attorney, Donald H. Segretti. He denied knowing anything about such an operation and called the report "ridiculous."

But that was only the first of many reports alleging "that Segretti was involved in undercover rascality." The allegations of sabotage and espionage were regularly denounced as false by spokesmen for the White House and the re-election committee.

The Post reported on Oct. 15 that Segretti, one of more than 50 alleged undercover operators for the Nixon campaign, had named Dwight L. Chapin, then the President's appointments secretary, as one of his contacts. The source of the charges was a sworn statement from another California attorney, Lawrence Young. Segretti, Young and Chapin had been college classmates. Chapin said the story was "based on hearsay and is fundamentally inaccurate."

Time magazine Oct. 23, citing Justice Department files, wrote that:

- Segretti was hired by Chapin and Gordon Strachan, a White House staff aide, and was paid by Herbert W. Kalmbach, Nixon's personal attorney.
- Segretti received more than $35,000 between Sept. 1, 1971, and March 15, 1972, "to subvert and disrupt Democratic candidates' campaigns."
- The FBI began an investigation after discovering a record of phone calls between Segretti and Howard Hunt, one of the seven Watergate defendants.

Records showed that Segretti had made calls to the White House and Chapin's home, *The New York Times* reported Oct. 18. A Times report Oct. 19 said that Segretti apparently volunteered to work for Democratic candidate McGovern in the California primary campaign in June. Although there was evidence that a man named Segretti had appeared at McGovern headquarters, there was no evidence that he actually had worked on the campaign, the Times said.

The Los Angeles Times reported on Oct. 23 that Segretti had told a San Francisco attorney that "he was trying to develop an organization to infiltrate the primary campaigns of two candidates for the Democratic nomination, Senators Muskie of Maine and Henry M. Jackson of Washington." His purpose, it was reported, was to prevent a sweep of the primaries by one candidate.

Segretti Investigation. A Justice Department investigation of Segretti was confirmed by an administration source on Feb. 11, *The New York Times* reported. Earlier, the department had said that Segretti's efforts appeared to be legal and did not warrant an investigation. But the Times quoted a source as saying that Segretti might have violated a statute making it illegal to distribute political literature that is unsigned or contains an unauthorized signature.

Attorney General Richard G. Kleindienst told reporters on Feb. 12 that his department's Watergate investigation was continuing because such an investigation is never closed. "You can just assume it's going on, and I'm not going to tell you what is," he said.

Other Incidents. James McCord, one of the defendants in the criminal case, investigated syndicated columnist Jack Anderson in the spring of 1972, *The Washington Post* reported on Sept. 27. An alleged confidential memorandum from McCord dealt with Anderson's business and social relationship with Anna Chennault of Washington, D.C., a member of the Republican National Finance Committee.

Another Watergate defendant, E. Howard Hunt Jr., had tried to recruit a government employee to investigate the private life of Sen. Edward M. Kennedy (D Mass.), the Post reported on Feb. 10. Clifton DeMotte, a General Services Administration employee at Davisville, R.I., said the incident had occurred in July 1971, when Kennedy was considered a leading contender for his party's presidential nomination.

The GAO said on March 12 that it would investigate some $150-a-week payments reportedly made to Theodore T. Brill, chairman of the Young Republicans at George Washington University. Brill told the Post that he had been paid to infiltrate radical groups in 1972 for Nixon's re-election committee.

Criminal and Civil Trials

> The trial of the five burglars and two others associated with the break-in marked an important moment in the Watergate investigation. Most of the defendants pleaded guilty, and they declined to implicate the White House in the break-in. Judge John J. Sirica appeared frustrated over the narrow focus of the trial, which did not reveal who had orchestrated the burglary.

The criminal trial of the seven Watergate defendants began on Jan. 8 and ended on Jan. 30. Sentencing was March 23. Still to be tried are three civil suits related to the Watergate. The U.S. District Court in Washington is where the criminal trial was held and where the civil suits will be tried. Chief Judge John J. Sirica tried the criminal case. Judge Charles R. Richey will try the civil cases.

Pre-trial Activity. A federal grand jury indicted Liddy, Hunt, McCord, Barker, Martinez, Sturgis and Gonzalez on eight counts Sept. 15. The seven were charged with breaking into the Watergate offices for the purpose of stealing documents and installing electronic listening devices to intercept telephone and oral communications.

Sirica on Oct. 4 enjoined all parties connected with the bugging from making public statements about it. His injunction covered law enforcement officials, defendants, witnesses, alleged victims and attorneys. Sirica's order was greeted with a protest from several Democratic officials. He responded by amending the order to remove references to "witnesses, potential witnesses, complaining witnesses and alleged victims." And he said, "It is not the intention of this court to affect congressional activity, political debate or news media reporting."

On Oct. 11, the final day for filing motions, attorneys for Liddy, Hunt and McCord filed affidavits charging that they had been followed and their telephones had been tapped. They asked for a change of venue, which was denied.

The trial was supposed to start on Nov. 15. But on Oct. 27, Sirica postponed the trial until Jan. 8, 1973. The judge had a pinched nerve, and his doctor advised the postponement.

Trial Opening. A jury was chosen in two days. Sirica warned prospective jurors that he expected the trial to last four to six weeks. Jurors were sequestered from the start.

Defense and government attorneys made their opening statements on Jan. 10. Earl J. Silbert, the chief prosecutor, charged that a broadly ranging political espionage operation had been ordered by top officials of the Committee for the Re-election of the President in 1972. He said Liddy had received $235,000 in cash from the re-election committee to carry out various assignments. Only $50,000 of the money could be accounted for by the prosecution, Silbert said. He also described the hiring by Hunt of a Brigham Young University student, Thomas J. Gregory, to infiltrate the campaign organizations of candidates McGovern and Muskie.

Two defense attorneys, Gerald Alch and Henry Rothblatt, acknowledged in their opening statements that their clients had been in the Watergate the night of June 17. But both said their clients were innocent of the charges.

Guilty Pleas. Within a few days, the seven defendants had been reduced to two. On Jan. 11, Sirica accepted a guilty plea from Hunt on all six counts with which he was charged. On Jan. 15, Barker, Sturgis, Martinez and Gonzalez pleaded guilty. Hunt was freed after posting $100,000 bond. The other four remained in the District of Columbia jail.

Gerald Alch, McCord's attorney, made a motion for a mistrial after the guilty pleas had been made. The absence of the five men from the courtroom would lead the jurors to conclude that guilty pleas had been made and would prejudice the rights of McCord and Liddy, the two men still on trial, he argued. Sirica denied Alch's motion and advised him that he could appeal the ruling to the U.S. Court of Appeals.

Few Answers. Several times during the trial, Sirica personally questioned defendants and witnesses in an effort to get to the bottom of the Watergate affair. He interrogated Barker, Sturgis, Martinez and Gonzalez Jan. 15 about who had planned the bugging and where the money to pay for it had come from.

The four denied press reports that they had been under pressure to plead guilty, that they still were being paid by an unnamed source and that they had been promised a cash settlement as high as $1,000 a month if they pleaded guilty and went to jail.

Anti-communism and anti-Castroism figured in the testimony of the four, two of whom had been linked to the Bay of Pigs invasion. "When it comes to Cuba and the communist conspiracy involving the United States, I will do anything to protect this country," Sturgis said. Gonzalez said he had been told by Barker and Hunt that "we're solving the Cuban situation" by breaking into the Watergate.

'Law of Duress.' Alch, McCord's lawyer, wrote in a memorandum to the court Jan. 17 that his client's participation in the break-in and other activities had been justified because McCord feared violence against Nixon and other Republicans. He explained the "law of duress" to reporters in these words: "If one is under a reasonable apprehension—regardless of whether that apprehension is in fact correct—he is justified in breaking a law to avoid the greater harm. . . ." Alch cited "potentially violent groups" that supported Democratic candidates in 1972 and might have indicated their plans to the Democrats.

Baldwin Testimony. A key government witness, Alfred Baldwin, testified in secret session Jan. 17 about the persons whose conversations he had overheard while tapping phones at the Democratic National Committee. Before the trial went into secret session, Baldwin described how McCord had hired him in May 1972 and how his wiretapping apparatus had been set up in the motel room across from the Watergate. He said he was instructed to take notes on monitored conversations through the day and into the evening, turning over his logs to McCord.

Sloan Testimony. Hugh Sloan, the former treasurer of the President's re-election finance committee, said John Mitchell and Maurice Stans had approved spending money that the government claimed was used for espionage against the Democrats.

In testimony Jan. 23, Sloan said that he had given $199,000 in cash to Liddy at the direction of Jeb Stuart Magruder, deputy campaign chairman for the President. Magruder testified that the committee budgeted about $235,000 for intelligence operations directed by Liddy. He said he knew nothing about illegal bugging activities.

Convictions. Liddy and McCord were found guilty on Jan. 30 of conspiracy, burglary and wiretapping violations. Liddy was convicted on six counts, McCord on eight. Their attorneys said they would appeal.

Alch, McCord's attorney, was bitingly critical of Sirica on the trial's last day. Sirica, he said, "did not limit himself to acting as a judge. He has become, in addition, a prosecutor and an investigator. Not only does he indicate that the defendants are guilty, but that a lot of other people are guilty. The whole courtroom is permeated with a prejudicial atmosphere." Alch claimed on Jan. 31 that Sirica had committed at least nine errors providing grounds for the reversal of McCord's conviction.

The judge had been critical of the prosecution for failing to ask more questions about the motivation of the men. He had sought to compensate for what he felt was this shortcoming by doing extensive interrogating of his own. Questions left unanswered by the trial would, he said, have to be answered by the Senate investigation.

Sentencing. Liddy was given the heaviest sentence by Sirica on March 23. He was sentenced to a minimum of six years and eight months to a maximum of 20 years in prison and was fined $40,000.

The judge left open the final sentence, pending a three-month study by the U.S. Bureau of Prisons, for Barker, Hunt, Sturgis, Martinez and Gonzalez. The five were jailed until the study was completed, at which time Sirica would, he said, uphold the "provisional" maximum sentences he had imposed, reduce the sentences or place the men on probation. For Barker, Sturgis, Martinez and Gonzalez, the potential maximum sentence was 40 years; for Hunt, 35.

One of the most unusual twists of the trial occurred the day of sentencing, when Sirica read a letter written to him by McCord earlier that week. In the letter, McCord wrote that other persons besides those convicted had been involved. Perjury had been committed, he charged. And he claimed that political pressure had been applied to make the defendants plead guilty.

Sirica postponed sentencing of McCord for one week and freed him on $100,000 bond. On March 30, Sirica deferred sentencing until June 15 so that McCord would have the opportunity to testify further before a federal grand jury and before the Senate investigating committee.

Civil Suits. Remaining to be tried before Judge Richey are three civil suits, one filed by Democrats against Republicans and two by Republicans against Democrats. The actions:

- Attorneys for the Democratic National Committee filed suit against the President's re-election committee on June 20, 1972—three days after the break-in—seeking $1 million in damages. Damages sought were increased to $3.2 million on Sept. 11 and increased again to $6.4 million on Feb. 28, 1973. Defendants were expanded to include Liddy, Hunt, former campaign treasurer Sloan, finance chairman Stans, Magruder and Herbert L. Porter, a former Nixon campaign aide.
- Stans and Francis I. Dale, chairman of Nixon's re-election committee, filed a $2.5-million countersuit on Sept. 11.
- Stans filed a $5-million libel suit against former Democratic Chairman O'Brien on Sept. 14 on the grounds that O'Brien had falsely accused him of political espionage on Sept. 11.

Probes, Leaks, Denials

The longest and most penetrating probe of the Watergate and related matters is expected to be conducted by the Senate select committee. But, in the months since the bugging arrests, other investigations as well as those by the House Banking and Currency Committee have been conducted by the FBI, the GAO, the White House and a federal grand jury. Leakage of information from these probes has led to denials, countercharges and recriminations. As the Senate committee was preparing for public hearings, Chairman Ervin and the White House appeared to be headed toward a showdown over the right of White House staff members to refuse to testify before congressional committees.

White House. At an Aug. 29 news conference, Nixon said that no one then employed in his administration had been involved in the Watergate bugging. He said that a complete investigation of the incident by John W. Dean III, his counsel, permitted him to declare "categorically that his investigation indicates that no one in the White House staff, no one in this administration, presently employed, was involved in this very bizarre incident."

The President claimed that "technical violations" of the federal election campaign law had "occurred and are occurring, apparently, on both sides." He refused to discuss what possible violations had been committed by the Democrats, saying only that "I think that will come out in the balance of this week."

Nixon added, "What really hurts in matters of this sort is not the fact that they occur, because overzealous people in campaigns do things that are wrong. What really hurts is if you try to cover it up."

At a news conference the next day, Aug. 30, Nixon said he would not comply with a Democratic suggestion that a special, nonpartisan prosecutor instead of a Justice Department attorney be assigned to the Watergate case.

Ronald L. Ziegler, the White House press secretary, said on Sept. 8 that the report on Dean's Watergate investigation would not be released. Lawrence O'Brien, then McGovern's campaign manager, had requested its release.

Justice Department. Attorney General Richard Kleindienst pledged Aug. 28 that the FBI investigation of Watergate would be "the most extensive, thorough and comprehensive investigation since the assassination of President Kennedy." When completed, he said, "no credible, fair-minded person is going to be able to say that we whitewashed or dragged our feet on it."

Nixon expressed confidence in the FBI investigation on Oct. 5. He said it made the 1948 Alger Hiss probe, which had helped him build a reputation as a young representative, look like "a Sunday school exercise."

The Washington Post reported on Oct. 11 that FBI investigators in the Watergate case had been hindered by resistance from middle- and lower-level White House officials and by witnesses who gave incorrect or incomplete information.

Judiciary Committee. The Senate Judiciary Committee began confirmation hearings Feb. 28 on L. Patrick Gray III, Nixon's nominee for permanent director of the FBI. Out of the hearings came new disclosures about espionage and the Watergate. FBI records submitted by Gray to the committee sometimes corroborated some earlier news reports. These were among the statements in the records:

- Herbert Kalmbach, Nixon's personal attorney, told the FBI he and Dwight Chapin, then the President's appointments secretary, arranged to pay between $30,000 and $40,000 to Donald Segretti, the alleged saboteur.
- Re-election committee officials tried to impede an FBI investigation of the Watergate.
- Dean, the President's counsel, sat in on all interviews of White House personnel conducted by FBI investigators. Gray told the committee on March 6 that he had opposed Dean's presence at the interviews but had permitted him to be present because the alternative would have been to have no interviews.
- Liddy and Hunt, two former White House consultants, "traveled around the United States contacting former CIA employees for the purpose of

setting up a security organization for the Republican Party dealing with political espionage."

- An unnamed official of the Republican re-election committee told the FBI that Hugh Sloan "allegedly disbursed large sums to various committee officials for unknown reasons." The disbursements included $50,000 to Jeb Stuart Magruder, $100,000 to Herbert Porter and $89,000 to Liddy.

The Judiciary Committee hearings resulted in the withdrawal of Gray's nomination, at Gray's request, by the President on April 5. Confirmation of the nominee had appeared increasingly unlikely.

Among the factors that damaged Gray's chances were his testimony before the committee that he had turned over FBI files to John Dean and his statement to the committee that Dean probably had lied to the FBI in saying he did not know that E. Howard Hunt had a White House office. Gray also was damaged by Dean's refusal to testify before the committee, claiming executive privilege.

Congress has broad powers to investigate the executive branch. Lawmakers can call on presidential aides to testify on Capitol Hill or turn over important documents. This helps ensure that lawmakers perform their checks-and-balances role, reining in possible instances of abuse by members of a presidential administration. However, Congress's authority is limited. Presidents can decline to disclose information under certain circumstances. For example, a president who claims "executive privilege" can refuse to allow his aides to cooperate if he believes the investigation could endanger national security.

Nixon, throughout the Watergate scandal, would claim executive privilege to block congressional investigations. In some respects, he set the tone for later clashes between Congress and the White House. Bill Clinton claimed executive privilege to thwart congressional investigations into several cases of alleged wrongdoing. George W. Bush in 2005 declined to share some memos written by John Roberts, a former Justice Department lawyer who had been nominated to the Supreme Court.

Select Committee. The executive privilege issue is an important one in the impending hearings of the Senate investigating committee, too, and it has yet to be resolved. Chairman Ervin, considered the Senate's foremost constitutional expert, has threatened to subpoena White House staff members and have them arrested by the Senate sergeant at arms if they do not appear.

The White House has promised to cooperate with the committee by answering questions in writing. Ervin

has rejected that offer and a later White House suggestion that informal testimony, not under oath, might be permitted. "That is not executive privilege," said Ervin at a news conference April 2. "That is executive poppycock."

As a result of the letter he had written to Judge Sirica, conspirator James McCord had arranged to meet with the judge several days after the sentencing. Instead, he met privately with Samuel Dash, the committee counsel, on March 23 and 24. Dash briefed reporters on the meeting on March 25 but would not discuss the substance of the conversations.

Quoting unidentified sources, *The Los Angeles Times* said that McCord had told Dash that Magruder and Dean had prior knowledge of the Watergate bugging. The report was denied—as it had been before—and Nixon reaffirmed his confidence in Dean.

McCord testified in secret before the select committee on March 28. Another leak, again attributed to an unidentified source by *The Washington Post,* quoted McCord as telling the committee that John Mitchell had approved the bugging personally and that Charles W. Colson, former special counsel to Nixon, knew in advance of the plot. More denials were forthcoming.

The White House responded in a fury, accusing the committee of allowing "irresponsible leaks in tidal wave proportions." Responding to Ervin's rejection of the White House offer of informal testimony by its staffers, press secretary Ziegler said: "I would encourage the chairman to get his own disorganized house in order so that the investigation can go forward in a proper atmosphere of traditional fairness and due process."

Ervin announced on April 3 that the full committee would suspend closed hearings. Colson reinforced his assertion of innocence by taking a lie detector test, which indicated, according to press reports April 8, that he was telling the truth.

Grand Jury. While the select committee was conducting its leaky investigation, the federal grand jury was continuing to hear witnesses in secret. E. Howard Hunt Jr. invoked the 5th Amendment (against self-incrimination) when he appeared before the jury on March 27. The next day, Judge Sirica granted the government's request to grant Hunt immunity from further prosecution, and he testified for nearly four hours.

G. Gordon Liddy, too, had been granted immunity and ordered by Sirica on March 30 to testify before the grand jury. He refused to answer the jury's questions and was sentenced to an additional jail term for contempt of court. Sirica sentenced Liddy to serve until the end of the grand jury term—the end of 1973 unless extended—or 18 months, whichever came first.

Four other conspirators—Barker, Martinez, Sturgis and Gonzalez—were ordered to testify after being given immunity. Sirica indicated their cooperation, and McCord's, would be a factor when he sentenced them and McCord in June.

Partisan Repercussions

Nixon had been a leading figure in the Republican Party for more than two decades when the Watergate investigations began. He won kudos for his staunch anti-communist views, which he leavened with such innovative decisions as pursuing arms control agreements with the Soviet Union. But many Democrats despised him for his conservative views and hard-edged political tactics.

At the beginning of the Watergate scandal, Republicans generally defended the president, while many Democrats criticized him. This was hardly surprising. Politicians tend to stand by those in their party. As investigators uncovered more and more misbehavior by White House officials, however, Republicans began to waver in their support of Nixon. Their second thoughts may have been the result of a genuine distaste for his actions or the public's increasing skepticism of the president. As long as Nixon enjoyed the support of those in his own party, his hold on the presidency was secure. But when Republicans began to bolt, he faced deep political peril.

It is noteworthy that American government was divided during the Watergate scandal. Even though the nation had just re-elected a Republican president, Democrats held majorities in both chambers of Congress. Such division tends to accentuate the checks-and-balances nature of our government, since a Congress controlled by one party usually acts as an adversary to a president of the opposing party. Would lawmakers have investigated Nixon so aggressively if a single political party had controlled both Congress and the White House? Such a question is impossible to answer.

If the Watergate scandal dropped any ominous fallout on Republican candidates in the 1972 elections, it apparently did no damage to the President, who won a second term by a landslide. Watergate simply was not an important issue in most places.

McGovern. George McGovern made several speeches about it. In a Los Angeles speech Oct. 16, he called the Republican activities "the shabbiest undercover operations in the history of American politics." On Oct. 25, in a nationwide television speech, he accused the administration of corruption and sabotage and said the nation was confronted with "a moral and a constitutional crisis of unprecedented dimensions." Earlier that day in Cleveland, McGovern had said a report linking White House staff chief Haldeman with the affair "places the whole ugly mess of corruption, espionage and sabotage squarely in the lap of Richard Nixon."

Republicans. As the Senate investigation drew closer and the administration-Congress disagreement grew sharper, Republican leaders showed more signs of worry.

Senate Republicans were becoming more concerned about the political impact, said Senate Minority Leader Hugh Scott (R Pa.) on March 29. The same day, Senators Robert W. Packwood (R Ore.) and Charles McC. Mathias Jr. (R Md.) urged Nixon to appoint a prominent outsider to head a special White House investigation. "The most odious issue since the Teapot Dome," said Packwood in describing the matter.

George Bush, the Republican national chairman, called the Watergate bugging "grubby" and said the incident should be "promptly and fully cleared up" to prevent adverse effects on the party.

But the shrillest attack on the White House was launched by Sen. Lowell P. Weicker Jr. (R Conn.), the junior Republican on the investigating committee. He said in a television interview April 1 that a paid agent of the Nixon re-election committee had spied on nine congressional offices in 1972. Two days later, he called for Haldeman's resignation because, said Weicker, he "clearly has to accept responsibility" for a broad range of alleged espionage activities during the 1972 campaign.

Senators Ervin and Howard H. Baker Jr. (R Tenn.), the select committee's vice chairman, issued a statement on April 4 saying that the committee had "received no evidence of any nature" connecting Haldeman with illegal activities. To which Weicker responded: "I concur with the statement."

Public opinion proved an important factor throughout Watergate. As Nixon's popularity dropped, Congress came under more and more pressure to investigate the scandal aggressively. This situation contrasted with the 1998 impeachment of President Bill Clinton. Even though Americans disapproved of Clinton's personal behavior, most did not want to see him removed from office. This helped shore up Democratic support for the beleaguered president and protect him from being forced out of the White House.

Public opinion, especially in this day of scientific polling, can be an important check on the actions of our elected officials. Republicans who may have wanted to stand by Nixon during Watergate were concerned by polls showing that their party could be punished in the 1974 elections.

Martha Mitchell's Phone Calls

Former Attorney General John N. Mitchell resigned as President Nixon's campaign manager on July 1, 1972. He said he had been spending too much time away from his wife, Martha, and their daughter.

His resignation came a week after Mrs. Mitchell had telephoned a wire service reporter twice. In both calls, she threatened to leave Mitchell if he did not give up politics.

Mrs. Mitchell phoned *The New York Times* on March 27, 1973, and said, according to the Times' report: "I fear for my husband. I'm really scared. I have a definite reason. I can't tell you why. But they're not going to pin anything on him. I won't let them, and I don't give a damn who gets hurt. I can name names. . . . If you hear that I'm sick or can't talk, please, please, get your reporters out to find me. Somebody might try to shut me up."

Mrs. Mitchell was quoted as saying, in another call to the wire service on March 31: "I think this administration has turned completely against my husband. In other words, they're desperate, and I will not under any circumstances let them pin it on my husband. I think my husband has become the whipping boy for the whole administration, and they want to hide who is really involved."

Newspaper Poll. A poll conducted by Political Surveys and Analyses Inc., Princeton, N.J., and commissioned by *The Wall Street Journal,* indicated that the Republicans might find the Watergate affair a serious liability. The poll, published April 6, found, in 501 telephone interviews around the country:

- Ninety-one per cent of those questioned had heard or read about the Watergate incident.
- Thirty-eight per cent believed some top Nixon aides knew in advance about the bugging; 33 per cent did not; 29 per cent were unsure.
- Seventy-one per cent said the affair would not affect their votes; 29 per cent said they would be less likely to vote Republican in 1974.

- Fifty-three per cent thought Nixon was unaware of the bugging plans; 21 per cent thought he was; 26 per cent were unsure.
- Fifty-four per cent believed the White House had tried to prevent a full investigation of the case; 23 percent thought the White House had done "everything it should to bring out all the facts"; 23 per cent were unsure.
- Fifty-four per cent felt press coverage had been fair; 30 per cent thought the press had been "making too much" of it.
- Sixty per cent wanted the congressional investigation continue; 26 per cent thought the case should be dropped; 14 per cent were unsure.

Bouts with the Press

The Nixon White House tended to lash out at its critics. One of its main targets was the press. Aggressive reporters uncovered stunning instances of abuse of power, both by administration officials and by campaign aides. Those accused often responded by denying the stories and heatedly assailing the press for printing them. They denounced reporters for being biased. But reporters for leading newspapers, such as The Washington Post *and* The New York Times, *went to great lengths to make sure they got their details correct.*

Tensions between reporters and politicians were hardly new. In the early 1960s, a handful of reporters based in South Vietnam began filing stories that the war was going badly for the United States. Military officials and some elected officials criticized the reporters, charging them with reckless and biased coverage. In the end, however, it turned out that the reporters were correct in their assessment of the war.

But Watergate seemed to mark a new low in relations between the White House and the Fourth Estate. Nixon rarely held news conferences. He personally accused journalists of distorting the truth. If this strategy was meant to encourage the public to distrust critical stories in the press, it failed. Ultimately, Nixon lost public support as the stories proved to be largely accurate.

The nature of the news media has changed greatly in the decades since Watergate. A proliferation of cable and online news services means that politicians face greater scrutiny than ever. Some of these news services take little time to check their facts. Often, their reporting is driven by political bias.

Larger and more established organizations, however, continue to emphasize careful, unbiased reporting. One thing that hasn't changed is the tension between reporters and the politicians they cover. When a reporter publicly charges a politician with wrongdoing, a politician's first response is often to attack the reporter. Polls show that the public has little confidence in either politicians or reporters—perhaps because of the attacks and allegations.

Two court tests involving the press coverage have been byproducts of the Watergate affair.

Los Angeles Times. The first test resulted from the tape-recorded interview of Alfred Baldwin in October by two *Los Angeles Times* reporters, Jack Nelson and Ronald J. Ostrow. The Times had promised Baldwin that it would not divulge details of the interview without his approval.

In December, attorneys for E. Howard Hunt sought the tapes for use in the forthcoming criminal trial. Judge Sirica rejected the Times' contention that being forced to turn over the tapes would inhibit its ability to report the news and would violate the constitution's 1st Amendment protection for free press.

Sirica cited the newspaper for contempt of court and ordered its Washington bureau chief, John F. Lawrence, jailed. He was in jail for only a few hours before the impasse was broken by an agreement between Baldwin and the court. Baldwin and his attorneys agreed to make the recordings available to Sirica for private inspection, with the understanding that Sirica would edit out any remarks by Baldwin's attorneys or the two reporters.

Civil Suits. The second court action against the press occurred on Feb. 26, when attorneys for Nixon's re-election committee subpoenaed nine reporters, two newspaper executives and three other persons with knowledge of the Watergate. The publications involved were *The Washington Post, The Washington Star-News, The New York Times* and *Time* magazine.

The re-election committee attorneys sought materials such as notes, tapes and other private records from the reporters. The material was sought in connection with the three civil suits before the U.S. District Court.

Judge Richey quashed the subpoenas on March 20. "This court cannot blind itself to the possible chilling effect the enforcement of these subpoenas would have on the flow of information to the press and, thus, to the public," he said.

Steady Friction. The refusal of many potential sources of information to talk to reporters about the Watergate has forced the press to rely heavily on statements from unidentified persons. This situation has brought about frequent denials of unattributed accusations and occasional castigation of the press by administration and re-election committee spokesmen. Their favorite target has been *The Washington Post.*

One of the strongest attacks came from campaign manager Clark MacGregor on Oct. 16, just after the reports on Donald Segretti and his alleged associations with the White House. "Using innuendo, third-person hearsay, unsubstantiated charges, anonymous sources and huge scare headlines—the Post has maliciously sought to give the appearance of a direct connection between the White House and the Watergate—a charge which the Post knows—and half a dozen investigations have found—to be false," MacGregor said.

MacGregor accused the Post of "hypocrisy" for not investigating allegations that the McGovern campaign organization was responsible for isolated incidents of violence at Nixon campaign offices. The Post reported on Oct. 18 that police and both parties' campaign workers had failed to link the McGovern organization with the incidents.

After a Post report on Oct. 25 linked Haldeman, the White House staff chief, with the secret cash fund, press secretary Ziegler accused the Post of "character assassination" and "the shoddiest kind of journalism."

Points to Ponder

Congressional Power

- What are some of the formal powers Congress has to check the president's actions?

- What recourse does the president have to resist Congress?

The Press

- Why do reporters often rely on unnamed sources? What do you think would happen if the use of unnamed sources was curtailed? What risks do the news media take by relying on these sources?

Additional Questions

- Does our legal system ensure that a political official will be fully investigated in the face of credible allegations of wrongdoing? What political strategies and tactics might a politician use to counterattack when accused of wrongdoing?

- Can campaign funds corrupt the political system? Why does the United States allow campaign contributions?

- What do you think about campaign organizations uncovering dirt on political opponents? At what point do such aggressive tactics cross a legal or ethical line?

WATERGATE PERSONALITIES

The seven senators who served on the Watergate committee would play an important role in history. The Democratic chairman, Sam J. Ervin Jr. of North Carolina, had a folksy style that sometimes led his opponents to underestimate his determination. Like many southern Democrats of the time, Ervin was a political moderate who worked well with both Republicans and Democrats. He also was an expert on the Constitution. Ervin took a tough stance during the Watergate investigation, insisting that the White House cooperate fully with the committee's demands for testimony and documents.

The vice chairman was Republican Howard H. Baker Jr. of Tennessee. Baker was an ambitious politician who would later become the Senate Republican leader and an unsuccessful candidate for president. He was highly respected among his Senate colleagues for his ability to craft legislative compromises. Famously, he asked during the Watergate hearings, "What did the President know and when did he know it?"

The committee's staff was instrumental in gathering evidence and developing lines of questioning. Fred D. Thompson, the Republican counsel, would later become a Republican senator from Tennessee.

Major investigative committees, such as the Watergate committee, typically have a chairman from one party and a vice chairman from another. Such a bipartisan combination is important for winning public confidence. Ideally the chairman and vice chairman should be viewed as moderates who have open minds. For example, the 9/11 Commission, created in 2002 to look into the events that led to the September 11 terrorist attacks, had two highly regarded and relatively moderate politicians at the helm. Both the Republican chairman, former New Jersey governor Howard Kean, and the Democratic vice chairman, former representative Lee H. Hamilton, worked hard to investigate the issues fairly. Thanks to their efforts, the commission's report was treated with great respect.

Biographies of Senate Select Committee's Members, Counsels

For profiles of the House Judiciary Committee members, see p. 182.

Sen. Sam J. Ervin Jr. (D N.C.), 76, chairman of the committee, is considered the Senate's leading constitutional scholar. In his nearly 19 years in the Senate, he has sided sometimes with the conservatives, sometimes with the liberals. He was chosen to head the committee because of his reputation for fairness and nonpartisanship. Ervin is a member of the Judiciary and Armed Services Committees and chairman of the Government Operations Committee.

When President Nixon ordered presidential aides not to honor subpoenas issued by the select committee,

Ervin responded by saying, "I'd recommend to the Senate they send the sergeant at arms of the Senate to arrest a White House aide or any other witness who refuses to appear and . . . let the Senate try him."

Sen. Howard H. Baker Jr. (R Tenn.), 47, the committee vice chairman and ranking minority member, was elected to the Senate in 1966. His father was the late Rep. Howard H. Baker (R Tenn. 1951–64), and his father-in-law was the late Sen. Everett McKinley Dirksen (R Ill. 1951–69).

Baker unsuccessfully challenged Sen. Hugh Scott (R Pa.) for the minority leadership in 1969 and 1971 as the candidate of Senate conservatives. He serves on the Commerce and Public Works Committees, the Republican Committee on Committees and the Republican Personnel Committee.

Baker has said he favors "a full, thorough and fair investigation with no holds barred, let the chips fall where they will."

Sen. Edward J. Gurney (R Fla.), 59, elected in 1968, is the first Republican senator from Florida since Reconstruction. He is a member of the Government Operations, Judiciary and Select Small Business Committees. In 1972, Gurney was the chief defender of the Nixon administration during the Judiciary Committee's investigation of the International Telephone and Telegraph Corporation.

He has said of the Watergate investigation, "I want to see that it is as nonpartisan as possible, but I certainly want to bring out every last piece of information." When the investigation resolution was debated Feb. 7, Gurney read information from political polls indicating that the public did not have much interest in the Watergate matter.

Sen. Daniel K. Inouye (D Hawaii), 48, has represented Hawaii in Congress since the islands gained statehood in 1959. He served in the House for four years and has been a senator since 1963. He is a member of the Appropriations, Commerce and District of Columbia Committees.

In 1972, as chairman of the D.C. Appropriations Subcommittee, he conducted full-scale investigations of the District of Columbia government. He is one of four assistant majority whips and vice chairman of the Democratic Senatorial Campaign Committee.

Sen. Joseph M. Montoya (D N. M.), 57, came to the Senate in 1964 after spending eight years in the House. He is a member of the Appropriations and Public Works Committees.

When first appointed to the investigating committee, he said he expected that the members "will be able to sift through the facts and come up with a complete story of just what was involved and just who was involved, in addition, if any, to those already named."

Sen. Herman E. Talmadge (D Ga.), 59, a senator since 1957, was governor of Georgia for the nine years preceding his election to the Senate. In the Senate, he is chairman of the Agriculture and Forestry Committee and ranking Democrat on the Finance Committee. He also serves on the Veterans' Affairs, Select Standards and Conduct and Select Nutrition and Human Needs Committees and is a member of the Democratic Policy Committee.

Talmadge, considered by some senators to be one of their most intelligent colleagues, has said he plans to do no investigating on his own but will depend on the committee's hearings for his knowledge. "I see myself as a juror," he said, "and a juror doesn't background himself."

Sen. Lowell P. Weicker Jr. (R Conn.), 41, was elected to the Senate in 1970 after spending one term in the House. He is a member of the Banking, Housing and Urban Affairs and Aeronautical and Space Sciences Committees. He is also on the Republican Senatorial Campaign Committee.

Weicker has been particularly outspoken about the Watergate investigation and has said he is conducting his own studies on the matter. He has charged that offices of members of Congress were next in line to be bugged. Weicker said he sought membership on the investigating committee because "I'm a professional politician. Because of things like the Watergate, people have lost faith in politicians, and I want to see that changed. The only thing that will convince them to respect politicians is to bring dirty business like the Watergate out in the open."

Samuel Dash, 48, a Georgetown University criminal law professor, is the majority counsel for the select committee. He is director of Georgetown's Institute of Criminal Law and Procedure and is considered a leading authority on wiretapping. He is a former Philadelphia district attorney and was a trial attorney for the Justice Department's criminal division in 1951 and 1952.

Dash has characterized the Watergate investigation as "the most important ever undertaken by the Senate because it goes to the heart of the democratic process."

Fred D. Thompson, 30, a Nashville lawyer, is the committee's minority counsel. Thompson is a former U.S. attorney for Tennessee's middle district and served as Sen. Baker's re-election campaign manager for that area in 1972. As a federal prosecutor, Thompson was known chiefly for his handling of bank robbery and moonshine whisky cases.

Thompson said he views his role as minority counsel as ensuring that the committee staff "keeps within the scope of the investigation" and does not delve into matters unrelated to political espionage.

Watergate Cast of Characters: Similar Backgrounds

As this Congressional Quarterly article points out, the men who were associated with the Watergate scandal came from diverse backgrounds. Many of them—including such high-ranking officials as former attorney general John N. Mitchell and White House chief of staff H. R. Haldeman—would ultimately serve prison terms for their roles in Watergate.

Lawyers, businessmen, media specialists, non-politicians—these are the words that characterize the men whose names have been prominently mentioned in news accounts of the Watergate case.

The common denominator appears to be lack of experience as candidates for public office. With the exception of convicted conspirator G. Gordon Liddy, not one ever sought office. Liddy made an unsuccessful try for the Republican nomination for the U.S. House from New York in 1968—on a law-and-order theme.

The only political background attributable to any of the other Watergate personalities comes from managing or participating in the campaigns of others—particularly President Nixon. Former Attorney General John N. Mitchell was Nixon's campaign manager in 1968. White House aides H. R. Haldeman and John D. Ehrlichman were advance men in past Nixon campaigns, as was Dwight L. Chapin, the President's former appointments secretary. Maurice H. Stans was Nixon's chief fundraiser in 1968 as well as 1972.

Occupations. The legal profession claims Ehrlichman; Liddy; Mitchell; John W. Dean III, the President's former counsel; Gordon C. Strachan, Haldeman's former deputy, and Charles W. Colson, the President's former special counsel.

From business come Maurice Stans, a former commerce secretary; Jeb Stuart Magruder, a former Haldeman deputy, and James W. McCord Jr., another convicted conspirator.

Media specialists have been plentiful in the Nixon White House, most of them former colleagues of Haldeman at the Los Angeles office of the J. Walter Thompson advertising agency, which he managed. Among them are Ronald L. Ziegler, the President's press secretary, and Chapin. Magruder also has a background in advertising and business.

Recruitment. Haldeman, one of the prime recruiters of White House talent, was responsible for bringing in Ziegler, Chapin, Magruder and Ehrlichman. Mitchell's efforts brought Dean and Strachan to the executive mansion.

The ages of the Watergate personalities range from Strachan (29) to Stans (65). Most of them are in their 40s and 50s.

Liddy, McCord and E. Howard Hunt are three of seven men convicted in the Watergate affair. None of the men subsequently linked to Watergate or other campaign excesses has been indicted, but all have been or are likely to be called before the Watergate grand jury to explain their roles.

(Ziegler is not a suspect in the affair, nor has his name been mentioned in connection with any other campaign efforts that might come under the grand jury's scrutiny. He is included in the biographical sketches because of his prominence as the White House's spokesman.)

Accusations. According to testimony leaked from the grand jury probe, Haldeman kept a $350,000 fund in his White House office, some of which allegedly was channeled to convicted Watergate conspirators through Strachan to buy their continued silence. He has denied such charges.

Ehrlichman was not publicly connected to Watergate until April 26, when it was disclosed that he had been present when Dean gave former acting FBI Director L. Patrick Gray III documents allegedly taken from E. Howard Hunt's White House office. The documents later were destroyed by Gray, it was reported. Ehrlichman has confirmed that he was present when the documents were turned over to Gray, but insists that he did not know their contents and did not order their destruction.

Mitchell has admitted attending three meetings at which the Watergate bugging was discussed, but has insisted that he did not approve such plans. Magruder reportedly told the grand jury that Mitchell and Dean approved the bugging and that Colson knew about it.

Kalmbach reportedly controlled a $500,000 fund that helped pay for alleged sabotage activities by Donald H. Segretti. Chapin, in turn, has been named as Segretti's contact in the White House.

Stans, according to testimony at the Watergate trial, kept large sums of cash in his safe at the re-election committee, some of which helped pay for the bugging.

Dwight L. Chapin

Dwight L. Chapin, 32, had worked on and off for Nixon ever since his graduation from the University of Southern California in 1962. As the President's appointments secretary from 1969 until his Feb. 28 departure for private business, Chapin was one of the few White House staff members with easy access to the President. He charted the President's schedule and coordinated all trips, including the 1972 China visit. He was born Dec. 2, 1940, in Wichita, Kan.

Described as utterly loyal to the President, Chapin worked as an advance man for Nixon in his 1964 and 1968 presidential campaigns. From 1963 to 1966, he worked under H. R. Haldeman at the J. Walter Thompson advertising agency in Los Angeles. Although unofficially involved in the 1972 campaign, Chapin has been named as a contact for Donald H. Segretti, an alleged operative in undercover espionage activities for the Republicans.

Charles W. Colson

Charles W. Colson, 41, special counsel to the President from late 1969 until last February, was known

Charles "Chuck" Colson, former special counsel to President Richard Nixon

in White House circles as a tough troubleshooter and key political adviser. In charge of liaison with outside groups, Colson hammered out agreements between administration officials and lobbies and took charge of public relations efforts to garner support for presidential policies.

He was born Oct. 16, 1931, in Boston, graduated from Brown University and took a law degree from George Washington University. From 1956–61, Colson was administrative aide to former Sen. Leverett Saltonstall (R Mass. 1945–67), and after several years in private law practice, he played a marginal role in Nixon's 1968 presidential campaign.

During the 1972 campaign, Colson rode herd on the campaign efforts of White House staff members, while reportedly trying to influence re-election committee activities. Watergate conspirator E. Howard Hunt worked as a consultant for Colson in early 1972. In an August 1972 memo to White House staffers, Colson wrote that it was correct he once said "I would walk over my grandmother if necessary" to assure the President's re-election.

John W. Dean III

John W. Dean III, 34, the President's counsel since July 1970, is one of the bright, young—but politi-

Source: AP Images

John W. Dean III, counsel to President Richard Nixon

cally inexperienced—aides Nixon surrounded himself with after taking office. Dean was largely responsible for the legal work on the unprecedented positions the President has taken on executive privilege and impoundment of funds voted by Congress.

It was Dean who conducted the first Watergate investigation for the President in the summer of 1972 and reported that no one then at the White House was involved. Later events, however, led Nixon to ask for Dean's resignation, which he received and accepted April 30. Dean was born Oct. 14, 1938, in Akron, Ohio. He attended three undergraduate schools and graduated from Georgetown University Law School in 1965.

Dean's rise to the important job of the President's White House lawyer was rapid. He was minority counsel for the House Judiciary Committee in 1967, associate director of the National Commission on Reform of the Criminal Laws from 1967 to 1969, and associate deputy attorney general from 1969 to 1970 before replacing John D. Ehrlichman as counsel to the President.

John D. Ehrlichman

John D. Ehrlichman, 48, directed the White House organization for domestic policy that parallels Dr. Henry Kissinger's foreign affairs staff. Described as efficient, brusque and a stickler for punctuality, Ehrlichman rose rapidly in the Nixon administration. He was counsel to the President from January to November 1969, when he became assistant to the President for domestic affairs. He was born in Tacoma, Wash., on March 20, 1925.

Ehrlichman—like White House staff chief H. R. Haldeman, another principal in the Watergate case who also resigned April 30—was an advance man during Nixon's 1960 presidential campaign. He was a classmate of Haldeman at the University of California at Los Angeles.

Ehrlichman served as Nixon's "tour director" during the 1968 campaign. Before joining the campaign, he was associated with the law firm of Hullin, Ehrlichman, Roberts and Hodge in Seattle, Wash. He held no official post in the 1972 Nixon re-election campaign.

Source: AP Images

John D. Ehrlichman, adviser to President Richard Nixon

H. R. Haldeman

H. R. Haldeman, 46, was generally considered the most powerful man in the White House after the Presi-

H. R. Haldeman, assistant to President
Richard Nixon

dent until his resignation April 30. The crew-cut Haldeman, who had been an assistant to the President since 1969, was charged with running the White House, passing the President's ideas to subordinates and jealously guarding the President's schedule. He was born Oct. 27, 1926, in Los Angeles, and graduated from the University of California at Los Angeles.

Haldeman was an advance man in Nixon's 1960 presidential campaign, managed his 1962 try for the governorship of California and was chief of staff in Nixon's 1968 presidential campaign. Although he took no official part in the 1972 campaign, it has been reported Haldeman played a major role in directing the Committee for the Re-election of the President from the White House.

Many of the personalities connected to the Watergate affair either worked for Haldeman when he managed the J. Walter Thompson advertising agency's Los Angeles office in the 1960s or were recruited by him. Among them are John D. Ehrlichman, Haldeman's college classmate, and Dwight Chapin and Ronald Ziegler from the advertising firm.

E. Howard Hunt Jr.

E. Howard Hunt Jr., 54, is a former Central Intelligence Agency operative who pleaded guilty to all charges against him in the Watergate break-in and bugging trial. He served as White House consultant to his friend, Charles W. Colson, one of President Nixon's chief aides.

Born in Hamburg, N.Y., Oct. 9, 1918, he graduated from Brown University in 1940. After graduation he worked as a war correspondent, editorial writer and screenwriter before beginning a 21-year global career as a CIA agent. Over the years he also wrote 42 short stories and spy novels under several pseudonyms. He faces a maximum possible sentence of 35 years in jail and a $40,000 fine as a result of his Watergate conviction.

Hunt's wife died in a Dec. 8, 1972, plane crash in Chicago. Authorities examining the wreckage found $10,000 in $100 bills in Mrs. Hunt's purse.

E. Howard Hunt Jr., former CIA operative

Herbert W. Kalmbach

Herbert W. Kalmbach, 51, is President Nixon's personal attorney. A partner in the Los Angeles firm of Kalmbach, De Marco, Knapp and Chillingsworth, Kalmbach is a longtime associate of Nixon and Robert H. Finch, the former Nixon aide. He was born Oct. 19, 1921, in Port Huron, Mich., and graduated from the University of Southern California and its law school.

Kalmbach was the associate finance chairman of the 1968 Nixon for President campaign under Maurice H. Stans and acted as an unofficial fundraiser for President Nixon until the Committee for the Re-election of the President was organized.

G. Gordon Liddy

G. Gordon Liddy, 42, is probably the most flamboyant personality known to have been involved in the

Source: AP Images

G. Gordon Liddy, former counsel to President Richard Nixon's campaign finance committee

break-in at Democratic party headquarters. A former FBI agent, assistant district attorney and law-and-order candidate for Congress, Liddy was at one time considered to be the organizer of the ill-fated bugging attempt. He was convicted Jan. 3 by a U.S. district court jury of conspiracy, burglary and illegal wiretapping, and later refused to testify before the Watergate grand jury.

Born in New York City Nov. 30, 1930, Liddy is a graduate of Fordham University and Fordham law school. He spent five years with the FBI before joining the Dutchess County, N.Y., district attorney's office in 1965. In 1968 Liddy ran unsuccessfully for the Republican nomination in what was then New York's 28th congressional district.

After practicing law in his father's New York firm, Liddy became special assistant in the Treasury Department in 1969, where he gained his reputation for stubborn independence. An unauthorized speech on gun control led to his dismissal in 1971. Liddy joined the staff of the White House Domestic Council under John D. Ehrlichman in June 1971, but left that post in December 1971 to become general counsel to the Committee for the Re-election of the President. Four months later he moved to the finance committee as counsel.

Jeb Magruder

Jeb Magruder, 38, the first administration official to resign over the Watergate affair, was another of the California advertising and management types who populated the White House in the first Nixon term. He was in line for a high administration job in the second term, but assumed the vague position of planning director for the Commerce Department after being tainted by the Watergate trial. He testified at the trial that he helped establish what he thought to be a "legal" intelligence-gathering operation.

At the White House, which he joined in 1969, Magruder worked for Haldeman and Herbert G. Klein, communications director for the executive branch. He left the executive mansion in late 1971 to become deputy director of the Committee for the Re-election of the President.

The boyish-looking Magruder was born Nov. 5, 1934, in New York City. He graduated from Williams College and attended the University of Chicago's business school. He was regarded as a top-notch administrator, having worked in advertising and management before heading a small cosmetics firm in Santa Monica, Calif. He was a volunteer for Nixon, Sen. Barry Goldwater (R Ariz.) and former Rep. Donald Rumsfeld (R Ill.).

James W. McCord Jr.

When James Walter McCord Jr. was arrested along with four other men inside the Democratic headquarters last June 17, he was serving as security co-ordinator for the Nixon re-election committee and the Republican National Committee. He was fired the next day.

From 1951 until his retirement in 1971 McCord worked for the CIA, and before that, as a clerk and special agent at the FBI.

At his arrest McCord listed his birthday as Oct. 9, 1918, but *The New York Times* reported that bail records showed it to be July 26, 1924. News reports have quoted sources as saying he was born in Texas, and that he holds degrees from the University of Texas and George Washington University.

After retiring from the CIA, McCord started his own security consulting business, McCord Associates Inc., in Rockville, Md. In 1971 he taught a seminar entitled "Industrial and Retail Security" at Montgomery College in Maryland.

McCord was convicted Jan. 30 on eight counts of conspiracy, burglary and wiretapping. On March 23 Judge John J. Sirica read in court a letter McCord had written him charging that persons besides those convicted were involved in the Watergate case, that perjury had been committed during the trial and that political pressure had been applied to make the defendants plead guilty. On March 30 Sirica deferred McCord's sentencing until June 15. McCord testified March 28 in closed session before the Ervin committee investigating the Watergate.

John N. Mitchell

John N. Mitchell, 59, the President's former law partner, was Nixon's closest adviser on domestic and political affairs during his term as attorney general (1969–72) and director of the Committee for the Re-election of the President (March 1–July 1, 1972). Mitchell left the re-election committee after his wife, Martha, demanded publicly that he leave politics and "all those dirty things that go on."

Mitchell and Nixon were partners in the New York law firm of Mudge, Rose, Guthrie, Alexander and Mitchell, which Nixon joined after losing the 1962 California governor's race. Mitchell specialized in municipal bonds. He was born Sept. 5, 1913, in Detroit, and graduated from Fordham University and its law school.

Mitchell ran Nixon's 1968 campaign and served as an unofficial adviser in the 1972 campaign after he left the re-election committee. Mitchell was credited with developing the tough law-and-order stance which was a major campaign issue for Nixon in 1968. His famous watchword to reporters in the early days of Nixon's first term was, "Watch what we do, not what we say."

Source: AP Images

John N. Mitchell, former attorney general and director of the Committee for the Re-election of the President (CREEP).

Ken Rietz

Ken Rietz, 32, headed President Nixon's youth campaign in 1972. On March 1, 1973, he was named director of the Republican National Committee's "New Majority Campaign for 1974," a position he resigned from April 23, 1973. He was born May 3, 1941, in Oshkosh, Wis., and graduated from George Washington University.

Rietz first gained prominence as Sen. Bill Brock's (R Tenn.) campaign manager in 1970. Prior to that, he was active with the Wisconsin Republican organization in 1965 and 1966 and served as campaign director in 1966 and 1968 and legislative assistant in 1966–68 to Rep. William A. Steiger (R Wis.). In 1969, he was named assistant communications director and information director of the Republican National Committee.

Reitz's deputy on the campaign staff, George K. Gorton, reportedly has admitted that he hired and paid a George Washington University student last year to infiltrate radical groups. Gorton, 25, was hired March 19 by the Interior Department's Bicentennial Commission, but was removed from the job April 21. The appointment had been temporary, a department spokesman said.

Donald H. Segretti

Donald H. Segretti, 31, a California lawyer, has been under Justice Department investigation for reportedly directing a campaign of political sabotage on behalf of the Republican party during the 1972 presidential campaign. Segretti reportedly was paid at least $20,000 by the President's personal attorney, Herbert Kalmbach, with money from a secret fund kept in the office of former Secretary of Commerce Maurice Stans.

Born Sept. 17, 1941, in San Marino, Calif., a Los Angeles suburb, Segretti received a degree in finance from the University of Southern California in 1963. At USC he met Dwight Chapin, former appointments secretary to President Nixon and a Watergate figure.

After graduation, Segretti studied in Cambridge, England, for a year and then graduated from the University of Southern California law school. After a brief stint with the Treasury Department in Washington, he served as a captain in the Army Judge Advocate General's Corps and was discharged in 1971.

Maurice H. Stans

Maurice H. Stans, 65, was the chief fundraiser for the 1968 and 1972 Nixon-Agnew campaigns and is currently chairman of the Finance Committee to Re-elect the President. From Aug. 23, 1972, to Jan. 17, Stans served concurrently as chairman of the Republican National Finance Committee.

Stans resigned Feb. 15, 1972, as secretary of commerce, a post he had held since the start of the Nixon administration. He was born March 22, 1908, in Shakopee, Minn., and attended Northwestern and Columbia Universities.

Stans held several positions in the Eisenhower administration, including director of the Bureau of the Budget from 1958–60. Before heading the 1968 fundraising campaign, Stans was a New York investment banker.

Gordon C. Strachan

Gordon C. Strachan, 29, was staff assistant to presidential aide H. R. Haldeman from August 1970 until December 1972. In January 1973, Strachan became general counsel of the United States Information Agency. He resigned April 30, the same day as Haldeman. He was born July 24, 1943, in Berkeley, Calif., graduated from the University of Southern California and received his law degree from the University of California.

Strachan was an associate with Nixon's law firm of Mudge, Rose, Guthrie & Alexander from 1968 to 1970 and served as the liaison between Haldeman's office and the Committee for the Re-election of the President.

Ronald L. Ziegler

Ronald L. Ziegler, 33, the President's press secretary since 1969, has taken much of the heat from reporters over the Watergate affair—mainly because he is the only administration spokesman on the subject. His credibility was damaged badly by 10 months of denials of Watergate news stories as "fiction," "shabby journalism" and "character assassination," only to turn around after the President's April 17 statement and declare his past remarks "inoperative."

But Ziegler always did a good job of fending off the press and is believed to be a favorite of the President.

The press secretary is a protege of H. R. Haldeman, for whom he worked at the J. Walter Thompson advertising agency in Los Angeles.

Ziegler was born May 12, 1939, in Covington, Ky. He graduated from the University of Southern California in 1961 and immediately went to work as press secretary to California Republican legislators. He worked on Nixon's unsuccessful gubernatorial campaign in 1962 and was campaign press secretary for Nixon in 1968. He also aided in the 1964 campaign of former Sen. George Murphy (R Calif. 1965–71).

WATERGATE:

A Dramatic Switch by the White House

On April 17, Nixon announced a new policy at a brief news conference. He said that members of the White House staff would appear if the Senate Watergate Committee asked them to testify. The president, without going into detail, also said he was looking intensively into the Watergate affair because he had learned about serious new charges. He explained that any person in the government who was indicted by the grand jury would be suspended, and any person who was convicted would be fired. (An indictment is a formal charge of serious criminal wrongdoing.) This was a change from some of Nixon's earlier statements. Previously he had expressed absolute confidence that no one who was currently employed in his administration had any involvement in Watergate.

Even with his change of heart, Nixon said that witnesses could avoid certain questions by asserting executive privilege. Senate Watergate Committee chairman Sam Ervin, however, said his committee, rather than the president, would decide what questions must be answered.

As more evidence of wrongdoing came to light during the early spring, newspapers reported on evidence that former attorney general John N. Mitchell and John W. Dean III, the White House counsel, had approved and helped plan the Watergate break-in and bugging of June 17, 1972. Mitchell denounced the allegations. In another sign of the deepening scandal, the new attorney general, Richard G. Kleindienst, said he was disqualifying himself from further involvement in the Watergate case. He did not want to prosecute his colleagues in the Nixon administration.

By the end of April the capital was obsessed with Watergate. Some of Nixon's top aides had come under investigation. They included White House chief of staff H. R. Haldeman and Nixon's top domestic advisor, John D. Ehrlichman. Several grand juries, or special investigatory bodies, were looking into the scandal.

If public hearings on the Watergate scandal begin May 15 before a Senate investigating committee, as scheduled, some of the star witnesses will be members of the White House staff. Their willingness to testify was signaled by a dramatic reversal by President Nixon.

"All members of the White House staff will appear voluntarily when requested by the committee," Nixon said at a brief news conference on April 17. "They will testify under oath and they will answer fully all proper questions."

The President also told reporters that he had begun "intensive new inquiries" into the Watergate affair on March 21 "as a result of serious charges which came to my attention." Without further elaboration, he said there had been "major new developments in the case."

Sen. Sam J. Ervin Jr. (D N.C.), chairman of the committee, indicated April 19 that the hearings may have to be postponed if key witnesses are indicted.

Magruder Statements. *The Washington Post* April 19 reported that Jeb Stuart Magruder, former deputy director of the Committee for the Re-election of the President, had accused former Attorney General John N. Mitchell and John W. Dean III, the White House counsel, of approving and helping plan the Watergate break-in and bugging of June 17, 1972. Mitchell and Dean "later arranged to buy the silence of the seven convicted Watergate conspirators," according to the Post.

Mitchell denounced the report as "nonsense" April 19. But on April 20, *The New York Times* reported that Mitchell has told friends he attended three early-1972 meetings at which Watergate bugging proposals were discussed. He reportedly said he rejected the idea.

The Post said Magruder, former special assistant to Nixon and now a Commerce Department official, made the statements to federal prosecutors April 14.

Several news accounts said that testimony by Magruder and other Republicans was expected to result in criminal indictments of high-ranking Nixon re-election campaign officials. One source was quoted by the Post as saying Mitchell and Dean would be among those indicted.

Presidential Position. Indicating that some indictments might come out of the grand jury investigation in Washington, Nixon said at his news conference: "If any person in the executive branch or in the government is indicted by the grand jury, my policy will be to immediately suspend him. If he is convicted, he will, of course, be automatically discharged."

The President did not answer questions at the hastily summoned meeting with reporters. After the conference ended, his press secretary, Ronald L. Ziegler, said that all previous statements from the White House were "inoperative . . . the President's statement today is the operative statement."

WATERGATE ANNOUNCEMENT TEXT

The president said he had reached an agreement with the Senate Watergate Committee to allow his staffers to testify in front of the committee. This agreement, he said, would not violate the government's separation of powers. (The doctrine of separation of powers means that all three branches of government have equivalent powers, and no branch can be made subservient to the others. For more about the separation of powers, see p. 81.)

Nixon also said that he had made extensive inquiries into the scandal. He had met recently with his attorney general, who was the top law enforcement official in his administration. Without going into detail, Nixon said investigators were making great progress in uncovering the truth. He also pledged to suspend anyone in his administration who was indicted of a crime. Anyone convicted of a crime would be fired.

Following is the text of President Nixon's announcement on the Watergate scandal April 17.

I have two announcements to make. Because of their technical nature, I shall read both of the announcements to the members of the press corps.

The first announcement relates to the appearance of White House people before the Senate select committee, better known as the Ervin committee.

For several weeks. Sen. Ervin and Sen. Baker and their counsel have been in contact with White House representatives John Ehrlichman and Leonard Garment. They have been talking about ground rules which would preserve the separation of powers without suppressing the facts.

I believe now an agreement has been reached which is satisfactory to both sides. The committee ground rules as adopted totally preserve the doctrine of separation of powers. They provide that the appearance by a witness may, in the first instance, be in executive session, if appropriate.

Second, executive privilege is expressly reserved and may be asserted during the course of the questioning as to any questions.

Now, much has been made of the issue as to whether the proceedings could be televised. To me, this has never been a central issue, especially if the separation of powers problem is otherwise solved, as I now think it is.

All members of the White House staff will appear voluntarily when requested by the committee. They will testify under oath and they will answer fully all proper questions.

I should point out that this arrangement is one that covers this hearing only in which wrongdoing has been charged. This kind of arrangement, of course, would not apply to other hearings. Each of them will be considered on its merits.

My second announcement concerns the Watergate case directly.

On March 21, as a result of serious charges which came to my attention, some of which were publicly reported, I began intensive new inquiries into this whole matter.

Last Sunday afternoon, the Attorney General, Assistant Attorney General Petersen and I met at length in the EOB (Executive Office Building) to review the facts which had come to me in my investigation and also to review the progress of the Department of Justice investigation.

I can report today that there have been major developments in the case concerning which it would be improper to be more specific now, except to say that real progress has been made in finding the truth.

If any person in the executive branch or in the government is indicted by the grand jury, my policy will be to immediately suspend him. If he is convicted, he will, of course, be automatically discharged.

I have expressed to the appropriate authorities my views that no individual holding, in the past or at present, a position of major importance in the administration should be given immunity from prosecution.

The judicial process is moving ahead as it should; and I shall aid it in all appropriate ways and have so informed the appropriate authorities.

As I have said before and I have said throughout this entire matter, all government employees and especially White House staff employees are expected fully to cooperate in this matter. I condemn any attempts to cover up in this case, no matter who is involved.

Ervin Response. Nixon's reversal of position apparently averted a showdown with the chairman of the Senate select committee on the Watergate, Sam J. Ervin Jr. (D N.C.). Ervin had insisted that past and present members of the White House staff be available to testify under oath before the committee. Nixon had refused to permit his staff to testify, arguing that they were protected from doing so by the doctrine of executive privilege.

BACKGROUND OF EXECUTIVE PRIVILEGE

Executive privilege refers to the right of a president to withhold certain information from Congress and the courts. Otherwise, presidents would not be able to keep any documents private. Although the Constitution does not mention executive privilege, every president has asserted it.

The concept of executive privilege dates back to George Washington. In 1791 the government was embarrassed by a disastrous military operation along the frontier. Congress launched an investigation. Lawmakers demanded that the president turn over any documents about the decision to launch the operation.

In response, Washington declared that he had the constitutional right to refuse to turn over the information—but only if withholding it was in the best interest of the public. In other words, he could not refuse to turn over documents simply to protect himself from being embarrassed for bad leadership. In this case, he decided there was

no public harm in cooperating with Congress. Accordingly, he gave Congress all the information it had requested.

With his actions, Washington established two important precedents. First, he determined that presidents have the right to keep certain documents from becoming public. Second, presidents should use executive privilege only to protect the nation, rather than themselves.

Executive privilege is based on the doctrine of separation of powers. In our government, each of the three branches—the executive, legislative, and judiciary—has certain responsibilities. No branch can become more powerful than the others. Without executive privilege, a president would not be able to stop the other branches from taking his private papers, and he would lose some power. Presidents have always conducted much of their work out of the public eye because they deal with such sensitive issues as protecting the national security, negotiating foreign treaties, and weighing economic decisions that can affect entire industries.

The right of executive privilege has evolved over the nation's history. Washington himself, later in his presidency, refused to turn over certain diplomatic letters to Congress because he felt the full disclosure of the private letters would be inappropriate. Other early presidents, including Thomas Jefferson and James Madison, also classified certain correspondence as secret. Congress did not challenge their right to do so.

In the twentieth century, President Dwight Eisenhower greatly expanded the concept of executive privilege. In the past, presidents had defined it as applying only to themselves and to high-level White House officials. But Eisenhower at one point seemed to say it applied to the entire executive branch.

Nixon went far beyond any of his predecessors in invoking executive privilege. He repeatedly refused to turn over Watergate documents to investigators. His lawyers at one point implied that, regardless of how a court might rule, the president alone had the authority to decide which documents were protected by executive privilege. Nixon even went as far as to use executive privilege to try to protect low-ranking officials in his administration.

These tactics frustrated investigators who wanted to get to the bottom of Watergate. Critics accused Nixon of abusing his power to protect himself and his staff from criminal charges. Nixon's actions became so controversial that the next several presidents were careful not to use executive privilege very often.

In recent years, however, presidents have started using executive privilege more expansively. President Bill Clinton, for example, lost a court battle when he tried to invoke executive privilege to block an investigation into alleged misdeeds by his agriculture secretary. President George W. Bush aggressively used executive privilege to limit public access to presidential papers even years after a president has left office. (See p. 60 for another look at executive privilege.)

Nixon said on April 17 that discussions had been going on for several weeks among Ervin; Sen. Howard H. Baker Jr. (R Tenn.), vice chairman of the investigating committee; the majority and minority counsels to the committee, and John D. Ehrlichman and Leonard Garment of the White House staff. The ground rules adopted in the discussions "totally preserve the doctrine of separation of powers," the President said. He added that "the appearance by a witness may, in the first instance, be in executive session, if appropriate," and that "executive privilege is expressly reserved and may be asserted during the course of the questioning as to any questions."

Ervin called Nixon's decision to allow his staff to testify before the committee "a victory for constitutional government." But he made clear that the committee would be the final judge of whether White House witnesses could refuse to answer questions. "Somebody has to rule on that point," Ervin said, "and these guidelines expressly say that the committee's going to do the ruling. If the committee rules adversely to the witness on any question of privilege, the committee shall require the witness to testify."

Kleindienst Withdrawal. Attorney General Richard G. Kleindienst disqualified himself from further involvement in the Watergate case on April 19 so that he would not have to put himself in the position of prosecuting present or former colleagues in the Nixon administration. His decision, he said, "relates to persons with whom I have had personal and professional relationships."

Kleindienst announced that Assistant Attorney General Henry Peterson would take full control of the Justice Department's criminal investigation of the Watergate. Petersen had been in charge of the investigation, reporting to Kleindienst.

Mitchell, who resigned as attorney general to become Nixon's campaign manager in March 1972, was quoted by *The New York Times* as praising Kleindienst's decision as "entirely appropriate and correct." Mitchell told the Times that if Kleindienst had stayed with the investigation, "no matter what he did he would be accused of playing politics, because he knew so many of the people who have been mentioned in this thing."

Dean's Role. John Dean, the President's counsel, was not involved in the discussions between the White House and the Senate committee. Nixon made no reference to him in his April 17 statement. Dean had come under attack for his refusal to testify at Senate confirmation hearings on L. Patrick Gray III as permanent FBI director, claiming executive privilege.

In response to the attacks, Nixon had phoned Dean from Key Biscayne, Fla., on March 26 to express his personal confidence in him. In his April 17 statement, the President said he had met on April 15, as part of his investigation, with Kleindienst and Petersen. Ziegler, pressed by reporters about Dean's role, said the President "felt it was not appropriate that any member of the White House staff be involved in further investigation." Dean had conducted the first investigation for the White House in 1972.

In its April 19 story, *The Washington Post,* quoting White House sources, said that Dean's resignation was considered imminent.

But Dean himself cast doubt on that prediction when he issued this statement the same day:

"To date I have refrained from making any public comments whatsoever about the Watergate case. I shall continue that policy in the future, because I believe that the case will be fully and justly handled by the grand jury and the Ervin select committee.

"It is my hope, however, that those truly interested in seeing that the Watergate case is completely aired and that justice is done will be careful in drawing any conclusions as to the guilt or involvement of any persons until all the facts are known and until each person has had an opportunity to testify under oath in his own behalf.

"Finally, some may hope or think that I will become a scapegoat in the Watergate case. Anyone who believes this does not know me, know the true facts nor understand our system of justice."

As early as August 1972 and as late as March 1973, the President had expressed confidence in his staff. On Aug. 29, 1972, he said at a news conference, "I can say categorically that his (Dean's) investigation indicates that no one in the White House staff, no one in this administration, presently employed, was involved in this very bizarre incident."

Civil Suits

Apart from the criminal investigation into Watergate, the courts also dealt with a number of civil lawsuits. A civil lawsuit takes place when a person or an organization sues another, usually for a sum of money. In this case, the chairman of the Democratic Party sued the Republican Party over the Watergate break-in. Several other lawsuits also had been filed during the 1972 election campaign. Although these lawsuits were not nearly as important as the criminal investigation, they reveal that political organizations often turn to the courts to defeat their opponents.

In addition to the President's new attitude of cooperation with Senate investigators, the Republican Party reportedly was making some moves of its own toward settling one of three civil suits pending in U.S. District Court in Washington, D.C. The suit, filed just after the June 1972 break-in at Democratic national headquarters, charges the Republican Party with conspiring to violate the civil rights of Lawrence F. O'Brien, then Democratic national chairman, and other Democratic officials. The suit seeks $6.4 million in damages.

The Washington Post reported April 18 that conversations had been held between attorneys for the Democrats and Republicans concerning possible out-of-court settlement of the suit. The amount reportedly involved in the conversations was $525,000. Lawyers and party officials did not deny the report, and Democratic Chairman Robert S. Strauss confirmed that conversations had been held.

"We are not in accord," Strauss said on April 18, "but we have talked both in person and on the telephone within the last couple of weeks." Strauss was under considerable pressure from some state chairmen, it was learned, not to settle out of court for the amount reportedly discussed.

Points to Ponder

- If a congressional committee wanted to obtain all the president's documents dealing with an important threat to national security, should the president turn them over? What about documents touching on a sensitive political issue, such as policies about abortion? Under what situations should a president be required to turn over documents?

- If a president is elected by the people and answerable to the people, why should he or she have the right to refuse to share information with them or with Congress?

- If Congress wants documents that might show wrongdoing by one of the president's top aides, should it have the power to force the president to turn them over?

- What worries you more—a top presidential aide evading justice or the nation's well-being being put at risk by documents that are shared with Congress?

WATERGATE:

Traumatic Week for the Administration

In late April and early May, the administration was buffeted by a torrent of disclosures and charges. By the end of April, a number of President Nixon's top aides resigned. Nixon tried to put a brave face on the situation. He met with members of his cabinet and told them, "We've had our Cambodias before." This was a reference to the bitter public criticism he faced in 1970 for his decision to invade Cambodia.

But *The Washington Post, The New York Times,* and other newspapers reported a remarkable series of allegations on April 20 and for the next several days. These allegations indicated that top Nixon aides may have tried to protect the Watergate conspirators and blocked investigations into the break-in:

- Former attorney general and former Nixon campaign manager John N. Mitchell testified before a grand jury in Washington. He allegedly said that he had approved payments of Nixon's campaign funds to the seven Watergate conspirators after their arrests.
- John W. Dean III, the White House counsel, was reported to have supervised cash payments of $175,000 in Republican campaign funds to the seven Watergate defendants and their lawyers after the break-in. The alleged purpose of the payments was to silence the defendants.
- The federal grand jury was said to be investigating the possibility that H. R. Haldeman, the White House chief of staff, had a role in the Watergate bugging or in later attempts to block investigations into the case. Government prosecutors were trying to determine whether a secret $350,000 fund had been used by Haldeman's office to pay off the defendants and their lawyers. The grand jury was said to be investigating whether Haldeman had received transcripts obtained through the wiretapping of Democratic national headquarters.
- Government prosecutors reportedly established that most of the payments to the conspirators were made by Frederick C. LaRue, an aide to Mitchell when Mitchell was Nixon's campaign manager. Haldeman's former political aide was said to have testified that

Haldeman had ordered him to give $350,000 to LaRue to pay the conspirators.
- During the winter and spring of 1972–73, members of the presidential staff were said to have warned Nixon that some of his aides, including Mitchell and Dean, were involved in the Watergate bugging and subsequent coverup.
- Newspapers disclosed the existence of a secret fund of up to $500,000. At least part of that money had been used to pay for Republican sabotage and espionage operations in the 1972 campaign. The fund was allegedly controlled by the president's personal lawyer, Herbert W. Kalmbach.
- Federal investigators were believed to have determined that significant political information obtained from the Watergate wiretaps was turned over to White House officials.

A SERIES OF RESIGNATIONS

Shortly before the end of April, the administration suffered two high-profile resignations. The first former White House or campaign official to resign from the administration was Jeb Stuart Magruder. On April 26, he quit his job as director of policy development at the Commerce Department.

On April 27, the acting director of the FBI, L. Patrick Gray III, resigned one day after the press reported that he had destroyed documents belonging to a Watergate conspirator. The reports said White House advisor John D. Ehrlichman and Dean told Gray to destroy the documents, which "should never see the light of day." One group of documents may have included phony State Department cables that were designed to implicate former president John F. Kennedy, a Democrat, in the 1963 assassination of the South Vietnamese president. Other documents contained material on a 1969 automobile accident involving Democratic senator Edward M. Kennedy of Massachusetts, who was viewed by many as a potential rival to Nixon. Ehrlichman denied that he knew the contents of the files and had told Gray what to do with them. Gray said he had not examined the papers and did not know their contents.

WHITE HOUSE RESIGNATIONS

"Today, in one of the most difficult decisions of my Presidency, I accepted the resignations of two of my closest associates in the White House—Bob Haldeman, John Ehrlichman—two of the finest public servants it has been my privilege to know.

"I want to stress that in accepting these resignations, I mean to leave no implication whatever of personal wrongdoing on their part, and I leave no implication tonight of implication on the part of others who have been charged in this matter. But in matters as sensitive as guarding the integrity of our democratic process, it is essential not only that rigorous legal and ethical standards be observed, but also that the public, you, have total confidence that they are both being observed and enforced by those in authority and particularly by the President of the United States. They agreed with me that this move was necessary in order to restore that confidence. . . . The Counsel to the President, John Dean has also resigned."

—*President Nixon in address to the nation,*
April 30, 1973

Damaging as these resignations were, they were but a taste of what was to come. On April 30, Nixon announced the resignations of four of his top advisors: Haldeman, Ehrlichman, Dean, and Attorney General Richard G. Kleindienst. Addressing the nation that night, Nixon said he took full responsibility for any improper activities connected with his 1972 presidential campaign. He pledged that "justice will be pursued fairly, fully and impartially." But a Gallup Poll published May 4 found that large percentages of Americans did not think Nixon had told the whole truth in this speech, and that he had participated in a coverup.

CRIMINAL CHARGES

Nixon, losing several of his most trusted advisors, faced the difficult task of filling key White House positions. At the same time, several of his former aides faced criminal charges. On May 10, a federal grand jury indicted two past members of Nixon's Cabinet: Attorney General John N. Mitchell and Secretary of Commerce Maurice H. Stans. The men were accused of obstructing justice by interfering with a federal investigation and lying to the Watergate grand jury. They allegedly had obtained a secret $200,000 cash contribution to the Nixon campaign. In return for the contribution, they allegedly had promised to help the contributor, Robert L. Vesco, who was being investigated by the government for financial swindling.

Many members of Congress worried about the Justice Department investigation of Watergate. They did not believe the executive branch should be investigating itself. Instead, they wanted an investigator who would be independent of the president. On May 1, the Senate passed a resolution asking Nixon to appoint a special prosecutor to head the investigation.

The press continued to report damaging allegations. On May 1, it was disclosed that the president had directed Ehrlichman in 1971 to investigate the Pentagon Papers leak. (See box on Pentagon Papers, p. 44.) The result was the hiring of two men who were later convicted conspirators in the Watergate break-in: E. Howard Hunt and G. Gordon Liddy. In a bizarre turn of events, it was revealed that the two men allegedly burglarized the office of the psychiatrist of Pentagon Papers defendant Daniel Ellsberg.

The Justice Department on May 2 filed criminal charges against the Finance Committee to Re-elect the President for allegedly concealing Vesco's $200,000 contribution. Perhaps most damaging, government investigators appeared to be gathering evidence implicating high-ranking officials in the White House and the president's re-election committee in a coverup of the Watergate break-in.

The burgeoning Watergate scandal unreeled with breathtaking speed in the week ending May 5. The week's developments in the many-faceted drama led to partial paralysis of the Nixon administration. The President himself publicly accepted responsibility for any wrongdoing in the affair. A cabinet officer and three of Nixon's top assistants resigned. The taint of corruption reached into the Pentagon Papers trial in Los Angeles.

PENTAGON PAPERS

The Pentagon Papers, a 47-volume study of U.S. involvement in the Vietnam War, led indirectly to the Watergate scandal. Portions of the documents were leaked to *The New York Times* in 1971. The *Times* published excerpts and summaries, which painted a highly critical picture of the U.S. government. The documents revealed, for example, that President Lyndon B. Johnson, Nixon's predecessor, had deliberately expanded the war even while he was assuring the public that he would not expand it.

The Nixon administration had nothing to do with the Pentagon Papers, and it could have rejected their depiction of the war. But Nixon fiercely opposed leaks by government officials. He directed the Justice Department to stop the *Times* from publishing the documents on the grounds that they could harm national security. An epic legal battle ensued, with the Supreme Court eventually allowing the *Times* and other newspapers to print the documents.

But Nixon would not let the issue go. The White House looked into the leak and determined that Daniel Ellsberg, a Pentagon employee, had been the culprit. In a wide-ranging investigation of Ellsberg, the White House learned he had been seeing a psychiatrist in Los Angeles. FBI agents tried to question the psychiatrist, but he refused to cooperate because a doctor's dealings with a patient are typically confidential.

At this point, "the plumbers" unit in the White House took over. The plumbers got their name because their task was to prevent leaks. On the orders of John Ehrlichman, they broke into the psychiatrist's office on September 2, 1971, to find Ellsberg's file. After they didn't find anything, they scattered pills on the floor so that police would assume the break-in was related to drugs. The real motive for the break-in was not disclosed until the Watergate scandal was being investigated.

Because the plumbers were able to break in without being caught, high White House officials believed such tactics could be successfully used in the 1972 presidential campaign. G. Gordon Liddy, who was one of the plumbers, proposed a $1 million plan that included wiretaps and break-ins of key Democratic officials. White House officials who examined the plan included Attorney General John N. Mitchell, who later resigned to run Nixon's campaign, and John Dean, the counsel to the president. Eventually, a scaled-back version of Liddy's plan was approved for $250,000. This plan would result in the Watergate break-in.

Climactic Events

These were the highlights of the week's climactic events:

- The President April 30 announced the resignation of four men: H. R. Haldeman, White House chief of staff; John D. Ehrlichman, chief counselor for domestic affairs; John W. Dean III, presidential counsel; and Attorney General Richard G. Kleindienst. At the same time, Nixon announced the nomination of Defense Secretary Elliot L. Richardson as attorney general and the appointment of Leonard Garment as presidential counsel.
- Alexander M. Haig Jr., Army vice chief of staff and former chief deputy to Henry A. Kissinger, Nixon's national security adviser, was appointed interim White House chief of staff May 4.
- Addressing the nation the night of April 30, Nixon said he took full responsibility for any improper activities connected with his 1972 presidential campaign and pledged that "justice will be pursued fairly, fully and impartially." The President said Richardson would have full charge of the administration's Watergate investigations and would have authority to appoint a special prosecutor in the case.
- A Gallup Poll published May 4 found that 40 per cent of the 456 persons questioned did not think Nixon had told the whole truth in this speech. Fifty per cent said they thought he had participated in a coverup.

POLL REPORT: DAMAGE TO NIXON FROM WATERGATE AFFAIR

Watergate has taken a serious toll with the public in President Nixon's popularity and credibility ratings, according to the latest Harris Survey. The survey was conducted among 1,537 households April 18–23, before the President's television speech April 30.

These were the questions and responses in the Harris poll, published April 29:

"Do you feel that the White House has been frank and honest on the Watergate affair, or do you feel they have withheld important information about it?"

Frank and honest	9%
Withheld important information	63
Not sure	28

"How would you rate President Nixon on his handling of the Watergate political spying case—excellent, pretty good, only fair, or poor?"

Excellent to pretty good (positive)	17%
Only fair to poor (negative)	61
Not sure	22

"How would you rate President Nixon on his handling of corruption in government—excellent, pretty good, only fair, or poor?"

	April	February	October 1972
Positive	25%	32%	32%
Negative	64	55	55
Not sure	11	13	13

"How would you rate President Nixon on inspiring confidence personally in the White House—excellent, pretty good, only fair, or poor?"

	April	March	February	January
Positive	50%	59%	60%	53%
Negative	49	39	39	45
Not sure	1	2	1	2

- It was disclosed on May 1 that Ehrlichman had told FBI interviewers on April 27 that the President had directed him in 1971 to undertake an independent investigation of the Pentagon Papers leak. Ehrlichman hired E. Howard Hunt and G. Gordon Liddy—convicted conspirators in the Watergate break-in—to conduct the probe, which led to the burglary of the office of Pentagon Papers defendant Daniel Ellsberg's psychiatrist. Ehrlichman said he had not authorized the burglary and that when he learned about it, he instructed Hunt and Liddy "not to do this again."

- The judge in the Pentagon Papers trial, W. Matthew Byrne Jr., confirmed May 2 that he had discussed a possible job offer as FBI director with Ehrlichman on April 5 and April 7. Byrne said he refused to "discuss or consider" the offer until the Pentagon Papers trial had been concluded.

- Ehrlichman's name had surfaced April 27 in connection with allegations that he had promised on at least two occasions to help accused mutual fund swindler Robert L. Vesco, a big contributor to the 1972 Nixon campaign, take over a scandal-ridden Lebanese bank. Ehrlichman said he had met once with Vesco's representatives, but he denied providing any assistance.

A similar intercession on behalf of Vesco by John N. Mitchell was reported May 1. The intercession allegedly took place while Mitchell was still attorney general; it was the third alleged intercession by Mitchell on behalf of Vesco.

The Justice Department May 2 filed criminal charges against the Finance Committee to Re-elect the President for allegedly concealing a $200,000 contribution made by Vesco.

- *The New York Times* reported May 2 that government investigators had gathered evidence implicating high-ranking officials in the White House and the President's re-election committee in an elaborate coverup of White House involvement in the June 17, 1972, Watergate break-in.

- Donald H. Segretti, a California lawyer, was indicted by a grand jury in Orlando, Fla., May 4 on charges of distributing a phony letter on the stationery of Sen. Edmund S. Muskie (Maine), a 1972 candidate for the Democratic presidential nomination. The letter accused two other candidates, Senators Henry M. Jackson (Wash.) and Hubert H. Humphrey (Minn.), of sexual misconduct.

Scandals for Harding, Truman, Eisenhower

The following article summarizes three major presidential scandals in the twentieth century that occurred before Watergate. By the end of the century, two additional presidents, Ronald Reagan and Bill Clinton, faced significant scandals:

Iran-contra. In late 1986, the administration of President Ronald Reagan was shaken by serious allegations. White House officials were said to have sold arms to Iran, an enemy of the United States. They also were said to have used money from the sales to fund a right-wing guerilla group in Nicaragua known as the contras. Both actions violated laws passed by Congress.

The charges sparked a series of investigations. Eventually a special prosecutor charged 14 people with crimes, of whom 11 were convicted. The group included Secretary of Defense Caspar W. Weinberger, as well as two national security advisors, the assistant secretary of state, and several CIA officers. Two of the convictions were overturned on legal grounds. A special review board that included former senator John Tower issued a highly critical report that blamed Reagan for failing to properly supervise the National Security Council.

In 1987, Reagan went on national television to express regret for what happened. His poll ratings dropped briefly to below 50 percent. But by the time he left the presidency in 1989, his popularity had rebounded.

Clinton impeachment. In 1998, President Bill Clinton faced the gravest crisis of his presidency. A special investigator looking into an unrelated charge came across evidence that Clinton lied when he was questioned before a grand jury about his relationship with a White House intern, Monica Lewinsky. Lying under oath is a serious crime known as perjury.

Republican members of Congress, who were frequently at odds with the Democratic president, demanded his ouster. With a majority in the House, they moved quickly to impeach him. Democrats, however, opposed impeachment. While they agreed that Clinton acted improperly, they argued that he had lied about a personal matter and therefore should not face impeachment.

The House narrowly passed two counts of impeachment in December 1998. One count was for perjury and the second was for obstruction of justice. Clinton thus became the second president in history, after Andrew Johnson in 1868, to be impeached. The Senate held a trial in early 1999. It acquitted Clinton, with every Democrat and several

Republicans voting against removing him from office.

Polls showed that most Americans opposed impeachment. Clinton remained popular until he left office in 2001. However, Clinton faced disciplinary action from the legal community, including a $90,000 fine. He was banned from practicing law in his native state of Arkansas for five years.

Scandals involving cabinet officers or high level presidential assistants have shaken at least three previous administrations in this century. In contrast to the Watergate affair, the earlier affairs involved allegations of bribery or influence peddling for economic favors.

Presidents Warren G. Harding, Harry S Truman and Dwight D. Eisenhower all faced crises involving alleged wrongdoing by those close to them. Harding died just as the massive scandals which became the hallmark of his administration were beginning to break into the open. His Vice President and successor, Calvin Coolidge, moved quickly to deal with the corruption and his actions have been credited with saving his new administration and the Republican Party from much of the onus.

But Presidents Truman and Eisenhower attempted for a time to defend their aides, thereby incurring political damage for seeming to be reluctant to take corrective actions. Republican promises to clean up the Truman administration's "mess in Washington" were used effectively in the 1952 presidential campaign. And the huge Democratic gains in the 1958 mid-term elections have been attributed in part to the influence-peddling charges made against President Eisenhower's chief assistant, Sherman Adams.

Key elements in all the scandals were vigorous congressional investigations and widespread press coverage.

Following is an account of the three major episodes of scandal in modern American political history.

Harding: Teapot Dome

The Harding administrations scandals—which actually broke in full force after the President's death on Aug. 2, 1923—resulted in the resignations of Attorney General Harry M. Daugherty and Secretary of the Navy Edwin Denby, the dismissal of William J. Burns as head of the Bureau of Investigation (subsequently re-named the Federal Bureau of Investigation), and the later conviction and imprisonment of Secretary of the Interior Albert B. Fall.

The central scandal, known as Teapot Dome, involved leases of naval oil reserves. Congress in 1920 had enacted the General Leasing Act, which authorized the secretary of the Navy under certain conditions to lease naval oil reserves on public lands to private oil operators.

Harding on May 31, 1921, signed an executive order at the urging of Interior Secretary Fall and Navy Secretary Denby by transferring jurisdiction over the naval oil reserves from the Navy to the Interior Department. Then, early in 1922, Fall leased the Elk Hills reserve in California to Edward L. Doheny of the Pan-American Petroleum and Transport Company and the Teapot Dome reserve in Wyoming to Harry F. Sinclair's Mammoth Oil Company. The leases were granted without public notice or competitive bidding.

When Senate hearings opened on Oct. 25, 1923, they concentrated at first on the legality and expediency of the two leases. Then Sen. Thomas J. Walsh (D Mont. 1913–33) began probing the sudden wealth of former Interior Secretary Fall who had resigned in March 1923. The investigation revealed that Fall had accepted bribes from Doheny and Sinclair. Doheny had given Fall at least $100,000 and Sinclair had given the interior secretary at least $300,000. Fall was later convicted of accepting a bribe in connection with the Elk Hills lease and was sentenced to prison and fined $100,000.

Fall became the first cabinet officer to serve a prison term for illegal activities connected with government service. Navy Secretary Denby also resigned, but was never charged with criminal acts.

Justice Department Inaction. The Justice Department also came under fire for its handling of Teapot Dome. Attorney General Harry M. Daugherty's failure to prosecute Fall, Sinclair, Doheny and others led President Coolidge on March 28, 1924, to demand Daugherty's resignation.

To replace Daugherty as attorney general, Coolidge appointed Harlan Fiske Stone, former dean of Columbia University's Law School, with instructions to clean up the Justice Department. Stone later went on to become an associate justice of the United States Supreme Court, and served as chief justice from 1941 to 1946.

One of Stone's first moves as attorney general was to revamp the Bureau of Investigation. William J. Burns, founder of the detective agency that bears his name, was serving as head of the bureau. Stone later wrote, "When I became attorney general, the Bureau of Investigation was . . . in exceedingly bad odor. . . . The head of the Bureau . . . had himself participated in serious infractions of the law and obstructions of justice." As a replacement, Stone appointed the young assistant director, J. Edgar Hoover.

Truman: Vaughan and Caudle

The last years of President Harry S Truman's administration were rocked by a series of scandals involving White House aides and Justice Department officials. The abrupt dismissal of Attorney General J. Howard McGrath and his replacement by federal judge James P. McGranery of Philadelphia in the spring of 1952 was the most dramatic event in a string of events that began in 1949.

The first Truman aide to come to public attention in connection with possible wrongdoing was Gen. Harry Vaughan, the President's military aide as well as a personal friend. Charges were made before a special Senate investigation subcommittee that Vaughan had used his influence to gain quick action on a number of projects for clients of friends. Vaughan came under congressional fire for accepting a present of a deep freeze from a Chicago company, a gift that became widely used by editorial cartoonists as a symbol of corruption in Washington. Despite the allegation, Vaughan remained in Truman's favor throughout the administration.

> *"In this job I am not worried about my enemies. It is my friends that are keeping me awake nights."*
> —Warren G. Harding, 1923

A second scandal involved the Reconstruction Finance Corporation (RFC) and Donald Dawson, special assistant to President Truman for personnel affairs. The RFC, established in 1932 under the Hoover administration to provide easy credit terms to failing businesses, was kept going after World War II as a hedge against a possible recession. A subcommittee of the Senate Banking and Currency Committee headed by freshman Sen. J. William Fulbright (D) of Arkansas cited Dawson as wielding undue influence on who received loans from the RFC. No criminal charges were brought, and like Vaughan, Dawson was kept on in the White House despite implications of questionable activities.

The most serious corruption in Truman's presidency, and the one which led to large-scale resignations and eventual jail terms for some of those implicated, involved the Justice Department and the Bureau of Internal Revenue (now known as the Internal Revenue Service). Among the senior officials implicated in charges of fixing tax cases were T. Lamar Caudle, assistant attorney general in charge of the Tax Division; Charles Oliphant, general counsel to the Bureau of Internal Revenue; George J. Schoenman, Internal Revenue Commissioner; Joseph Nunan, a former Internal Revenue Commissioner; Jess Larson, chief of the General Services Administration, and Matthew H. Connelly, Truman's appointments secretary. Much of the evidence in the cases was uncovered by a special investigating subcommittee of the House

Ways and Means Committee. Altogether, 66 persons in the Bureau of Internal Revenue and the Justice Department were ousted, and nine—including Caudle and Connelly—ended up in prison.

In the face of these charges, Truman appointed Attorney General McGrath to head a cleanup drive. Truman's announcement met with opposition because McGrath was a former chairman of the Democratic National Committee (1947–49) and was the head of the Justice Department when much of the alleged activity had occurred. The House Judiciary Committee reacted by voting to investigate McGrath and the Justice Department.

Independent Prosecutor Appointed. Truman finally appointed Newbold Morris, a prominent liberal Republican lawyer from New York, as a special prosecutor. When McGrath and Morris feuded, the attorney general let the special prosecutor go, and was in turn fired by Truman. Truman brought in Judge McGranery as his new attorney general, but no successor to Morris was named. The Justice Department's handling of the case, concluded a House Judiciary subcommittee, raised "additional doubts in the public mind as to the honesty of those in public office."

Eisenhower: Sherman Adams

In 1958, President Eisenhower's White House chief of staff, Sherman Adams, stood accused of interference in the activities of federal regulatory agencies. The controversy culminated in Adams' resignation.

On Feb. 17, 1958, evidence was presented to a special House Legislative Oversight Subcommittee that Adams had attempted to influence a case pending before the Civil Aeronautics Board in 1953. On May 26, the subcommittee heard testimony regarding a 1953 letter sent by then FCC Chairman Rosel H. Hyde to Adams reporting on the status of contests for TV licenses in St. Louis, Mo., and Flint, Mich.

Then on June 5, acting Chairman John Bell Williams (D Miss. 1947–68) said the subcommittee had authenticated information that Adams had occupied hotel rooms in Boston paid for by Bernard Goldfine, a Boston textile magnate who was involved in cases before the Federal Trade Commission and the Securities and Exchange Commission. Revelations followed concerning gifts of a $700 vicuna coat and a $2,400 oriental rug Adams had received from Goldfine.

Press coverage of the relationship between Adams and Goldfine prompted President Eisenhower to issue a statement of support for Adams on June 18, 1958. While admitting that Adams may have been "imprudent" in his relations with Goldfine, the President said Adams was an "invaluable public servant, doing a difficult job efficiently, honestly, and tirelessly." "I need him," the President said.

But the furor did not subside. Republicans concerned about the impact of the Adams affair on the upcoming mid-term election began voicing their fears. Senate Republican leader William F. Knowland (R Calif. 1945–59) said Adams "has so hurt his usefulness in his position that it will be harmful to the broad policies" of the President.

> *"The trouble with Republicans is that when they get in trouble they start acting like cannibals."*
> —Richard M. Nixon, 1958

Rep. Richard M. Simpson (R Pa.), chairman of the Republican Congressional Campaign Committee, said Adams' activities "can only be harmful" to the GOP at election time.

Throughout the summer, the subcommittee's investigations continued to keep the case in the public mind.

On Sept. 22, 1958, Adams resigned his position in a nationwide radio and television address. He said he "must give full consideration to the effect of (his) continuing presence on the public scene." He referred to "a campaign of vilification by those who seek personal advantage by my removal from public life." Adams said testimony before the subcommittee had established that he had done "no wrong."

President Eisenhower, in a letter accepting his assistant's resignation, commended Adams for his "self-less and tireless devotion to the work of the White House and to me personally. . . ."

Goldfine served a jail sentence for contempt of court and income tax evasion. Adams continued to deny any wrongdoing and retired to New Hampshire. No charges were ever pressed against him.

Points to Ponder

The resignation of high-profile presidential aides, allegations of improprieties in the White House, and falling poll numbers were a blow to President Nixon's credibility.

- If you were the president's chief of staff, what advice would you give him on managing a political crisis like Watergate, or Monicagate, or Iran-contra?

- How did President George W. Bush respond to low public opinion ratings in his second term? How was President Clinton boosted by high ratings in most of his second term?

- What steps can a president take to restore the public's confidence in his honesty and integrity after a crisis has faded?

- Do you believe that public approval of a president is a good barometer of how the president is doing? Or is the public often wrong? Can you think of a decision that a president might make that would be unpopular at the time but in retrospect would emerge as the right thing to do?

- Given that each branch of our government is considered equally powerful, who should investigate the executive branch if it is suspected of wrongdoing? Can an executive agency, such as the FBI, conduct a fair and thorough investigation of the executive branch? If not, do Congress or the courts have the authority to investigate the executive branch? What if another branch of government, such as Congress, is accused of violating the law? Could the FBI investigate Congress without undermining the independence of the legislative branch?

WATERGATE:

Indictments, High-Level Reorganization

The news media, Congress, and federal grand juries all had significant roles in uncovering the Watergate scandal. But they went about it in very different ways.

Investigative journalism came of age during Watergate. A number of reporters doggedly unearthed key documents, found sources who could tell them about the scandal, and wrote electrifying articles about misdeeds at high levels of government. Without the efforts of these reporters—especially Bob Woodward and Carl Bernstein of *The Washington Post*—the full story of the scandal may not have been revealed.

The news media, however, did not have the power to force Nixon out of the White House. That role fell to Congress, which has the constitutional power to impeach a president and remove him from office. Both the House of Representatives and the Senate launched in-depth investigations of the White House, often building on the groundwork laid by the press. Once sufficient evidence was gathered, the House of Representatives began impeachment proceedings. Such a move was extraordinary. Only once before in American history had a president been impeached.

Federal grand juries also figured prominently during the scandal. Grand juries, composed of private citizens, have broad powers to investigate alleged crimes under the guidance of prosecutors. They can interview witnesses under oath and issue subpoenas, or legal orders, to gain access to important evidence. The Watergate grand jury in Washington, and several grand juries elsewhere, concluded that top executive branch officials had committed serious crimes in connection with the Watergate break-in. They issued indictments (formal criminal charges) against some of Nixon's most powerful aides.

Thanks to the Constitution's guarantee of a free press, reporters have always played an important role in the nation's political history. But newspapers were especially important during the early days of the Watergate scandal. *The Washington Post, The New York Times,* and other leading papers broke many stories about the scandal, raising charges of serious wrongdoing by high government officials. Reporters developed excellent sources in the Nixon administration who helped them expose corrupt activities. These sources in many cases were officials who were dismayed by the extent of wrongdoing taking place around them. Not surprisingly, Nixon and his most trusted aides issued barbed attacks on reporters. But they could not stop the stream of damaging articles.

The coverage of Watergate has influenced political reporting to this day. Before Watergate, reporters typically treated high-ranking officials deferentially. During the 1933–45 administration of President Franklin D. Roosevelt, for example, reporters did not reveal the extent to which the president had lost the ability to walk because of polio. They felt that was a private matter. But after Watergate, reporters became increasingly aggressive. They derailed the careers of several aspiring politicians. In 1987, for example, reporters with the *Miami Herald* revealed that Sen. Gary Hart of Colorado, a leading Democratic presidential contender, was having an out-of-wedlock affair. The coverage forced Hart out of the race, and his political career never recovered.

The Press and Watergate: How Fair Has It Been?

The role of the press in covering the Watergate scandal came in for both praise and censure during the week ended May 12. Of greatest significance was the award of a Pulitzer Prize to *The Washington Post* for its leadership in the coverage. But the same day the prizes were announced, the Vice President, several senators and a leading political columnist were among those who had critical things to say about the performance of the press.

Pulitzer Award. The Post won a gold medal "for a distinguished example of meritorious service" from the trustees of Columbia University, who issue the Pulitzer Prizes. "*The Washington Post* from the outset refused to dismiss the Watergate incident as a bad political joke, a mere caper," said the material accompanying the award, announced May 8.

"It mobilized its total resources for a major investigation, spearheaded by two first-rate investigative reporters, Carl Bernstein and Robert Woodward. As their disclosures developed the Watergate case into a major political scandal of national proportions, the Post backed them up with strong editorials, many of them written by Roger Wilkins, and editorial cartoons drawn by the two-time Pulitzer Prize winner, Herbert A. Block (Herblock)."

Agnew Criticism. Vice President Agnew, long an outspoken critic of media performance, attacked some of the press, including the Post, on May 8 in a speech at the University of Virginia in Charlottesville. While acknowledging a contribution from "some elements of the press," he went on to say that the contribution had been "overblown by self-adulating rhetoric."

Among Agnew's complaints, according to the news coverage of his speech, were these: Some of the media had "transgressed the boundaries of propriety" . . . it is a "very short jump to McCarthyistic techniques from what's going on now" . . . some of the press has been guilty of "double hearsay," "undisclosed source rumor" and "character assassination."

Proxmire Attack. Democrat William Proxmire, the man who replaced the late Republican Joseph McCarthy as the senator from Wisconsin, took the Senate floor on May 8 to denounce "the McCarthyistic destruction of President Nixon that is now going on with increasing vehemence daily in the press." While giving the media credit for doing "a tremendous job in covering one of the most important scandals in American history," Proxmire, a former newspaperman, said that some statements about Nixon had become "grossly unfair" to the President.

Proxmire was especially critical of reports that former White House counsel John W. Dean III had privately charged the President with being directly involved in a coverup of Watergate. "President Nixon is being tried, sentenced and executed by rumor and allegation," said Proxmire. Such unattributed information—"a reckless momentum of reporting innuendo and rumor," Proxmire called it—"may well have gone a long way toward destroying the President of the United States," he said.

Scott, Mansfield. Proxmire was joined by the Senate's two floor leaders, Republican Hugh Scott (Pa.) and Democrat Mike Mansfield (Mont.). "The media, when they are responsible, are the finest press in the world," said Scott. "But when they ride momentum and suddenly decide that a whisper can be turned into a charge, or a rumor into a fact, or a wrongful deed by one person into an alleged wrongful deed by another, up to that point unconnected, then the media are acting irresponsibly as well."

Mansfield noted that "rumors and innuendos flourish and take hold. From the seed comes plants of various kinds. But rumors, innuendos and the like are not facts, and the innocence or guilt of any individual involved in this messy, sordid situation will have to be determined on that basis and that basis only."

Reston's Rebuttal. *New York Times* columnist James Reston, in his column May 9, challenged Proxmire to come up with a solution to stem the flow from the "undergound geyser" of Watergate information.

"There is obviously a serious problem here," he wrote, "but it raises some fundamental questions: Would this scandal have reached the present point of disclosure if the press had not reported the secret testimony of witnesses in this case? Is a government which had knowledge of this kind of political espionage and sabotage, and then tried to conceal the facts, entitled to bar reporters from getting beyond the screen of secrecy?"

Broder's Advice. Another columnist to discuss the issue of the press and Watergate was David S. Broder, a political reporter for *The Washington Post,* who had just won a Pulitzer Prize for his 1972 commentary.

Broder was critical in his May 8 column of his Washington colleagues for their general failure to pursue the Watergate story. He quoted Ben H. Bagdikian, a press critic who had told the newspaper editors' convention in Washington the week before that no more than 14 of the 2,200 regularly employed reporters in the capital "did any substantial work on the Watergate case, and the number of publications that pursued it with any vigor can be counted on one hand."

Broder remarked that only nine easily deflected questions about campaign practices had been asked the President at press conferences between the break-in and the White House resignations. He called for the revival of the presidential press conference, "a vital, irreplaceable institution—which the press itself has allowed to wither into disuse under the antagonism of the last two Presidents."

Impeachment: An Infrequent and Often Political Move

This article summarizes the constitutional provisions of impeachment and gives a short overview of impeachments in American history.

Congress is the branch of government with the power to impeach and remove public officials. A majority of the House of Representatives may vote to impeach someone. But that person remains in office unless two-thirds of the Senate votes to convict.

As of 1973, just one president had been impeached: Andrew Johnson in 1868. The Senate, by a single vote, acquitted him, thereby allowing him to serve out his term. Nixon almost undoubtedly would have been impeached by the House, and he faced probable conviction in the Senate. But he chose instead to resign.

By the end of the twentieth century, the House had impeached a second president: Bill Clinton. The House passed two counts of impeachment because Clinton lied under oath about a relationship he had with a White House intern. The Senate, however, acquitted Clinton by a wide margin. Most of the votes were cast along party lines, with Republican members of Congress voting to impeach or convict Clinton, and Democrats voting against impeachment or conviction.

The Clinton impeachment has spurred a lot of discussion about which types of offenses should be considered impeachable. The Constitution lists "treason, bribery or other high crimes and misdemeanors" as grounds for impeaching members of the executive branch and removing them from office. But it does not define the types of offenses that might fall under "high crimes and misdemeanors." Some commentators have suggested that impeachment is a subjective decision that can be made only by Congress.

In the cases of both Johnson and Clinton, many of the members of Congress who voted to impeach or convict were political opponents of the president. They may have been motivated as much by their political views as by their judgment of whether a major crime had been committed. In the case of Nixon, however, the evidence of major wrongdoing became so strong that even his allies seemed to be leaning toward removing him from office.

The founders wrote the Constitution before the creation of political parties. But Democrats and Republicans are often very much at odds with each other—a division that has grown since Watergate. It is not clear whether members of Congress can put aside their political feelings and make an objective decision about whether a public official should be impeached. In recent years, Republicans have held a majority in Congress. They have generally declined to investigate charges that President George W. Bush, a Republican, may have violated the Constitution through such actions as collecting information about private phone conversations without obtaining a warrant. Democrats called for such investigations, but they were accused of acting in a partisan manner.

The constitutional language for removing judges is different from the language for removing members of the executive branch. The Constitution states that judges remain in office "during good behavior." Some observers believe that Congress may remove a judge for bad behavior. One of the more interesting conflicts over impeaching a judge occurred in 1970. Gerald R. Ford, the Republican leader of the House, proposed impeaching a liberal Supreme Court justice, William O. Douglas. Ford pointed to Douglas's financial ties to a foundation, but he also disagreed with some of Douglas's judicial rulings. He failed to find proof of criminal wrongdoing, and the effort to impeach Douglas fizzled.

Despite revelations, accusations and denials surrounding the Watergate scandal and alleged coverup attempts, congressional leaders of both parties have been reluctant to discuss the subject of presidential impeachment. This reluctance may in part reflect an awareness of the sensationalism and partisan politics that have historically been associated with impeachment proceedings.

Senate Majority Leader Mike Mansfield (D Mont.) May 8 expressed hope that both the press and members of Congress would not make hasty judgments, adding that "rumors, innuendos and the like are not facts." He pointed out that broad investigations were in progress.

Rep. John E. Moss (D Calif.) April 30 urged House Democratic leaders to start a formal inquiry into possible impeachment of President Nixon. (The House must initiate impeachment proceedings.) But House Democratic floor leader Thomas P. O'Neill (Mass.) publicly termed the Moss proposal "premature."

Constitutional Provisions

Impeachment, the process by which legislatures may remove public officials from office for certain proscribed actions, dates from 14th-century England. The subject of much controversy at the Constitutional Convention in 1787, the impeachment provisions of the U.S. Constitution are scattered in the first three articles:

- The House of Representatives . . . shall have the sole power of impeachment. (*Article I, section 2.*)

- The Senate shall have the sole power to try all impeachments. When sitting for that purpose, they shall be on oath or affirmation. When the President of the United States is tried, the Chief Justice shall preside. And no person shall be convicted without the concurrence of two-thirds of the Members present. Judgment in cases of impeachment shall not extend further than to removal from office, and disqualification to hold and enjoy any office of honor, trust or profit under the United States; but the party convicted shall, nevertheless, be liable and subject to indictment, trial, judgment and punishment, according to law. *(Article I, section 3.)*
- The President . . . shall have power to grant reprieves and pardons for offenses against the United States, except in cases of impeachment. *(Article II, section 2.)*
- The President, Vice President and all civil officers of the United States shall be removed from office on impeachment for, and conviction of, treason, bribery or the other high crimes and misdemeanors. *(Article II, section 4.)*
- The trial of all crimes, except in cases of impeachment, shall be by jury. . . . *(Article III, section 2.)*

Congressional Procedures. Congress has dealt with impeachment under such widely varying circumstances that few uniform procedures have been established. The House, which must initiate the process, usually refers a resolution proposing impeachment of an official to its Judiciary Committee or to a special investigating committee. If the committee approves the resolution and reports it to the floor, the House must adopt it by a majority vote in order to impeach the official.

The House then selects several managers from its membership to present the articles of impeachment to the Senate, and to serve as prosecutors during the Senate trial proceedings.

Senate rules adopted in 1868 allow both sides to present witnesses and evidence, and the defendant to have benefit of counsel and the right of cross-examination.

Impeachment in U.S. History

Impeachment proceedings have been initiated more than 50 times in the House since 1789, but only 12 cases have reached the Senate. Of these 12 cases, only one involved a President. Two of the cases were dismissed on jurisdictional grounds, six ended in acquittal and four in conviction. Nine of the 12 cases, including the four convictions, involved federal judges.

In 1805, Supreme Court Justice Samuel Chase was impeached on charges of partisan conduct on the bench but was acquitted by the Senate after a sensational trial.

The three nonjudicial officials impeached and then acquitted were Sen. William Blount (D Tenn. 1796–97) in 1797; William W. Belknap, President Grant's secretary of war, in 1876; and President Andrew Johnson in 1868.

Andrew Johnson. The only President to be impeached, Andrew Johnson, survived several Senate roll calls on conviction by a one-vote margin.

The first of two impeachment attempts came as the culmination of a post–Civil War battle between Johnson, who favored a lenient attitude toward the Confederate states, and Radical Republicans in Congress, who favored more repressive policies. In 1867 the House rejected a Judiciary Committee resolution impeaching Johnson.

Johnson's dismissal of his secretary of war without Senate concurrence in 1868, however, gave his enemies another opportunity. A few days later the House voted to impeach the President on charges of violating the Tenure of Office Act and attacking Congress in a series of political speeches.

After weeks of argument and testimony, the Senate took a test vote on one of the 11 articles of impeachment, falling one vote short of conviction. After two more votes produced the same result, the Senate adjourned *sine die*, abruptly ending the trial.

Other Presidents. Resolutions to impeach or investigate the possibility of impeaching at least five Presidents had been introduced in the House prior to 1973. The resolutions named Nixon (1972), Harry S Truman (1952), Herbert Hoover (1932 and 1933), Grover Cleveland (1896) and John Tyler (1843).

THE GRAND JURY

Federal grand juries played a key role throughout the Watergate scandal. Grand juries in Washington, D.C., New York City, Los Angeles, and elsewhere conducted extensive investigations into wrongdoing by prominent officials. In many cases, they issued indictments, or formal accusations of a crime.

Numerous states, as well as the federal government, use grand juries to examine criminal actions. Federal grand juries are composed of 23 citizens. They may spend months listening to a prosecutor question witnesses and examining other evidence gathered by the prosecutor. The grand jury determines whether the evidence warrants an indictment. Once a grand jury issues an indictment, the case then moves to court.

Grand jury proceedings differ from a court trial in important ways. No judge is allowed during the proceedings, which are kept secret. Witnesses must testify or face the threat of being jailed for contempt of court. They are not allowed to have lawyers present.

Some experts criticize the grand jury system. They worry about a lack of legal safeguards. As a result, they warn, overzealous prosecutors can win indictments against defendants without much evidence of wrongdoing.

Grand juries play an important role in political investigations. Since Watergate, grand juries have been convened to investigate top officials in the presidential administrations of Ronald Reagan and Bill Clinton. Grand juries are also frequently deployed to investigate government scandals at the state and local levels.

WATERGATE:

Committee Hearings of 'Utmost Gravity'

Meeting in a majestic room adorned with chandeliers and marble walls, Congress began the historic task of formally investigating the Watergate scandal in May 1973. A special committee of seven senators, known as the Senate Select Committee on Presidential Campaign Activities, held its first hearing on May 17. (See profiles in Watergate Personalities, p. 26.) Its chairman, Sen. Sam J. Ervin Jr. of North Carolina, a Democrat, warned in his opening statement that the Watergate scandal may have represented "a very serious subversion" of the U.S. electoral process.

The first round of hearings looked into the wiretapping, break-in, and alleged coverup of the incident. They began slowly. The former director of administration for the Committee for the Re-election of the President, Robert C. Odle Jr., described hiring and decision-making processes at the re-election committee. Odle said that key Nixon aides, including former White House chief of staff H. R. Haldeman and former attorney general John N. Mitchell, played important roles on the campaign. He also described events on June 17, 1972, the day that five men were arrested at the Watergate office building. One of Odle's more intriguing recollections concerned G. Gordon Liddy, the former re-election committee counsel, who shredded a stack of papers that afternoon. Liddy would later be convicted for his role in the break-in.

The hearings took a dramatic turn on the second day when convicted Watergate conspirator James W. McCord Jr. gave testimony that implicated President Nixon himself.

McCord said he was advised to plead guilty at the January criminal trial of seven Watergate defendants and go quietly to prison. In exchange, he would receive executive clemency—that is, a presidential pardon or a reduction of his sentence. McCord said he was promised financial aid, rehabilitation, and a job. His electrifying testimony detailed meetings with a former presidential staff assistant and a series of cloak-and-dagger conversations with an unidentified person using a highway telephone.

Other revelations in May raised troubling questions about attempts by the White House to make use of the Central Intelligence Agency (CIA). The deputy director of the CIA testified to the Senate Armed Services Committee that the White House tried to pressure the CIA into assisting with a coverup of the Watergate scandal. The acting Armed Services Committee chairman, Democrat Stuart Symington of Missouri, said that several former Nixon aides were directly involved in the efforts to pressure the CIA. He named Haldeman, White House advisor John D. Ehrlichman, White House counsel John W. Dean III, and former acting director of the FBI L. Patrick Gray. Adding to the controversy, former CIA director Richard M. Helms appeared before a Senate appropriations subcommittee May 16 and reportedly said that several White House aides used Nixon's name in requesting CIA help in the Watergate coverup. Such action appeared to violate the 1947 National Security Act, which prohibited the CIA from engaging in domestic intelligence operations.

Exactly 11 months after the break-in and bugging of Democratic national headquarters, a Senate committee opened hearings on the Watergate scandal "in an atmosphere of the utmost gravity." The incident on June 17, 1972, was only a pebble at the center of a still-widening circle of disclosures of governmental and political corruption. The seven-member Senate Select Committee on Presidential Campaign Activities began its public hearings on May 17.

Chairman Sam J. Ervin Jr. (D. N.C.) described the atmosphere as testimony began in front of the television floodlights that filled the pillared, chandeliered, marble-walled caucus room of the Russell Senate Office Building. "If the allegations that have been made in the wake of the Watergate affair are substantiated, there has been a very serious subversion of the integrity of the electoral process," he said, "and the committee will be obliged to consider the manner in which such a subversion affects the continued existence of this nation as a representative democracy, and how, if we are to survive, such subversions may be prevented in the future."

The hearings got off to a slow start the first day. But they sprang vividly to life on the second day with testimony from convicted Watergate conspirator James W. McCord Jr. His testimony implicated President Nixon himself in alleged offers of executive clemency in return for a guilty plea by McCord at the January criminal trial of seven Watergate defendants.

McCord, a stocky, balding veteran of 19 years with the Central Intelligence Agency (CIA), read a statement to the committee. The presidential pressure, he said, was conveyed to him in January by John J. Caulfield, a former presidential staff assistant whose immediate supervisor was former White House counsel John W. Dean III. At midnight May 18, Caulfield went on administrative leave from the Treasury Department.

Caulfield told him, McCord said, "to remain silent, take executive clemency by going off to prison quietly, and I was told that while there I would receive financial aid and later rehabilitation and a job. I was further told in a January meeting in 1973 with Caulfield that the President of the United States was aware of our meeting, that the results of the meeting would be conveyed to the President, and that at a future meeting there would likely be a personal message from the President himself."

Hearings May 17

The first round of hearings dealt with the planning and execution of the wiretapping and break-in and the alleged coverup of the incident. A second round of hearings was to explore allegations of broader campaign espionage and sabotage. And a third will probe alleged violations of campaign spending laws.

Odle. The lead-off witness May 17 was Robert C. Odle Jr., 28-year-old former director of administration for the Committee for the Re-election of the President. He informed the senators and the standing-room-only crowd of press and public:

- H. R. Haldeman, former White House chief of staff, and former Attorney General John N. Mitchell had a great deal to do with hiring the re-election committee staff, many of whom were recruited from the White House and the executive branch.
- As early as May 1971, soon after the nucleus of a campaign organization had been formed and 10 months before he left the Justice Department

to become President Nixon's re-election campaign director, Mitchell was involved in major campaign decisions. A confidential White House memorandum dated Feb. 9, 1972, was released at the hearing by Samuel Desh, the Senate committee's chief counsel. The memo indicated that Mitchell had final decision-making authority on the re-election committee.

- Odle and Robert Reisner, then an aide to Jeb Stuart Magruder, deputy director of the re-election committee, took some committee files home, on Magruder's orders, for safekeeping the weekend after the break-in and returned them to Magruder the next Monday. Sen. Howard H. Baker Jr., vice chairman of the investigating committee, questioned whether the file taken by Odle contained records of "Operation Gemstone," the code phrase for alleged espionage and sabotage plans.

Odle, who admitted repeatedly that he had "a very hard time reconstructing the chronology of that day," said he had not looked at the file, knew nothing in advance about the break-in and did not learn until later that "things which have no place in a political campaign were in it (the files)."

- Odle's first hint of the break-in came in a phone call the afternoon of June 17 from Mrs. James W. McCord Jr., wife of one of five men arrested at the Watergate office building early that morning. According to Odle, she told him, "Jim has been involved in a project that's failed. He's in jail."
- The other man convicted—five others pleaded guilty—G. Gordon Liddy, former re-election committee counsel, approached Odle the afternoon of June 17 and, according to Odle, "asked where the paper shredder was. I said, 'It's in there.'" After being told how to work the machine, said Odle, Liddy returned with a foot-high stack of papers. Odle said he presumed Liddy shredded the papers.
- In May 1972, at the time of Nixon's decision to bomb Haiphong harbor, Odle was given between $3,000 and $4,000 to finance a public demonstration of support. The money was spent partly to bring people to Washington in buses for rallies, he said.

Dismissing criticisms of the tactics used, Odle told the Senate committee that the re-election committee "did it publicly, they did it overtly and they did it honestly." The committee of 400 employees "kind of came together that week," he said. "Everybody worked hard."

Other Witnesses. Three other witnesses appeared before the select committee on May 17. They were Bruce A. Kehrli, special assistant to the President, and Sgt. Paul W. Leeper and Officer John Barrett of the Metropolitan Police Department in Washington.

Hearings May 18

McCord, the former security coordinator for the President's re-election committee, dominated the May 18 hearing with his electrifying allegations of White House involvement. In his statement, he described not only the alleged approaches by Caulfield, but a series of cloak-and-dagger conversations with an unidentified person from a highway telephone booth near his Rockville, Md., home.

On Jan. 8, the first day of the criminal trial, McCord said his attorney, Gerald Alch, told him that William O. Bittman, the attorney for another defendant, E. Howard Hunt Jr., wanted to meet with him and with a third defendant, Bernard Barker, to discuss clemency. "I had no intention of accepting executive clemency," McCord said. "But I did want to find out what was going on, and by whom, and exactly what the White House was doing now."

McCord said that Alch, not he himself, met with Bittman. Alch, he added, informed him that Bittman had sent word that McCord would be called that night by "a friend I had known from the White House."

That night, McCord continued, he was phoned by an unidentified person—he later said the caller had a New York accent—who instructed him to go to a pay phone booth near an inn on a highway. McCord said he followed the instructions and was advised by the same person in the second telephone conversation to plead guilty and not to accept immunity from a grand jury in exchange for his testimony. The voice, according to McCord, promised him executive clemency, care for his family, "rehabilitation" after his release from prison, and a job.

McCord described later meetings and conversations with Caulfield. He said he refused to discuss clemency or pleading guilty but was glad to talk with him in order to make his position clear.

Caulfield, according to McCord, said the clemency offer came "from the very highest levels of the White House." He quoted Caulfield as saying that the President, who was in Key Biscayne, Fla., at that time, "had been told of the forthcoming meeting with me and would be immediately told of the results of the meeting. I may have a message to you at our next meeting from the President himself."

Earlier in his testimony before the Senate committee McCord had reported that he had been told of strategy meetings on bugging and espionage by the re-election committee that had been held in the office of then Attorney General John N. Mitchell, who resigned on March 1, 1972, to become Nixon's campaign director. Also involved in the meetings, he said, were Jeb Stuart Magruder, deputy campaign director, and presidential counsel Dean. The source of McCord's information on the meetings, he said, was G. Gordon Liddy, another Watergate conspirator.

Clemency offers were made to him by Caulfield several times, at meetings on a parkway near Washington and on a drive into the country, McCord said. He quoted Caulfield as telling him that "the President's ability to govern is at stake. Another Teapot Dome scandal is possible and the government may fall. Every body else is on track but you. You are not following the game plan. Get closer to your attorney."

At their final meeting, a Jan. 25 drive into the countryside near Warrenton, Va., McCord said he was told when he repeated his refusal to plead guilty: "You know that if the administration gets its back to the wall it will have to take steps to defend itself." And according to McCord, Caulfield offered White House assistance in providing $100,000 in cash to bail him out of jail.

"The testimony of Mr. McCord as to what was told him by John Caulfield would not be accepted in a court of law, to connect the President with what Mr. Caufield was doing," Ervin said. "But it is admissible to show whether or not Mr. Caufield is a party to any agreement to attempt to suppress information about what is popularly known as the Watergate affair at this stage," Ervin continued.

Policeman's Testimony. A second witness, who testified briefly at the opening of the May 18 hearing, was Washington policeman Carl M. Shoffler. He described his part in apprehending five men in the Watergate building at the time of the June 1972 break-in.

CIA SAYS WHITE HOUSE PRESSURED IT TO ASSUME ROLE

In testimony before the Senate Armed Services Committee May 14, Lt. Gen. Vernon Walters, deputy director of the Central Intelligence Agency (CIA), revealed that the White House tried to pressure the CIA into assisting in a coverup of the Watergate scandal.

During a closed session of the committee, the CIA deputy told members that he had twice threatened to resign and seek a private meeting with the President if the pressure from top Nixon aides on the CIA to assist in the coverup did not stop.

Walters' testimony was revealed by acting Armed Services Committee Chairman Stuart Symington (D Mo.). Symington said that it was "very clear . . . that there was an attempt to unload major responsibility for the Watergate bugging and coverup on the CIA."

Symington said that former Nixon aides H. R. Haldeman, John D. Ehrlichman, John W. Dean III and former acting director of the FBI L. Patrick Gray were directly involved in the attempts to pressure the CIA into assisting with a coverup of the Watergate break-in and its connection with the Nixon re-election committee.

The three White House aides, Symington said, "were doing everything in the world to obstruct justice." According to Symington, Walters was summoned on numerous occasions to White House meetings designed to pressure the CIA deputy into obligating the agency in efforts to cover up the Watergate scandal.

Symington said in a statement issued after Walters appeared before the committee that "under these difficult circumstances and heavy pressures, I believe that (CIA) Director (Richard M.) Helms and General Walters . . . behaved very well with respect to this attempt."

Helms. Meanwhile, former CIA Director Helms appeared before a Senate appropriations subcommittee May 16 and reportedly told the committee that several White House aides used Nixon's name in requesting CIA help in the Watergate coverup.

Following the closed hearing, Sen. John L. McClellan (D Ark.) told reporters that Helms resisted the attempts to involve the CIA in a coverup, but did not disclose the attempts to Congress or the President because the requests came from top levels in the White House.

The CIA "wanted to go as far as they could to accommodate the President," McClellan said, but "some things went too far and they put a stop to it."

McClellan accused the White House of violating the 1947 National Security Act, which prohibits the CIA from engaging in domestic intelligence operations. The conservative Democrat called the attempts by Haldeman, Ehrlichman and Dean to involve the CIA in the coverup "beyond impropriety."

Ellsberg. On May 16, Daniel Ellsberg told a joint subcommittee looking into government secrecy that the Pentagon Papers case was "part of a scheme to reelect the President."

Ellsberg, recently acquitted of charges in the case, told the subcommittee that the scheme involved an attempt to associate certain Democratic presidential candidates with the release of the Pentagon Papers and Ellsberg.

Acting Subcommittee Chairman Edmund S. Muskie listened as Ellsberg said the Nixon administration had hoped to "establish a link between me and the Democratic candidates, specifically you, Mr. Muskie."

Ellsberg's statement prompted a heated exchange between Muskie and Sen. Strom Thurmond (R S.C.). Thurmond accused Muskie of using the subcommittee and Ellsberg's appearance as a political forum.

"You brought him (Ellsberg) here to criticize the President. . . ," Thurmond shouted at Muskie. "You are not fit to be a presidential candidate."

Muskie apologized to Ellsberg for the "senatorial temper" displayed at the hearing. Thurmond declined comment on the exchange with Muskie.

Dean Statement

John W. Dean III, the former White House counsel, would emerge as a pivotal figure during the investigations of Watergate. He would provide sworn testimony implicating top White House officials, including President Nixon himself, in the Watergate coverup. Before Dean testified, he worried that Nixon's allies would find ways to discredit him. In this statement, released before his much-anticipated testimony, Dean sought to squash rumors about his testimony and his motives.

Dean was neither the first nor the last person in U.S. history to come under attack for providing damaging information about a leading political figure. More recently, Paula Jones endured attacks on her character when she accused President Clinton of making unwanted sexual advances to her. (For more about the Clinton scandals, see p. 46.) And, in 2004, former White House anti-terrorism advisor Richard A. Clarke came under fire after publicly alleging that the Bush White House had made serious mistakes in its war against terrorism.

Following is the text of a statement issued on May 10, through his attorney, by John W. Dean III, former presidential counsel.

In light of unfounded reports and persistent rumors concerning me and my testimony, I feel compelled to present what I earnestly hope will be kept in mind by all who are interested in the complete truth concerning the Watergate case.

The news stories quoting unidentified sources and speculating on the nature of my testimony do not come from me, have not been authorized by me, nor have they come from my attorneys.

The information contained in these stories is neither complete nor accurate. I have not, and will not, leak my testimony to the media.

There have been discussions within the White House during the past four to five months as to how to end the Watergate matter, but these discussions always ended with an unwillingness to accept the truth for what it meant.

That unwillingness to accept the truth still prevails among some who are affected by the truth. I have always been—as I am now—prepared to have the truth emerge, but I am not willing to see the truth distorted further, nor am I willing to shoulder the blame for those unwilling to accept the truth.

I am very aware that there is an ongoing effort to limit or prevent my testifying fully and freely.

Efforts have been made to prevent me from obtaining relevant information and records; attempts have been made to influence the handling of my testimony by the prosecutors; restrictions have been placed on the scope of my testimony as it relates to the White House; and blatant efforts have been made to publicly intimidate me.

Finally, I am, of course, aware of efforts to discredit me personally in the hope of discrediting my testimony.

In fact, I have learned from several good friends that there is a concerted effort to "get me." Indeed, this is a most unfortunate attitude, for I seek to "get" no one, rather, I seek to get only the truth.

This infamous matter has already lingered too long and done too much damage to the processes of government. It will only end when the truth is told.

Those who believe that they can "get me" and discredit my testimony with absurd or personal attacks are forgetting what I believe is a basic fact of life—ultimately the truth always emerges. The truth will emerge in the Watergate case.

I am a lawyer and have full faith in our judicial process. The taxpayers, who have been my employers for the last several years, deserve from me the full facts as I know them.

And I, too, believe that justice must be pursued fairly, fully, and impartially no matter who is involved.

Points to Ponder

- Is John Dean right? Does the truth ultimately always emerge when powerful politicians break the law?

- What can presidents do to suppress information they want to keep hidden?

- Should you believe a witness who provides sworn testimony to Congress about alleged government misdeeds? What do you look for when trying to decide whether such a witness is being truthful?

WATERGATE:
A Presidential Counterattack

Facing mounting criticism, Nixon began a counterattack to protect his presidency. He issued a statement on May 22 denying that he was personally guilty of any wrongdoing in the Watergate scandal. But he admitted for the first time that some people in the White House had attempted to cover it up. In his defense, Nixon linked his intervention in the Watergate scandal to the need to protect national security information from being leaked to the press.

He said that in 1971, after the press published excerpts from the so-called Pentagon Papers—which were top-secret Department of Defense documents about America's political and military involvement in Vietnam—he had organized a Special Investigations Unit (known as "the plumbers") to probe leaks to reporters. When the Watergate scandal broke in June 1972, he feared an investigation might lead to that unit as well as to the CIA. Nixon said his priority was to avoid disclosure of national security matters, although he had not wanted the investigation of the break-in to be impeded. Sounding contrite, the president added that, in hindsight, he should have paid more attention to warnings about a coverup. "To the extent that I may in any way have contributed to the climate in which they [Watergate and other illegal campaign activities] took place, I did not intend to; to the extent that I failed to prevent them, I should have been more vigilant," Nixon said. (For more about the Pentagon Papers and their relationship to Watergate, see page 44.)

He also said the administration would not try to invoke executive privilege in any matter concerning criminal conduct. Executive privilege refers to the right of the officials in the executive branch to refuse to turn over certain private papers or testify about certain matters. (For more about executive privilege, see below and page 39.)

EXECUTIVE PRIVILEGE

Reprinted from *Congressional Quarterly Weekly Report*, May 19, 1973

*Presidents sometimes claim "executive privilege" to avoid turning over certain information to Con-*gress. *If a president always had to share private memos, correspondence, and other information with Congress, he would find it hard to do his job. His advisors would be reluctant to share their opinions because anything they said or wrote could become public. Foreign diplomats would have trouble negotiating treaties because sensitive details could get leaked. For that reason, every president since George Washington has claimed executive privilege on occasion to protect the national interest.*

Nixon, however, faced accusations that he used executive privilege to protect himself from being investigated. Under criticism, he began backing off from broad claims of executive privilege in May.

Presidential counsel Leonard Garment May 16 characterized the President's new executive privilege guidelines as less than rigid and promised that they would not be used to cover up the Watergate scandal.

The guidelines, as released May 3 by the White House, said past and present presidential aides questioned regarding Watergate should invoke the privilege in connection with conversations with the President, conversations among themselves involving communications with the President and as to presidential papers.

Asked by White House reporters if the guidelines effectively barred past and present presidential aides from testifying about Watergate, Garment replied that the application of the guidelines in individual cases could not be predicted.

"We're not dealing with a static set of rules," he said, emphasizing that the guidelines offered only "general guidance," and their adequacy would become clear as the investigations by the Senate special committee and the grand jury moved forward.

He noted that there was no way to force an aide to invoke executive privilege if he did not want to, and pointed out that certain former aides already had violated the guidelines in talks with the press.

If the guidelines prove unworkable, "they'll be addressed again, reviewed and appropriate changes will be made," Garment said. The guidelines "do not represent attempts to restrict or suppress information," he said.

Asked if he could give assurances that executive privilege would not be used to cover up the Watergate affair, Garment replied, "I think you can be sure of that."

> Nixon's explanations failed to satisfy administration critics. A New York Times *editorial, for example, said his lengthy statement revealed that he and his White House aides were far more involved in the Watergate scandal than had previously been acknowledged. The editorial stated, "The President attempts to justify this involvement by asserting the claims of national security and internal security, but what comes through is the picture of Government frighteningly out of control."*

President Nixon issued a statement denying any personal complicity in the Watergate scandal but admitting for the first time that some persons in the White House had attempted to cover it up. As talk of his possible resignation increased, the President said he would "continue to do the job I was elected to do."

Nixon did not read the 4,000-word May 22 statement himself. Several members of his staff submitted to an intensive and occasionally acrimonious grilling by reporters.

The Central Intelligence Agency (CIA) was at the forefront of Watergate developments during the week ending May 26. It turned up as a focal point of interest at the second week of hearings by the Senate Watergate investigating committee and in several other committees of both the House and Senate.

As Watergate disclosures continued to unreel on several fronts, U.S. Attorney Harold H. Titus Jr. said in Washington May 24 that more indictments were expected in two to three months. A key figure in the case had agreed to plead guilty and become a government witness, he said. Government sources identified the witness as former White House aide Jeb Stuart Magruder, according to press reports.

Nixon's Statement on Coverup

President Nixon admitted May 22 that there had been a White House coverup in the Watergate affair, but asserted he was innocent of any planning or knowledge of it.

The White House had been buffeted for weeks by charges of complicity in the Watergate break-in and coverup, particularly from grand jury testimony, the Senate special Watergate committee and other congressional hearings. As a result, there were calls for Nixon's resignation.

The President, in a 4,000-word statement and another summary statement, his first public remarks on Watergate since May 9, sought to explain his and the White House's roles in the Watergate affair and related activities.

Nixon did not meet with reporters on the statements. They were released by his press office and questions were taken by presidential aides.

Discussing his actions that may have led to the coverup, Nixon said that in 1971, after publication of the Pentagon Papers, he had organized a Special Investigations Unit in the White House headed by John D. Ehrlichman and Egil Krogh, to probe leaks to newsmen.

When the Watergate scandal broke in June 1972, Nixon said he feared that a Watergate investigation might lead to a probe of the Special Investigations Unit (also known as the "plumbers") and from there to the CIA, which he said he mistakenly believed may have been involved in Watergate.

"In this area," Nixon said, "I felt it was important to avoid disclosure of the details of the national security matters with which the group was concerned. I knew that once the existence of the group became known, it would lead inexorably to a discussion of these matters, some of which remain, even today, highly sensitive.

Nixon and National Security

President Nixon made a ringing defense of government secrecy in national security affairs May 24 before an audience of more than 500 cheering former Vietnam POWs. Confidentiality and secrecy were essential to the conduct of administration policies aimed at promoting world peace, the President said. "It is time to quit making national heroes out of those who steal national secrets and publish them in the newspapers," Nixon said in a remark that drew a standing ovation at a reception in the State Department auditorium. "If a document is classified, keep it classified."

The President did not mention his current troubles over the Watergate affair, but the issue of governmental secrecy has been central to Watergate and related activities that have caused him much embarrassment. On May 22, the President issued a statement saying his intervention in the Watergate scandal was aimed at protecting national security information from leaks to the press.

"I wanted justice done with regard to Watergate; but in the scale of national priorities with which I had to deal—and not at that time having any idea of the extent of political abuse which Watergate reflected—I also had to be deeply concerned with ensuring that neither the covert operations of the CIA nor the operations of the Special Investigations Unit should be compromised.

"Therefore, I instructed Mr. (H. R.) Haldeman and Mr. Ehrlichman to ensure that the investigation of the break-in not expose either an unrelated covert operation of the CIA or the activities of the White House investigations unit—and to see that this was personally coordinated between General (Vernon A.) Walters, the deputy director of the CIA, and Mr. (L. Patrick) Gray of the FBI. It was certainly not my intent, nor my wish, that the investigation of the Watergate break-in or of related acts be impeded in any way.

"It now seems that later, through whatever complex of individual motives and possible misunderstandings, there were apparently wide-ranging efforts to limit the investigation or to conceal the possible involvement of members of the administration and the campaign committee."

In a tone of contrition, the President said that hindsight made it apparent he "should have given more heed to the warning signals I received along the way about a Watergate coverup and less to the reassurances.

"To the extent that I may in any way have contributed to the climate in which they (the Watergate and other illegal campaign activities) took place, I did not intend to; to the extent that I failed to prevent them, I should have been more vigilant."

In order to assure that justice is done, Nixon said, he was amending his earlier positions on executive privilege. Henceforth, he said, the doctrine will not be invoked in any matter concerning criminal conduct, and he specifically mentioned Watergate and the coverup.

Concerning the Dean documents, Nixon said they included "authorization for surreptitious entry—breaking and entering, in effect—on specified categories of targets in specified situations related to national security."

Nixon said the plans were drawn up in 1970 under his supervision by the directors of the FBI, CIA, Defense Intelligence Agency and National Security Agency.

The President said the plans were approved July 23, 1970, but five days later, on July 28, approval was rescinded because FBI Director J. Edgar Hoover in the meantime had objected to them.

"It was this unused plan and related documents that John Dean removed from the White House and placed in a safe deposit box," Nixon said. He added that the documents were "extremely sensitive" because they were based upon and included assessments of foreign intelligence capabilities which must remain secret.

Nixon said he organized the "plumbers" in 1971 after publication of the Pentagon Papers. "It created a situation in which the ability of the government to carry on foreign relations . . . could have been severely compromised," he said.

When Daniel Ellsberg was identified as the papers "leak," Nixon said he told Krogh that the unit "should find out all it could about Mr. Ellsberg's associates and his motives. I did impress upon Mr. Krogh the vital importance to the national security of his assignment," Nixon said.

But the President denied any authorization or knowledge of the break-in at the office of Ellsberg's psychiatrist that later resulted in the dismissal of espionage charges against Ellsberg.

"Because of the emphasis I put on the crucial importance of protecting the national security, I can understand how highly motivated individuals could have felt justified in engaging in specific activities that I would have disapproved had they been brought to my attention," Nixon said. He added that he had to assume responsibility for those actions.

The work of the unit "tapered off" at the end of 1971, but its activities cannot be revealed because of the "highly sensitive" nature of its efforts, Nixon said.

Editorial Comment on Nixon's May 22 Statement

Following are excerpts from editorials commenting on President Nixon's May 22 statement on the Watergate situation:

The Washington Evening Star and News, May 23:

Mr. Nixon would have us believe that, in actions he may have taken as regards Watergate, he was motivated by nothing but concern for the national security.

It may be so. But there are a few matters which still confuse us and upon which we would welcome further presidential elucidation. For example, Mr. Nixon admits that the White House Special Investigations Unit ("The Plumbers") was set up [in June] 1971, with his approval. He describes it as "a small group" under John Ehrlichman, consisting of Egil Krogh, David Young, E. Howard Hunt and G. Gordon Liddy, a unit known only to "a very few persons at the White House."

Mr. Nixon says the task of The Plumbers was two-fold: to stop security leaks and to "investigate other sensitive security matters." We can understand the group's first function. But we find it a trifle hard to understand that, with a huge federal intelligence establishment at his beck and call, Mr. Nixon felt compelled to turn to this small group of buccaneers to undertake tasks of grave national security. Was the FBI really that useless? Could no one in the Secret Service be trusted? What about the National Security Agency, the CIA, the Department of Justice, the Treasury, the Defense Department? What qualities had Hunt and Liddy that were lacking in these great departments and agencies?

The New York Times, May 24:

President Nixon's lengthy statement on the Watergate scandals reveals more of the truth than he or any of his senior associates had previously been willing to put on the record. The involvement of the President and of his White House aides in the tangled events that led to these assorted crimes and conspiracies and the subsequent attempt to cover them up is much more extensive than had previously been acknowledged.

The President attempts to justify this involvement by asserting the claims of national security and internal security, but what comes through is the picture of Government frighteningly out of control and directed by men seemingly incapable of making the most elementary distinctions between foreign affairs and domestic affairs, between the interests of the nation and the interests of a particular President or political party, between what is legal and illegal and between what might be permissible in a grave emergency and what is routine procedure. . . .

Although the President's latest statement discloses more of the truth, only the statements of other principals can show whether the whole truth has yet been revealed. Mr. Nixon has reiterated several specific denials about the extent of his knowledge of and therefore his culpability for various misdeeds. Those denials have to stand the test of time. Meanwhile, it is abundantly clear that an inflated and erroneous conception of "national security" led to criminal behavior which has brought the office of the President into grave disrepute.

The Wall Street Journal, May 24:

President Nixon's latest statement on Watergate offers a plausible and even persuasive explanation of events leading up to the break-in and bugging. His explanation of events after the bugging is far less persuasive, and most of all it's a pity the same statement was not made long ago. Coming as it does it reinforces an impression of Greek tragedy, with the President carried by the Fates and the nation dragged along.

We find it absolutely fascinating, in fact, to read of how the Watergate conspirators were first hired to plug the leaks that led to the Pentagon Papers and other disclosures of classified information. And how once started, this rather seamy business became steadily more so, escalating first into illegality in the name of national security, then into illegality in the name of partisan politics.

It in no way excuses any of the offenses, or ignores that those in charge of enforcing laws have a special responsibility to observe them, to note that in this chain of events the Watergate conspirators were neither the only ones nor the first ones to conclude that their purposes were more important than the law. It is a lesson in how much the law depends on a climate of civility, on a consensus that certain offenses are unthinkable, that erodes when the nation becomes politically polarized.

A certain teleology is evident in the sequence leading to the bugging, and one suspects something similar prevailed after the arrests as well. But the President was far less detailed and specific in describing how the coverup came about, though he was more willing than before to admit personal failing, as opposed to mere institutional responsibility. But this admission was wrung out under tremendous pressure, and after one supposedly final explanation. The context can only add to the impression that the President is acting like a man with something to hide.

The Washington Post, May 24:
On Tuesday the President suddenly issued (via Mr. Ziegler) a document of several thousand words seeking to clarify his role in the Watergate crime and coverup and in the related squalors that have come to public attention. It is interesting—and it is also heartbreaking. For appalling as many of the revelations have been that have come to us through the press, the courts and the Ervin Committee hearings, none has provided so damning an indictment of the Nixon presidency as does Mr. Nixon's own attempt to defend it. The President's lengthy statement is—by turn—pathetic, unconvincing, confused. What emerges, however, is all too clear. If you take Mr. Nixon's explanations at face value, there emerges the picture of a kind of incompetence bordering on the criminally negligent, a failure of authority and responsibility and plain sense that all but defies belief. . . .

Presidents of the United States over the past couple of decades have been granted by the people considerable license to invoke national security needs as a justification for all manner of activities that otherwise would not be permitted and which certainly would not be permitted to go on in secrecy. This is an enormous trust, and from time to time, our Presidents have abused it. You could argue—and many people do—that President Johnson abused it in the course of escalating the American Vietnam involvement. But nobody argues that he abused it for small or personal or political reasons: the dissembling was undertaken, he believed, to fulfill a genuine, if unpopular, national security imperative abroad. Whether he was right or wrong, that is a distinction of some importance. For what we must reluctantly suspect now is not just that Mr. Nixon's campaign and government appointees abused the prerogatives of White House power, but that the President himself is invoking the sacred and serious national security claim frivolously and to ends for which it was never intended. Trust me, the President says. With every effort of his own to maintain such trust, he makes it harder.

The investigation into the Watergate scandal picked up steam in late May after Archibald Cox was sworn in as special prosecutor. Cox, a Harvard University law professor, pledged to fully investigate charges arising from Watergate and the 1972 presidential campaign. But he soon found himself embroiled in a high-profile conflict with the Senate that tested the powers of the executive and legislative branches. At the same time, the government faced the potential of an even more serious constitutional battle. Nixon said he would resist demands for information from both the Senate and the Watergate grand jury.

Cox was the choice of Elliot L. Richardson, who was nominated to be the new attorney general. As special prosecutor, Cox would have full authority for investigating and prosecuting offenses related to the Watergate break-in. Members of the Senate Judiciary Committee questioned both Cox and Richardson about Cox's autonomy. They wanted to make sure he would be truly independent from the administration, allowing him to conduct a thorough investigation of Watergate.

Cox had served in the administrations of three Democratic presidents. He assured senators that he felt no obligation to consult with the attorney general about the investigation. Referring to Richardson's oversight, Cox told the Judiciary Committee, "The only authority he's retained is the authority to give me hell if I don't do the job." He also said that he would not feel obligated to respond if the president asked for a report. Cox promised that he would pursue the trail of any federal crime involved in the Watergate scandal—even if that trail might lead to the Oval Office itself.

For his part, Richardson told senators that his oversight of the special prosecutor would include giving him full authority, providing him with all possible staff support, and, if necessary, removing him. He explained, however, that he could only remove the special prosecutor for "extraordinary improprieties." He stressed that he could not conceive of Cox ever committing major misdeeds.

Cox's appointment did not require Senate approval, but Richardson agreed that he would withdraw the appointment if the Senate opposed it. Richardson, however, did require a majority vote of the Senate in order to become attorney general. He served as Nixon's secretary of defense. Even though he was widely respected in Washington, some senators worried about the administration choosing one of its own men to have responsibility for the Watergate investigation. The senators queried him especially closely about an allegation that Richardson had wanted to conceal the CIA's role in the break-in into the office of Daniel Ellsberg's psychiatrist. (For more about Ellsberg and the Pentagon Papers, see p. 44.) They also asked him about his recent contacts with figures implicated in the Watergate case. After two days of detailed questioning, Richardson won Senate confirmation on May 23.

Cox and the Senate committee shared the same goal in investigating Watergate. But they almost immediately found themselves at odds. Cox, in one of his first moves as special prosecutor, urged the committee to postpone its public hearings. He said he was concerned that the hearings would interfere with his investigation and prevent those guilty of serious crimes from ever being brought to justice. He pointed out several potential problems if the committee proceeded. For example, witnesses who were granted some immunity in exchange for testifying before the committee might escape from being convicted. Also, witnesses might be reluctant to fully disclose all the facts in front of televised Senate hearings.

But the committee resisted taking directions from the special prosecutor. It voted unanimously on June 5 to reject Cox's request. Ervin disagreed that the courts might allow guilty parties to go free because of the hearings. He also believed that the committee, which had been authorized by the Senate to conduct the investigation, had no authority to postpone it.

COX'S EFFORTS TO DELAY, LIMIT SENATE INVESTIGATION

Reprinted from *Congressional Quarterly Weekly Report*, June 9, 1973

In one of his first moves as Watergate special prosecutor, Archibald Cox June 4 urged the Senate committee investigating the case to call off its public hearings for one to three months. "The continuation of hearings at this time would create grave danger that the full facts about the Watergate case and related matters will never come to light and that many of those who are guilty of serious wrong-doing will never be brought to justice," Cox said in a letter to Committee Chairman Sam J. Ervin Jr. (D N.C.).

Elaborating on his reasons for requesting a delay, Cox told reporters that "public hearings prior to the investigation will increase the risk that major guilty parties will go unpunished. . . . Quite possibly all would go free." Other reasons he offered were:

- "Immediate public hearings would impede the investigation" and "make it impossible to get at the truth from bottom to top."
- All the facts about Nixon's involvement should be brought out "at one time and in a comprehensive presentation. . . ."
- A grant of partial immunity for certain witnesses before the committee might prevent them from being convicted later.
- Witnesses might be less likely to make full disclosures before television cameras than privately to prosecutors.
- The committee lacks some powers held by the prosecution, such as a promise of access to all documents and files in the executive branch.
- Persons inclined to fabricate explanations might be aided by premature disclosure of testimony by other witnesses.

Ervin responded promptly with a 300-page rebuttal to Cox's argument, and the committee resumed televised hearings the following day. Its members met behind closed doors June 5 to consider Cox's recommendation and voted unanimously to reject it.

When the hearings convened later that day, Ervin listed these reasons for pressing ahead without delay:

- The committee had been authorized by the Senate to conduct the investigation and had no authority to postpone it.
- The committee did not agree with Cox's contention that the courts will permit guilty parties to escape justice because of the hearings.
- There was a greater chance for indicted persons to get a fair trial "in an atmosphere of judicial calm after rather than before" the hearings.

Pretrial Publicity. Undaunted, Cox moved June 6 to require that the committee take testimony from two key witnesses—Jeb Stuart Magruder and John W. Dean III—in closed session, or at least without live media coverage. In a motion submitted to U.S. District [Court] judge John J. Sirica, Cox asked for the restriction because "widespread pretrial publicity . . . might prevent bringing to justice those guilty of serious offenses in high government offices."

Magruder and Dean, who were scheduled to appear before the committee the following week, were known to be under consideration for indictment in connection with the Watergate scandal. They reportedly were prepared to offer evidence of the involvement of top White House officials, including the President.

Senate Response. The Senate committee's lawyers went to work immediately preparing a 15-page legal brief opposing Cox's request. Filed with the court June 7, it argued that under the doctrine of separation of powers the court had no jurisdiction over the committee's actions.

It also countered Cox's contention that the televised hearings would create damaging pretrial publicity, saying that such a threat was minimized by the fact that "indictments in the Watergate case are not expected for three months and . . . consequently, trial must be six months to a year away. . . ."

"It is our view that we would be unpardonably remiss if, in this time of national emergency, we did not push forward to full revelation of the facts," the brief stated.

This second assault on their proceedings enflamed members of the Senate investigating committee. "To try to get the judicial branch of the government to enjoin the legislative from functioning is without precedent in the history of the republic," said Sen. Herman E. Talmadge (D Ga.), who earlier had publicly urged the committee to call key witnesses promptly.

Chairman Ervin, always mindful of the Constitution, declared that "no agency of the government has the power to dictate . . . how (the committee) should exercise the constitutional powers of the Senate."

Immunity Hearing. Judge Sirica heard arguments June 8 on his power to deny the Senate committee's request for immunity for Dean and Magruder, and on Cox's request for limited coverage of their testimony. In his June 6 motion, Cox acknowledged that there was no legal way to prevent the immunity grants, which the committee unanimously voted in May.

The Justice Department, however, had exercised its power to delay the grants for the legal limit of 30 days. The waiting period expired June 8 in Magruder's case, and was due to expire June 12 in Dean's case. Under the law, the two men could still be prosecuted if the evidence against them was gathered independently of their Senate testimony. *(See Delay, p. 65.)*

The question of whether the court had the power to block immunity grants of the Senate committee was closely connected to the question of whether it could modify the committee's procedures. The committee's position was that since even Cox agreed there were no grounds for denying the grants, there was no basis for any other sort of court interference in its operations. Sirica said he would announce his decision June 12.

Cox promptly escalated the battle by going to court. He asked U.S. District Court judge John J. Sirica to require the committee to take testimony from two key witnesses behind closed doors, or at least without live media coverage. Otherwise, Cox warned, all the publicity might prevent successful prosecutions of government officials who had committed crimes. The two witnesses—Jeb Stuart Magruder and John W. Dean III—were both facing indictment. But they reportedly were prepared to offer evidence of the involvement of top White House officials, including the president.

Members of the Senate investigating committee were furious with Cox. They believed that a member of another branch of government had no right to try to tell Congress what to do. "To try to get the judicial branch of the government to enjoin the legislative from functioning is without precedent in the history of the republic," said Sen. Herman E. Talmadge (D Ga.). The committee responded with its own court filing, arguing that because of the constitutional separation of powers, the court had no jurisdiction over the committee's actions. (The separation of powers doctrine holds that the three branches of government—legislative, executive, and judicial—are equal. For more about the separation of powers, see p. 81.) The committee's legal brief also contended that, at a time of national emergency, it was critical to continue to push toward a full revelation of the facts.

Judge Sirica heard arguments on June 8. He focused on Cox's request for limited coverage of the testimony. He also looked into the related question of whether the courts had the authority to tell the Senate committee that it could not request immunity for Dean and Magruder. Four days later, Sirica denied Cox's request. He also granted limited immunity to Dean and Magruder. He said the court lacked the power to intervene in the case. Cox decided against appealing the decision, and he stressed the importance of cooperation between his office and the committee.

About the same time, an even more critical conflict appeared to be brewing. The government was potentially edging toward one of the most dramatic showdowns in the nation's history over the separation of powers between the three branches of government. Amid reports that Watergate prosecutors had sufficient evidence to summon the president before the grand jury, Nixon on May 29 said he would not provide oral or written testimony to the Watergate grand jury or to the Senate select committee. He claimed that testimony would be "constitutionally inappropriate" and violate the separation of powers. Nixon believed that the executive branch would be weakened if Congress could order a president to testify. His critics, however, suspected he was just trying to evade responsibility for Watergate.

Neither the independent prosecutor nor the Senate had asked Nixon for testimony yet. But it appeared they disagreed with the president's interpretation. Sen. Sam J. Ervin Jr. (D N.C.), chairman of both the Senate investigating committee and the Senate Judiciary Subcommittee on Separation of Powers, took a sharply different position. He said White House officials were not above the law. Instead they had an obligation, like other citizens, to provide information about possible crimes to grand juries.

Ervin cited a historical case to buttress his position. Looking all the way back to 1807, he noted that the chief justice of the United States at the time agreed that a court could subpoena President Thomas Jefferson in order to obtain an important letter. Ervin also pointed out that Jefferson, setting a "magnificent example," agreed to turn over the letter without a subpoena.

Throughout this period, evidence mounted of White House involvement in serious crimes. The New York Times on June 4 published CIA memos that described discussions between top White House aides and officials of the FBI and CIA beginning shortly after the 1972 break-in. The memos appeared to imply that White House officials did not see the bugging as a possible threat to national security, as Nixon had argued. Instead, the officials worried about the political implications. The memos also detailed meetings in which top White House aides had pressured the CIA to assist in a coverup of the scandal. Two of those aides, Haldeman and Ehrlichman, denied wrongdoing and gave much different versions of events.

Reprinted from *Congressional Quarterly Weekly Report*, June 2, 1973

Presidential Subpoena: Violation of Constitution?

Continuing concern and uncertainty about the President's role in the Watergate scandal appeared to be moving the concept of separated powers to one of its most severe tests.

The White House made its position clear May 29. President Nixon said he would not provide information through oral or written testimony to the Watergate grand jury or to the Senate select committee. For him to do so, he said through press secretary Ronald L. Ziegler, would be "constitutionally inappropriate" and a violation of the separation of powers.

Thus the limits of inquiry were apparently set, both for the co-equal judicial branch within which the grand jury investigation was continuing and for the co-equal legislative branch within which the select committee was working. The White House statement followed reports that the prosecutors working with the grand jury had informed the Justice Department that they had sufficient evidence to call Nixon to appear. The Justice Department was said to support the White House position that the only way in which the President could be compelled to answer questions was by a summons from the House of Representatives as part of impeachment proceedings.

Ervin Position. The Supreme Court, said Sen. Sam J. Ervin Jr. (D N.C.), has ruled that Congress can issue a subpoena to a witness, but it has not ruled that Congress can subpoena anyone except White House aides—the decision does not exempt anyone. White House officials, said Ervin—chairman of the Senate investigating committee and of the Senate Judiciary Subcommittee on Separation of Powers—are not royalty; they retain the obligations of other citizens. And one of those obligations—as the administration pointed out to Ervin's subcommittee earlier in 1973 when the subcommittee was considering bills to protect newsmen from grand jury demands for testimony—is to provide information concerning possible crimes to grand juries.

During one of the first days of the Watergate hearings, Ervin directed attention on this question back to 1807, when former Vice President Aaron Burr was on trial for treason. Burr asked Chief Justice John Marshall, who was presiding over the trial at the circuit level, to subpoena President Thomas Jefferson. Burr contended that Jefferson had a letter which would contradict testimony that had been given against Burr.

Ervin related that Marshall found that without doubt the court could issue a subpoena to the President. The only question was, he said, whether or not the subpoena could require the President to produce the letter referred to. The uncertainty lay, Ervin said, not in the character of the witness but in the testimony he was being asked to give. Eventually,

Marshall ruled that the subpoena requiring the letter from the President could be issued.

'Magnificent Example.' Setting a "magnificent example which has been honored as much in the breach as in the observance," noted Ervin, Jefferson said he would produce the letter without the compulsion of a subpoena. In a footnote to the 1972 Supreme Court ruling that newsmen had to answer grand jury subpoenas, Justice Byron R. White noted that the Burr case resolved the point concerning the President: "Chief Justice Marshall, sitting on circuit, opined that in proper circumstances, a subpoena could be issued to the President of the United States."

The question of proper circumstances may have been what Jefferson was concerned about when he wrote to the prosecutor in the Burr case, explaining why he himself would not bring the letter to the trial at Richmond, Va. For him to do so, he wrote, "would leave the nation without an executive branch . . . the sole branch which the Constitution requires to be always in function. It could not then intend that it should be withdrawn from its station by any coordinate authority."

Richardson, Cox Win Approval

After two more days of questioning, the Senate Judiciary Committee May 23 voted unanimously to approve the move of Elliot L. Richardson, currently serving as secretary of defense, from the Pentagon to the Justice Department, where he would serve as attorney general. Within two hours, the Senate had voted to confirm Richardson as well.

The vote of approval from the Senate committee also endorsed Richardson's selection of Harvard Law Professor and former Solicitor General Archibald Cox as the special prosecutor for the executive branch investigation of the charges arising from the Watergate affair and the 1972 presidential campaign.

Cox did not have to be confirmed by the Senate, but Richardson had earlier agreed that he would withdraw any nomination for that post which the committee failed to approve.

After questioning both men May 21 concerning the guidelines under which Cox would operate, the committee seemed satisfied that Richardson had met their demands for true independence for the special prosecutor, a major point of disagreement between the committee and the nominee during the first days of the confirmation hearings. An executive session was set for the morning of May 22 to vote on the Richardson nomination.

But after telephone calls from former Pentagon Papers defendant Daniel Ellsberg to certain committee members, the executive session became another public hearing. Summoned on short notice from the Pentagon, Richardson was subjected to another lengthy interrogation session by committee members concerned by Ellsberg's claim that Richardson had encouraged the concealment of the role of the CIA in the break-in into the office of Ellsberg's psychiatrist.

Cox: Even to the Oval Office

"The only authority he's retained is the authority to give me hell if I don't do the job," Cox stated to the committee May 21, dealing with the touchy question of Richardson's ultimate responsibility—as attorney general—for the special prosecutor. Cox, who had served as solicitor general in the Kennedy and Johnson administrations, expressed his full satisfaction with the guidelines drawn up by Richardson for the work of the special prosecutor. (*See Cox biography, this page.*)

The guidelines, which were made public in final form May 21, gave him "the best of both worlds," said Cox—independence from, but strong support by, Richardson and the Justice Department. "I'll have the whip hand," said Cox. "And you won't hesitate to use it?" asked Assistant Senate Majority Leader Robert C. Byrd (D W.Va.). "No, sir," replied Cox.

PROSECUTOR ARCHIBALD COX

Harvard Law Professor Archibald Cox received an important telephone call on his 61st birthday. Calling May 17 was a former student, Attorney General–designate Elliot L. Richardson.  He asked Cox—who had served three Democratic Presidents—to come back to Washington to head the government's investigation of the spreading scandals surrounding the Watergate break-in and the 1972 presidential election.

The next day Cox agreed. On May 21, he and Richardson faced the Senate Judiciary Committee, which was considering Richardson's nomination and had been given a virtual veto over the selection of the special prosecutor. There was little doubt that Cox would win their approval.

Born in New Jersey in 1912, Cox has spent all of his adult life either in Richardson's own home-state of Massachusetts or in Washington. A graduate of Harvard College and Harvard Law School, Cox began teaching law there in 1945 after serving for two years in the office of the solicitor general and then for two more years as associate solicitor for the Labor Department.

Only a year after he began his teaching career, Cox was named a full professor at Harvard. Serving for a year as co-chairman of the Construction Industry Stabilization Commission in 1951–1952, he then accepted the post of chairman of the Truman administration's Wage Stabilization Board. Demonstrating his strong-minded independence, he resigned that post after only four months, when Truman overruled one of the board's decisions. Cox returned to teaching labor law at Harvard.

In 1961, Cox was again summoned to Washington. This time he served President Kennedy as solicitor general. After Kennedy's death, Cox served President Johnson in that same post until the summer of 1965 when he again returned to Cambridge.

In 1968, he headed a commission which inquired into the causes of student disorders at Columbia University. In 1972, he was counsel to a committee of the Massachusetts legislature which studied charges of wrongdoing against two state judges.

Declaring that he felt no obligation to inform or consult with the attorney general on matters arising during the investigation, Cox said that should Richardson demand information he would revert to his professional role and say to his former student: "Look, Elliot, that isn't the way we understood it." If the disagreement continued, he said, the only alternative for Richardson would be to fire him.

Promising the committee that he would have no compunctions in pursuing the trail of any federal crime involved in the Watergate-presidential campaign scan-

…

…

…

…

…

…

PART I: Break-In and Senate Inquiry

dal, Cox agreed that he would follow all leads to their conclusion. "Even if that trail should lead . . . to the Oval Office of the White House itself?" pressed Byrd. "Wherever that trail may lead," responded Cox.

And what if the President should ask for a report on the work of the special prosecutor, continued Byrd. Richardson replied that such a request would be referred to the special prosecutor. Cox said that he would feel no obligation to respond affirmatively and would simply exercise his own judgment in responding to such an "extraordinary request."

Noting his own lack of prosecutorial experience, Cox said he would select as his chief deputy someone with such a background. Asked when he would name this assistant, Cox replied that he would look for one as soon as the committee advised him that "it's safe to begin . . . I wish I could have done it two months ago."

Duties and Responsibilities of the Special Prosecutor

Following are guidelines relating to the special Watergate prosecutor issued by Attorney General–designate Elliot L. Richardson May 19:

The Special Prosecutor

There will be appointed by the attorney general, within the Department of Justice, a special prosecutor to whom the attorney general shall delegate the authorities and provide the staff and other resources described below.

The special prosecutor shall have full authority for investigating and prosecuting offenses against the United States arising out of the unauthorized entry into Democratic National Committee headquarters at the Watergate, all offenses arising out of the 1972 presidential election for which the special prosecutor deems it necessary and appropriate to assume responsibility, allegations involving the President, members of the White House staff, or presidential appointees, and any other matters which he consents to have assigned to him by the attorney general.

In particular, the special prosecutor shall have full authority with respect to the above matters for:

- Conducting proceedings before grand juries and any other investigations he deems necessary.
- Reviewing all documentary evidence available from any source, as to which he shall have full access.
- Determining whether or not to contest the assertion of "executive privilege" or any other testimonial privilege.
- Determining whether or not application should be made to any federal court for a grant of immunity to any witness, consistently with applicable statutory requirements, or for warrants, subpoenas, or other court orders.
- Deciding whether or not to prosecute any individual, firm, corporation or group of individuals.
- Initiating and conducting prosecutions, framing indictments, filing informations, and handling all aspects of any cases within his jurisdiction (whether initiated before or after his assumption of duties), including any appeals.
- Coordinating and directing the activities of all Department of Justice personnel, including United States attorneys.
- Dealing with and appearing before congressional committees having jurisdiction over any aspect of the above matters and determining what documents, information, and assistance shall be provided to such committees.

In exercising this authority, the special prosecutor will have the greatest degree of independence that is consistent with the attorney general's statutory accountability for all matters falling within the jurisdiction of the Department of Justice. The attorney general will not countermand or interfere with the special prosecutor's decisions or actions. The special prosecutor will determine whether and to what extent he will inform or consult with the attorney general about the conduct of his duties and responsibilities. The special prosecutor will not be removed from his duties except for extraordinary improprieties on his part.

STAFF AND RESOURCE SUPPORT

Selection of Staff. The special prosecutor shall have full authority to organize, select, and hire his own staff of attorneys, investigators, and supporting personnel, on a full- or part-time basis, in such numbers and with such qualifications as he may reasonably require. He may request the assistant attorneys general and other officers of the Department of Justice to assign such personnel and to provide such other assistance as he may reasonably require. All personnel in the Department of Justice, including United States attorneys, shall cooperate to the fullest extent possible with the special prosecutor.

Budget. The special prosecutor will be provided with such funds and facilities to carry out his responsibilities as he may reasonably require. He shall have the right to submit budget requests for funds, positions, and other assistance, and such requests shall receive the highest priority.

Designation and Responsibility. The personnel acting as the staff and assistants of the special prosecutor shall be known as the Watergate special prosecution force and shall be responsible only to the special prosecutor.

Continued Responsibilities of Assistant Attorney General, Criminal Division. Except for the specific investigative and prosecutorial duties assigned to the special prosecutor, the assistant attorney general in charge of the criminal division will continue to exercise all of the duties currently assigned to him.

Applicable Departmental Policies. Except as otherwise herein specified or as mutually agreed between the special prosecutor and the attorney general, the Watergate special prosecution force will be subject to the administrative regulations and policies of the Department of Justice.

Public Reports. The special prosecutor may from time to time make public such statements or reports as he deems appropriate and shall upon completion of his assignment submit a final report to the appropriate persons or entities of the Congress.

Duration of Assignment. The special prosecutor will carry out these responsibilities, with the full support of the Department of Justice, until such time as, in his judgment, he has completed them or until a date mutually agreed upon between the attorney general and himself.

Richardson described to the committee the elements of the statutory authority he would retain over the special prosecutor as attorney general. He would retain this responsibility, he said, in order to avoid having to amend the law spelling out the duties and functions of the attorney general. His residual authority as attorney general in regard to the special prosecutor would consist, he said, of the power to appoint the special prosecutor, to delegate full authority to him, to provide him with full back-up and all possible staff support, and the power to remove the special prosecutor. He noted that the exercise of this last power was limited by the language of the guidelines which said that the special prosecutor could only be removed for "extraordinary improprieties." It was "inconceivable" to him, said Richardson, that his former professor, Cox, would ever be guilty of such misdeeds.

Richardson: Maximum Disclosure

The committee probed Richardson's memory further about recent contacts with figures implicated in the Watergate case. Again Richardson related the fact of his luncheon meeting on May 1 with Egil Krogh Jr., at the latter's request, to discuss the course of action Krogh should take with his knowledge of the break-in at the office of Ellsberg's psychiatrist. As he had previously testified, Richardson said that he counseled Krogh to make the information available to the judge in the Pentagon Papers case. Krogh, who had received contrary counsel from his own attorney, said Richardson, did so.

Richardson said that his only other recent contact with persons named in the spreading allegations was a telephone conversation on April 30 with former White House aide John D. Ehrlichman. Ehrlichman had called, said Richardson, only to say that Krogh wanted to talk with Richardson. Ehrlichman did not say what Krogh wanted to talk about, Richardson said.

Called unexpectedly from the Pentagon May 22 to appear again before the judiciary panel, Richardson was questioned about Ellsberg's claim that Richardson knew of—and condoned concealment of—CIA involvement in the break-in at the office of Ellsberg's psychiatrist. With some vehemence, Richardson replied that he had participated in no coverup, that on the contrary, he had advised "maximum disclosure" by Krogh.

Krogh's statement to the Pentagon Papers judge did not mention CIA involvement in the break-in, but Richardson's own notes of their earlier conversation revealed that Krogh had mentioned to him the use of CIA documents and disguises by some of the White House "plumbing" crew whose work it was to find and stop security leaks.

Krogh's omission of this information left the impression, John V. Tunney (D Calif.) said, that he was covering up CIA involvement. Richardson protested this interpretation of the omission: he said his own reading of the statement found it quite in keeping with what Krogh had told him at their meeting.

Nixon had indicated concern, Richardson said, at their April 29 meeting that disclosure of the Ellsberg break-in not bring full disclosure of the work of the "plumbers," a disclosure which the President felt would endanger national security. But on May 2 Krogh told Richardson that he had received a message from Nixon through Ehrlichman, whose resignation had been announced by Nixon two days earlier, that this national security concern had been resolved and that no claim of executive privilege would be made in regard to information concerning the "plumbers'" break-in.

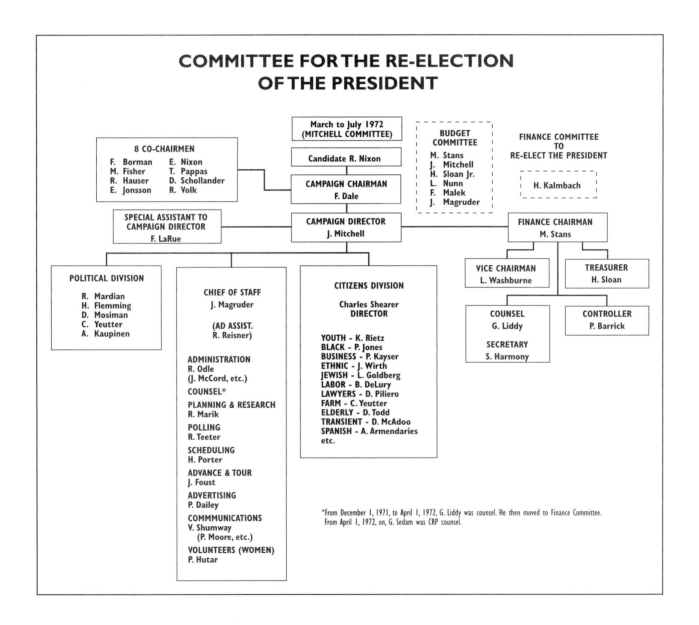

WATERGATE: Magruder Implicates Top Officials
and MOST DAMAGING CHARGES YET BY DEAN

In the second half of June 1973, two important witnesses gave highly damaging testimony to the Senate Watergate Committee. Their accounts implicated top-ranking administration officials, and even President Nixon himself.

The first witness was Jeb Stuart Magruder. He had been the deputy director of the Committee for the Re-election of the President. Magruder described events leading up to the Watergate break-in and bugging, as well as the subsequent coverup. He implicated high-ranking officials, including John N. Mitchell, who had been Nixon's former attorney general and was later his campaign director. Magruder also cast blame on John W. Dean III, the former White House counsel, and H. R. Haldeman, the president's former chief of staff. But he did not accuse the president of criminal actions. Instead, Magruder stated repeatedly that, as far as he knew, Nixon did not know anything about the break-in or the coverup.

In exchange for his testimony, the Senate committee gave Magruder a grant of partial immunity. This meant Magruder's testimony could not later be used to convict him in a criminal trial. However, Magruder could still be convicted if other evidence was found that implicated him. (Prosecutors often grant immunity to witnesses to get valuable testimony that uncovers criminal conspiracies.)

At the end of June, John W. Dean III was the star of the Watergate show for a whole week. His testimony marked a major turning point in the Watergate saga because he directly implicated Nixon. Dean began with a 245-page statement that took him six hours to read. It contained comprehensive allegations against Nixon's closest aides.

Perhaps most remarkably, Dean accused the president himself of having known since September 1972, before the presidential election in November, about attempts to suppress the scandal.

Dean also turned over 50 documents to the committee. These documents revealed that the administration audited the tax returns of its political enemies in order to harass them. They also showed that the administration kept a list of people who were targeted because they opposed the administration.

After a few days of Dean's testimony, the committee received a memorandum from J. Fred Buzhardt, a lawyer for the president. Buzhardt rebutted some of Dean's statements. He also accused Dean and Mitchell of being chiefly to blame for the scandal. Buzhardt backpedaled a bit one day later. He said the memo was not actually a White House position but rather could serve as the basis for asking Dean questions.

The contradiction between Dean's testimony and White House statements worried senators. The committee's Democratic chairman and Republican vice chairman said it might be helpful to get testimony from the president. If the president did not appear before the committee, he might instead submit a written statement. The White House, however, resisted the idea.

With evidence mounting against Nixon, nine members of the House of Representatives formally discussed impeachment in speeches on the House floor. Moreover, the chairman of the House committee that oversaw taxes said he might launch an investigation into White House use of the Internal Revenue Service for political purposes.

The most detailed account so far of high-level Nixon administration involvement in the Watergate affair and its coverup emerged from testimony before a Senate investigating committee during the week ending June 16. The most damaging statements came from Jeb Stuart Magruder, the former deputy director of the Committee for the Re-election of the President.

Magruder, now a private consultant in Washington, related to the seven-member committee his version of the events leading up to the June 17, 1972, break-in and bugging and the calculated planning to keep the facts from coming out.

He named names. Implicated most strongly in Magruder's testimony, both in the planning and coverup, was John N. Mitchell, Nixon's former attorney general and law partner who later became his campaign director.

John W. Dean III, the former White House counsel who has become a vital figure in the various investigations of the scandal, received prominent mention in Magruder's statements. Magruder testified under a grant of partial immunity from further prosecution. Dean, with a similar grant, was expected to follow Magruder in appearing before the committee when it reconvened.

In a full day of testimony June 14, Magruder freely admitted his own complicity in the well-financed scheme to spy on the Democrats. His implications reached as high in the White House hierarchy as H. R. Haldeman, the President's former chief of staff. But they stopped at the door of the Oval Office. Magruder stated repeatedly that, to his knowledge, Nixon was unaware of the crimes or their coverup.

Magruder was preceded in the witness chair June 12 and 13 by Maurice H. Stans, Nixon's former commerce secretary and later his campaign finance director. Stans denied any advance knowledge of the Watergate, describing himself as only a fundraiser and a conduit for money that went to the political side of the operation.

But Stans was contradicted by Magruder. June 24, 1972, became a date of contention, because Magruder claimed Stans had been briefed by Mitchell that day on the burglary at Democratic national headquarters. Stans could recall no such briefing.

Other Developments. These were among the week's other highlights in the Watergate case.

- A federal judge refused to bar television and radio coverage of the Senate hearings. Special prosecutor Archibald Cox had asked that they be removed.
- Convicted conspirator James W. McCord Jr. asked for a new trial. His sentencing, scheduled for June 15, was postponed indefinitely.
- Nine representatives took the House floor to discuss presidential impeachment proceedings.
- Morton Halperin, a former consultant to the National Security Council, sued Henry Kissinger and other officials for wiretapping.
- Vice President Agnew and Interior Secretary Rogers C. B. Morton criticized the Senate Watergate hearings. Republican National Chairman George Bush defended them.
- Convicted Watergate conspirator E. Howard Hunt Jr. was paid more than $200,000 after blackmailing the White House with threats to expose administration officials for involvement in illegal activities, *The Washington Post* reported.

- David Young, a former member of the White House investigations unit, or "plumbers," refused to testify before a Los Angeles County grand jury June 14 in connection with the 1971 burglary of the office of Daniel Ellsberg's former psychiatrist. Egil Krogh Jr., former head of the "plumbers," was ordered to appear before the grand jury on July 5.
- Financier Robert L. Vesco, already under criminal indictment for donating an unreported $200,000 to the Nixon campaign, was charged with illegal use of a telegram to order the transfer of $250,000 from the Bahamas to New York City. The United States is trying to extradite Vesco from Costa Rica. Vesco reportedly left Costa Rica for the Bahamas.

McGovern on Watergate

Reprinted from *Congressional Quarterly Weekly Report*, June 17–22, 1973

Some good news is coming out of the Watergate affair, said Sen. George McGovern, paraphrasing historian Charles Beard's statement that "it gets darkest just before the stars come out." The South Dakota Democrat, who lost to President Nixon in 1972, spoke June 15 at a high school commencement in Gaithersburg, Md.

He called Watergate "the most serious scandal in the 200-year life of our nation. It symbolized a rapid and dangerous drift toward an official secrecy and intrigue that would spell certain death for freedom and representative government."

But he found hope in some developments. It is good news, he said, that:

- The political system "is demonstrating a capacity to identify and correct its own evil."
- "Persistent, courageous journalists have exposed the crimes that powerful men attempted to hide."
- "A clear-headed, responsible judge has insisted that justice be done."
- The Senate investigating committee is "moving with dignity and fairness to

> develop the essential facts and to clarify the central issues."
>
> - Indictment, interrogation and possible conviction of high government officials demonstrates that the rule of law includes "the mighty as well as the small."
>
> - Congress has been challenged "to insist on its rightful check on the executive. . . . Hopefully, we will never again accept the notion that the President has either a divine or a man-made mandate to rule behind closed doors without reference to the Congress, the press and the people."

John W. Dean III was the star of the Watergate show for a whole week, and the customers got their money's worth. From Monday through Friday, June 25–29, the former White House counsel made statements and answered questions before the televised hearings of the Senate Select Committee on Presidential Campaign Activities.

He began with a 245-page statement that took him six hours to read. It contained the most comprehensive indictment yet heard against the men who had been closest to President Nixon, and Dean accused the President himself of having known since September 1972 about attempts to suppress the scandal.

Much of the cross-examination by committee lawyers and senators the rest of the week was devoted to trying to break down Dean's testimony. But the 34-year-old attorney, fired by Nixon on April 30, stood by his original statement. He remained unflustered in the face of sometimes open hostility from the senators, often appearing to control the situation with his somber composure.

Accompanying Dean's testimony were dozens of documents, some 50 altogether, that he turned over to the committee as supporting evidence. One set of papers opened up a new area of alleged administration political pressure: the use of tax audits to harass its opponents. Lists of political enemies, persons singled out for retribution because of their opposition to the administration, were revealed.

The White House began the week with a terse statement that it would have nothing to say about Dean's testimony. But a few days later, a memorandum from J. Fred Buzhardt, special counsel to the President, was given to the committee, rebutting some of Dean's statements and accusing him and his "patron," former Attorney General John N. Mitchell, of being the chief culprits in the scandal. A day after releasing the memo, Buzhardt issued a statement describing it as "an hypothesis prepared as a basis for cross-examination" but not a "White House position."

Presidential Testimony. The clear conflict between Dean and the White House prompted both the Democratic chairman and the Republican vice chairman of the Senate investigating committee to raise the question of seeking presidential testimony. Neither suggested specifically that Nixon should appear before the committee in person.

Chairman Sam J. Ervin Jr. (D N.C.) asked Dean on June 28, "Is there any way whatsoever to test the credibility of anybody when the credibility has to be judged merely on the basis of a written statement?" Dean said there was not.

Vice Chairman Howard H. Baker Jr. (R Tenn.) made reference to an important meeting of Dean, the President and others on Sept. 15, 1972. "I'm not prepared to say at this point how we may be able to gain access to the President's knowledge of that meeting," said Baker. He expressed hope that, at a later hearing, the committee could obtain "statements from the President—in whatever manner can be arranged."

The White House continued its resistance to direct presidential testimony. Deputy press secretary Gerald L. Warren said in San Clemente, Calif., June 28 that Nixon would not testify voluntarily and that it would be "constitutionally inappropriate" for him to respond to a subpoena.

Weicker Charge. The most emotional episode of the hearings so far was provided by a committee member, Sen. Lowell P. Weicker (R Conn.), who accused the White House of trying to smear him. Weicker has been a leading Republican critic of administration handling of the scandal. He asked special prosecutor Archibald Cox to investigate the alleged smear.

To enthusiastic applause from spectators in the hearing room, Weicker said heatedly on June 28: "Let me make it clear, because I've got to have my partisan moment. Republicans do not cover up, Republicans do not go ahead and threaten, Republicans do not go ahead and commit illegal acts, and God knows Republicans don't view their fellow Americans as enemies to be harassed; but rather I can assure you that Republicans and those that I serve with look upon every American as a human being to be loved and won."

Plans for 'Political Enemies'— and Mills' Response

One of the most remarkable moments in the whole Watergate scandal occurred when Dean produced a White House "enemies list." The list included liberal fundraisers, prominent journalists, and even a couple of Democratic members of Congress.

Dean said the White House goal was to use the federal government against people who opposed the administration. That could include Internal Revenue Service audits, which can cause a lot of time and expense for the person being audited even if the person has legally complied with all tax requirements. Other tactics, Dean said, could include denying federal grants for people on the list, or even investigating them for crimes.

Such tactics would be illegal. Government officials, such as tax auditors and prosecutors, are required to make decisions based on evidence, not politics. The alleged tactics were aimed to weaken Nixon's political opponents and thereby undercut the nation's two-party system.

Members of Congress were outraged. The powerful chairman of the House tax committee threatened an investigation.

One of the documents given to the Senate Watergate Committee by former White House counsel John W. Dean III was a copy of a confidential memorandum written by Dean on "dealing with our political enemies." Another of the documents was a copy of a memo to Dean from former special White House counsel Charles Colson containing the names of 20 persons to be given priority in that "dealing."

Dean said in his memo and in testimony to the committee that "available federal machinery" was to be used against persons opposed to the Nixon administration. Techniques such as audits by the Internal Revenue Service (IRS), denial of federal grants, prosecution and litigation were included.

The disclosure of the scheme June 27 brought an immediate threat of a congressional investigation of IRS activities by Rep. Wilbur D. Mills (D Ark.). He is chairman of the House Ways and Means Committee and the Joint Committee on Internal Revenue Taxation.

Mills said June 27 he had directed the staff of the joint committee to begin preliminary checks into the charges that the IRS was used for political purposes. If evidence indicated that the charges might be true, Mills said, he would give priority to that investigation and set aside work on trade and tax reform bills which are important to the administration. "I want to know more before we decide" whether to go ahead with a full-scale inquiry, Mills said.

Following are excerpts from the memos. The one by Dean was to John D. Ehrlichman, former White House domestic affairs adviser, and was dated Aug. 16, 1971. Colson's was written Sept. 9, 1971.

'Dealing With. . .Enemies'

This memorandum addresses the matter of how we can maximize the fact of our incumbency in dealing with persons known to be active in their opposition to our Administration. Stated a bit more bluntly—how we can use the available federal machinery to screw our political enemies.

After reviewing this matter with a number of persons possessed of expertise in the field, I have concluded that we *do not* need an elaborate mechanism or game plan, rather we need a good project coordinator and full support for the project. In brief, the system would work as follows:

- Key members of the staff [e.g., Colson, (Harry) Dent, (Peter) Flanigan, (Patrick) Buchanan] should be requested to inform us as to who they feel we should be giving a hard time.
- The project coordinator should then determine what sorts of dealings these individuals have with the federal government and how we can best screw them (e.g., grant availability, federal contracts, litigation, prosecution, etc.).
- The project coordinator then should have access to and the full support of the top officials of the agency or department in proceeding to deal with the individual.

I have learned that there have been many efforts in the past to take such actions, but they have ultimately failed—in most cases—

because of lack of support at the top. Of all those I have discussed this matter with, Lyn Nofziger appears the most knowledgeable and most interested. If Lyn had support he would enjoy undertaking this activity as the project coordinator. You are aware of some of Lyn's successes in the field, but he feels that he can only employ limited efforts because there is a lack of support.

THE PRIORITY LIST

1. **Picker, Arnold M.**, United Artists Corporation: Top Muskie fundraiser. Success here could be both debilitating and very embarrassing to the Muskie machine. If effort looks promising, both Ruth and David Picker should be programmed and then a follow-through with United Artists.

2. **Barkan, Alexander E.**, National Director of AFL-CIO's Committee on Political Education: Without a doubt the most powerful political force programmed against us in 1968. ($10 million dollars, 4.6 million votes, 115 million pamphlets, 176,000 workers—all programmed by Barkan's C.O.P.E.—So says Teddy White in The Making of the President '68). We can expect the same effort this time.

3. **Guthman, Ed**, Managing Editor L.A. Times: Guthman, former Kennedy aide, was a highly sophisticated hatchetman against us in '68. It is obvious he is the prime mover behind the current Key Biscayne effort. It is time to give him the message.

4. **Dane, Maxwell**, Doyle, Dane and Bernbach: The top Democratic advertising firm—They destroyed Goldwater in '64. They should be hit hard starting with Dane.

5. **Dyson, Charles**, Dyson-Kissner Corporation: Dyson and Larry O'Brien were close business associates after '68. Dyson has huge business holdings and is presently deeply involved in the Businessmen's Educational Fund which bankrolls a national radio network of 5 minute programs—Anti-Nixon in character.

6. **Stein, Howard**, Dreyfus Corporation: Heaviest contributor to McCarthy in '68.

If McCarthy goes, will do the same in '72. If not, Lindsay or McGovern will receive the funds.

7. **Lowenstein, Allard**: Guiding force behind the 18 year old "dump Nixon" vote drive.

8. **Halperin, Morton**, leading executive at Common Cause: A scandal would be most helpful here.

9. **Woodcock, Leonard**, UAW: No comments necessary.

10. **S. Sterling Munro, Jr.**, Senator Jackson's AA: We should give him a try. Positive results would stick a pin in Jackson's white hat.

11. **Feld, Bernard T.**, President, Council for Livable World: Heavy far left funding. They will program an "all court press" against us in '72.

12. **Davidoff, Sidney**: (Mayor) Lindsay's top personal aide: A first class S.O.B., wheeler-dealer and suspected bagman. Positive results would really shake the Lindsay camp and Lindsay's plans to capture youth vote. Davidoff in charge.

13. **Conyers, John**, Congressman, Detroit: Coming on fast. Emerging as a leading black anti-Nixon spokesman. Has known weakness for white females.

14. **Lambert, Samuel M., President**, National Education Association: Has taken us on vis a vis federal aid to parochial schools—a '72 issue.

15. **Mott, Stewart Rawlings**: Nothing but big money for radic-lib candidates.

16. **Dellums, Ronald**, Congressman, California: Had extensive EMK-Tunney support in his election bid. Success might help in California next year.

17. **Schorr, Daniel**, Columbia Broadcasting System: A real media enemy.

18. **Dogole, S. Harrison**, President of Globe Security Systems: Fourth largest private detective agency in U.S. Heavy Humphrey contributor. Could program his agency against us.

19. **Newman, Paul**, Radic-Lib causes. Heavy McCarthy involvement '68. Used effectively in nationwide T.V. commercials. '72 involvement certain.

20. McGrory, Mary, Columnist: Daily hate Nixon articles.

CONSPIRACY, OBSTRUCTION LAWS

The legal case against White House officials focused on laws dealing with conspiracy and obstruction of justice. These laws are considered vital to maintaining a healthy justice system. Legal experts agree that anyone who tries to block, or obstruct, the criminal justice system should be punished severely.

Following are some of the sections of the United States Code pertaining to conspiracy and obstruction of justice. All are part of Title 18, "Crimes and Criminal Procedure."

Section 201 (h): "Whoever, directly or indirectly, gives, offers, or promises anything of value to any person, for or because of the testimony under oath or affirmation given or to be given by such person as a witness upon a trial, hearing, or other proceeding, before any court, any committee of either House or both Houses of Congress, or any agency, commission, or officer authorized by the laws of the United States to hear evidence or take testimony, or for or because of his absence therefrom. . . . Shall be fined not more than $10,000 or imprisoned for not more than two years, or both."

Section 371: "If two or more persons conspire either to commit any offense against the United States, or to defraud the United States, or any agency thereof in any manner or for any purpose, and one or more of such persons do any act to effect the object of the conspiracy, each shall be fined not more than $10,000 or imprisoned not more than five years, or both. . . . If, however, the offense, the commission of which is the object of the conspiracy, is a misdemeanor only, the punishment for such conspiracy shall not exceed the maximum punishment provided for such misdemeanor."

Section 1503: "Whoever corruptly, or by threats or force, or by any threatening letter of communication, endeavors to influence, intimidate, or impede any witness, in any court of the United States or before any United States magistrate or other committing magistrate, or any grand or petit juror, or officer in or of any court of the United States, or officer who may be serving at any examination or other proceeding before any United States magistrate or other committing magistrate, in the discharge of his duty, or injures any party or witness in his person or property on account of his attending or having attended such court or examination before such officer, magistrate, or other committing magistrate, or on account of his testifying or having testified to any matter pending therein, or injures any such grand or petit juror in his person or property on account of any verdict or indictment assented to by him, or on account of his being or having been such juror, or injures any such officer, magistrate, or other committing magistrate in his person or property on account of the performance of his official duties, or corruptly or by threats or force, or by any threatening letter of communication, influences, obstructs, or impedes, or endeavors to influence, obstruct, or impede, the due administration of justice, shall be fined not more than $5,000 or imprisoned not more than five years, or both."

PRESIDENTIAL RESIGNATION: NO HISTORIC PRECEDENTS

Reprinted from *Congressional Quarterly Weekly Report,* July 7, 1973

Before Nixon, no president had ever resigned. But several had died while holding office. If a president left office for any reason, the Constitution called for the vice president to take over. During the early stages of the Watergate investigation, the vice president was Spiro Agnew. (Agnew would actually resign before Nixon because of another scandal.) But some political experts called for the administration to be replaced altogether.

Debate over whether President Nixon should resign because of the Watergate affair has sent participants on both sides back to the text of the Constitution to bolster their arguments.

No President has ever resigned—and only one Vice President, John C. Calhoun, stepped down voluntarily. He left Andrew Jackson's administration in 1832 to become a senator. Article II of the Constitution addresses the possibility of presidential resignation:

"In Case of the Removal of the President from Office, or at his Death, Resignation, or Inability to discharge the Powers and Duties of the said Office, the Same shall devolve on the Vice President, and the Congress may by Law provide for the Case of Removal, Death, Resignation or Inability, both of the President and Vice President, declaring what Officer shall then act as President, and such Officer shall act accordingly, until the Disability be removed, or a President shall be elected." (Section I, Clause 6)

25th Amendment. The ambiguity of that language—particularly the term "disability"—had provoked occasional debate ever since the Constitutional Convention of 1787. Prompted by President Eisenhower's 1955 heart attack and the Kennedy assassination, Congress in 1965 proposed the 25th Amendment to the Constitution, which prescribed a method for determining presidential disability and a procedure to follow in such cases. The amendment was ratified Feb. 10, 1967.

The 25th Amendment also remedies the constitutional silence on the question of a vacant vice presidency. The first two sections deal with that possibility and with presidential resignation.

"Section 1. In case of the removal of the Presdent, from office or his death or resignation, the Vice President shall become President.

"Section 2. Whenever there is a vacancy in the office of the Vice President, the President shall nominate a Vice President who shall take office upon confirmation by a majority vote of both houses of Congress."

Clifford Plan. Clark Clifford, who served as presidential counsel in the Truman administration and as secretary of defense in the Johnson administration, based an argument for the resignation of both Nixon and Agnew on those sections of the amendment.

In an article in *The New York Times* June 4, Clifford proposed the following chain of events: Agnew would resign; Nixon would ask Congress for a list of three qualified individuals to replace him; Nixon would name one of the three as the replacement; Congress would confirm the new Vice President; Nixon would resign, and the newly confirmed Vice President would become President.

"Although we do not have the parliamentary system, there is more flexibility in our Constitution than first meets the eye," Clifford argued. He added that Congress should insist that the person chosen to succeed Nixon promise not to try for a second term in 1976.

In a speech on the Senate floor June 25, Charles H. Percy (R Ill.) disputed the Clifford plan, saying, "Any suggestion that President Nixon resign in favor of a coalition-caretaker government uses obtuse reasoning to support a preposterous mechanism to achieve what the Democratic Party failed to achieve in the last election." Percy, himself a vocal administration critic on the Watergate issue, warned that such proposals "distort constitutional principles to fit the needs of the moment."

Truman. Historical examples of proposals such as Clifford's—for presidential resignation because of political, rather than physical, disability—are rare. One example occurred after the mid-term congressional election of 1946, when a Democratic President faced Republican majorities in both houses of Congress.

Sen. J. W. Fulbright (D Ark.) suggested that President Truman appoint Sen. Arthur Vandenberg (R Mich.) to be secretary of state and then step down. In the absence of a Vice President and under the existing order of succession, Vandenberg then would have become President, and the Republicans would have controlled both the legislative and executive branches of government.

Points to Ponder

President Nixon was not the first executive official to use wiretapping and other secret surveillance tactics. In the name of national security, President Franklin Roosevelt and several of his successors ordered the use of listening devices to monitor suspected subversives, including spies. The FBI even eavesdropped on Martin Luther King Jr., claiming he could pose a security threat. However, Nixon went far beyond other presidents in systematically trying to use federal agencies to punish his enemies.

- Do you think a president should ask the CIA or FBI to monitor a person whom he suspects of trying to undermine the national security?

- Would you trust the White House to impartially investigate organizations that may be violating the law? Or are presidential aides likely to target political adversaries?

WATERGATE:

Testimony from Taciturn John Mitchell

By early July, the Nixon White House and Congress were nearing a historic showdown. The Senate Watergate Committee wanted to hear testimony from Nixon about the Watergate scandal and review some presidential papers. But Nixon wrote a letter to committee chairman Sam J. Ervin Jr. on July 6 saying he would not cooperate with such a request. Nixon justified his refusal by citing the Constitution and its doctrine of separation of powers between the three branches of government. (See box on separation of powers.)

Ervin responded cautiously. He believed that the committee had the authority to issue a subpoena that, under the legal system, would force Nixon to testify as well as turn over papers. But he preferred to work cooperatively with the White House. He wrote Nixon a letter warning that the nation could be facing "a fundamental constitutional confrontation" between Congress and the White House. The Watergate committee also adopted a resolution supporting its chairman.

Introductory text continues at top of p. 83

SEPARATION OF POWERS: A CONTINUOUS STRUGGLE

Separation of powers, a concept that dates back to ancient Greece, means that responsibilities are divided into several governmental units instead of concentrated in one. The goal is to prevent a single person or government office from accumulating total power and turning the country into a dictatorship.

When the founders wrote the Constitution, they were careful to divide the government into three branches: the legislative (Congress), which writes the laws; the executive (president), which implements the laws; and the judicial (courts), which interprets the law. Moreover, they created a system of checks and balances to make sure that each branch could be constrained by the other two. If a president became corrupt, for example, Congress could impeach him. If Congress passed laws that violated basic rights, the courts could throw out the laws by ruling them unconstitutional.

President Nixon, in 1973, referred to the separation of powers when he refused to testify before Congress or turn over certain papers to it. He believed that Congress was trying to exceed its constitutional authority by putting itself on a higher level than the presidency. If the president had to answer to Congress in such a way, Nixon worried that the executive branch would be forever weakened.

Many in Congress saw the issue differently. They believed that it was Nixon, not Congress, who was amassing too much power. If a president violated the law, Congress needed to have the authority to fully investigate the matter. That included questioning the president and examining documents that might contain evidence about a crime. Otherwise, lawmakers believed, the president would not be answerable to the law.

The clash between Nixon and his congressional investigators provides a vivid illustration of the importance of the separation of powers. But it was hardly the first time that a president or members of Congress were accused of seizing too much power. The history of the United States is full of examples when one branch of government appeared to overstep its authority. The other branches of government would often respond by restoring the government to its balance.

Some of our most influential presidents have pushed the limits of their office. During the Civil War, Abraham Lincoln ordered the arrests of thousands of northern citizens who were suspected of sympathizing with the Confederacy. He suspended the writ of habeas corpus, which meant that these arrests could not be challenged in courts. Critics denounced Lincoln as a dictator. The chief justice of the United States said that only Congress had the authority to take such an action. But Lincoln argued that Congress was out of session, and it was up to him to save the country.

In the twentieth century, a number of presidents also took actions that appeared to threaten the separation of powers. For example, President Harry S Truman sent troops into the Korean War without a single vote in Congress. Yet the Constitution says that only Congress has the right to declare war. Similarly, John F. Kennedy and Lyndon B. Johnson led the country into the Vietnam War without a declaration of war by Congress. And Nixon did not inform Congress before he ordered the Air Force to bomb Cambodia.

The other two branches of government have also been accused from time to time of violating the separation of powers. Amid the turmoil following the Civil War, Congress attempted to establish itself as the most powerful branch in government. In 1867, it passed a law making it much harder for the president to get rid of his own top advisors. When President Andrew Johnson removed his secretary of war, congressional leaders said he had broken the new law and tried to force him out of office. This touched off one of the gravest constitutional crises in the history of the country. If Congress had succeeded, it would have set a precedent that the president was inferior to the legislative branch. Although the House did impeach Johnson, the Senate decided by a one-vote margin against convicting him. This allowed him to retain the presidency.

The Supreme Court is not above stretching its power. Beginning in the late nineteenth century, justices consistently interpreted the Constitution to stop legislators from passing laws that protected workers from unsafe conditions or very low pay. The Court believed that such laws violated the property and contract rights of companies. As a result, even when a majority of lawmakers wanted to help workers through such steps as establishing a minimum wage, judges allowed companies to pay workers as little as possible.

The Court's more conservative views sparked one of the most dramatic separation of power showdowns in our history. President Franklin D. Roosevelt and Congress, trying to bring the nation out of the Great Depression of the 1930s, passed a series of laws to spur the economy and help workers. The Supreme Court repeatedly ruled the laws unconstitutional by votes of 5–4. The Court said the federal government had exceeded its authority.

A frustrated Roosevelt announced in 1937 that he was going to ask Congress to add six new justices to the Court. The new justices, presumably, would be allies of Roosevelt and tilt the Court his way. The president was able to propose this "court-packing" plan, as it was known, because the Constitution was silent on whether more than nine justices could serve on the Court. But critics were furious. They accused Roosevelt of abusing his power and attempting to take over the judicial branch. As it turned out, the crisis was averted when the Court, by a narrow margin, began to support some of the new laws.

Separation of powers is not a simple matter of right and wrong. Sometimes, officials who appear to overstep their bounds act to help the nation. In 1962, the Supreme Court ruled that states have to count the votes of all citizens equally, regardless of whether the votes were cast in cities or rural areas. This "one-person, one-vote" concept is obviously important for democracy. But before the Court acted, state legislators had the right to decide how to count votes cast in different places. Some observers felt the Court was exceeding its authority.

Since Nixon, the tug and pull between the branches of government has continued. Perhaps that is natural because people in positions of power often try to extend their power, even if they mean well. In 2006, for example, President George W. Bush was accused of exceeding his authority by authorizing wiretapping without notifying either Congress or the courts. Bush said his actions were needed to protect the nation from terrorists.

Separation of powers is a concept that extends beyond Washington, D.C. Under the Constitution, the states can act as a check on federal power. They have broad authority over many issues that affect our day-to-day lives, such as education and health care. In fact, the Constitution gives an especially vast power to the states. If three-quarters of the states were ever to join forces, they could call a special constitutional convention and entirely rewrite the Constitution. Throughout history, however, that has never happened.

Ervin suggested that the two sides meet to discuss the situation. Nixon and Ervin appeared to be interested in meeting, but the plan fell through when Nixon was hospitalized for pneumonia. Whether a meeting would have changed anything was not clear. A White House spokesman indicated that the president's position was firm.

Meanwhile, the Watergate committee continued to take testimony. Former attorney general John N. Mitchell appeared before the Senate Watergate Committee in early July. His account of events was much different from that given by some other witnesses who had accused top White House officials of participating in an illegal coverup of the Watergate break-in. Mitchell, who kept most of his answers short, said he had no prior knowledge of the break-in and bugging of the Democratic national headquarters. He also said he had not informed the president of any coverup.

Mitchell faced some skeptical questioning. In particular, the committee's chief lawyer, Samuel Dash, pointed out that Mitchell had given false testimony under oath in the past. Dash asked Mitchell whether the committee had a good reason to believe him now.

The next witness after Mitchell was Richard A. Moore, who was Nixon's special counsel. Moore also disagreed with Dean. He said he was convinced that the president did not know about the coverup until March 21. That was when, according to Moore, Dean told everything he knew to Nixon. As soon as that happened, Moore said he had advised Nixon to respond quickly and seek legal advice from outside the White House.

In other developments, former Nixon advisor John D. Ehrlichman said parts of Dean's testimony were entirely untrue. And 10 Senate conservatives had cocktails with Nixon and assured him they continued to support him. But in another damaging revelation, *The New York Times* said some of Nixon's most influential aides had approved sabotaging Democratic operations in 1972. The sabotage reportedly was paid for with $100,000 of unreported campaign contributions.

John N. Mitchell told his side of the story to the Senate Select Watergate Committee during the week ending July 14. His story conflicted repeatedly with the accounts of previous witnesses at the televised hearings, especially those of John W. Dean III and Jeb Stuart Magruder, his former close associates.

The former attorney general and campaign director spent 2 1/2 days on the witness stand. Appearing under a subpoena from the committee, he made no opening statement. He volunteered little information, and most of his answers were terse.

Sometimes Mitchell's testimony appeared to contradict the record of his responses to earlier interrogations. This obviously strained the credulity of some committee members and counsel, reflected in a new testiness between the questioned and the questioner.

Mitchell, who is under indictment by a federal grand jury in New York City for obstruction of justice involving an illegal campaign contribution, denied prior knowledge of the break-in and bugging of Democratic national headquarters on June 17, 1972. He admitted he had a hand in the subsequent coverup (although he refused to label it thus) and that he had not informed Nixon of his knowledge. He defended his decision not to tell the President what he knew on grounds that to do so would have hampered Nixon's re-election chances.

As Mitchell neared the conclusion of his testimony on July 12, Samuel Dash, chief counsel for the committee, asked in some exasperation: "What I have to say on that (the conflicting statements), Mr. Mitchell, is that since you may have given false testimony under oath on prior occasions, is there really any reason for this committee to believe your testimony before this committee?"

Presidential Testimony. Outside the hearings themselves, a conflict was building between the committee and the White House. In a letter to Committee Chairman Sam J. Ervin Jr. (D N.C.) July 6 (made public July 7), the President refused to appear before the committee in person or to make presidential files available to it. Nixon cited the constitutional doctrine of separation of powers as his reason for refusing.

Ervin disagreed. He said the committee had the authority to subpoena Nixon and his papers, but he opposed using that authority. The committee went into executive session July 12 and adopted a resolution supporting Ervin's position. The same day, Ervin wrote Nixon a letter warning of "the very grave possibility of a fundamental constitutional confrontation between the Congress and the presidency."

Both the resolution and the letter urged a meeting between the two sides. Nixon and Ervin conferred briefly by telephone and agreed to meet. No date was set, but Nixon's illness would be a delaying factor.

The prospective value of the meeting also remained uncertain because of White House intransigence on the documents issue. Gerald L. Warren, deputy White House press secretary, told reporters the meeting would cover procedural matters and that "there will be no change" in the President's position. The meeting, said Warren, would be "a matter of courtesy."

Moore Testimony. The next witness after Mitchell was Richard A. Moore, special counsel to Nixon, a 59-year-old former West Coast broadcasting executive. Moore, too, disagreed with Dean's testimony. He was convinced, he said, that the President had no knowledge of Watergate or its coverup until March 21.

In his second day on the stand, July 13, Moore told the committee that he did not tell Nixon what he had learned from former White House counsel Dean about Watergate because he felt that the Dean account lacked credibility. Dean, Moore said, "never told me of an actual criminal situation" until March 20, when, according to Moore, Dean informed him of E. Howard Hunt Jr.'s money requests. Hunt at that time had been convicted in the break-in and was awaiting sentencing. On March 20, Dean told Moore he was going to tell everything he knew to the President, and did so the next day.

Moore said he suggested that Nixon move quickly on the scandal, particularly urging him to get legal advice from outside the White House. Moore quoted the President as responding: "I understand, thank you."

Nixon did meet with an outside counsel in Key Biscayne, Fla., on April 20, according to a White House announcement, but the name of the adviser has never been revealed. Moore said that at a May 8 meeting, the President told him he had racked his mind over the scandal and asked, "Were there any clues I should have seen?" Moore said he reassured him that there had been none.

Nixon Letter to Ervin

Following is a letter written July 6 by President Nixon to Sam J. Ervin Jr. (D N.C.), chairman of the Senate Watergate investigating committee, in response to the committee's request for presidential testimony and access to presidential papers:

On July 6, Nixon sent a historic letter to the chairman of the Senate Watergate Committee. The president said he would not turn over presidential papers prepared for, or received by, his former staff members. The reason, Nixon said, is that no future president would be able to function if staff members worried that their confidential advice would become public. Other presidents have advanced similar arguments. In 2005, for example, President George W. Bush refused to turn over internal Justice Department memos during a political battle over a Supreme Court nomination. Bush argued that allowing such

memos to become public would inhibit administration lawyers from expressing their views frankly.

What was unusual about Nixon's situation, however, was that Congress was investigating possible misdeeds by top White House officials. Some lawmakers wondered if Nixon was using constitutional arguments to protect his aides from prosecution.

Nixon also said he would refuse to testify before the committee. Such testimony, he believed, would violate the constitutional doctrine of separation of powers. Each of the three branches of government was designed to have equal power, and it would not be appropriate for the president to be forced to appear before another branch of government. He cited a 1953 letter by former president Harry S Truman, who refused to appear before a House committee.

Dear Mr. Chairman:

I am advised that members of the Senate Select Committee have raised the desirability of my testifying before the Committee. I am further advised that the Committee has requested access to Presidential papers prepared or received by former members of my staff.

In this letter I shall state the reasons why I shall not testify before the Committee or permit access to Presidential papers.

I want to strongly emphasize that my decision, in both cases, is based on my Constitutional obligation to preserve intact the powers and prerogatives of the Presidency and not upon any desire to withhold information relevant to your inquiry.

My staff is under instructions to cooperate fully with yours in furnishing information pertinent to your inquiry. On 22 May 1973, I directed that the right of executive privilege, "as to any testimony concerning possible criminal conduct or discussions of possible criminal conduct, in the matters presently under investigation," no longer be invoked for present or former members of the White House staff. In the case of my former Counsel, I waived in addition the attorney-client privilege.

These acts of cooperation with the Committee have been genuine, extensive and, in the history of such matters, extraordinary.

The pending requests, however, would move us from proper Presidential cooperation with a Senate Committee to jeopardizing the fundamental Constitutional role of the Presidency.

This I must and shall resist.

No President could function if the private papers of his office, prepared by his personal staff, were open to public scrutiny. Formulation of sound public policy requires that the President and his personal staff be able to communicate among themselves in complete candor, and that their tentative judgments, their exploration of alternatives, and their frank comments on issues and personalities at home and abroad remain confidential. I recognize that in your investigation as in others of previous years, arguments can be and have been made for the identification and perusal by the President or his Counsel of selected documents for possible release to the Committees or their staffs. But such a course, I have concluded, would inevitably result in the attrition, and the eventual destruction, of the indispensable principle of confidentiality of Presidential papers.

The question of testimony by members of the White House staff presents a difficult but different problem. While notes and papers often involve a wide-ranging variety and intermingling of confidential matters, testimony can, at least, be limited to matters within the scope of the investigation. For this reason, and because of the special nature of this particular investigation, I have agreed to permit the unrestricted testimony of present and former White House staff members before your Committee.

The question of my own testimony, however, is another matter. I have concluded that if I were to testify before the Committee irreparable damage would be done to the Constitutional principle of separation of powers. My position in this regard is supported by ample precedents with which you are familiar and which need not be recited here. It is appropriate, however, to refer to one particular occasion on which this issue was raised.

In 1953 a Committee of the House of Representatives sought to subpoena former President Truman to inquire about matters of which he had personal knowledge while he had served as President. As you may recall, President Truman declined to comply with the subpoena on the ground that the separation of powers forbade his appearance. This position was not challenged by the Congress.

It is difficult to improve upon President Truman's discussion of this matter. Therefore, I request that his letter, which is enclosed for the Committee's convenience, be made part of the Committee's record.

The Constitutional doctrine of separation of powers is fundamental to our structure of government. In my view, as in the view of previous Presidents, its preservation is vital. In this respect, the duty of every President to protect and defend the Constitutional rights and powers of his Office is an obligation that runs directly to the people of this country.

The White House staff will continue to cooperate fully with the Committee in furnishing information relevant to its investigation except in those instances where I determine that meeting the Committee's demands would violate my Constitutional responsibility to defend the Office of the Presidency against encroachment by other Branches.

At an appropriate time during your hearings, I intend to address publicly the subjects you are considering. In the meantime, in the context of Senate Resolution 60, I consider it my Constitutional responsibility to decline to appear personally under any circumstances before your Committee or to grant access to Presidential files.

I respect the responsibilities placed upon you and your colleagues by Senate Resolution 60. I believe you and your Committee colleagues equally respect the responsibility placed upon me to protect the rights and powers of the Presidency under the Constitution.

Truman Letter to Velde

Following is the text of the letter written Nov. 12, 1953, by President Truman to Harold H. Velde (R Ill. 1949–57), chairman of the House Un-American Activities Committee, that was referred to in the Nixon letter to Ervin:

Dear Sir:

I have your subpoena dated November 9, 1953, directing my appearance before your committee on Friday, November 13, in Washington. The subpoena does not state the matters upon which you seek my testimony, but I assume from the press stories that you seek to examine me with respect to matters which occurred during my tenure of the Presidency of the United States.

In spite of my personal willingness to cooperate with your committee, I feel constrained by my duty to the people of the United States to decline to comply with the subpoena.

In doing so, I am carrying out the provisions of the Constitution of the United States; and am following a long line of precedents, commencing with George Washington himself in 1796. Since his day, Presidents Jefferson, Monroe, Jackson, Tyler, Polk, Fillmore, Buchanan, Lincoln, Grant, Hayes, Cleveland, Theodore Roosevelt, Coolidge, Hoover and Franklin D. Roosevelt have declined to respond to subpoenas or demand for information of various kinds by Congress.

The underlying reason for this clearly established and universally recognized constitutional doctrine has been succinctly set forth by Charles Warren, one of our leading constitutional authorities, as follows:

"In this long series of contests by the Executive to maintain his constitutional integrity, one sees a legitimate conclusion from our theory of government. *** Under our Constitution, each branch of the Government is designed to be a coordinate representative of the will of the people. *** Defense by the Executive of his constitutional powers becomes in very truth, therefore, defense of popular rights—defense of power which the people granted to him.

"It was in that sense that President Cleveland spoke of his duty to the people not to relinquish any of the powers of his great office. It was in that sense that President Buchanan stated the people have rights and prerogatives in the execution of his office by the President which every President is under a duty to see 'shall never be violated in his person' but 'passed to his successors unimpaired by the adoption of a dangerous precedent.' In maintaining his rights against a trespassing Congress, the President defends not himself, but popular government; he represents not himself but the people."

President Jackson repelled an attempt by the Congress to break down the separation of powers in these words:

"For myself I shall repel all such attempts as an invasion of the principles of justice as well as of the Constitution, and I shall esteem it my sacred duty to the people of the United States to resist them as I would the establishment of a Spanish Inquisition."

I might commend to your reading the opinion of one of the committees of the House of Representatives in 1879, House Report 141, March 3, 1879, Forty-fifth Congress, Third Session, in which the House Judiciary Committee said the following:

"The Executive is as independent of either house of Congress as either house of Congress is independent of him, and they cannot call for the records of his actions, or the action of his officers against his consent, any more than he can call for any of the journals or records of the House or Senate."

It must be obvious to you that if the doctrine of separation of powers and the independence of the Presidency is to have any validity at all, it must be equally applicable to a President after his term of office has expired when he is sought to be examined with respect to any acts occurring while he is President.

The doctrine would be shattered, and the President, contrary to our fundamental theory of constitutional government, would become a mere arm of the Legislative Branch of the Government if he would feel during his term of office that his every act might be subject to official inquiry and possible distortion for political purposes.

If your intention, however, is to inquire into any acts as a private individual either before or after my Presidency and unrelated to any acts as President, I shall be happy to appear.

COMMITTEE RESOLUTION, ERVIN LETTER

The Senate Watergate Committee disagreed with Nixon about access to presidential papers. Committee members unanimously felt they were entitled to review every document that pertained to the Watergate scandal. However, the senators did not want to provoke a constitutional showdown. Therefore, they suggested that the committee chairman, Sam J. Ervin Jr., meet with Nixon to work out a compromise.

Meeting in executive session July 12, the Senate Watergate Committee took steps to avoid a confrontation with the Nixon administration over the availability to the committee of White House documents. This is the text of a resolution adopted by the committee:

Resolved by the Senate Select Committee on Presidential Campaign Activities:

1. That the Committee is of the unanimous opinion that the Committee is entitled to have access to every document in the possession of the White House or any Department or agency of the Executive Branch of the Federal Government, which is relevant to prove or disprove any of the matters the Committee is authorized by Senate Resolution 60 to investigate.
2. That the Committee is anxious to avoid any confrontation with the White House in respect to this matter and for this reason authorizes the Chairman to meet with the President to ascertain whether there is any reasonable possibility of working out any reconciliation between the position of the Committee in this respect and that announced by the President in his letter to the Chairman bearing date July 6, 1973, which will enable the Committee to gain access to documents necessary to enable it to make the inquiry which it is authorized by Senate Resolution 60 to make.

Following is the text of a letter written by Sen. Sam J. Ervin Jr. (D N.C.), the committee chairman, to Nixon July 12 (*See Nixon letter to Ervin, p. 84*):

Dear Mr. President:

I acknowledge receipt of your letter of July 6, addressed to me with a copy to Senator Baker.

The Committee feels that your position as stated in the letter, measured against the Committee's responsibility to ascertain the facts related to the matters set out in Senate Resolution 60, present (sic) the very grave possibility of a fundamental constitutional confrontation between the Congress and the Presidency. We wish to avoid that, if possible. Consequently, we request an opportunity for representatives of this Committee and its staff to meet with you and your staff to try to find ways to avoid such a confrontation.

We stand ready to discuss the matter with you at your convenience. We would point out that the hearings are ongoing and that time is of the essence. We trust that this may be done very promptly.

Points to Ponder

- What if the president had nothing to hide? Should he still refuse to appear to testify before a congressional committee? Why or why not?

- Why do you think the committee proceeded cautiously rather than demanding that the president comply with their requests for testimony and records?

WATERGATE:

Near Showdown on White House Records

One of the most important turning points of the Watergate investigation took place in late July 1973. A witness revealed that President Nixon had taped private conversations with top aides.

The testimony by Alexander P. Butterfield, the head of the Federal Aviation Administration and a former White House aide, changed the course of the scandal. Investigators quickly realized that the tapes could demonstrate conclusively whether Nixon had participated in an illegal coverup. Their top priority turned to obtaining the tapes and listening to the president's conversations with key players in the Watergate scandal. First, however, they would have to persuade the White House to turn over the tapes.

Maneuvering over the tapes began almost immediately. Senators on the Watergate committee were particularly interested in recordings of Nixon's conversations with former White House counsel John W. Dean III. They wanted to find out if Dean had been truthful when he testified that

the president had been involved with the coverup. But the White House balked at turning over the tapes. Nixon, who spent a week in the hospital with pneumonia, even ordered the Secret Service to withhold information from the committee.

The news about the tapes had a secondary impact: it weakened support for Nixon in Congress. The president's conservative supporters were unhappy that their conversations with Nixon had been secretly recorded.

Meanwhile, the Senate committee kept taking testimony. Robert C. Mardian, a former assistant attorney general and political coordinator of the 1972 Nixon re-election campaign, appeared for two days. He told the committee that Nixon authorized the removal of wiretap materials from the office of an FBI official. The materials had resulted in the mistrial of Daniel Ellsberg, a former Defense Department staffer who had faced espionage charges for leaking national security documents known as the Pentagon Papers. (For more about the Pentagon Papers, see p. 44.)

Despite a prank that offered temporary hope for reconciliation, the Senate Select Committee on Presidential Campaign Activities seemed to be headed toward a showdown with the Nixon administration over the release of presidential tapes and records.

The conflict intensified during the week ended July 21 with the unexpected testimony of Alexander P. Butterfield, head of the Federal Aviation Administration and former White House aide. Butterfield revealed, and the White House confirmed, that President Nixon's private conversations had been taped since the spring of 1971.

Sources on Capitol Hill reported that the revelation, more than any other development in the Watergate scandal, eroded support for Nixon in Congress. Even among some conservatives who had been his strongest supporters, according to the sources, feelings of betrayal ran strong over the realization that conversations presumed to be private had been secretly recorded.

The immediate concern of the Watergate investigating committee was obtaining tapes of Nixon's personal and telephone conversations with key witnesses who had appeared before the committee. The chief interest was in John W. Dean III, the former White House counsel who had put his word against Nixon's by linking the President directly to the Watergate coverup.

Disclosure of the presidentially ordered bugging, for historical purposes, intensified the dilemma of a Chief Executive already weakened by Watergate. Either he could turn the tapes over to the Senate committee or he could refuse to do so. If he turned them over, he could be absolved or implicated. If he did not, he would be suspected of having something to hide.

All indicators pointed toward refusal. White House sources told reporters July 19 that Nixon would stand by his position, expressed in a letter to Watergate Committee Chairman Sam J. Ervin Jr. (D N.C.) July 6, that

White House documents are protected by the doctrine of separation of powers.

Nixon spent the week in the hospital, recuperating from viral pneumonia. After Butterfield's disclosure July 16, he ordered the Secret Service, which has custody of the tapes, to withhold all information from the committee. The date of a previously scheduled meeting with Ervin was in doubt. An official White House statement on the tapes was expected to be made public on July 23.

Meanwhile, the pressure on Nixon continued to build. After his release from Bethesda Naval Hospital July 20, he spoke briefly and informally to members of the White House staff in the rose garden. Talk of his resigning before the end of his term, he told them, was "just plain poppycock." He promised to "work right up to the hilt" and suggested: "Let others wallow in Watergate. We're going to do our job."

Committee Hearings. Chairman Ervin's job was made embarrassing by a prankster who, representing himself as Treasury Secretary George P. Shultz, phoned Ervin July 19 to say that Nixon was ready to release the tapes. Ervin happily announced the news to the nationally televised hearings.

A few minutes later, after a call from the White House, he announced, with reddened face, that he had been taken in. The Bible-quoting, 76-year-old southerner denounced the telephone as an "instrument of the devil." The FBI started an investigation of who made the call.

Testifying before the committee July 19 and 20 was Robert C. Mardian, a former assistant attorney general and political coordinator of the 1972 Nixon re-election campaign. Mardian told the committee July 20 that Nixon authorized the removal of wiretap materials from the office of an FBI official that ultimately resulted in the mistrial of Daniel Ellsberg on espionage charges in the Pentagon Papers case.

The logs, summaries and correspondence making up the wiretap materials stemmed from national security taps placed on 17 National Security Council officials and newsmen in 1970 and 1971. One of those tapped was Morton S. Halperin, a member of the National Security Council at that time. Ellsberg, a friend of Halperin, was overheard on Halperin's telephone.

The revelation in April at Ellsberg's trial that he had been overheard, plus the government's inability to quickly locate the logs of the Ellsberg conversation, resulted in a mistrial and dismissal of all charges against Ellsberg and a codefendant, Anthony Russo. The wiretap materials eventually were located in the office of John D. Ehrlichman, a former presidential aide, who resigned April 30.

Mardian said he first learned of the existence of the wiretaps in June or July 1971 from a friend, William C. Sullivan, then an associate director of the FBI. Mardian said Sullivan told him he had "very sensitive" national security logs, which he had removed from bureau files, in his safe in his FBI office.

Mardian, who was an assistant attorney general at the time, said Sullivan was concerned that if he were fired—he later was—the materials would be found in his safe, and he wanted to know what to do with them. Mardian told Sullivan he would report the conversation to then Attorney General John N. Mitchell.

Mardian said that he told Mitchell what he had learned, but that the attorney general gave him no instructions about what to do with the materials. Sometime in July 1971, Mardian said, he got a call from either Ehrlichman or another former presidential aide, H. R. Haldeman. The caller told him to go to San Clemente, Calif., immediately to tell the President what he knew of the materials. Mardian said he did this, and the President ordered him to get the materials from Sullivan and give them to Ehrlichman. Mardian said the materials concerned electronic surveillance authorized by the President and undertaken at the direction of the National Security Council.

BUTTERFIELD'S EXPLANATION OF PRESIDENTIAL WIRETAPS

Following are excerpts from the transcript of an exchange between Fred D. Thompson, minority counsel of the Senate Watergate Committee, and Alexander P. Butterfield, administrator of the Federal Aviation Administration and former deputy assistant to President Nixon. Thompson was questioning Butterfield about the taping of presidential conversations. The exchange occurred at committee hearings July 16.

Thompson: Mr. Butterfield, are you aware of the installation of any listening devices in the oval office of the President?

Butterfield: I was aware of listening devices, yes, sir.

Thompson: When were those devices placed in the oval office?

Butterfield: Approximately the summer of 1970. I cannot begin to recall the precise date.

My guess, Mr. Thompson, is that the installation was made between—and this is a very rough guess—April or May of 1970 and perhaps the end of the summer or early fall 1970.

Thompson: Are you aware of any devices that were installed in the Executive Office Building office of the President?

Butterfield: . . . They were installed at the same time.

Thompson: Would you tell us a little bit about how those devices worked, how they were activated, for example?

Butterfield: I don't have the technical knowledge, but I will tell you what I know about how those devices were triggered. They were installed, of course, for historical purposes, to record the President's business, and they were installed in his two offices, the oval office and the EOB (Executive Office Building) office. . . .

Butterfield: . . . In that the oval office and the Executive Office Building office were indicated on this locator box, the installation was installed in such a way that when the light was on "oval office," the taping device was at least triggered. It was not operating, but it was triggered—it was spring-loaded, if you will, then it was voice-actuated.

So when the light was on "oval office," in the oval office and in the oval office only, the taping device was spring-loaded to a voice-actuating situation. When the President went to the EOB office, the EOB light was on. In the EOB office, there was the same arrangement.

Thompson: . . . . What about the cabinet room? Was there a taping device in the cabinet room?

Butterfield: Yes, sir, there was.

Thompson: Was it activated in the same way?

Butterfield: No, sir, it was not, and my guess is, and it is only my guess, is because there was no cabinet room location per se on the locator box.

To ensure the recording of business conversations in the cabinet room, a manual installation was made. . . .

Thompson: There were buttons on the desk in the cabinet room there that activated that device?

Butterfield: There were two buttons. . . . There was an off-on button, one said "Haldeman" and one that said "Butterfield" that was on and off respectively, and one on my telephone.

Thompson: So far as the oval office and the EOB office is concerned, would it be your testimony that the device would pick up any and all conversations no matter where the conversations took place in the room and no matter how soft the conversations might have been?

Butterfield: Yes, sir. . . .

Thompson: Was it a little more difficult to pick up in the cabinet room?

Butterfield: Yes, sir, it was a great deal more difficult to pick up in the cabinet room.

Thompson: All right. We talked about the rooms now, and if we could move on to telephones, are you aware of the installation of any devices on any of the telephones, first of all, the oval office?

Butterfield: Yes, sir.

Thompson: What about the Executive Office Building office of the President?

Butterfield: Yes, sir. The President's business telephone at his desk in the Executive Office Building.

Thompson: What about the Lincoln Room?

Butterfield: Yes, sir, the telephone in the Lincoln sitting room in the residence.

Thompson: What about Aspen cabin at Camp David?

Butterfield: Only in, on the telephone at the President's desk in his study in the Aspen cabin, his personal cabin.

Thompson: It is my understanding this cabin was sometimes used by foreign dignitaries. Was the device still present during those periods of time?

Butterfield: No, sir, the device was removed prior to occupancy by chiefs of state, heads of government and other foreign dignitaries.

Thompson: All right. Would you state who installed these devices, all of these devices, so far as you know?

Butterfield: . . . The Secret Service. The technical security division of the Secret Service.

Thompson: Would you state why, as far as your understanding is concerned, these devices were installed in these rooms?

Butterfield: There was no doubt in my mind they were installed to record things for posterity, for the Nixon library. The President was very conscious of that kind of thing. We had quite an elaborate setup at the White House for the collection and preservation of documents, and of things which transpired in the way of business of state.

Thompson: On whose authority were they installed, Mr. Butterfield?

Butterfield: On the President's authority by way of Mr. Haldeman and Mr. Higby. (H. R. Haldeman, then White House chief of staff, and Lawrence M. Higby, deputy assistant to the President). . . .

Thompson: Where were the tapes of those conversations kept, maintained?

Butterfield: I cannot say where. I am quite sure in the Executive Office Building in some closets or cupboards or files which are maintained by the technical security division of the U.S. Secret Service.

Thompson: Were these tapes checked periodically?

Butterfield: Yes, they were checked at least daily. . . . I think some were used more frequently than others. The Secret Service knew this; they made sure that they were checked periodically and sufficiently. . . .

Thompson: Were any of these tapes ever transcribed, reduced to writing or typewritten paper, so far as you know?

Butterfield: To my recollection, no.

Thompson: Mr. Butterfield, as far as you know from your own personal knowledge, from 1970 then until the present time all of the President's conversations in the offices mentioned . . . were recorded as far as you know?

Butterfield: That is correct, until I left. Someone could have taken the equipment out, but until the day I left I am sure I would have been notified.

Thompson: And as far as you know, those tapes are still available?

Butterfield: As far as I know, but I have been away for four months, sir. . . .

CQ CONGRESSIONAL QUARTERLY WEEKLY REPORT, JULY 28, 1973

With features from August 4, 1973

WATERGATE:
A Historic Constitutional Confrontation

July 1973 was a unique month in American history. Both the Senate Watergate Committee and special prosecutor Archibald Cox issued subpoenas, or legal orders, to the president. They wanted to obtain White House tapes of private conversations.

Only once before in American history had a president been served with a subpoena. In that case, which involved President Thomas Jefferson in 1807, Jefferson decided to comply without a court order. In the case of Watergate, however, President Nixon dug in his heels. He said the investigators did not have the right to private presidential papers—a position that provoked an unprecedented court battle over the power of a president to resist a criminal investigation.

Both Nixon and his adversaries were determined to win the legal battle. The Senate Watergate Committee issued a pair of subpoenas directing him to hand over certain papers and tapes. When Nixon refused to comply with the subpoenas, the committee members took the extraordinary step of going to court to try to force him to turn over the documents.

Meanwhile, U.S. District Court judge John J. Sirica, who was presiding over the Watergate case, asked Nixon's lawyers to explain why the White House was resisting another subpoena. That subpoena had come from Cox, and it also sought tapes and documents related to Watergate. In Nixon's response to the judge, he claimed that the judicial branch of the government could not give an order to the head of the executive branch. A skeptical Sirica gave Nixon two weeks to explain more fully why he was not complying with Cox's subpoena.

It was clear to all sides that this remarkable showdown would eventually make its way to the Supreme Court, once it wound its way through lower courts. Even then, though, it was not clear whether Nixon would obey the high court if it ruled that he had to turn over the tapes. The White House sent mixed signals on this question.

Meanwhile, the Senate Watergate Committee continued to hold hearings. The main witness at the end of July was John D. Ehrlichman, Nixon's former domestic affairs adviser. Ehrlichman said he was innocent of any wrongdoing. He justified the Watergate break-in as necessary for national security. He also defended Nixon as a strong and competent politician.

Sen. Sam J. Ervin Jr., the bushy-browed old North Carolinian who heads the Senate select committee that is investigating the Watergate affair, called it "the greatest tragedy this country has ever suffered." The committee vice chairman, Howard H. Baker Jr. of Tennessee, described it as a "historic conflict" between the legislative and executive branches of government.

With the five other members of the committee, Ervin and Baker concluded on July 26 that the best way to break the deadlock with President Nixon over his refusal to grant the committee access to certain records would be to take him to court. The committee was expected to seek a declaratory judgment ordering the President to turn over the tapes and documents.

The constitutional confrontation was arrived at when Nixon refused to hand over the tapes and papers sought in two subpoenas from the committee on July 23. Arguing the doctrines of executive privilege and separation of powers, he replied: "I cannot and will not consent to giving any investigatory body private presidential papers."

The same day the committee was moving toward court action, a U.S. District Court judge in Washington, D.C., signed an order directing Nixon's lawyers to "show cause why there should not be full and prompt compliance" with another subpoena. That subpoena, also seeking tapes and documents related to Watergate, was served on White House lawyers by attorneys working with Archibald Cox, the government's special prosecutor of the case.

In a letter to the judge explaining his reasons for resisting the third subpoena, Nixon wrote that he was following "the example of a long line of my predecessors as President of the United States who have consistently adhered to the position that the President is not subject to compulsory process from the courts."

And so the issue edged toward eventual solution by the Supreme Court, with both sides claiming faith in their legal and ethical positions. Nixon became the second President in U.S. history to be served with a subpoena. The first was Thomas Jefferson, in 1807.

The next step in the litigation probably would be the filing of a petition by the Senate committee in U.S. District Court. Attorneys for the President had until Aug. 7 to reply to the "show cause" order.

A final decision by the Supreme Court, after the appeals processes had been exhausted, was expected within a few months. "The President, just as in other matters, would abide by a definitive decision of the highest court," said a White House spokesman.

As the dispute over records raged on, the Watergate committee hearings continued. The week ended July 28 started with testimony from Gordon C. Strachan, assistant to former White House chief of staff H. R. Haldeman, and continued through four days of testimony by John D. Ehrlichman, Nixon's former domestic affairs adviser. Ehrlichman claimed innocence of wrongdoing in the Watergate scandal and defended an administration-sponsored burglary as legal and justified on national security grounds.

In his opening statement July 24, Ehrlichman spoke of the tumultuous events that led to White House emphasis on security. "Some of these events in 1969 and 1970 included hundreds of bombings of public buildings, a highly organized attempt to shut down the federal government, intensive harassment of political candidates and violent street demonstrations which endangered life and property," he testified.

He defended his old boss, the President: "From close observation I can testify that he is not paranoid, weird, psychotic on the subject of demonstrators or hypersensitive to criticism. He is an able, tough international politician, practical, complex, able to integrate many diverse elements and to see the interrelationships of minute and apparently disassociated particles of information and events."

Part of Ehrlichman's testimony was devoted to refuting claims made earlier before the committee by former White House counsel John W. Dean III. Ehrlichman charged that Dean's statement that Watergate was the "major thing" occurring in the White House from June 17 to Sept. 15, 1972, was "false than all the other falsehoods" in his testimony.

CONFLICT ISSUE IS JOINED: ON TO THE SUPREME COURT

For the first time in 166 years, on July 23 an American President was subpoenaed. Richard M. Nixon and Thomas Jefferson are the only two Presidents to share the distinction.

Jefferson was subpoenaed by Chief Justice John Marshall in the treason trial of Aaron Burr in 1807. He was ordered to testify at the trial in Richmond, Va., and to provide certain correspondence. He did not testify, but said he would if the trial were in Washington. And he gave Marshall a letter that the chief justice sought.

Nixon has outdone Jefferson. He was served with three subpoenas from two sources. Two of the subpoenas, one for tape-recorded conversations and the other for written records, came from the Senate Select Committee on Presidential Campaign Activities. The third, for both tapes and papers, came from Archibald Cox, the government's special prosecutor in the Watergate case.

Court Action. White House lawyers were ordered to respond to the subpoenas by 10 a.m. July 26. That morning, Douglas M. Parker of the White House counsel's staff delivered a letter from Nixon to Chief Judge John J. Sirica of [the] U.S. District Court in Washington. The letter was in response to the Cox subpoena.

"I must decline to obey the command of that subpoena," Nixon wrote. "In doing so I follow the example of a long line of my predecessors as President of the United States who have consistently adhered to the position that the President is not subject to compulsory process from the courts.

"The independence of the three branches of our government is at the very heart of our constitutional system. It would be wholly inadmissible for the President to seek to compel some particular action by the courts. It is equally inadmissible for the courts to seek to compel some particular action from the President."

Besides the separation of powers doctrine, the letter declined the command of the subpoena on the basis of executive privilege.

Nixon quoted from an 1865 attorney general's opinion to support his position.

He noted that he was voluntarily giving the federal grand jury in Washington a memorandum from W. Richard Howard to Bruce Kehrli, two White House aides, which the jury wanted, and several political memos from former aide Gordon C. Strachan to his boss, former White House chief of staff H. R. Haldeman. But Nixon refused to turn over the requested tapes. "Like all of my predecessors," he wrote, "I have always made relevant material available to the courts except in those rare instances when to do so would be inconsistent with the public interest."

After reading Nixon's letter to the court, Judge Sirica was asked by Cox to sign an order directing the President to "show cause why there should not be full and prompt compliance" with the subpoena. Sirica polled the 20 members of the grand jury who were present, and they unanimously approved the order. Nixon's lawyers were given until Aug. 7 to reply.

Committee Action. At the same time the letter was being delivered to the court, a similar letter was in the hands of Sam J. Ervin Jr. (D N.C.), chairman of the Senate Watergate Committee. "I cannot and will not consent to giving any investigatory body private presidential papers," the letter concluded, reaffirming what Nixon had written in letters July 6 and July 23. (*See text of letter, p. 95.*)

As in his letter to Sirica, Nixon left open the possibility that he would provide other specific materials upon request of the committee.

On a motion from Vice Chairman Howard H. Baker Jr. (R Tenn.), the committee voted unanimously to authorize its lawyers to go to court. Sometime in the next week, the committee was expected to seek a declaratory judgment in U.S. District Court that would order Nixon to comply with its subpoenas.

"The chair recognizes that there is no precedent for litigation of this nature, but there originally was no precedent for any litigation," said Ervin. "And I think this litigation is essential if we are to determine whether the President is above the law and whether the President is immune from all of the duties and responsibilities in matters of this kind which devolve upon all the other mortals who dwell in this land."

Baker held out hope that "there is some way to ameliorate the situation." He suggested again that a small panel of persons outside government be formed for the purpose of going over tapes and documents and deciding which ones could be given to the committee. This suggestion had been rejected by the committee previously.

The committee action deliberately avoided another course that could have been followed: asking the full Senate to cite Nixon for contempt. Seeking a declaratory judgment would, Baker explained, be quicker and cleaner and "gets away from the emotional issue" of a contempt proceeding.

Supreme Court. The conflict between the administration and its investigators would be resolved eventually by the Supreme Court, weeks or months later. Deputy White House press secretary Gerald L. Warren said July 26 that Nixon would abide by a "definitive" decision of the court. But Charles A. Wright, a White House consultant and University of Texas law professor who was expected to argue the case before the court, said the Supreme Court rulings are not always definitive. Failure of the court to treat the separation of powers issue fully could lead to Nixon's continued refusal to release tapes and documents, he suggested.

Wright said he would like to see the case concluded as quickly as possible. "The sooner we can get to the bottom of Watergate," he said, "the better off the country will be."

"The President is very confident of his constitutional position as outlined in the letters," said deputy press secretary Warren. And, Warren added, he "fully expects his position to be upheld in the courts."

Cox, quoting from an 1803 Supreme Court decision (*Marbury v. Madison*), differed. Nixon's position "is not legally sound" he said, "Separation of powers from the beginning of history has not disabled a court from issuing orders to the executive branch."

Nixon Letter on Subpoenas

In the following letter, Nixon said he would not turn over the documents sought by the subpoenas, or legal orders. As in previous letters, he said it would be inappropriate for a president to hand over private White House papers to Congress. Such an action would violate the separation of powers doctrine, which holds that the three branches of government—executive, legislative, and judicial—are equal. (For more about the separation of powers, see p. 81.)

Following is the text of a letter written on July 25 by President Nixon to Chairman Sam J. Ervin Jr. of the Senate Watergate Committee in response to the two subpoenas served on the White House by the committee on July 23.

Dear Mr. Chairman:

White House counsel have received on my behalf the two subpoenas issued by you, on behalf of the Select Committee, on July 23rd.

One of these calls on me to furnish to the Select Committee recordings of five meetings between Mr. John Dean and myself. For the reasons stated to you in my letters of July 6th and July 23rd, I must respectfully refuse to produce those recordings.

The other subpoena calls on me to furnish all records of any kind relating directly or indirectly to the "activities, participation, responsibilities or involvement" of 25 named individuals "in any alleged criminal acts relating to the Presidential election of 1972." Some of the records that might arguably fit within that subpoena are Presidential papers that must be kept confidential for reasons stated in my letter of July 6th. It is quite possible that there are other records in my custody that would be within the ambit of that subpoena and that I could, consistent with the public interest and my Constitutional responsibilities, provide to the Select Committee. All specific requests from the Select Committee will be carefully considered and my staff and I, as we have done in the past, will cooperate with the Select Committee by making available any information and documents that can appropriately be produced. You will understand, however, I am sure, that it would simply not be feasible for my staff and me to review thousands of documents to decide which do and which do not fit within the sweeping but vague terms of the subpoena.

It continues to be true, as it was when I wrote you on July 6th, that my staff is under instructions to cooperate fully with yours in furnishing information pertinent to your inquiry. I have directed that executive privilege not be invoked with regard to testimony by present and former members of my staff concerning possible criminal conduct or discussions of possible criminal conduct. I have waived the attorney-client privilege with regard to my former Counsel. In my July 6th letter I described these acts of cooperation with the Select Committee as "genuine, extensive and, in the history of such matters, extraordinary." That cooperation has continued and it will continue. Executive privilege is being invoked only with regard to documents and recordings that cannot be made public consistent with the confidentiality essential to the functioning of the Office of the President.

I cannot and will not consent to giving any investigatory body private Presidential papers. To the extent that I have custody of other documents or information relevant to the work of the Select Committee and that can properly be made public, I will be glad to make these available in response to specific requests.

Nixon Rose Garden Speech

Nixon delivered a rousing speech to his staff after spending a week in the hospital for pneumonia. Despite his illness and the problems with Watergate, the president appeared fit and determined. He dismissed any talk of resigning. He said he would continue to work hard and focus on tackling the nation's most pressing problems.

Following is a transcript of the remarks President Nixon made to about 200 members of his staff on July 20 in the White House rose garden after his release from Bethesda Naval Hospital, where he had spent a week for treatment of viral pneumonia:

Thank you very much for your very warm welcome.

I had heard that while I was out at Bethesda that you were all working, and here you are outside. (Laughter)

However, I do want you to know that, after a week away from the White House, it is very good to be back, and particularly good to be back to see all of you.

As I was at Bethesda, I realized that this was the first time in 13 years I had been in the hospital except for my physical examinations. The other time was in the year 1960 when, some of you may recall, I had a knee infection and was at Walter Reed for two weeks.

I told the staff at Bethesda that I got out perhaps a day or two earlier, not because their medication, which was excellent, and their competence, which was superb, but because their spirit lifted me. And I can assure you another reason I am back a little bit early is that your spirit lifts me and I am most grateful for the fact that while I was there, a few papers used to come out, you know, the things you send out to me that I sign without looking at. (Laughter)

In any event, I do want you to know that just the thought that while I was away that the White House was going forward, that all the work was being done, that everything that needed to be done for this country was going forward as I would have wanted it to go forward, and as the people would want it to go forward, that really helped me get back. And I thank you very much for all those extra hours so many of you put in during that time.

As you can imagine, while I was there, I had a lot of chance to think, to sleep, to rest. It is a little difficult, I must say, to do some of those things when you are not used to it. I mean I am used to thinking but—(laughter)—not sleeping and resting.

Also, I had a chance to go through some of the mail Rose sent out to me, selected mail and wires from all over the country. It seems that nothing really touches people more than illness. You know, if you want to talk to somebody and you say, "How are you feeling?" they usually tell you. Then things really get going. So, as far as this was concerned, I found that I must have heard from everybody in this country who had pneumonia, and believe me, there are a lot of them that have had pneumonia. (Laughter)

All of them touched me, but I, as usual, tried to pick one out I thought was particularly interesting. It would come from California, as you might imagine, Livermore, Calif., up north. I campaigned it many years ago, in 1950, when it was a small town. It has grown up a little now. It is from an 8-year-old and he prints it.

He writes: "Dear President Nixon: I heard you were sick with pneumonia. I just got out of the hospital yesterday with pneumonia and I hope you did not catch it from me." (Laughter and applause)

"Now you be a good boy and eat your vegetables like I had to." I hate vegetables, but I will eat them. "If you take your medicine and your shots, you will be out in eight days like I was. Love, John W. James III, 8 years old."

Well, John W. James III, I got out in seven days, so did a little bit better than he did. But perhaps my case of pneumonia was not as difficult as his. I will take his advice. I will eat my vegetables. Try now and then to take the shots—maybe not the kind of shot that he takes, but who knows—(laughter)—Walter Tkach is my adviser in that respect.

But in any event, there is one bit of advice I am not going to take, and I will not take too much of your time to tell you about that advice, because this is a very serious vein—it will be of interest to our friends in the press, to the whole nation and to the thousands who have writ-

ten me, and it will disturb my very good corps of doctors who were advising me to do this, do that, and so forth and so on—that is, they said, "Mr. President, now look, you have excellent health, you have been very fortunate that you have established a modern record of 4½ years in the White House without having missed a day because of illness, but you have got to realize you are human. You can't press yourself so much, and what you have to do is to slow down a little now and take some time off and relax a little more."

I just want you to know what my answer to them was and what my answer to you is. No one in this great office at this time in the world's history can slow down. This office requires a President who will work right up to the hilt all the time. That is what I have been doing. That is what I am going to continue to do, and I want all of you to do likewise.

I know many say, "But then you will risk your health." Well, the health of a man is not nearly as important as the health of the nation and the health of the world.

I do want you to know that I feel that we have so little time in the positions that all of us hold, and so much to do. With all that we have to do and so little time to do it, at the end of the next 3½ years to look back and think: But for that day, something went undone that might have been done that would have made a difference in whether we have peace in the world or a better life at home. That would be the greatest frustration of all.

I don't say this heroically, because I know that every man who has ever been in this position feels exactly the same way and has felt as I do.

So, I want you to know when I come back from Camp David Monday morning, it is going to be full tilt all the way, and we want all of you to work that way, too.

Another bit of advice, too, that I am not going to take—oh, it really isn't advice. I was rather amused by some very well-intentioned people who thought that perhaps the burdens of the office, you know, some of the rather rough assaults that any man in this office gets from time to time, brings on an illness and, after going through such an illness, that I might get so tired that I would consider either slowing down or even, some suggested, resigning.

Well, now, just so we set that to rest, I am going to use a phrase my Ohio father used to use. Any suggestion that this President is ever going to slow down while he is President or is ever going to leave this office until he continues to do the job and finishes the job he was elected to do, anyone who suggests that, that is just plain poppycock.

We are going to stay on this job until we get the job done. (Applause)

Because after all, you see, when we put all of the events that we read about, the things we see on television, in perspective and then we think of the ages, we think of the world, and not just our own little world. We think of the nation, and not only our little part of that nation. We realize that here in this office is where the great decisions are going to be made that are going to determine whether we have peace in this world for years to come. We have made such great strides toward that goal.

It is going to determine whether there is a chance that this nation can have a prosperity without war and without inflation, something we have not had since President Eisenhower was President, and we are making progress toward the goal.

It is going to determine whether or not this nation is going to be on a course that we all worked for, a course in which, rather than having the rate of crime escalating in this nation, the use of dangerous drugs destroying our young people, that we win those battles which we have launched and carried on. It is going to determine whether programs we have to provide fair and better opportunity for all Americans are going to have a chance, whether they are carried forward.

There are these and other great causes that we were elected overwhelmingly to carry forward in November of 1972. And what we were elected to do, we are going to do, and let others wallow in Watergate. We are going to do our job. (Applause)

Cox Request for Tapes

Following is the text of the letter written July 18 by special prosecutor Archibald Cox to presidential counsel J. Fred Buzhardt. Cox requested access to the tapes of eight conversations between Nixon and top aides who had been accused of wrongdoing. The prosecutor believed the tapes would shed light on the guilt or innocence of important White House officials.

In this letter, Cox argued that the separation of powers doctrine was irrelevant because he did not work for Congress. Therefore, turning over tapes to his office would not set a precedent for future relations between the White House and Congress.

Dear Mr. Buzhardt:

I am writing to request access to the recordings of certain conversations between the President and various members of the White House staff and others whose conduct is under investigation in connection with the

alleged coverup of the break-in at the Democratic National Committee offices. The conversations are listed below.

May I emphasize three essential aspects of this request:

First, the request is part of an investigation into serious criminal misconduct—the obstruction of justice. The tapes are material and important evidence—quite apart from anything they show about the involvement of the President—because the conversations recorded in all probability deal with the activities of other persons under investigation. Indeed, it is not implausible to suppose that the reports to the President on these occasions may themselves have been made pursuant to a conspiracy and as part of a coverup.

Second, furnishing the tapes in aid of an investigation into charges of criminal conspiracy plainly raises none of the separation-of-powers issues you believe to be involved in furnishing so-called "Presidential Papers" to the Select Committee. The Select Committee is seeking information—as I understand the position—solely in order to recommend legislation. Whatever fears you may entertain that furnishing the tapes in aid of the Select Committee's legislation function would set a precedent for furnishing presidential papers to other legislative committees are plainly irrelevant to my request. For my request involves only a grand jury investigation resulting from highly extraordinary circumstances. No question of precedent arises because the circumstances almost surely will never be repeated.

Third, I would urge that the tapes be furnished for use in my investigation without restriction. This procedure strikes me as the method of establishing the truth which is most fair to everyone concerned, including the President. It is proper to point out, however, that if you thought it essential to furnish the papers only to the grand jury under the rules pertaining to grand jury documents, an appropriate procedure could be devised. This is an additional circumstance distinguishing the present investigation from the situation before the Select Committee.

The particular conversations to which my present request pertains have been carefully selected as those material to the investigation, to wit:—

1. Meeting of June 20, 1972, in the President's EOB Office between the President and Messrs. Ehrlichman and Haldeman from 10:30 a.m. to 1:00 p.m. (time approximate).

2. Telephone conversation of June 20, 1972, between the President and Mr. Mitchell from 6:08 to 6:12 p.m.

3. Meeting of June 30, 1972, in the President's EOB Office between the President and Messrs. Haldeman and Mitchell from 12:55 to 2:10 p.m.
4. Meeting of September 15, 1972, in the President's Oval Office between the President and Mr. Dean from 5:15 to 6:17 p.m. Mr. Haldeman joined this meeting at 5:27 p.m.
5. Meeting of March 13, 1973, in the President's Oval Office between the President and Mr. Dean from 12:42 to 2:00 p.m. Mr. Haldeman was present from 12:43 to 12:55 p.m.
6. Meeting of March 21, 1973, in the President's Oval Office between the President and Messrs. Dean and Haldeman from 10:12 to 11:55 a.m.
7. Meeting of March 22, 1973, in the President's EOB Office between the President and Mr. Dean from 1:57 to 3:43 p.m. Mr. Ehrlichman joined this meeting at 2:00 p.m., and Messrs. Haldeman and Mitchell joined at 2:01 p.m.
8. Meeting of April 15, 1973, in the President's EOB Office between the President and Mr. Dean from 9:17 to 10:12 p.m. (you will recall that this is the conversation the recording of which I requested as early as June 11 and which you declined to furnish under the misapprehension that this was only a subsequent memorandum).

You will realize that as the investigation proceeds it may be necessary to request additional recordings.

Sincerely,
Archibald Cox
Special Prosecutor

POLL REPORT

Reprinted from *Congressional Quarterly Weekly Report*, August 4, 1973

As Watergate investigations progress, confidence in the Nixon presidency decreases, according to the latest Harris Survey. But a tiny plurality thinks he should remain in office even if he ordered a coverup.

In the poll, conducted among 1,485 households July 18–22, Harris found the overall rating of Nixon was not at an all-time low (that was in March 1971). But personal confidence in the President was. These were the questions and the responses:

"In view of what has happened in the Watergate affair, do you think President Nixon should resign as President or not?"

	July	June	May
Should resign	22%	22%	14%
Should not resign	66	62	75
Not sure	12	16	11

"If it is proven that President Nixon ordered the coverup of White House involvement in Watergate, after Republican agents were caught there, do you think he should resign or not?"

	July	June
Should resign	44%	46%
Should not resign	45	40
Not sure	11	14

"How would you rate President Nixon on inspiring confidence personally in the White House—excellent, pretty good, only fair, or poor?"

	July	June	May
Good/excellent	21%	24%	32%
Only fair/poor	69	65	57
Not sure	10	11	11

"How would you rate the job President Nixon is doing as President—excellent, pretty good, only fair, or poor?"

	July	June	February
Good/excellent	42%	48%	60%
Only fair/poor	54	49	39
Not sure	4	3	1

Baker vs. Kennedy. Persons in the same Harris sample who voted in the 1972 election were also asked their preference for President in a trial heat between Sen. Howard H. Baker Jr. (R Tenn.), vice chairman of the Senate Watergate Committee, and Sen. Edward M. Kennedy (D Mass.).

Baker	45%
Kennedy	44
Not sure	11

Wright Letter to Cox

> *Here is the White House response to Cox's request. This is the text of a letter to Cox written on July 23 by Charles Alan Wright, a consultant to Buzhardt.*
>
> *In his letter, Wright explained that the president would not turn over the tapes. He disagreed with Cox's argument that the separation-of-powers argument did not apply. The reason, in his view, was that Cox might use the tapes to prosecute White House officials in the courts. The courts are part of the judicial branch of government, which meant the separation of powers argument applied.*
>
> *Wright agreed that prosecuting lawbreakers was an important goal. But he maintained that other national interests were even more important, such as making sure the president had the right to keep certain documents private. Otherwise, the power of the presidency could be undermined.*
>
> *In his conclusion, Wright said that only the president could determine whether releasing the tapes would be in the public interest. And, he said, the president decided that releasing the tapes would not meet that standard.*

Dear Mr. Cox:

Mr. Buzhardt has asked that I respond to your letters to him of June 20th, July 18th and July 20th in which you make certain requests with regard to tape recordings of or about conversations between the President and various members of the White House staff and others.

The President is today refusing to make available to the Senate Committee material of a similar nature. Enclosed is a copy of his letter of this date to Senator Ervin stating his position about the tapes. I am instructed by the President to inform you that it will not be possible to make available to you the recordings that you have requested.

In general the reasons for the President's decision are the same as those that underlie his response to the Senate Committee. But in your letter of July 18th you state that furnishing the tapes in aid of an investigation into charges of criminal conspiracy raises none of the separation-of-powers issues that are raised by the request from the Senate Committee. You indicated a similar position when we met on June 6th. At that time you suggested that questions of separation of powers did not arise since you were within the Executive Branch, though, as I recall, you then added that your position is a little hard to describe since, in your view, you are not subject to direction by the President or the Attorney General.

I note that in your subsequent letters, and particularly that of July 18th in which you argue that the sepa-

ration-of-powers argument is inapplicable, there is no suggestion that you are a part of the Executive Branch. Indeed, if you are an ordinary prosecutor, and thus a part of the Executive Branch as well as an officer of the court, you are subject to the instructions of your superiors, up to and including the President, and can have access to Presidential papers only as and if the President sees fit to make them available to you.

But quite aside from the consideration just stated, there is an even more fundamental reason why separation-of-powers considerations are fully as applicable to a request from you as to one from the Senate Committee. It is clear, and your letter of the 18th specifically states, that the reason you are seeking these tapes is to use some or all of them before grand juries or in criminal trial. Production of them to you would lead to their use in the courts, and questions of separation-of-powers are in the forefront when the most confidential documents of the Presidency are sought for use in the Judicial Branch. Indeed most of the limited case law on executive privilege has arisen in the context of attempts to obtain executive documents for use in the courts.

The successful prosecution of those who have broken the laws is a very important national interest, but it has long been recognized that there are other national interests that, in specific cases, may override this. When Congress provided in the Jencks Act, 18 U.S.C. (subsection) 3500 (d), that the United States may choose to refuse to disclose material that the court has ordered produced, even though in some instances this will lead to a mistrial and to termination of the prosecution, it was merely recognizing that, as the courts had repeatedly held, there are circumstances in which other legitimate national interests requiring that documents be kept confidential outweigh the interest in punishing a particular malefactor. Similarly in civil litigation the United States may feel obliged to withhold relevant information, because of more compelling governmental interests, even though this may cause it to lose a suit it might otherwise have won. The power of the President to withhold confidential documents that would otherwise be material in the courts comes from "an inherent executive power which is protected in the constitutional system of separation of power." *United States v. Reynolds,* 345, U.S. 1, 6 n. 9 (1953).

In your letter to Mr. Buzhardt of July 10th you quoted Mr. Richardson's statement to the Senate Judiciary Committee in which he concluded that it was the President's intention "that whatever should be made public in terms of the public interest in these investigations should be disclosed."

That is, of course, the President's view, but it is for the President, and only for the President, to weigh whether the incremental advantage that these tapes would give you in criminal proceedings justifies the serious and lasting hurt that disclosure of them would do to the confidentiality that is imperative to the effective functioning of the President. In this instance the President has concluded that it would not serve the public interest to make the tapes available.

Cox Statement on Subpoenas

Here is the text of the statement issued on July 23 by Cox in response to Wright's letter. Cox said he would seek subpoenas to force the White House to turn over the tapes. He asserted that "no man is above the law."

This afternoon I received from the White House a letter declining to furnish tapes of conversations on the President's telephone or in his office. Eight specific tapes were requested by me in a letter dated July 18, 1973, a copy of which is attached.

Careful study before requesting the tapes convinced me that any blanket claim of privilege to withhold this evidence from a grand jury is without legal foundation. It therefore becomes my duty promptly to seek subpoenas and other available legal procedures for obtaining the evidence for the grand jury. We will initiate such legal measures to secure the eight tapes and certain other evidence as soon as proper papers can be prepared.

The effort to obtain these tapes and other documentary evidence is the impartial pursuit of justice according to law. None of us should make assumptions about what the tapes will show. They may tend to show that there was criminal activity—or that there was none. They may tend to show the guilt of particular individuals—or their innocence. The one clear point is that the tapes are evidence bearing directly upon whether there were criminal conspiracies, including a conspiracy to obstruct justice, among high government officials.

Happily, ours is a system of government in which no man is above the law. Since Chief Justice Marshall's decision in Marbury vs. Madison in 1803, the judicial branch has ruled upon the legal duties as well as the constitutional privileges of the Chief Executive. I dispute the constitutionality of the President's claim of privilege as applied to the administration of the criminal laws, but I do not question its bona fides. In seeking and obeying a constitutional ruling with respect to these papers and records, we would promote the rule of law essential to both liberty and order.

Nixon Letter to Ervin

Following is the text of a letter written July 23 by President Nixon to Sam J. Ervin Jr. (D N.C.), chairman of the Senate Watergate investigating committee. In this letter, Nixon rejected the committee's request for tape recordings of presidential conversations.

The president argued that Congress did not have the right to private presidential conversations. He also said he had listened to the tapes, and they would not help the committee determine wrongdoing in the Watergate scandal. He was concerned that the tapes contained a number of private comments about various people and issues that had nothing to do with Watergate. Moreover, the conversations referred to other documents and tapes. They could not be understood unless the White House turned over a wide number of presidential records, mostly unrelated to Watergate. Most of the records, Nixon said, were highly confidential and should be kept private.

Dear Mr. Chairman:

I have considered your request that I permit the Committee to have access to tapes of my private conversations with a number of my closest aides. I have concluded that the principles stated in my letter to you of July 6th preclude me from complying with that request, and I shall not do so. Indeed the special nature of tape recordings of private conversations is such that these principles apply with even greater force to tapes of private Presidential conversations than to Presidential papers.

If release of the tapes would settle the central questions at issue in the Watergate inquiries, then their disclosure might serve a substantial public interest that would have to be weighed very heavily against the negatives of disclosure.

The fact is that the tapes would not finally settle the central issues before your Committee. Before their existence became publicly known, I personally listened to a number of them. The tapes are entirely consistent with what I know to be the truth and what I have stated to be the truth. However, as in any verbatim recording of informal conversations, they contain comments that persons with different perspectives and motivations would inevitably interpret in different ways. Furthermore, there are inseparably interspersed in them a great many very frank and very private comments, on a wide range of issues and individuals, wholly extraneous to the Committee's inquiry. Even more important, the tapes could be accurately understood or interpreted only by reference to an enormous number of other documents and tapes, so that to open them at all would begin an endless process of disclosure and explanation of private Presidential records totally unrelated to Watergate, and highly confidential in nature. They are the clearest possible example of why Presidential documents must be kept confidential.

Accordingly, the tapes, which have been under my sole personal control, will remain so. None has been transcribed or made public and none will be.

On May 22nd I described my knowledge of the Watergate matter and its aftermath in categorical and unambiguous terms that I know to be true. In my letter of July 6th, I informed you that at an appropriate time during the hearings I intend to address publicly the subjects you are considering. I still intend to do so and in a way that preserves the Constitutional principle of separation of powers, and thus serves the interests not just of the Congress or of the President, but of the people.

ERVIN, BAKER RESPONSES TO NIXON DENIAL OF RECORDS

The Senate Watergate Committee's chairman, Sam J. Ervin Jr., and vice chairman, Howard H. Baker Jr. (R Tenn.), made these comments at a July 23 public hearing. They had just received Nixon's letter rejecting the committee's request for access to White House records and tapes.

Ervin pointed out that the president made contradictory statements about the tapes. On the one hand, Nixon claimed that the tapes supported his position, but on the other hand, he said they could be misinterpreted. Ervin also disagreed with Nixon's interpretation of the separation of powers. He said the separation of powers could not protect illegal activities. Nixon, he said, should show moral leadership and help determine whether criminal acts were committed in a coverup of Watergate instead of refusing to cooperate with the committee.

Baker, a member of the president's own party, was also concerned. He said he continued to believe the president should turn over the records so that the committee could get to the bottom of Watergate. But he was less critical of the president than Ervin.

ERVIN
…This is a rather remarkable letter about the tapes. If you will notice, the President says he has heard the tapes, or some of them, and they sustain his position. But he says he's not going to let anybody else hear them for fear they might draw a different conclusion. (*Letter text, p. 100*)

In other words, the President says that they are susceptible of, the way I construe it, two different interpretations, one favorable to his aides and one not favorable to his aides.

I deeply regret this action of the committee (voting to issue subpoenas of the tapes and records). I have very different ideas of separation of powers from those expressed by the President. If such a thing as executive privilege is created by the doctrine of separation of powers, it has these attributes. First, if it exists at all, it only exists in connection with official duties.

Second, under no circumstances can it be involved in either alleged illegal activities or political campaign activities.

I am certain that the doctrine of separation of powers does not impose upon any President either the duty or the power to undertake to separate a congressional committee from access to the truth concerning alleged criminal activities.

I was in hopes that the President would accede to the request of this committee for these tapes and these papers.

I love my country. I venerate the office of the President, and I have the best wishes for the success of the … present incumbent of that office, because he is the only President this country has at this time.

A President not only has constitutional powers which require him to see to it or to take care that the law be faithfully executed, and I think it's his duty under those circumstances to produce information which would either tend to prove or disprove that criminal activities have occurred. But beyond that, the President of the United States, by reason of the fact that he holds the highest office in the gift of the American people, owes an obligation to furnish a high standard of moral leadership to this nation and his constitutional duties, in my opinion, and undoubtedly his duty of affording moral leadership of the country place upon him some obligation under these circumstances.

We have evidence here that during the time the President was running for re-election to the highest office in the gift of the people of this nation that some of his campaign funds were found in the possession of burglars in the headquarters of the opposition political party. And I think that high moral leadership demands that the President make available to this committee any information in the form of tapes or records which will shed some light on that crucial question: How did it happen that burglars were caught in the headquarters of the opposition party with the President's campaign funds in their pockets and in their hotel bedrooms at the time? And I don't think the people of the United States are interested so much in abstruse arguments about the separation of powers or executive privilege as they are in finding the answer to that question.

I deeply regret that this situation has arisen, because I think that the Watergate tragedy is the greatest tragedy this country has ever suffered. I used to think that the Civil War was our country's greatest tragedy, but I do remember that there were some redeeming features in the Civil War in that there was some spirit of sacrifice and heroism displayed on both sides. I see no redeeming features in Watergate.

BAKER

Mr. Chairman, it is difficult for me to express my disappointment that we arrive at the place where at least the leading edge of a confrontation of the question of separation of powers between the Congress and the White House is before us. You have pointed out, I am sure, that this committee has authorized by unanimous vote the issuance of a subpoena *duces tecum* for certain documents and certain portions of the so-called Butterfield tapes relevant to the inquiry of this committee.

As my colleagues on the committee know, I have tried as hard as I know how to find a way around this confrontation. I have suggested various and several alternative possibilities. Even now, I don't despair of hope that we can find a way to reconcile our differences in the conflict that impends between the Congress and the executive department. But I concur with my colleagues on the committee in the evaluation that there was no other practical course of action except to authorize the action which has now been described, and I voted for it and I support it.

I think the material sought by the subpoena *duces tecum* or, more accurately, by the subpoenas *duces tecum*, are essential, if not vital, to the full, thorough inquiry mandated and required of this committee.

I shall refrain from expressing my evaluation of the entire situation, that is, the totality of the testimony and the inferences to be drawn from it, until we have heard all of the information, all the witnesses, all of the testimony, and examined all of the documents that are made available to us. On Feb. 24, 1974, or prior thereto, if the committee files its report at an earlier date, I will express my conclusions, but not before.

It is my fond hope, however, that when we do finally get to the business of writing a report, that we have all of the available information and that we can in fact write a definitive statement on Watergate—not trying to indict or persecute anyone nor to protect anyone.

The committee has been criticized from time to time for its absence of rules of evidence, the right of confrontation, of cross-examination by counsel, and a number of other legal concepts that we do not have. But we do not have defendants, either, and we are not trying to create defendants. We are trying to find fact, to establish circumstances, to divine the causes, to ascertain the relationships that make up in toto the so-called Watergate affair.

I am unhappy that it is necessary for us to come to the brink of a constitutional confrontation, and although that is a hackneyed phrase, it is an accurate phrase, a constitutional confrontation between the Congress and the White House, a confrontation that has never been resolved in its totality by the courts, a principle and doctrine that has never been fully elaborated and spelled out, in order to fully discharge our obligation as a committee. But I think that is precisely where we are.

I have no criticism of any person. I will not sit in judgment of any person or the conduct of any person until all of the evidence is taken, but I can do no less than try to gain all of the information available on which to base such a conclusion later.

Drinan Impeachment Resolution

Reprinted from *Congressional Quarterly Weekly Report*, August 4, 1973

Rep. Robert F. Drinan (D Mass.) introduced a resolution (H Res 513) July 31 for the impeachment of President Nixon for "high crimes and misdemeanors." It appeared to be regarded as premature by many members of the House and Senate, who said they awaited the conclusion of Senate Watergate hearings.

Drinan, a Roman Catholic priest and former law school dean, cited these reasons for introducing the resolution, the first introduced against Nixon in either house:

- Secret bombing of Cambodia, financed by money obtained from Congress "under false pretenses and spent in an unconstitutional manner."
- Nixon's taping of conversations in his offices without the knowledge of other persons being taped.
- Refusal to spend appropriated funds, despite court rulings against the administration on impoundment.
- Establishment of a "super-secret security force within the White House."

Points to Ponder

- In hindsight, one might ask why President Nixon taped conversations in his office. It seems like an odd thing to do. But compare that action with more commonplace ways of communicating today. Would it be appropriate for Congress or the courts to make the White House turn over emails between the president and his staff? What about digital video shot by the president or his staff?

- The investigation of the Watergate scandal would depend largely on whether Congress and the independent prosecutor would win access to the White House tapes. Can you think of a scenario in which it would harm the national interest if a president were to turn over records of private conversations? What about a scenario in which it would harm only the president's political career, but not the nation?

WATERGATE COMMITTEE HEARS 33RD WITNESS, RECESSES and THE 34TH WATERGATE WITNESS:

Nixon Restates His Case

On Aug. 7, the Senate Watergate Committee began a month-long recess after hearing from its 33rd witness. Committee members would need to figure out how to proceed in the fall on their planned investigation into campaign contributions and political espionage (dirty tricks intended to damage opposition candidates). They were under pressure to wrap up their investigation so that the Senate could get on to other business.

The committee's work was overshadowed at times by the power struggle over tapes of Nixon's private conversations. The White House continued to wage a court battle against demands that it turn over the tapes. Nixon said he was worried about establishing a precedent that private White House documents could become public. But on Aug. 29, he suffered a significant legal setback when U.S. District Court judge John J. Sirica ordered the White House to give him the tapes for his review.

The administration also faced trouble on a new front. Vice President Spiro T. Agnew learned that he was under a federal investigation into allegations that he had taken money from contractors in exchange for funneling government contracts to them. Investigators believed he had accepted bribes both as governor of Maryland and as vice president of the United States. Agnew vigorously denied the allegations.

LAST WITNESSES

The final two witnesses in August before the Senate Watergate Committee were Assistant Attorney General Henry E. Petersen and his ex-boss, former attorney general Richard G. Kleindienst. The two men defended the Justice Department's handling of Watergate. Petersen even criticized the decision to take away the investigation from the Justice Department and hand it over to a special prosecutor, arguing that the original prosecution team could have gotten to the bottom of the affair. (Many observers had worried that the Justice Department had a conflict of interest because it reported to Nixon. Independent prosecutor Archibald Cox was hired partly because he pledged to pursue the case even if the evidence led to the president.)

Both witnesses said that they had not received instructions from Nixon in March to report new facts about Water-

gate to him. This testimony was viewed as somewhat damaging to Nixon, who had maintained that he was trying to get information on the scandal.

With polls showing him losing public confidence, Nixon held a televised press conference on Aug. 15. His remarks got mixed reviews. He did little more than repeat his earlier claims of non-involvement in Watergate. He also maintained that releasing tapes of private conversations with White House aides would dangerously weaken the office of the presidency.

BATTLES OVER TAPES

Meanwhile, the White House escalated the battle over the tapes. First, White House chief of staff Alexander M. Haig Jr. argued that the Senate Watergate Committee's request to obtain just a few tapes was unworkable. Then White House lawyers filed a legal argument in federal court opposing the demand by Cox for the tapes and related documents. Nixon's lawyers argued that the president had a right to withhold the tapes even if they dealt with a criminal plan. They said that the president had the right to keep his communications confidential. They also argued that the courts could not order the president to turn over the documents because of the doctrine of separation of powers. (For more on the separation of powers, see p. 81.)

The Senate Watergate Committee filed its own lawsuit for the tapes on Aug. 9. This made the legal situation highly complicated. All three branches of government now were involved in the critical constitutional question of whether a president could be forced to hand over private documents that might provide clues to a crime. One Supreme Court justice, Harry A. Blackmun, warned that the "very glue of our ship of state seems about to become unstuck." Some prominent members of Nixon's own party thought he should release the tapes and other documents. Otherwise, he would continue to face political problems. Sen. Robert Dole of Kansas, a former Republican national chairman, said that "with the exception of a very few, Republicans in the Senate and Republicans in the House feel the tapes should be released."

On Aug. 22, Cox and the president's attorney, Charles Alan Wright, brought their competing arguments into Sirica's courtroom. The two lawyers clashed over whether Sirica should enforce the grand jury subpoena, or legal order, that sought to force the president to turn over the tapes. Wright cited "the simple fact of history" that no court had ever attempted to do what Cox asked. It would undermine the privacy of future presidents and dangerously weaken the executive branch. "There are times when other national interests are more important even than the fullest administration of criminal justice," Wright said.

He claimed that only the president could decide what documents could be made public and what should be protected by executive privilege. But Sirica appeared troubled by this argument. If the president alone could decide what evidence should be revealed, "there is potential for grave abuse then," he told Wright.

Cox, for his part, argued that the government would be weakened if Nixon was allowed to keep the tapes secret. "Public confidence in our institutions is at stake," he said.

On Aug. 29, Sirica ordered Nixon to turn over tapes of nine conversations so that he could review them. If he determined they did not contain information related to national security, he would forward them to the Watergate grand jury. But his ruling hardly settled the matter. White House lawyers immediately rejected it, even hinting they might ignore it altogether. Several days later, however, Nixon met with his lawyers and decided on a more standard legal strategy. He would appeal Sirica's ruling to the U.S. Court of Appeals in the District of Columbia.

Thus, the president seemed to opt for a prolonged legal duel that would likely end at the U.S. Supreme Court. Even then, some observers worried that the battle might result in a deadlock. Nixon had stated earlier that he would comply only with a "definitive" Supreme Court ruling. He did not say how he would determine whether the court's ruling met that standard. Nor was it clear what might happen if the president refused to comply with a Supreme Court decision.

OTHER DEVELOPMENTS

Nixon's poll numbers sank slowly through the late summer amid a steady drumbeat of accusations. One of the most damaging legal developments took place in early September in Los Angeles. There, a grand jury issued indictments, or formal charges, against four members of a secret White House task force for burglary. The men were charged with breaking into the office of the psychiatrist of Daniel Ellsberg, a former Pentagon staffer who had leaked a top-secret report known as the Pentagon Papers. (For more about Ellsberg and the Pentagon Papers, see p. 44.) The indictments were issued against John D. Ehrlichman, Nixon's former domestic affairs advisor; Egil (Bud) Krogh Jr., former deputy assistant to the president; David R. Young, another former White House aide; and convicted Watergate conspirator G. Gordon Liddy.

The administration also faced other controversies:

- Several companies admitted illegal contributions to Nixon's re-election campaign of up to $100,000 each.
- James W. McCord Jr., convicted Watergate conspirator, said he destroyed critical documents related to the Watergate break-in. He also said he thought the FBI had been blocked from thoroughly investigating the case before the destruction of evidence.
- Documents revealed that U.S. Army intelligence units in 1972 spied on a group of supporters of George McGovern, the Democratic presidential nominee. This appeared to violate a 1970 law prohibiting the army from conducting civilian spying.
- G. Gordon Liddy, convicted Watergate conspirator, was cited for contempt of Congress for refusing to testify before two congressional committees.
- *The New York Times* identified several government officials, including ambassadors based overseas, whose phones had been tapped under Nixon's authority. Nixon had earlier said he authorized wiretapping to stop news leaks that were jeopardizing sensitive foreign policy matters.
- Although not directly related to Watergate, the Senate Watergate Committee released a controversial memo by Charles W. Colson, a former aide to Nixon. The memo appeared to show that Nixon and former attorney general John N. Mitchell improperly intervened in the settlement of a government anti-trust case against the International Telephone and Telegraph Company.

T he Senate Watergate Committee recessed its hearings Aug. 7 after zeroing in for two days on the Justice Department and FBI's early handling of the case. The stories told by its final two witnesses, Assistant Attorney General Henry E. Petersen and his ex-boss, former Attorney General Richard G. Kleindienst, were not startling. Nevertheless, they provided fascinating insights into two areas: the inside workings of a department whose halting progress in the Watergate investigation had been widely criticized, and the severe tensions the probe induced within the top ranks of the Nixon administration.

With a final ripple of his now-famous eyebrows, Committee Chairman Sam J. Ervin Jr. (D N.C.) unceremoniously gaveled the hearings closed at 4:45 p.m. Tuesday after finishing with Petersen, the committee's 33rd witness. Seven more witnesses were due to appear beginning Sept. 10 before the panel moved beyond the first phase: the break-in itself.

The conflict between the legislature and executive branches of government seemed to be advancing inexorably toward a constitutional crisis, which many observers warned could juggle the balance of authority between the branches of government. Speaking generally on the moral issues of Watergate in an address before the American Bar Association Aug. 5, Nixon Supreme Court Justice appointee Harry A. Blackmun warned that the "very glue of our ship of state seems about to become unstuck." The observation seemed to apply with special aptness to the tapes controversy.

The White House position grew increasingly obdurate as the week progressed. In a CBS television interview Aug. 3, White House chief of staff Alexander M. Haig Jr. argued that selective release of tapes of White House conversations sought by the committee would encourage Watergate defendants to insist on complete disclosure so as to exonerate themselves of perjury charges.

Then, on Aug. 7, White House lawyers filed a 34-page brief with federal judge John J. Sirica opposing the subpoena filed by Special Prosecutor Archibald Cox for the tapes and related documents. Nixon's lawyers argued that the President had a right to withhold the tapes in order to safeguard the confidentiality of presidential communications—even if they dealt with a criminal plan—and that under the separation-of-powers doctrine the court had no business enforcing the subpoena. The committee filed its own suit Aug. 9.

Petersen and Kleindienst. Assistant Attorney General Petersen, 52, was a registered Democrat who described himself as "non-partisan." His ex-boss, Kleindienst, who described himself as "a hard-nosed 50-year-old geezer", was a creature of Republican politics. He had directed the 1964 presidential campaign of fellow-Arizonian Barry Goldwater and had been national field director for Richard Nixon's 1968 campaign.

Both witnesses made persuasive cases for the propriety of their handling of Watergate, if not entirely for their effectiveness. However, Petersen bitterly disputed the decision to hand the investigation over to a special prosecutor, arguing that the switch reflected unjustly on the integrity of the Justice Department. Given time, he said, the original prosecution team "could have made the case."

So far as the President was concerned, perhaps the most damaging testimony offered by the two witnesses was their agreement that neither had received instructions from Nixon on or after March 21 to report new facts to him, as Nixon had maintained.

Nixon seemed about ready to reply. As the hearings recessed he was huddling with top advisers and speechwriters at his Camp David retreat in Maryland's Catoctin Mountains, preparing his long-promised statement on the Watergate hearings.

SUMMARY OF NIXON'S REPLY IN COURT TEST OVER TAPES

Throughout the summer, President Nixon engaged in legal battles to avoid having to turn over tapes of private White House conversations. In his reply to special prosecutor Archibald Cox, Nixon argued that the office of the presidency would be forever weakened if Cox succeeded in forcing the White House to turn over the tapes. A president and his aides would not be able to have frank discussions if they had to worry about their private memos and other documents becoming public. Nixon also said that the president had the right to withhold information if he believed that disclosing the information could harm the public. This was an extremely broad view of executive privilege. (For more about executive privilege, see p. 39.) Nixon argued that the White House had the right to keep documents private even if those documents were associated with criminal activity. Moreover, he said the president was not answerable to the courts because the courts were not a superior branch of government. He concluded, "the judicial branch lacks power to compel the President to produce information that he has determined it is not in the public interest to disclose."

Following is the text of the summary of Nixon's reply to Special Prosecutor Archibald Cox's subpoena seeking taped conversations in the Watergate case. The Nixon brief was filed Aug. 7 in U.S. District Court in Washington, D.C.

The present proceeding, though a well-intentioned effort to obtain evidence for criminal prosecutions, represents a serious threat to the nature of the presidency as it was created by the Constitution, as it has been sustained for 184 years, and as it exists today.

If the special prosecutor should be successful in the attempt to compel disclosure of recordings of presidential conversations, the damage to the institution of the presidency will be severe and irreparable. The character of that office will be fundamentally altered and the total structure of government—dependent as it is upon a separation of powers—will be impaired.

The consequence of an order to disclose recordings or notes would be that no longer could a President speak in confidence with his close advisers on any subject. The threat of potential disclosure of any and all conversations would make it virtually impossible for President Nixon or his successors in that great office to function. Beyond that, a holding that the President is personally subject to the orders of a court would effectively destroy the status of the executive branch as an equal and coordinate element of government.

There is no precedent that can be said to justify or permit such a result. On the contrary, it is clear that while courts and their grand juries have the power to seek evidence of all persons, including the President, the President has the power and thus the privilege to withhold information if he concludes that disclosure would be contrary to the public interest.

The breadth of this privilege is frequently debated. Whatever its boundaries it must obtain with respect to a President's private conversations with his advisers (as well as to private conversations by judges and legislators with their advisers). These conversations reflect advisory opinions, recommendations, and deliberations that are an essential part of the process by which presidential decisions and policies are formulated. Presidential privacy must be protected, not for its own sake, but because of the paramount need for frank expression and discussion among the President and those consulted by him in the making of presidential decisions.

The privilege with regard to recordings was not waived by the decision of the President, in the interest of having the truth about Watergate come out, to permit testimony about portions of those conversations by persons who participated in them. Testimony can be limited, as recordings cannot, to the particular area in which privilege is not being claimed. Nor does the privilege vanish because there are claims that some of the statements made to the President by others in these conversations may have been pursuant to a criminal conspiracy by those other persons. That others may have acted in accordance with a criminal design does not alter the fact that the President's participation in these conversations was pursuant to his constitutional duty to see that the laws are faithfully executed and that he is entitled to claim executive privilege to preserve the confidentiality of private conversations he held in carrying out that duty.

In the exercise of his discretion to claim executive privilege the President is answerable to the nation but not to the courts. The courts, a co-equal but not a superior branch of government, are not free to probe the mental processes and the private confidences of the President and his advisers. To do so would be a clear violation of the constitutional separation of powers. Under that doctrine the judicial branch lacks power to compel the President to produce information that he has determined it is not in the public interest to disclose.

The issue here is starkly simple: will the presidency be allowed to continue to function?

FOUR VERSIONS ON NOTIFICATION

The question of what President Nixon knew about the Watergate coverup and when he learned it is one that committee Vice Chairman Howard H. Baker Jr. (R Tenn.) asked repeatedly during the hearings. It never was finally settled. As the committee recessed for a month-long vacation, there were four versions of when Nixon first got word of the coverup:

Nixon: "Until March of this year, I remained convinced that the . . . charges of involvement by members of the White House staff were false. However, new information then came to me which persuaded me that there was a real possibility that some of these charges were true, and suggesting further that there had been an effort to conceal the facts. . . ." (*Statement issued April 30*)

Dean: On March 21, "I began by telling the President that there was a cancer growing on the presidency" and "then proceeded to tell him some of the highlights that had occurred during the coverup." (*Statement to the committee June 25*)

Ehrlichman: The former domestic adviser to the President said he gave Nixon a complete report on the coverup April 14, based on his inquiry that began March 30. "I have great difficulty believing" Dean's testimony that he gave the President a complete report March 21, Ehrlichman said. (*Testimony July 27*)

Kleindienst: "I would say that the information, the nature that I described with (Nixon on April 15) would have come to his attention contemporaneously. If Mr. Ehrlichman is talking to Magruder all afternoon the day before, I would just assume, although he didn't say, that Mr. Ehrlichman would have made a report like this to the President. But I would gather from my meeting with the President that he had no such knowledge until immediately prior to my meeting." (*Testimony Aug. 7*)

Agnew Revealed as Target of Federal Investigation

Just when it seemed that things could not get any worse for the administration, Vice President Spiro T. Agnew learned that he was under criminal investigation. He faced allegations that he had steered government contracts to companies that had paid him money. It the allegations were true, it would mean that the vice president was accepting bribes.

Vice President Spiro T. Agnew, one of the few major administration figures to survive without a taint of the Watergate scandal, was informed Aug. 2 that he is under federal investigation on charges of bribery, extortion and tax fraud. The charges were reported to relate to the award of state contracts during Agnew's two years (1967–1968) as governor of Maryland, and to the award of federal building contracts in Maryland since he became vice president in 1969.

Agnew met with President Nixon for almost two hours Aug. 7, and on the following day told a press conference that he was defending himself, instead of "spending my time looking around to see who's supporting me." The White House refused to comment on the charges.

On Aug. 6, as *The Wall Street Journal* was printing its editions containing the first major story on the Agnew investigation, Agnew released a brief statement: "I have been informed that I am under investigation for possible violations of the criminal statues. I will make no further comment until the investigation has been completed, other than to say that I am innocent of any wrongdoing, that I have confidence in the criminal justice system of the United States and I am equally confident that my innocence will be affirmed."

The Knight newspaper chain on Aug. 8 reported that Agnew had received $50,000 from private contractors after he became vice president. *The Los Angeles Times* the same day quoted a source close to the investigation as saying that an indictment of Agnew was expected within weeks.

In response to these allegations which Agnew denied and labeled "damn lies," the vice president called an afternoon press conference on Aug. 8. Saying that he had no intention of being "skewered" by "defamatory statements . . . leaked to the news media by sources that the news reports refer to as close to the federal investigators," Agnew responded to questions from a packed auditorium of newsmen. He labeled the allegations which went beyond the bare statement that he was being investigated as "false and scurrilous and malicious." He said he had "no expectation of being indicted" and that he had given no consideration to leaving the post of vice president, even temporarily.

He indicated a willingness to cooperate with the investigators, who had begun their inquiry early in 1973 concerning reported kickbacks to Baltimore County officials by contractors and architectural firms. Agnew served as Baltimore county executive from 1962 until he moved to the governor's mansion in 1967. There were "highly unprecedented constitutional questions" which were involved in such an investigation, Agnew noted, but he said he would make available whatever—including "my own body for interrogation"—was needed and whatever was considered advisable by his legal counsel.

BLACKMUN: 'GRAVE DAMAGE'

Supreme Court Justice Harry A. Blackmun Aug. 5 told 750 members of the American Bar Association (ABA) and their families that the Watergate scandal had created an atmosphere whereby the "very glue of our ship of state seems about to come unstuck."

Blackmun told the assembled lawyers and judges there was a fear that "grave damage" had been done to the democratic process because of the scandal. "The pall of Watergate, with all its revelations of misplaced loyalties, of strange measures of the unethical, of unusual doings in high places, and by lawyer after lawyer after lawyer, is upon us," he said.

Appointed to the court in 1970 by President Nixon and generally considered a member of the court's conservative wing, Blackmun noted that every administration in recent times had been affected by scandals—large and small. "One senses a laxness in public life that 20 years ago, if indulged in, could not be politically surmounted," he said.

Speaking before the bar association's annual prayer breakfast, Blackmun chose as his text the Old Testament book of Nehemiah, which describes the rebuilding of the walls of Jerusalem in 446 B.C. against what seemed to be overwhelming odds. "One may say that our Jerusalem is in ruins," he said. One might question, he added, whether American society's "foundations are eroding, and whether the walls, after all, are only rubble.

"Perhaps we need to make our own solitary inspection of the walls," he concluded, "to plan; to cooperate; to resolve that it is worth doing; to provide leadership; to engage, if necessary, in activity that simultaneously is both defensive and constructive; to rededicate—or should I say dedicate—ourselves to what this bar association and this nation stand for."

The justice received a standing ovation.

President Nixon went on national television on Aug. 15 to give his side of the Watergate story. In essence, he was appearing as the 34th witness, after 33 official witnesses appeared before the Senate Watergate Committee. But Nixon offered little new information about the scandal, and he left many questions unanswered. He said he regretted the events associated with the Watergate scandal, emphasized that he would not turn over the tapes, and urged Congress to get back to major legislative issues.

The 34th Witness

To many it seemed anticlimactic. Instead of adding new information to that already accumulated during eight weeks of Senate Watergate Committee hearings—and wave upon wave of sensational White House secret-baring—President Nixon in his Aug. 15 response to the testimony for the most part only repeated earlier claims of non-involvement. Nixon declared he was telling "the simple truth" and asked the public to let him return to running the country.

"We must not stay so mired in Watergate that we fail to respond to challenges of surpassing importance to America and the world," the President said near the end of his nationally televised speech. "We cannot let an obsession with the past destroy our hopes for the future."

At another place Nixon directed a pointed barb toward Congress, blaming preoccupation with Watergate for lack of attention to legislative programs. "Legislation vital to your health and well-being sits unattended on the Congressional calendar," Nixon told the viewers.

Early reaction to Nixon's statement was mixed.

In working on his speech with advisers earlier in the week at Camp David, Md., the President seemed to face a clearly defined challenge: to win back the confidence of the American people, who had elected him less than 10 months earlier by the third largest electoral vote in history. Nixon's public support had fallen dizzily since the beginning of the Watergate hearings: a late public opinion poll showed that had the election been held in late July or early August 1973, former opponent George McGovern might have defeated him.

By choosing national television as a vehicle for his statement, Nixon had decided to employ a tactic he had used before: to go over the heads of Congress and the press and appeal directly to the public. But the tactic had two edges. In using television, Nixon would be appearing in the same forum, on the same video screen that 33 Watergate committee witnesses had already flashed across, each with his own version of events. Each had offered his own rationale, and each had asked for belief, even though some of their statements were completely incompatible.

Thus, in a sense, the President would be the 34th witness, and instead of seven men, an unseen grassroots panel would be deciding his credibility in a most profound way.

Nixon's approach to them came in several parts.

First, he surprised some observers who had been predicting an attack on the Watergate committee by offering only oblique criticism. While complaining that the committee had become "increasingly absorbed in an effort to implicate the President personally" in Watergate, Nixon asserted, "I do not question the right of a Senate committee to investigate charges made against the President to the extent that this is relevant to their legislative duties." And, he said, it was the duty of the committee—along with the courts—to decide who told the truth during the hearings.

Nixon also repeated an earlier position that "because the abuses occurred under my administration and in the campaign for my re-election, I accept full responsibility for them." Looking directly at the camera he added, "I regret that these events took place."

It was a brisk, business-like apology, but an apology nonetheless. Having said that, the President briefly reiterated earlier statements in which he had maintained his own innocence.

And he repeated arguments already made by White House lawyers, that releasing tapes of his private conversations with White House aides in order to prove his truthfulness would violate the presidential privilege of confidentiality. This principle "is absolutely essential to the conduct of the presidency, in this and future administrations," Nixon claimed, and to violate it "would cripple all future presidents by inhibiting conversations between them and those they look to for advice."

Nixon said he recognized that the term Watergate had taken on a number of definitions, including abuse of the political process, and of investigational authority in the name of national security. However, he stated an argument similar to that of Watergate witness Jeb Stuart Magruder, that those transgressions had arisen from the same devotion to a "higher morality" that had been invoked by liberal political activists in the 1960s.

"That attitude can never be tolerated in this country," Nixon said. ". . . The notion that the end justifies the means proved contagious. Thus it is not surprising, even though it is deplorable, that some persons in 1972 adopted the morality that they themselves had rightly condemned and committed acts that have no place in our political system."

Saying that those acts should be punished, Nixon called for "a renewed respect for the mutual restraints that are the mark of a free and civilized society."

The President admitted that "instances have now come to light in which a zeal for (national) security did go too far, and did interfere impermissibly with individual liberty." However, he cautioned against an over-reaction that would place unreasonable limits on the President's duty to protect the nation's security.

In a more detailed statement released in conjunction with the speech, Nixon corrected his May 22 declaration that he had not learned of the break-in at the office of Pentagon Papers figure Daniel Ellsberg's psychiatrist until after Nixon had begun his own investigation March 21. He actually learned of the burglary March 17, Nixon said. However, he did not explain exactly how he found out, nor did he say why he had erred on May 22, other than to suggest an oversight. The point was but one of a number of questions he left unanswered.

SUMMARY OF COX ARGUMENT FOR TAPES SUBPOENA

After Nixon's lawyers said he was not obligated to turn over tapes of private conversations, Watergate special prosecutor Archibald Cox filed a long argument in court. Cox claimed that the president, like every other citizen, has to respond to a grand jury. He said that the public has a right to hear all evidence that may shed light on a crime. He also argued that if Nixon turned over the tapes it would not weaken the presidency. The grand jury was only looking for certain conversations related to possible crimes, he pointed out, and was not interested in most of Nixon's meetings.

Looking back at history, Cox discussed the 1807 treason trial of Aaron Burr. He noted that President Thomas Jefferson complied with a subpoena in that case, which in Cox's view meant that presidents in general must obey subpoenas. He also argued that the courts, not the president, have the power to determine what evidence should be turned over for a criminal investigation.

Following is the text of the summary of Watergate Special Prosecutor Archibald Cox's memorandum filed in U.S. District Court in Washington on Aug. 13 in support of his suit to compel President Nixon to turn over to the grand jury investigating the Watergate affair recordings of certain taped conversations relating to the case.

The 68-page memorandum responded point-by-point to the Aug. 7 White House reply to the Cox subpoena in which President Nixon was held "answerable to the nation but not to the courts."

Arguments in the case to obtain release of the tapes and documents were scheduled to begin in U.S. District Court in Washington on Aug. 22.

I

The President has an enforceable legal duty not to withhold material evidence from a grand jury. The grand jury occupies a fundamental position in the administration of public justice. There is no exception for the President from the guiding principle that the public, in the pursuit of justice, has a right to every man's evidence. These propositions were recognized as early as 1807 in *United States v. Burr*, 25 Fed. Cas. 30 (No. 14,692d) (C.C.D. Va. 1807). They have critical importance in a grand jury inquiry into gross misconduct by high officials in the Executive Offices of the President.

The decision in *United States v. Burr* is but a specific application of two historic constitutional principles: (1) even the highest executive officials are subject to the rule of law, which it is emphatically the province and duty of the courts to declare; and (2) the rights and obligations of the President and other high executive officers are defined and judicial orders are entered on the premise that these officials, rather than interpose their naked power, will obey the law's explicit and particularized commands. Accordingly, the Court of Appeals for this Circuit, like every other Federal court, has rejected the claim that absolute executive privilege flows from the constitutional separation of powers. It has ruled that it is for the Judiciary—not the Executive—to determine what materials may be held confidential because of a particular exigency and what evidence must be produced. *Committee for Nuclear Responsibility,*

Inc. v. Seaborg, 463 F2d 788, 792–94 (D.C. Cir. 1971).

The subpoena was properly directed to the President, and the Court has power to enforce it. Counsel's claim that the President, because of his great powers, has immunity from orders enforcing legal obligations is inconsistent with our entire constitutional tradition. The President cannot be limited by judicial intrusion into the exercise of his constitutional powers under Article II. Here, however, the grand jury is not seeking to control the President in the exercise of his constitutional power to withhold the evidence sought by the subpoena merely by his own declaration of the public interest. The grand jury is seeking evidence of criminal conduct that the respondent happens to have in his custody—largely by his personal choice. All the Court is asked to do is hold that the President is bound by legal duties in appropriate cases just as other citizens—in this case, by the duty to supply documentary evidence of crime. In the language of the authoritative precedents, this is a "ministerial duty."

Contrary to counsel's argument, enforcement of the subpoena would not create the threat of "potential disclosure of any and all conversations" (Brief in Opposition 2-3), nor does our submission suggest that every participant in a Presidential conversation would have to speak "in continual awareness that at any moment any Congressional committee, or any prosecutor working with a grand jury, could at will command the production of the verbatim record of every word written or spoken" (Brief in Opposition 16-17). Not only are the facts of the case much narrower, but a settled rule of evidence protects a broad range of Presidential papers and conversations against disclosure *when the Court decides*—after *in camera* inspection when necessary—that the public interest in the secrecy of the particular items outweighs the need for the evidence in the administration of justice.

II

The present case does not fall within the traditional rule of executive privilege as administered by the courts. Counsel for respondent wisely refrain from pressing such a claim. Under the usual rule, the Court—not the President—determines whether particular documents are privileged by weighing the need for the evidence against any governmental interest in secrecy. Here, the only possible governmental interest in secrecy is encouraging openness and candor in giving advice and promoting the free flow of discussion in deliberations upon executive policy by assuring a measure of confidentiality. Preservation of secrecy is unwarranted in the present case for two independent reasons. First, the interest in confidentiality is never sufficient to support an official privilege where there is reason to believe that the deliberations may have involved criminal misconduct. Second, under the particular circumstances of the present case, the need of the grand jury for the critically important evidence provided by the recordings upon a question of wrongdoing by high officials and party leaders easily outweighs the slight risk to the freedom of executive discussions. There will be few occasions upon which a grand jury will have similar cause to believe there may be material evidence of the criminality of high officials in the papers and documents in the Executive Office of the President. The aides of future Presidents are not likely to be timid because of this remote danger of disclosure. If there be some small risk of greater reticence, it is not too great a price to pay to preserve the integrity of the Office of the President.

III

Even if the tape recordings might once have been covered by a privilege, any such claim to continued secrecy has been waived by the extensive testimony, given with respondent's consent, publicizing individual versions of the conversations. In his public statement of May 22, 1973, respondent announced that "Executive privilege will not be invoked as to any testimony concerning possible criminal conduct, in the matters presently under investigation, including the Watergate affair and the alleged cover-up." In accordance with that statement, Dean, Mitchell, Ehrlichman and Haldeman already have testified extensively before the Senate Committee and/or in other proceedings concerning the conversations specified in the subpoena. Haldeman even was allowed access to various tapes after he left government office and gave testimony based upon his listening to the tapes denied the grand jury. Respondent and his counsel themselves have made comments for publication upon the content of the conversations. Under familiar legal principles those disclosures waive any right to further confidentiality. Not even a President can be allowed to select some accounts of a conversation for public disclosure and then to frustrate further grand jury inquiries by withholding the best evidence of what actually took place.

WATERGATE BOX SCORE: OVER 20 INVESTIGATIONS . . . LAWSUITS, TRIALS—AND SEVERAL MORE THREATENED

By early August, Watergate had triggered eight civil suits, seven congressional inquiries, six grand jury investigations, three trials and numerous federal agency investigations. Still more actions were planned.

While it may seem strange to have so many different legal actions, each type of action had a different purpose:

In a civil suit, a person or an organization claims to have been injured. That party files a lawsuit to get monetary compensation for the injury. In the aftermath of Watergate, for example, Democrats and Republicans filed suits against each other, each claiming the other side had injured them in some way.

Congress typically launches hearings or inquiries to get information that can lead to legislation. After Watergate, Congress passed several laws intended to prevent future presidents from abusing their power.

Grand juries investigate alleged crimes. They have the power to take sworn testimony from witnesses and to gather information by issuing subpoenas. If members of a grand jury believe a person is guilty of a crime, they can issue an indictment.

Once a person is indicted, he or she faces a criminal trial. It is at a trial that a defendant is found guilty or innocent.

Federal agency investigations tend to be less formal than investigations by Congress or grand juries. They are designed to zero in on wrongdoing within an agency and often result in recommendations for improvements.

Here is a summary of the various legal proceedings that had taken place by August.

CONGRESSIONAL

- The House Banking and Currency Committee on Oct. 3, 1972, voted to reject a probe of Nixon campaign finances. According to House committee sources, Chairman Wright Patman (D Texas) directed the staff to stay on top of the case for possible future hearings.
- Sen. Edward M. Kennedy (D Mass.), chairman of a Senate Judiciary subcommittee, reported on Jan. 22 the results of a staff investigation of Watergate.
- Sen. Sam J. Ervin Jr.'s (D N.C.) Senate Select Committee on Presidential Campaign Activities opened hearings on Watergate May 17.
- The full Senate Judiciary Committee heard Watergate-related testimony during the confirmation hearings of L. Patrick Gray III for FBI director and of Elliot L. Richardson for attorney general.
- The House and Senate Armed Services Committees and the Senate Appropriations Committee held extensive hearings on CIA involvement in the Watergate coverup.

Planned. In an interview published in *The New York Times* June 16, Rep. Peter W. Rodino Jr. (D N.J.), chairman of the House Judiciary Committee, said he was planning a broad investigation into Justice Department and FBI operations as a result of Watergate.

Possible. Rep. Wilbur D. Mills (D Ark.), chairman of the House Ways and Means Committee and the Joint Committee on Internal Revenue Taxation, said June 27 he had directed the staff of the Joint Committee to begin preliminary checks into charges that the Internal Revenue Service was used for political purposes.

GRAND JURIES

Washington, D.C. The original Watergate grand jury was first impaneled June 5, 1972, in Washington as a regular grand jury. It began its investigation of the Watergate break-in immediately after the crime had occurred. After handing down the indictments of the original seven defendants on Sept. 15, 1972, the jury reconvened on March 26, 1973, to consider new charges.

Although still in session, the jury was to be joined on Aug. 13 by a special grand jury requested by Watergate special prosecutor Archibald Cox to probe new areas. The new jury was to consider charges of campaign corruption, focusing on illegal contributions by corporations, extortion by federal officials, conspiracy and obstruction of justice.

New York City. A federal grand jury in New York City on May 10 indicted four men, including two former Nixon cabinet officers, on charges of conspiring to arrange a secret $200,000 contribution to the 1972 campaign. Indicted were former Attorney General John N. Mitchell, former Commerce Secretary Maurice H. Stans, New Jersey financier Robert L. Vesco (who made the contribution) and New Jersey attorney Harry L. Sears. Mitchell, Stans and Sears pleaded not guilty on May 21. A bench warrant was issued for the arrest of Vesco, who was believed to be out of the country.

Los Angeles. A federal grand jury in Los Angeles on June 7 opened an investigation into the break-in at the office of Pentagon Papers defendant Daniel Ellsberg's psychiatrist.

Orlando, Fla. A federal grand jury in Orlando, Fla., on May 4 indicted Los Angeles attorney Donald H. Segretti and Tampa accountant George Hearing on charges of distributing a bogus letter under the letterhead of 1972 Democratic presidential candidate Edmund S. Muskie. Hearing pleaded guilty to one count of a two-count indictment and was sentenced on June 15 to a maximum of one year in prison. Segretti, who pleaded innocent on May 17, was scheduled for trial in Tampa the week of Oct. 8.

Houston. A federal grand jury in Houston, Texas, was investigating a $100,000 contribution made by Gulf Resources and Chemical Corporation to the Nixon campaign. Part of the money allegedly went through Mexico into the Miami bank account of convicted Watergate conspirator Bernard L. Barker and was used to help finance the Watergate bugging.

Anne Arundel County. A grand jury in Anne Arundel County, Maryland, on June 13 indicted Blagden H. Wharton, a Maryland banker and 1972 Republican campaign official, on four counts of violating state election laws by falsifying campaign contribution reports on a dinner held for Vice President Agnew in May 1972.

CIVIL SUITS

Democrats. Three days after the Watergate break-in, then Democratic Chairman Lawrence F. O'Brien announced a $1-million invasion-of-privacy suit against the Nixon re-election committee. On Sept. 11, 1972, the Democrats announced they would file an amended complaint that would add to the defendants finance chairman Stans, re-election committee treasurer Hugh W. Sloan, finance committee counsel G. Gordon Liddy and former part-time White House consultant E. Howard Hunt Jr., as well as the five men arrested on June 17. The Democrats also raised the damages sought from $1 million to $3.2 million and charged the defendants with political espionage dating back to March 1972. However, a federal district judge dismissed the five burglars from the suit on Sept. 20, 1972.

The Democrats doubled the damages sought to $6.4 million and added Jeb Stuart Magruder and Herbert L. Porter, two former officials of the re-election committee, as defendants, on Feb. 28, 1973.

The Washington Post reported April 18 and Aug. 1 discussions of an out-of-court settlement of the suit.

Republicans. Two days after the Democrats added Stans to their suit, Stans and re-

election committee chairman Francis I. Dale on Sept. 13, 1972, filed a $2.5 million abuse-of-process suit against the Democrats, charging them with using the courts "as an instrument for creating political headlines."

The next day, Stans filed a $5-million libel suit against O'Brien on grounds that O'Brien on Sept. 11 had falsely accused him of political espionage.

McCord. Convicted conspirator James W. McCord Jr. on April 20 filed a $1.5-million cross claim against the President's re-election committee and three campaign officials: Magruder, Liddy and E. Howard Hunt Jr. McCord claimed the defendants had entrapped him in activities that resulted in his conviction.

Common Cause. The so-called citizens' lobby filed suit Sept. 6, 1972, to compel the President's re-election finance committee to make full disclosure of its income and expenditures before April 7, 1972, the date such disclosures became mandatory. On July 24 a U.S. district court judge in Washington, D.C., ordered the committee to comply.

McCarthy. The California Committee for Eugene McCarthy on May 18 filed suit in San Francisco Superior Court against officials of the Nixon campaign and others, charging that a bogus letter had been sent out under the committee's letterhead during the 1972 California primary campaign. Named in the suit were Segretti, former Nixon lawyer Herbert W. Kalmbach, Stans, Mitchell, the President's re-election committee and 15 others.

Halperin. Morton H. Halperin, a former consultant to the National Security Council, on June 14 filed suit in U.S. District Court in Washington, D.C., for the bugging of his telephone from 1969 to 1971 for as long as 25 months. Halperin, a senior fellow at the Brookings Institution, named as defendants national security adviser Henry A. Kissinger; former White House aides H. R. Haldeman and John D. Ehrlichman; White House chief of staff and former Kissinger deputy Alexander Haig; John Mitchell; former FBI official William C. Sullivan; former acting FBI Director William D. Ruckelshaus; the Chesapeake and Potomac Telephone Company, and unnamed agents of the FBI and other government agencies.

Oliver. Democratic party official R. Spencer Oliver, whose telephone at Democratic National Committee headquarters was tapped, on June 15 filed a $5-million suit against Nixon campaign officials and others.

FEDERAL INVESTIGATIONS

Justice Department. Watergate special prosecutor Archibald Cox inherited the original Justice Department investigation of Watergate. A Cox spokesman told Congressional Quarterly that the Cox team was dealing directly with the FBI and was receiving "full cooperation."

GAO. The General Accounting Office had been investigating Watergate since August 1972, when it released a report citing Republicans for apparent violations of the campaign spending law—which the GAO helps police. By the beginning of August 1973, the GAO had referred seven Watergate-related reports to the Justice Department for action out of a total of 21 reports of apparent election law violations.

BAR ASSOCIATION

The state bar of California was planning an investigation of Nixon and five California lawyers for possible disciplinary action, *The San Francisco Examiner* reported July 29. The lawyers named were Ehrlichman, Kalmbach, Segretti, former White House aide Gordon C. Strachan and former Nixon re-election committee official Robert C. Mardian.

TRIALS

For all the legal maneuvering that surrounded Watergate, it had produced only three trials by the summer of 1973.

- Two of the seven men tried on criminal charges in the Watergate break-in, McCord and Liddy, were convicted Jan. 30, 1973, in U.S. District Court in Washington, D.C. The other five pleaded guilty.
- Bernard L. Barker, one of the convicted conspirators, was convicted in Florida Nov. 1, 1972, on a charge that he had misused a notary public seal to indicate that a campaign check was endorsed in his presence. Barker received a 60-day sentence, which was suspended on the condition that he surrender his notary's license.
- The President's re-election finance committee June 20 was found guilty of concealing a $200,000 cash contribution from indicted financier Robert L. Vesco. A U.S. district court judge in Washington fined the committee $3,000. It was the second conviction for the Nixon campaign organization and the second under the Federal Election Campaign Act of 1971. The finance committee had been fined $8,000 on Jan. 26 after pleading no contest to charges of not reporting to the GAO cash sums given by treasurer Hugh Sloan to G. Gordon Liddy.

Points to Ponder

The dispute over releasing records of private conversations became a major flash point in the Watergate scandal. Few of us would be able to persuade a judge that our personal records were so important that prosecutors should not have access to them. But a president may be able to argue that turning over records could endanger the security of the nation and permanently weaken the office of the presidency.

- Do you agree with Nixon that he had the right to refuse to comply with subpoenas or other court orders? Do presidents have some responsibilities that put their actions above the law? Or do you think the courts should be able to inspect presidential communications when reviewing evidence of a crime? What if no crime were alleged, but instead a private citizen was suing the president for misdeeds in his personal life?

- Would you want the president to turn over records even if you thought that it could strengthen the nation's enemies? Or do you think it is so important to hold the president accountable for possibly illegal actions that he should comply with court orders, regardless of the risks to the nation?

PART II: THE WHITE HOUSE TAPES

INTRODUCTION:
'Saturday Night Massacre' Precipitates House Impeachment Inquiry

Richard M. Nixon was losing his hold on the presidency. No one should have known it better than he as he watched it crumble away.

From the late summer of 1973 through the spring of 1974, Nixon appealed repeatedly to the public to "put Watergate behind us" and turn toward the more constructive business of government. But it was too late. Watergate had engulfed the Nixon administration. Defense had become the White House's principal preoccupation, draining its ability to govern.

At stake by mid-May was Nixon's very survival in office. For the first time in 106 years, an American president was subject to a formal impeachment inquiry.

BATTLE OVER TAPES

Increasingly during this period, the story of Watergate became the battle over access to tapes of private White House conversations. Investigators—the Watergate grand jury and the special prosecutor, the Senate committee, and later the House impeachment inquiry—sought them. First they made requests for the tapes, and then they issued subpoenas. Nixon, with legal arguments developed by his White House defense team, resisted releasing them.

Nixon based his refusal to cooperate on executive privilege and the separation of powers. Essentially, he argued that the office of the presidency would be undermined if he knuckled under to the investigators' demands. Explaining his concept of presidential confidentiality, Nixon said at one press conference, "Once it is known that a conversation that is held with a president can be subject to a subpoena by a Senate committee, by a grand jury, by a prosecutor, and be listened to by anyone, the principle of confidentiality is thereby irreparably damaged."

But Nixon's continued resistance to subpoenas for the tapes slowly turned public opinion against him. Not only did Nixon lose in the courts, but his credibility would suffer

with the disclosures that some subpoenaed tapes did not exist. In addition, a mysterious blank space would be discovered in one critical tape, which apparently had been tampered with.

The battle over the tapes began in July 1973. The Watergate grand jury issued a subpoena for them only days after their existence was revealed. This sparked a legal fight that was waged in federal courts in August and September. Charles Alan Wright, an attorney for Nixon, argued that it was in the best interests of the nation to protect a president's right to confidentiality. "There are times when other national interests are more important even than the fullest administration of criminal justice," he said.

Watergate special prosecutor Archibald Cox disagreed. "There is strong reason to believe that the integrity of the executive offices has been corrupted," he said. "Public confidence in our institutions is at stake."

Federal judge John J. Sirica essentially sided with Cox. In his decision, he said he would privately inspect the nine tapes that the federal grand jury had subpoenaed. If he decided that divulging the conversations would not harm the nation, he would turn over the tapes to the grand jury.

The White House rejected the order and appealed Sirica's ruling to the federal appeals court in Washington. Wright and Cox filed briefs Sept. 10 and argued their cases the next day. On Oct. 12, the appeals court upheld Sirica's order,

SATURDAY NIGHT MASSACRE

The losses in court led to the "Saturday night massacre" of Oct. 20, 1973.

No single incident cost Nixon more dearly than the shattering events of that evening. The reverberations that followed included a surge of demands for Nixon's resignation or impeachment.

The events leading up to Oct. 20 began when the president and his lawyers tried to work out a deal with Watergate special prosecutor Archibald Cox. Having lost in court, Nixon offered to turn over written summaries of the tapes to Sen. John C. Stennis (D Miss.). Stennis would verify them against the actual tapes and then give the summaries to both the special prosecutor and the Ervin committee. As part of the compromise, Nixon ordered Cox to cease further attempts to obtain data on presidential conversations.

Cox rejected what he considered a limitation on his investigative authority. Nixon retaliated by ordering Attorney General Elliot L. Richardson to fire him. Richardson resigned rather than do so. His deputy, William D. Ruckelshaus, followed suit. Cox finally was fired by U.S. Solicitor General Robert H. Bork, who became acting attorney general after the resignations and was ordered by Nixon to get rid of Cox.

MISSING TAPES AND GAPS

Cox's dismissal was, as the White House later acknowledged, a miscalculation. The incident ignited what Nixon's chief of staff, Alexander M. Haig Jr., described as a "firestorm." Public and congressional response was immediately and decisively negative. Four days after the "massacre," House Judiciary Committee chairman Peter W. Rodino Jr. (D N.J.) announced plans for the committee to "proceed full steam ahead" with an impeachment investigation.

The judiciary committees of both chambers also set to work almost immediately on legislation to create the position of another special prosecutor, this time to be independent of the executive branch. But by Nov. 1, Bork had appointed a replacement for Cox and had pledged him greater independence than his predecessor had had. The new prosecutor was Leon Jaworski, a wealthy Texas lawyer.

Meanwhile the White House, backpedaling quickly, agreed to turn over the tapes. Wright announced that Nixon "does not defy the law, and he has authorized me to say he will comply in full with the orders of the court." He promised to turn over the nine subpoenaed tapes "as expeditiously as possible."

But two of the nine tapes did not exist, a White House lawyer told Sirica Oct. 31. Moreover, a White House aide testified Nov. 2, the president had discovered that the tapes did not exist nearly a month before the White House publicly acknowledged their non-existence. "I have passed the point of reacting," said House Speaker Carl Albert (D Okla.).

The next uproar over tapes arose in late November, when White House spokesmen disclosed that an 18-minute gap had been discovered in an important conversation

between Nixon and his former chief of staff, H. R. Haldeman, on June 20, 1972, three days after the Watergate break-in. Rose Mary Woods, the president's personal secretary, changed her earlier story and said she might have caused the gap accidentally. A six-man panel of court-appointed electronics experts examined the tape and reported that the gap apparently was no accident.

JUDICIARY COMMITTEE ACTION

With only four dissenting votes, the House in February gave the Judiciary Committee full authority to investigate the possible impeachment of the president. Attempting to appear fair and bipartisan, the committee agreed, after initial Democratic resistance, to permit Nixon's new lawyer, James D. St. Clair, to participate in the inquiry and to ask questions of witnesses. In recognition of the historic nature of the proceedings, the committee voted to open its investigation to the public and to allow television cameras in the hearing room.

More often than not, the committee was able to maintain at least a surface appearance of bipartisanship. One basic point of disagreement was the definition of an impeachable offense. Committee Democrats took the view that an impeachable offense need not be equated with an indictable crime. Committee Republicans took the narrower position that a president must be accused of a crime to be impeached.

Both Republicans and Democrats on the committee agreed that Nixon had to cooperate with their requests for information. The committee, and Jaworski, issued additional subpoenas to the White House seeking materials and tapes thought to be relevant to ongoing investigations of Watergate. Nixon steadfastly resisted these demands, refusing to comply.

Finally, on the night before the deadline set by the House Judiciary Committee for his response to its first subpoena for Watergate tapes, Nixon announced that he would release more than 1,200 pages of edited transcripts of certain Watergate-related conversations. "The materials I make public tomorrow," he said in a nationally televised speech April 29, "will provide all the additional evidence needed to get Watergate behind us, and to get it behind us now."

He could hardly have been more wrong. The general reaction to the release of the transcripts was overwhelmingly negative. The edited transcripts revealed many contradictions and raised many questions. And they intensified the Judiciary Committee's search for the truth.

CONGRESS EXAMINES PRESIDENTIAL IMPEACHMENT

On one of the most dramatic days in the Watergate scandal, President Nixon on Oct. 20 got rid of his attorney general and deputy attorney general and fired special prosecutor Archibald Cox. He also abolished the special prosecutor's office.

The president's actions sent shock waves across the country. Many feared he was placing himself above the law by firing the man who was investigating his administration. Dozens of members of Congress called for his impeachment.

The remarkable turn of events was sparked by a legal battle over White House tapes of private conversations. Cox wanted to review nine of the tapes for evidence of criminal actions by administration officials. The White House resisted, arguing that the office of the presidency could be weakened permanently if private presidential conversations became subject to review. A federal appeals court suggested that the two sides try to reach an out-of-court compromise. Accordingly, Cox and Charles A. Wright, Nixon's lawyer, met three times to negotiate. But neither man was willing to back down, and they informed the court that they had failed to come to terms.

On Oct. 12, the appeals court, on a 5–2 vote, ruled that Nixon had to turn over the tapes. The judges stated that a president is not immune from judicial orders, such as subpoenas. "The Constitution makes no mention of special presidential immunities," they said. The president "is not above the law's commands."

The ruling upheld the decision of U.S. District Court judge John J. Sirica. Under the ruling, Sirica would first listen to the tapes to make sure they did not contain confidential information that could harm the national interest. He would then turn them over to the Watergate grand jury.

Nixon, reluctant to obey the court order, offered an alternative on Oct. 15. Instead of producing the tapes, he would prepare summaries of them. He would allow a member of the Senate—Democrat John C. Stennis of Mississippi—to listen to them and verify the accuracy of the summaries. Under Nixon's plan, Cox would be barred from trying to force the White House to turn over additional tapes, notes, or memos of presidential conversations.

After several days of negotiations, Cox rejected this compromise. He held a televised news conference on the afternoon of Oct. 20. He explained that the summaries of the tapes would probably not help him prosecute wrongdoers because a court would likely reject such summaries as evidence. Furthermore, he could not continue to conduct his investigation without being allowed to obtain additional records from the White House. As a result, he said he had decided to go back to court to force Nixon to turn over the tapes.

On the same day, Attorney General Elliott Richardson told Nixon that he agreed with Cox. He did believe that one part of the president's plan was reasonable: providing summaries and allowing Stennis to review the tapes. But he opposed the idea of barring Cox from obtaining additional records.

Within hours of Cox's news conference, Nixon asked Richardson to fire Cox. Richardson resigned rather than carry out the order. Nixon next asked the deputy attorney general, William D. Ruckelshaus, to fire Cox. Ruckelshaus responded with a letter of resignation, but Nixon fired him before receiving it. The number-three man in the Justice Department, Solicitor General Robert H. Bork, was then directed to fire Cox. Bork carried out the order. Bork also ordered the FBI to seal off the special prosecutor's offices and prevent any files from being removed.

CALLS FOR IMPEACHMENT

These actions outraged both Congress and the public. Lawmakers returned after the Veterans Day weekend to take steps to impeach a president for the first time in more than a century. Some 84 members of the House of Representatives introduced bills that called either for impeachment or for an investigation of impeachment proceedings, which could lead to impeachment. Also, 98 representatives favored a measure to create a new special prosecutor's office that would be independent of the White House.

Amid the turmoil, a new figure emerged to spearhead impeachment proceedings. Peter W. Rodino Jr., a New Jersey Democrat, chaired the House Judiciary Committee. He pledged to "proceed full steam ahead" and initiate a broad investigation. It would look not only at Watergate but also at other possible offenses, such as Nixon's secret bombing of Cambodia in 1970. The focus was turning from the Senate to the House because the Constitution gives authority to the House to impeach a president. Only after a president is impeached does the Senate step in and decide whether to convict the president and remove him from office, or to acquit him and allow him to finish his term.

Rodino hinted at a more partisan approach than that taken by the Senate Watergate Committee. The Democrats on the House Judiciary Committee would have their own chief counsel and staff. Rodino also wanted the authority to issue subpoenas, or legal orders, without the support of the full committee. This meant that Republicans would not have the ability to block him. Some Republicans said they opposed these procedures.

Republicans and Democrats generally seemed to have different views of the Watergate scandal. Democratic representatives reported that their constituents heavily favored impeachment. Republicans said their constituents also disapproved of Nixon's actions but were not calling for impeachment.

IMPEACHMENT

One of the common misconceptions about American government is that impeaching a president removes him from office.

The Constitution, however, lays out a two-step process for removing a president or other high public official. Impeachment is merely the first step. The House of Representatives has the power to impeach a president with a majority vote. Such an act may be thought of as a formal criminal charge against the president, much as a citizen may be formally charged, or indicted, by a grand jury. The Constitution says that a president may be impeached for "treason, bribery, or other high crimes and misdemeanors." It is up to members of the House to decide what sort of crimes, in addition to bribery and treason, may be punishable by impeachment.

Only after impeachment does the Senate become involved. It holds a trial to determine whether the president should be convicted or acquitted. The chief justice of the United States oversees the trial. Two-thirds of the Senate must vote to convict the president in order to remove him from office.

Because of the two-thirds requirement, removing a president from office is far more difficult than impeaching him. As of the end of the twentieth century, the House of Representatives had successfully impeached just two presidents: Andrew Johnson and Bill Clinton. In each case, the Senate failed to muster the two-thirds majority needed for conviction.

Had Nixon not resigned in August 1974, he would have almost certainly been impeached as well. The Watergate scandal was so grave that his prospects in the Senate also appeared bleak, with opponents appearing to have more than the two-thirds votes needed to remove him.

Complicating the situation, Vice President Spiro Agnew had resigned Oct. 10. He was under investigation for allegedly accepting payments from contractors and then steering federal work to them. With Agnew gone, the next person in line for the presidency was the Democratic Speaker of the House, Carl Albert of Oklahoma. Some Republicans accused Democrats of trying to take over the White House by driving Nixon out of

Source: Library of Congress

Vice President Spiro T. Agnew

office. "What they couldn't win by election, they're trying to do by other means," said Rep. Samuel L. Devine, an Ohio Republican. But Albert insisted he did not want to become president. He said the House should handle Nixon's nomination of Republican Gerald R. Ford for vice president before turning to impeachment.

A REVERSAL ON THE TAPES

Perhaps because of the talk of impeachment, or perhaps for other reasons, Nixon reversed his position on the tapes. At an Oct. 23 court hearing, Nixon's lawyer, Charles A. Wright, said the president would turn over the tapes to Sirica after all. "The president does not defy the law, and he has authorized me to say he will comply in full with the orders of the court," Wright told Sirica. There was no more talk of the proposed compromise under which Nixon would merely provide summaries of the tapes. Wright explained the reversal by saying the events of the weekend had shown that the compromise would not have ended the crisis engulfing the government.

Some observers wondered if Nixon's goal all along had been to get rid of Cox. The special prosecutor's aggressive investigation was reaching into many White House activities, including large political contributions that had been made in cash. He also was looking into the possible abuse of power by the Internal Revenue Service and other agencies. But Alexander M. Haig Jr., who became the president's chief of staff after H. R. Haldeman's resignation, said Nixon had changed his mind over the tapes partly because of the controversy that broke out, and partly because the disunity could weaken the United States overseas. Both Haig and Wright said the White House had not anticipated the reaction to its compromise. "We all miscalculated," said Haig.

Cox had secured his first indictment, or formal criminal charge, days before he was fired. The Watergate grand jury that he worked with voted to indict a former White House aide, Egil (Bud) Krogh Jr., for lying under oath during the initial Watergate investigation in 1972. Krogh was the former head of the White House unit, known as "the plumbers," that had attempted to stop leaks to the press.

With Cox gone, Assistant Attorney General Henry E. Peterson took over the investigation into Watergate. Both Peterson and Bork pledged a vigorous and swift investigation. Assistants to Cox, who were now Justice Department employees, said they would resign if Peterson did not continue to obtain all the information that could shed light on the scandal.

Meanwhile, the Senate Watergate Committee kept pondering ways to obtain its own copies of the tapes. Judge Sirica had ruled on Oct. 17 that he did not have the authority to order the president to turn over the tapes to the committee. He explained that Congress had never passed a law to give federal courts jurisdiction over such a case. The committee appealed Sirica's ruling to a higher court. Senators also raised the possibility of passing a bill that would give the Senate the power to subpoena the tapes.

At the same time, the committee took testimony about the political dirty tricks that the Nixon campaign had used to weaken the candidacies of prominent Democratic politicians. Witnesses told about fake campaign literature, disrupted rallies, and lesser pranks. All these tactics had been designed to create confusion and dissension among Democratic presidential contenders. Some of the most riveting testimony came from Donald H. Segretti, a former Nixon campaign official. Segretti testified on Oct. 3 that he had attempted to undermine the campaign of Democratic senator Edmund S. Muskie of Maine. His tactics included placing stink bombs in Muskie's headquarters and sending out letters with false statements on Muskie's stationery. Before testifying, Segretti pleaded guilty in court to political espionage.

Responding to an enormous outpouring of public rage over the firing of special prosecutor Archibald Cox, Congress moved for the first time in more than a century toward consideration of the impeachment of a president.

Rep. Peter W. Rodino Jr. (D N.J.), chairman of the House Judiciary Committee, told reporters Oct. 24 the committee would "proceed full steam ahead" with an impeachment investigation. He said the panel would investigate any allegation of "impeachable offenses," a phrase which other committee sources said included the secret bombing of Cambodia in 1970, an aborted administration plan for burglary and wiretapping of suspected subversives and President Nixon's refusal to spend funds appropriated by Congress.

The Democratic majority on the committee, Rodino said, had decided to hire a separate chief counsel and staff to investigate any charges that might bear on the President's impeachment. This group also would seek authority for Rodino to subpoena, without a vote of the full committee, any documents, tapes or other materials bearing on the investigation.

It was apparent that Nixon, despite a dramatic admission of defeat on the question of court access to secret White House tape recordings, had failed to stem the determination of many Democrats in the House to push forward with, at the least, an impeachment inquiry. Some Republican members of the Judiciary Committee said they opposed the procedures announced by Rodino.

Public Outcry. Public pressure to impeach the President struck Congress with tornado-like velocity after the President, on Oct. 20, ordered the firing of special prosecutor Cox, a Harvard law professor who until his discharge had almost unlimited, independent authority to investigate charges of illegal acts by any member of the administration—including the President and his staff. Attorney General Elliot L. Richardson and Deputy Attorney General William D. Ruckelshaus resigned rather than carry out Nixon's order to fire Cox. The prosecutor was then fired—and the office of special prosecutor was abolished—by Solicitor General Robert H. Bork, who had become acting attorney general. (Bork would later be nominated to the Supreme Court in 1987 by President Reagan. After one of the stormiest confirmation battles in the nation's history, the Senate rejected the nomination by a vote of 58–42, with opponents claiming that he was too conservative.)

"Whether we shall continue to be a government of laws and not of men is now for Congress and ultimately the American people to decide," said Cox.

Public response to the President's action was overwhelmingly negative. A Congressional Quarterly poll of House members showed telephone calls, telegrams and mail received by most Democratic representatives to be heavily in favor of impeachment. Most Republican representatives said their constituents strongly opposed Nixon's action but generally stopped short of calling for impeachment.

Congressional Reaction. On the first two days after Congress returned from its Veterans Day recess, 84 representatives introduced legislation calling for impeachment of the President or an investigation of impeachment procedures.

In addition, 98 representatives—including four Republicans—sponsored legislation to establish a special prosecutor's office that would be independent of administration restrictions. A number of House and Senate Republicans urged the President to appoint a new special prosecutor to forestall passage of such legislation.

Protection of Records. Assistant Attorney General Henry E. Petersen, to whom the task of investigating Watergate and other cases had reverted, Oct. 26 petitioned U.S. District Court Chief Judge John J. Sirica to declare all investigative records the property of the court. The petition noted that "within a few minutes" of Cox's ouster, "agents of the FBI acting on direct instructions of the White House 'sealed' the offices of the Watergate Special Prosecution Force, as well as of the former Attorney General and deputy attorney general."

The Cox-Richardson Drama

Nixon's confrontation with Congress first surfaced to public view at 8:25 p.m. Oct. 20 when presidential spokesman Ronald L. Ziegler announced the firing of Cox and the departure of Richardson and Ruckelshaus. Nixon also ordered all investigations of Cox's office returned to the jurisdiction of the Justice Department.

It was the greatest administration upheaval since April 30, when White House aides H. R. Haldeman, John D. Ehrlichman, John W. Dean III and Attorney General Richard G. Kleindienst resigned in the wake of the broadening Watergate scandal.

The issue was, as Richardson told a news conference Oct. 23, "presidential authority versus the independence and public accountability of the special prosecutor"—a historic confrontation between the principle of executive privilege, or presidential confidentiality, as stated by President Nixon, and the right of other parties to investigate the executive branch when there is apparent evidence of wrongdoing by members of that branch.

Order to Cox. The "firestorm," as Nixon's chief of staff, Alexander M. Haig Jr., described it, began the evening of Oct. 19.

Nixon, who had been ordered by the U.S. Circuit Court of Appeals to turn over nine tape recordings of White House conversations to the special Watergate prosecutor, let the deadline expire for an appeal to the Supreme Court. Then he offered a compromise.

Rather than giving Cox the tapes, the President said, he would prepare summaries of their contents and then permit Sen. John C. Stennis (D Miss.) to listen to the tapes to verify the President's account. He would do so "with the greatest reluctance," he said, because he considered even this offer a violation of the principle of the presidential confidentiality he had vowed to uphold.

Nixon also ordered Cox "as an employee of the executive branch to make no further attempts by the judicial process to obtain tapes, notes or memoranda of presidential conversations." It was understood that the President was prepared to fire Cox if he did not acquiesce.

The President decided on his proposal Monday afternoon, Oct. 15, Richardson said, and negotiations proceeded throughout the week. The chairman and vice chairman of the Senate Select Watergate Committee, Senators Sam J. Ervin Jr. (D N.C.) and Howard H. Baker Jr. (R Tenn.), reportedly agreed to the tapes plan, although they later disagreed on their interpretation of its exact details. Cox, however, had questions about it, and refused to accept the limitation on his future investigative efforts. Richardson sided with Cox, and was not informed in advance of the President's decision to order Cox to cease and desist.

Cox's Statement. Cox held a televised Saturday afternoon news conference Oct. 20. He denied he was "looking for a confrontation," and said he was "certainly not out to get the President of the United States." But, he said, he could not accept the President's proposal and would go back into court for a decision on Nixon's apparent noncompliance with the court's order—a decision which could have resulted in a contempt of court citation against the President.

"I think it is my duty as the special prosecutor, as an officer of the court and as the representative of the grand jury, to bring to the court's attention what seems to me to be noncompliance," Cox said.

To accept Nixon's proposal would create "insuperable difficulties" for him as prosecutor, Cox said. He doubted summaries of the tapes would be admissible as evidence in court, and said barring him from seeking further White House tapes and documents would prevent him from conducting his investigation. He complained of "repeated frustration" in his attempts to get information from the White House about Watergate, the alleged coverup, the "White House plumbers" activities and related matters.

Cox contended Nixon's instructions were "inconsistent with pledges that were made to the United States Senate and through the Senate to the American people before I was appointed and before Attorney General Richardson's nomination was confirmed"—pledges to appoint and guarantee the independence of a special Watergate prosecutor.

Richardson's Position. Richardson agreed. He wrote the President Oct. 20 that while he considered the Stennis part of the proposal to be reasonable and constructive and hoped U.S. District Court Judge John J. Sirica would accept it, he could not accept the ban on any future attempts by Cox to obtain records from the White House.

"As you point out, this instruction does intrude on the independence you promised me with regard to Watergate when you announced my appointment," Richardson wrote.

The two men talked. The President was "very deliberate, very restrained in tone . . . but he was absolutely firm on the course he had determined upon," Richardson later told a news conference.

"When, therefore, Mr. Cox rejected that position, and gave his objections to the Stennis proposal, as well as his reasons for insisting on assured access to other tapes and memoranda, the issue of presidential authority versus the independence and public accountability of the special prosecutor was squarely joined," Richardson said.

"The President, at that point, thought he had no choice but to direct the attorney general to discharge Mr. Cox. And I, given my role in guaranteeing the independence of the special prosecutor, as well as my belief in the public interest embodied in that role, felt equally clear that I could not discharge him. And so I resigned," Richardson said.

"At stake, in the final analysis, is the very integrity of the governmental processes I came to the Department of Justice (in May) to help restore," Richardson noted. He did not dispute the President's right to change the rules of the game, but said he could not abide by the change.

After Richardson offered his resignation, Deputy Attorney General Ruckelshaus was called by Haig and asked to fire Cox. "I simply could not do it," Ruckelshaus told *The New York Times*. And so he wrote out a letter of resignation. The White House did not wait to receive it

before announcing that Ruckelshaus had been fired for refusing to obey the President's orders.

Solicitor General Robert H. Bork then was informed that under the law he was acting attorney general and must fire Cox. He did so.

At 8:25 p.m. Oct. 20, in an unusual Saturday night news conference, White House press secretary Ronald L. Ziegler stunned newsmen with the announcements of the firing of Cox and abolition of his special prosecutor's office, the resignation of Richardson and the firing of Ruckelshaus.

Ziegler also announced that Bork had ordered the FBI to seal off the special prosecutor's offices to prevent the removal of any files. This act, with the firings, set off cries of outrage across the country, and protests began to mount immediately, along with cries for impeachment of the President.

Some critics doubted that the issue of confidentiality was as important to the President as getting rid of Cox, and Nixon's capitulation on the tapes issue Oct. 23 heightened those feelings. Some felt the entire tapes issue had been contrived to fire Cox.

Cox himself said he had the impression he was being deliberately "confronted with things that were drawn in such a way that I could not accept them." Richardson said the possibility of firing Cox was first raised with him by presidential aides earlier in the week as "one way of mooting the (tapes) case, and thereby in effect resolving the constitutional impasse." Richardson said he rejected the suggestion as "totally unacceptable."

The Washington Post reported the President had wanted to abolish the special prosecutor's office since last June because Cox's investigation was "hitting too close to the President and his friends and former aides, and was probing too deeply into every aspect of White House activity going back to 1969."

Cox acknowledged in a CBS television interview Oct. 24 that at the time he was fired, his staff was looking into large political contributions, chiefly in cash, raised by White House aides in 1970, and "possible abuses" of national security and other government agencies, including the Internal Revenue Service. Cox declined to say whether he had evidence sufficient to compel Congress to impeach the President.

Richardson News Conference. Richardson acknowledged that there had been "continuing arguments" with the President's lawyers on the scope of Cox's investigation, but denied any attempts had been made to head off the investigation. He defended Cox against charges that he was conducting a "witch hunt" or was trying to "get Nixon," but conceded that "many people" in the Republican Party, on the Hill and on the President's staff felt there was partisanship because Cox and some of his top aides are Democrats and formerly served in Democratic administrations. Cox was solicitor general in the Kennedy administration. He also was a law professor of Richardson's at Harvard Law School, and was picked by Richardson for the special prosecutor's job.

Richardson spoke at a packed news conference in the Great Hall of the Department of Justice Oct. 23. He had asked Acting Attorney General Bork for use of the room. He had praise for the Nixon administration and said he strongly believed in its general purposes and priorities, but "I have been compelled to conclude that I could better serve my country by resigning my public office than by continuing in it."

Both Richardson and Ruckelshaus stressed their belief that an independent special prosecutor was necessary in the Watergate investigation. They praised the integrity of Assistant Attorney General Henry E. Petersen, chief of the criminal division, who will now take charge of the investigation, but, Richardson said, "I think the situation is fraught with great difficulty for him, and I think that whoever is attorney general and Mr. Petersen would both be in a better position if a new special prosecutor were appointed."

"The problem really is not, in my view, the problem of the real integrity or the courage or the determination of Mr. Petersen and those working with him to do this job," Richardson said. "The problem is one of public perception and public confidence. . . . These were the reasons why, in the first place, I believed that the special prosecutor should be appointed. And certainly I think that both problems remain and therefore point again to the same result."

There was no indication the White House would name a special prosecutor, but there were demands in Congress that one be appointed, either by Congress or by the courts.

Bork and Petersen pledged a vigorous, swift investigation. Bork said Oct. 24 that the White House had agreed on "regularized procedures" for turnover of evidence. He stopped short of saying he would go to court if necessary to get information, but said he would "go wherever we need to get the evidence."

Members of the special prosecutor's staff, now Justice Department employees, indicated they would resign in protest if real efforts did not continue to seek out all necessary information.

Ruckelshaus News Conference. Ruckelshaus said that since he was picked by Richardson to be his deputy, he felt bound by the same agreement regarding the special prosecutor, and when he was asked to violate it, he had no choice but to refuse. "These were not heroic acts" by Richardson and himself, he added. Since Bork

was not a party to the agreement, Ruckelshaus said, he urged Bork that "if he could find it in himself to comply (and fire Cox), it would probably be a good thing."

However, Ruckelshaus reiterated his belief that a special prosecutor is needed. He spoke at a news conference Oct. 23 at the National Press Club.

Like Richardson, Ruckelshaus said that in Cox's shoes, he would have done the same thing Cox did, and, also like Richardson, he declined to give his own judgment of whether Nixon should be impeached. That judgment was up to the American people, Ruckelshaus said.

On hearing just before the end of the news conference that the President had decided to comply with the court decision on the tapes, Ruckelshaus said, "I am very glad he has complied. I certainly applaud his action. It remains to be seen to what extent the investigation can be carried forward."

Cox's Reaction. Cox, on hearing of Nixon's actions Oct. 20, said: "Whether we shall continue to be a government of laws and not of men is now for Congress and ultimately the American people to decide." He appeared at the special prosecutor's office Oct. 23 for a farewell party given by his staff. On hearing of the President's decision to turn over the tapes, Cox said: "I know that all citizens will be as happy as I am that the President chose to respect the rule of law."

Nixon's Reversal on Tapes

The dramatic announcement came quietly. "I am . . . authorized to say that the President of the United States would comply in all respects with the order of Aug. 29 as modified by the order of the court of appeals," said Charles Alan Wright, special White House counsel, standing stiffly before Judge John J. Sirica. That crisis had passed: no longer did the President stand in direct conflict with the federal courts.

That Aug. 29 order, issued by Sirica to President Nixon, directed that the taped recordings of specific presidential conversations—subpoenaed by the original grand jury investigating Watergate—be surrendered to Sirica. In order to ascertain whether the tapes were properly protected from disclosure to the grand jury by the President's claim of executive privilege, Sirica then would privately examine them. On Oct. 12, the court of appeals, District of Columbia circuit, upheld Sirica's order with modifications allowing the President to withhold any portions of the tapes which related to national security—and to have those specific claims of executive privilege examined individually. The effect of the order was delayed by the court of appeals until Oct. 19 in order that Nixon—who had repeatedly made clear his determination not to release the tapes—might appeal the ruling to the Supreme Court.

The week passed, and late on Friday evening, Oct. 19, no appeal had been filed. The Sirica order thus became effective. The President then announced his compromise—he would release to the grand jury and to the Senate Watergate Committee summaries of the tapes, validated and certified by Sen. John C. Stennis (D Miss.) as accurate and complete. Special Watergate prosecutor Archibald Cox rejected this compromise and was fired; his firing was followed by the resignations of Attorney General Elliot L. Richardson and Deputy Attorney General William Ruckelshaus. Public reaction to these weekend events was strongly hostile.

On Monday, Oct. 22, a summary of the compromise proposal was delivered to Sirica's court in preparation for a hearing during which Wright would try to convince Sirica to accept this as a satisfactory response to his order. A hearing was set for the following day.

Grand Jury Session. On the morning of Oct. 23 Sirica met in public session with the original Watergate grand jury and the newly convened additional grand jury investigating Watergate-related matters. He spoke to them, he said, in an effort to alleviate the anxiety concerning their role which might have developed as a result of the weekend's events.

"You are advised first," he said, "that the grand juries of which you serve remain operative and intact. . . . You are not dismissed and will not be dismissed except as provided by law upon the completion of your work or the conclusion of your term. . . . You may rely on the court to safeguard your rights and to preserve the integrity of your proceedings," he concluded.

Nixon's Change. The rusty machinery of impeachment, shaken loose by a surge of grassroots sentiment in favor of congressional action against the President, was beginning to move on Capitol Hill early in the afternoon of Oct. 23 even as Sirica's courtroom at the foot of that hill was filling with spectators. Law students, members of the press and interested citizens overflowed the room expecting to hear Wright's arguments that the compromise was a satisfactory response to Sirica's order.

Without drama, the bespectacled Sirica began to read to the courtroom the pertinent documents: the Oct. 12 appeals court order; his original Aug. 29 order—already in effect—and the relevant sections of the appeals court opinion outlining the procedure which that court had approved.

When he completed the reading, Sirica asked: "Are counsel for the President prepared at this time to file

with the court the response of the President to the modified order of the court?"

Rising from his chair and walking slowly to the podium facing Sirica, Wright began to speak. But instead of launching into an expected explanation of the President's compromise proposal, he said in a low voice: "I am not prepared at this time to file a response.

"I am, however, authorized," he continued, "to say that the President of the United States would comply in all respects with the order. . . . It will require some time . . . to put those materials together, to do the indexing, itemizing as the court of appeals calls for."

As if fearful that he had not heard correctly, Sirica asked: "As I understand your statement, that will be delivered to this court?"

"To the court *in camera* (in chambers)," replied Wright.

"You will follow the decisions or statements delineated by me," repeated Sirica.

"Will comply in all respects with what your honor has just read," said Wright. The previous day, he noted, the White House had filed a response "along different lines, along the lines indicated in the statement to the country on Friday. That statement . . . is now withdrawn."

Explaining the sudden decision to surrender the tapes and scuttle the compromise, Wright continued: "The President's statement on Friday was what we hoped would be a satisfactory method of accommodating the needs that led your honor and the court of appeals to rule as they did while minimizing the danger to confidentiality. We had hoped that that kind of solution would end a constitutional crisis." (Wright later told newsmen that he had left Washington on Saturday after the compromise was announced, thinking that his work for the White House was over.)

Referring to the public uproar arising from the President's decision to fire Cox, Wright continued: "The events of the weekend, I think, have made it very apparent that it would not (end the constitutional crisis). Even if I had been successful, as I hoped I would be in persuading you, Mr. Chief Judge, that this did adequately satisfy the spirit of the court of appeals ruling, there would be those who would have said that the President is defying the law.

"This President does not defy the law, and he has authorized me to say he will comply in full with the orders of the court."

"The court is very happy that the President has reached this decision," Sirica responded, asking for an approximate idea of the time when the tapes might actually be delivered to the court. Wright replied that he did not know the timetable, except to say that it would be done "as expeditiously as possible."

After thanking Wright, Sirica adjourned the hearing.

White House Briefing

The President's dramatic reversal of position on the Watergate tapes was the outgrowth of a miscalculation on the part of Nixon and his top advisers, two presidential aides told the press Oct. 23. According to Alexander M. Haig, the President's chief of staff, and Charles A. Wright, his special counsel, no one in the White House expected that the President's compromise on the tapes would lead to the dismissal of special prosecutor Archibald Cox and the resignations of Attorney General Elliot L. Richardson and Deputy Attorney General William Ruckelshaus, or to the "firestorm" of protest and demands for the President's impeachment.

"We all miscalculated Friday night (Oct. 19)," Wright said at a White House press conference two hours after he had announced in court that Nixon would comply with the judicial order to turn over the Watergate tapes. He said his own mood had been one of "euphoria" that the President apparently had averted a constitutional crisis with an "extraordinarily generous proposal" to turn over summaries of the tapes to the Senate Watergate Committee after they were checked by Sen. John C. Stennis (D Miss.). As to the Justice Department shakeup, Haig said "it was not preplanned, not desired and probably not too well visualized on Friday morning by all of the participants."

Asked if the talk of impeachment in Congress had caused Nixon to change his mind about the tapes, Haig replied that it did not stem solely from the threat of impeachment, but from the "whole milieu" of concerns that arose over the weekend. The nation could not continue to be torn by the disruptive events of the last few days, he said, adding that he did not believe Congress would have impeached Nixon if he had not given in. When the confusion of the people, press and Congress had been cleared away and the truth had emerged, he said, impeachment would have died as an issue. Haig added that the President never considered resigning over the latest series of events.

Haig denied reports that the President's intent all along was to fire Cox because the special prosecutor's investigation was getting too broad. He admitted, however, that there was concern in the White House about the "political alignment" of Cox's staff and because it appeared to be "roaming" outside the special prosecutor's purview. While he specifically exempted Cox from criticism, he said there had been "occasions where we haven't been especially pleased" with the investigation.

Pending Investigations. Haig also said that the President would allow Cox's investigations of the ITT affair and the Howard Hughes–Charles (Bebe) Rebozo campaign contribution to continue under Justice Department auspices, but he declined to say whether Nixon would resist attempts to get presidential documents relating to those circumstances. The ITT matter concerned allegations that the Justice Department made a favorable antitrust settlement with International Telephone and Telegraph Corporation in exchange for a corporate contribution to the 1972 Republican national convention.

The Hughes-Rebozo matter concerned a reported $100,000 cash contribution after the 1968 campaign from millionaire industrialist Hughes which Rebozo, a close friend of the President, admitted keeping in a safe deposit box for three years before returning the money to Hughes.

In answer to other questions, Haig said it was he who ordered FBI agents to seal Cox's offices after his firing. Haig explained that he had been given reports that some of Cox's staff were removing materials from their offices. Wright, asked why it was necessary to abolish Cox's office in addition to firing the special prosecutor, said "it made much more sense" to move the Watergate investigation into the institutional framework of the Justice Department.

Wright also was asked how people could believe in the President's assurances of a continued impartial investigation now that three highly respected legal officials had left in protest. "I don't see what the departures have to do with the credibility of the President," he replied.

The press conference began with Haig giving the White House's side of the events that led to the crisis weekend of Oct. 20–21. (*See Richardson's and Cox's versions, p. 122.*)

Unfolding Drama. Haig said the President decided on the weekend of Oct. 13 to make a "herculean effort" to resolve the tapes controversy. At that time the President had a choice of turning over the tapes to U.S. District Court Chief Judge John J. Sirica by midnight Oct. 19 or appealing an appellate court's decision upholding Sirica to the Supreme Court.

Two factors led to Nixon's decision to resolve the issue, Haig related. One was the domestic "storm of controversy" that surrounded the issue and which would have "polarized the body politic" if the case had been appealed to the Supreme Court, he said. The other was "international implications of some gravity." He explained that any foreign leader, friend or foe, would note the disunity in America and make his calculations based on his perceptions of the strength and permanency of the Nixon administration.

"For these two reasons and no others" the President acted, Haig said.

Stennis was chosen as the go-between for four reasons, Haig said: he was a Democrat and a former judge, he had an impeccable reputation and no one was more highly qualified to assess the national security implications of the tapes. After getting Stennis' consent, Richardson was instructed to get Cox's agreement.

Haig said Richardson spent Oct. 15–18 trying to get Cox to agree to the compromise, but that it became apparent by the evening of Oct. 18 that Cox would not comply. Haig cited Cox's "strong desire" for access to documents and memorandums covering "private conversations of the President," in addition to the tapes.

That was not the kind of cooperation the White House expected from Cox, Haig stated, so efforts were made the evening of Oct. 19 to get the approval of Chairman Sam J. Ervin Jr. (D N.C.) of the Senate Watergate Committee and Vice Chairman Howard H. Baker Jr. (R Tenn.). When Ervin and Baker agreed, "we set in train the chain of events that brought us to Saturday's firestorm," Haig said.

The President believed he was making an important concession in the national interest, Haig said, and he instructed Richardson to inform Cox that he was going through with his plan.

"We all assumed" Cox had three options, Haig said. He could have accepted the fact that he was receiving the information he wanted, he could have delayed his decision or resigned, or he could have rebutted and challenged the President.

When he took the latter course in a televised news conference Oct. 20, the President had no choice but to fire him, Haig stated.

Both Haig and Wright said they had not heard the tapes, but felt certain they would support the President's position that he knew nothing about the Watergate break-in or coverup.

Congressional Action

By the time most members of Congress returned Oct. 23 from their Veterans Day weekend holiday, the impeachment process had begun. Shortly before noon that day, House Speaker Carl Albert (D Okla.) told a crowded press briefing that he would refer all impeachment resolutions to the Judiciary Committee, headed by Peter W. Rodino Jr. (D N.J.).

Albert urged that the unity of the nation be kept in mind. "For the Congress to act in a reckless or hasty manner," he said, "would further engender disunity." Rodino, standing next to him at the briefing, promised that the impeachment controversy would not delay action on the

nomination of Gerald R. Ford as vice president, which the Judiciary Committee was also considering.

Three hours later, the mood of Congress was changed somewhat by the announcement of the President's decision to surrender the tapes. But the plans to go ahead with a study of impeachment remained intact. A spokesman for Rodino's committee said the committee would be "basically unaffected" by the President's reversal.

On Oct. 24, Albert followed up on his call for action on the Ford nomination by telling reporters that the Judiciary Committee should handle that first, before working on presidential impeachment. Committee leaders were saying, meanwhile, that if necessary it could do both at once.

For Albert, the issue of Ford's nomination was of more than casual significance. Without a vice president, the speaker was next in line for the presidency. If he pushed hard for impeachment, critics would charge that he was acting more out of ambition than out of principle.

PRESIDENTIAL SUCCESSION

As if the possibility of Nixon facing impeachment wasn't enough to rock the government, Vice President Spiro Agnew resigned on Oct. 10. He faced a federal investigation into mishandling government contracts. Agnew was the first vice president in the nation's history to resign as a result of scandal. The only previous vice president to resign, John C. Calhoun, had stepped down to return to the Senate.

Agnew's departure meant there was no vice president to assume the presidency in case Nixon left office. The next in line for the presidency was the Speaker of the House, Carl Albert. Unlike Nixon and Agnew, Albert was a Democrat.

Years earlier, a president in Nixon's situation would not have been able to name a new vice president. The Constitution, as originally written, did not discuss the issue of what to do if a vice president died or resigned. But this issue was addressed in 1967 with a constitutional amendment. Under the Twenty-fifth Amendment, a president must nominate a new vice president. That person assumes the vice presidency upon approval by both the House of Representatives and the Senate.

Nixon moved swiftly. Two days after Agnew's resignation, Nixon nominated Gerald R. Ford to the vice presidency. Ford, a veteran Michigan representative, was the leader of the House Republicans. His nomination was generally praised. The Senate approved the nomination on Nov. 27 by a vote of 92–3. The House followed suit on Dec. 6, approving him by 387–35.

Republican Reaction. Within minutes of Albert's Oct. 24 briefing, some Republicans were already talking of impeachment as a partisan power grab. "What they couldn't win by election, they're trying to do by other means," said Rep. Samuel L. Devine (R Ohio). "They're trying to create a Democratic government."

Those closer to Albert insisted, however, that the presidency was the last thing on the 65-year-old Speaker's mind. There were reports that Albert had been so reluctant to appear ambitious that he refused even to send the impeachment resolutions to committee until other members of the leadership convinced him that national feeling required it.

"The speaker is conscious that he might by some remote degree become president," explained Rep. John J. McFall (D Calif.), the majority whip. "He wants it to be clear that he doesn't want to undermine or destroy anybody." McFall had urged Albert to press on with the impeachment study.

Another member of the leadership, Democratic caucus chairman Olin E. Teague (Texas), said that the Judiciary Committee would have to handle the Ford nomination carefully to avoid a negative reaction. "If we go too fast on Ford," Teague told Congressional Quarterly, "we'll be accused of rubber-stamping a colleague. If we go too slow, we'll be accused of trying to keep Carl Albert in succession. We want to do it right."

Senate Role. For the time being, the House was the focus of the fight. The Senate, ultimate jury in an impeachment case, had no constitutional role to play at the outset of the impeachment process. But there was some action.

PRESIDENTIAL DISABILITY

In the crush of Watergate and Middle East events, the problem was hardly noticed. But a handful of legislative experts on Capitol Hill began quietly worrying about a particularly disturbing aspect of the vacancy in the vice presidency and the pressures President Nixon had been under.

The question: What would happen if Nixon were to become physically or mentally incapable of continung his duties as President before Congress confirmed vice presidential nominee Gerald R. Ford? The answer, these experts said, was clear: until Ford was confirmed, there was no provision in the Constitution for removing the President from office on grounds of disability—even if he were to suffer a clearly disabling heart attack, stroke or other catastrophe.

"It could very easily be a hairy situation," said Karl O'Lessker, Sen. Birch Bayh's (D Ind.) legislative assistant. Bayh is chairman of the Senate Judiciary Constitutional Amendments Subcommittee, which helped draft the 25th Amendment dealing with presidential disability.

The chief counsel of the subcommittee, William J. Heckman, told Congressional Quarterly that the disability part of the amendment is "inoperative" in the absence of a vice president to take over as acting president. "Nothing could be done about it," Heckman said. "Essentially I suppose somebody at the White House would still issue instructions in (Nixon's) name."

The 25th Amendment was designed to make clear the mechanics of who could declare a president disabled. Once the determination had been made, the vice president would become the "acting president" until the period of disability ended. However, if there is no vice president to take over the job, the amendment cannot be invoked, Heckman said.

Would Speaker of the House Carl Albert (D Okla.), who under the laws of succession was next in line after the vice president for the presidency, step into the job? Not so long as the President remained alive, said Heckman—no matter what the degree of his disability. "It is clear in the legislative history (of the amendment) and in the Succession Act that Albert is not eligible to become the acting president," he said.

A dissenting view on this point came from Nicholas deB. Katzenbach, who was the acting attorney general when the 25th

Amendment was being debated in Congress in 1965. Katzenbach said he believed that, in the absence of a vice president, the procedure would revert to the Succession Act and that Albert could become president in the event Nixon became disabled.

Katzenbach agreed that a less clear-cut case of presidential disability, in which a president refused to allow himself to be removed, could lead to a constitutional crisis that could dwarf those threatened by Watergate.

The Senate Judiciary Committee met in closed session Oct. 24 and agreed to begin a public investigation of the firing of Cox. The former prosecutor himself was scheduled to appear before the committee in its first day of hearings, expected Oct. 28. The committee rejected arguments by Sen. Edward M. Kennedy (D Mass.) and other liberal Democrats to begin the hearings immediately. Action also was delayed on a resolution calling on the President to reinstate Cox. Republican leaders of the Senate urged the President Oct. 24 to appoint a new special prosecutor.

The Senate hearings were expected to include testimony by Richardson and Ruckelshaus. James O. Eastland (D Miss.), the Judiciary Committee chairman, said he would favor calling both as witnesses.

Senate Watergate Committee

At the same time that Cox was pursuing the White House tapes of private presidential conversations, the Senate Watergate Committee also wanted the tapes for its own investigation. U.S. District Court judge John J. Sirica had concluded he lacked the authority to order the president to hand over the tapes to the committee. The committee subsequently appealed the decision to a higher court.

If the committee lost in court, it could look into another strategy. It could introduce legislation stating that the committee had the authority to issue a subpoena for the tapes. If Congress passed such legislation, the courts probably would agree that the president had to obey it.

For the Senate Select Watergate Committee, the week was like a ride on a roller coaster. The committee's investigatory hopes rose to a peak Oct. 19 with a White House promise of access to summaries and transcripts of Watergate-

related presidential tapes. But these hopes hit bottom Oct. 23 when the senators learned they would get nothing at all.

While the committee was disappointed that it would not receive the transcripts or summaries, the seven members appeared to be in agreement that the President had made a wise decision in obeying a court order to release the tapes to the Watergate grand jury. As a result of the events, the committee canceled a scheduled meeting for Oct. 25, at which it would have voted on the President's offer. It was to meet instead on Oct. 29 or 30 to discuss future courses of action.

One route, according to Deputy Chief Counsel Rufus L. Edmisten, was for the committee to call for the testimony of the three officials who left the government in the wake of the tapes controversy: special prosecutor Archibald Cox, Attorney General Elliot L. Richardson and Deputy Attorney General William D. Ruckelshaus. This had been proposed by Committee Vice Chairman Howard H. Baker Jr. (R Tenn.) and was being considered by the staff, Edmisten told Congressional Quarterly. Another proposal reportedly being considered by the staff was to subpoena millionaire industrialist Howard Hughes and Charles G. (Bebe) Rebozo, a close friend of the President. Rebozo was reported to have accepted a cash contribution of $100,000 from Hughes in 1969 and 1970, and to have kept it in a safe deposit box for three years before returning the money to Hughes.

Committee Chief Counsel Samuel Dash told Congressional Quarterly the up and down events of the week changed nothing as far as the committee was concerned. The hearings would continue as scheduled. He added, however, that the committee might delve more deeply into the Watergate break-in and coverup because "I don't really have confidence that the Department of Justice can act independently under the President." He said the committee "felt comfortable" with Cox in charge of the government's investigation. The White House said Cox's probe would be carried on by the Justice Department.

At week's end, the committee was scheduled to resume its hearings Oct. 30 with further testimony into campaign "dirty tricks."

Tape Disclosure Reaction. Baker and Committee Chairman Sam J. Ervin Jr. (D N.C.) expressed pleasure at the President's Oct. 23 decision to yield the tapes to the grand jury, even though it meant the deal with the committee was off. Baker said Nixon made "a tough decision that will spare the nation the agony and grief of a constitutional confrontation." At the same time he asked the White House to work out an arrangement that would allow "pertinent information" on the tapes to be given to the committee. According to a spokesman for the senator, Baker was, in effect, asking for the resurrection of the President's Oct. 19 offer.

Sen. Herman E. Talmadge (D Ga.) said the President's decision "should remove the cloud of doubt, suspicion and uncertainty" that hovered over his head for the last several months. Sen. Daniel K. Inouye (D Hawaii) said he hoped Nixon would follow up his latest tapes decision with the rehiring of Cox, Richardson and Ruckelshaus.

Inouye, speaking to the AFL-CIO convention Oct. 22, had called for Nixon's resignation. "Like many of you," he told the delegates, "I have sadly concluded that President Nixon can no longer effectively lead our nation." He added that Congress should consider impeaching the President if he refused to resign. Inouye, responding through a spokesman Oct. 25, told Congressional Quarterly he would retract his call for the resignation or impeachment of the President only if Nixon rehired Cox, Richardson and Ruckelshaus.

Sen. Lowell P. Weicker Jr. (R Conn.), who angrily rejected the President's original deal with the committee, told Congressional Quarterly after Nixon reversed himself on the tapes issue that he was "delighted the President has put himself on the same footing as all the rest of us" by obeying the court order. "It wouldn't have happened without the firings and resignations and the U.S. people's protests. They tried to float one out of the White House and it just didn't work," he said in reference to the Oct. 19 tapes proposal.

Court Action. On the legal front, the committee was continuing its court battle to get the tapes on its own. The committee filed a motion Oct. 23 in the U.S. Court of Appeals in Washington asking for an expedited appeal of the decision by U.S. District Court Chief Judge John J. Sirica rejecting the committee's subpoena to obtain the tapes. Sirica ruled Oct. 17 that he lacked jurisdiction to order the President to hand over the tapes to the committee.

Edmisten told CQ that an unfavorable ruling by the appellate court would result in the committee introducing legislation establishing its jurisdiction for the tapes. The President probably would veto it, he said, but he expressed confidence Congress would override the veto.

The President's Oct. 19 proposal to turn over summaries and transcripts of the tapes to the committee and the grand jury came as a complete surprise to Ervin and Baker. Each was out of town and had to return to Washington to meet with Nixon. There was speculation that the senators had been "used" by the President to fire Cox, the theory being that their acceptance of the proposal while Cox had rejected it made it easier for Nixon to isolate the special prosecutor and dismiss him.

But Edmisten, who is very close to Ervin, denied this. He said Ervin "felt he'd won a victory for the committee and the country." In any case, he added, Ervin and

Baker had nothing to lose. The committee still could appeal Sirica's decision and had a chance to get the tapes themselves rather than White House summaries.

Dash, however, had a different view. He told CQ there probably was "never a good faith offer in the first place. After flying in Senators Baker and Ervin to the Oval Office it now appears to have been a basis of an offer to Cox, and Cox was fired," he said.

Weicker was the only member of the committee who publicly rejected the tapes offer outright. He issued a statement Oct. 20 calling it a compromise of investigative procedure. "Rather than appearing wise and honorable," he said, "last night's compromise looks like what it is—a deal between an evasive President and an easily diverted Congress. I am glad the special prosecutor had no part of it. I will have no part of it."

Nixon Order, Richardson Reply

Following are the texts of letters exchanged between President Nixon and Attorney General Elliot L. Richardson on Oct. 19 and 20 and released by Richardson on Oct. 23. In his letter Nixon instructs Richardson to direct the Watergate special prosecutor to cease all attempts to obtain presidential documents or tapes by the judicial process. Richardson responds that he cannot carry out the order.

Nixon Instruction

October 19, 1973

Dear Elliot:

You are aware of the actions I am taking today to bring to an end the controversy over the so-called Watergate tapes and that I have reluctantly agreed to a limited breach of Presidential confidentiality in order that our country may be spared the agony of further indecision and litigation about those tapes at a time when we are confronted with other issues of much greater moment to the country and the world.

As a part of these actions, I am instructing you to direct special prosecutor Archibald Cox of the Watergate Special Prosecution Force that he is to make no further attempts by judicial process to obtain tapes, notes, or memoranda of Presidential conversations. I regret the necessity of intruding, to this very limited extent, on the independence that I promised you with regard to Watergate when I announced your appointment. This would not have been necessary if the Special Prosecutor had agreed to the very reasonable proposal you made to him this week.

Sincerely,

RICHARD NIXON

Richardson Response

Dear Mr. President:

Thank you for your letter of October 19, 1973, instructing me to direct Mr. Cox that he is to make no further attempts by judicial process to obtain tapes, notes or memoranda of Presidential conversations.

As you point out, this instruction does intrude on the independence you promised me with regard to Watergate when you announced my appointment. And, of course, you have every right as President to withdraw or modify any understanding on which I hold office under you. The situation stands on a different footing, however, with respect to the role of the special prosecutor.

Acting on your instruction that if I should consider it appropriate, I would have the authority to name a special prosecutor, I announced a few days before my confirmation hearing began that I would, if confirmed, "appoint a special prosecutor and give him all the independence, authority, and staff support needed to carry out the tasks entrusted to him."

I added, "Although he will be in the Department of Justice and report to me—and only to me—he will be aware that his ultimate accountability is to the American people."

At many points throughout the nomination hearings, I reaffirmed my intention to assure the independence of the special prosecutor, and in my statement of his duties and responsibilities I specified that he would have "full authority" for "determining whether or not to contest the assertion of 'executive privilege' or any other testimonial privilege."

And while the special prosecutor can be removed from office for "extraordinary improprieties," his charter specifically states that "the Attorney General will not countermand or interfere with the special prosecutor's decisions or actions."

Quite obviously, therefore, the instruction contained in your letter of October 19 gives me serious difficulty. As you know, I regarded as reasonable and constructive the proposal to rely on Senator Stennis to prepare a verified record of the so-called Watergate tapes and I did my best

to persuade Mr. Cox of the desirability of this solution of that issue.

I did not believe, however, that the price of access of the tapes in this manner should be the renunciation of any further attempt by him to resort to judicial process, and the proposal I submitted to him did not purport to deal with other tapes, notes, or memoranda of Presidential conversations.

In the circumstances I would hope that some further accommodation could be found along the following lines:

First, that an effort be made to persuade Judge Sirica to accept for purposes of the grand jury the record of the Watergate tapes verified by Senator Stennis. In that event, Mr. Cox would, as he has, abide by Judge Sirica's decision.

Second, agreement should be sought with Mr. Cox not to press any outstanding subpoenas which are directed merely to notes or memoranda covering the same conversations that would have been furnished in full through the verified record.

Third, any future situation where Mr. Cox seeks judicial process to obtain the record of Presidential conversations would be approached on the basis of the precedent established with respect to the Watergate tapes. This would leave to be handled in this way only situations where a showing of compelling necessity comparable to that made with respect to the Watergate tapes had been made.

If you feel it would be useful to do so, I would welcome opportunity to discuss this matter with you.

Respectfully,

ELLIOT L. RICHARDSON

Richardson Statement

In the following statement, Richardson explains why he resigned three days earlier after being told by the president to fire special prosecutor Archibald Cox.

Following is the text of a statement read by for Attorney General Elliot L. Richardson at the start news conference Oct. 23:

There can be no greater privilege and there is no greater satisfaction than the opportunity to serve one's country. I shall always be grateful to President Nixon for giving me that opportunity in several demanding positions.

Although I strongly believe in the general purposes and priorities of his administration, I have been compelled to conclude that I could better serve my country by resigning public office than by continuing in it. This is true for two reasons

(1) Because to continue would have forced me to carry out a direct order of the President.

(2) Because I did not agree with the decisions which brought about the necessity for the issuance of that order.

In order to make clear how this dilemma came about, I wish to set forth as plainly as I can the facts of the unfolding drama which came to a climax last Saturday afternoon. To begin, I shall go back to Monday of last week. Two courts—District Court and the Court of Appeals of the District of Columbia—had ruled that the privilege protecting presidential communications must give way to the criminal process, but only to the extent that a compelling necessity had been shown. The President had a right of further review in the Supreme Court the United States; he had a right, in other words, to try to persuade the Supreme Court that the long-term public interest in maintaining the confidentiality of presidential communications is more important than the public interest in the prosecution of a particular criminal case, especially where other evidence is available. Had he insisted on exercising that right, however, the issue would have been subject to continuing litigation and controversy for a prolonged additional period and this at a time of acute international crisis.

Against this background, the President decided on Monday afternoon to make a new effort to resolve the impasse. He would ask Sen. John Stennis, a man of impeccable reputation for truthfulness and integrity, to listen to the tapes and verify the completeness and accuracy of a record of all pertinent portions. This record would then be available to the grand jury and for any other purpose for which it was needed. Believing however, that only the issue of his own involvement justified any breach of the principle of confidentiality and wishing to avoid continuing litigation, he made it a condition of the offer to provide a verified record of the subpoenaed tapes that access to any other tapes or records would be barred.

I regarded the proposal to rely on Sen. Stennis for a verified record (for the sake of brevity I will call it "the Stennis proposal") as reasonable, but I did not think it should be tied to the foreclosure of the right of the special prosecutor to invoke judicial process in future cases. Accordingly, I outlined the Stennis proposal to Mr. Cox later on Monday afternoon and proposed that the question of other tapes and documents be deferred. Mr. Cox and I discussed the Stennis proposal again on Tuesday morning.

On Wednesday afternoon, responding to Mr. Cox's suggestion that he could deal more concretely with the proposal if he had something on paper, I sent him the

document captioned "A Proposal," which he released in his Saturday press conference. On the afternoon of the next day he sent me his comments on the proposal, including the requirement that he have assured access to other tapes and documents. The President's lawyers regarded Mr. Cox's comments as amounting to a rejection of the Stennis proposal, and there followed the break-off of negotiations reflected in the correspondence with Charles Alan Wright released by Mr. Cox.

My position at that time was that Sen. Stennis' verified record of the tapes should nevertheless be presented to the district court for the court's determination of its adequacy to satisfy the subpoenas, still leaving other questions to be dealt with as they arose. That was still my view when at 8 p.m. Friday evening the President issued his statement directing Mr. Cox to make no further attempts by judicial process to obtain tapes, notes or memoranda of presidential conversations.

A half hour before this statement was issued, I received a letter from the President instructing me to give Mr. Cox this order. I did not act on the instruction, but instead, shortly after noon on Saturday, sent the President a letter restating my position. The President, however, decided to hold fast to the position announced the night before. When, therefore, Mr. Cox rejected that position and gave his objections to the Stennis proposal, as well as his reasons for insisting on assured access to other tapes and memoranda, the issue of presidential authority versus the independence and public accountability of the special prosecutor was squarely joined.

The President at that point thought he had no choice but to direct the attorney general to discharge Mr. Cox. And I, given my role in guaranteeing the independence of the special prosecutor, as well as my belief in the public interests embodied in that role, felt equally clear that I could not discharge him. And so I resigned.

At stake in the final analysis is the very integrity of the governmental processes I came to the Department of Justice to help restore. My own single most important commitment to this objective was my commitment to the independence of the special prosecutor. I could not be faithful to this commitment and also acquiesce in the curtailment of his authority. To say this, however, is not to charge the President with a failure to respect the claims of the investigative process: given the importance he attached to the principle of presidential confidentiality, he believed that his willingness to allow Sen. Stennis to verify the subpoenaed tapes fully met these claims.

The rest is for the American people to judge. On the fairness with which you do so may well rest the future well-being and security of our beloved country.

IMPEACHMENT OF PRESIDENTS
BILL CLINTON AND ANDREW JOHNSON

When the following Congressional Quarterly article was published in 1973, only one president in history—Andrew Johnson—had been impeached. By the end of the twentieth century, however, the House of Representatives had impeached a second president: Bill Clinton. He was accused of trying to cover up his relationship with a White House intern. Clinton was the only man elected to the presidency to be impeached. (Johnson was elected vice president, and he assumed the presidency after the assassination of Abraham Lincoln.) Clinton, like Johnson, was acquitted by the Senate and went on to finish his term.

BILL CLINTON

The Watergate scandal led, indirectly, to the Clinton impeachment. In the wake of Watergate, Congress passed a number of laws to prevent government misconduct. One of these laws empowered a three-judge panel to appoint an "independent counsel" with broad powers when high-ranking officials were suspected of criminal actions. Unfortunately for Clinton, a three-judge panel in 1994 appointed a particularly relentless independent counsel to look into allegations that the president had taken part in illegal land deals.

The independent counsel was Kenneth W. Starr, a staunch Republican with extensive legal experience. He failed to implicate either Clinton or first lady Hillary Rodham Clinton in any criminal acts involving the Whitewater land deals, as they were known. Meanwhile, however, Clinton was being sued by an Arkansas woman, Paula Jones, who accused him of sexually harassing her while he was governor of Arkansas. Jones's lawyers began looking into other instances of misconduct by Clinton, and they learned about his affair with a young White House intern, Monica Lewinsky.

Just as Nixon had tried to avoid legal scrutiny, Clinton engaged in a court battle to delay the Jones case until after he left office. But the Supreme Court unanimously voted to let the case proceed. Never before had a sitting president faced a lawsuit for alleged wrongdoing that occurred before he entered the White House.

The civil lawsuit and the Starr investigation came together with disastrous consequences for the president. As Jones's lawyers became interested in Lewinsky's story, Starr questioned Lewinsky for hours and persuaded her to cooperate with his investigation.

Lies and Calls for Impeachment

On Jan. 17, 1998, Clinton gave a pretrial deposition in the Jones case—meaning he answered questions under oath. He was surprised when Jones's lawyers began asking him whether he had a sexual relationship with Lewinsky. He denied such a relationship. By lying under oath, he opened himself up to be charged with perjury, a serious crime.

Clinton, in meetings with his top aides and interviews with reporters, continued to deny the relationship. He even went on national television with his denials. "I did not have sexual relations with that woman, Miss Lewinsky," he said. "I never told anybody to lie, not a single time—never," he said. "These allegations are false. And I need to go back to work for the American people."

But Starr kept investigating the case until, during the summer of 1998, he produced clear evidence that Clinton and Lewinsky had engaged in a sexual relationship. On Aug. 17, Clinton appeared voluntarily before Starr's grand jury, against the advice of his lawyers. He repeatedly refused to answer specific questions about his relationship with Lewinsky. That night, he made a remarkable appearance on national television to admit that he had lied to the American people. "Indeed, I did have a relationship with Ms. Lewinsky that was not appropriate. In fact, it was wrong," he said. "I misled people, including even my wife. I deeply regret that."

The following month, Starr delivered a lengthy report and dozens of boxes of evidence to the Republican-controlled House of Representatives, accusing Clinton of having committed serious offenses. Clinton faced humiliation as the House Judiciary Committee publicly released the Starr report, which detailed the president's sexual activities with Lewinsky and his attempts to conceal the affair. The very prestige of the presidency and even America's status among other nations seemed to suffer amid the many jokes made at the president's expense. Numerous newspaper editorials called on Clinton to resign. Most ominously for Clinton, the House started the impeachment process.

The impeachment of Clinton became sharply politicized, more so than the Watergate scandal. Republicans on the House Judiciary Committee, who were in the majority, accused the president of making deceptive statements under oath. Democrats did not defend Clinton's behavior, but they argued that his conduct was not so egregious as to warrant impeachment. The Constitution says "high crimes and misdemeanors" are punishable by impeachment, but it does not define what types of transgressions would meet that standard.

Throughout this period, Clinton remained enormously popular with the American public. This contrasted with Nixon, who sunk in the polls as the Watergate scandal deepened. Polls during the Clinton investigation also showed that most Americans opposed impeachment. Democrats unexpectedly scored gains in the congressional elections in November.

Nevertheless, Republicans on the committee passed four articles of impeachment in early December 1998. They accused Clinton of having committed perjury by lying under oath in both the Jones case and before Starr's grand jury, of obstructing justice, and of making false statements in response to 81 written questions that the committee had sent him. Democrats battled for an alternative approach that called for Congress to censure the president, which was a type of reprimand. But they were outvoted.

Impeachment Debate and Trial

One day before the House of Representatives planned to begin considering the four articles of impeachment, Clinton ordered a series of air strikes against Iraq. The timing infuriated Republicans. They accused him of trying to distract attention from his troubles, which Clinton denied. But after delaying the proceedings for just 24 hours, the House launched into a debate over impeachment. On Saturday, Dec. 19, the House narrowly approved two counts of impeachment. The counts accused Clinton of committing perjury by having lied to Starr's grand jury and of obstructing justice through such actions as encouraging Lewinsky to provide misleading information. The votes closely followed party lines, with Republicans overwhelmingly supporting impeachment and Democrats overwhelmingly opposing it.

Despite the high drama of impeachment, it was clear that Clinton would almost certainly be acquitted in the Senate. Although Republicans had a 55–45 majority, they needed 67 votes—two-thirds of the Senate—to remove the president from office. Every Democrat, and several Republicans, opposed taking such a step.

The historic trial in the Senate began on Jan. 7, 1999. William H. Rehnquist, the chief justice of the United States, presided over it. A team of 13 House Republicans made their case for convicting Clinton. They argued that he had corrupted the nation's system of justice. Seven lawyers defended the president. They maintained that the Republicans' case did not meet the constitutional standard needed to remove a president from office. Senators also viewed videotaped depositions, or formal questioning, of Lewinsky and other witnesses.

On Feb. 8, each side made its closing arguments. White House counsel Charles Ruff asked the senators, "Would it put at risk the liberties of the people to retain the president in office? Putting aside partisan animus, if you can honestly say that it would not, that those liberties are safe in his hands, then you must vote to acquit." Chief prosecutor Henry Hyde (R Ill), however, said, "A failure to convict will make the statement that lying under oath, while unpleasant and to be avoided, is not all that serious."

On Feb. 12, on live television, senators cast their votes on whether to convict or acquit the president. On the charge of perjury, the Senate voted not guilty by a margin of 55–45. On the charge of obstruction of justice, senators were divided, 50–50. In both cases, Republicans fell far short of the required 67 votes needed to convict.

Hours after the votes, Clinton made a brief statement in the White House rose garden. He said he was "profoundly sorry" for his actions. He remained highly popular and served out the rest of his term, which ended on Jan. 20, 2001. But the scandal may have cast a shadow on Democrats. In the close 2000 presidential election, Vice President Al Gore fell short in his quest to succeed Clinton in the White House.

Many historians view Clinton's transgressions as far less serious than those of Nixon. Clinton lied about his personal activities, whereas Nixon sought to cover up crimes that involved the abuse of power and even threatened the country's democratic system. Nevertheless, Clinton's actions were more troubling than those of President Johnson. Congress impeached John-

son for trying to remove a cabinet member from office, which is generally considered within a president's authority.

ANDREW JOHNSON

The impeachment and trial of President Andrew Johnson in 1868 . . . was based on the charge of his violation of a federal statute, the Tenure of Office Act. But in addition, the procedure was a profoundly political struggle between irreconcilable forces.

Questions such as control of the Republican Party, how to deal with the South, in a state of chaos following the Civil War, and monetary and economic policy all had an effect on the process.

Johnson as President was an anomaly. Lincoln's running mate in 1864, he was a southerner at a time when the South was out of the union; a Jacksonian Democrat who believed in states' rights, hard money, and minimal federal government activity running with an administration pursuing a policy of expansion both in the money supply and the role of government; a man who had little regard for the Negro in the midst of a party many of whose members were actively seeking to guarantee the rights of the newly freed slaves.

In these contradictions lay the basis for an inevitable conflict. The interplay of personalities and policies decreed that the conflict would result in an impeachment process.

Johnson had been the only member of the U.S. Senate from a seceding southern state (Tennessee) to remain loyal to the Union in 1861. Lincoln later made him military governor of Tennessee and chose him as his running mate in 1864 as a southerner and Democrat who was also a loyalist and in favor of prosecuting the war.

Sources

Michael Les Benedict, *The Impeachment and Trial of Andrew Johnson*, W. W. Norton and Company Inc., New York, 1973.

Raoul Berger, *Impeachment: The Constitutional Problems*, Harvard University Press, Cambridge, 1973.

James G. Blaine, *Twenty Years of Congress, 1861–1881*, The Henry Hill Publishing Company, Norwich, Conn., 1886.

On Lincoln's death in 1865, this outsider without allies or connections in the Republican Party succeeded to the presidency. Johnson's ideas on what should have been done to reconstruct and readmit the southern states to representation clashed with the wishes of a majority of Congress, overwhelmingly controlled by the Republicans.

Among the latter, there was a strong desire to secure the Negroes in their rights. Some had selfish motives: black votes and support were necessary for the Republicans to maintain their political hegemony. Others were more idealistic: the ex-slaves were helpless and had to be protected by the federal government, or they would quickly lose their new freedom.

Congress was divided into roughly three groups. The small minority of Democrats supported the President. About half the Republicans were known as "radicals," because they favored strong action to revolutionize southern society, by harsh military means if necessary. The other half of the Republicans were more conservative; while unwilling to go as far as the radicals, they wanted to make sure the South did not return to the unquestioned control of those who ruled it before the Civil War.

Over the years 1866–69, the conservative Republicans were repeatedly thrown into coalition with the radicals, often against their wishes. The radicals always counted on Johnson to help them out by behaving aggressively and uncompromisingly. They were usually confirmed in their expectations.

Upon taking office, Johnson began to pursue Lincoln's mild and tolerant reconstruction plans. The new President felt that a few basics were all that needed to be secured: abolition of slavery; ratification of the 13th Amendment, which abolished slavery in all states; repudiation of all state debts contracted by the Confederate governments; nullification of secession. When the southern states had done these things, Johnson felt they should be readmitted.

But Republicans wanted more: a Freedmen's Bureau, to protect and provide services for the ex-slaves; a civil rights bill, guaranteeing the Negroes their rights, and an over-all plan of reconstruction providing for temporary military governments in the South.

Throughout 1866, Johnson and Congress battled over these issues. In February, the President vetoed the Freedmen's Bureau bill. The Senate failed to override, but this was the last Johnson veto to be sustained. For the rest of the year, bill after bill was passed over Johnson's veto, including a second Freedmen's Bureau bill, a civil rights bill and, in early 1867, a reconstruction bill and the Tenure of Office Act.

The Tenure of Office Act, the violation of which was to be the legal basis for Johnson's impeachment, was passed over his veto March 2, 1867. The act forbade the President to remove civil officers (appointed with the consent of the Senate) without the approval of the Senate. Its purpose was to protect incumbent Republican officeholders from executive retaliation if they did not support the President. Johnson had made wholesale removals from rank-and-file federal offices both during and after the election campaign of 1866.

UNSUCCESSFUL ASHLEY RESOLUTION

About the time the Tenure of Office Act was being debated, the first moves toward impeachment began. On Jan. 7, 1867, two Missouri representatives, Benjamin F. Loan (R Mo. 1863–69) and John R. Kelso (R Mo. 1865–67), attempted in turn to introduce resolutions in the House proposing impeachment, but each was prevented by parliamentary maneuver.

But later the same day, Rep. James M. Ashley (R Ohio 1859–69) rose on a question of privilege and formally charged the President with high crimes and misdemeanors. (Ashley was the great-grandfather of Rep. Thomas L. Ashley (D Ohio), who was elected in 1954 in the same district as his ancestor.)

Ashley made general charges, and no specific violations of law were mentioned. Most members recognized the charges as basically political grievances rather than illegal acts. The matter was referred to the House Judiciary Committee, which reported on March 2, 1867, two days before the expiration of the 39th Congress, that the committee had reached no conclusion. Its members recommended that the matter be given further study by the next Congress.

On March 7, 1867, the third day of the 40th Congress, Ashley again introduced his resolution, and it was referred to the Judiciary Committee for further investigation. The committee studied the matter throughout the year and issued a report on Nov. 25, 1867. A majority of the committee reported an impeachment resolution. When the House voted on the matter Dec. 7, the radicals suffered a crushing defeat. The resolution calling for impeachment was turned down, 57 to 108.

SUCCESSFUL SECOND TRY

Johnson appeared to have won. But, observed James G. Blaine in his memoirs, "Those best acquainted with the earnestness of purpose and the determination of the leading men who had persuaded themselves that the safety of the Republic depended upon the destruction of Johnson's official power, knew that the closest watch would be kept upon every action of the President, and if an apparently justifying cause could be found the project of his removal would be vigorously renewed." Within a month, the radicals found their issue.

Johnson had long wanted to rid himself of Secretary of War Edwin M. Stanton. Stanton was a close ally of the radical Republicans. After repeatedly trying to get him to resign, Johnson suspended him on Dec. 12, 1867. On Jan. 13, 1868, the Senate refused to concur, thus, under the terms of the Tenure of Office Act, reinstating Stanton.

Apparently flushed by his recent victory on the impeachment issue in the House, Johnson decided to force the issue. He dismissed Stanton on Feb. 21, citing the power and authority vested in him by the Constitution. In effect, he was declaring the Tenure of Office Act unconstitutional and refusing to abide by it.

This action enraged Congress, driving conservative Republicans into alliance with the radicals on impeachment. A House resolution on impeachment was immediately offered and was referred to the Committee on Reconstruction, headed by Rep. Thaddeus Stevens (R Pa. 1859–68; Whig 1849–53), one of the radical Republican leaders. The next day, Feb. 22, the committee reported a resolution favoring impeachment. The House vote, taken two days later, was 126 to 47 in favor, on a strict party-line basis.

TRIAL IN THE SENATE

The House took the next step of drawing up the specific articles of impeachment and appointing managers to present and argue the charges before the Senate. There were 11 articles in all, the main one concerning Johnson's removal of Stanton in contravention of the Tenure of Office Act.

Between the time of the House action and the beginning of the trial in the Senate, the conservative Republicans had time to reflect. One of the main objects of their reflection was fiery Ben Wade of Ohio. Wade was president pro tem of the Senate and, under the succession law then in effect, was next in line for the presidency. He was also one of the most radical of the radical Republicans, a hard-liner on southern reconstruction and a monetary expansionist—anathema to conservatives.

Another concern of both factions of Republicans was the upcoming national convention and presidential election. Conservatives were in favor of nominating Gen. Ulysses S. Grant, a hero in the North after the Civil War. They viewed him as the most likely candidate to win and were confident they could control him and keep him from adopting radical policies. Radicals were anxious to gain control of the presidency to prevent Grant's nomination and dictate the party's platform.

The trial started March 30, when one of the House managers made the opening argument. Although other charges were presented against the President, the House managers relied mainly on Johnson's removal

of Stanton as a direct violation of the Tenure of Office Act. One of the House managers revealed the bitter emotions prevailing at the time when he said, "The world in after times will read the history of the administration of Andrew Johnson as an illustration of the depth to which political and official perfidy can descend."

By May 11, the Senate was ready to ballot. The first vote was taken on the 11th article, which was a summary of many of the charges set forth in some of the preceding articles. The result was 35 guilty, 19 not guilty. If one vote had switched, the necessary two thirds would have been reached. Seven Republican senators joined the 12 Democrats in supporting the President.

After the first vote, the Senate adjourned as a court of impeachment until May 26. When they reconvened on that date, two more ballots were taken, on the second and third articles of impeachment. The results were the same as on the first ballot, 35 to 19. The Senate then abandoned the remaining articles and adjourned as a court of impeachment.

UNCONSTITUTIONAL GROUNDS

The Tenure of Office Act was virtually repealed early in Grant's administration, once the Republicans had control of the appointing power, and was entirely repealed in 1887. And in 1926, the Supreme Court declared, "The power to remove . . . executive officers . . . is an incident of the power to appoint them, and is in its nature an executive power" (*Myers vs. United States*). The opinion, written by Chief Justice William Howard Taft, himself a former president, referred to the Tenure of Office Act and declared that it had been unconstitutional.

Administration Officials Who Have Quit or Been Fired

Congressional Quarterly in October 1973 published the following list of government officials who had resigned or been fired in connection with Watergate. Among the most important of these was John W.

Dean III, the former White House counsel. He was the only high-ranking administration official to come before the Senate Watergate Committee and accuse Nixon of involvement in the Watergate coverup.

On Oct. 19, Dean pleaded guilty to a charge of conspiracy to obstruct justice and defraud the United States because of his past attempts to hide the truth about Watergate. He also agreed to testify for the prosecution in future trials of other White House officials. This was regarded as a major development. Dean was viewed as a potential key witness against such former administration leaders as John N. Mitchell, H. R. Haldeman, and John D. Ehrlichman. He might have even testified against Nixon himself had criminal charges ever been brought against the president.

Archibald Cox, Elliot L. Richardson and William D. Ruckelshaus joined the list of Watergate-related departures from the Nixon administration on Oct. 20, when special prosecutor Cox was fired by President Nixon and Attorney General Richardson and his deputy, Ruckelshaus, resigned over the dismissal. At least five of Richardson's aides and four of Ruckelshaus' assistants resigned or announced they would do so, and more Justice Department officials were expected to step down as a result of Nixon's abolition of the special prosecutor's office.

Before the dramatic weekend events, at least 12 persons had resigned or been fired from government posts because of the Watergate scandals. They were, in chronological order in 1973:

- Dwight L. Chapin, Nixon's appointments secretary since 1969, resigned Feb. 28 to join United Air Lines as an executive after being named in press reports as a link to political saboteur Donald H. Segretti. In Senate testimony Oct. 3, Segretti confirmed that Chapin had hired him to play dirty tricks on Democrats in the 1972 presidential campaign.
- Jeb Stuart Magruder, who had served as deputy director of the Nixon re-election campaign, resigned as director of policy development in the Commerce Department on April 26. Testifying before the Senate Watergate Committee June 14, Magruder admitted his involvement in the Watergate break-in and coverup and implicated other administration officials. He pleaded guilty Aug. 16 to a reduced one-count charge and promised to testify against others allegedly involved in the scandal.
- L. Patrick Gray III resigned as acting FBI director April 27 after it was reported that he had destroyed documents belonging to convicted

Watergate conspirator E. Howard Hunt at the orders of presidential aides. Gray confirmed the reports during his Aug. 3 and 6 testimony before the Senate Watergate Committee.

- John W. Dean III resigned under fire as presidential counsel on April 30, saying he would not become a "scapegoat" in the Watergate case. Dean, who pleaded guilty Oct. 19 to one conspiracy count for his role in the coverup, was the only administration official to accuse President Nixon of involvement in the scandal.
- John D. Ehrlichman, the President's chief domestic affairs adviser, resigned April 30. Ehrlichman denied any wrongdoing in testimony before the Senate committee July 24–27, but he was indicted Sept. 4 in connection with the 1971 burglary of the office of Daniel Ellsberg's psychiatrist.
- H. R. Haldeman, White House chief of staff who also resigned April 30, denied during Senate testimony July 30–Aug. 1 Dean's charges that he participated in the coverup.
- Richard G. Kleindienst, whose resignation as attorney general was announced by Nixon April 30 along with those of Dean, Ehrlichman and Haldeman, cited "close personal and professional associations" with others implicated in the scandal as his reason for leaving.
- David R. Young, who had first joined the White House as an assistant on Henry A. Kissinger's National Security Council staff and later was transferred to the domestic council, resigned April 30. He was indicted Sept. 4 in connection with the Ellsberg break-in.
- Gordon C. Strachan, former staff assistant to Haldeman, resigned April 30 as general counsel of the United States Information Agency. He told the Senate committee July 20 and 23 of his duties as liaison between Haldeman and the re-election committee.
- Robert C. Odle Jr., former director of administration for the re-election committee, was fired from his consultant's job at the Agriculture Department May 7. He had been named by the General Accounting Office as one of several persons who handled "unrecorded" campaign funds.
- Egil (Bud) Krogh Jr., who joined the White House staff in 1969 and became transportation under secretary in 1973, resigned May 9, taking "full responsibility" for the Ellsberg break-in. Krogh was indicted Sept. 4 for his role in that incident and again on Oct. 11 for lying during the initial Watergate investigation in 1972.

- John J. Caulfield, a retired New York City undercover policeman who had worked at the White House, resigned May 24 as assistant director for criminal enforcement in the Treasury Department's Bureau of Alcohol, Tobacco and Firearms. He told the Senate investigating committee May 22–23 that he had relayed an offer of executive clemency to conspirator James W. McCord Jr., under instructions from Dean.
- In addition to the government departures, Kenneth Rietz, director of the Republican National Committee's "new majority" campaign for the 1974 elections, resigned unexpectedly on April 24 to join a private business. News reports had linked Rietz with an effort to recruit campaign spies while he was running the Nixon youth campaign in 1972.

Texts of Oct. 20 Resignation Statements, Letters

Following are the White House text of Press Secretary Ronald L. Ziegler's Oct. 20 announcement of the resignation or dismissal of Attorney General Elliot L. Richardson, Deputy Attorney General William D. Ruckelshaus and Watergate special prosecutor Archibald Cox and the texts of letters from Richardson to Nixon, Nixon to Richardson, Ruckelshaus to Nixon, Nixon to acting Attorney General Robert H. Bork and Bork to Cox.

Ziegler Statement

I know many of you are on deadline. I have a brief statement to give at this time, and following the reading of the statement we will have an exchange of a series of letters relating to action which President Nixon has taken tonight.

President Nixon has tonight discharged Archibald Cox, the Special Prosecutor in the Watergate case. The President took this action because of Mr. Cox's refusal to comply with instructions given Friday night through Attorney General Richardson that he was not to seek to invoke the judicial process further to compel production of recordings, notes or memoranda regarding private Presidential conversations.

Further, the office of the Watergate special prosecution force has been abolished as of approximately 8:00 p.m. tonight. Its function to investigate and prosecute those involved in the Watergate matter will be transferred back into the institutional framework of the Department of Justice, where it will be carried out with thoroughness and vigor.

In his statement Friday night, and in his decision not to seek Supreme Court review of the Court of Appeals decision with regard to the Watergate tapes, the President sought to avoid a constitutional confrontation by an action that would give the Grand Jury what it needs to proceed with its work with the least possible intrusion of Presidential privacy. That action taken by the President in the spirit of accommodation that has marked American constitutional history was accepted by responsible leaders in Congress and the country. Mr. Cox's refusal to proceed in the same spirit of accommodation, complete with his announced intention to defy instructions from the President and press for further confrontation at a time of serious world crisis, made it necessary for the President to discharge Mr. Cox and to return to the Department of Justice the task of prosecuting those who broke the law in connection with Watergate.

Before taking this action, the President met this evening with Attorney General Richardson. He met with Attorney General Richardson at about 4:45 today for about thirty minutes.

The Attorney General, on hearing of the President's decision, felt obliged to resign, since he believed the discharge of Professor Cox to be inconsistent with the conditions of his confirmation by the Senate.

As Deputy Attorney General, Mr. William Ruckelshaus, refused to carry out the President's explicit directive to discharge Mr. Cox. He, like Mr. Cox, has been discharged of further duties effective immediately.

We have available for you now the exchange of letters between Attorney General Richardson and the President and the other correspondence.

Richardson Resignation

October 20, 1973

The President
The White House

Dear Mr. President:

It is with deep regret that I have been obliged to conclude that circumstances leave me no alternative to the submission of my resignation as Attorney General of the United States.

At the time you appointed me, you gave me the authority to name a special prosecutor if I should consider it appropriate. A few days before my confirmation hearing began, I announced that I would, if confirmed, "appoint a special prosecutor and give him all the independence, authority, and staff support needed to carry out the tasks entrusted to him." I added, "Although he will be in the Department of Justice and report to me— and only to me—he will be aware that his ultimate accountability is to the American people."

At many points throughout the nomination hearings, I reaffirmed my intention to assure the independence of the special prosecutor, and in my statement of his duties and responsibilities, I specified that he would have "full authority" for "determining whether or not to contest the assertion of 'Executive Privilege' or any other testimonial privilege." And while the special prosecutor can be removed from office for "extraordinary improprieties," I also pledged that "The Attorney General will not countermand or interfere with the Special Prosecutor's decisions or actions."

While I fully respect the reasons that have led you to conclude that the Special Prosecutor must be discharged, I trust that you understand that I could not in the light of these firm and repeated commitments carry out your direction that this be done. In the circumstances, therefore, I feel that I have no choice but to resign.

In leaving your Administration, I take with me lasting gratitude for the opportunities you have given me to serve under your leadership in a number of important posts. It has been a privilege to share in your efforts to make the structure of world peace more stable and the structure of our own government more responsive. I believe profoundly in the rightness and importance of those efforts, and I trust that they will meet with increasing success in the remaining years of your Presidency.

Respectfully,

ELLIOT L. RICHARDSON

Nixon to Richardson

October 20, 1973

Dear Elliot:

It is with the deepest regret and with an understanding of the circumstances which brought you to your decision that I accept your resignation.

Sincerely,

RICHARD NIXON

Honorable Elliot L. Richardson
The Attorney General
Justice Department
Washington, D.C.

Ruckelshaus to Nixon

Dear Mr. President,

It is with deep regret that I tender my resignation. During your Administration, you have honored me with four appointments—first in the Justice Department's Civil Division, then as administrator of the Environmental Protection Agency, next as acting director of the Federal Bureau of Investigation, and finally as Deputy Attorney General. I have found the challenge of working in the high levels of American Government an unforgettable and rewarding experience.

I shall always be grateful for your having given me the opportunity to serve the American people in this fashion.

I am, of course, sorry that my conscience will not permit me to carry out your instruction to discharge Archibald Cox. My disagreement with that action at this time is too fundamental to permit me to act otherwise.

I wish you every success during the remainder of your Administration.

Respectfully,

William D. Ruckelshaus

Nixon to Bork

October 20, 1973

Dear Mr. Bork:

I have today accepted the resignations of Attorney General Richardson and Deputy Attorney General Ruckelshaus. In accordance with Title 28, Section 508(b) of the United States Code and of Title 28, Section 0.132(a) of the Code of Federal Regulations, it is now incumbent upon you to perform both the duties as Solicitor General, and duties of and act as Attorney General.

In his press conference today Special Prosecutor Archibald Cox made it apparent that he will not comply with the instruction I issued to him, through Attorney General Richardson, yesterday. Clearly the Government of the United States cannot function if employees of the Executive Branch are free to ignore in this fashion the instructions of the President. Accordingly, in your capacity of Acting Attorney General, I direct you to discharge Mr. Cox immediately and to take all steps necessary to return to the Department of Justice the functions now being performed by the Watergate Special Prosecution Force.

It is my expectation that the Department of Justice will continue with full vigor the investigations and prosecutions that had been entrusted to the Watergate Special Prosecution Force.

Sincerely,

RICHARD NIXON

Honorable Robert H. Bork
The Acting Attorney General
Justice Department
Washington, D.C.

Bork to Cox

October 20, 1973

Dear Mr. Cox:

As provided by Title 28, Section 508(b) of the United States Code and Title 28, Section 0.132(a) of the Code of Federal Regulations, I have today assumed the duties of Acting Attorney General.

In that capacity I am, as instructed by the President, discharging you, effective at once, from your position as Special Prosecutor, Watergate Special Prosecution Force.

Very truly yours,

ROBERT H. BORK
Acting Attorney General

Honorable Archibald Cox
Special Prosecutor
Watergate Special Prosecution Force
1425 K Street, N.W.
Washington, D.C.

Text of Nixon's Oct. 19 Watergate Tapes Compromise

Following is the White House text of President Nixon's Oct. 19 statement announcing his decision not to appeal the Watergate tapes decision of the U.S. Court of Appeals and his compromise plan for revealing a summary of the tapes' contents:

For a number of months, there has been a strain imposed on the American people by the aftermath of Watergate, and the inquiries into and court suits arising out of that incident. Increasing apprehension over the possibility of

a constitutional confrontation in the tapes cases has become especially damaging.

Our Government, like our Nation, must remain strong and effective. What matters most, in this critical hour, is our ability to act—and to act in a way that enables us to control events, not to be paralyzed and overwhelmed by them. At home, the Watergate issue has taken on overtones of a partisan political contest. Concurrently, there are those in the international community who may be tempted by our Watergate-related difficulties at home to misread America's unity and resolve in meeting the challenges we confront abroad.

I have concluded that it is necessary to take decisive actions that will avoid any possibility of a constitutional crisis and that lay the groundwork upon which we can assure unity of purpose at home and end the temptation abroad to test our resolve.

It is with this awareness that I have considered the decision of the Court of Appeals for the District of Columbia. I am confident that the dissenting opinions, which are in accord with what until now has always been regarded as the law, would be sustained upon review by the Supreme Court. I have concluded, however, that it is not in the national interest to leave this matter unresolved for the period that might be required for a review by the highest court.

Throughout this week, the Attorney General, Elliot Richardson at my insistence, has been holding discussions with Special Prosecutor Archibald Cox, looking to the possibility of a compromise that would avoid the necessity of Supreme Court review. With the greatest reluctance, I have concluded that in this one instance I must permit a breach in the confidentiality that is so necessary to the conduct of the Presidency. Accordingly, the Attorney General made what he regarded as a reasonable proposal for compromise, and one that goes beyond what any President in history has offered. It was a proposal that would comply with the spirit of the decision of the Court of Appeals. It would have allowed justice to proceed undiverted, while maintaining the principle of an independent Executive Branch. It would have given the Special Prosecutor the information he claims he needs for use in the grand jury. It would also have resolved any lingering thought that the President himself might have been involved in a Watergate cover-up.

Stennis Choice

The proposal was that, as quickly as the materials could be prepared, there would be submitted to Judge Sirica, through a statement prepared by me personally from the subpoenaed tapes, a full disclosure of everything contained in those tapes that has any bearing on Watergate. The authenticity of this summary would be assured by giving unlimited access to the tapes to a very distinguished man, highly respected by all elements in American life for his integrity, his fairness, and his patriotism, so that that man could satisfy himself that the statement prepared by me did indeed include fairly and accurately anything on the tapes that might be regarded as related to Watergate. In return, so that the constitutional tensions of Watergate would not be continued, it would be understood that there would be no further attempt by the Special Prosecutor to subpoena still more tapes or other Presidential papers of a similar nature.

I am pleased to be able to say that Chairman Sam Ervin and Vice Chairman Howard Baker of the Senate Select Committee have agreed to this procedure and that at their request, and mine, Senator John Stennis has consented to listen to every requested tape and verify that the statement I am preparing is full and accurate. Some may ask why, if I am willing to let Senator Stennis hear the tapes for this purpose, I am not willing merely to submit them to the court for inspection in private. I do so out of no lack of respect for Judge Sirica, in whose discretion and integrity I have the utmost confidence, but because to allow the tapes to be heard by one judge would create a precedent that would be available to 400 district judges. Further, it would create a precedent that Presidents are required to submit to judicial demands that purport to override Presidential determinations on requirements for confidentiality.

Special Prosecutor

To my regret, the Special Prosecutor rejected this proposal. Nevertheless, it is my judgment that in the present circumstances and existing international environment, it is in the overriding national interest that a constitutional confrontation on this issue be avoided. I have, therefore, instructed White House counsel not to seek Supreme Court review from the decision of the Court of Appeals. At the same time, I will voluntarily make available to Judge Sirica—and also to the Senate Select Committee—a statement of the Watergate-related portions of the tapes, prepared and authenticated in the fashion I have described.

I want to repeat that I have taken this step with the greatest reluctance, only to bring the issue of Watergate tapes to an end and to assure our full attention to more pressing business affecting the very security of the nation. Accordingly, though I have not wished to intrude upon the independence of the Special Prosecutor, I have

felt it necessary to direct him, as an employee of the Executive Branch, to make no further attempts by judicial process to obtain tapes, notes, or memoranda of Presidential conversations. I believe that with the statement that will be provided to the court, any legitimate need of the Special Prosecutor is fully satisfied and that he can proceed to obtain indictments against those who may have committed any crimes. And I believe that by these actions I have taken today America will be spared the anguish of further indecision and litigation about tapes.

Our constitutional history reflects not only the language and inferences of that great document, but also the choices of clash and accommodation made by responsible leaders at critical moments. Under the Constitution it is the duty of the President to see that the laws of the Nation are faithfully executed. My actions today are in accordance with that duty, and in that spirit of accommodation.

Cox Response

Following is the Oct. 19 statement of Watergate Special Prosecutor Archibald Cox in response to President Nixon's compromise plan on the Watergate tapes:

In my judgment, the President is refusing to comply with the court decrees. A summary of the context of the tapes lacks the evidentiary value of the tapes themselves. No steps are being taken to turn over the important notes, memoranda and other documents that the court orders require. I shall bring these points to the attention of the court and abide by its decision.

The President's directions to make no further attempts by the judicial process to obtain tapes, notes or memoranda of presidential conversations will apply to all such matters in the future.

These directions would apply not only to the so-called Watergate investigation but all matters within my jurisdiction.

The instructions are in violation of the promises which the Attorney General made to the Senate when his nomination was confirmed. For me to comply to those instructions would violate my solemn pledge to the Senate and the country to invoke judicial process to challenge exaggerated claims of executive privilege. I shall not violate my promise.

Acceptance of these directions would also defeat the fair administration of criminal justice. It would deprive prosecutors of admissible evidence in prosecuting wrongdoers who abused high government office. It would also enable defendants to go free, by withholding material a judge ruled necessary to a fair trial. The President's action already threatens this result in the New York prosecution of John Mitchell and Maurice Stans. I cannot be a party to such an arrangement.

I shall have a more complete statement in the near future.

Points to Ponder

After Nixon left office, Congress tried to make it easier to investigate presidents and other high-ranking executive branch officials. A new law gave judges the power, under certain circumstances, to appoint independent counsels. Such counsels, unlike Cox, were protected from being fired by the president. But controversy would eventually arise over these powerful prosecutors, some of whom were accused of being overly zealous. Instead of fixing the problem, the independent counsel law appeared to expose presidents to unfair investigations.

- Do you think it is possible to create a system under which presidents can be scrutinized thoroughly without being subjected to an unfair investigation?

- If a prosecutor is investigating a high-ranking political official, who can make sure that a prosecutor is acting fairly, and not out of political motives? How important is it to strike a proper balance between an independent prosecutor and the White House?

APPOINTMENTS AND HEARINGS; TWO TAPES DO NOT EXIST and CONGRESS CONTINUES HEARINGS ON TAPES, PROSECUTOR

During the fall of 1973, President Nixon came under increasing criticism on a number of fronts. Suspicions mounted that the White House was trying to cover up crimes by refusing to cooperate with court orders to hand over tapes of presidential conversations. The White House announced that two of the nine tapes sought by the Watergate grand jury did not exist. Later, it revealed that a third tape contained an 18-minute gap. Nixon also faced questions about a number of matters unrelated to Watergate. He came under allegations that he had underpaid taxes and had improperly interfered with a Justice Department investigation into the International Telephone and Telegraph Corporation (ITT).

MISSING TAPES

In one of the most troubling developments, the White House announced on Oct. 31 that two of the nine tapes that it had been ordered to hand over to U.S. District Court judge John J. Sirica did not exist. One of the tapes would have contained the first conversation between the president and Attorney General John N. Mitchell after the Watergate break-in. The other tape would have contained a conversation between Nixon and John W. Dean III. This conversation was considered important because Dean had claimed that he and the president discussed granting executive clemency to a key Watergate witness at that meeting. The implication by Dean was that Nixon wanted to stop the witness from testifying about Watergate by promising to shorten his prison sentence or taking certain other steps to help him.

J. Fred Buzhardt, special White House counsel, claimed that the president failed to record his telephone conversation with Mitchell because he used a telephone extension that was not hooked up to the automatic White House taping system. Regarding the missing conversation with Dean, Buzhardt's first explanation was that the tape recording system was malfunctioning. Later, he said that the six-hour tape had run out before Dean and Nixon met.

Many wondered why Nixon had not spoken out earlier about the missing tapes. Nixon said he was first informed on Sept. 29 or 30 that the tapes might not exist, but that this was not confirmed to him until about Oct. 27. The president said, however, that he would provide the grand jury with a

special recording that contained references to the Mitchell conversation and his notes on the Dean meeting.

The tapes were to have been submitted to Sirica for his review. Unless they contained information that had to remain secret to protect the nation, they would then be turned over to the grand jury that was looking into Watergate. Many officials responded with shock and skepticism when the White House announced that the two tapes were missing. "I have passed the point of reacting," said House Speaker Carl Albert, an Oklahoma Democrat.

CALLS FOR RESIGNATION

Two senators responded to the news by asking Nixon to resign. The first, Republican Edward R. Brooke of Massachusetts, said that Nixon might not be guilty of impeachable offenses. But he said he had reluctantly concluded that Nixon should step down because "I don't think the country can stand the trauma that it has been going through for the past few months." Some congressional leaders urged Nixon to publicly disclose all information about his role in the Watergate scandals. The president "must appear before an appropriate forum and lay his cards on the table," said Democratic senator Henry M. Jackson of Washington.

Although Nixon's fellow Republicans would be expected to defend him, many tried to distance themselves from the White House. In the Senate, Colorado Republican Peter H. Dominick advised Republicans to begin acting independently of Nixon. However, the Senate's senior Republican, George D. Aiken of Vermont, appeared impatient with Nixon's critics. He said the House should either move ahead with impeaching Nixon or "get off his back." On the Senate Watergate Committee, Republican Edward J. Gurney emerged as Nixon's strongest defender.

Congress took steps to continue the scrutiny of Watergate. It extended the term of the Watergate grand jury, which had been scheduled to expire in December 1973. It passed a law giving Sirica's court the power to enforce subpoenas issued by the Senate Watergate Committee. (Sirica in October had declined to rule on a committee subpoena for White House tapes, saying he did not have authority over the matter.) The House also voted overwhelmingly to grant the Judiciary Committee $1 million to investigate

Watergate. However, some Republicans bitterly opposed the measure. They wanted written guarantees that Republican members of the committee would have input into choosing staff members who would handle the investigation.

Lawmakers also considered legislation to create a special prosecutor who would be entirely independent of the White House. The idea was that a panel of judges, rather than the Justice Department, would appoint the prosecutor. The president would not have any authority over the prosecutor's actions. However, the legislation lost momentum as confidence grew in the new special prosecutor, Leon Jaworski. Many in Congress continued to feel that Nixon had abused his power by firing Cox. Their view was reinforced by federal district judge Gerhard A. Gesell, who ruled that the administration had acted illegally in firing Cox. But the judge did not order Cox reinstated, and Cox said he would not use the ruling to try to regain his former post.

A number of editorial writers, both Republicans and Democrats, suggested that the time had come for Nixon to step down. The editors of Time Inc., who had previously endorsed Nixon for president, wrote: "Richard Nixon and the nation have passed a tragic point of no return. It now seems likely that the President will have to give up his office: he has irredeemably lost his moral authority, the con-

fidence of most of the country, and therefore his ability to govern effectively."

Nixon, however, said he would not resign. On Nov. 7, he declared: "I have no intention whatever of walking away from the job I was elected to do. As long as I am physically able, I am going to continue to work 16 to 18 hours a day for the cause of a real peace abroad and for the cause of prosperity, without inflation and without war, at home." Although Nixon declined to meet with the Senate Watergate Committee, he mounted a counteroffensive to restore his credibility. In November, he met with all 234 Republican members of Congress, as well as some moderate and conservative Democrats. In those meetings, he reiterated that he would not resign.

In addition to legal actions by the Watergate grand jury, investigations elsewhere around the country raised new questions about improper White House activities. On Dec. 27, for example, a Las Vegas grand jury indicted billionaire Howard Hughes. He was charged with illegal stock manipulation and conspiracy in connection with an airline merger. Senators wanted to know if there was a connection between Nixon's approval of the merger and a $100,000 campaign contribution for Nixon that Hughes gave to a close friend of Nixon, Charles G. Rebozo.

Congress, as if numbed by exposure to too many major, unexpected developments that could affect the course of the nation, appeared to look to the people for guidance on how far to assert itself to resolve a continuing crisis of confidence in the nation's leadership.

"I have passed the point of reacting," said House Speaker Carl Albert of the week's events. Other members of Congress said the situation boiled down to what the people of the country believed.

It was a week in which the administration attempted to repair damage to its Justice Department by filling two important vacancies but saw its credibility challenged when it reported two secret White House tape recordings did not exist. It also was a week in which Congress moved toward confirmation of a new vice president but saw its efforts to establish a special prosecutor's office slowed by wrangling. The major events:

- Senate and House Judiciary Committees began hearings on legislation to establish a special prosecutor with complete independence from the President and power to investigate and prosecute charges against the President, his staff and former aides.
- Attorneys for the President announced that two of the nine tape recordings sought by ousted spe-

cial prosecutor Archibald Cox and the U.S. District Court did not exist.

- President Nixon announced the nomination of Sen. William B. Saxbe (R Ohio) to become attorney general, succeeding Elliot L. Richardson, who resigned rather than fire Cox.
- Acting Attorney General Robert H. Bork announced the selection of Texas attorney Leon Jaworski to become special prosecutor.
- The Senate Rules Committee began hearings on the vice presidential nomination of Gerald R. Ford.
- After a 20-day recess, the Senate Watergate Committee resumed its hearings with testimony from Democratic and Republican campaigners.

The Missing Tapes

Two of the long-sought tapes of presidential conversations related to the Watergate case did not exist, J. Fred Buzhardt, special White House counsel, told Judge John J. Sirica Oct. 31.

The two conversations which Buzhardt said were never recorded at all were the President's first conversation with Attorney General John N. Mitchell after the

Watergate break-in and his meeting with John W. Dean III in which Dean said the subject of executive clemency for E. Howard Hunt was discussed.

The first conversation was by telephone on June 20, 1972; Buzhardt said that the President was using a telephone extension not connected to the automatic recording system, and hence the conversation was not recorded. The meeting with Dean took place in the President's office in the Executive Office Building next door to the White House on April 15, 1973; Buzhardt said at first that this conversation was not recorded due to a malfunctioning of the system. On Nov. 1, the explanation was revised to say that a six-hour tape had run out before the conversation began.

Sirica had announced Oct. 30: "The White House will prepare as soon as possible an analysis of the materials which will be transmitted to the court together with the tapes and documents themselves." The announcement followed a lengthy meeting between Sirica, Buzhardt and two members of the Watergate prosecution force, Henry S. Ruth Jr. and Philip A. Lacovara.

All parties, Sirica said, agreed to procedures for submitting the tapes for him to examine privately and determine whether any part of them was protected from disclosure to the Watergate grand jury by the claim of executive privilege. The procedures were developed within the guidelines set forth by the appeals court ruling backing Sirica's initial order.

Sirica said that, before he examined the materials, he would hear arguments in a closed session on the various claims of privilege relevant to particular parts of the tapes. Then, he said, he would examine the tapes and other material and decide individually on each portion for which executive privilege was claimed. His rulings would be handed down one at a time, he said.

Another meeting was set by Sirica with Buzhardt, Ruth and Lacovara for the afternoon of Nov. 2. At that time, he indicated, a timetable for turning over the materials and for hearing arguments would be set up.

Profile: Leon Jaworski, the New Special Prosecutor

Bowing to the public outcry over the firing of special prosecutor Archibald Cox, the White House on Nov. 1 announced the appointment of a new special prosecutor. Leon Jaworski was a prominent Texas trial lawyer and a veteran Democrat. Nixon also announced a new attorney general: Republican senator William B. Saxbe of Ohio.

Nixon praised Jaworski as "the best we could get for this very important position." Acting attorney general Bork said Jaworski would have as much independence as Cox. Bork also said that Jaworski would have complete cooperation from the White House and full access to presidential documents. Furthermore, Nixon would not fire Jaworski without the agreement of top members of Congress.

These promises failed to reassure many members of Congress who were upset over the firing of Cox. Some lawmakers wanted U.S. District Court judge Sirica to appoint a prosecutor who would not be answerable in any way to the White House. Jaworksi, however, seemed comfortable with the arrangement. He told reporters that there would be no restraints on his investigation.

For his part, Nixon continued to blame Cox for the actions that led to Cox's dismissal. He said the special prosecutor had been unreasonable in rejecting a compromise that would have given him summaries of tapes of presidential conversations, rather than the tapes themselves. At a press conference, he said that a special prosecutor should not take a president to court, as Cox had done. Asked repeatedly how he would respond if the new special prosecutor insisted on access to more tapes, Nixon said he thought a compromise could be worked out. This seemed to be a sign that his level of cooperation would not necessarily increase with the new special prosecutor.

The search for a new special prosecutor to replace ousted Archibald Cox officially ended Nov. 1, with the announcement that a well-known Texas trial lawyer had been asked and had agreed to take over the beleaguered post. The announcement of the selection of Leon Jaworski, 68, as the new Watergate special prosecutor was coupled with the nomination of Sen. William B. Saxbe (R Ohio) to succeed Elliot L. Richardson as attorney general.

Appearing briefly before newsmen to announce the Saxbe nomination, President Nixon did not mention Jaworski by name, but said acting Attorney General Robert H. Bork had selected a man who is "the best we could get for this very important position." A highly successful trial lawyer, Jaworski has been president of the American Bar Association (1971–72), a special assistant to the U.S. attorney general (1962–65), a member of two presidential commissions and a close friend of President Lyndon B. Johnson. He is a Democrat.

Immediately following the President's appearance, acting Attorney General Bork said Jaworski would have

*Special Prosecutor
Leon Jaworski*

the same broad mandate and independence which had been given Cox. He said Jaworski had been "promised the full cooperation of the executive branch," and, should he decide that he needs presidential documents, "there will be no restrictions placed on his freedom. . . ."

In addition, Bork said, Nixon had given his personal assurance that he would not fire Jaworski without the agreement of a "substantial majority" of an eight-member congressional group: majority and minority leaders of the House and Senate, chairmen and ranking minority members of the Judiciary Committees of both houses. It was Nixon's dismissal of Cox Oct. 20 that had triggered an outburst of criticism, demands for impeachment, and calls for a new prosecutor independent of the executive branch.

Bork said he did not expect that court battles over access to White House tapes and documents would continue. "I anticipate reasonableness on both sides," he said. It will be up to Jaworski, Bork added, to decide whether to pursue such investigations as the reported probe of presidential friend C. G. "Bebe" Rebozo's handling of a $100,000 campaign contribution from billionaire Howard Hughes—a matter that Cox had been investigating.

Speaking to newsmen in Houston Nov. 1, Jaworski confirmed that "there are no restraints on what I'll be permitted to do." He said he was first approached about the job before the appointment of Cox in May, but he turned it down because "I did not think at the time the independence was there that is there now." Jaworski said he was accepting the position since "it was put on the basis of duty to one's country which I felt I must perform."

Congressional Reaction. Initial congressional reaction to the Jaworski appointment was mixed. Despite assurances of independence, skepticism persisted that the office of special prosecutor could only be truly independent if it were not tied to the executive branch.

Career Highlights

The son of a rural Baptist minister, Jaworski was born in Waco, Texas, Sept. 19, 1905. After graduating from high school at age 15, he went on to Baylor University, where he received an LL.B. at age 19. He then went to George Washington University, where he received a master of laws degree—also working part-time for Rep. Thomas (Tom) Connally (D Texas 1917–29).

Jaworski made his courtroom debut at age 20, defending a man accused of moonshining in Waco. He won an acquittal for his client, even though the trial took place in a bone-dry Baptist county during Prohibition.

Following World War II, he served as a colonel in the war crimes section of the Judge Advocate General's department of the Army, prosecuting major war criminals in Nuremberg. In 1961, he published a book, "After Fifteen Years," describing his experiences as a war-crimes prosecutor. The late President Johnson wrote the introduction to the book, referring to Jaworski as "my friend and counselor." Jaworski had represented Johnson in 1960, defending him successfully in two suits filed by Republicans who sought to enjoin Johnson from running simultaneously for senator and vice president.

In 1962, at Johnson's suggestion, Attorney General Robert F. Kennedy appointed Jaworski to serve as special prosecutor in the contempt case against Gov. Ross R. Barnett of Mississippi for Barnett's attempt to prevent the registration of black student James H. Meredith at the University of Mississippi. One year later, he was named special state counsel in a Texas court of inquiry into the assassination of President Kennedy. Later, he was retained as special counsel by the Warren Commission investigating the assassination.

Jaworski was a member of the President's Commission on the Causes and Prevention of Violence (1968–69), established after the assassinations of the Rev. Martin Luther King Jr. and Robert F. Kennedy. He also served on President Johnson's Commission on Law Enforcement and the Administration of Justice, and in 1967 joined four other commission members in partial dissent from the final commission report, arguing that the Supreme Court had gone too far in some of its decisions regarding defendants' rights.

In 1969, Jaworski said the violence commission's report should have taken a stronger stand against campus disorders.

Since 1951, Jaworski has been a senior partner in the Houston-based law firm of Fulbright, Crooker and Jaworski. The firm, which employs more than 150 lawyers, also has offices in Washington, D.C., and Mexico City.

Jaworski has long been associated with leading Texas Democrats, among them former Gov. John B. Connally (1963–69). Married in 1931 to Jeannette Adam, Jaworski has three children and several grandchildren.

Nixon: 'Outrageous, Vicious, Distorted Reporting'

In his first press conference since firing special Watergate prosecutor Archibald Cox, President Nixon Oct. 26 portrayed himself as a strong, decisive leader in his efforts to help settle the Middle East crisis. He characterized press coverage of the Cox firing as "frantic" and "hysterical," and declared, "I have never heard or seen such outrageous, vicious, distorted reporting in 27 years of public life."

However, Nixon said, public and congressional reaction to Cox's firing and demands that he resign or be impeached had not affected his Middle East performance.

"I have a quality which is—I guess I must have inherited it from my Midwestern mother and father—which is that the tougher it gets the cooler I get," Nixon said. At another point he asserted, ". . . even in this week, when many thought that the President was shell-shocked, unable to act, the President, acted decisively in the interest of peace, in the interest of the country, and I can assure you that whatever shocks gentlemen of the press may have or others—political people—these shocks will not affect me in doing my job."

The press conference lasted 38 minutes, including an eight-minute opening statement. The President had postponed planned television appearances twice during the week. The first had been billed as an address to the people, but that was cancelled in favor of a press conference the following day. That press conference was postponed, however, because of the Middle East crisis.

Watergate. Concerning Watergate, the President defended his firing of Cox and announced that Acting Attorney General Robert H. Bork would appoint a replacement. But Nixon added that the new prosecutor would not be allowed to go to court to obtain evidence from his own files.

The President also endorsed the handling by his longtime friend, C. G. (Bebe) Rebozo, of a $100,000 cash contribution from an emissary of billionaire Howard Hughes, saying Rebozo had exercised "very good judgment in doing what he did."

Middle East. In an opening statement, Nixon outlined the chronology of negotiations between the United States and the Soviet Union for enforcing the settlement of the Israeli-Arab war.

A "very significant and potentially explosive crisis developed" on Oct. 24, Nixon said. "We obtained information which led us to believe that the Soviet Union was planning to send a very substantial force into the Mideast—a military force."

As a result, the President continued, he ordered a "precautionary" world-wide military alert for American forces shortly after midnight to signal to the Soviets that the United States "could not accept any unilateral move on their part to move military forces into the Mideast." Shortly thereafter, Nixon sent Soviet Communist Party Leader Leonid I. Brezhnev "an urgent message" asking him not to send troops, and urging instead that the Soviets join the United States in supporting a United Nations resolution that would exclude major powers from participating in a peacekeeping force.

During the "several exchanges" that followed, Nixon said, "we reached the conclusion that we would jointly support the resolution, which was adopted in the United Nations."

> Criticism from the press "has been my lot throughout my political life, and I suppose because I have been through so much, that may be one of the reasons that when I have to face an international crisis, I have what it takes."
>
> —Richard M. Nixon, 1973

The "outlook for a permanent peace is the best that it has been in 20 years" as a result of the two powers having agreed to "participate in trying to expedite the talks between the parties involved," Nixon said. He added that he was optimistic for a permanent settlement, since "what the developments of this week should indicate to all of us is that the United States and the Soviet Union, who admittedly have very different objectives in the Mideast, have now agreed that it is not in their interests to have a confrontation there—a confrontation which might lead to a nuclear confrontation."

In response to questions, Nixon denied inferences that he had orchestrated the crisis to take attention away from public and congressional criticism of his firing of Cox. "It was a real crisis," he said. "It was the most difficult crisis we've had since the Cuban confrontation in 1962."

News Conference Text

Following is the White House text of President Nixon's Oct. 26 news conference.

THE PRESIDENT: Will you be seated, please?

Ladies and gentlemen, before going to your questions, I have a statement with regard to the Mideast which I think will anticipate some of the questions, because this will update the information which is breaking rather fast in that area, as you know, for the past two days.

The cease-fire is holding. There have been some violations, but generally speaking it can be said that it is holding at this time. As you know, as a result of the U.N. resolution which was agreed to yesterday by a vote of 14 to 0, a peacekeeping force will go to the Mideast, and this force, however, will not include any forces from the major powers, including, of course, the United States and the Soviet Union.

The question, however, has arisen as to whether observers from major powers could go to the Mideast. My up-to-the-minute report on that, and I just talked to Dr. Kissinger five minutes before coming down, is this: We will send observers to the Mideast if requested by the Secretary General of the United Nations, and we have reason to expect that we will receive such a request.

With regard to the peacekeeping force, I think it is important for all of you ladies and gentlemen, and particularly for those listening on radio and television, to know why the United States has insisted that major powers not be part of the peacekeeping force, and that major powers not introduce military forces into the Mideast. A very significant and potentially explosive crisis developed on Wednesday of this week. We obtained information which led us to believe that the Soviet Union was planning to send a very substantial force into the Mideast, a military force.

When I received that information, I ordered, shortly after midnight on Thursday morning, an alert for all American forces around the world. This was a precautionary alert. The purpose of that was to indicate to the Soviet Union that we could not accept any unilateral move on their part to move military forces into the Mideast. At the same time, in the early morning hours, I also proceeded on the diplomatic front. In a message to Mr. Brezhnev, an urgent message, I indicated to him our reasoning and I urged that we not proceed along that course, and that, instead, that we join in the United Nations in supporting a resolution which would exclude any major powers from participating in a peacekeeping force.

As a result of that communication, and the return that I received from Mr. Brezhnev—we had several exchanges, I should say—we reached the conclusion that we would jointly support the resolution which was adopted in the United Nations.

We now come, of course, to the critical time in terms of the future of the Mideast. And here, the outlook is far more hopeful than what we have been through this past week. I think I could safely say that the chances for not just a cease-fire, which we presently have and which, of course, we have had in the Mideast for some time, but

the outlook for a permanent peace is the best that it has been in 20 years.

The reason for this is that the two major powers, the Soviet Union and the United States, have agreed—this was one of the results of Dr. Kissinger's trip to Moscow—have agreed that we would participate in trying to expedite the talks between the parties involved. That does not mean that the two major powers will impose a settlement. It does mean, however, that we will use our influence with the nations in the area to expedite a settlement.

The reason we feel this is important is that first, from the standpoint of the nations in the Mideast, none of them, Israel, Egypt, Syria, none of them can or should go through the agony of another war.

The losses in this war on both sides have been very, very high. And the tragedy must not occur again. There have been four of these wars, as you ladies and gentlemen know, over the past 20 years. But beyond that, it is vitally important to the peace of the world that this potential troublespot, which is really one of the most potentially explosive areas in the world, that it not become an area in which the major powers come together in confrontation.

What the developments of this week should indicate to all of us is that the United States and the Soviet Union, who admittedly have very different objectives in the Mideast, have now agreed that it is not in their interest to have a confrontation there, a confrontation which might lead to a nuclear confrontation and neither of the two major powers wants that.

We have agreed, also, that if we are to avoid that, it is necessary for us to use our influence more than we have in the past, to get the negotiating track moving again, but this time, moving to a conclusion. Not simply a temporary truce, but a permanent peace.

I do not mean to suggest that it is going to come quickly because the parties involved are still rather far apart. But I do say that now there are greater incentives within the area to find a peaceful solution and there are enormous incentives as far as the United States is concerned, and the Soviet Union and other major powers, to find such a solution.

Turning now to the subject of our attempts to get a ceasefire on the home front, that is a bit more difficult.

Today White House Counsel contacted Judge Sirica. We tried yesterday but he was in Boston, as you know, and arrangements were made to meet with Judge Sirica on Tuesday to work out the delivery of the tapes to Judge Sirica.

Also, in consultations that we have had in the White House today, we have decided that next week the Acting Attorney General, Mr. Bork, will appoint a new special prosecutor for what is called the Watergate matter. The special prosecutor will have independence. He will have total cooperation from the Executive Branch, and he will have as a primary responsibility to bring this matter which has so long concerned the American people, bring it to an expeditious conclusion, because we have to remember that under our Constitution it has always been held that justice delayed is justice denied. It is time for those who are guilty to be prosecuted, and for those who are innocent to be cleared. I can assure you ladies and gentlemen, all of our listeners tonight, that I have no greater interest than to see that the new special prosecutor has the cooperation from the Executive Branch and the independence that he needs to bring about that conclusion.

And now I will go to Mr. Cormier.

Role of New Prosecutor

Q: Mr. President, would the new special prosecutor have your go-ahead to go to court if necessary to obtain evidence from your files that he felt were vital?

A: Mr. Cormier, I would anticipate that that would not be necessary. I believe that as we look at the events which led to the dismissal of Mr. Cox, we find that these are matters that can be worked out and should be worked out in cooperation and not by having a suit filed by a special prosecutor within the Executive Branch against the President of the United States.

This, incidentally, is not a new attitude on the part of a President. Every President since George Washington has tried to protect the confidentiality of Presidential conversations and you remember the famous case involving Thomas Jefferson where Chief Justice Marshall, then sitting as a trial judge, subpoenaed the letter which Jefferson had written which Marshall thought or felt was necessary evidence in the trial of Aaron Burr. Jefferson refused to do so but it did not result in a suit. What happened was, of course, a compromise in which a summary of the contents of the letter which was relevant to the trial was produced by Jefferson and the Chief Justice of the United States, acting in his capacity as Chief Justice, accepted that.

That is exactly, of course, what we tried to do in this instant case.

I think it would be well if I could take just a moment, Mr. Cormier, in answering your question to point out what we tried to do and why we feel it was the proper solution to a very aggravating and difficult problem.

The matter of the tapes has been one that has concerned me because of my feeling that I have a Constitutional responsibility to defend the Office of the Presidency from any encroachments on confidentiality which might affect future Presidents in their abilities to conduct the kind of conversations and discussions they need

to conduct to carry on the responsibilities of this Office. And, of course, the special prosecutor felt that he needed the tapes for the purpose of his prosecution.

That was why, working with the Attorney General, we worked out what we thought was an acceptable compromise, one in which Judge Stennis, now Senator Stennis, would hear the tapes and would provide a complete and full disclosure, not only to Judge Sirica, but also to the Senate Committee.

Attorney General Richardson approved of this proposition. Senator Baker, Senator Ervin approved of the proposition. Mr. Cox was the only one that rejected it.

Under the circumstances, when he rejected it and indicated that despite the approval of the Attorney General, and, of course, of the President and of the two major Senators on the Ervin Committee, when he rejected the proposal, I had no choice but to dismiss him.

Under those circumstances, Mr. Richardson, Mr. Ruckelshaus felt that because of the nature of their confirmation that their commitment to Mr. Cox had to take precedence over any commitment they might have to carry out an order from the President.

Under those circumstances, I accepted with regret the resignations of two fine public servants.

Now we come to a new special prosecutor. We will cooperate with him, and I do not anticipate that we will come to the time when he would consider it necessary to take the President to court. I think our cooperation will be adequate.

Prosecutor and Presidential Documents

Q: This is another way of asking Frank's question, but if the special prosecutor considers that information contained in Presidential documents is needed to prosecute the Watergate case, will you give him the documents, beyond the nine tapes which you have already turned over?

A: I have answered that question before. We will not provide Presidential documents to a special prosecutor. We will provide, as we have in great numbers, all kinds of documents from the White House, but if it is a document involving a conversation with the President, I would have to stand on the principle of confidentiality. However, information that is needed from such documents would be provided. That is what we have been trying to do.

Congressionally Mandated Prosecutor

Q: Mr. President, you know in the Congress there is a great deal of suspicion over any arrangement which will permit the Executive branch to investigate itself or which will establish a special prosecutor which you may fire again. As 53 Senators, a majority, have now co-sponsored a resolution which would permit Judge Sirica to establish and name an independent prosecutor, separate and apart from the White House Executive branch, do you believe this arrangement would be constitutional and would you go along with it?

A: I would suggest that the action that we are going to take of appointing a special prosecutor would be satisfactory to the Congress, and that they would not proceed with that particular matter.

Response to Impeachment Talk

Q: Mr. President, I wonder if you could share with us your thoughts and tell us what goes through your mind when you hear people who love this country, and people who believe in you, say reluctantly that perhaps you should resign or be impeached.

A: Well, I am glad we don't take the vote of this room, let me say. And I understand the feelings of people with regard to impeachment and resignation. As a matter of fact, Mr. Rather, you may remember when I made the rather difficult decision, I thought the most difficult decision of my first term on December 18th, the bombing by B-52s of North Vietnam, that exactly the same words were used on the networks—I don't mean by you, but they were quoted on the networks—that are used now: tyrant, dictator, he has lost his senses, he should resign, he should be impeached.

But I stuck it out, and as a result of that, we not only got our prisoners of war home, as I have often said, on their feet rather than on their knees, but we brought peace to Vietnam, something we haven't had and didn't for over 12 years.

It was a hard decision, and it was one that many of my friends in the press who had consistently supported me on the war up to that time disagreed with. Now, in this instance I realize there are people who feel that the actions that I have taken with regard to the dismissal of Mr. Cox are grounds for impeachment.

I would respectfully suggest that even Mr. Cox and Mr. Richardson have agreed that the President had the right, constitutional right, to dismiss anybody in the Federal Government, and second, I should also point out that as far as the tapes are concerned, rather than being in defiance of the law, I am in compliance with the law.

As far as what goes through my mind, I would simply say that I intend to continue to carry out, to the best of my ability, the responsibilities I was elected to carry out last November. The events of this past week—I know, for example, in your head office in New York, some

thought that it was simply a blown-up exercise; there wasn't a real crisis. I wish it had been that. It was a real crisis. It was the most difficult crisis we have had since the Cuban confrontation of 1962.

But because we had had our initiative with the Soviet Union, because I had a basis of communication with Mr. Brezhnev, we not only avoided a confrontation, but we moved a great step forward toward real peace in the Mideast.

Now, as long as I can carry out that kind of responsibility, I am going to continue to do this job.

Cox Motives

Q: Mr. President.

A: Mr. Lisagor.

Q: There have been reports that you felt that Mr. Cox was somehow out to get you. I would like to ask you if you did feel that, and if so, what evidence did you have?

A: Mr. Lisagor, I understand Mr. Cox is going to testify next week under oath before the Judiciary Committee, and I would suggest that he perhaps would be better qualified to answer that question.

As far as I am concerned, we had cooperated with the Special Prosecutor. We tried to work out in a cooperative way this matter of the production of the tapes. He seemed to be more interested in the issue than he was in a settlement, and under the circumstances, I had no choice but to dismiss him. But I am not going to question his motives as to whether or not he was out to get me. Perhaps the Senators would like to ask that question.

'Vicious, Distorted Reporting'

Q: Mr. President, in 1968, before you were elected, you wrote that too many shocks can drain a nation of its energy and even cause a rebellion against creative change and progress. Do you think America is at that point now?

A: I think that many would speculate. I have noted a lot on the networks particularly and sometimes even in the newspapers. But this is a very strong country, and the American people, I think, can ride through the shocks they have.

The difference now from what it was in the days of shocks, even when Mr. Lisagor and I first met 25 years ago, is the electronic media. I have never heard or seen such outrageous, vicious, distorted reporting in 27 years of public life. I am not blaming anybody for that. Perhaps what happened is what we did brought it about, and therefore, the media decided that they would have to take that particular line.

But when people are pounded night after night with that kind of frantic, hysterical reporting, it naturally shakes their confidence. And yet, I should point out that even in this week, when many thought that the President was shell-shocked, unable to act, the President acted decisively in the interest of peace, in the interest of the country, and I can assure you that whatever shocks gentlemen of the press may have, or others, political people, these shocks will not affect me in my doing my job.

Tapes: No Public Disclosure

Q: Mr. President, after the tapes are presented to Judge Sirica and they are processed under the procedure outlined by the U.S. Court of Appeals, will you make those tapes public?

A: No, that is not the procedure that the court has ordered, and it would not be proper. Judge Sirica, under the Circuit Court's order, is to listen to the tapes, and then is to present to the Grand Jury the pertinent evidence with regard to its investigation. Publication of the tapes has not been ordered by the Circuit Court of Appeals, and Judge Sirica, of course, would not do anything that would be in contravention of what the Circuit Court of Appeals has ordered.

Bearing Up Under Stress

Q: Mr. President—

A: Mr. ter Horst.

Q: Mr. President, Harry Truman used to talk about the heat in the kitchen—

A: I know what he meant. (Laughter)

Q: —and a lot of people have been wondering how you are bearing up emotionally under the stress of recent events. Can you discuss that?

A: Those who saw me during the Middle East crisis thought I bore up rather well, and, Mr. ter Horst, I have a quality which is—I guess I must have inherited it from my Midwestern mother and father—which is that the tougher it gets, the cooler I get. Of course, it isn't pleasant to get criticism. Some of it is justified, of course. It isn't pleasant to find, for example, that, speaking of my friend Mr. Rebozo, that despite the fact that those who printed it, and those who said it, knew it was untrue—said that he had a million-dollar trust fund for me that he was handling—it was nevertheless put on one of the networks, knowing it was untrue. It isn't pleasant, for example, to hear or read that a million dollars in campaign funds went into my San Clemente property, and even after we had a complete audit, to have it repeated.

Those are things which, of course, do tend to get under the skin of the man who holds this office. But as far as I am concerned, I have learned to expect it. It has been my lot throughout my political life, and I suppose because I have been through so much, that may be one of the reasons that when I have to face an international crisis, I have what it takes.

Watergate and Mideast

Q: Mr. President, I would like to ask you a question about the Mideast. To what extent do you think your Watergate troubles influenced Soviet thinking about your ability to respond in the Mideast, and did your Watergate problems convince you that the U.S. needed a strong response in the Mideast to convince other nations that you have not been weakened?

A: Well, I have noted speculation to the effect that the Watergate problems may have led the Soviet Union to miscalculate. I tend to disagree with that, however.

I think Mr. Brezhnev probably can't quite understand how the President of the United States wouldn't be able to handle the Watergate problems. He would be able to handle it all right, if he had them. (Laughter) But I think what happens is that what Mr. Brezhnev does understand is the power of the United States. What he does know is the President of the United States.

What he also knows is that the President of the United States, when he was under unmerciful assault at the time of Cambodia, at the time of May 8, when I ordered the bombing and the mining of North Vietnam at the time of December 18, still went ahead and did what he thought was right; the fact that Mr. Brezhnev knew that regardless of the pressures at home, regardless of what people see and hear on television night after night, he would do what was right. That is what made Mr. Brezhnev act as he did.

Television Anger

Q: Mr. President, you have lambasted the television networks pretty well. Could I ask you, at the risk of reopening an obvious wound, you say after you have put on a lot of heat that you don't blame anyone. I find that a little puzzling. What is it about the television coverage of you in these past weeks and months that has so aroused your anger?

A: Don't get the impression that you arouse my anger. (Laughter)

Q: I'm afraid, sir, that I have that impression. (Laughter)

A: You see, one can only be angry with those he respects.

Regaining Confidence

Q: Mr. President, businessmen are increasingly saying that many chief executive officers of corporations do not get the latitude you have had, if they have the personnel problems that you have had, to stay in the job and correct them. You have said you are going to stay. Do you have any plan set out to regain confidence of people across the country, and these businessmen who are beginning to talk about this matter? Do you have any plans, besides the special prosecutor, which looks backward, do you have any plan that looks forward for regaining the confidence of the people?

A: I certainly have. First, to move forward in building a structure of peace in the world, in which we have made enormous progress in the past and which we are going to make more progress in the future: our European initiative, our continued initiative with the Soviet Union, with the People's Republic of China. That will be the major legacy of this Administration.

Moving forward at home in our continuing battle against the high cost of living, in which we are now finally beginning to make some progress, and moving forward also on the matters that you referred to, it is true that what happened in Watergate, the campaign abuses, were deplorable. They have been very damaging to this Administration; they have been damaging certainly to the country as well.

Let me say, too, I didn't want to leave an impression with my good friend from CBS over here that I don't respect the reporters. What I was simply saying was this: That when a commentator takes a bit of news and then, with knowledge of what the facts are, distorts it, viciously, I have no respect for that individual.

Executive Privilege

Q: Mr. President—

A: You are so loud, I will have to take you.

Q: I have to be, because you happen to dodge my questions all of the time.

A: You had three last time.

Q: Last May you went before the American People and you said, "Executive privilege will not be invoked as to any testimony concerning possible criminal conduct or discussing of possible criminal conduct, including the Watergate affair and the alleged cover-up."

If you have revised or modified this position, as you seem to have done, could you explain the rationale of a law-and-order Administration covering up evidence, prima facie evidence, of high crimes and misdemeanors?

A: I should point out that perhaps all of the other reporters in the room are aware of the fact that we have waived Executive privilege on all individuals in the Administration. It has been the greatest waiver of Executive privilege in the whole history of this Nation.

And as far as any other matters are concerned, the matters of the tapes, the matters of Presidential conversations, those are matters in which the President has a responsibility to defend this office, which I shall continue to do.

THE PRESS: Thank you, Mr. President.

Question of Tapes' Quality

The quality of the recordings of White House conversations was a subject of disagreement between two of President Nixon's closest aides, both of whom testified before Judge Sirica Nov. 8.

Nixon's longtime personal secretary and executive assistant, Rose Mary Woods, told the court of her month-long struggle to get the "gist" of the subpoenaed conversations down in type for the President's review. She described the job as very difficult, at times almost impossible, due to the location of the microphones and of the persons speaking, the acoustic qualities of the rooms in which the recordings were made and the intervening noise. "Sometimes the President puts his feet up on the desk," she said. "Then you hear a noise (on the tape) like a bomb. Boom!"

H. R. Haldeman, Nixon's former chief of staff until his resignation under fire on April 30, agreed that intervening noise was somewhat of a problem. Noting that the microphones in one of the presidential offices were buried in the top of the desk, he warned Sirica that when china coffee cups were set down on the desk, it was "ear-splitting" for the person listening to the tapes. The tapes were not "great," he continued, but he said he had no particular trouble understanding them. They were of "fair" quality, he said, "a quite adequate record of the conversations" they were designed to preserve.

Hard Listening. Woods, who has worked with Nixon since 1951, said that she had "no knowledge whatsoever" about the existence of the White House recording system until former White House aide Alexander Butterfield disclosed it to the Senate Watergate Committee in mid-July. She said she first saw one of the tapes on Sept. 29, when, at the request of the President, she went to Camp David, Md., to try to listen to the subpoenaed tapes and write down what was audible.

Her work on the initial eight tapes she was given continued during the first week in October, the weekend of Oct. 4–7 at Key Biscayne, Fla., and subsequent weeks in Washington, being completed only on Oct. 23–24, she said. The original (and only) typed record of the tapes was given to the President, she said.

Woods said that the eight tapes were still in her office safe and that she alone possessed the combination to the safe. In addition, she said, in that safe were six tapes she had been given Nov. 5. Explaining the "gap" which she reportedly had found in one of those tapes on which she had worked most recently, Woods said that she had been searching for a conversation on April 16 between Nixon and former presidential counsel John W. Dean III—and that the tape she had been using apparently began after the time of that conversation—so she feared a gap. She said she found a tape containing that conversation Nov. 8.

Wong Testimony. Following Woods, Alfred Wong, deputy assistant director of the Secret Service and former chief of the White House technical security unit, continued his testimony, begun Nov. 7. Wong said that it should be possible for the exact equipment used in making each set of tapes to be located and identified. Sirica asked him to do so, in case such knowledge might be helpful in evaluating the tapes.

A Memory Problem. Haldeman, the first witness to appear at the hearings at the behest of the special prosecution force, appeared under subpoena. Until he himself received tapes to listen to on April 25–26, Haldeman said, he was not aware that anyone else had heard the tapes—apart from one time that Butterfield had checked to ascertain that the system was operating.

The first tapes that he received were related to the March 21 meeting of Dean, Nixon and himself, he said. He listened to them twice at the request of the President. Haldeman could not recall any explanation for the fact that 22 tapes were provided to him in order for him to find that specific conversation. Nor could he remember why Secret Service records showed that the tapes, after their second delivery to him, were not returned to their vault until May 2, after his departure from the White House staff. Also lost from Haldeman's memory, he said, was the origin of the idea of his listening in mid-July to several more tapes, particularly that of the Sept. 15, 1972, meeting of Dean, Nixon and himself.

NIXON ON RESIGNING

As the Watergate scandal deepened, Nixon repeatedly rejected calls for his resignation. No president had ever resigned in U.S. history. Nixon was determined to follow in the footsteps of his predecessors and serve out his term.

Following is the statement President Nixon made Nov. 7 at the conclusion of his televised statement on the energy crisis:

As a result of the deplorable Watergate matter, great numbers of Americans have had doubts raised as to the integrity of the President of the United States. I've even noted that some publications have called on me to resign the office of President of the United States.

Tonight I would like to give my answer to those who have suggested that I resign.

I have no intention whatever of walking away from the job I was elected to do.

As long as I am physically able, I am going to continue to work 16 to 18 hours a day for the cause of a real peace abroad and for the cause of prosperity, without inflation and without war, at home.

And in the months ahead, I shall do everything that I can to see that any doubts as to the integrity of the man who occupies the highest office in this land—to remove those doubts where they exist.

And I am confident that in those months ahead, the American people will come to realize that I have not violated the trust that they placed in me when they elected me as President of the United States in the past.

And I pledge to you tonight that I shall always do everything that I can to be worthy of that trust in the future.

CONGRESSIONAL REACTION TO NIXON ON MISSING TAPES

The revelation that two of the presidential tapes were missing severely weakened Nixon's standing with Congress. For the first time, a Republican senator called on Nixon to resign. Other promi-

nent lawmakers in both parties urged Nixon to turn over all information pertaining to Watergate and to disclose everything he knew about the scandal. Although a number of Democrats had criticized Nixon, the misgivings among congressional Republicans were an ominous sign. Nixon needed to hold on to the support of his party's leaders in order to save his presidency.

In the wake of the surprise announcement Oct. 31 that two of the nine White House tape recordings ordered turned over to a federal district court did not exist, two senators asked President Nixon to resign. Several congressional leaders urged Nixon to restore public confidence in his leadership by publicly disclosing all information regarding his role in the Watergate scandals.

Resignation Requests. Sen. Edward W. Brooke (R Mass.) became the first Republican senator to ask the President to step down. Appearing Nov. 4 on ABC's "Issues and Answers," Brooke was asked if he had come to believe that Nixon should resign. "I have reluctantly come to that conclusion," Brooke replied. "I don't think that the country can stand the trauma that it has been going through for the past few months. It has been like a nightmare, and I know that he doesn't want to hurt the country, and I certainly don't want to prejudge the case. He might not be guilty of any impeachable offense.

"On the other hand, there is no question that President Nixon has lost his effectiveness as the leader of this country, primarily because he has lost the confidence of the people of the country, and I think therefore that in the interests of this nation that he loves that he should step down, should tender his resignation." Brooke actively campaigned for Nixon in 1968 and 1972.

Later in the day on Oct. 31, White House deputy press secretary Gerald L. Warren said Nixon had "absolutely no intention of resigning. . . . The President intends to pursue his objectives in foreign policy, national policy and in clearing up the Watergate matter."

Walter F. Mondale (D Minn.) became the second senator within the week to urge Nixon to resign. Mondale, who was considering running for the presidency in 1976, said Nov. 6 that Nixon's moral credibility was gone and the chances that he could restore it were "pretty remote."

Mondale and Brooke both urged Congress to confirm Gerald R. Ford as vice president, although Mondale said he was "not particularly impressed" by Ford.

Two other senators had called for Nixon's resignation before the announcement that the two tapes did not exist—John V. Tunney (D Calif.) and Daniel K. Inouye (D Hawaii), a member of the Senate Watergate Committee.

Aiken Advice. The Senate's senior Republican, George D. Aiken of Vermont, passed along to Congress some advice he had received from a constituent: "Either impeach him or get off his back." Aiken, in a Senate speech Nov. 7, said it was the duty of the House to "set a deadline, of weeks or months, in which to come up with an impeachment charge." It was, he said, "the President's duty to his country not to resign," although resignation would relieve Congress of its duty.

Disclosure Demands. Pressure on the President to make public all his knowledge related to the Watergate incidents came from three Republicans and one Democrat who had generally supported the President. In a statement Nov. 1, Sen. Barry Goldwater (R Ariz.) said that Nixon's credibility had "reached an all-time low from which he may not be able to recover" and urged the President to appear before the Senate select Watergate committee to answer questions. "I feel now more than ever that this may offer the only way out," Goldwater said.

"As one schooled in electronics," Goldwater said, he could understand the circumstances under which the two tapes were not made, "but as a practical person in close touch with the American people, I doubt that they will accept this."

The strongest statement came from Sen. Peter H. Dominick (R Colo.) in a speech to the Denver Bar Association Nov. 5. Declaring that there was a "crisis of confidence in our leadership," Dominick urged the President to release all tapes, documents, papers, files and memorandums requested by the Senate Watergate Committee and the special prosecutor's office. Nixon should also "make available voluntarily all other information within his control—whether in or out of the executive branch—which he feels will have a strong bearing on the issues that have been raised," Dominick continued. "The breadth of this disclosure should be limited only by constraints imposed by the national interest."

Dominick, who was chairman of the Republican Senate Campaign Committee in 1972 and who himself would be up for re-election in 1974, also advised Republicans to "follow a more independent course from here on. I think a good place to start would be for the Republican Party to take the leadership in resolving the crisis of confidence in our government."

Senate Minority Leader Hugh Scott (R Pa.) Nov. 5 also urged Nixon to "give the people all the information and let them judge. . . . A forum has to be found to make the information available."

Similar sentiments were expressed by Sen. Henry M. Jackson (D Wash.) in a Nov. 4 interview on CBS's "Meet the Press." "I believe we have reached the point where the President must appear before an appropriate forum and lay his cards on the table," he said. He added that the Senate Watergate Committee would be an appropriate forum. Jackson, who had usually supported the President on questions of national security and defense, said that if the President did not divulge the information, he would face "an unchallengeable demand for impeachment or the possibility of a direct request for resignation, and I think the push will come from the Republican leadership, not just from Democrats."

While reiterating his belief that Nixon was innocent of any wrong-doing, Vice President-designate Ford (R Mich.) told the Senate Rules Committee Nov. 5 that he thought the President should produce all documents necessary to clear up questions of his involvement in Watergate.

EXCERPTS OF MEDIA DEMANDS FOR NIXON'S RESIGNATION

The missing tapes marked an important turning point in the Watergate scandal. A number of prominent news organizations called on Nixon to resign. Even some conservative publications turned against him. This development signaled deep trouble for Nixon. To a greater extent than today, the editorial pages of publications such as The New York Times *and* Time *magazine in the early 1970s were highly influential, and political leaders of both parties often looked to editorial writers for guidance.*

Following are excerpts from several editorials demanding or suggesting that President Nixon resign:

TIME MAGAZINE NOV. 12
Richard Nixon and the nation have passed a tragic point of no return. It now seems likely that the President will have to give up his office: he has irredeemably lost his moral authority, the confidence of most of the country, and therefore his ability to govern effectively. . . .

The editors of Time Inc., speaking on the editorial pages of *Time's* sister publication *Life*, have endorsed Nixon for President three times, in 1960, 1968 and 1972. . . . Thus we come with deep reluctance to our conclusion that he must leave office. We consider the situation so unprecedented, the issue so crucial to the country, that we publish this first editorial in *Time's* 50-year history.

In two centuries, no American President has been removed from office other than by death or the voters' will. Once the spell is broken, would it become too easy for political opponents of any future president to oust him? We think not. Watergate is unique. In fact, the really dangerous precedent would be the opposite: to allow a President with Nixon's record to continue in office. This would be a terrible circumstance to lodge in our history, a terrible thing to explain to our children and their children. . . .

A President's "big decisions" cannot be put into a compartment separate from his other actions, his total behavior. His integrity and trustworthiness are perhaps the most important facts about him to his country and to the world. And these Nixon has destroyed. The nightmare of uncertainty must be ended.

THE NEW YORK TIMES NOV. 4

The visible disintegration of President Nixon's moral and political authority, of his capacity to act as chief executive, of his claim to leadership and to credibility leads us to the reluctant conclusion that Mr. Nixon would be performing his ultimate service to the American people—and to himself—by resigning his office before this nation is forced to go through the traumatic and divisive process of impeachment. . . .

The gravity of the case against him rests . . . on his deliberate violations of the letter and the spirit of the Constitution and, flowing out of this, the collapse of public confidence in the integrity of the man who only one year ago was elected to the presidency by the largest popular majority in history. . . .

The one last great service that Mr. Nixon can now perform for his country is to resign. He has been trying to "tough it out" for too long at too great a cost to the nation. As long as he clings to office, he keeps the presidency swamped in a sea of scandal and the American public in a morass of concern and confusion. The state of the union requires nothing less than a change in the sorry state of the presidency.

THE DETROIT NEWS NOV. 4

After Rep. Gerald Ford has been confirmed as vice president, President Richard Nixon should resign. . . . This newspaper has been one of Mr. Nixon's strongest supporters. Watergate aside, we still agree with many of his basic policies. . . .

However, unless the present crisis of authority is resolved . . . the country must endure 38 more months of the doubts, charges and recriminations which have destroyed the President's ability to lead. . . .

The White House's assertion that two key Watergate tapes never existed and can't be delivered sinks President Nixon's credibil-

ity to an all-time low. Someone in the White House is guilty of either unbelievable stupidity or outright lies. In either case, public confidence in this administration suffers the final shattering blow. . . .

We hope Mr. Nixon will see this suggestion (to resign) as a wise one for himself and as a necessary one for the national welfare. If he does not see it that way, the next step in the unfolding tragedy of Richard Nixon may be impeachment. Distressing as that procedure might be, it would be less distressing than three more years of political vendetta. Enough is enough.

THE DENVER POST NOV. 4

Ironically, it was just a year ago this Sunday that The Post wrote its final editorial supporting Mr. Nixon for the presidency because among other reasons we believed he was the better man to produce effective national unity. . . .

But in a time of national crisis, such as the recent alerting of our military forces in the Middle Eastern situation, the people must be able to trust automatically the President's integrity. And on simpler matters, it is intolerable that on a question of whether or not the tapes were really lost, a great number of people simply don't take the word of their President. . . .

When the vice presidency is filled, the Republican party must live up to its responsibilities. . . . The Republican party should try to persuade the President to resign. . . . History would think well of a Nixon decision to step down, not as an admission of guilt, but as a recognition that the needed trust essential to the conduct of his office has been lost. . . .

If, however, resignation is not in the cards, then this newspaper has come to the reluctant conclusion that only an impeachment proceeding will heal our hemorrhaging of national confidence in the presidency.

NATIONAL REVIEW NOV. 9

Richard Nixon is still the legal head of government, but is he, in the meaning proper to a constitutional, republican society, still a legitimate ruler? . . . Perhaps the surrender on the tapes will prove a turning point but . . . if the public distrust and rejection of Mr. Nixon persists, deepens further, and hardens, the country will be facing the crippling and possibly catastrophic prospect of three years without—a legitimate government. . . .

The one way and the only way to close out that crisis would be by Richard Nixon's departure. . . . If Mr. Nixon becomes convinced—and by a few more months at most it will be sure, one way or another—that he has irretrievably lost the support and trust of a solid majority of the people, it will then be his duty to resign his office as the only act able to heal the grievous wound.

This would be, under the circumstances, the highest act of loyalty and patriotism on his part, and we therefore feel that Richard Nixon, facing the reality, would see resignation as his duty; and if he did not, it would become the duty of his closest friends and associates to persuade him so to see it.

But if, by the New Year say, no charge of criminal conduct against the President takes unequivocal and public form . . . it will then be time for his critics, and especially his critics in Congress, to put up or shut up.

Points to Ponder

- By the fall of 1973, Nixon was losing support in Congress, the news media, and the general public. Once a president loses the trust of Americans, how can he win it back? Can an unpopular president improve his standing by ignoring his opponents and instead concentrate on firming up support among members of his own party?

- Nixon and his aides often lambasted the media. They regarded reporters as enemies who misstated facts and presented a slanted version of the news. Do you feel that newspapers brought about the decline in Nixon's popularity? Or were newspapers merely reflecting the increased antagonism that the public felt toward Nixon?

WATERGATE:

Vital Work Ahead for Senate Committee

The Senate Watergate Committee continued its work during the fall amid mounting concerns in Congress and among the public about the Watergate scandal. The committee's witnesses late in the year were little-known political contributors and people who used unscrupulous methods to try to undermine competing campaigns.

On Nov. 21 came the shocking news that one of the Watergate tapes contained an 18-minute inaudible portion. The gap, discovered by President Nixon's personal secretary while transcribing the tape, spurred speculation that the administration was suppressing evidence related to Watergate.

Amid sinking poll numbers, Nixon faced questions not only about Watergate but about other potential scandals as well. In particular, he was battered by allegations that he had underpaid his taxes. He also faced questions about his role in a Justice Department investigation of the International Telephone and Telegraph Corporation. Watergate prosecutors had learned that Nixon may have ordered the Justice Department in 1971 to end legal action against the company. Some evidence indicated that Nixon was influenced by a pledge by the company to pay as much as $400,000 to finance the Republican National Convention in 1972.

The administration also was coming under growing fire over contributions to Nixon's 1972 re-election campaign. By mid-November, six large corporations had pleaded guilty to breaking the law by contributing as much as $100,000 apiece to the Nixon campaign without public disclosure.

By the end of the year, many basic questions about the Watergate scandal remained unanswered. Investigators wondered when Nixon found out about the coverup and whether his top aides had participated in wrongdoing. Because of the concerns about Watergate, polls now showed that less than 30 percent of the American public approved of Nixon's performance as president. With his integrity in question, Nixon made a remarkable statement at a late November news conference. "I am not a crook," he said in response to a question about his taxes.

Meanwhile the new special Watergate prosecutor, Leon Jaworski, won over critics in Congress who worried that he would not mount a thorough investigation. He promised to stand up to the White House and insist on gaining access to all critical documents. White House officials also promised that they would not interfere with Jaworski's investigation. As a result, Congress backed off from a plan that would have created a stronger type of prosecutor.

> "*I have an idea the greatest crisis the country faced has passed on Watergate.*"
> —Sen. Howard H. Baker Jr., Sept. 10, 1973

> "*It is entirely possible that Watergate will not be over any time soon.*"
> —Sen. Howard H. Baker Jr., Nov. 19, 1973

The contrast between Senator Baker's two observations was understandable. Ten weeks is a relatively short time, but Watergate disclosures came so quickly in the fall of 1973 that politicians and pundits alike found themselves eating their words.

In September, the Senate Watergate Committee was in recess after hearing from key witnesses: John W. Dean III, John N. Mitchell, John D. Ehrlichman and H. R. Haldeman. Meanwhile, the criminal investigation was

in the hands of special prosecutor Archibald Cox and the country seemed confident that justice would be done. So what more could be expected of a dramatic nature?

But Watergate had a life of its own. Like a snowball rolling downhill, it continued to grow until it created one constitutional and cabinet crisis after another—and ultimately the presidency itself was endangered. First there was the court battle over the President's refusal to hand over the tapes. Then came the firing of Cox and the resignations of Attorney General Elliot L. Richardson and his deputy, William D. Ruckelshaus. Then the President reversed himself and agreed to release the tapes. Then it was learned that two of the nine tapes never existed, and it developed that the seven remaining tapes were not distinct. And from it all emerged the threat of presidential impeachment.

Submerged in all the mind-boggling events were the hearings of the seven-member Senate Select Committee on Presidential Campaign Activities—the Watergate committee. Its witnesses since September were relatively unknown dirty tricksters and political contributors. They lacked the glamour and impact of their predecessors, so for many Americans the hearings became only a small part of the Watergate story.

But while the committee no longer remained in the limelight of Watergate events, some observers believed that its most important work lay ahead: the report and recommendations it was required to make to the Senate—and thus to the American people—on how to prevent another Watergate.

What corrective legislation would the members recommend? What had the hearings proved, if anything? What would the senators have done differently if they had it to do all over again? Why could not the entire matter have been left in the hands of the special prosecutor?

These and other questions were put to five of the seven committee members, top committee staffers and Senate leaders by Congressional Quarterly before the committee recessed for Thanksgiving. Senators Edward J. Gurney (R Fla.) and Daniel K. Inouye (D Hawaii) were not available for interviews.

TAPE BLANK: 18 MINUTES

On Nov. 21 came the disturbing news that one of the Watergate tapes contained an 18-minute inaudible portion. Although President Nixon's personal secretary, Rose Mary Woods, claimed that she erased the tape by accident, the 18-minute gap fueled increased speculation that the president was suppressing evidence about Watergate.

The 18-minute gap remains a mystery to this day. Experts would spend years trying to recover the missing words of the conversation, which took place between Nixon and Haldeman just three days after the Watergate break-in. But, to date, no one has succeeded in recovering any intelligible conversation. (For more on the investigation into the gap, see p. 169.)

The revelation on Nov. 21 that an 18-minute portion of a subpoenaed Watergate tape was blank caused Federal District Judge John J. Sirica to order the remaining subpoenaed tapes to be turned over to the U.S. court for safekeeping.

The 18-minute blank occurred in the middle of a taped conversation between President Nixon and former presidential adviser H. R. Haldeman, recorded June 20, 1972, just three days after the Watergate break-in. In subpoenaing the tape, former special prosecutor Archibald Cox said "there is every reason to infer that the meeting included discussion of the Watergate incident."

Legislative Recommendations

In addition to investigating the White House, members of Congress wanted to make sure that nothing like Watergate would happen again. Many lawmakers focused on the need to regulate campaign contributions, which were at the heart of the Watergate scandal.

While a wide variety of remedies were suggested, almost all those interviewed agreed that some controls would have to be put on the use of cash in future campaigns. Free-flowing cash—hundreds of thousands of dollars of it—was at the heart of the Watergate scandal, it was believed. Cash in large, untraceable quantities bought the Watergate burglars and paid for the coverup.

There was a secret $350,000 cash fund in the White House that helped get things going and, according to testimony by Frederick C. LaRue, a Nixon re-election committee official, and Anthony T. Ulasewicz, a money courier, $449,000 was raised on quick order to maintain the burglars and pay their lawyers' fees. Herbert W. Kalmbach, a Nixon lawyer and fund-raiser, told the committee of getting $75,000 in $100 bills from a California businessman by telling him it was for a "special assignment."

REGULATING CAMPAIGN CONTRIBUTIONS

Since the early days of the nation, politicians have collected money from private citizens and companies to fund their campaigns. This has long created concerns that money was corrupting the political process. Might an elected official take actions to help leading donors, even if those actions run counter to the public interest?

The Watergate scandal brought criticism over campaign financing to the fore. Large campaign contributions, even hundreds of thousands of dollars in cash (enormous sums at the time), were used to pay the Watergate burglars and finance the coverup. Many of the contributions were never reported as required by law.

Watergate intensified calls to overhaul campaign funding. As far back as President Theodore Roosevelt in the early twentieth century, reformers had tried to clean up the system of campaign finance and limit contributions. In 1971 Congress passed the Federal Election Campaign Act, requiring that campaigns publicly disclose large contributions and certain types of spending. After the Watergate scandal, Congress came under pressure to take additional steps. Over the following decades, however, reformers would face a fundamental problem. No matter how hard they tried to take money out of the political process, donors would find ways to skirt the intent of the law. Even so, the new laws helped shed light on the campaign finance system. Much of the money contributed for political activities was publicly disclosed.

In 1974 Congress provided for the public funding of presidential campaigns. Instead of raising money from private sources, presidential candidates could receive money from the Treasury. In exchange, they had to agree to certain limits on spending. The 1974 law also imposed certain limits on campaign contributions to prevent a single individual from donating more than a few thousand dollars to a particular candidate. It limited contributions to outside groups and expenditures by candidates. And it created a new agency, the Federal Election Commission, to enforce campaign finance laws.

Questions arose over whether the new law was constitutional. Could Congress limit contributions and the amount of money spent by campaigns? Or did that violate the free speech rights of individuals who wanted to spend their money on political activities? In an important 1976 case, *Buckley v. Valeo*, the Supreme Court upheld key portions of the law. It approved the system for publicly funding presidential cam-

paigns, limiting campaign contributions, and disclosing the contributions. But it also ruled that Congress could not limit the amount of money spent by campaigns. In one of the most significant parts of their ruling, the justices also said Congress could not stop spending by independent individuals and groups. In other words, if a local business organization wanted to run television ads extolling the virtues of its preferred candidate, it had the constitutional right to do so.

Over time, this led to a massive shift in political spending. Instead of giving large amounts of money to candidates, donors began channeling more money to outside organizations, known as political action committees, or PACs. These PACs could not run ads with such overt messages as "Vote for John Smith" or "Vote against Mary Jones." But they could tout Smith's considerable political experience or castigate Jones for alleged incompetence or unwise political positions. Donors also could give large amounts of money to political parties. The parties could then use the money to boost voter turnout or to drum up support on important political issues.

Critics denounced the new system. They worried that PACs did not have to disclose the sources of their contributions. In effect, the law had failed to either fully rein in campaign spending or force public disclosure of contributions.

After years of debate, Congress returned to the issue in 2002. Two senators—Republican John McCain of Arizona and Democrat Russ Feingold of Wisconsin—won passage of an ambitious campaign finance law. It raised the limits for direct contributions from individuals to candidates. But it cracked down on spending by outside organizations, such as PACs. Opponents of the new law went to court to block it, but the Supreme Court upheld most of its provisions.

While the new law may have curbed certain abuses, it became clear during the 2004 presidential campaign that the political finance system was hardly perfect. New types of organizations spent millions of dollars for ads about candidates and issues. These organizations were known as "527s," after a section in the tax code. Officially, they were not affiliated with either political party. Many of their ads raised questionable allegations about the candidates.

In addition, the system of publicly financing presidential campaigns appeared to be on the verge of collapse. Both the Republican candidate, President George W. Bush, and the Democratic candidate, Sen. John F. Kerry, decided to opt out of public financing during the presidential primaries. This enabled them to raise and spend far more money than they could if they had agreed to the public financing limits. As a result, they spent much of their time raising money from individuals and organizations with political agendas. Critics worried that this could enable wealthy donors to buy an electoral victory. They also wondered if the winning candidate could feel beholden to major contributors.

Cash and Corruption. Chairman Sam J. Ervin Jr. (D N.C.), Vice Chairman Baker (R Tenn.) and Sen. Joseph M. Montoya (D N.M.) said they wanted to see tight limits placed on cash contributions and disbursements. Checks or some other traceable notes were what Ervin had in mind. "Big amounts (of cash) tend to breed corruption, and Watergate was part of that," said Montoya. According to Ervin, there was only one reason for the use of cash: "Funds are received and disbursed in cash to conceal transactions," he said. Congress, he asserted, "should outlaw any substantial contribution of cash and disbursement of cash" in future campaigns.

While agreeing that a ban or limit on the use of cash in campaigns was desirable, Sen. Lowell P. Weicker Jr. (R Conn.) said a law along those lines would be difficult to enforce. Such a law might be a deterrent, he noted, but "if enforcement is difficult, it's not that much of a deterrent."

Public Funding. Public financing of federal elections was an issue that had been around for a while and could get the boost it needed to succeed if backed by the committee. But no member seemed interested in that route. None volunteered any thoughts along those lines, and Rufus L. Edmisten, the committee's deputy chief counsel, said he detected "no movement on the part of anyone on the committee" for public campaign financing. All the members supported a motion on the Senate floor July 26 that tabled a public campaign financing amendment.

Baker, who had steadfastly opposed public campaign financing, said only that he was keeping an "open mind" on the subject.

Nevertheless, several witnesses—all Democrats—had urged such legislation. Berl Bernhard, Sen. Edmund S. Muskie's (D Maine) presidential campaign manager in 1972, said that was one reform most urgently needed,

because candidates were being forced to devote too much time to "passing the hat. America deserves candidates who have enough time to consider the issues, enough funds to present their views to the voters and to compete equally on the merits, not men who make the best fund-raisers because they appeal to a particular interest group or because they are in a position to put pressure on people with money."

Election Commission. Another legislative idea, boosted by Ervin and Senate Minority Leader Hugh Scott (R Pa.), was an independent commission to supervise federal elections. Ervin said the commission should have the power to obtain injunctions against certain activities and to prosecute law violators. He said he believed it should be composed of equal numbers of Republicans and Democrats—serving staggered terms by presidential or congressional appointment—and be given most of the Justice Department's legal responsibilities regarding elections.

PHASE I OF COMMITTEE HEARINGS: UNANSWERED QUESTIONS

Even after months of listening to testimony and studying evidence, investigators had failed to answer many questions about the Watergate scandal. The reasons had to do with both the complexity of the scandal and the administration's skill in parrying questions. This article summarizes what was known, and not known, by the end of 1973.

After the first phase of the Senate investigating committee's hearings—the phase dealing with the Watergate break-in and coverup—there were enough conflicts of testimony to keep students of Watergate busy for months. These were some key questions raised by the witnesses:

When did President Nixon learn about the Watergate coverup—and what, if anything, was his role in it?

No witness directly disputed Nixon's May 22 statement that "the burglary and bugging of the Democratic National Committee headquarters came as a complete surprise to me." But former Acting FBI Director

L. Patrick Gray III said he had warned the President during a phone conversation July 6, 1972, that "people on your staff are trying to mortally wound you" by interfering with the bureau's Watergate investigation. Asked if he thought a reasonable person would have inferred that his staff was engaging in illegal conduct, Gray replied: "I do. . . ."

Nixon's two former top assistants, John D. Ehrlichman and H. R. Haldeman, and former Attorney General John N. Mitchell, all insisted on the President's innocence of the coverup. Against them stood John W. Dean III, former presidential counsel, who testified that Nixon knew of the coverup as early as Sept. 15, 1972.

Nixon set out his version of the meeting in an Aug. 15 television address. He said Dean gave him "no reason . . . to believe any others were involved. Not only was I unaware of any coverup, but at that time, and until March 21, I was unaware that there was anything to cover up."

Did former Attorney General John N. Mitchell approve the bugging plan in advance?

Jeb Stuart Magruder, former deputy director of the Nixon re-election committee, said Mitchell approved the plan at a meeting in Key Biscayne, Fla., on March 30, 1972. Mitchell said he rejected it. Frederick C. LaRue, another committee official, said Mitchell had been vague, neither rejecting nor approving the plan. Magruder also testified that he had shown Mitchell reports on the first wiretaps on the Democratic headquarters—an allegation Mitchell described as "a palpable, damnable lie."

What was the involvement, if any, of Haldeman and Ehrlichman in the break-in or coverup?

Both denied any participation or early awareness. But Gordon C. Strachan, Haldeman's former assistant, testified that Haldeman told him to "make sure our files are clean" shortly after the break-in. Dean said Ehrlichman told him to shred documents taken from Hunt's White House safe after the break-in. Nixon's former personal attorney, Herbert W. Kalmbach, testified that

Ehrlichman assured him in July 1972 that making payments to the Watergate defendants was a proper and approved activity.

One week after the break-in, on June 23, 1972, Haldeman and Ehrlichman met with then CIA Director Richard M. Helms and then CIA Deputy Director Vernon A. Walters. According to Helms and Walters, Haldeman told Walters to talk to Acting FBI Director Gray about limiting his agency's Watergate probe. "Mr. Haldeman said there was a lot of flak about the Watergate burglary, that the opposition was capitalizing on it," Helms related.

Highlights of Senate Watergate Committee Actions, 1973

Feb. 7: The Senate unanimously approved S Res 60, establishing a select committee "to conduct an investigation and study of the extent, if any, to which illegal, improper, or unethical activities were engaged in by any persons, acting individually or in combination with others, in the presidential election of 1972, or any campaign, canvass, or other activity related to it."

May 17: The committee opened its hearings with testimony from Robert C. Odle Jr., a former office manager at the Nixon re-election committee.

May 18: Convicted conspirator James W. McCord Jr. testified that he had been offered executive clemency in exchange for his silence, on Nixon's authority. But the man who made the offer, John J. Caulfield, later testified he had no proof that Nixon had approved it.

June 13: Chairman Sam J. Ervin's questioning of Nixon's chief 1972 fund-raiser, Maurice H. Stans, led to the first open conflict among committee members, as Sen. Edward J. Gurney (R Fla.) charged Ervin with harassing the witness.

June 14: Jeb Stuart Magruder, former deputy director of the re-election committee, gave the first inside look at events leading up to and following the Watergate break-in. He said former Attorney General John N. Mitchell approved the break-in plans and participated in the coverup along with Stans and other high administration officials. Mitchell and Stans denied the allegations.

June 15: Nixon's former counsel, John W. Dean III, began five days of explosive testimony. He read for six hours from a 245-page statement, which included allegations that Nixon knew of the coverup as early as Sept. 15, 1972, and had discussed hush money for Watergate defendants.

June 27: Dean revealed the names on a secret White House political "enemies list," in testimony to the Senate Watergate Committee.

July 6: Nixon wrote to Ervin refusing to appear in person before the committee or to provide it with any presidential files.

July 10: Former Attorney General Mitchell testified that he had rejected the break-in plan, but deliberately kept Nixon ignorant of its true dimensions later in order to ensure the President's re-election.

July 16: Surprise witness Alexander P. Butterfield, a former White House aide who had become head of the Federal Aviation Administration, disclosed that an automatic recording system had been taping presidential conversations at the White House and Executive Office Building since the spring of 1971. The next day, the committee asked for access to some of the tapes in an effort to clear up conflicts in testimony.

July 23: After receiving a written refusal from Nixon, the committee voted unanimously to subpoena tapes and other White House documents in his possession—making him the first president since Thomas Jefferson to be subpoenaed.

July 24: Former White House domestic affairs adviser John D. Ehrlichman testified he had approved a "covert operation" that led to the 1971 attempted burglary of the office of Daniel Ellsberg's psychiatrist—but had not approved the burglary.

July 30: H. R. Haldeman, Nixon's former chief of staff, testified that the President had authorized him in July to take some of the crucial White House tapes home for a private listening. Haldeman echoed Ehrlichman's denials of involvement in the break-in or coverup.

Aug. 3: Former Acting FBI Director L. Patrick Gray III testified that he had warned Nixon July 6, 1972, that "people on your staff are trying to mortally wound you" by using the FBI and CIA in a coverup. Gray acknowledged having lied about Watergate-related documents he destroyed, at what he thought was the bidding of Ehrlichman and Dean.

Sept. 24: When the hearings resumed after a seven-week recess, conspirator E. Howard Hunt Jr. testified that former special White House counsel Charles W. Colson knew of the plan that led to the Watergate break-in.

Sept. 26: The committee began its second phase of hearings, on political sabotage, with witness Patrick J. Buchanan, a White House speechwriter who vigorously defended Nixon and attacked the committee staff as "character assassins."

Oct. 3: Donald H. Segretti, who conducted a political sabotage program against Democrats in 1972, said he reported frequently on his activities to former White House appointments secretary Dwight L. Chapin.

Oct. 17: U.S. District Judge John J. Sirica rejected the committee's suit for access to White House tapes on grounds that the court lacked jurisdiction.

Nov. 7: The committee began its third and final phase of hearings, exploring campaign financing. John J. Priestes, a Miami homebuilder, testified that officials of Nixon's re-election finance committee promised to help solve his problems with the Federal Housing Administration (FHA) in exchange for a $100,000 contribution—a deal that eventually fell through.

Nov. 13: The committee adopted a resolution calling on the president to meet with all seven members to answer questions about the Watergate case.

Nov. 13–15: Executives for several large corporations testified that Nixon fund-raiser Stans had pressured them into making illegal corporate contributions in 1972. The men and the companies had pleaded guilty and been fined for violating a federal law prohibiting corporate contributions to political campaigns.

DIRTY TRICKS

Dirty tricks, political sabotage, negative campaigning, black advance, pranks—those were some of the terms used to describe activities examined in the Senate investigating committee's second phase of hearings. The key witness was Donald H. Segretti, a 32-year-old California lawyer who said he was hired in 1971 by former White House aides Dwight L. Chapin and Gordon C. Strachan to coordinate "activities tending to foster a split between the various Democratic hopefuls and to prevent the Democratic Party from uniting behind one candidate."

At one time or another during the campaign, Segretti said, he had a total of 28 agents working either directly or indirectly for him in 12 states. His testimony centered on the "tricks" he and his collaborators played during the 1972 Florida and California primaries. These ranged from sophomoric but disruptive stunts—such as setting off stink bombs at political events—to clearly illegal acts such as distributing phony campaign literature.

Three of Segretti's Florida tricks brought him a six-month prison sentence for violation of federal election laws. Working with two others, he:

- Mailed out letters on the stationery of Sen. Edmund S. Muskie (D Maine), falsely accusing Senators Henry M. Jackson (D Wash.) and Hubert H. Humphrey (D Minn.) of sexual improprieties and excessive drinking.
- Distributed flyers at a rally for Gov. George C. Wallace (D Ala.) that said: "If you liked Hitler, you'll love Wallace— Vote for Muskie."
- Printed and put up posters, attributed to a fictitious "Mothers for Busing" committee, that said: "Help Muskie Support Busing More Children Now."

Segretti's California activities, as he outlined them for the committee, were similar. One was a phony press release sent out on Humphrey stationery saying that another candidate, Rep. Shirley Chisholm (D N.Y.), had once been a patient in a mental institution.

Despite the serious implications of Segretti's sabotage operation, which he ruefully admitted, some of his tales evoked smiles in the hearing room. At one point, the poker-faced witness described how he and another agent, posing as organizers of a planned Muskie fund-raising dinner in Washington, D.C., arranged for a number of uninvited African diplomats to be delivered to the gala in rented limousines. Segretti said he and his associates ordered large quantities of pizza, flowers and liquor for the real organizers of the event, and hired a magician who showed up to entertain. "We also made inquiries about renting an elephant, but were unable to make the necessary arrangements," Segretti added.

His final act of the 1972 political campaign, Segretti said, was to hire a small plane to fly over the Miami Beach, Fla., convention center during the Democratic national convention in July, trailing a sign that read: "Peace, pot, promiscuity. Vote McGovern."

Nixon Counterattacks: 'I Have Earned Every Cent'

Often when politicians sink in the polls, they become more vulnerable to charges of misdeeds. This appeared to have been the case with Nixon. In addition to the Watergate scandal, he faced pointed criticism on several other fronts. They included:

- *Income taxes. The media reported that Nixon paid only $1,670 in income taxes in 1970 and 1971 on an income of $400,000. Nixon did not dispute the media reports. But he claimed that he was entitled to pay the low amounts because he had donated his vice presidential papers to the government. This enabled him to make a deduction of $500,000, thereby lowering his taxes.*
- *Milk prices. Nixon faced questions over whether his administration had rewarded the dairy industry in exchange for a $422,500 donation to his re-election campaign. Specifically, critics pointed to a decision by the former agriculture secretary to increase price supports for milk producers. This decision boosted the income of dairy farmers by hundreds of millions of dollars. Nixon, however, denied any wrongdoing. He said he only agreed to the new price supports when it became clear that Congress had the votes to increase them.*

Trying to boost his popularity, Nixon vigorously attacked his critics and defended his actions. But this approach, known as "Operation Candor," was undercut by new allegations of White House wrongdoing. Nixon tried to project a forceful image, but he found himself fending off questions about Watergate. (For more on Operation Candor, see p. 174.)

"I am not a crook." The remark by Nixon before an Associated Press Managing Editors press conference Nov. 17 was an extraordinary comment from a President, but it came at an extraordinary time, when allegations of impropriety and illegality against him were rampant.

With Nixon's popularity at a record low, he sought to bring himself and his case before the public during the week ended Nov. 23 with speeches and visits to former Rep. Carl Vinson (D Ga. 1914–65) in Macon, Ga., and the Republican Governors' Conference in Memphis, Tenn., in addition to the press conference in Orlando, Fla. "Operation Candor," the White House was calling it. The President had spent the previous week in private meetings with members of Congress, explaining his actions and urging their support.

But Watergate did not recede as a presidential problem. And Nixon was being buffeted by criticism over his handling of his personal income taxes, a 1971 case involving milk price supports, the energy crisis and White House charges that former Attorney General Elliot L. Richardson lied before the Senate Judiciary Committee in explaining his motives for resigning. All these matters except the Richardson episode came up at the press conference.

Tax Payments. The televised, hour-long press conference was held at Walt Disney World near Orlando, with about 400 Associated Press managing editors in attendance. The "I am not a crook" remark came in answer to a question about Nixon's personal finances and tax payments. Press reports had noted that Nixon paid only $1,670 in income taxes in 1970 and 1971 on income of $400,000. In his answer, Nixon did not confirm or deny the figures, stating only that he paid "nominal amounts" in taxes for those years.

He said this situation resulted from the $500,000 worth of income deductions he claimed by donating his vice presidential papers to the government. This decision, he said, had been recommended to him by former President Johnson and had not been questioned by the Internal Revenue Service.

The President then detailed some of his personal finances, saying he left the office of vice president in 1961 with a $47,000 net worth, but during the next eight years earned between $100,000 and $250,000 annually from his law practice and from a book he wrote.

"I made my mistakes," the President went on, "but in all my years of public life, I have never profited, never profited from public service. I have earned every cent. . . . Well, I am not a crook. I have earned everything I have got."

Watergate Questions. Half of the 20 questions at the press conference concerned Watergate and related events. The President repeated his innocence of any wrong-doing and promised to supply more evidence to prove his case. While conceding he had made a mistake in not more closely supervising his 1972 campaign, he refused to blame subordinates.

Asked if he still considered former White House aides John D. Ehrlichman and H. R. Haldeman the "finest public servants" he had ever known, as he had characterized them when they quit under fire in April, Nixon replied that they were "dedicated, fine public servants" who eventually would be proven innocent of any wrong-doing.

The President was questioned about two of nine tape recordings of his conversations that were not turned over to the Watergate grand jury under a court order. The

White House had explained Oct. 31 that the tapes never existed (*See p. 145*).

(*See p. 145*)

Nixon repeated the reasons for the missing June 20, 1972, conversation with former Attorney General John N. Mitchell and an April 15, 1973, talk with former presidential counsel John W. Dean III. The Mitchell telephone conversation was held on a phone that was not hooked up to the automatic recording device, and the Dean conversation took place after the recording machine had run out of tape, Nixon stated.

He said he was first informed on Sept. 29 or 30 that the tapes might not exist, but that this was not confirmed to him until about Oct. 27. Nixon repeated, however, that he would provide the grand jury with a Dictabelt recording that contained references to the Mitchell conversation and his notes on the Dean meeting.

As additional explanation for the missing tapes, Nixon characterized the recording devices as unsophisticated. He called one "a little Sony" with "little lapel mikes" in his desk, and said the system cost about $2,500. This was a contradiction of testimony before the Senate Watergate Committee by Alexander P. Butterfield, a former White House aide, who told of an elaborate arrangement of tapes, microphones and triggering devices in Nixon's offices and telephones.

JAWORSKI'S COMMITTEE TESTIMONY

Some of Nixon's critics were skeptical of Leon Jaworski when he was first appointed special Watergate prosecutor. They worried that the Texas trial lawyer, who was appointed by the Nixon administration, would not investigate the scandal aggressively. Some in Congress pressed for legislation that would change the way independent prosecutors were appointed. They wanted an entity outside the White House, such as a panel of federal judges, to appoint an independent prosecutor.

Over time, however, Jaworski's stock rose. He pledged a thorough and fair investigation. In particular, he would not be deterred from seeking documents just because the White House might claim that the documents contained secret national security information. At the same time, the White House assured Congress that it would not interfere with Jaworski's investigation. For example, administration officials said they would not try to limit his authority without the agreement of top congressional leaders.

As a result of such pledges, Congress backed off from changing the appointment system for independent prosecutors. However, lawmakers would return to the issue after Nixon's resignation and grant independent prosecutors more power.

Special Watergate prosecutor Leon Jaworski told the Senate Judiciary Committee Nov. 20 that he would not allow White House claims of national security [to] stand in the way of his Watergate investigation. However, he added that he did not expect he would have to review White House tapes or see documents relating to national security, which he said White House aides had offered.

During committee questioning about special prosecutor legislation, Jaworski acknowledged that presidential assistants the preceding week had brought a "national security" problem involving the "plumbers" team to his attention. He assured the committee that "my analysis was I could proceed, and I told them I expected to proceed."

"What assurances do you have that the veil of national security won't be drawn over the matter?" Sen. Edward M. Kennedy (D Mass.) asked.

"One, much as I respect the issue of national security, I'm not going to be blinded by it," Jaworski replied, "and two, there was no resistance (from White House special counsel J. Fred Buzhardt and chief of staff Alexander M. Haig Jr.) when I said I thought some indictments could be brought, and I was going to pursue them."

The "plumbers" unit, set up in 1971 to plug news leaks of national security information, was in charge of the break-in of the office of Pentagon Papers figure Daniel Ellsberg's psychiatrist.

In earlier testimony, former Attorney General Elliot L. Richardson told the committee that Buzhardt had informed him during the summer of 1973 of a "very significant national security problem" involving the break-in case. Depending on "how it is handled," Richardson said, the problem could be a serious impediment to Jaworski's efforts to bring federal indictments.

New Regulation. On the same day that Jaworski testified, his boss, Acting Attorney General Robert H. Bork, issued a departmental regulation designed to strengthen Jaworski's independence. The regulation ordered that the special prosecutor's jurisdiction would not be limited without approval of eight congressional leaders. An earlier regulation had required the consensus of the eight leaders before President Nixon could fire Jaworski. The leaders included majority and minority leaders of the House and Senate and the chairmen and ranking minority members of the House and Senate Judiciary Committees.

POLL REPORT

Reprinted from *Congressional Quarterly Weekly Report*, December 1, 1973

The publicity about missing and erased tapes took a toll on Nixon's popularity. This Harris poll showed that a plurality of Americans felt that Nixon would ultimately be found to have violated the law.

Note the question about potential Democratic presidential candidates in 1976. One man who was not mentioned in the poll was Jimmy Carter—who would, in fact, win his party's nomination and go on to become president. At the time of the poll, Carter had been the governor of Georgia for just two years, and he was unknown to many Americans.

Confidence in President Nixon continued to erode as Watergate developments unfolded, according to the latest Harris Survey. Interviewing of 1,459 households for the poll, published Nov. 26, was conducted Nov. 12–15.

These were the questions and answers:

"When all of the investigations and crises have finished, do you think that President Nixon will be found to have violated the law, as was true of Vice President Agnew, or don't you think this will happen?"

	Latest	October
Violated law	44%	39%
Won't happen	34	36
Not sure	22	25

"Do you tend to agree or disagree that President Nixon is a man of high integrity?"

	Latest	October	September 1972
Agree	39%	39%	76%
Disagree	46	44	13
Not sure	15	17	11

"Do you tend to agree or disagree that President Nixon does not inspire confidence as a president should?"

	Latest	October	September 1972
Agree	65%	58%	49%
Disagree	29	30	40
Not sure	6	12	11

Democrats on Presidency. For a Gallup Poll published Nov. 25, 627 persons who call themselves Democrats (in a total sample of 1,550 adults), in interviews Nov. 2–5, were shown a list of 11 men and asked: "Which one would you like to see nominated as the Democratic candidate for president in 1976?"

Sen. Edward M. Kennedy (Mass.)	41%
Gov. George C. Wallace (Ala.)	15
Sen. Edmund S. Muskie (Maine)	9
Sen. Henry M. Jackson (Wash.)	6
Sen. George McGovern (S.D.)	6
Sen. Adlai E. Stevenson III (Ill.)	4
Sen. Birch Bayh (Ind.)	3
Sen. Walter F. Mondale (Minn.)	2
Sen. William Proxmire (Wis.)	2
Sen. Robert C. Byrd (W.Va.)	1
Sen. John V. Tunney (Calif.)	1
Undecided	10

POSSIBLY A 'SINISTER FORCE' BLANKED OUT THE TAPE and WATERGATE: An Inconclusive Report on Gap in Tape

By the end of 1973, Watergate investigators were focusing almost entirely on the tapes of White House conversations. U.S. District Court judge John J. Sirica finally obtained seven White House tapes on Nov. 26—about four months after the Watergate grand jury had issued a subpoena for them. He turned over four of the tapes to the grand jury. Nixon had not made a special claim of executive privilege for those tapes—that is, he had not argued that they contained sensitive information that could hurt the nation if made public. In December, Sirica declined to give most of the remaining three tapes to the grand jury. He said most of the conversations on the tapes were not relevant to Watergate. However, one segment that was relevant to the investigation was a 39-minute conversation that contained an 18-minute gap.

The gap occurred in the middle of a conversation between Nixon and former presidential advisor H. R. Haldeman shortly after the Watergate break-in. There was a tone but no audible conversation. Rose Mary Woods, Nixon's personal secretary, said she discovered the gap while transcribing the tape. Woods subsequently testified that she made a mistake by pressing the "record" button when she meant to press the "stop" button. She also said that she immediately told Nixon about the gap. He advised her "not to worry" because he thought that it was not on one of the subpoenaed tapes, Woods said.

A panel of experts in New York City began reviewing the mysterious gap to determine the cause of the hum on the tape. They also wanted to know if any information on the tape could be recovered. The experts had been selected by both the White House and the special prosecutor's office. In a preliminary report in December, they dismissed a theory by the White House that the hum might have been caused by Woods's high-intensity lamp or electric typewriter.

By the first week of December, the growing Watergate scandal had claimed a number of victims. Some 18 men had either been indicted (formally charged with lawbreaking) in connection with Watergate or had pleaded guilty. Eight had been convicted and sentenced. The indictments and guilty pleas encompassed both those who had participated in the original break-in and those who had participated in the coverup. In an end-of-year report, special prosecutor Leon Jaworski also listed eight corporations that had pleaded guilty to making campaign contributions. He predicted more indictments in the coming year.

Nixon struggled to sustain his presidency in the face of the scandal. Trying to shore up his political base, Nixon mounted "Operation Candor," a campaign to clear up confusion about Watergate. As part of this operation, he planned to release transcripts or summaries of presidential tapes. But he changed his mind. In December, *The Washington Post* reported that part of the reason for the change was that the White House had realized the tapes would reveal the president knew about the Watergate coverup before March 21. Previously, Nixon had said that was the date when he first learned about it.

An exotic new brand of electronic demonology was offered as a possible explanation for the inexplicably missing segment of 18 minutes and 15 seconds from a tape recording of a Watergate-related presidential conversation. A "devil theory" was the description given by Alexander M. Haig Jr., the White House chief of staff. Haig testified Dec. 6 at a hearing on the erased tape before Chief Judge John J. Sirica in U.S. District Court in Washington, D.C.

The tape he referred to was one of those subpoenaed by the court. It was made on June 20, 1972, three days after the break-in at Democratic national headquarters in Washington's Watergate complex. The blank segment contained a conversation, sought by investigators of the Watergate scandal, between President Nixon and his former chief of staff, H. R. Haldeman. For two weeks, the court had been trying to determine what caused the mysterious 18-minute hum, preceded and followed by other conversations, in the tape.

One possible explanation was that Rose Mary Woods, Nixon's personal secretary, had accidentally erased all or part of the 18 minutes by pushing the wrong button on the recorder while she took a phone call. White House lawyers had expressed skepticism about an accidental erasure of the tape.

Haig told the court that attorneys assigned to the case had informed him on Nov. 20 that they had been unable to recreate the buzz that had replaced conversation during the gap in the tape. That evening, he recounted, he learned of two tones in the prolonged hum—a lower-volume tone starting about five minutes into the segment.

He and the lawyers, Haig said, discussed the possibility that "perhaps there had been one tone applied by Miss Woods" and that perhaps later, "some sinister force had come in and applied the other energy source and taken care of the information on the tape."

LISTENING AND TESTING

Investigators continued to turn their energies to the subpoenaed tapes. Sirica turned over four of the tapes to the Watergate grand jury at the end of November. Experts also began studying the 18-minute gap in another subpoenaed tape, hoping to determine how it was erased and whether it could be restored.

Four months after the Watergate grand jury subpoenaed certain presidential tapes, four of those tapes were cleared for presentation to that body. John J. Sirica, chief U.S. District Court judge in Washington, D.C., Nov. 30 agreed with a motion by special prosecutor Leon Jaworski that the four tapes, to which no particular claim of executive privilege had been raised, could be turned over to the grand jury.

On Dec. 3, Sirica began listening to the other tapes in a heavily guarded jury room. He was listening to the conversations for which executive privilege had been claimed, and he would decide whether or not those tapes should also go to the grand jury.

Meanwhile, in New York City, the June 20, 1972, tape containing the mysterious 18-minute hum was undergoing intensive examination by a panel of experts selected jointly by the White House and the special prosecutor's office. The tape was carried to New York by armed federal marshals the night of Nov. 29 along with the machines related to its pro-

duction and, perhaps, to the origin of the hum. Experts were seeking the cause of the hum and were working to discover if the original signals of the conversation first recorded there—and covered or erased by the hum—could be electronically enhanced and thus recovered.

The examination and testing were taking place in Manhattan at the Federal Scientific Corporation Laboratory, whose vice president for acoustics research, Mark R. Weiss, was one of the agreed-upon panel of experts. The panel also included Richard H. Bolt of Cambridge, Mass.; Franklin Cooper, professor of linguistics at the University of Connecticut; James L. Flanagan, a digital coding expert from Bell Laboratories; Thomas G. Stockham Jr., professor of computer sciences at the University of Utah; and John G. McKnight, an audio systems consultant.

Sirica asked Haig if he knew who the "sinister force" might be. Haig replied that he did not. According to White House records, only Woods, presidential assistant Stephen Bull and the President had access to the tape.

After the court hearing, reporters asked Haig if he had ever asked Nixon if he could have erased anything on the tape. Woods had testified earlier that the President had "pushed some buttons back and forth" while listening to excerpts of the tape as she was making a summary of its contents the weekend of Sept. 29 at Camp David, Maryland. Haig shook his head in the negative in response to the question.

White House lawyers said they discovered the 18-minute gap on Nov. 14. Haig said he told Nixon about it the next day. The court was notified of the erasure on Nov. 21.

Haig said in his testimony Dec. 6 that the White House had been reluctant to make public the new discrepancy in the tapes because of the earlier disclosure that two tapes did not exist. "We had just had two nonrecordings, which was fairly traumatic from our perspective, and it was important we not have a repeat of that kind of thing, which led to perceptions by the American people which I don't think were justified by the facts," he testified.

After the introduction of the new conspiratorial element in the already cloudy issue of the tapes, Sirica announced that a panel of experts scrutinizing the partially blank tape in New York City were expected to report to the court the next week. If necessary, Sirica said, he then would resume the hearings.

Haldeman Influence. In earlier court testimony, the inference was left by another witness that former staff chief Haldeman continued to exert considerable influence on White House policy. Haldeman resigned April 30 as a result of pressure from Watergate.

Haig tersely dismissed such speculation. "Mr. Haldeman does not influence what we do in the White House," he said.

Ford and Nixon. A few hours after the court recessed on Dec. 6, Gerald R. Ford was sworn in as Vice President before a joint session of Congress.

Ford's accession to the vice presidency immediately opened up a new round of speculation on Capitol Hill about the survivability of Nixon as President. With the vice presidency no longer vacant, some Republican members of Congress were speaking more candidly than before about impeachment or resignation of the scandal-damaged President.

One Republican senator, Jacob K. Javits of New York, spoke out publicly Dec. 5, the day before Ford's confirmation and swearing in. When Ford was sworn in, said Javits, "there will exist a new situation concerning any call on the President to resign in the interest of the country. . . . I and others will have to give every thoughtful consideration to that possibility."

Other Republicans on the Hill disagreed with Javits, or were more circumspect. But even some Nixon loyalists were anxious for the President to make a full report on his personal finances, as he had promised to do as part of his "Operation Candor." (*See p. 174.*)

Continuing Tapes Riddles

Presidential secretary Woods made her fourth appearance in Sirica's court on Dec. 5. She had testified previously that she might have caused part of the 18-minute hum through an accident while she was working on the tapes Oct. 1. She told the President immediately, but no one else. The President was not concerned, because at the time, reportedly, he did not believe the hum to be in a subpoenaed tape.

Special White House counsel J. Fred Buzhardt Jr., appearing before Sirica Nov. 30, said that he had first learned of the full extent and import of the missing conversation on Nov. 14, six weeks after Woods had informed the President of her mistake and a week before Sirica was informed of the gap. He said that the official White House explanation, included in the documents given to Sirica with the tapes themselves on Nov. 26—

that the hum was produced by the current of a high-intensity lamp and an electric typewriter—was "just a possibility," not a certainty.

Buzhardt said that the day after he learned of the gap, he and White House attorney Samuel J. Powers met with Woods. But to his recollection, he added, he did not ask her how her mistake, during a five-minute telephone call, could have created a gap more than three times as long in the recorded conversations.

A week later, on Nov. 22, Buzhardt discovered that Woods had nine other original presidential tapes in her possession, the lawyer testified. These tapes covered the period Jan. 3–4, 1973, and special prosecutor Leon Jaworski had requested some of them from the White House Nov. 15. The tapes included conversations of the President with John D. Ehrlichman and former White House special counsel Charles W. Colson. Former White House counsel John W. Dean III had testified before the Senate Watergate Committee in June that Ehrlichman had told him Jan. 4 that discussions were under way concerning the possibility of executive clemency for Watergate defendant E. Howard Hunt Jr.

Woods obtained the nine additional tapes on Nov. 19, according to records kept by deputy presidential assistant John C. Bennett. As soon as he realized that Woods was working with the original tapes, Buzhardt said, he had copies made for her that she could use to compile a digest of the conversations included. The nine tapes were returned to Bennett on the morning of Nov. 26.

UNTANGLING SUBPOENA CONFUSION

Lawyers, including criminal prosecutors, are trained to be extremely precise when writing legal arguments. Otherwise, their words may be misinterpreted. This article shows the consequences of a vaguely written legal order. One of the Watergate subpoenas called for tapes and other documents relating to a three-way meeting between Nixon and two of his top aides on the morning of June 20, 1972. But since there had been no three-way meeting that morning, Nixon's lawyers were able to cast doubt on which tapes had to be turned over.

"He told me not to worry, because that was not one of the subpoenaed tapes," said Rose Mary Woods Nov. 28. She was relating to U.S. District Judge John J. Sirica what President Nixon's reaction had been on Oct. 1

when she had informed him that she feared she had mistakenly erased some conversation on the June 20, 1972, tape.

But, as it turned out, that conversation between Nixon and H. R. Haldeman was indeed one of those sought by the grand jury in its subpoena of July 23, 1973. Testimony from various White House lawyers attributed their confusion over the specific conversations of June 20 included in the subpoena to its ambiguous language.

The subpoena sought: "All tapes and other electronic and/or mechanical recordings or reproductions, and any memoranda, papers, transcripts and other writings relating to (the) meeting of June 20, 1972, in the President's Executive Office Building office involving Richard Nixon, John Ehrlichman and H. R. Haldeman from 10:30 a.m. to noon (time approximate)."

White House lawyers said that there was no three-way meeting of Nixon, Ehrlichman and Haldeman on the morning of June 20, but instead two consecutive meetings, one with Ehrlichman from 10:25 to 11:30 and then one with Haldeman from 11:26 to 12:45. Because the first meeting occurred at times closer to those mentioned in the subpoena, White House attorneys assumed that was the only conversation desired, they said.

More precise language, contained in a memorandum filed by former special prosecutor Archibald Cox with Sirica Aug. 13, resulted, when read by the White House attorneys in November, in the realization that both conversations were desired. The memorandum described the meeting as follows:

"Respondent (Nixon) met with John D. Ehrlichman and H. R. Haldeman in his old Executive Office Building office, on June 20, 1972, from 10:30 a.m. until approximately 12:45. . . . Early on the morning of June 20, Haldeman, Ehrlichman, Mitchell, Dean and Attorney General Kleindienst met in the White House. This was their first opportunity for full discussion of how to handle the Watergate incident. . . . From there, Ehrlichman and then Haldeman went to see the President. . . ."

Haldeman Role. Haldeman's continuing role in White House activities, more than six months after his departure April 30 as chief of staff, was further detailed in testimony Dec. 4 before Sirica. Lawrence M. Higby, an official in the Office of Management and Budget and Haldeman's former deputy, said that he learned Nov. 14 or 15, in a telephone call from his former boss, that Haldeman was already aware of the 18-minute gap in the June 20 tape.

During the conversation, Higby said, he received the clear impression that someone at the White House had asked Haldeman for his handwritten notes taken during the conversation the hum eliminated. Haig said Dec. 5 that he had telephoned Haldeman. Buzhardt said that when he told the President Nov. 14 about the long gap, Nixon suggested that Haldeman's notes of that meeting be obtained. The notes indicated that the missing portion of the conversation between Haldeman and Nixon dealt with Watergate.

Those notes and other files that Haldeman had left at the Executive Office Building were in a locked file cabinet, and only Haldeman knew the combination to the lock, Higby said. On Nov. 15, Haldeman gave Higby precise instructions about how to find and remove the notes, making clear that any deviation from the instructions should be reported to him, according to Higby. Higby said that he read the notes to Haldeman over the telephone before handing them over, with Haldeman's acquiescence, to Buzhardt.

Repeat Performance. Rose Mary Woods made a surprise repeat performance Dec. 5 in court, upstaging the star witness of the day, Alexander Haig. Judge Sirica recalled Woods to "get to the bottom" of complaints by her attorney, Charles S. Rhyne, that White House lawyers had placed the President's interests ahead of hers.

Woods said that she had the impression before her first court appearance Nov. 8 that Leonard Garment, Buzhardt and Samuel J. Powers of the White House legal staff were her lawyers. However, she testified that the three had counseled her not to volunteer information and to answer questions "yes" or "no," without otherwise coaching her.

Haig recommended that she obtain her own lawyer late Thanksgiving Day, Woods said. Haig telephoned Rhyne, when she suggested him, and he accepted her as a client the next day.

Sirica Skepticism. Woods said that she had been "terribly worried" that she might have accidentally caused a 4 1/2-minute hum in the June 20 taped conversation between Nixon and Haldeman. But she added that she "could see no way at all I could have caused an 18-minute gap." Buzhardt had informed Sirica Nov. 21 of an 18-minute blank in the recording.

Sirica expressed skepticism about Woods' earlier explanation of the erasure. "I'm not saying I don't believe you," he said. "I haven't made up my mind." The judge assured her that she was not on trial and that the hearing gave her the "greatest forum you'll ever have to speak in" to provide information about what might have caused the hum.

Woods replied that she was on trial by the press, although "I'm not supposed to say that. . . . If I could offer any idea, any proof, any knowledge of how that 18-minute gap happened, there is no one on earth who would rather. I'm doing the very best I can." Woods said that the President or Haig had first informed her that a full 18 minutes of the conversation consisted of the hum.

Jill Volner, assistant Watergate prosecutor, asked, "Do you have any knowledge, direct or indirect, of anyone tampering [with] or obliterating any of the tapes?"

"No, ma'am, I have not," Woods replied.

Box Score of Watergate Indictments and Convictions

By the end of 1973, investigators had advanced cases against 18 men in connection with the Watergate scandal—and the investigation was still in its early stages. A year later, virtually all of the president's most trusted aides would be facing prison sentences, and Nixon himself would be implicated in the cover-up. Watergate would far surpass any other political scandal in American history. Even the Teapot Dome scandal of the early 1920s—regarded as the worst twentieth century scandal before Watergate—resulted in the conviction of just one top presidential aide, although others resigned in disgrace.

By the first week of December, 18 men had been indicted for or pleaded guilty to criminal offenses related to the Watergate scandal. Eight had been convicted and sentenced.

The first indictment since Leon Jaworski was named Watergate special prosecutor in October was returned on Nov. 29, when Dwight L. Chapin, President Nixon's former appointments secretary, was accused of lying to a federal grand jury.

Jaworski was quoted by the Dec. 10 *U.S. News & World Report* magazine as saying that he expected more indictments in the first few weeks of 1974. "I would be very disappointed if the trials themselves were not completed within a year's period of time," he said.

These were the indictments and convictions in the Watergate and related cases—not including campaign contribution violations:

Watergate Break-In. Seven men were indicted Sept. 15, 1972, for the June 17, 1972, break-in at the Watergate complex. They were E. Howard Hunt Jr., G. Gordon Liddy, James W. McCord Jr., Bernard L. Barker, Eugenio R. Martinez, Virgilio R. Gonzalez and Frank A. Sturgis.

Liddy and McCord were the only ones to plead not guilty and stand trial. They were convicted Jan. 30, 1973, of conspiracy, burglary and wiretapping violations. Judge John J. Sirica sentenced all but Liddy on Nov. 9; Liddy was sentenced March 23 to from six years and eight months to 20 years.

Watergate Coverup. Three men who participated in the attempt to keep the lid on the Watergate scandal agreed to cooperate with prosecutors in exchange for reduced charges for their coverup roles. None had been sentenced by Dec. 8.

- Frederick C. LaRue, once an aide to former Attorney General John N. Mitchell and an official of the Nixon re-election committee, pleaded guilty June 27 in U.S. District Court in Washington, D.C., to charges of conspiracy to obstruct justice.
- Jeb Stuart Magruder, a former White House aide who became deputy director of the Nixon re-election committee in late 1971, pleaded guilty Aug. 16 to a charge of conspiracy to obstruct justice, unlawfully intercept wire and oral communications and defraud the United States.
- John W. Dean III, Nixon's chief counsel until he was dismissed April 30, pleaded guilty Oct. 19 to a single felony count of conspiracy to obstruct justice and defraud the United States.

Plumbers Break-In. Four former members of the secret White House investigations unit known as the "plumbers" were indicted Sept. 4 by a Los Angeles, Calif., county grand jury for their roles in the 1971 break-in at the office of Dr. Lewis Fielding, a psychiatrist who had treated Pentagon Papers defendant Daniel Ellsberg.

They were John D. Ehrlichman, Nixon's former domestic affairs adviser; David R. Young, a former White House aide; G. Gordon Liddy, former counsel to the Nixon re-election finance committee and convicted Watergate conspirator, and Egil Krogh Jr., former White House aide and leader of the plumbers.

All four were charged with state counts of burglary and conspiracy. Ehrlichman was also cited for perjury because of conflicts in his testimony before the Senate Watergate investigating committee and the California grand jury. All four pleaded not guilty. The California charges against Krogh were dropped Dec. 3, after he pleaded guilty Nov. 30 in U.S. District Court in Washington, D.C., to violating Fielding's civil rights. An Oct. 11 federal indictment brought against Krogh for allegedly lying about his role in the burglary also was dropped in light of his plea.

Political Sabotage. In addition to Dwight Chapin, two men were charged in connection with a 1972 political sabotage campaign directed against the Democrats.

- Donald H. Segretti, a California lawyer, pleaded guilty Oct. 1 in U.S. District Court in Washington to three misdemeanor charges for his political activities in the Florida primary. An earlier federal indictment in Tampa, Fla., to which Segretti had pleaded not guilty, was dropped. He was sentenced Nov. 5 to six months in prison.

- George Hearing, who worked for Segretti in Florida, was indicted May 4 by a federal grand jury in Tampa. He pleaded guilty to one count of violation of campaign laws for distributing a phony campaign letter and was sentenced to a maximum prison term of one year.

Vesco Case. Former Attorney General John N. Mitchell and former Commerce Secretary Maurice H. Stans were indicted May 10 by a federal grand jury in New York City on obstruction of justice and perjury charges.

They allegedly attempted to block a government investigation of the activities of financier Robert L. Vesco in exchange for a $200,000 contribution to the Nixon campaign. Their trial was scheduled to begin Jan. 7, 1974.

'Operation Candor': Still Considerable Confusion over Various Aspects of the Watergate Scandal

> Nixon created "Operation Candor" in the fall. His goal was to mount a public relations offensive that would address concerns about his role in Watergate, as well as in other possible scandals. However, the operation failed to answer many troubling questions. For example, why did the president feel that he was unable to reveal the substance of the tapes that the special prosecutor was seeking? Why did it take so long for the White House to announce that two of the nine tapes sought by the prosecutor may not exist? Why did another tape contain an 18-minute gap?
>
> The White House also did not fully answer questions about campaign contributions and the administration's use of wiretaps.

"Operation Candor," President Nixon's campaign to clear up confusion about his role in the Watergate and other alleged scandals, had raised new questions and left many of the old ones unanswered one month after its initiation in early November.

Tapes

In a television appearance Nov. 17, Nixon told a group of newspaper editors that he hoped there would be some way to make public "the substance" of the subpoenaed White House tapes. That, he said, would prove he did not know about the Watergate break-in or coverup.

But nothing seemed to be preventing the President from releasing his transcripts of the taped conversations, as his remark implied. U.S. District Judge John J. Sirica, who had jurisdiction over the tapes, said Nov. 14 that Nixon was free to "waive any privilege and make tapes or other materials public" whenever he wished.

Also at the Nov. 17 question-and-answer session at Disney World, Fla., Nixon said he "voluntarily waived privilege with regard to turning over the tapes." He had not surrendered the tapes, however, until two federal courts ordered him to do so.

Nonexistent Tapes. Why, the President was asked during the session, did his spokesmen wait so long to tell Judge Sirica that two of the nine tapes subpoenaed by the special prosecutor might not exist? Nixon replied that he was informed of the possibility on Sept. 29 or 30 and that the tapes' absence was definitely determined Oct. 26 after a thorough search.

Nixon did not explain why his legal adviser, Charles Alan Wright, who told Sirica Oct. 23 that the President would "comply in all respects" with the subpoena, had not been kept informed of those developments. Wright later said he did not learn that the two tapes could not be found until Oct. 31, when it was announced in open court.

Tape Gap. The 18-minute gap discovered in one of the subpoenaed tapes, and conflicting explanations of it offered by White House aides and attorneys in Sirica's court, were other murky areas.

White House counsel J. Fred Buzhardt publicly announced Nov. 21 that a gap existed in a subpoenaed June 20, 1972, tape. The revelation came only a day after Nixon had assured a group of Republican governors in Memphis, Tenn., that he knew of no "bombshells" still to explode in the Watergate case.

The part of the tape obliterated by a humming sound covered a discussion on Watergate between Nixon and his then chief of staff, H. R. Haldeman. According to Haldeman's notes of the talk, Nixon instructed him to begin a public relations effort to offset the effects of the Watergate break-in three days earlier. It was the only discussion on the tape that touched on the Watergate case.

White House attorneys suggested, in a statement filed with the court Nov. 26, that the gap had been caused accidentally by Rose Mary Woods, the President's personal secretary, while she was transcribing the tape on Oct. 1. In testimony the same day, Woods apologized to Judge Sirica for not mentioning her "terrible mistake" Nov. 8, when she first testified on the handling of the tapes.

Woods later modified her testimony to say that she might have caused only about five minutes of the gap while taking a phone call. Buzhardt conceded Nov. 29 that his original Nov. 26 explanation for the erasure was "not a certainty at all," but "just a possibility."

Alexander M. Haig Jr., the President's chief of staff, told Sirica Dec. 6 that he and others at the White House had theorized that the gap might have been created by some mysterious "sinister forces." Outside the court,

Haig suggested the more mundane possibility that Woods had misjudged the length of her phone call.

When the hearings recessed Dec. 7 to await the judgment of technical experts examining the tape, the White House had come up with no explanation for the 18-minute gap. A preliminary report by the experts to Sirica Dec. 13 indicated that the gap probably was not caused by Woods.

Woods testified that she told the President of her Oct. 1 mistake on the tape immediately, and that he shrugged it off, saying the Haldeman conversation was not included in the subpoena. The White House statement of Nov. 26 said Buzhardt was informed of the erasure "shortly thereafter."

Buzhardt said he and another White House attorney played the tape Nov. 14 and realized for the first time that the gap lasted 18 and not five minutes. It was also then, he said, that he realized for the first time that the subpoena did cover the partially obliterated conversation. Buzhardt said Nixon was informed of this new information right away. The next day, when Haldeman's notes mentioning the public relations offensive turned up, the President was told of them also, Buzhardt testified.

The puzzle remained: Why did Buzhardt wait for more than a month to assess the extent of damage supposedly done to the tape by Woods on Oct. 1 and to inform the court about it? And why were he and Nixon unclear in October on the details of a subpoena issued by the special prosecutor in July?

Campaign Financing

In the 1972 presidential election, Nixon told the newspaper editors, "Neither party was without fault with regard to the financing. They (the Democrats) raised $36-million, and some of that, like some of ours, came from corporate sources and was illegal, because the law had been changed, and apparently people didn't know it."

By the time Nixon said that, six corporations had been fined in federal court for making illegal contributions to his campaign. In contrast, the special prosecutor had disclosed no such illegal contributions to the McGovern campaign. A law prohibiting corporate gifts in federal campaigns was first passed in 1907, and the restriction had never been lifted.

Milk Deal. Throughout the first month of "Operation Candor," Nixon did not defuse charges that his 1972 campaign officials and others had solicited illegal corporate contributions with the promise of favorable government treatment or the threat to withhold favors. One of the most publicized cases was the alleged "milk deal," in which the administration had been accused of receiving more than $400,000 in contributions from three milk cooperatives in return for raising price supports paid to milk producers.

Nixon and some of his top aides met with representatives of the dairy industry on March 23, 1971. They reportedly discussed the price support issue at another meeting among themselves later the same day. Two days later, the administration reversed its policy and announced a large increase in milk price supports.

In his Nov. 17 briefing, Nixon denied that the decision represented a "quid pro quo" for a campaign contribution. The real reason behind it, he said, was that "Congress put a gun to our head" in the form of a petition demanding the increase, signed by 102 members, mostly Democrats.

Nixon said his advisers warned him that if he did not act, Congress would pass legislation raising the support payments even higher, and that Congress would override a veto. Some Senators expressed skepticism that the President would capitulate so readily on that matter, when his usual policy had been to veto, with little fear of an override, any legislation he thought inflationary.

ITT Case. Another alleged case of quid pro quo involved a favorable out-of-court settlement of an antitrust suit against the International Telephone and Telegraph Corporation (ITT), reportedly arranged after the company pledged at least $100,000 to the Nixon re-election campaign.

A White House statement confirmed Oct. 30 that Nixon had ordered then Deputy Attorney General Richard G. Kleindienst in April 1971 to delay appealing the suit—but denied that the action was politically motivated. Kleindienst never mentioned the call from Nixon during extensive questioning on the matter by the Senate Judiciary Committee in 1972, and the call was not acknowledged by the White House until a newspaper wrote about it in October.

Nixon's role in the ITT settlement was also brought into question by an internal White House memo, released Aug. 1 by the Senate Watergate Committee, warning of the existence of documents that could "directly involve the President" in the case.

Hughes-Rebozo Transaction. Nixon's close friend, Charles G. Rebozo, received $100,000 in cash from billionaire Howard Hughes in two installments in 1969 and 1970. The money was returned in June 1973. Nixon and Rebozo said it was intended as a 1972 campaign contribution but eventually was returned because of an internal dispute at the Hughes company that might have made the gift embarrassing to acknowledge.

Two former Hughes aides had submitted court depositions with differing versions of the contribution, one of them alleging that part of it was given in exchange for Justice Department approval of a proposed Hughes acquisition.

"If this was a campaign contribution," Nixon was asked at a press conference Oct. 26, "who authorized Mr. Rebozo to collect campaign contributions for your re-election or for the Republican Party?" Nixon answered that a finance chairman for his campaign had not been appointed when Rebozo first received the gift, and that the internal dispute had erupted by the time the chairman took office.

Nixon said Rebozo showed "very good judgment" in the matter, but did not explain why his friend kept the cash in a strongbox so long before returning it to Hughes.

National Security Issue

The President's definition of national security—a doctrine he had invoked to justify a number of his actions—remained unclear. His former top aides, H. R. Haldeman and John D. Ehrlichman, had testified before the Senate Watergate Committee that the President was justified in ordering illegal activities to protect national security.

Nixon did not answer a Nov. 17 question on whether he had discussed the legality or illegality of plans by the White House "plumbers" unit to gather information on Pentagon Papers defendant Daniel Ellsberg. He said only that he had not authorized the 1971 break-in at the office of Ellsberg's psychiatrist—and that the plumbers were set up to prevent "leaks which were seriously damaging to the national security." Nixon also said he had blocked an earlier investigation of the plumbers because it might have jeopardized sensitive national security matters.

Wiretaps. Nixon confirmed Nov. 17 that the Secret Service had maintained a surveillance of his brother, F. Donald Nixon, "for security reasons." He did not explain those reasons, beyond indicating there was concern that people "who might be in a foreign country" might attempt "to use improper influence." Nixon did not say what legal authority the Secret Service acted on in conducting the surveillance.

There were also unanswered questions about wiretaps of 13 government officials and four newsmen conducted by the administration from 1969 to 1971, supposedly in order to find the sources of national security news leaks.

WATERGATE: Indications of Deliberate Tape Erasures
and SIX MONTHS IN PRISON FOR 'PLUMBER' EGIL KROGH

The beginning of 1974 brought little respite to the embattled administration of President Nixon. A panel of electronic experts concluded in January that an 18-minute gap in a tape recording of a White House conversation did not occur by accident. Instead, it was caused by at least five separate, manual erasures. This was potentially grave news for the president. The tape contained a conversation between him and White House chief of staff H. R. Haldeman that took place shortly after the Watergate break-in. It was considered crucial evidence to determining whether Nixon was being truthful when he denied participating in the Watergate coverup.

The panel's report contradicted testimony by Nixon's personal secretary, Rose Mary Woods. She had said she must have accidentally erased the tape in the process of transcribing it. It also sparked questions about any role that Nixon played in creating the gap. The White House denied that Nixon himself had erased the tapes, either accidentally or deliberately. It warned against making any "premature judgments" about the panel's report.

Tampering with evidence can be a serious crime. U.S. District Court judge John J. Sirica held four days of hearings on the tape. Then he sent the case to a grand jury for further investigation.

Nixon's troubles deepened with subsequent revelations that two other tapes of presidential conversations contained gaps. In both cases, the gaps occurred during conversations that may have dealt with Watergate.

Members of Congress were almost unanimous in warning that the news about the tapes could seriously damage Nixon. Some lawmakers said that any evidence that Nixon participated in the Watergate cover-up or tampered with the tapes would lead to impeachment. A few Republicans, however, such as Vice President Gerald R. Ford and Sen. Barry Goldwater of Arizona, defended the president.

Nixon also found himself embroiled in a new battle over White House tapes. On Jan. 4, he rejected demands by the Senate Watergate Committee that he turn over hundreds of additional tapes and other documents. Nixon denounced the committee's demands as an "unconstitutional usurpation of power" that would elevate Congress over the executive branch. Sen. Herman E. Talmadge, a Georgia Democrat on the Watergate committee, shot back that the president's refusal made people think "he has something to hide." Despite the sharp words, the White House and the committee continued to negotiate over the issue, seeking a compromise.

Meanwhile, the Senate Watergate Committee began to look into allegations that the president had improperly based decisions on campaign contributions. Nixon vigorously defended himself against the charges. He denied that his administration's 1971 approval of higher milk price supports had anything to do with dairy industry groups contributing more than $400,000 to his 1972 campaign. Instead, he said the decision to raise prices was made to help the nation's economy. The decision was also spurred by Congress, which was moving to raise the prices if the administration did not act. Nixon pointed out that dairy contributions amounted to less than 1 percent of the total contributions to his reelection campaign.

Similarly, Nixon defended his attempt to block the Justice Department in 1971 from pursuing an antitrust suit against the International Telephone and Telegraph Corporation. A subsidiary of the corporation had promised to help pay for the 1972 Republican national convention. Nixon said his preference not to pursue action against the corporation had nothing to do with political contributions. Instead, he was philosophically opposed to taking antitrust actions against companies that were big but not necessarily hurting economic competition.

The long-awaited results of a study by experts of what caused the celebrated 18½-minute gap in a tape recording of a Watergate-related presidential conversation were made public the week ending Jan. 19. They were bad news for President Nixon.

The six-man panel of electronics specialists reported on Jan. 15 that the hum on the June 20, 1972, tape had been caused by at least five separate, manual erasures. The missing segment contained a conversation between the President and H. R. Haldeman, then the White House chief of staff. It was considered crucial evidence in proving whether or not Nixon knew of or participated in the Watergate coverup. He denied that he did.

The experts made their report to Chief Judge John J. Sirica of U.S. District Court in Washington, D.C. Sirica started four days of hearings the day he received the report. At the conclusion of the hearings, Sirica announced that he would send the case to a federal grand jury for action.

But the bad news for Nixon did not end with the disclosures about the June 20 tape. On Jan. 18, it was brought out that two other tapes of presidential conversations also contained gaps.

One was a 57-second blank space in a cassette recording of the President's recollection of a March 21, 1973, meeting with John W. Dean III, then the White House counsel and later the man who first alleged White House involvement in the Watergate coverup.

The other was a 38-second blank in Nixon's taped recollection of a telephone conversation with former Attorney General John N. Mitchell on June 20, 1972, three days after the Watergate break-in and the same day as the conversation containing the 18½-minute gap.

Experts' Report. The possibility that the Nixon-Haldeman conversation was deliberately erased was raised after the court-appointed panel of technical experts reported that the gap resulted from a manual process of repeated erasures and re-recording.

The experts said the gap could not possibly have been caused accidentally by Nixon's personal secretary, Rose Mary Woods, in the process of transcribing the tapes, as she had testified "must have" happened. Woods also said, however, that she could not have caused more than four or five minutes of the gap.

The panel's report shook the nation, already shocked by previous disclosures of missing or inaudible White House tapes.

The report and succeeding days of conflicting court testimony by White House aides and Secret Service agents set off a quick chain of reactions:

- The FBI entered the case of the Watergate tapes for the first time, at the request of Watergate Special Prosecutor Leon Jaworski. The White House said Jan. 17 that it would cooperate with the investigation, but would not say what would happen if agents tried to interview the President on the subject. FBI Director Clarence M. Kelley did not rule out the possibility that this would be necessary. Kelley said that only Jaworski would receive the results of the FBI inquiry.
- Congressional reaction was quick and almost unanimous in the belief that the latest disclosures represented a damaging blow to the President. Any evidence of his involvement in the Watergate coverup or tampering with tapes would make impeachment almost inevitable, some members said.

  Rep. Jerome R. Waldie (D Calif.), a member of the House Judiciary Committee, which was considering impeachment, said that if Nixon refused to turn over materials needed by the committee, he would demand an immediate House vote on impeachment.
- The disclosures probably helped give a new lease on life to the Senate Select Watergate Committee and its hearings, which some committee members reportedly had wanted to end. The committee was to decide after the opening of Congress Jan. 21 whether or not to continue public hearings into Watergate-related matters, including campaign contributions made to Nixon by the milk producers and by billionaire Howard Hughes.
- The White House denied Jan. 16 that Nixon himself had erased the tapes, either accidentally or deliberately, and said any "premature judgments" about the report of erasures on the tapes were "unwarranted." Gerald L. Warren, the deputy White House press secretary, refused to answer any other questions about the reports.
- Vice President Gerald R. Ford said Jan. 17 that it would be "premature to jump in on the testimony of six witnesses, who may or may not be upheld, and call for impeachment."
- Sen. Barry Goldwater (R Ariz.) also defended the President, saying the technical experts' report "doesn't mean a thing." But most of the reaction to the news was grim and indicated serious damage to the President, who already was at the lowest point of his career in public opinion polls.

DEFENDERS OF THE PRESIDENT

Two Republican leaders, Vice President Gerald R. Ford and Arizona Sen. Barry Goldwater, coupled strong defenses of President Nixon with harsh attacks on his critics.

Ford. On Jan. 15, two hours before new information damaging to the administration was disclosed in a Washington, D.C., court hearing, Ford told the American Farm Bureau Federation in Atlantic City, N.J., that "powerful pressure organizations" were engaged in "an all-out attack" on the President and his policies.

Ford declined to comment later in the day on the report of technical experts that an 18½-minute gap in the crucial spot on one of the subpoenaed White House tapes was caused by erasing and re-recording at least five segments of the tape. But an aide said the Vice President had no information about the report before he spoke.

Two of the groups Ford cited were the AFL-CIO and Americans for Democratic Action (ADA), both of which had been lobbying publicly for Nixon's impeachment. "If they can crush the President and his philosophy, they are convinced that they can then dominate the Congress and, through it, the nation," he said.

Ford lashed out at "the relatively small group of activists who are out to impeach the President." If they cannot succeed immediately, he said, "they will try to stretch out the ordeal, to cripple the President by dragging out the preliminaries to impeachment for as long as they can, and to use the whole affair for maximum political advantage."

The uncharacteristically combative tone of Ford's speech led to speculation that it had been written by White House speech writers. *The Washington Star-News* printed such a report Jan. 16, and Ford acknowledged that White House writers had worked with him to draft the speech, because he had not yet hired writers of his own. But he insisted that he initiated and approved its substance.

Goldwater. Barry Goldwater, who earlier had emerged as a leading Republican critic of Nixon's handling of the Watergate scandals, echoed Ford's attacks on administration critics during a party fund-raising dinner Jan. 15. Speaking in Hunt Valley, Md., he charged that "liberal Democrats do not have what it takes either in evidence or guts" to impeach Nixon.

Goldwater said he would not lead a delegation of Republicans to ask Nixon to resign, as some rumors had suggested. But he repeated his earlier characterization of [the] Watergate affair as "one of the most scandalous and stupid in the history of this country." Goldwater had first changed direction on the issue in a Jan. 13 appearance on "Meet the Press," where he defended the President and attacked his critics.

Asked about the technical experts' report on the Watergate tape, Goldwater said the new information "doesn't mean a thing to me."

AN IMPEACHABLE OFFENSE IS. . . .

The Constitution does not clearly spell out the types of offenses that are punishable by impeachment. It states that a president (or certain other high-ranking officials) may be impeached for "treason, bribery, or other high crimes and misdemeanors." But what sorts of offenses are included under "high crimes and misdemeanors"?

Because the language in the Constitution is so vague, some experts believe that impeachment is as much a political matter as a legal matter. When Gerald R. Ford served in the House, he defined an impeachable offense as "whatever a majority of the House of Representatives considers it to be at a given moment in history." Inevitably, this means that a president whose party controls Congress is safer from impeachment than a president who is facing a hostile opposition party in Congress.

The first president in history to be impeached, Andrew Johnson in 1868, was associated with the Democratic Party. Progressive Republicans controlled Congress. They fought with Johnson over a range of issues following the Civil War, including rights for blacks and reconstruction for the defeated Southern states. Then they impeached him for violating a new, and highly questionable, law. Many historians view the impeachment of Johnson as an attempt by the Republicans to depose a political enemy rather than to punish an alleged criminal. Johnson finished out his term when the Senate narrowly voted to acquit him.

The second impeachment of a president, in 1998, also became a highly politicized battle. Clinton, a Democrat, was accused of lying under oath and attempting to obstruct a criminal investigation. Republicans, who controlled Congress, charged that his offenses met the "high crimes and misdemeanors" standard in the Constitution. But Democrats disagreed. They contended that Clinton's attempts to cover up an affair with a White House intern failed to meet the constitutional standard for impeachment, because his misbehavior was personal rather than an abuse of his office. The House vote to impeach Clinton largely followed party lines. The Senate then acquitted him, with a few Republicans joining all Democrats to keep Clinton in office.

The Watergate scandal pitted a Republican president against a Democratic Congress. It is uncertain whether a Republican Congress would have investigated Nixon so aggressively. Initially, many Republicans defended Nixon, saying his offenses did not meet the standard for impeachment. But as investigators uncovered more and more evidence of serious White House crimes, many of Nixon's defenders changed their minds.

In theory, Congress could impeach a president for a minor offense. The Constitution, after all, does not say that a president has to commit specific crimes to be impeached. And the House of Representatives needs only a majority vote to impeach. But it would be very difficult to remove a president from office unless he is guilty of substantial wrongdoing. It takes a two-thirds vote of the Senate to convict a president and force him out of office. Rarely in history has the opposition party controlled both a majority of the House and two-thirds of the Senate. Even if an opposition party was to amass that many seats, many in the House and Senate would likely be uncomfortable with removing a president from office for minor transgressions because it could permanently weaken the presidency.

- . . . "treason, bribery, or other high crimes and misdemeanors."—*The Constitution*
- . . . "one in its nature or consequences subversive of some fundamental or essential principle of government, or highly prejudicial to the public interest . . . a violation of the Constitution, of law, of an official oath, or of duty, by an act committed or omitted, or, without violating a positive law, by the abuse of discretionary powers from improper motives, or for any improper motives, or for any improper purpose."—*Benjamin F. Butler* (R Mass.), one of the House managers of the impeachment case against Andrew Johnson, March 30, 1868
- . . . "of such a character to commend itself at once to the minds of all right thinking men, as beyond all question, an adequate cause (for impeachment). It should . . . leave no reasonable ground of suspicion upon the motives of those who inflict the penalty. . . ."—*William Pitt Fessenden* (Whig Maine), one of the seven "Republicans" in the Senate who voted against the conviction of Andrew Johnson
- . . . actions "as an individual and such judge. . . . (which brought) his court into scandal and disrepute, to the prejudice of said court and public confidence in the administration of justice therein, and to the prejudice of public respect and confidence in the federal judiciary and to render him unfit to serve as such judge."—*Articles of Impeachment against Federal District Judge Halsted Ritter*, 1936
- . . . "whatever a majority of the House of Representatives considers it to be at a given moment in history; conviction results from whatever offenses two-thirds of the other body considers to be sufficiently serious to require removal of the accused from office. . . . There are few fixed principles among the handful of precedents."—*Rep. Gerald R. Ford*, speech on the House floor, April 15, 1970

Experts' Report to Court on 18-Minute Hum in Tape

Following are excerpts of the report made to Chief Judge John J. Sirica Jan. 15 by the advisory panel of electronics specialists that studied the June 20, 1972, presidential tape containing an 18½-minute gap:

In response to your request we have made a comprehensive technical study of the White House tape of June 20, 1972, with special attention to a section of buzzing sounds that lasts approximately 18.5 minutes. Paragraphs that follow summarize our findings and indicate the kinds of tests and evidence on which we base the findings.

Magnetic signatures that we have measured directly on the tape show that the buzzing sounds were put on the tape in the process of erasing and re-recording at least five, and perhaps as many as nine, separate and contiguous segments. Hand operation of keyboard controls on the Uher 5000 recorder was involved in starting and again in stopping the recording of each segment. The magnetic signatures observed on the tape show conclusively that the 18.5-minute section could not have been produced by any single, continuous operation. Further, whether the footpedal was used or not, the recording controls must have been operated by hand in the making of each segment.

The erasing and recording operations that produced the buzzing section were done directly on the tape we received for study. We have found that this tape is 1814.5 feet long, which lies within a normal range for tapes sold as 1800 feet in length. We have examined the entire tape for physical splices and have found none. Other tests that we have made thus far are consistent with the assumption that the tape is an original and not a re-recording.

A Uher 5000 recorder, almost surely the one designated as Government Exhibit #60, was used in producing the 18.5-minute section. Support for this conclusion includes recorder operating characteristics that we measured and found to correspond to signal characteristics observed on the evidence tape.

The buzzing sounds themselves originated in noise picked up from the electrical power line to which the recorder was connected. Measurements of the frequency spectrum of the buzz showed that it is made up of a 60 cycles per second fundamental tone, plus a large number of harmonic tones at multiples of 60. Especially strong are the third harmonic at 180 and the fifth harmonic at 300 cycles per second. As many as forty harmonics are present in the buzz and create its "raucous" quality. Variations in the strength of the buzz, which during most of the 18.5-minute section is either "loud" or "soft," probably arose from several causes including variations in the noise on the power line, erratic functioning of the recorder, and changes in the position of the operator's hand while running the recorder. The variations do not appear to be caused by normal machine operations.

Can speech sounds be detected under the buzzing? We think so. At three locations in the 18.5-minute section, we have observed a fragment of speech-like sound lasting less than one second. Each of the fragments lies exactly at a place on the tape that was missed by the erase head during the series of operations in which the several segments of erasure and buzz were put on the tape. Further, the frequency spectra of the sounds in these fragments bear a reasonable resemblance to the spectra of speech sounds.

Can the speech be recovered? We think not. We know of no technique that could recover intelligible speech from the buzz section. Even the fragments that we have observed are so heavily obscured that we cannot tell what was said. . . .

In developing the technical evidence on which we have based the findings reported here, we have used laboratory facilities, measuring instruments, and techniques of several kinds, including: digital computers located in three different laboratories, specialized instruments for measuring frequency spectra and waveforms, techniques for "developing" magnetic marks that can be seen and measured directly on the tape, techniques for measuring the performance characteristics of recorders and voice-operated switches, and statistical methods for analyzing experimental results.

In summary we have reached complete agreement on the following conclusions:

1. The erasing and recording operations that produced the buzz section were done directly on the evidence tape.
2. The Uher 5000 recorder designated Government Exhibit #60 probably produced the entire buzz section.
3. The erasures and buzz recordings were done in at least five, and perhaps as many as nine, separate and contiguous segments.
4. Erasure and recording of each segment required hand operation of keyboard controls on the Uher 5000 machine.
5. Erased portions of the tape probably contained speech originally.
6. Recovery of the speech is not possible by any method known to us.
7. The evidence tape, in so far as we have determined, is an original and not a copy.

Respectfully submitted,
Richard H. Bolt
Franklin S. Cooper
James L. Flanagan
John G. (Jay) McKnight
Thomas G. Stockham, Jr.
Mark R. Weiss

Profiles of the 38 Judiciary Committee Members

For profiles of the Senate select committee's members and counsels and the Watergate cast of characters, see p. 26.

By early 1974, the spotlight had turned to the House Judiciary Committee. Since the House of Representatives has the power of impeachment, the Judiciary panel would make preliminary recommendations on whether to impeach Nixon.

After their work investigating Watergate, several members of the Judiciary Committee moved on to increasingly prominent political careers. Paul S. Sarbanes and William S. Cohen both won election to the Senate, with Cohen then serving as secretary of defense under President Clinton. Trent Lott also moved to the Senate. He took over one of the most powerful posts in Washington—Senate majority leader—until he resigned under fire in 2002 after making a joke that was interpreted as supporting segregation.

Others remained in the House more than 30 years later. John Conyers Jr. and Charles B. Rangel moved up the ranks to occupy leadership positions on powerful committees. Another Democrat, Barbara C. Jordan, gained national attention during the Watergate hearings for a riveting speech supporting the impeachment of Nixon. An impassioned orator, her keynote speech at the 1976 Democratic convention is considered one of the great speeches in recent history.

Following are profiles of all 38 members of the House Judiciary Committee—21 Democrats and 16 Republicans. Included are district descriptions, presidential support scores for 1973 and any comments each member may have made concerning the impeachment investigation. There is one vacancy on the Republican side.

The Democrats

Peter W. Rodino Jr., 64, represents New Jersey's 10th district (Newark), which was in 1974 about 52 per cent black. A member of the House since 1949 and chairman of the committee since 1973, he faces the possibility of a strong primary challenge from a black candidate in 1974. A liberal, he supported Nixon on 28 per cent of the votes on which the President took a position during 1973. He has commented: "I must say that the consideration of resolutions relating to the possible impeachment of the President is a task I would have preferred not to undertake."

Harold D. Donohue, 72, represents Massachusetts' heavily industrialized 3rd district (central, Worcester). First elected to the House in 1947, Donohue did not go on the Judiciary Committee until the early 1950s, after Rodino. A quiet man who heads the Subcommittee on Claims, Donohue has a liberal voting record, supporting Nixon on 28 per cent of the votes in 1973.

Jack Brooks, 51, represents Texas' industrial 9th district (Beaumont-Port Arthur, Galveston). Brooks was first elected to the House in 1952 at the age of 29. He is a tough and outspoken liberal, was close to Lyndon Johnson and active on civil rights issues. He chairs the government operations subcommittee which investigated federal spending on the presidential homes at San Clemente, Calif., and Key Biscayne, Fla. He supported Nixon on 34 per cent of the votes in 1973.

Robert W. Kastenmeier, 49, represents Wisconsin's 2nd district, which includes the University of Wisconsin at Madison (southern). He has been a member of the House since 1959, is a highly regarded, issue-oriented liberal, and serves as chairman of the Subcommittee on Courts, Civil Liberties, and the Administration of Justice. He supported Nixon on 26 per cent of the votes in 1973. Kastenmeier has not said that he favors impeachment, but commented that before the "Saturday night massacre" firing of Archibald Cox, impeachment was "really unthinkable in practical terms. That is no longer the case."

Don Edwards, 58, represents the blue-collar suburbs of California's 9th district (Oakland to San Jose). He has been a member of the House since 1963, is a former FBI agent and national chairman of the Americans for Democratic Action. Edwards has gained the reputation of a hard-working liberal and is chairman of the Subcommittee on Civil Rights and Constitutional Rights. In 1973, he supported Nixon on 21 per cent of the votes. "We plan to prepare through our staff the most honest hard-hitting bill of particulars we can get," he has said, "and then present it to the American people."

William L. Hungate, 51, represents the rural and small-town 9th district of Missouri (northeast, St. Charles). A moderately liberal member of the House since 1964, Hungate heads the hard-working Subcommittee on Criminal Justice. He supported Nixon on 34 per cent of the votes during 1973.

John Conyers Jr., 44, represents Michigan's predominantly black 1st district (residential areas of Detroit). A member of the House since 1966 and a forceful proponent of civil rights measures, Conyers heads the Subcommittee on Crime. He supported Nixon on 20 per cent of the votes during 1973.

Joshua Eilberg, 52, represents Pennsylvania's middle-income residential 4th district (Philadelphia). He is a former majority leader in the state house of representatives, and was elected to the House in 1966. Liberal, quiet and hard-working, he heads the Subcommittee on Immigration, Citizenship, and International Law. He supported Nixon on 28 per cent of the votes in 1973. Eilberg has said that he would define an impeachable offense as a presidential action "which shocks the conscience," not necessarily a criminal action.

Jerome R. Waldie, 48, represents California's heavily industrial 14th district (most of Contra Costa County). Former majority leader of the state legislature, Waldie was elected to the House in 1966. He is regarded as very liberal and independent, and as one of the best lawyers on the committee. He is planning to run for governor of California in 1974. Waldie supported Nixon's position on 20 per cent of the votes during 1973. Sponsor of the first impeachment resolution introduced after the Cox firing, Waldie has said that "gross abuse of the office of the presidency, whether it is criminal or not, could be proper grounds for impeachment."

Walter Flowers, 40, represents the conservative Democratic 7th district of Alabama (west central, Tuscaloosa, Birmingham suburbs). He is a moderately conservative third-term member of the House, supporting Nixon's position 50 per cent of the time in 1973. Flowers has said that Congress has great latitude in defining an impeachable offense, but that it should not impeach a president simply because of "a lot of small things" or mere "distaste" for his actions.

James R. Mann, 53, represents the heavily industrialized 4th district of South Carolina (Greenville/Spartanburg). He is a former prosecutor, was elected to the House in 1969, and is regarded as one of the most conservative Democrats on the committee, supporting Nixon on 59 per cent of the votes in 1973. "Impeachment merely reveals the failure of the Judiciary Committee to exercise its oversight function," Mann has noted. "Congress is merely doing its duty to police executive power."

Paul S. Sarbanes, 40, represents the Baltimore suburbs of Maryland's 3rd district. Son of Greek immigrants, a Rhodes scholar and former state legislator, Sarbanes was elected to the House in 1970. He is a liberal with strong labor backing, and is respected by colleagues for his thoughtful intelligence. In 1973 he supported Nixon on 28 per cent of the votes.

John F. Seiberling, 55, represents Ohio's 14th district, which includes Akron and Kent State University. He is a decorated veteran of World War II, and was an attorney for the Goodyear Rubber Company—which his grandfather founded—before winning election to the House in 1970. Considered very liberal, he supported Nixon's position 25 per cent of the time in 1973.

George E. Danielson, 58, represents California's 29th district, which includes eastern Los Angeles. He is a former FBI agent and state legislator, and was elected to the House in 1970 with labor backing. Danielson has a tenuous hold on his seat because of recent redistricting, which placed him in the same district as Chet Holifield (D Calif.), chairman of the Government Operations Committee. Danielson, a liberal, supported Nixon's position 22 per cent of the time in 1973. He has said that an impeachable offense should be defined narrowly as an indictable offense.

Robert F. Drinan, 53, represents Massachusetts' suburban and small-town 4th district (Boston suburbs, small industrial towns). Drinan is a Jesuit priest and former dean of Boston College Law School. He was elected to the House in 1970 and 1972 by narrow margins, has been highly critical of Nixon and was the first member of Congress (on July 31, 1973) to introduce an impeachment resolution. He has been a flamboyant spokesman for liberal causes, supporting Nixon on 33 per cent of the votes in 1973. "The first illusion we have to break is that you have to prove a criminal offense (to impeach the President). This is a political offense."

Charles B. Rangel, 43, represents New York's 19th district (Manhattan, Harlem). He is a former state legislator who defeated Adam Clayton Powell Jr. in a 1970 primary. In June 1973, he proposed that a special committee should be formed "to see if the President's role in the events surrounding the Watergate bugging and its subsequent coverup constituted grounds for impeachment." Rangel supported Nixon on 27 per cent of the votes in 1973.

Barbara C. Jordan, 36, represents Texas' primarily black 18th district (central Houston). She is a former state senator, was elected in 1972 as the first black woman to serve in Congress from the South and is an articulate and well respected member of the committee. She supported Nixon on 30 per cent of the votes in 1973.

Ray Thornton, 45, represents Arkansas' agricultural 4th district. A former state attorney general, he was elected to the House in 1972. He supported Nixon on 45 per cent of the votes in 1973 and has avoided making public statements concerning impeachment.

Elizabeth Holtzman, 32, represents New York's 16th district (Brooklyn) after upsetting former House dean and Judiciary Committee Chairman Emanuel Celler in the 1972 primary. She is a former state committee-woman, a liberal and is regarded as highly intelligent and hard-working. She supported Nixon's position 29 per cent of the time during 1973. She has commented: "We don't help to restore public confidence in the processes of government if we don't act expeditiously, with thoroughness, fairness and justice."

Wayne Owens, 36, represents Utah's 2nd district (Salt Lake City). A liberal who worked in the Robert F. Kennedy 1968 presidential primary campaign, Owens is expected to run for a Senate seat in 1974. He supported Nixon's position 32 per cent of the time in 1973.

Edward Mezvinsky, 36, was elected in 1972 over an incumbent Republican to represent Iowa's rural and rapidly growing industrial first district. He is a consumer advocate, a strong liberal, and a freshman spokesman in the House. He supported Nixon on 34 per cent of the votes in 1973.

The Republicans

Edward Hutchinson, 59, represents Michigan's rural and small-town 4th district. He is a former state legislator who was elected to the House in 1963. He is conservative and quiet, preferring to stay out of the public eye. He supported Nixon's position 75 per cent of the time in 1973. "We've only got one president," he has said, "and impeachment of a president is something the country can't afford."

Robert McClory, 65, represents the outer Chicago suburbs of Illinois' 13th district. He is a former state legislator and has served in the House since 1963. Although he is of equal seniority as Hutchinson, he ranks second on the Republican side because of a draw for position. He has won re-election by wide margins in the past, but faces an energetic challenger for his seat in the March primary. McClory is regarded by some as one of the most partisan Republicans on the committee. He supported Nixon's position 67 per cent of the time in 1973. "There should be some kind of criminal offense (to justify impeachment)," he has said, "and there has to be direct evidence of (the President's) involvement."

Henry P. Smith III, 62, represents New York's 36th district (Niagara County). He is a conservative, a former mayor and county judge, who was elected to the House in 1964. He could face a strong Democratic challenger in 1974. In 1973, Smith supported Nixon on 68 per cent of the votes.

Charles W. Sandman Jr., 52, represents the rural areas and resorts in the 2nd district of New Jersey. Former majority leader of the state senate and a member of the House since 1967, Sandman was soundly defeated in a 1973 race for governor. He is very conservative, supporting Nixon on 44 per cent of the votes in 1973.

Tom Railsback, 41, represents Illinois' 19th district (western). He is a former state legislator and popular moderate conservative with labor support. He was first elected to the House in 1967 and is one of the more outspoken Republicans on the committee. He supported Nixon on 51 per cent of the votes in 1973. "You have an impeachment by the Democrats without any Republican participation," he has asserted, "and it's going to divide the country."

Charles E. Wiggins, 46, represents the primarily blue-collar suburbs of California's 25th district (eastern Los Angeles county), essentially the district Nixon once represented (1947–50). A thoughtful conservative considered by many the best legal mind on the committee, Wiggins was first elected to the House in 1967. He supported Nixon's position 64 per cent of the time in 1973.

The President would be impeachable, he has said, for "conduct which, exposed to the light of day, produces moral outrage among the people that causes them to believe that he is no longer fit to serve."

David W. Dennis, 61, represents the industrial and agricultural 10th district of Indiana (Muncie and Richmond). He is a criminal defense lawyer and former state legislator who was elected to the House in 1969. Considered a "feisty" and tenacious advocate, Dennis is expected to face a tough fight for his seat in 1974. He supported Nixon on 76 per cent of the votes in 1973.

Hamilton Fish Jr., 47, represents the Hudson River communities of New York's 25th district (outer New York City suburbs, farms and small industrial towns). A moderate Republican first elected to the House in 1968, Fish supported Nixon on 49 per cent of the votes in 1973. He has said that an impeachable offense is not necessarily an indictable offense.

Wiley Mayne, 56, represents Iowa's agricultural 6th district (northwest). He is a former FBI agent and trial attorney who was elected to the House in 1966. He won with only 52 per cent of the vote in 1972, and is likely to face a strong challenge in the 1974 election. He supported Nixon on 70 per cent of the votes in 1973. Mayne feels that an impeachable offense must be a crime.

Lawrence J. Hogan, 45, represents the Washington, D.C., suburbs of Maryland's 5th district. A former FBI agent, elected to the House in 1968, Hogan is a strong conservative and supported Nixon on 67 per cent of the votes in 1973. He has stated: "We ought to disqualify those members from the grand jury (the House Judiciary Committee considering impeachment charges) who have said that the President ought to be impeached."

M. Caldwell Butler, 48, represents the traditionally Republican 6th district of Virginia (western, Roanoke). He is a former Republican leader in the state assembly and campaign manager for former Rep. Richard H. Poff (R 1952–72), who also was a Judiciary Committee member. Butler was elected in 1972 to fill Poff's seat. He supported Nixon's position 75 per cent of the time in 1973. "The time has come to impeach or cease fire," he has said.

William S. Cohen, 33, represents Maine's 2nd district, which includes Bangor, a city of which he was formerly mayor. Elected in 1972 to his first House term after a walking campaign, he has been mentioned as a possible gubernatorial candidate. He is an articulate and independent-thinking Republican, and is considered by his colleagues as one of the brightest young members on the committee. Cohen supported Nixon on 53 per cent of the votes in 1973. In defining an impeachable offense, he has said: "It's like Robert Frost on love. It's indefinable and unmistakable—I know it when I see it."

Trent Lott, 32, represents the rapidly growing resort and industrial areas of Mississippi's 5th district (southeast). Formerly administrative assistant to now-retired Rep. William M. Colmer (D Miss. 1933–1973), Lott became a Republican and won Colmer's seat in 1972. A very conservative member, he supported Nixon's position 69 per cent of the time in 1973.

Harold V. Froehlich, 41, represents Wisconsin's rural 8th district (northeast). He is former speaker of the state assembly, and has maintained his reputation as an extreme fiscal conservative. He was elected to the House by a narrow margin in 1972 and faces a hard contest in 1974 to hold his seat. He supported Nixon's position 60 per cent of the time in 1973.

Carlos J. Moorhead, 51, represents the conservative white-collar 20th district of California (Los Angeles). A former state assemblyman, he supported Nixon on 70 per cent of the votes during 1973. Impeachment should only come for criminal acts, he maintains.

Joseph J. Maraziti, 61, represents the new rural 13th district in New Jersey (west). He is a former judge and state legislator. A moderate, he supported Nixon's position 61 per cent of the time in 1973.

Delbert L. Latta, 53, represents the largely agricultural 5th district of Ohio (northwest). Latta, a veteran Republican legislator, was first elected to the House in 1958. A conservative, Latta supported President Nixon's position 72 per cent of the time in 1973. Latta says "all impeachment proceedings must be defined within the confines of the Constitution, nothing more, nothing less."

Points to Ponder

- How does the issue of tape erasure make you feel about President Nixon's defense of his actions in Watergate? Even if Nixon didn't have anything to do with the erasure, do you think he was working with others to obstruct justice?

- By early 1974, Congress was looking into allegations that Nixon acted improperly in a number of incidents. Lawmakers wanted to know whether Nixon raised milk price supports and intervened in a federal anti-trust case in exchange for campaign contributions. Do you think that Watergate was just one piece of a pattern of improper behavior by Nixon? Or had members of Congress become so suspicious of Nixon that they began to question many of his actions?

CQ CONGRESSIONAL QUARTERLY WEEKLY REPORT, FEBRUARY 9, 1974

With features from February 23 and March 2, 9, 16, 23, and April 6, 1974

APPROVAL OF SUBPOENA POWER FOR JUDICIARY COMMITTEE

In the early months of 1974, support grew in Congress for launching impeachment proceedings against a president for the first time in more than a century. Even former supporters of Nixon grew impatient with his refusal to cooperate with Congress and turn over important documents. Members of the House Judiciary Committee threatened to issue subpoenas, or legal orders, to try to force the president to cooperate. At the same time, top White House aides were formally charged with crimes in court.

In perhaps the most dangerous challenge to Nixon, the House of Representatives overwhelmingly gave support for the House Judiciary Committee to examine impeachment. The 410–4 vote on Feb. 6 granted the committee special power to issue subpoenas to obtain information from the White House. The legislation would enable committee members to look at a wide range of alleged administration abuses.

Some Republicans tried to modify the legislation by imposing a deadline on the committee's efforts to consider impeachment and giving more clout to committee Republicans. But Democrats, who were in the majority in the House, successfully resisted such efforts. They did, however, accede to some Republican requests, such as granting the senior Republican on the Judiciary Committee the authority to issue subpoenas.

By March, the committee had made plans to examine six types of alleged White House misdeeds:

- Domestic surveillance, such as using wiretaps to listen in on conversations by government officials and reporters.
- Political campaign tactics, including so-called dirty tricks that Nixon's re-election campaign used against popular Democratic candidates in 1972.
- The Watergate break-in and coverup, including the possible use of "hush money" to prevent the seven original Watergate defendants from speaking out. The Watergate investigation would also look into the firing of the first Watergate special prosecutor, Archibald Cox, and the tapes of private presidential conversations.
- Nixon's personal finances, including his apparent underpayment of taxes.

- Campaign fund abuses, such as allegations that Nixon gave political favors to special interests that made large donations to his re-election campaign.
- Other misconduct, especially the administration's secret orders to bomb Cambodia in 1971.

NIXON'S RESISTANCE

Despite facing growing criticism, Nixon vowed to fight his critics. He repeatedly ruled out the option of resigning. He also predicted that he would not be impeached. In his State of the Union speech at the end of January, he urged the nation to put Watergate behind it. "One year of Watergate is enough," he declared. (The State of the Union speech is an annual address by the president that lays out top priorities for the coming year.) He also vowed to "fight like hell" to keep his office. One reason that Nixon gave for battling the allegations is that he said he was innocent of any wrongdoing. Another reason was that no president had ever resigned. For him to step down after winning re-election by an overwhelming margin could weaken the office of the presidency, Nixon warned. "If the President resigned when he was not guilty of charges, then every president in the future could be forced out of office by simply leveling the charges and getting the media to carry them, and getting a few congressmen and senators who were on the other side to exploit them," he said.

Nixon promised to work with Watergate investigators. In his State of the Union speech, he said he would cooperate "in any way I consider consistent with my responsibility to the office of the presidency." But he exasperated both his supporters and his opponents by repeatedly ruling out turning over critical documents, including tapes of White House conversations. When Judiciary Committee leaders asked for tapes of more than 40 conversations between Nixon and his aides about the Watergate scandal, the president refused. He also rejected requests for documents from special prosecutor Leon Jaworski.

Nixon made the same arguments he had raised the previous year when the Watergate grand jury and the Senate Watergate Committee requested tapes and other documents. He said many of the documents contained private information. If they were made public, it could damage the national interest. "The reason we cannot go that far" in turning over documents, explained Nixon on March 15, "isn't a question that the President has something to hide. It is the fact that every president, Democrat and Republican, from the founding of this republic, has recognized the necessity of protecting the confidentiality of presidential conversations. . . . And if that confidentiality principle is completely destroyed, future presidents will not have the benefit of the kind of advice an executive needs to make the right decisions."

The president offered to meet with members of the Judiciary Committee. But he said he would not consent to being cross-examined, or questioned under oath. He also said the courts had no power to force him to turn over confidential information.

Although Nixon was trying to protect himself, his stubbornness actually weakened his position. Democrats and Republicans on the Judiciary Committee had clashed for months over how to handle impeachment. But they closed ranks in the face of Nixon's repeated refusals to turn over documents. They believed he was challenging the right of Congress to conduct a thorough investigation. Many Democrats on the House Judiciary Committee, as well as a number of Republicans, began warning the White House that they would vote to issue subpoenas if Nixon did not cooperate. A subpoena could put Nixon in a difficult corner. If he refused to comply with it, the House might impeach him for contempt of Congress. But if he did comply, he would be turning over evidence that could show he or his top aides participated in criminal activities.

By March, leading Republicans were warning Nixon that he had to cooperate or face impeachment. Republican Rep. Lawrence J. Hogan of Maryland, a member of the Judiciary Committee, warned that the president "will lose even those on the committee who are trying to keep an open mind." Republican Sen. Charles H. Percy of Illinois said he would vote to convict Nixon if the president defied a Supreme Court ruling to comply with a Judiciary Committee subpoena. Even Sen. James L. Buckley, a conservative Republican from New York and one-time staunch Nixon supporter, called on the president to resign.

CHARGES AGAINST WHITE HOUSE AIDES

As Nixon battled to keep his office, many of his top aides were brought before criminal courts. At the end of January, former White House aide Egil Krogh was sentenced to six months in prison for approving the burglary of the office of a psychiatrist who had treated Daniel Ellsberg. (Ellsberg

was a former Pentagon staffer who leaked the Pentagon Papers. For more about him and the Pentagon Papers, see page 44.) The following month, former attorney general John N. Mitchell and former commerce secretary Maurice H. Stans—both of whom worked on Nixon's re-election campaign—went on trial in New York City. They faced charges of obstruction of justice, perjury, and conspiracy. Mitchell and Stans were the first former cabinet members in 50 years to be tried on criminal charges.

Nixon's credibility suffered another blow on March 1. The Watergate grand jury indicted seven men, including three of Nixon's former top aides: H. R. Haldeman, John D. Ehrlichman, and Mitchell. The men were charged with misleading FBI agents and the Senate Watergate Committee, concealing or destroying documents, secretly paying cash to help the defendants, and trying to block the FBI, CIA, and Justice Department from working honestly and impartially. Much attention focused on the grand jury's conclusion that Haldeman had lied about a conversation with Nixon in 1973. According to Haldeman, Nixon was told in this conversation that one of the Watergate burglars had threatened to reveal key details of the Watergate scandal unless he was paid $120,000. Haldeman had testified that Nixon said it would be wrong to buy the defendant's silence. The fact that the grand jury concluded that Haldeman was lying raised questions about Nixon's handling of the so-called "hush money." The press also noted that Nixon had publicly backed Haldeman's recollection of the conversation.

Even as he was trying to survive Watergate, Nixon faced difficulties on another front. Both the Internal Revenue Service and a congressional tax committee concluded that he had underpaid his income taxes by hundreds of thousands of dollars. Eager to avoid a drawn-out battle, Nixon quickly agreed to pay $467,000 in back taxes.

Meanwhile, the Senate Watergate Committee began fading from the scene. It lost a court battle to obtain additional White House tapes in early February because a judge worried that any publicity arising from the tapes could make it harder to put Watergate defendants on trial. On Feb. 19, the seven-member committee decided to hold no more public hearings. It did not want to interfere with the impeachment proceedings in the House or with criminal trials in court. Instead, the committee would continue its work in private. It would put its energy into issuing its final report on Watergate and recommendations for legislation to prevent future scandals. From now on, the focus would be on the House of Representatives, with its powers of impeachment.

With only four members voting "nay," the House Feb. 6 formally granted the Judiciary Committee power to investigate the conduct of President Nixon to determine whether there were grounds for his impeachment.

By a 410–4 vote, the House approved H Res 803, explicitly authorizing the committee to conduct the inquiry—already under way—and granting it special subpoena power during the inquiry. Voting against approval were four Republicans: Ben B. Blackburn of Georgia, Earl F. Landgrebe of Indiana, Carlos J. Moorhead of California, the only Judiciary Committee member of the four, and David C. Treen of Louisiana.

Republican committee members tried to amend the resolution to add a deadline for the committee's action, to limit the scope of the subpoena power and to secure an equal right for the Republican minority to subpoena witnesses. All amendment efforts failed when the House, by a 342–70 vote, approved a procedural motion, offered by Peter W. Rodino Jr. (D N.J.), chairman of the committee, moving the resolution directly to a vote and thereby barring any amendments.

The committee had reported the resolution unanimously on Jan. 31.

Committee Views

"The committee's investigative authority is intended to be fully coextensive with the power of the House in an impeachment investigation—with respect to the persons who may be required to respond, the methods by which response may be required, and the types of information and materials required to be furnished and produced," stated the Judiciary Committee's report (H Rept 93-774) on H Res 803, filed Feb. 1.

Emphasizing the intention of the investigation to proceed "in all respects on a fair, impartial and bipartisan basis," the report emphasized the joint exercise of subpoena power by the chairman and ranking minority member to ensure maximum flexibility and bipartisanship.

Deadline Opposed. On the matter of a deadline, the report stated: "It is not now possible to predict the course and duration of its inquiry. . . . Establishment of dates would be unrealistic and thus misleading. The committee was anxious to avoid an arbitrary deadline that might ultimately operate as an unnecessary hindrance to an early and just conclusion to its inquiry."

In additional views, Robert McClory (R Ill.), Lawrence J. Hogan (R Md.) and Joseph J. Maraziti (R N.J.) explained the need for a deadline and expressed the hope that Rodino would yield for such an amendment.

Relevance of Inquiry. Setting forth his case for an amendment restricting to those which were relevant to the inquiry the materials and witnesses which the committee could compel, Charles E. Wiggins (R Calif.) said that without such an amendment the resolution would authorize the committee "to engage in a politically motivated witch hunt. . . . It is not enough that good-faith disclaimers of any such intention have been repeatedly made by the chairman. . . . Rules must be fashioned which require the future performance which now is only promised."

In separate views, Moorhead (R Calif.) disapproved of "this overly broad grant of the subpoena power" which, he said, "can only precipitate a constitutional confrontation."

Fairness. David W. Dennis (R Ind.), Wiggins, Wiley Mayne (R Iowa), Hogan, M. Caldwell Butler (R Va.), Trent Lott (R Miss.), Maraziti and Robert F. Drinan (D Mass.) urged an amendment to allow either the chairman or the ranking minority member to exercise the subpoena power without fear of being overridden by the full committee.

Their amendment would have deleted language in H Res 803 authorizing the full committee to resolve any disagreement between the two men over a subpoena. If the amendment were not adopted, said its proponents, the inquiry would be launched "under ground rules which deliberately build in an inherent bias and inequity."

Floor Debate

"Whatever the result, we are going to be just and honorable and worthy of the public trust," said Committee Chairman Rodino in opening debate on the resolution. "We cannot turn away, out of partisanship or convenience, from problems that are now . . . our inescapable responsibility to consider. It would be a violation of our own public trust if we . . . chose not to inquire, not to consult, not even to deliberate, and then to pretend that we had not, by default, made choices."

After Rodino explained the contents and purpose of the resolution, he yielded small portions of the hour of debate under his control to various members on each side of the aisle "for the purposes of debate only." Because of the privileged nature of H Res 803, amendments could only be offered to it under two circumstances: if Rodino agreed to yield time for an amendment or if the House rejected the move to bring the resolution to an immediate vote.

"I will not join" in a subpoena of the President, announced ranking Republican committee member

Edward Hutchinson (R Mich.). The question of such a subpoena was to be referred to the full committee for a decision, under an agreement previously reached between Hutchinson and Rodino. Furthermore, Hutchinson made clear that he would join in issuing subpoenas only if he knew exactly what they sought and if the information had been requested previously and sought by less coercive means.

TEXT OF H RES 803

Following is the text of H Res 803, as approved by the House Feb. 6:

Resolved, That the Committee on the Judiciary, acting as a whole or by any subcommittee thereof appointed by the chairman for the purposes hereof and in accordance with the rules of the committee, is authorized and directed to investigate fully and completely whether sufficient grounds exist for the House of Representatives to exercise its constitutional power to impeach Richard M. Nixon, President of the United States of America. The committee shall report to the House of Representatives such resolutions, articles of impeachment, or other recommendations as it deems proper.

SEC. 2. (a) For the purpose of making such investigation, the committee is authorized to require—

(1) by subpoena or otherwise—

(A) the attendance and testimony of any person (including at a taking of a deposition by counsel for the committee); and

(B) the production of such things; and

(2) by interrogatory, the furnishing of such information; as it deems necessary to such investigation.

(b) Such authority of the committee may be exercised—

(1) by the chairman and the ranking minority member acting jointly, or, if either declines to act, by the other acting alone, except that in the event either so declines, either shall have the right to refer to the committee for decision the question whether such authority shall be so exercised and the committee shall be

convened promptly to render that decision; or

(2) by the committee acting as a whole or by subcommittee.

Subpoenas and interrogatories so authorized may be issued over the signature of the chairman, or ranking minority member, or any member designated by either of them, and may be served by any person designated by the chairman, or ranking minority member, or any member designated by either of them. The chairman, or ranking minority member, or any member designated by either of them (or, with respect to any deposition, answer to interrogatory, or affidavit, any person authorized by law to administer oaths) may administer oaths to any witness. For the purpose of this section, "things" includes, without limitation, books, records, correspondence, logs, journals, memorandums, papers, documents, writings, drawings, graphs, charts, photographs, reproductions, recordings, tapes, transcripts, printouts, data compilations from which information can be obtained (translated if necessary, through detection devices into reasonably usable form), tangible objects, and other things of any kind.

SEC. 3. For the purpose of making such investigation, the committee, and any subcommittee thereof, are authorized to sit and act, without regard to clause 31 of rule XI of the Rules of the House of Representatives, during the present Congress at such times and places within or without the United States, whether the House is meeting, has recessed, or has adjourned, and to hold such hearings, as it deems necessary.

SEC. 4. Any funds made available to the Committee on the Judiciary under House Resolution 702 of the Ninety-third Congress, adopted November 15, 1973, or made available for the purpose hereafter, may be expended for the purpose of carrying out the investigation authorized and directed by this resolution.

"The majority of this committee is doing everything possible to avoid partisanship," said Walter Flowers (D Ala.). Jack Brooks (D Texas) admonished the Republican to cooperate with the committee leadership, describing Rodino's sharing of the subpoena power with Hutchinson as "unprecedented" and indicating "bipartisan intent."

But Republicans still complained about the implementation of the inquiry and the subpoena power. McClory argued for inclusion of some deadline date in H Res 803. Wiggins described as "inherently unfair" the provisions allowing the full committee by majority vote to resolve any disputes between Hutchinson and Rodino over the issuance of a subpoena, an argument in which Drinan expressed support. Wiggins also pointed out the need for ensuring that all material subpoenaed was relevant to the inquiry and obtained from Rodino and Hutchinson assurances that relevance was implicit in the word "necessary" as used in H Res 803.

But Minority Leader John J. Rhodes (R Ariz.) stated that he would vote for Rodino's procedural motion and thus oppose any amendments, saying that the chairman's promise of a report by April 30 was sufficient for him. And committee Republican Tom Railsback (R Ill.) said he would not seek to amend the resolution: "We fought the procedural battle in committee, and we lost it. The amendments I supported then are not essential."

The House then adopted Rodino's motion on a 342–70 vote, and followed this vote with the 410–4 approval of H Res 803.

"This power authorizes the appearance of the President under compulsion if necessary," said Jerome R Waldie (D Calif.), a committee member and sponsor of one of many impeachment resolutions. "No other forum can do so during his tenure. . . . Only through his appearance can he be required to disclose what he has so far refused to disclose; his appearance is essential."

Nixon's Refusal on Tapes: 'Not in National Interest'

President Nixon refused during the week ending Feb. 9 to turn over any more tapes to either the Watergate special prosecutor or the Senate Watergate Committee.

Special Prosecutor. The battle continued between Nixon's lawyers and special prosecutor Leon Jaworski over whether Jaworski had all the evidence he needed to complete his Watergate investigation. Nixon said in his state of the union message Jan.

30 that he had. The President's special Watergate counsel, James D. St. Clair, hinted the next day that the time had come to halt the flow of White House material to the prosecutor.

Jaworski said Feb. 3 in a television interview that the White House had not turned over all the materials he had requested, and he indicated he would not hesitate to subpoena them if necessary. The White House responded with a lengthy communication, reportedly a refusal to turn over more material, but neither side would discuss the contents until a meeting between Jaworski and St. Clair had been held.

Watergate Committee. Nixon's refusal to give the Senate Watergate Committee five tapes it sought was explained in a letter Feb. 6 from the President to U.S. District Judge Gerhard A. Gesell. Gesell on Jan. 25 had directed Nixon to explain personally why he had refused.

Nixon wrote that "out of respect for the court" he would answer, but reiterated his position that the courts had no power to force him to give up material he wanted to keep confidential. He said disclosure of the contents of the five tapes "would not be in the national interest."

The President said that giving the tapes to the Watergate committee would amount to giving them to "the world at large," violating the principle of confidentiality of presidential communications. He said the committee's request was a political question and "inappropriate for resolution by the judicial branch."

In addition, Nixon said, disclosing the contents of the tapes could have adverse effects on criminal proceedings in Watergate-related cases.

Jaworski, who was asked by the judge to comment on that question, said four of the tapes contained material to be used as evidence in forthcoming trials, but indicated their release would have only marginal effects on pretrial publicity. He suggested they could be turned over to the Watergate committee on the condition that they may not be made public.

Letter Text. The text of Nixon's letter follows:

I have been advised by special counsel to the President of the order issued by you on January 25, 1974, in which you solicited my personal response with reference to five specified taped conversations.

As indicated in the various briefs, pleadings and other papers filed in this proceeding, it is my belief that the issue before this court constitutes a nonjusticiable political question.

Nevertheless, out of respect for this court, but without in any way departing from my views that the issues presented here are inappropriate for resolution by the judicial branch, I have made a determination that the entirety of the five recordings of Presidential conversations described on the subpoena issued by the Senate Select Committee on Presidential Campaign Activities contains privileged communications, the disclosure of which would not be in the national interest.

I am taking this position for two primary reasons. First, the Senate select committee has made known its intention to make these materials public. Unlike the secret use of four out of five of these conversations before the grand jury, the publication of all of these tapes to the world at large would seriously infringe upon the principle of confidentiality, which is vital to the performance of my constitutional responsibilities as President.

Second, it is incumbent upon me to be sensitive to the possible adverse effects upon ongoing and forthcoming criminal proceedings should the contents of these subpoenaed conversations be made public at an inappropriate time. The dangers connected with excessive pretrial publicity are as well known to this court as they are to me. Consequently, my constitutional mandate to see that the laws are faithfully executed requires my prohibiting the disclosure of any of these materials at this time and in this forum.

IMPEACHABLE OFFENSE: OPINION OF INQUIRY STAFF

Reprinted from *Congressional Quarterly Weekly Report,* February 23, 1974

A major task for Congress was determining whether Nixon had a role in the Watergate coverup. That involved learning more about Nixon's actions. But another key issue had to do with the Constitution. What sort of presidential misdeeds should be punishable by impeachment? The Constitution is vague on this matter. It states that impeachment may be triggered by "Treason, Bribery, or other high Crimes and Misdemeanors." Nowhere does it give any further detail about the types of high crimes and misdemeanors that should be considered grounds for impeachment.

Staff members of the House Judiciary Committee conducted an in-depth study of the issue. They concluded that impeachment is intended for an officeholder who had violated his public duties or seriously undermined public confidence. Such an official might have misused government funds, abused his power, or neglected his duties. Whether the officeholder actually broke the law may be a secondary consideration, the report said. "Some of the most grievous offenses against our constitutional form of government may not entail violations of the criminal law," stated the report.

Nixon's lawyers reached a different conclusion. They contended that the Constitution was meant to replace arbitrary political decisions with a system of laws. For that reason, the Constitution stipulated that a president could be removed only for violating the law, not for political actions. They pointed out that the Constitution specifically uses the word "crimes" in its description of impeachment. "American impeachment was not designed to force a President into surrendering executive authority," they argued, "but to check overtly criminal actions as they are defined by law."

This was not just an academic debate. Under the interpretation of the Constitution put forward by the Judiciary Committee, Nixon was in grave peril. He faced multiple allegations of having misused his office. Nixon's actions had unquestionably undermined public trust in the presidency. But under the interpretation of

Nixon's lawyers, the House would have a much harder time impeaching Nixon. That is because doubt existed over whether Nixon had actually engaged in a crime. Proving that Nixon had broken the law would be difficult, especially if the president refused to turn over vital evidence such as tapes of White House conversations.

Democrats and Republicans generally had differing views of impeachment. To Peter J. Rodino of New Jersey, the Democratic chairman of the House Judiciary Committee, there was no need to prove that Nixon broke the law. "It has been my view all along that grounds for impeachment need not arise out of criminal conduct." But the committee's senior Republican, Edward Hutchinson of Michigan, said the president could be impeached only if he had been personally involved in criminal acts.

The impeachment of President Bill Clinton in 1998 sparked a similar debate. But the issues were largely reversed. Clinton was accused of making false statements under oath about a private matter: his relationship with a White House intern. That would be a violation of the law. But it was debatable whether he had misused his office. For more about the Clinton impeachment, see page 133.

Following are excerpts from a Feb. 20 memorandum prepared by the impeachment inquiry staff of the House Judiciary Committee:

THE HISTORICAL ORIGINS OF THE IMPEACHMENT PROCESS

"The Constitution provides that the President '... shall be removed from Office on Impeachment for, and Conviction of, Treason, Bribery, or other high Crimes and Misdemeanors.' The framers could have written simply 'or other crimes'.... They did not do that.... They adopted instead a unique phrase used for centuries in English parliamentary impeachments....

"Two points emerge from the 400 years of English parliamentary experience with the phrase.... First, the particular allegations of misconduct, alleged damage to the state in such forms as misapplication of funds, abuse of official power, neglect of duty, encroachment on Parliament's prerogatives, corrup-

tion, and betrayal of trust. Second, the phrase ... was confined to parliamentary impeachments; it had no roots in the ordinary criminal law, and the particular allegations of misconduct under that heading were not necessarily limited to common law or statutory derelictions or crimes.

"**The Intention of the Framers.** The debates on impeachment at the Constitutional Convention ... focus principally on its applicability to the President.... Impeachment was to be one of the central elements of executive responsibility....

"The framers intended impeachment to be a constitutional safeguard of the public trust, the powers of government conferred upon the President ... and the division of powers....

"**The American Impeachment Cases.** ... Does Article III, Section 1 of the Constitution, which states that judges 'shall hold their Offices during good Behavior,' limit the relevance of the ten impeachments of judges with respect to presidential impeachment standards as has been argued...? It does not....

"Each of the thirteen American impeachments involved charges of misconduct incompatible with the official position of the officeholder. This conduct falls into three broad categories: (1) exceeding the constitutional bounds of the powers of the office in derogation of the powers of another branch of government; (2) behaving in a manner grossly incompatible with the proper function and purpose of the office; and (3) employing the power of the office for an improper purpose or for personal gain....

"In drawing up articles of impeachment, the House has placed little emphasis on criminal conduct. Less than one-third of the eighty-three articles the House has adopted have explicitly charged the violation of a criminal statute or used the word 'criminal' or 'crime' to describe the conduct alleged....

"Much more common in the articles are allegations that the officer has violated his duties or his oath or seriously undermined public confidence in his ability to perform his official functions....

"All have involved charges of conduct incompatible with continued performance of the office; some have explicitly rested upon a 'course of conduct'.... Some of the individual articles seem to have alleged conduct that, taken alone, would not have been considered serious....

THE CRIMINALITY ISSUE

"The central issue ... is whether requiring an indictable offense as an essential element of impeachable conduct is consistent with the purposes and intent of the framers....

"Impeachment and the criminal law serve fundamentally different purposes. Impeachment is the first step in a remedial process.... The purpose ... is not personal punishment; its function is primarily to maintain constitutional government....

"The general applicability of the criminal law also makes it inappropriate as the standard.... In an impeachment proceeding a President is called to account for abusing powers which only a President possesses.

"Impeachable conduct ... may include the serious failure to discharge the affirmative duties imposed on the President by the Constitution. Unlike a criminal case, the cause for removal ... may be based on his entire course of conduct in office.... It may be a course of conduct more than individual acts that has a tendency to subvert constitutional government.

"To confine impeachable conduct to indictable offenses may well be to set a standard so restrictive as not to reach conduct that might adversely affect the system of government. Some of the most grievous offenses against our constitutional form of government may not entail violations of the criminal law....

"To limit impeachable conduct to criminal offenses would be incompatible with the evidence ... and would frustrate the purpose that the framers intended....

CONCLUSION

"In the English practice and in several of the American impeachments, the criminality issue was not raised at all. The emphasis has

been on the significant effects of the conduct.... Impeachment was evolved ... to cope with both the inadequacy of criminal standards and the impotence of the courts to deal with the conduct of great public figures. It would be anomalous if the framers, having barred criminal sanctions from the impeachment remedy ... intended to restrict the grounds for impeachment to conduct that was criminal.

"The longing for precise criteria is understandable.... However, where the issue is presidential compliance with the constitutional requirements and limitations on the presidency, the crucial factor is not the intrinsic quality of behavior but the significance of its effects upon our constitutional system or the functioning of our government.

IMPEACHABLE OFFENSE: OPINION OF NIXON ATTORNEYS

Reprinted from *Congressional Quarterly Weekly Report*, March 23, 1974

Following are excerpts from a Feb. 28 analysis prepared by James D. St. Clair, John J. Chester, Michael A. Sterlacci, Jerome J. Murphy and Loren A. Smith, attorneys for President Nixon:

ENGLISH BACKGROUND OF CONSTITUTIONAL IMPEACHMENT PROVISIONS

"The Framers felt that the English system permitted men ... to make arbitrary decisions, and one of their primary purposes in creating a Constitution was to replace this arbitrariness with a system based on the rule of law.... They felt impeachment was a necessary check on a President who might commit a crime, but they did not want to see the vague standards of the English system that made impeachment a weapon to achieve parliamentary supremacy....

"To argue that the President may be impeached for something less than a criminal offense, with all the safeguards that definition implies, would be a monumental step backwards into all those old English practices that our Constitution sought to eliminate. American impeachment was not designed to force a President into surrendering executive authority . . . but to check overtly criminal actions as they are defined by law. . . .

"The terminology 'high crimes and misdemeanors' should create no confusion or ambiguity. . . . It was a unitary phrase meaning crimes against the state, as opposed to those against individuals. . . . It is as ridiculous to say that 'misdemeanor' must mean something beyond 'crime' as it is to suggest that in the phrase 'bread and butter issues' butter issues must be different from bread issues. . . .

THE CONSTITUTIONAL CONVENTION
"It is evident from the actual debate and from the events leading up to it that Morris' remark that 'An election of every four years will prevent maladministration,' expressed the will of the Convention. Thus, the impeachment provision adopted was designed to deal exclusively with indictable criminal conduct. . . . The Convention rejected all non-criminal definitions of impeachable offenses. . . . To distort the clear meaning of the phrase 'treason, bribery or other high crimes and misdemeanors' by including non-indictable conduct would thus most certainly violate the Framers' intent."

LEGAL MEANING OF IMPEACHMENT PROVISION
"Just as statutes are to be construed to uphold the intent of the drafters . . . so should we uphold the intent of the drafters of the Constitution that impeachable offenses be limited to criminal violations. Also as penal statutes have been strictly construed in favor of the accused, so should we construe the impeachment provisions of the Constitution. . . .

AMERICAN IMPEACHMENT PRECEDENTS
"Some of the proponents of presidential impeachment place great emphasis on the cases involving federal judges to support the proposition that impeachment will lie for conduct which does not of itself constitute an indictable offense. This view is appar-

ently most appealing to those broad constructionists who favoring a severely weakened Chief Executive argue that certain non-criminal 'political' offenses may justify impeachment. . . .

"The Framers . . . distinguished between the President and judges concerning the standard to be employed for an impeachment. Otherwise the 'good behavior' clause is a nullity. . . .

"The precedent . . . asserted by the House in 1804 that a judge may be impeached for a breach of good behavior was reasserted again with full force over one hundred years later in 1912. . . .

"The fact that the House . . . felt it necessary to make a distinction in the impeachment standards between the Judiciary and the Executive reinforces the obvious—that the words 'treason, bribery, and other high crimes and misdemeanors' are limited solely to indictable crimes and cannot extend to misbehavior. . . .

"The acquittal of President Johnson over a century ago strongly indicates that the Senate has refused to adopt a broad view of 'other high crimes and misdemeanors'. . . . Impeachment of a President should be resorted to only for cases of the gravest kind—the commission of a crime named in the Constitution or a criminal offense against the laws of the United States. If there is any doubt as to the gravity of an offense or as to a President's conduct or motives, the doubt should be resolved in his favor. This is the necessary price for having an independent executive. . . .

CONCLUSION: PROPER STANDARD FOR PRESIDENTIAL IMPEACHMENT
"Any analysis that broadly construes the power to impeach and convict can be reached only . . . by placing a subjective gloss on the history of impeachment that results in permitting the Congress to do whatever it deems most politic. The intent of the Framers, who witnessed episode after episode of outrageous abuse of the impeachment power by the self-righteous English Parliament, was to restrict the *political* reach of the impeachment power.

"Those who seek to broaden the impeachment power invite the use of power 'as a means of crushing political adversaries or ejecting them from office.'.... The acceptance of such an invitation would be destructive to our system of government and to the fundamental principle of separation of powers.... The Framers never intended that the impeachment clause serve to dominate or destroy the executive branch of the government...."

NIXON ON IMPEACHMENT

Reprinted from *Congressional Quarterly Weekly Report*, March 2, 1974

President Nixon declared at his Feb. 25 White House news conference that he did not believe he would be impeached and that he would not resign to save Republicans from losses at the polls in November.

"I want my party to succeed," Nixon said, "but more important, I want the presidency to survive. And it is vitally important in this nation that the presidency of the United States not be hostage to what happens to the popularity of a president at one time or another."

Nixon said he thought 1974 would be a good year for Republican candidates who stood behind the administration's record of peace and prosperity.

The President was less combative than at previous meetings with the press when questioned about Watergate-related matters.

Nixon revealed that he had refused a request to testify before a Watergate grand jury and that his counter-offer, to respond to questions in writing or to meet with the Watergate special prosecutor, had been turned down.

Impeachment. The President said he accepted the opinion of his White House counsel and some other constitutional lawyers that "a criminal offense on the part of the President is the requirement for impeachment," rather than some other criteria such as dereliction of duty.

Asked if it would not be in his best interest and that of the country to have the question of his involvement in Watergate resolved by impeachment, Nixon said: "Well, a full impeachment trial in the Senate under our Constitution comes only when the House determines that there is an impeachable offense. It is my belief that the House, after it conducts its inquiry, will not reach that determination. I do not expect to be impeached."

Nixon reiterated his position that he would cooperate with the House Judiciary Committee's staff investigation of impeachment charges so long as this did not interfere with his concept of executive privilege.

Taxes. Nixon said he would pay California income taxes if required to do so. He added that he would withdraw the federal income tax deduction he claimed for donating his vice presidential papers if it were determined that the deduction was improper. The President asserted at another point that similar deductions had been claimed in the past by a number of other public figures.

Kalmbach. Nixon denied that he had been consulted about an offer by his personal lawyer, Herbert W. Kalmbach, to a 1970 Republican campaign contributor, of a European ambassadorship in return for a $100,000 contribution. However, Nixon said, he had begun an inquiry at the White House to determine who was responsible for approving the offer. "I would go further and say that ambassadorships cannot be purchased, and I would not approve an ambassadorship unless the man or woman was qualified, clearly apart from any contributions," Nixon said.

AREAS OF INQUIRY

Reprinted from *Congressional Quarterly Weekly Report*, March 9, 1974

These were the six major areas of charges against President Nixon that were under investigation by the special staff assembled by the House Judiciary Committee:

- **Domestic surveillance**—which included the activities of the investigative unit known as the White House "plumbers," the use of wiretaps to overhear the conversations of newsmen and White House personnel, and the offer of a possible post as FBI director, made by former presidential assistant John D. Ehrlichman to the federal judge who presided over the Pentagon Papers case. As of March 1, the inquiry staff reported that arrangements for interviewing witnesses on these charges had begun.
- **Intelligence operations related to the 1973 presidential election**—which included the "dirty tricks" campaign and coverup. A preliminary report on the information gathered on these matters was under review for a decision on "precisely what additional evidence and witness interviews are needed . . . to complete these investigations," the staff reported March 5.
- **Watergate break-in and coverup**—which included the possible use of "hush money" for the seven original Watergate defendants, the firing of the first Watergate special prosecutor, Archibald Cox, and the presidential tapes and their gaps. The preliminary reports in this area were under review; "testimony and exhibits sealed by court order in Watergate-related litigation have not yet been obtained," the staff reported March 5.
- **Personal finances**—which included the President's gift of his vice presidential papers to the government, the sale of his New York apartment and improvements to Key Biscayne, Fla., and San Clemente, Calif., homes and grounds. "For several months the federal income tax affairs of the President have been the subject of an extensive investigation by the Joint Committee on Internal Revenue Taxation. . . . The results . . . will become available shortly," the report stated. "The inquiry staff is prepared to begin immediately to assimilate the results. . . . Meanwhile, the inquiry staff is preparing tentative lists of witnesses. . . and documents to be sought."
- **Political use of executive agencies; campaign fund abuses**—which included 26 individual allegations, among them those concerning the contributions from milk producers and from financier Robert L. Vesco. Requests for information concerning these charges had gone from the committee to several executive departments and independent agencies, said the staff.
- **Other misconduct**—which included the bombing of Cambodia, the impoundment of funds and the dismantling of the Office of Economic Opportunity. The legal issues involved and past practices of other administrations in similar circumstances were under study, the staff reported. "Within the next two weeks senior members of the staff will determine which matters should be pursued further," the report said.

NIXON ON RESIGNATION: NO PLANS FOR 'AN EASY COP-OUT'

Reprinted from *Congressional Quarterly Weekly Report*, March 16, 1974

In a question-and-answer session before the Executives Club of Chicago March 15, President Nixon was asked: "Do you not think that the entire incident (Watergate) has begun to affect the quality of life in this country, particularly the great deal of uncertainties that people have about it, and also has begun to affect the concept of ethics, particularly in our young people? And for these reasons alone, would it not be better if you resigned at this time and allowed yourself the public forum as a private citizen to answer all accusations on all parts?"

This was Nixon's answer, as transcribed by Congressional Quarterly from a tape recording:

"Let me respond . . . first, by saying that of course Watergate has had a disturbing effect not only on young people but on other people. It was a wrong and very stupid action, to begin with. I have said that, I believe it now.

"Second, as far as Watergate is concerned, it has been carried on, it has been, I believe, over-publicized, and a lot of charges have been made that frankly have proved to be false. I'm sure that many people in this audience have read at one time or other either in your news magazines, possibly in a newspaper, certainly heard on television and radio, such charges as this:

- "That the President helped to plan the Watergate thing before and had knowledge of it.
- "That the President was informed of the coverup on September the 15th of 1973 (sic).
- "That the President was informed that payments were being made on March the 13th, and that a blackmail attempt was being made in the White House on March the 13th rather than on March 21st, when I said was the first time that those matters were brought to my attention.
- "That the President had authorized the issuance of clemency or a promise of clemency to some of the defendants, and that the President had ordered the burglarizing, again a very stupid act, part in the fact of its being wrong and illegal, of Dr. Ellsberg's psychiatrist's office in California.

"Now all of those charges have been made. Many of the Americans, perhaps the majority, believe them. They are all totally false, and the investigations will prove it. Whatever the Congress does, the tapes, etc., when they all come out, will establish that they are false.

"The President learned for the first time on March 21 of 1973 that the blackmail attempt was being made in the White House—not on March 13.

"The President learned for the first time at that time that payments had been made to the defendants, and let me point out that payments had been made. But correcting what may have been a misapprehension when I spoke to the press on March the 6th in Washington, it was alleged that the payments that had been made to defendants were made for the purpose of keeping them still. However, Mr. Ehrlichman, Mr. Haldeman, Mr. Mitchell have all denied that that was the case, and they certainly should be allowed the right in court to establish their innocence or guilt without our concluding that that was the case.

"Be that as it may, Watergate has hung over the country, and it continues to hang over the country. It will continue to as the Judiciary Committee continues its investigation, not only of the voluminous documents that we have already presented to the special prosecutor; not only of all the material they have from the Ervin committee that has conducted months of hearings—and they have access to that—but in addition, scores of tapes and thousands of documents more, which would mean that not just one year, but two years or three years we're going to have this hanging over the country.

"That's why I want a prompt and just conclusion and will cooperate . . . with the committee, consistent with my responsibilities to defend the office of the presidency, to get that prompt and just conclusion.

"Now under these circumstances, because the impression has been created, as you have very well indicated, doubts, mistrust of the President. I recognize that. Why doesn't the President resign? Because if the President resigned when he was not guilty of charges, then every president in the future could be forced out of office by simply leveling the charges and getting the media to carry them, and getting a few congressmen and senators who were on the other side to exploit them.

"Why doesn't the President resign because his popularity is low? I already have referred to that question, because if the time comes in this country when a president makes decisions based on where he stands in the polls rather than what is right or what is wrong, we'll have a very weak president. The nation and the world needs a strong president.

"Now, personally, I will say finally, from a personal standpoint, resignation is an easy cop-out. Resignation, of course, might satisfy some of my good, friendly partisans who would rather not have the problem of Watergate bother them. On the other hand, apart from the personal standpoint, resignation of this President on charges of which he is not guilty, resignation simply because he happened to be low in the polls, would forever change our form of government. It would lead to weak and unstable presidencies in the future, and I will not be a party to the destruction of the presidency of the United States."

TELEVISING AN IMPEACHMENT: A DISPUTED PROPOSITION

Reprinted from *Congressional Quarterly Weekly Report*, April 6, 1974

At the time of the Watergate scandal, the public could not count on watching Congress on television. C-Span coverage of House and Senate proceedings did not begin until the 1980s. On occasion, particularly important congressional hearings did receive live television coverage. As long ago as 1954, millions of Americans watched Senate hearings on Wisconsin senator Joseph R. McCarthy, who faced questions about possible misconduct in the so-called Army McCarthy Hearings. McCarthy's reputation collapsed when a lawyer at the hearing assailed him for unfairly accusing officials of Communist sympathies.

Senate Majority Leader Mike Mansfield's (D Mont.) March 28 assertion that a Senate impeachment trial should be televised touched off a controversy over the role of television in impeachment proceedings.

The immediate response from several Republicans was that Mansfield's statement was premature. "We are not addressing that issue until someone sends a resolution deal-

ing with it to the Senate Rules Committee," a spokesman for Senate Minority Leader Hugh Scott (R Pa.) told Congressional Quarterly.

"I think we ought to wait until we know if there's going to be a Senate trial before we talk about that," said Rep. David W. Dennis (R Ind.), a member of the House Judiciary Committee. "I'm not crazy about televising any proceedings, because I think they tend to lend a circus atmosphere."

Mansfield made the statement during a breakfast meeting with reporters at which he also said some members of the House had told him they believed there were enough votes to impeach Nixon.

A spokesman for Assistant Majority Leader Robert C. Byrd (D W.Va.) said he endorsed Mansfield's suggestion that the Senate proceedings be televised. Byrd, a long-time advocate of opening the Senate to television cameras, had suggested that any impeachment trial should be televised during a March 3 interview on NBC-TV's "Meet the Press."

Rep. Charles E. Wiggins (R Calif.), another member of the Judiciary Committee, told Congressional Quarterly he was doubtful that television coverage in the Senate would be proper. "The most important consideration is that this trial be fair and it ascertain the truth under a mechanism that insulates it from outside pressures and passions," Wiggins said. "That's much more important in my opinion than the value of some public access to the proceedings through television."

Senate sources noted that a resolution calling for televising an impeachment trial probably would not be introduced until after the House Judiciary Committee had acted on its staff's impeachment inquiry. "It would be anticipatory to act before that," said one source.

HOUSE ATTITUDES

In the meantime, support for televising a House floor debate on impeachment gathered strength in the wake of Mansfield's statement.

Rep. Sidney R. Yates (D Ill.) introduced a resolution (H Res 1028) April 4 calling for televising of House proceedings. Yates originally introduced a resolution (H Res 802) Jan. 31, 1973, seeking to open the chamber to radio and television. Since then he had been joined by 43 cosponsors, 36 Democrats and seven Republicans.

"Putting the House on the air would prove to be an invaluable way of enlightening our constituents on the meaning and importance of the constitutional process of impeachment," Yates said in an April 2 "Dear Colleague" letter seeking more cosponsors for his resolution. "Broadcasting the proceedings will provide a sense of immediacy and an all-pervasive eye and ear on the events which will transpire; thereby, giving our citizens a sense of participating in the operation of their government."

While he was firmly opposed to televising the Judiciary Committee's impeachment proceedings, Wiggins said he was less concerned about opening the floor of the House to television. "Television coverage of the House might prejudice a Senate trial," Wiggins said. "But the reality is, whether it's covered by television or not, it's going to be given such broad coverage that a senator would have to be literally isolated in an igloo somewhere to not be affected and be aware of what's going on. We're ultimately going to have to be confident that senators mean their oath when they take the oath to be guided solely by the evidence."

No Precedents

Live radio and television coverage of House or Senate proceedings, except for some joint sessions, apparently was unprecedented.

The Senate long had consented to live broadcasts of committee proceedings. The House banned such coverage from 1952 until late 1970, when the Legislative Reorganization Act carried a provision authorizing it at the discretion of a majority of each House committee.

Rule 4 of the Senate Manual's guidelines for the regulation of the Senate wing states, "The taking of pictures of any kind is prohibited in the Senate chamber, the Senate reading rooms, the Senate cloak rooms and the private dining room of the Senate." A Senate Rules Committee spokesman said that rule had been waived only twice in recent years, both times for the taking of still pictures of sessions for historical purposes.

Under existing rules, televising of Senate committee proceedings had to be cleared with the chairman of the committee involved and with the Senate Rules Committee. The Senate sergeant at arms had to give permission for filming anywhere in the Senate wing of the Capitol building itself.

There were two areas on the grounds of the Capitol where television crews could operate without specific permission: a grassy triangle across from the Senate steps and an area at the bottom of the hill on which the Capitol building is located.

Points to Ponder

Although congressional Republicans and Democrats often clash, they can close ranks in a hurry if they feel that the authority of Congress is threatened. This is what happened when Nixon challenged the right of Congress to force him to turn over documents. It happened again in 2006, when Democratic and Republican leaders at a bitterly partisan time abruptly joined forces. In that instance, they said the FBI had no right to raid the office of a member of Congress—Democratic Rep. William J. Jefferson of Louisiana—in a search for evidence of criminal wrongdoing.

- Is it healthy in our democracy for Democrats and Republicans to defend the authority of Congress while clashing so much over other issues that they accomplish comparatively little legislation? Do you think Congress overstepped its authority during Watergate? Can you point to a time since Watergate that Congress abused its power?

- President Nixon justified his refusal to cooperate with Congress by saying he had to protect the integrity of his office. Do you think his behavior accomplished that goal? Or did he actually undermine the office of the presidency?

- Does it strengthen our government when the two political parties clash over a president's actions, with members of the president's party defending them while members of the opposition party are critical? Or do such divisions indicate that politicians are putting their party loyalty above their duty to make sure the president is acting appropriately?

WATERGATE: A Historic Subpoena to the President and
JAWORSKI SUBPOENAS 60 ADDITIONAL CONVERSATIONS

In a stunning challenge to President Nixon, the House Judiciary Committee on April 11 issued a subpoena to try to force the White House to turn over records of conversations related to Watergate. Just five days later, Watergate special prosecutor Leon Jaworski issued his own subpoena, seeking tapes and records of more than 60 conversations.

The committee's subpoena represented a particularly dangerous threat to Nixon's presidency. Congressional leaders predicted to Nixon that he could be forced out if he did not cooperate. Even fellow Republicans broke ranks with the president. Six prominent Senate Republicans warned Nixon that he needed to give the committee all the materials it requested. If not, they said, "the first article in the bill of impeachment very well could be contempt of Congress."

On the Judiciary Committee, Democrats and Republican joined forces. They were frustrated that the White House had declined to cooperate even though the committee had first requested the records almost two months earlier. The committee voted 33–3 to issue a subpoena, or legal order, to the White House for tapes and other records of more than 40 presidential conversations. The conversations were viewed as vital to determining whether Nixon or his top aides participated in an illegal coverup of the Watergate burglary. The committee gave the president two weeks to comply, but it later agreed to extend the deadline to April 30.

White House press secretary Ronald L. Ziegler said the White House would turn over materials by the deadline. But he did not state whether all the tapes would be submitted. Instead, he said the president would comply "consistent with his constitutional responsibilities." That indicated Nixon might continue to claim executive privilege and refuse to cooperate fully with the subpoena. Executive privilege refers to the right of a president to refuse to hand over documents that might damage the national interest. (For more about executive privilege, see page 60.)

Members of the Judiciary Committee were further outraged by reports that the administration was screening the tapes. The White House, according to the reports, was eliminating irrelevant sections. Committee chairman Peter W. Rodino Jr., a New Jersey Democrat, warned the president to comply entirely. A lack of cooperation, Rodino warned, would be grounds for impeachment.

On April 22, the committee asked Nixon for additional materials. Some of the newly requested tape recordings and documents concerned Watergate. Others had to do with allegations that the president allowed himself to be influenced by campaign contributions in decisions regarding milk price supports and an antitrust suit against the International Telephone and Telegraph Corporation.

On another front, the Judiciary Committee also began looking into Nixon's tax situation. The Internal Revenue Service and a congressional committee had both concluded that Nixon owed almost $500,000 in back taxes. Committee staff raised the possibility that the president had committed tax fraud by deliberately trying to cheat.

The Judiciary Committee staff issued a report on April 25. It recommended focusing the investigation on Watergate, domestic surveillance and intelligence operations, allegations that the administration had improperly used its power to help its friends or harm its critics, and tax fraud. It suggested ending the investigation into other matters. For example, the staffers had studied questions about whether Nixon acted illegally when he impounded funds—that is, refused to spend money appropriated by Congress. The staff felt the issue of impoundment could be handled by the courts instead of by the investigation into impeachment. The staff also said it needed more time to look into evidence that Nixon had acted illegally in ordering the secret bombing of Cambodia.

In his subpoena, Jaworski sought some of the same materials the committee wanted. But he also wanted to obtain records of different conversations, some of which took place in the White House during the week following the June 1972 break-in. Jaworski said the materials were needed by both his office and Watergate defendants as both sides prepared for trial.

In a grim sign of Nixon's plight, a poll taken in late March indicated that a plurality of Americans favored impeachment. Some 43 percent of Americans in the poll favored impeachment, compared to 41 percent who opposed it. The remainder were undecided.

Marking out clear limits to Republican support for President Nixon on Capitol Hill, key Republicans in both chambers sent strong warnings to the White House during the week ending April 13, climaxed by a bipartisan subpoena to the President from the House Judiciary Committee.

The dilatory tactics of the White House in dealing with the request of the committee's impeachment inquiry for information "make it very difficult for minority members," said Rep. Hamilton Fish Jr. (R N.Y.) before voting for the subpoena April 11. Fish described the White House response as "outrageous." Nixon supporter Edward Hutchinson (R Mich.) agreed regretfully that it was "offensive to the House."

Earlier in the week, six Senate Republicans, all holding leadership posts, warned Nixon that "the first article in the bill of impeachment very well could be contempt of Congress," if Nixon did not quickly furnish the impeachment inquiry with all the materials it needed. Minority Leader Hugh Scott (Pa.), Assistant Minority Leader Robert P. Griffin (Mich.), John G. Tower (Texas), Wallace F. Bennett (Utah), Norris Cotton (N.H.) and Bill Brock (Tenn.) sent their message April 9 through Dean Burch, counselor to the President.

The President was running his own case, said a former member of the White House defense team, implying that the delaying moves in supplying the House with information originated with Nixon, not his counsel, James D. St. Clair.

After the White House received the subpoena, Press Secretary Ronald L. Ziegler said that by April 25 the White House would give the inquiry materials which would be "comprehensive and conclusive in regard to the President's actions," and that compliance would be as full as "consistent with his constitutional responsibilities."

"Realistically," noted an inquiry staff memo, "the President cannot be compelled to comply with a subpoena." If the President did not comply, it was unlikely that the House would move to attempt to enforce the subpoena, but would simply take into account, along with the other charges against Nixon, his noncompliance.

A Committee Subpoena

Undeterred by a last-minute telephone call from St. Clair, the Judiciary Committee on the afternoon of April 11 voted 33–3 to subpoena the President in order to obtain the records of certain conversations which the staff judged would be potentially helpful in determining Nixon's knowledge of or participation in the Watergate coverup.

After several hours of heated discussion, including two party-line votes on related matters, the committee united to adopt a Republican amendment making the subpoena more specific in describing the items at which it was directed. Then the committee voted to authorize issuance of the subpoena. Voting against issuance were the ranking committee Republican, Hutchinson, who cast the proxy vote of Charles E. Wiggins (R Calif.) against the subpoena as well, and Trent Lott (R Miss.). Absent and not voting were Charles W. Sandman Jr. (R N.J.) and Harold V. Froehlich (R Wis.).

It was the first time in history that a President had been subpoenaed to furnish information to an inquiry investigating impeachment charges against him. In 1973, when the special prosecutor and the Senate Watergate Committee issued subpoenas to Nixon, he became the first president since Thomas Jefferson to be served with a subpoena.

Demanded by the subpoena—which contained a deadline of 10 a.m. April 25, exactly two months after the original request for the information—were tapes and other records of more than 40 presidential conversations. They were described by the committee as conversations:

- Between the President and H. R. Haldeman, then White House chief of staff, on Feb. 20, 1973, concerning the possible appointment of campaign aide Jeb Stuart Magruder to a government post.
- Among Nixon, Haldeman and John D. Ehrlichman, then Nixon's domestic affairs adviser, on Feb. 27, 1973, concerning the assignment of White House counsel John W. Dean III to work with the President on Watergate.
- Between the President and Dean on March 17, 1973.
- Between Nixon and Ehrlichman on March 27 and March 30, 1973.
- All conversations between Nixon and Haldeman and Nixon and Ehrlichman April 14–17, 1973.
- All conversations between Nixon and then Attorney General Richard G. Kleindienst and between Nixon and Assistant Attorney General Henry E. Petersen April 15–18, 1973.

St. Clair Response. In a belated response to the committee deadline of April 9 for a White House response to the Feb. 25 request for this information, St. Clair wrote that "a review of the materials was underway" and probably would be completed by April 22, when Congress returned from its Easter recess. "We expect . . . that the additional materials furnished at that time will permit the committee to complete its inquiry promptly," he wrote.

Republican committee members joined their Democratic colleagues in making plain their disappointment at this reply. "This is an additional dilatory tactic by the President's lawyers . . . an unconscionable delay," said Lawrence J. Hogan (R Md.). "We don't want to be unreasonable, but this response is unacceptable," agreed Tom Railsback (R Ill.). "It certainly creates a presumption that the President is withholding damaging evidence," said M. Caldwell Butler (R Va.).

Forty-five minutes before the April 11 committee meeting began—to consider a subpoena—St. Clair called special committee counsel John M. Doar and asked whether a subpoena would be avoided if the White House, within a day or two, gave the committee the first four items requested. Doar said he could not reply for the committee but would deliver the message.

The last-minute compromise offer swayed a number of committee Republicans who had come ready to back a subpoena. Democrats were not so influenced. "It's a little late to make a deal," said Robert W. Kastenmeier (D Wis.).

Amendments. In a party-line vote of 21–17, the Democrats overruled Republican opposition to a rule limiting debate on the subpoena to one minute per member. David W. Dennis (R Ind.) then proposed to amend the subpoena to limit it to the four items the White House appeared ready to provide, to avoid a "blanket subpoena" and the risk of "getting slapped down." But the committee rejected this amendment, 22–16, with Butler joining the Democrats in opposition.

Delbert L Latta (R Ohio), a senior member of the House who had recently joined the Judiciary Committee to fill a vacancy, then proposed an amendment to make more specific the dates and times of the known conversations sought by the committee within the last two categories. Latta also moved to recess until after lunch; the committee agreed by voice vote.

Republican committee members, led by Robert McClory (Ill.), tried during the luncheon recess to obtain more specific assurances from St. Clair concerning the furnishing of needed materials. Their failure assured bipartisan support for the subpoena. When the committee reconvened, the Latta amendment was quickly adopted by voice vote after Rodino expressed his support for it. The subpoena was then approved, with only three dissenting votes.

Re-emphasizing committee determination to move ahead, Rodino announced that during the first week after the recess, the committee would discuss narrowing the scope of the inquiry by dropping some of the matters under investigation. The week of April 29, he said, the committee would consider the rules needed to guide its evidentiary proceedings.

Counsel's Role. Even as the committee readied a subpoena for the White House, some agreement was reached on the role for the President's counsel in the evidentiary proceedings.

Although the committee Democrats had at first reacted negatively to St. Clair's request for full participation in the proceedings, they agreed, at a committee caucus April 9, to allow St. Clair a certain role. Rodino said April 11 he would support granting the President's counsel:

- The privilege of attending the initial presentation of the evidence to the committee and of receiving copies of whatever documents and materials committee members were given.
- The opportunity, at the end of the presentation, to make his views known to the committee concerning the evidence and to recommend that certain witnesses be called.
- The opportunity to question witnesses "as the committee deems appropriate," if and when the committee called any witnesses.

Nixon's Taxes. Any hope that Nixon's pledge to pay his back taxes would end the matter was proved vain during the week after the Internal Revenue Service (IRS) and a joint congressional committee had presented him with reports assessing his back-tax bill at almost $500,000. The question of whether fraud was involved in the preparation of the tax returns was clearly within the scope of the impeachment inquiry, said special committee counsel John M. Doar April 8. And so the IRS had been asked to turn over the records of its investigation to the inquiry staff.

The President's involvement in possible tax fraud was "an area that the Judiciary Committee must dispose of," said Attorney General William B. Saxbe April 9. But he acknowledged that weeks or months before the IRS and congressional reports on presidential taxes, information on the matter had gone to the special Watergate prosecutor.

The New York Times reported April 11 that Donald C. Alexander, commissioner of internal revenue, had asked the special prosecutor to begin a federal grand jury investigation into a possible criminal conspiracy concerning Nixon's disallowed claim of a $576,000 tax deduction for his vice presidential papers.

In California, the executive officer of the state franchise board announced April 12 that Nixon owed $4,263.72 in back taxes to the state for 1969 and 1970, plus a penalty of $39.17 for 1970.

Mitchell-Stans Trial

Precisely two years after $200,000 in $100 bills was delivered to Nixon's re-election campaign finance chairman, Maurice H. Stans, former Attorney General John N. Mitchell took the witness stand in a federal courtroom. Mitchell denied charges that he and Stans, in return for the secret contribution from financier Robert L. Vesco, had tried to block an investigation of Vesco by the Securities and Exchange Commission (SEC).

Mitchell, taking the stand April 10 in U.S. District Court in New York City, said that he did not recall meeting Vesco until late spring 1972, after the contribution had been made.

Former New Jersey Republican leader Harry L. Sears had testified earlier that he had introduced Vesco and Mitchell a year before that.

"With regard to cooperation, as you probably are aware, we have cooperated with the Rodino committee, the Judiciary Committee of the House of Representatives, by my directing that all of the materials that were furnished to the special prosecutor have been turned over to the Judiciary Committee. . . . Being reasonable, it seems to me, would be that the committee should first examine what it has, because Mr. Jaworski, the special prosecutor, said that he had what he considered to be the full story of Watergate, and we want the full story out."

—President Nixon during question-and-answer session before the Executives' Club of Chicago, March 15, 1974

"On March 12, 1974, I wrote to you requesting access to certain taped conversations. . . . If the President declines to produce these materials. . . . I am compelled by my responsibilities to seek appropriate judicial process."

—Watergate Special Prosecutor Leon Jaworski in an April 11, 1974, letter to special presidential counsel James D. St. Clair

The efforts of investigators to obtain information from the White House became a triangular tug-of-war April 18 when, at the request of Watergate special prosecutor Leon Jaworski, Judge John J. Sirica issued a subpoena ordering President Nixon to furnish Jaworski with the tapes and records of more than 60 conversations that took place between June 1972 and June 1973.

Jaworski made the request April 16, stating that the information contained in the records was needed in order for the government and the defendants in the

Watergate coverup case to build their cases. The White House said it would have no comment until its lawyers had studied the request. Two of the defendants in the coverup case, Charles W. Colson and Robert C. Mardian, joined Jaworski's request for the subpoena. The case was scheduled for trial Sept. 9.

Weary of three months of fruitless negotiations to obtain the information without a subpoena, Jaworski had asked that Sirica set April 23—one week from the date of the request—as the deadline for a White House reply to the subpoena. Sirica, issuing the order two days later, set a deadline of May 2, two weeks from the date of the subpoena. The subpoena to Nixon issued April 11 by the House Judiciary Committee for records of more than 40 conversations contained a deadline of April 25.

Turning inside out his pledge in March that he would give the House committee everything he had given the special prosecutor, Nixon apparently had told Jaworski in early April, through St. Clair, that he would receive any materials that Nixon had given the House committee. And he apparently added that he would not consider other materials Jaworski had requested until he had decided what to give the Judiciary Committee.

Maintaining the committee's right to decide what was and was not relevant to its inquiry, Judiciary Committee Chairman Peter W. Rodino Jr. (D N.J.) reacted adversely April 18 to reports that the White House was screening the tapes requested in order to eliminate irrelevant portions from those that would be given to the committee. Such White House editing, said Rodino on the NBC-TV "Today" show, "would mean that the White House would be making the final determination. . . . This could not be a proper . . . comprehensive inquiry unless we were to make the determination as to what is necessary."

If the President did not fully comply with the committee subpoena, said Rodino, that noncompliance "could be considered as a possible ground of impeachment." A study prepared by the impeachment inquiry staff supported that statement after an analysis of the various ways in which the committee and the House could deal with presidential noncompliance.

Separate Requests. In a letter April 11 to presidential counsel James D. St. Clair, explaining why he would request the additional subpoena, the third from the special prosecutor's office to the White House, Jaworski tried to separate his request from that of the committee. "I have emphasized repeatedly that our request is in no way tied to the requests of the House Judiciary Committee," he wrote. "The requests are distinguishable both factually and legally. Nevertheless, you have refused to consider them separately, and you have been unable to tell us the criteria that will govern the President's response."

But some of the conversations in which the impeachment inquiry was interested, and for which Jaworski also sought records and recordings, were the same. Jaworski sought material related to:

- Conversations during the week after the June 17, 1972, break-in at Democratic national headquarters in Washington's Watergate office building, including three between Nixon and Colson and three between Nixon and his then chief of staff, H. R. Haldeman.
- A number of conversations between Nixon and Colson, former White House counsel John W. Dean III, Haldeman and former domestic affairs adviser John D. Ehrlichman during March and April 1973, including six conversations on April 14, seven on April 16, four on April 17 and six on April 25. Many of these also were sought by the subpoena from the House committee.
- Two conversations between Nixon and Haldeman on June 4, 1973, after Haldeman had left his White House post. It was the day that Nixon went to Camp David, Maryland, and listened to some of the tapes. Both conversations were telephone conversations.

Jaworski explained that he was asking for the subpoena, and the early reply date, "solely for the purpose of preventing any postponement of the trial or delay during the conduct of the trial." He said that if the requested material were supplied, it would have to be analyzed—"an arduous and time-consuming task." If the White House should contest the subpoena, Jaworski said, "it would be best for all concerned that such limitation be initiated promptly in order to avoid the possibility of postponing the trial."

Warning from Scott. Applying another spur to White House cooperation, Senate Minority Leader Hugh Scott (R Pa.) warned that Nixon's refusal to cooperate with the House committee could lead to his impeachment. In a letter to his constituents made public April 18, Scott stated: "It would be a grave danger and with serious consequences possibly leading to impeachment if the President would not cooperate with the committee and decided against furnishing the necessary facts requested by the committee." He said that he was urging both sides to cooperate in reaching an acceptable compromise on the necessary material.

Lowenstein Suit. In another Watergate-related development, former Rep. Allard K. Lowenstein (D N.Y. 1969–71) filed suit April 18 against five former White House officials for conspiring through an "enemies list"

to defeat him in 1972. He also accused the FBI of investigating him unlawfully and the Internal Revenue Service of auditing his tax returns to harass him.

The former White House officials named in the suit were H. R. Haldeman, John D. Ehrlichman, Charles W. Colson, John W. Dean III and Lawrence M. Higby. Among others named as defendants in the civil suit, filed in U.S. District Court in Brooklyn, were several FBI and IRS officials.

POLL REPORT

For the first time, a plurality of persons interviewed by the Harris Survey agreed that President Nixon should be impeached and removed from office. The poll was published April 13.

These were the percentages in the survey, conducted March 24–29 in 1,495 households nationwide:

Should be impeached	43%
Should not	41
Not sure	14

A majority agreed with a statement that if Nixon "fails to turn over the information the House Judiciary Committee wants, then that committee should vote to bring impeachment charges against the President."

Agreed	55%
Disagreed	33
Not sure	12

A majority said they did not expect Nixon to give the Judiciary Committee all the material it sought.

Expected	19%
Did not expect	67
Not sure	14

A larger majority gave the President, Harris wrote, "overwhelmingly negative marks . . . on the way he is cooperating with the impeachment proceedings."

Positive	21%
Negative	72
Not sure	7

The same survey found that more persons believed John W. Dean III, Nixon's chief accuser and a former presidential counsel, than believed the President. This was the question: "Who do you think has been more truthful about the Watergate coverup—President Nixon or John Dean?"

	Latest	July 1973
Nixon	29%	38%
Dean	46	37
Not sure	25	25

TRANSCRIPTS:

A Dramatic Disclosure by Nixon

In the spring of 1974, Nixon continued to resist demands for tapes of private White House conversations. Responding to a House Judiciary Committee subpoena for tapes, he instead released heavily edited transcripts of 46 tapes of discussions he had with his advisers about Watergate. Democrats on the committee denounced Nixon for refusing to comply with the subpoena, or legal order. Republicans also criticized the president because the transcripts appeared to reveal the president as a man willing to cut bargains for his political survival. The House Judiciary Committee and the Watergate special prosecutor demanded more documents from the White House. The Judiciary Committee threatened the president with impeachment if he didn't comply. But the president said the committee had everything it needed to investigate the Watergate scandal.

The White House claimed the transcripts proved that the president was innocent of any criminal involvement in the Watergate coverup. A White House summary stated, "In all of the thousands of words spoken, even though they often are unclear and ambiguous, not once does it appear that the President of the United States was engaged in a criminal plot to obstruct justice."

The president's approach temporarily split Democrats and Republicans in Congress. Many Democrats said they needed the tapes to make sure the White House had not tampered with them before making transcripts. They also fumed that Nixon was refusing to comply with the committee's subpoena. "The tapes which were subpoenaed and an expert analysis of the tapes are essential to obtain the whole truth," said James R. Mann of South Carolina, one of the more conservative Democrats on the Judiciary Committee. "How can anyone object to the whole truth? . . .

Unless I get it I am handicapped in my service to the American people in determining this issue."

Democrats were concerned that key conversations may have been deleted. Former White House counsel John W. Dean III, for example, reportedly said the transcripts left out a critical discussion between him and Nixon. The discussion focused on using the Internal Revenue Service to harass opponents of the administration, according to Dean.

At first, Republicans generally praised Nixon for providing the committee with vital information for its investigation. They opposed a move by Democrats on the Judiciary Committee to inform Nixon that he had not complied with the subpoena. "I view the submission of the President to be a good-faith effort on his part to comply with the legitimate demands of our committee for evidence," said Charles E. Wiggins of California, a Republican member of the Judiciary Committee.

But Republicans grew critical as they pored over the 1,254 pages of edited transcripts. Nixon emerged as a crude man who sprinkled his sentences with profanities and obscenities. He referred to "the thick skull" of a prominent Republican senator and suggested putting pressure on the Speaker of the House. He appeared highly suspicious of real or imagined political enemies. The transcripts also had many "unintelligible" words and phrases that left many wondering about the true meaning of the president's conversations.

Meanwhile, several of Nixon's top aides faced criminal trials. The results were mixed. One jury acquitted two former members of Nixon's cabinet, John N. Mitchell and Maurice H. Stans, who had been accused of engaging in a criminal conspiracy. But one of Nixon's former top aides, John D. Ehrlichman, was later convicted for his role in the Watergate burglary.

Breaking his own rule that private presidential conversations were protected by the doctrine of executive privilege, President Nixon April 30 turned over to the House Judiciary Committee heavily edited transcripts of 46 tapes of discussions between Nixon and his advisers concerning Watergate. The White House the same day also released to the public a 1,308-page volume containing the transcripts.

"I realize these transcripts will provide grist for many sensational stories in the press," Nixon said in announcing his decision during a nationwide television address April 29. "Parts will seem to be contradictory

President Richard Nixon announces in a nationally televised speech on April 29, 1974, that he will release edited transcripts of White House conversations between him and his aides regarding the Watergate break-in and coverup.

with one another, and parts will be in conflict with some of the testimony given in the Senate Watergate Committee hearings."

The President said he had been reluctant to release the tapes, "not just because they will embarrass me and those with whom I have talked, which they will—not just because they will become the subject of speculation and even ridicule—which they will—and not just because certain parts of them will be seized upon by political and journalistic opponents—which they will."

Nixon said he also was concerned with violating the confidentiality of presidential conversations and with "the human impact" that disclosure would have on those involved. However, he added, "the basic question at issue today is whether the President personally acted improperly in the Watergate matter," as charged by former White House counsel John W. Dean III during the 1973 Senate Watergate Committee hearings. "Month after month of rumor, insinuation and charges by just one Watergate witness—John Dean—suggested that the President did act improperly," said Nixon.

"From the beginning," he declared, "I have said that in many places on the tapes there were ambiguities—statements and comments that different people with different perspectives might interpret in drastically different ways. But although the words may be ambiguous—though the discussions may have explored many alternatives—the record of my actions is totally clear now, and I still believe it was totally correct then."

Judiciary Committee Role. The turnover of the transcripts was a response to an April 11 House Judiciary Committee subpoena for tapes of 42 conversations. The committee originally had requested the tapes on Feb. 25.

Although refusing to turn over the tapes themselves, Nixon offered to allow Committee Chairman Peter W. Rodino (D N.J.) and ranking Republican member Edward Hutchinson (R Mich.) to listen to the tapes and verify the accuracy of the transcripts.

The committee voted May 1, 20–18, to inform Nixon that he had not complied with the committee's subpoena. The vote split generally along party lines.

"The procedure suggested by the President for Mr. Hutchinson and me to come to the White House to review the subpoenaed tape recordings to determine the relevance and accuracy of the partial transcripts is not compliance with our subpoena," Rodino said May 1.

Republican Support. The President found some outspoken support for his position among Republicans. "I have no patience with people who whine and say, 'But the President didn't do it the way we wanted,'" said Sen. Barry Goldwater (R Ariz.). ". . . I believe the President has gone as far as he possibly could on the question of materials sought by the House Judiciary Committee."

Rep. Charles E. Wiggins (R Calif.), an influential member of the judiciary committee, declared April 30, "I view the submission of the President to be a good-faith effort on his part to comply with the legitimate demands of our committee for evidence."

Numerous Deletions. The transcripts were laced with parenthetical notes such as "materials unrelated to presidential actions deleted," "unintelligible," "inaudible" and "expletive omitted." Many of these deletions interrupted sections of the transcript so as to obscure meanings. In an interview with CBS news announcer Walter Cronkite, White House lawyer James D. St. Clair acknowledged that no attempts had been made to improve the quality of the tapes by electronic means.

Critics pointed out that without possession of the tapes themselves, the committee had no way of determining whether the tapes had been tampered with before the transcripts were made. This possibility was raised when CBS reported May 2 that friends of Dean quoted him as saying the transcripts did not contain a lengthy discussion on Sept. 15, 1972, between Dean and Nixon about using the Internal Revenue Service (IRS) to harass enemies of the administration and a report on an IRS investigation of Lawrence F. O'Brien, then chairman of the Democratic National Committee.

Other Actions. In other developments during the week ending May 4:

- White House lawyers May 1 moved to quash a special Watergate prosecution subpoena for tapes and records of 64 White House conversations relating to the coverup.
- White House chief of staff Alexander M. Haig Jr., appearing under subpoena at a May 2 closed meeting of the Senate Watergate Committee, presented a letter from Nixon instructing him not to answer any questions. Nixon had promised on May 22, 1973, that "executive privilege will not be invoked as to any testimony concerning possible criminal conduct or discussions of possible criminal conduct, in matters presently under investigation, including the Watergate affair and the alleged coverup."

Contents of Summary, Transcripts

To ensure that Nixon at least had a good first hearing in the press, the White House handed out a 50-page summary of the transcripts, giving the tapes an interpretation favorable to the President, shortly after the complete transcripts had gone to the House Judiciary Committee by station wagon at 10:30 a.m. April 30. Blue paperback copies of the transcripts, as thick as the Manhattan telephone directory, were not released at the White House press room until shortly after 3 p.m., less than two hours before deadlines for evening television newscasts.

Thus the nation's afternoon newspapers had only the interpretive summary, written in the style of a legal brief, to write about. And because of the volume of the complete transcripts and the timing of their release, the evening news programs and the next day's morning papers had time to prepare only cursory stories.

"Frankly, the President wanted to get his case out to the American people before the critics started in on the President," a White House official acknowledged to a *Washington Post* reporter. "We thought this was the best way to do it."

Claims of Innocence. The thrust of the summary was to substantiate Nixon's claims that he was innocent of criminal behavior and to discredit his former counsel, Dean.

"Throughout the period of the Watergate affair the raw material of these recorded confidential conversations establishes that the President had no prior knowledge of the break-in and that he had no knowledge of any cover-up prior to March 21, 1973," according to the summary. "In all of the thousands of words spoken, even

though they often are unclear and ambiguous, not once does it appear that the President of the United States was engaged in a criminal plot to obstruct justice."

One of the ambiguities the summary sought to resolve in Nixon's favor was part of a Sept. 15, 1972, conversation in which Nixon congratulated Dean for doing a good job. The transcript quoted Nixon as telling Dean, "Oh, well, this is a can of worms as you know a lot of this stuff that went on. And the people who worked this way are awfully embarrassed. But the way you have handled all this seems to me has been very skillful putting your fingers in the leaks that have sprung here and sprung there."

According to the summary, "This was said in the context not of a criminal plot to obstruct justice, as Dean alleges, but rather in the context of the politics of the matter, such as civil suits, counter-suits, Democratic efforts to exploit Watergate as a political issue and the like. The reference to 'putting your finger in the leaks' was clearly related to the handling of the political and public relations aspect of the matter. . . ."

However, critics were quick to point out that the passage could also be interpreted to show Nixon congratulating Dean on his handling of a coverup. The transcript showed that Nixon's comment was made after Dean had assured him that "Nothing is going to come crashing down to our surprise," and the summary deleted Nixon's question immediately after his remarks about "leaks": "The Grand Jury is dismissed now?"

Later in the conversation, Nixon commented, according to the transcript: "The worst may happen but it may not. So you just try to button it up as well as you can and hope for the best, and remember basically the damn business is unfortunately trying to cut our losses."

Discrediting Dean. In attempting to discredit Dean, the summary cited inconsistencies between his testimony before the Senate Watergate Committee and the transcribed conversations.

In one instance, Dean had testified that he told Nixon about money demands and threats of blackmail from Watergate defendants on March 13, 1973. "He said he was 'very clear' about this date," according to the summary. "It now develops that the conversations with the President, on the date of which Dean was so clear, did not in fact take place until the morning of March 21, 1973, as the President had always contended. . . . This discrepancy in Dean's testimony from the tapes of these two meetings is surprising in the light of Dean's self-professed excellent memory. . . ."

The summary claimed the transcripts disproved Dean's assertion that Nixon "never at any time" asked him during a March 22, 1973, meeting, also attended by

H. R. Haldeman, to deliver to Nixon a written report on his knowledge of Watergate.

In a more veiled attack on Dean, the summary referred to the trials of former Secretary of Commerce Maurice H. Stans and former Attorney General John N. Mitchell, whose acquittals were seen as damaging to Dean's credibility. Dean had been one of the prosecution's main witnesses.

The acquittals "demonstrate the wisdom of the President's actions in insisting that the orderly process of the judicial system be utilized to determine the guilt or innocence of individuals charged with crime, rather than participating in trials in the public media," according to the summary.

Hush Money to Hunt. While acknowledging that many of the transcribed exchanges between Nixon and his aides were ambiguous and that "someone with a motive to discredit the President could take (them) out of context and distort to suit his own purposes," the summary argued that a complete reading of the transcripts would show Nixon's innocence. However, the full transcripts showed that Nixon at least considered the option of paying hush money to Watergate defendant E. Howard Hunt Jr.

In a critical March 21 meeting, Dean told Nixon there would be "a continual blackmail operation" by the Watergate defendants, who were threatening to make public their involvement in the break-in of Daniel Ellsberg's psychiatrist's office. The "problem" of blackmail will not only go on now, but it will go on while these people are in prison, and it will compound the obstruction of justice situation," Dean told Nixon. This appeared in the edited transcript:

Dean: It will cost money. It is dangerous. People around here are not pros at this sort of thing. This is the sort of thing Mafia people can do: washing money, getting clean money, and things like that. We just don't know about those things, because we are not criminals and not used to dealing in that business.

Nixon: That's right.

Dean: It is a tough thing to know how to do.

Nixon: Maybe it takes a gang to do that.

Dean: That's right. There is a real problem as to whether we could even do it. Plus there is a real problem in raising some money. Mitchell has been working on raising some money. He is one of the ones with the most to lose. But there is no denying the fact that the White House, in (John D.) Ehrlichman, Haldeman and Dean are involved in some of the early money decisions.

Nixon: How much money do you need?

Dean: I would say these people are going to cost a million dollars over the next two years.

Nixon: We could get that. On the money, if you need the money you could get that. You could get a million dollars. You could get it in cash. I know where it could be gotten. It is not easy, but it could be done. But the question is who the hell would handle it? Any ideas on that?

Dean: That's right. Well, I think that is something that Mitchell ought to be charged with.

Nixon: I would think so too.

There followed a discussion of how the money might be raised and delivered. Later the conversation turned to what Dean called the likelihood that Hunt and the other defendants would demand clemency, which Nixon seemed to rule out for political reasons.

Dean: They all are going to expect to be out and that may put you in a position that is just untenable at some point. You know, the Watergate hearings just over, Hunt now demanding clemency or he is going to blow. And politically, it's impossible for you to do it. You know, after everybody—

Nixon: That's right!

Dean: I am not sure that you will ever be able to deliver on the clemency. It may be just too hot.

Nixon: You can't do it politically until after the '74 elections, that's for sure. Your point is that even then you couldn't do it.

Dean: That's right. It may further involve you in a way you should not be involved in this.

Nixon: No—it is wrong that's for sure.

Later in the same meeting Nixon seemed to rule out the payment of hush money as well.

Nixon: If, for example, you say look we are not going to continue to—let's say, frankly, on the assumption that if we continue to cut our losses, we are not going to win. But in the end, we are going to be bled to death. And in the end, it is all going to come out anyway. Then you get the worst of both worlds. We are going to lose, and people are going to—

Haldeman: And look like dopes!

Nixon: And in effect, look like a cover-up. So that we can't do.

A few moments later Nixon added, "First it is going to require approximately a million dollars to take care of the jackasses who are in jail. That can be arranged. That could be arranged. But you realize that after we are gone, and assuming we can expend this money, then they are going to crack and it would be an unseemly story. . . ."

Battle with Democrats. The transcripts shed light on Nixon's view of his Watergate troubles as a political vendetta on the part of the Democrats. In a Feb. 28, 1973, discussion with Dean on how to prepare for upcoming congressional hearings on Watergate, Nixon remarked, "It seems like a terrible waste of your time.

But it is important in the sense that all this business is a battle and they are going to wage the battle. A lot of them have enormous frustrations about those elections, state of their party, etc. And their party has its problems. . . ."

In the same discussion, Nixon acknowledged the importance of the affair but seemed to indicate belief that his lack of involvement in the actual break-in would keep him from harm.

Dean: We have come a long road on this thing now. I had thought it was an impossible task to hold together until after the election until things started falling out, but we have made it this far and I am convinced we are going to make it the whole road and put this thing in the funny pages of the history books rather than anything serious because actually—

Nixon: It will be somewhat serious but the main thing, of course, is also the isolation of the President.

Dean: Absolutely! Totally true!

Nixon: Because that, fortunately, is totally true.

Dean: I know that sir!

The Private Man. Besides illuminating matters of substance involving Watergate, the transcripts showed a picture of Nixon, the private man, in confidential discussions with aides, that differed dramatically from the decorous public image he had sought to project. In private, Nixon's language was often coarse and blunt, particularly in his characterizations of other public figures.

"I tried to get it through his thick skull," Nixon said of Sen. Howard Baker (R Tenn.) during a Feb. 28, 1973, discussion of Nixon's belief that hearsay evidence should not be permitted in the Senate Watergate Committee hearings. Baker was vice chairman of the committee.

During the Sept. 15, 1972, meeting with Haldeman and Dean, Nixon ordered that "the most comprehensive notes" be kept on "all those who tried to do us in," evidently referring to Democrats who were pressing the Watergate investigation.

"They didn't have to do it," Nixon said. "If we had had a very close election and they were playing the other side I would understand this. No—they were doing this quite deliberately and they are asking for it and now they are going to get it. We have not used the power in this first four years as you know. We have never used it. We have not used the Bureau (FBI) and we have not used the Justice Department but things are going to change now. And they are either going to do it right or go."

Dean asserted that the Nixon campaign team was then being audited by the General Accounting Office at the request of House Speaker Carl Albert (D Okla.)—the third man in line for the presidency.

"That surprises me," said Nixon.

"Well, (expletive deleted) the Speaker of the House," said Haldeman. "Maybe we better put a little heat on him."

"I think so too," said Nixon.

As embarrassing as some of these disclosures were, Nixon evidently was staking his presidency on the hope that the House of Representatives would not find impeachable offenses in any of them, or if they did, that the Senate would not find in them grounds for conviction.

A Finding of Non-Compliance

"There is no question that, whatever else the President may have done or been thought to have done on Monday evening, and whatever individual members of this committee may think of the merits of that action, the President has not complied with our subpoena," Judiciary Committee Chairman Rodino said May 1.

But there was a question within the Judiciary Committee as to the proper response from the committee to the President's move. At an unusual evening meeting May 1, which adjourned near midnight, this question was discussed at length.

Some Republicans felt that confrontation with the White House should be avoided at all costs. Ranking Republican Edward Hutchinson (R Mich.) warned that the men who constructed a government of separated powers never contemplated a confrontation between the branches of the government. "Confrontation never works," he said; "it produces only stalemates."

But there was a conflicting view, propounded by Jerome R. Waldie (D Calif.), that impeachment itself was the "ultimate confrontation of the legislative branch with the executive branch."

Middle Road. Following a middle road, the committee rejected a motion recommending that the President be found in contempt of Congress. Instead it authorized a terse letter to Nixon informing him that the committee found that he had not complied with its subpoena. The letter, from Rodino to Nixon, simply advised the President that the committee "finds that as of 10:00 a.m. April 30, you have failed to comply with the committee's subpoena of April 11, 1974."

Basic to the committee's decision was the members' feeling that they should have the best evidence possible on which to make a judgment on the charges against the President—and that the White House transcripts were not that best evidence. As James R. Mann (D S.C.), one of the more conservative Democratic members of the committee, explained it: "The tapes which were subpoenaed and an expert analysis of the tapes are essential to obtain the whole truth. . . . How can anyone object to the whole truth? . . . Unless I get it I am handicapped in my service to the American people in determining this issue."

The committee's position was further outlined by Rodino: "We did not subpoena an edited White House version of partial transcripts of portions of presidential conversations. We did not subpoena a presidential interpretation of what is necessary or relevant for our inquiry. And we did not subpoena a lawyer's argument presented before we have heard any of the evidence.

"Under the Constitution," Rodino reminded the committee, "it is not within the power of the President to conduct an inquiry into his own impeachment, to determine which evidence, and what version or portion of that evidence, is relevant and necessary to such an inquiry. These are matters which, under the Constitution, only the House has the sole power to determine. The President's suggestion that the committee have only the transcripts is not something that I or any member of the committee can explain to the American people. It would only raise questions about the committee's inquiry. The committee must follow the appropriate, the proper, the lawful way as it moves ahead."

Debate over Letters. The letter to the President—authorized by a motion proposed by Harold D. Donohue (D Mass.) as amended to include a text of the letter by Jack Brooks (D Texas)—was approved by the committee by a narrow margin, divided along party lines, 20–18. John Conyers Jr. (D Mich.) and Waldie, both in favor of citing the President for contempt, voted against the motion. Had they been joined by every Republican member, the motion would have failed on a tie vote, 19–19. But William S. Cohen (R Maine) crossed party lines to vote in favor of the Brooks-Donohue motion, providing the margin of approval.

Earlier, the committee had rejected, 11–27, a compromise letter proposed by Cohen which would have advised Nixon that the transcripts were not "full compliance" and that the committee should have the option of reviewing the original tapes, with the assistance of counsel and technical experts. But this proposal was objected to by members on both sides. Most Democrats found it too soft, while some Republicans opposed any such letter.

Voting with Cohen for his proposal were Walter Flowers (D Ala.), Mann, Wayne Owens (D Utah), Delbert L. Latta (R Ohio), Tom Railsback (R Ill.), Charles E. Wiggins (R Calif.), David W. Dennis (R Ind.), Hamilton Fish Jr. (R N.Y.), Wiley Mayne (R Iowa) and M. Caldwell Butler (R Va.). The committee then rejected, 18–20, a motion by Latta to table the Brooks-Donohue motion; Conyers joined the Republicans in voting to table it.

Pointing out that May 1 was "Law Day," Conyers then moved that the committee recommend to the House that Nixon be cited for contempt of Congress for failing to comply with the committee's lawful subpoena. "Law Day," suggested Conyers, was an appropriate occasion for the committee "to enforce the law on the President of the United States."

The committee rejected the motion, with only five members supporting it: Conyers, Waldie, Robert W. Kastenmeier (D Wis.), Charles B. Rangel (D N.Y.) and Elizabeth Holtzman (D N.Y.). Robert F. Drinan (D Mass.) abstained on the vote; the other 32 members opposed it. The committee then adjourned; it was almost midnight.

What Degree of Compliance? During hours of discussion on the evening of May 1 concerning the degree of compliance which the massive White House transcripts represented, no member of the committee suggested that they fully complied with the committee subpoena seeking tapes, dictabelts, notes, memoranda or other records of 42 presidential conversations. But there was a diversity of views on the degree of compliance.

No tapes of any of the conversations had been provided. The transcripts of most of the requested conversations had been provided, however, said special committee counsel John M. Doar. The sought-after conversations for which transcripts were not produced included a Feb. 20, 1973, conversation between the President and H. R. Haldeman, a Feb. 27, 1973, conversation between Nixon and John D. Ehrlichman and several of the conversations with Haldeman, Ehrlichman and other aides or officials during the period from April 15–18, 1973.

Furthermore, reported Doar, no notes, memoranda, dictabelts or other records of any of the conversations had been provided to the committee, and no explanation for the lack of these records had been given. Under questioning from several Republican members, Doar admitted that he had no personal knowledge of the existence of notes or dictabelts related to the specific conversations requested. He cited presidential statements and the testimony of various presidential aides concerning the existence of their notes, presidential notes and dictabelts produced by Nixon as part of his personal diary—in general, but not specifically related to the conversations sought.

If these records did not exist, Doar said, the President could have said so in his response to the subpoena. He did not.

Monitoring the Tapes. Referring to the President's suggestion that Rodino and Hutchinson listen to the tapes to verify the authenticity of the transcripts, Rodino asked Doar: "In your professional opinion, is it prudent for me and Mr. Hutchinson to make a judgment on the relevance of tapes not transcribed?"

"No," responded Doar, pointing to the need for those who listen to the tapes for that purpose to be thoroughly grounded in all the facts involved in the charges. Rodino agreed, calling it "absolutely impossible" for him to discharge adequately such a responsibility to the committee, to authenticate the tapes without the assistance of counsel and technical experts.

"These transcripts are not accurate," said Doar, referring to those provided by the White House. "I'm not suggesting intentional distortion," he said, "but with time, patience, energy and good equipment, they can be improved." With better equipment than the White House had, he said—and "superior diligence"—the impeachment inquiry staff had produced a better and more complete transcript of at least one tape already in the staff's possession, that of the March 21, 1973, meeting between Dean and Nixon.

"Do you mean that some of the 'deletions' and 'inaudibles' on the March 21 transcript have been deciphered with our equipment?" asked Waldie. "Yes," responded Doar, who emphasized to the committee that he felt there was "a very significant difference" between reading a transcript and listening to a tape.

Referring to the contents of the transcripts, Lawrence J. Hogan (R Md.) said that he had "come to the inescapable conclusion that he (Nixon) must have forgotten that the tapes were being made." Later he added that he felt that in many places the expletives deleted "seem to be essential to the meaning of the statement" from which they were removed.

Prevalent Dissatisfaction. Some dissatisfaction with the President's response was expressed by almost every committee member. But Wiggins urged that, although the form of the response was insufficient, the committee defer action on any response until its members had the opportunity to consider the substance of the transcripts. Since receiving the 1,300-page transcripts, he said, he had "diligently pursued the information" they contained, but was only through 200 pages. "We should not pursue form (the tapes)," he said, "if the substance meets needs."

Members of the committee were also disturbed by the medium that Nixon had chosen for his response. Mann chided Nixon for "mounting his electronic throne" of simply informing the committee of which materials it sought did or did not exist.

Flowers expressed similar concern about the forum by the President to respond. He pointed out that contents of the tapes still would be confidential if Nixon had just turned them over to the committee, instead of going public.

Procedural Plans. "We are going to go ahead," Rodino affirmed on the evening of May 1, informing committee members that the initial presentation of evidence would begin the next week, probably in closed session. Later he said that the committee members should expect to work mornings and afternoons, three days a week, hearing the evidence. Estimates of the time needed for this presentation ranged from five days to six weeks.

In preparation for receiving the evidence, the committee turned its attention to the rules of procedure that would guide the presentation. On May 1, the Judiciary Subcommittee on Courts, Civil Liberties and the Administration of Justice met to consider the rules drafted by the impeachment inquiry staff—and unanimously reported them to the full committee with several amendments.

The next day the full committee considered the rules and amendments at morning and afternoon sessions. The version adopted late on the afternoon of May 2 included several key points:

- The sessions at which the committee would receive from the staff a presentation of pertinent information would be hearings, open to the public unless closed by committee vote.
- Nixon as well as St. Clair would be invited to attend the presentation, and all hearings at which witnesses were heard by the committee, including any such hearings held in executive session.
- St. Clair could be invited to submit requests that the committee hear additional witnesses or receive additional evidence.
- St. Clair could raise objections relating to the examination of witnesses or the admissibility of evidence; such objections would be ruled on by the chairman, and his rulings would be final unless overruled by a majority of the committee members present.
- St. Clair could question any witness, subject to instructions from the chairman.

"The members . . . have leaned over backward to ensure fairness to St. Clair," said Rodino, noting the privileges the President's counsel could be granted under the rules. All attempts to expand or limit those privileges—through amendments suggested by committee members—were rejected.

By voice vote, the committee rejected an amendment proposed by George E. Danielson (D Calif.) removing from the rules the presidential counsel's right to object to the examination of a witness or the admissibility of evidence. Danielson proposed the amendment, he said, because of concern that giving St. Clair this right would allow him to obstruct the proceedings. Rodino made clear that he would not tolerate any such obstruction.

On the other hand, the committee also rejected, by a vote of 15–23, an amendment proposed by Dennis that would have given St. Clair the right to examine and cross-examine, not just question, any witness.

The committee by voice vote adopted an amendment allowing radio and television coverage of any open hearings, a proposal made by Robert McClory (R Ill.). By a vote of 19–17, an amendment was adopted setting 10 rather than 20 members as the number that would constitute a quorum for the hearings.

MITCHELL-STANS TRIAL: ACQUITTAL ON ALL 15 COUNTS

After deliberating four days, a U.S. District Court jury in New York City April 28 acquitted john N. Mitchell and Maurice H. Stans of all charges in their criminal conspiracy case. The verdict came on the 48th day of the trial of the two former Nixon cabinet officers and was reached after the nine men and three women deliberated for 26 hours.

Mitchell and Stans, former key figures in President Nixon's 1972 re-election campaign, had been charged with 15 counts of conspiracy, perjury and obstruction of justice.

Their trial, which began Feb. 21, marked the first time in the nation's history that two former cabinet officers had been tried together and the first trial of former cabinet officers since the Teapot Dome scandal of the 1920s.

The government had alleged that the two former Nixon aides attempted to impede a Securities and Exchange Commission (SEC) investigation of Robert L. Vesco, the fugitive financier, in return for a secret $200,000 cash contribution from Vesco to Nixon's 1972 re-election drive. The defense lawyers claimed that Mitchell and Stans never had attempted to "fix" the SEC investigation into Vesco's tangled financial dealings and that the prosecution's chief witnesses were not telling the truth.

In interviews after the verdicts were announced, the jurors said that they had voted to acquit Mitchell and Stans because they could not believe the testimony of key government witnesses. They used the words "incredible" or "unbelievable" when they talked about John W. Dean III, G. Bradford Cook, William J. Casey, Harry L. Sears and Laurence Richardson Jr., major prosecution witnesses.

"I don't want to say Mr. Dean was lying, but he was often unbelievable," said Sybil Kucharski, the 21-year-old forewoman of the jury. Referring to Mitchell and Stans, she said, "We didn't feel they had any reason to lie. We didn't feel they had the need. They were credible men."

Kucharski and five other jurors said in interviews that they saw nothing improper in what the two former administration officials had done for Vesco. "We didn't put them above the law," she said. "But we felt they were doing things in the course of the normal working day. They weren't sneaking around or anything."

The acquittal verdict emphasized the importance of the Watergate tape recordings in other criminal and impeachment proceedings. Dean, the former presidential counsel who was a key witness for the prosecution, was expected to be a major government witness in the forthcoming Watergate conspiracy trial of Mitchell, H. R. Haldeman, John D. Ehrlichman and four others. He also was the principal accuser of Nixon in the alleged White House effort to obstruct the Watergate investigation.

The White House said that "the President was very pleased for the two men and their families."

Vesco, too, expressed satisfaction.

District Court Action

On the second front of his battle of the tapes, Nixon sent his attorneys to court May 2 to seek the quashing of the Watergate special prosecutor's subpoena for tapes and documents relating to 64 post-Watergate conversations, most of them involving the President himself.

U.S. District Judge John J. Sirica set a hearing for May 8 on the motion to quash. He gave the special prosecutor and any of the seven defendants in the Watergate coverup case until 2 p.m. May 6 to reply to the President's motion, and the White House until May 8 to respond.

Sirica issued the subpoena April 18 at the request of special prosecutor Leon Jaworski. Jaworski said the information contained in the records was needed by both the government and the defendants to build their cases for the coverup trial, scheduled to begin Sept. 9. Two of the defendants, Charles W. Colson and Robert C. Mardian, joined in Jaworski's request for the subpoena.

Executive Privilege Question. The subpoenaed tapes and documents related to conversations between June 1972—the month of the Watergate break-in—and June 1973. In arguments before Sirica May 2, Philip A. Lacovara, counsel to the special prosecutor, pointed out that 20 of the tapes called for were among those for which the President released transcripts April 30. Therefore, Lacovara suggested, executive privilege had been waived regarding those conversations, and Sirica could rule immediately that those tapes should be turned over.

White House attorney John A. McCahill, however, said executive privilege had been waived only for the transcripts, not for the tapes themselves.

One possible exception was suggested in the President's motion. If any of the defendants in the coverup case could demonstrate that the presidential files contained information that would support their claims of innocence, the motion said, "the President would be willing to consider whether a defendant's need for access outweighs the public interest in maintaining confidentiality."

Transcripts' Impact. The presidential brief suggested that in view of the release of the 20 edited transcripts, Jaworski might want to "reassess his need" for the material. The prosecutors had argued in the past, however, that transcripts were not satisfactory as evidence as long as tapes themselves existed.

The brief also questioned whether many of the subpoenaed conversations would be admissible in a criminal trial. "For example, the recorded conversations between President Richard M. Nixon and John Dean, neither of whom are named parties in the current proceeding, can only be categorized as inadmissible hearsay," the brief stated.

The possibility that the President might appeal an unfavorable ruling on the subpoena request to the Supreme Court also was raised in the brief. He had not done so in past battles over subpoenas, always complying with them after seeking delays and compromises. He appealed to the U.S. Circuit Court of Appeals in the first subpoena case in the summer of 1973, but lost 5–2 and subsequently turned over the material.

The President's lawyers had argued that "a president is not subject to compulsory process from a court."

Nixon personally invoked executive privilege in the case of the latest subpoena. He said he had decided that disclosure of any more of his conversations "would be contrary to the public interest."

His special counsel, James D. St. Clair, said the Watergate prosecutors were plainly embarked on a "fishing expedition" and that "absolutely no attempt was made by the special prosecutor to establish either the admissibility or relevancy of any of the requested items."

Other Motions. Among a flurry of motions filed by the seven coverup defendants May 1 in U.S. District Court in Washington, D.C., was one by H. R. Haldeman, the former White House chief of staff, asking the court to permit him to "inspect and test" the original tapes of all his conversations with President Nixon to help him prepare his defense. He also asked to be allowed to inspect the machines used to record the conversations and later to transcribe the tapes, "to determine whether (they) were operating properly."

Haldeman and the other defendants also asked that the charges against them be dismissed on grounds of extensive pretrial publicity about the case. Several defendants asked to be tried separately and to have their trials moved out of Washington.

Jaworski was given until June 5 to respond to the defense motions. Similar motions were filed by the six defendants charged with conspiracy in the break-in at the office of Daniel Ellsberg's psychiatrist. That case was scheduled for trial June 17.

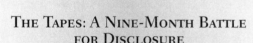

The Tapes: A Nine-Month Battle for Disclosure

The public revelation that many presidential conversations had been tape-recorded since early 1971 was made on July 16, 1973, at hearings of the Senate Watergate investigating committee. The man who opened up the stunning new chapter in the scandal was Alexander P. Butterfield, head of the Federal Aviation Administration and a former White House aide.

Butterfield's testimony triggered a continuing struggle over disclosure of the contents of the tapes. Following is a chronology of important dates in that struggle:

July 17–23, 1973: The Senate Watergate Committee and then Watergate special prosecutor Archibald Cox asked for certain Watergate-related tapes. After Nixon refused to release the tapes, the committee and Cox issued subpoenas demanding them.

Aug. 9: The Senate committee filed suit in U.S. District Court in Washington, D.C., in an attempt to gain access to the tapes.

Aug. 22: Cox and Charles Alan Wright, then consultant to the White House, argued before Sirica concerning the need for the subpoenaed tapes.

Aug. 29: Sirica ordered Nixon to make the tapes available to him for a decision on their use by the Watergate grand jury. The President refused.

Sept. 7: Cox asked the U.S. Court of Appeals to grant the grand jury direct access to the tapes.

Sept. 11: Wright, Cox and Sirica's two attorneys argued Sirica's Aug. 29 ruling before the Court of Appeals.

Sept. 13: The seven Court of Appeals judges issued a unanimous memorandum urging Nixon and Cox to settle the tapes dispute out of court.

Oct. 12: In a 5–2 decision, the appeals court upheld Sirica.

Oct. 19: Nixon said he would not comply with the order to give Sirica the tapes but would compromise by preparing summaries of the tapes' contents for Cox and the Senate committee—and would allow Sen. John C. Stennis (D Miss.) to listen to the tapes to verify the summaries.

Oct. 20: Cox refused the compromise because of the condition imposed by Nixon that he subpoena no more tapes or documents from the White House. Nixon ordered Richardson to fire Cox; Richardson and his deputy William D. Ruckelshaus resigned instead. Acting Attorney General Robert H. Bork then fired Cox.

Oct. 23: Wright announced that Nixon would turn over the tapes to the court.

Oct. 31: Buzhardt said two of the nine tapes requested never existed.

Nov. 21: White House attorneys told Sirica that an 18 1/2-minute segment was erased from the June 20, 1972, tape of a conversation between Nixon and H. R. Haldeman, his former chief of staff.

Nov. 26: White House attorneys turned over the existing subpoenaed tapes to the court.

Dec. 19: Sirica ruled that nearly all of two subpoenaed tapes and part of a third be

turned over to Leon Jaworski, Watergate special prosecutor.

Jan. 15, 1974: Technical experts reported to the court that the 18 1/2-minute gap was the result of five separate manual erasures.

Feb. 6: The House by a 410–4 vote approved H Res 803, authorizing the House Judiciary Committee to conduct an impeachment inquiry.

Feb. 25: The House Judiciary Committee sent James D. St. Clair, special White House counsel, a letter requesting tapes and documents related to presidential conversations, including some of those already provided to the special prosecutor.

March 6: St. Clair told Sirica that Nixon had decided to give the House committee all the tapes and documents submitted to the Watergate grand jury.

March 11: The White House leaked the committee's Feb. 25 letter requesting tapes of 42 additional conversations.

March 12: Ronald L. Ziegler, Nixon's press secretary, said that the President would be unwilling to supply additional tapes until the House Judiciary Committee defined impeachable offenses.

March 25: The Watergate grand jury's report on Nixon was turned over to the House committee.

April 4: The House Judiciary Committee gave Nixon until April 9 to decide whether to turn over the 42 presidential tape recordings.

April 9: White House attorneys told the committee that they needed more time to decide how to respond.

April 11: The House Judiciary Committee voted 33–3 to subpoena the tapes requested March 11.

April 18: Jaworski subpoenaed other tapes, memos and other materials relating to 64 conversations, needed as evidence for the Watergate coverup trial.

April 29: Nixon announced on national television that he would release the next day edited transcripts of certain tapes in response to the April 11 committee subpoena.

Points to Ponder

- How would members of Congress like it if their private conversations and strategy sessions with aides were transcribed and released to the public? Do you think their private conversations would match their public comments?

- Should a president be judged on what he says or does in private?

PART III: IMPEACHMENT THREAT AND RESIGNATION

INTRODUCTION:

Nixon Resigns under Threat of Certain Impeachment

Richard Nixon's hold on the presidency became ever more tenuous after his release on April 30, 1974, of transcripts of private White House conversations. The heavily edited version of the tapes that he made public failed to satisfy the demands of Watergate investigators. More damaging, it disenchanted many of his dwindling band of supporters.

The actual contents of the transcripts were just part of the story. The transcripts also gave the American people insights into the manner in which their president conducted himself in private. The transcripts, even as edited by Nixon and his staff, revealed a man willing to bargain for his political survival, and conferring with his advisers in an atmosphere of suspicion and hostility toward real or imagined enemies. The conversations between Nixon and his top aides were sprinkled liberally with profanity, much of it deleted from the transcripts. And the frequency of "unintelligible" words and phrases left many enigmas about the true meaning of conversations and remarks.

Indicative of the largely negative reaction to the transcripts was the editorial comment of *The Chicago Tribune*, which had endorsed Nixon's 1968 election and 1972 reelection. "We saw the public man in his first administration," the Tribune editorialized, "and we were impressed. Now in about 300,000 words we have seen the private man and we are appalled."

The transcripts became instant paperback bestsellers. To many readers, they appeared to show Nixon's conduct and attitude moving toward the "high crimes and misdemeanors" standard that the Constitution says is grounds for impeachment.

AN APPROACHING CONFRONTATION

On Capitol Hill, Republican conservatives began to express reservations about the future of their president. Party leaders in both houses had their doubts. "I see nothing that the President can do that would rehabilitate him in the public eye and restore confidence in him," said Rep. John B. Anderson of Illinois, chairman of the House Republican Conference.

As far as the White House was concerned, there would be no more tapes or transcripts. Nixon believed that neither the committee nor the Watergate special prosecutor had the authority to force him to turn over records of private conversations. His lawyer, James D. St. Clair, informed the House Judiciary Committee on May 7 that the president believed "that the full story is out now." "If the House wants to issue a subpoena, then we will have a constitutional confrontation," said St. Clair.

But lawmakers felt they needed additional evidence to fully investigate the Watergate coverup. Chairman Peter W. Rodino Jr. said he would be "adamant" in seeking additional material. Impeachment inquiry counsel John M. Doar said he would recommend that the committee subpoena additional tapes—and the committee agreed in mid-May to issue two more subpoenas.

On May 22, Nixon wrote Rodino that the committee's "never-ending" demands for tapes amounted to "such a massive invasion of presidential conversations that the institution of the presidency itself would be fatally compromised" if he complied with them.

Rodino, calling Nixon's response "a very grave matter," implied that the president's resistance could lead to impeachment.

On May 30, the Judiciary Committee subpoenaed 45 more tapes. Accompanying the subpoena was the sternest warning so far to the president, informing him that refusal to comply could be grounds for impeachment. A letter from the committee stated that "it is not within the power of the President to conduct an inquiry into his own impeachment, to determine which evidence . . . is relevant and necessary to such an inquiry."

Before departing for a trip to the Middle East June 10, Nixon responded with a letter to the committee. "I am determined," he wrote, "to do nothing which . . . would render the executive branch henceforth and forevermore subservient to the legislative branch, and would thereby destroy the constitutional balance."

A SUPREME COURT DECISION

The crucial demand for the tapes would come not from the Judiciary Committee, but rather from the special Watergate prosecutor, Leon Jaworski. He was seeking evidence from the president—in the form of White House tapes—for use in the trial of former Nixon aides charged in the Watergate coverup conspiracy. The confrontation over Jaworski's quest would reach a climax in the marble courtroom of the Supreme Court.

Jaworski on April 18 had issued a subpoena for tapes of 64 presidential conversations. On May 20, U.S. District Court judge John J. Sirica refused to quash the subpoena as Nixon had asked—ordering Nixon to turn over the subpoenaed tapes to the court.

Bypassing the appeals court, Jaworski asked the Supreme Court to hear arguments and rule as soon as possible on the validity of Nixon's claim of presidential privilege to withhold this evidence. White House attorneys opposed this request for immediate review. But on May 31, the justices agreed to hear the case in an extraordinary end-of-session argument July 8.

Jaworski and St. Clair made their arguments before a packed courtroom July 8. On July 24—hours before the televised impeachment debate began in the House Judiciary Committee—the court ruled. Unanimously, the justices rejected Nixon's claim of privilege in this case, upholding Sirica's order.

Failure to surrender the records, the court ruled, "would cut deeply into the guarantee of due process of law and gravely impair the basic function of the courts. . . . Without access to specific facts, a criminal prosecution may be totally frustrated." In a statement issued through St. Clair a few hours later, Nixon said he would "comply fully with the court's ruling. . . ."

COMMITTEE INVESTIGATION

Even as the court struggle for the tapes made its way toward the Supreme Court, the Judiciary Committee focused on its impeachment investigation. The 38-member committee began hearing evidence in private on May 9. Much of the material used in its investigation was the same as that used by the Senate Watergate Committee a year earlier. But there was one difference: the Judiciary Committee had access to some tape-recorded presidential conversations.

Reports began to gain momentum that Nixon had known about the coverup earlier than March 21, 1973, the date he had said he first learned of it. Other reports pointed to discrepancies between the White House transcripts and the actual tapes. Administration spokesmen decried the leaks as "a purposeful effort to bring down the President" and "trial by innuendo."

Rodino responded calmly, saying that the committee would not be diverted from its investigation. The committee's position was strengthened with the release of its own transcripts of eight tapes July 9. They differed markedly from the White House transcripts.

The committee version, for example, included a Nixon admonition to one of his top advisors, John Mitchell, on March 22, 1973. "I want you all to stonewall it, let them plead the Fifth Amendment, cover up or anything else," he had said. The White House version had not included Nixon's comment.

The White House called the release of the committee transcripts "a hyped public relations campaign."

In mid-July 1974, the Judiciary Committee completed its closed hearings. It began releasing volumes of evidence that would eventually total thousands of pages. Doar, backed by minority impeachment counsel Albert E. Jenner Jr., recommended impeachment. Presidential press secretary Ronald L. Ziegler described the committee inquiry as a "kangaroo court."

Amid mounting evidence of presidential wrongdoing, Democrats overwhelmingly seemed inclined to support impeachment. The unity among committee Republicans loyal to Nixon began to crack. On July 23, one of the Republicans, Lawrence J. Hogan of Maryland, said that he would vote for impeachment. He was the first Republican on the committee to break ranks.

COMMITTEE IMPEACHMENT DEBATE

The Judiciary Committee proceedings went public on the evening of July 24. The American people were given a chance to watch history as it happened in front of the television cameras.

As the committee members made their emotional, often painful opening statements, the eventual outcome was clear: a majority of the committee would vote for impeachment. Members of both parties believed Nixon had to go.

The committee debated five articles of impeachment exhaustively, often laboring into the night. Sometimes the debate was calm and thoughtful; sometimes it was strident and partisan. In the end, Democrats and a number of Republicans approved three articles of impeachment.

Conservative southern Democrats and Republicans eloquently expressed the difficulty of voting for impeachment. "I know for certain that I have nothing to gain politically or otherwise from what I must do here," said Democrat Walter Flowers of Alabama, "but after weeks of searching through the facts and agonizing over the constitutional requirements, it is clear to me what I must do."

The committee voted to impeach Nixon for obstructing justice, for abusing his presidential powers, and for contempt of Congress. They rejected two impeachment articles that accused the president of concealing the bombing of Cambodia and evading income taxes.

THE RESIGNATION

The end came quickly. The final Judiciary Committee vote was taken on July 30, 1974. The House prepared to start its impeachment proceedings in mid-August. While the outlook appeared doubtful for Nixon in both the House and Senate, a few loyalists remained hopeful.

In addition to his losses in the courts and in the Judiciary Committee, Nixon had suffered some other painful setbacks during the summer.

John D. Ehrlichman, his former domestic affairs adviser, was convicted in mid-July of conspiring to violate the civil rights of Dr. Lewis J. Fielding, Daniel Ellsberg's psychiatrist. He was sentenced to at least 20 months in prison.

Ehrlichman and H. R. Haldeman, Nixon's former closest adviser, who had resigned with Ehrlichman, were among the six men awaiting trial in the Watergate coverup. Also awaiting trial was John N. Mitchell, Nixon's former attorney general and campaign director.

Another former top adviser, Charles W. Colson, entered a surprise plea of guilty to charges of obstruction of justice in the Pentagon Papers trial of Ellsberg. He was fined and sentenced to one to three years in prison.

As the Judiciary Committee debated impeachment, John B. Connally, former secretary of the treasury and a man personally close to Nixon, was indicted for perjury, conspiracy to obstruct justice, and accepting bribes for his dealing with dairy industry lobbyists.

On Monday, Aug. 5, the remaining shreds of Nixon's defense fell away. That day, in response to the Supreme Court decision, he released three transcripts of conversations that took place on June 23, 1972—six days after the break-in. Nixon acknowledged that he had been withholding the three transcripts from his staff and his attorneys. The transcripts clearly contradicted Nixon's earlier claims of noninvolvement in the coverup. Nixon expressed regret for his "serious act of omission."

It was all over. Facing clear evidence of the president's guilt, congressional Republicans told Nixon that his support was gone. Impeachment in the House and conviction in the Senate appeared inevitable.

Nixon announced his resignation the night of Aug. 8 before the largest television audience up to that time. The next day, at noon, Vice President Gerald R. Ford was sworn in as president. Richard M. Nixon took his last trip aboard Air Force One to San Clemente, California, which would no longer be known as the Western White House.

GRAND JURY NAMES NIXON CO-CONSPIRATOR

The administration's decision to release transcripts of taped White House conversations did little to improve President Nixon's political standing. The transcripts revealed the president and his top advisors as focused on political survival and implacably hostile toward those who they regarded as enemies. The Senate Republican leader, Hugh Scott of Pennsylvania, described the contents of the transcripts as "disgusting" and "immoral." The House Republican leader, John J. Rhodes of Arizona, urged Nixon to consider resignation. *The Chicago Tribune*, formerly one of Nixon's staunchest supporters among major newspapers, suggested the House act quickly on a bill of impeachment. Despite these calls for Nixon to resign or face impeachment, the White House signaled that it had little interest in cooperating with investigators into the Watergate scandal. "As far as Watergate is concerned, the President has concluded . . . that the full story is now out," said Nixon's attorney, James D. St. Clair, a week after the transcripts were released.

The Judiciary Committee kept up the pressure. In mid-May, with virtually all its members convinced they needed tapes instead of transcripts, the committee issued two more subpoenas to Nixon by nearly unanimous votes. John M. Doar, the special committee counsel, believed some of these tapes would clarify Nixon's knowledge of the plan to bug the Democratic headquarters and the Watergate break-in. Testimony given to the Senate Watergate Committee had indicated that the Watergate plan had been approved by John N. Mitchell on March 30, 1972. Mitchell and H. R. Haldeman discussed the plan on April 4 and then met with the president shortly after to discuss campaign matters. Nixon and Haldeman then met privately. The committee sought records of these last two conversations.

The committee believed other conversations would shed light on Nixon's reaction in the days after the break-in. It also wanted more evidence about White House efforts to get CIA officials to limit the FBI's investigation of Watergate. And the committee requested information to determine whether the president had improperly helped the dairy industry and the International Telephone and Telegraph Corporation (ITT) in response to financial contributions.

But Nixon in late May rejected the subpoenas. He also said he would not honor future subpoenas. He said the panel's "never-ending" demands for tapes could be fatal to the presidency. Both Democrats and Republicans on the Judiciary Committee sharply criticized Nixon's refusal to cooperate.

Committee members also were alarmed by mounting indications of Nixon's wrongdoing. The evidence gathered by the committee's staff appeared to show that Nixon gave a direct command to raise money to pay off the Watergate burglars. According to committee members, Nixon spoke with Dean on March 21, 1973, about raising $120,000 for the Watergate defendants. Two members of the committee reported that Nixon said either "Well, for Christ sakes, get it" or "Goddamn it, get it."

At the end of May, the House Judiciary Committee sent Nixon a stern letter demanding the tapes. It also voted 37–1 to subpoena tapes of an additional 45 conversations. In its letter, the committee bluntly threatened Nixon with impeachment. "Your refusals in and of themselves might constitute a ground for impeachment," the letter warned. The letter also said that committee members may conclude that Nixon's failure to cooperate could mean the tapes contained incriminating statements.

Also in late May, U.S. District Court judge John J. Sirica ordered Nixon to turn over tapes and other records of 64 conversations. The records had been subpoenaed by Watergate special prosecutor Leon Jaworski. Sirica rejected an argument by St. Clair that Jaworski, who was appointed by the president, had no right to issue a subpoena to him. Sirica also rejected St. Clair's arguments that the special prosecutor already had all the evidence he needed, and that some of the tapes were covered by executive privilege. (Executive privilege is the president's right to withhold certain records that could damage the national interest. For more about executive privilege, see p. 60.) Instead of complying with Sirica's order, Nixon said he would appeal.

Reacting strongly, Jaworski asked the Supreme Court to step in. Normally, the case would first go to an appeals court, the route preferred by the White House. But that would take much more time than a direct ruling by the Supreme Court. Because of the gravity of the situation, the Supreme Court agreed on May 31 to hear the case. It scheduled oral arguments for July 8. Jaworski's motivation was slightly different than that of the House Judiciary Committee. He needed the tapes to prosecute Watergate defendants. He also wanted a definitive ruling from the high court to give him the power he needed to continue to investigate and prosecute crimes related to Watergate.

Nixon's refusal to cooperate was affecting other trials. The judge overseeing one Watergate-related case, for example, warned that Nixon's failure to supply documents might result in the dismissal of charges against the Watergate defendants. "The President must know," said Judge Gerhard A. Gesell, that "he is acting deliberately . . . in aborting this trial." St. Clair responded that the president's goal was not to have the charges dismissed. Instead, Nixon was determined to protect national security, which could be jeopardized by the disclosure of certain documents.

In early June, the press revealed that the original Watergate grand jury had voted unanimously to name Nixon as an unindicted co-conspirator. This meant the jurors believed that Nixon had broken the law by taking part in the Watergate coverup. The jurors, however, did not formally charge Nixon with a crime because Watergate special prosecutor Leon Jaworski told them that the Constitution did not permit the indictment of a president. Instead, it was up to the House to determine whether to impeach a president for committing crimes.

In another ominous sign for Nixon, one of his former top aides, Charles W. Colson, pleaded guilty to a charge that he had attempted to obstruct justice. Colson agreed to divulge everything he knew about Watergate. He was the first member of Nixon's inner circle of advisors to agree to cooperate with the special prosecutor. One month later, former White House aide John D. Ehrlichman was found guilty of four criminal charges. He had been the president's chief domestic advisor.

Text of Nixon's Letter on Subpoenaed Tapes, Diary

Reprinted from *Congressional Quarterly Weekly Report*, May 25, 1974

In this letter to the chairman of the House Judiciary Committee, Nixon stated that the committee already had documents detailing the full story of Watergate. He said that turning over additional records would dangerously weaken the presidency. However, Nixon said he would agree to answer questions under oath.

Following is the text of President Nixon's May 22 letter to Rep. Peter W. Rodino Jr., chair-

man of the House Judiciary Committee, indicating that the President would not comply with the committee's subpoenas for additional tapes and parts of his diary:

This letter is in response to two subpoenas of the House of Representatives dated May 15, 1974, one calling for the production of tapes of additional presidential conversations and the other calling for the production of my daily diary for extended periods of time in 1972 and 1973. Neither subpoena specifies in any way the subject matters into which the committee seeks to inquire. I can only presume that the material sought must be thought to relate in some unspecified way to what has generally been known as "Watergate."

On April 30, 1974, in response to a subpoena of the House of Representatives dated April 11, 1974, I submitted transcripts not only of all the recorded presidential conversations that took place that were called for in the subpoena, but also of a number of additional presidential conversations that had not been subpoenaed. I did this so that the record of my knowledge and actions in the Watergate matter would be fully disclosed, once and for all.

Even while my response to this original subpoena was being prepared, on April 19, 1974, my counsel received a request from the Judiciary Committee's counsel for the production of tapes of more than 140 additional presidential conversations—of which 76 were alleged to relate to Watergate—together with a request for additional presidential diaries for extended periods of time in 1972 and 1973.

The subpoenas dated May 15 call for the tapes of the first 11 of the conversations that were requested on April 19, and for all of the diaries that were requested on April 19. My counsel has informed me that the intention of the committee is to also issue a series of subpoenas covering all 76 of the conversations requested on April 19 that are thought to relate to Watergate. It is obvious that the subpoenaed diaries are intended to be used to identify even more presidential conversations, as a basis for yet additional subpoenas.

Thus, it is clear that the continued succession of demands for additional presidential conversations has become a never ending process and that to continue providing these conversations in response to the constantly escalating requests would constitute such a massive invasion into the confidentiality of presidential conversations that the institution of the presidency would be fatally compromised.

The committee has the full story of Watergate, in so far as it relates to presidential knowledge and presidential actions. Production of these additional conversations would merely prolong the inquiry without yielding significant additional evidence. More fundamentally, continuing ad infinitum the process of yielding up additional conversations in response to an endless series of demands would fatally weaken this office not only in this administration but for future presidencies as well.

Accordingly, I respectfully decline to produce the tapes of presidential conversations and presidential diaries referred to in your request of April 19, 1974, that are called for in part in the subpoenas dated May 15, 1974, and those allegedly dealing with Watergate that may be called for in such further subpoenas as may hereafter be issued.

However, I again remind you that if the committee desires further information from me about any of these conversations or other maters related to its inquiry, I stand ready to answer, under oath, pertinent, written interrogatories, and to be interviewed under oath by you and the ranking minority member at the White House.

Punctuated by events and revelations whose impact on his future would be defined behind the closed doors of grand juries and the House impeachment inquiry, the first week in June was not a comforting one for President Nixon.

It began early. On June 3, former White House special counsel Charles W. Colson pleaded guilty to a charge that he had attempted to obstruct justice by trying to destroy the public image of Pentagon Papers defendant Daniel Ellsberg. The first of Nixon's inner circle of advisers to agree to cooperate with the special prosecutor, Colson said he made his plea so that he could "tell everything I know about Watergate and Watergate-related matters."

As the House Judiciary Committee resumed its inquiry June 4, examining non-Watergate-related charges against Nixon, technical experts appointed by U.S. District Judge John J. Sirica reaffirmed their conclusions on the cause of the strategic gap in the tape of a June 20, 1972, conversation between Nixon and former chief of staff H. R. Haldeman: The gap was caused by at least five manual erasures of the tape.

"This report draws no inferences about such questions as whether the erasure and buzz were made accidentally or intentionally, or when, or by what person or persons," the experts' report stated. Those questions were left up to the grand jury to answer.

Nixon: Co-Conspirator

The most damaging of the week's disclosures, however, came June 6: *The Los Angeles Times* reported that the original Watergate grand jury had voted unanimously to name Nixon as an unindicted co-conspirator in the Watergate coverup case.

The meaning of such a grand jury action had been explained to Nixon on April 17, 1973, by Assistant Attorney General Henry E. Petersen.

Naming someone an unindicted co-conspirator, Petersen said, "just means that for one reason or another we don't want to charge them at the time. For example, I am indicted—you're named as an unindicted co-conspirator. You are just as guilty as I am but you are a witness— we are not going to prosecute you." It was widely assumed that the grand jury had taken this action after Watergate special prosecutor Leon Jaworski had informed them that it was not constitutionally proper to indict a sitting president—that impeachment proceedings should come first.

Special White House counsel James D. St. Clair, confirming the report, said that Nixon regretted the grand jury's action. St. Clair also pointed out that being named in this way by a grand jury did not prove that someone *was* a co-conspirator.

In response to a motion by defendants in the Watergate coverup case, Jaworski had agreed June 5 to supply to them a list of the persons named as unindicted co-conspirators in that case. St. Clair June 6 asked Sirica to make the list public, arguing that since the President's inclusion in the list was known, there was no longer any reason to keep the list secret. Sirica agreed to do so June 7, but actual disclosure required Supreme Court action.

CAN A PRESIDENT BE INDICTED?

Most people, when faced with a subpoena from Congress or from a grand jury, have little choice but to obey it. Otherwise, lawmakers can turn the case over to a prosecutor to pursue charges for contempt of Congress or contempt of court. Such a crime carries a penalty of up to one year in prison and a $1,000 fine.

When it came to President Nixon, however, the House Judiciary Committee could not easily throw him in jail. So instead it issued repeated demands to the president. Its main leverage was the threat of impeachment. That is part of the reason that the battle over the tapes took several months.

Neither the committee nor the Watergate special prosecutor attempted to issue an indictment, or formal criminal charge, against Nixon for contempt of Congress or for other crimes. Legal experts have been skeptical that a sitting president can be indicted. The Supreme Court has never been asked to rule on such an interesting constitutional question. Many analysts doubt that the court would uphold an indictment against a president. That is because if a president was removed from the White House and put in jail, it would effectively strip him of his power. And the Constitution gives Congress alone the right to impeach a president and remove him from office. The Watergate grand jury appeared to agree with this logic when it named Nixon as an unindicted co-conspirator, instead of issuing an indictment against him.

In contrast to Nixon, Congress dealt swiftly with another Watergate figure. G. Gordon Liddy, one of Nixon's top campaign officials, refused to answer questions on July 20, 1973, before a House Armed Services subcommittee. Less than two months later, the House voted 334–11 to cite him for contempt of Congress. The case was turned over the U.S. attorney in the District of Columbia. Liddy was found guilty on May 10, 1974.

Text of Nixon's June 9 Letter to Rodino

Reprinted from *Congressional Quarterly Weekly Report*, June 15, 1974

In this June 9 letter to the Judiciary Committee chairman, Nixon again refused to comply with the committee's subpoenas. The letter was a reply to the committee's May 31 subpoena for additional tapes and other materials. It also responded to a May 30 letter from the committee warning that Nixon's refusal to provide information could give the appearance that he had something to hide.

Nixon said the committee did not have the right to determine the confidentiality of presidential documents. He cited several historical examples of one branch of government refusing to comply with an investigation by another branch because of the constitutional separation of powers. He also said the committee had all the information it needed to wrap up its investigation into Watergate. The president dismissed the committee's conclusion that his refusal to cooperate might mean he had something to hide. That conclusion "flies in the face of established law" because a person who asserts his legal rights should not be penalized for doing so.

Members of the committee did not appear persuaded by the president's letter. "The doctrine of separation of powers has to yield to our inquiry," said Robert McClory of Illinois, one of the committee's senior Republicans.

Following is the text of a letter written by President Nixon to Rep. Peter W. Rodino Jr., chairman of the House Judiciary Committee, on June 9:

Dear Mr. Chairman:

In your letter of May 30, you describe as "a grave matter" my refusal to comply with the Committee's subpoenas of May 15. You state that "under the Constitution it is not within the power of the President to conduct an inquiry into his own impeachment," and add that "Committee members will be free to consider whether your refusals warrant the drawing of adverse inferences concerning the substance of the materials. . . ."

The question of the respective rights and responsibilities of the Executive and Legislative branches is one of the cardinal questions raised by a proceeding such as the one the Committee is now conducting. I believe, therefore, that I should point out certain considerations which I believe are compelling.

First, it is quite clear that this is not a case of "the President conduct[ing] an inquiry into his own impeachment." The Committee is conducting its inquiry; the Committee has had extensive and unprecedented cooperation from the White House. The question at issue is not who conducts the inquiry, but where the line is to be drawn on an apparently endlessly escalating spiral of demands for confidential Presidential tapes and documents. The Committee asserts that it should be the sole judge of Presidential confidentiality. I cannot accept such a doctrine; no President could accept such a doctrine, which has never before been seriously asserted.

What is commonly referred to now as "executive privilege" is part and parcel of the basic doctrine of separation of powers—the establishment, by the Constitution, of three separate and co-equal branches of Government. While many functions of Government require the concurrence or interaction of two or more branches, each branch historically has been steadfast in maintaining its own independence by turning back attempts of the others, whenever made, to assert an authority to invade, without consent, the privacy of its own deliberations.

Thus each house of the Congress has always maintained that it alone shall decide what should be provided, if anything, and in what form, in response to a judicial subpoena. This standing doctrine was summed up in a resolution adopted by the Senate on March 8, 1962, in connection with subpoenas issued by a Federal court in the trial of James Hoffa, which read: "Resolved, that by the privileges of the Senate of the United States no evidence under the control and in the possession of the Senate of the United States can, by the mandate of process of the ordinary courts of justice, be taken from the control or possession, but by its permission. . . ." More recently, in the case of Lt. William Calley, the chairman of the House Armed Services subcommittee refused to make available for the court-martial proceeding testimony that had been given before the subcommittee in executive session—testimony which Lt. Calley claimed would be exculpatory. In refusing, the subcommittee chairman, Representative Hebert, explained that the Congress is "an independent branch of the Government, separate from but equal to the Executive and Judicial branches," and that accord-

ingly only Congress can direct the disclosure of legislative records.

Equally, the Judicial branch has always held sacrosanct the privacy of judicial deliberations, and has always held that neither of the other branches may invade Judicial privacy or encroach on Judicial independence. In 1953, in refusing to respond to a subpoena from the House Un-American Activities Committee, Justice Tom C. Clark cited the fact that "the independence of the three branches of our Government is the cardinal principle on which our Constitutional system is founded. This complete independence of the judiciary is necessary to the proper administration of justice." In 1971, Chief Justice Burger analogized the confidentiality of the Court to that of the Executive, and said: "No statute gives this Court express power to establish and enforce the utmost security measures for the secrecy of our deliberations and records. Yet I have little doubt as to the inherent power of the Court to protect the confidentiality of its internal operations by whatever judicial means may be required."

These positions of the Courts and the Congress are not lightly taken; they are essential to maintaining the balances among the three branches of Government. Equal firmness by the Executive is no less essential to maintaining that balance.

The general applicability of the basic principle was summed up in 1962 by Senator Stennis, in a ruling upholding President Kennedy's refusal to provide information sought by a Senate subcommittee. Senator Stennis held: "We are now come face to face and are in direct conflict with the established doctrine of separation of powers. . . . I know of no case where the Court has ever made the Senate or the House surrender records from its files, or where the Executive has made the Legislative Branch surrender records from its files—and I do not think either one of them could. So the rule works three ways. Each is supreme within its field, and each is responsible within its field."

If the institution of an impeachment inquiry against a President were permitted to override all restraints of separation of powers, this would spell the end of the doctrine of separation of powers; it would be an open invitation to future Congresses to use an impeachment inquiry, however frivolously, as a device to assert their own supremacy over the Executive, and to reduce Executive confidentiality to a nullity.

My refusal to comply with further subpoenas with respect to Watergate is based, essentially, on two considerations.

First, preserving the principle of separation of powers—and of the Executive as a co-equal branch—

requires that the Executive, no less than the Legislative or Judicial branches, must be immune from unlimited search and seizure by the other co-equal branches.

Second, the voluminous body of materials that the Committee already has—and which I have voluntarily provided, partly in response to Committee requests and partly in an effort to round out the record—does give the full story of Watergate, insofar as it relates to Presidential knowledge and Presidential actions. The way to resolve whatever ambiguities the Committee may feel still exist is not to pursue the chimera of additional evidence from additional tapes, but rather to call live witnesses who can place the existing evidence in perspective, and subject them to cross-examination under oath. Simply multiplying the tapes and transcripts would extend the proceedings interminably, while adding nothing substantial to the evidence the Committee already has.

Once embarked on a process of continually demanding additional tapes whenever those the Committee already has fail to turn up evidence of guilt, there would be no end unless a line were drawn somewhere by someone. Since it is clear that the Committee will not draw such a line, I have done so.

One example should serve to illustrate my point. In issuing its subpoena of May 15, the Committee rested its argument for the necessity of these additional tapes most heavily on the first of the additional conversations subpoenaed. This was a meeting that I held on April 4, 1972, in the Oval Office, with then Attorney General Mitchell and H. R. Haldeman. The Committee insisted that this was necessary because it was the first meeting following the one in Key Biscayne between Mr. Mitchell and his aides, in which, according to testimony, he allegedly approved the intelligence plan that led to the Watergate break-in; and because, according to other testimony, an intelligence plan was mentioned in a briefing paper prepared for Mr. Haldeman for the April 4 meeting. Committee members made clear their belief that the record of this meeting, therefore, would be crucial to a determination of whether the President had advance information of the intelligence activities that included the break-in.

As it happens, there also was testimony that the ITT matter had been discussed at that April 4 meeting, and the Committee therefore also requested the April 4 conversation in connection with its ITT investigation. On June 5, 1974, a complete transcript was provided to the Committee for the purposes of the ITT probe, together with an invitation to verify the transcript against the actual tape. This transcript shows that not a word was spoken in that meeting about intelligence plans, or about anything remotely related to Watergate—as the Committee can verify.

I cite this instance because it illustrates clearly—on the basis of material the Committee already has—the insubstantiality of the claims being made for additional tapes; and the fact that a Committee demand for material does not automatically thereby convert the requested material into "evidence."

As for your declaration that an adverse inference could be drawn from my assertion of Executive privilege with regard to these additional materials, such a declaration flies in the face of established law on the assertion of valid claims of privilege. The Supreme Court has pointed out that even allowing comment by a judge or prosecutor on a valid Constitutional claim is "a penalty imposed by courts for exercising a Constitutional privilege," and that "it cuts down on the privilege by making its assertion costly." In its deliberations on the Proposed Federal Rules of Evidence, the House of Representatives—in its version—substituted for specific language on the various forms of privilege a blanket rule that these should "be governed by the principles of the Common law as they may be interpreted by the courts of the United States in light of reason and experience. . . . "But as adopted in 1972 by the Supreme Court—the final arbiter of "the principles of the Common law as. . .interpreted by the courts," and as codification of those principles—the Proposed Federal Rules clearly state: "The claim of a privilege, whether in the present proceeding or in a prior occasion, is not the proper subject of comment by judge or counsel. No inference may be drawn therefrom."

Those are legal arguments. The common-sense argument is that a claim of privilege, which is valid under the doctrine of separation of powers and is designed to protect the principle of separation of powers, must be accepted without adverse inference—or else the privilege itself is undermined, and the separation of powers nullified.

A proceeding such as the present one places a great strain on our Constitutional system, and on the pattern of practice of self-restraint by the three branches that has maintained the balances of that system for nearly two centuries. Whenever one branch attempts to press too hard in intruding on the Constitutional prerogatives of another, that balance is threatened. From the start of these proceedings, I have tried to cooperate as far as I reasonably could in order to avert a Constitutional confrontation. But I am determined to do nothing which, by the precedents it set, would render the Executive branch henceforth and forevermore subservient to the Legislative branch, and would thereby destroy the Constitutional balance. This is the key issue in my insistence that the Executive must remain the final arbiter of demands on its confidentiality, just as the Legislative and Judicial branches must remain the final arbiters of demands on their confidentiality.

EXCERPTS FROM JAWORSKI'S ARGUMENT TO SUPREME COURT . . . ASKING [FOR] WHITE HOUSE TAPES AS EVIDENCE FOR TRIAL

Reprinted from *Congressional Quarterly Weekly Report,* June 29, 1974

Watergate special prosecutor Leon Jaworski made a historic appeal to the Supreme Court on June 21, asking the justices to order President Nixon to turn over White House tapes and other documents. Jaworski asserted that the president could not withhold evidence merely by claiming it was confidential. He also said it was within the Supreme Court's power to decide the case. Jaworski disputed the White House contention that it could withhold the evidence because of executive privilege. He said there was a com-pelling public interest in disclosing the tapes and other documents. He also said Nixon had effec-tively waived executive privilege when he released transcripts of more than 40 presidential conversations.

Following are excerpts from the summary of Special Watergate Prosecutor Leon Jaworski's argument as filed with the Supreme Court June 21. He asked the court to order the Pres-ident to turn over White House tapes and other material for use as evidence in the trial of the former White House aides indicted for obstructing justice through the Watergate coverup:

The narrow issue presented to this Court is whether the President, in a pending prose-cution against his former aides and associ-ates being conducted in the name of the United States by a Special Prosecutor not subject to Presidential directions, may with-hold material evidence from the court merely on his assertion that the evidence involves confidential governmental deliberations. The Court clearly has jurisdiction to decide this issue. . . . This is only a specific application of the general but fundamental principle of our constitutional system of government that the courts, as the "neutral" branch of govern-ment, have been allocated the responsibility

to resolve all issues in a controversy properly before them, even though this requires them to determine authoritatively the powers and responsibilities of the other branches.

Any notion that this controversy, arising as it does from the issuance of a subpoena *duces tecum* to the President at the request of the Special Prosecutor, is not justiciable is wholly illusory. In the context of the most concrete and vital kind of case—the federal criminal prosecution of former White House officials—the Special Prosecutor, as the attorney for the United States, has resorted to a traditional mechanism to procure evi-dence for the government's case at trial. In objecting to the enforcement of the sub-poena, the President has raised a classic question of law—a claim of privilege—and the United States through its counsel and in its sovereign capacity, is opposing that claim. Thus, viewed in practical terms, it would be hard to imagine a controversy more appropri-ate for judicial resolution.

The fact that this concrete controversy is presented in the context of a dispute between the President and the Special Prosecutor does not deprive this Court of jurisdiction. Congress has vested in the Attorney General, as the head of the Department of Justice, the exclusive authority to conduct the govern-ment's civil and criminal litigation, including the exclusive authority for securing evidence. The Attorney General, with the explicit con-currence of the President, has vested that authority with respect to Watergate matters in the Special Prosecutor. These regulations have the force and effect of law and establish the functional independence of the Special Prosecutor. Accordingly, the Special Prose-cutor, representing the sovereign authority of the United States, and the President appear before the Court as adverse parties in the truest sense. The President himself has ceded any power that he might have had to control the course of the pending prosecu-tion, and it would stand the Constitution on its head to say that this arrangement, if respected and given effect by the courts, vio-lates the "separation of powers."

I

Throughout our constitutional history the courts, in cases or controversies before them, consistently have exercised final authority to determine whether even the highest executive officials are acting in accordance with the Constitution. . . . The courts have not abjured this responsibility even when the most pressing needs of the Nation were at issue.

In applying this fundamental principle, the courts have determined for themselves not only what evidence is admissible in a pending case, but also what evidence must be produced, including whether particular materials are appropriately subject to a claim of executive privilege. Indeed, this Court has squarely rejected the claim that the Executive has absolute, un-reviewable discretion to withhold documents from the courts.

The unbroken line of precedent establishing that the courts have the final authority for determining the applicability and scope of claims of executive privilege is supported by compelling arguments of policy. The Executive's legitimate interests in secrecy are more than adequately protected by the qualified privilege defined and applied by the courts. But as this Court has recognized, an absolute privilege which permitted the Executive to make a binding determination would lead to intolerable abuse. This case highlights the inherent conflict of interest that is presented when the Executive is called upon to produce evidence in a case which calls into question the Executive's own action. The President cannot be a proper judge of whether the greater public interest lies in disclosing evidence subpoenaed for trial, when that evidence may have a material bearing on whether he is impeached and will bear heavily on the guilt or innocence of close aides and trusted advisors.

In the framework of this case . . . the interests of justice as well as the interests of the parties to the pending prosecution require that the courts enter a decree requiring that relevant and unprivileged evidence be produced. The "produce or dismiss" option that is sometimes allowed to the Exec-

utive when a claim of executive privilege is overruled merely reflects a remedial accommodation of the requirements of substantive justice and thus has never been available to the Executive where the option could not satisfy these requirements. This is particularly true where the option would make a travesty out of the independent institution of the Special Prosecutor by allowing the President to accomplish indirectly what he cannot do directly—secure the abandonment of the Watergate prosecution.

II

There is nothing in the status of the President that deprives the courts of their constitutional power to resolve this dispute. The power to issue and enforce a subpoena *duces tecum* against the President was first recognized by Chief Justice Marshall in the *Burr* case in 1807, in accordance with two fundamental principles of our constitutional system: First, the President, like all executive officials as well as the humblest private citizens, is subject to the rule of law. Indeed, this follows inexorably from his constitutional duty to "take Care that the Laws be faithfully executed." Second, in the full and impartial administration of justice, the public has a right to every man's evidence. The persistent refusal of the courts to afford the President an absolute immunity from judicial process is fully supported by the deliberate decision of the Framers to deny him such a privilege.

Although it would be improper for the courts to control the exercise of the President's constitutional discretion, there can be no doubt that the President is subject to a judicial order requiring compliance with a clearly defined legal duty. The crucial jurisdictional factor is not the President's office, or the physical power to secure compliance with judicial orders, but the Court's ability to resolve authoritatively, within the context of a justiciable controversy, the conflicting claims of legal rights and obligations. The Court is called upon here to adjudicate the obligation of the President, as a citizen of the United States, to cooperate with a criminal prosecution by performing the solely ministerial task of producing specified, unprivileged evidence that he has taken within his sole personal custody.

III

The qualified executive privilege for confidential intra-governmental deliberations, designed to promote the candid interchange between officials and their aides, exists only to protect the legitimate functioning of government. Thus, the privilege must give way where, as here, it has been abused. There has been a *prima facie* showing that each of the participants in the subpoenaed conversations, including the President, was a member of the conspiracy to defraud the United States and to obstruct justice charged in the indictment in the present case, and a further showing that each of the conversations occurred in the course of and in furtherance of the conspiracy. The public purpose underlying the executive privilege for governmental deliberations precludes its application to shield alleged criminality.

But even if a presumptive privilege were to be recognized in this case, the privilege cannot be sustained in the face of the compelling public interest in disclosure. The responsibility of the courts in passing on a claim of executive privilege is, in the first instance, to determine whether the party demanding the evidence has made a *prima facie* showing of a sufficient need to offset the presumptive validity of the Executive's claim. The cases have held that the balance should be struck in favor of disclosure only if the showing of need is strong and clear, leaving the courts with a firm conviction that the public interest requires disclosure.

It is difficult to imagine any case where the balance could be clearer than it is on the special facts of this proceeding. The recordings sought are specifically identified, and the relevance of each conversation to the needs of trial has been established at length. The conversations are demonstrably important to defining the extent of the conspiracy in terms of time, membership and objectives.

On the other hand, since the President has authorized each participant to discuss what he and the others have said, and since he repeatedly has summarized his views of the conversations, while releasing partial transcripts of a number of them, the public interest in continued confidentiality is vastly diminished.

The district court's ruling is exceedingly narrow and, thus, almost no incremental damage will be done to the valid interests in assuring future Presidential aides that legitimate advice on matters of policy will be kept secret. The unusual circumstances of this case—where high government officials are under indictment for conspiracy to defraud the United States and obstruct justice—at once make it imperative that the trial be conducted on the basis of all relevant evidence and at the same time make it highly unlikely that there will soon be a similar occasion to intrude on the confidentiality of the Executive Branch.

IV

Even if the subpoenaed conversations might once have been covered by a privilege, the privilege has been waived by the President's decision to authorize voluminous testimony and other statements concerning Watergate-related discussion and his recent release of 1,216 pages of transcript from forty-three Presidential conversations dealing with Watergate. A privilege holder may not make extensive disclosures concerning a subject and then selectively withhold portions that are essential to a complete and impartial record. Here, the President repeatedly has referred to the conversations in support of his own position and even allowed defendant Haldeman access to the recordings after he left public office to aid him in preparing his public testimony. In the unique circumstances of this case, where there is no longer any substantial confidentiality on the subject of Watergate because the President has made far-reaching, but expurgated disclosures, the court may use its process to acquire all relevant evidence to lay before the jury.

V

The district court, correctly applying the standards established by this Court, found that the government's showing satisfied the requirements of Rule 17(c) of the Federal Rules of Criminal Procedure that items subpoenaed for use at trial be relevant and evidentiary. The enforcement of a trial subpoena *duces tecum* is a question for the trial court and is committed to the court's sound discretion. Absent a showing that the finding by the court is arbitrary and had no support in the record, the finding must not be disturbed by an appellate court. Here, the Special Prosecutor's analysis of each of the sixty-four conversations, submitted to the district court, amply supports that court's finding.

IMPEACHMENT:

Moving toward a Decision

Nixon's hold on power appeared to be fading quickly by late July. The House Judiciary Committee neared a historic vote on recommending impeachment. Meanwhile, a unanimous Supreme Court ordered Nixon to comply with a subpoena for tapes of 64 White House conversations.

Just a few weeks earlier, Nixon had departed for a successful trip in June to the Middle East. This set a pattern for many of his successors, who similarly would engage in high-profile meetings with foreign leaders to temporarily escape troubles at home. Nixon received a tumultuous welcome abroad. But impeachment made its impact even as far away as Salzburg, Austria. There, an angry Secretary of State Henry A. Kissinger threatened on June 11 to resign over allegations that he had initiated wiretaps on reporters and some of his own aides. He demanded that the allegations be withdrawn. Ultimately, the Senate Foreign Relations Committee would clear Kissinger of wrongdoing, and he would remain in his powerful post.

Nixon, although he enjoyed a brief respite from the scandal in mid-June, was not as fortunate. He returned to Washington buoyant and strengthened by his triumphant tour through the Middle East, and he made plans to fly to the Soviet Union. His lawyers filed legal arguments maintaining that the president was immune from certain subpoenas and grand jury actions. White House spokesmen also launched an attack on the House Judiciary Committee. They denounced it as "a clique of Nixon-hating partisans" for trying to destroy the president.

But evidence continued to point toward Nixon's guilt. Former White House special counsel Charles W. Colson testified about the president's role in obstructing justice. And the public learned that the Watergate grand jury, after its intensive investigation, had concluded that Nixon played a role in the scandal. Back in February, the jurors had secretly named the president as an unindicted co-conspirator. This meant that they believed he was guilty but decided to stop short of formally charging him with a crime. The grand jury's conclusion became public when the Supreme Court released this excerpt from the jury's proceedings:

"On February 25, 1974, in the course of its investigation . . . [the] grand jury, by a vote of 19–0, determined that there is probable cause to believe that Richard M. Nixon (among

others) was a member of the conspiracy to defraud the United States and to obstruct justice. . . . "

JUDICIARY COMMITTEE INVESTIGATION

The House Judiciary Committee, which had investigated Watergate for months, continued to forge ahead. It began hearing from Nixon attorney James D. St. Clair and other witnesses at the end of June. It planned to vote on a recommendation of impeachment by the end of July, after questioning witnesses and debating the issue. The House was expected to vote on impeachment by late August.

Committee Democrats and Republicans agreed to issue four more subpoenas to the White House. The subpoenas sought tapes of at least 49 White House conversations. The tapes could provide information about allegations of wrongdoing in four areas:

- A possible connection between campaign funds and the administration's reluctance to pursue an anti-trust case against a major company.
- The use of the Internal Revenue Service to harass administration opponents.
- A 1971 administration decision to increase milk price supports, which helped dairy producers that had made substantial campaign contributions.
- The president's involvement in illegal domestic surveillance activities, conducted chiefly by the White House "plumbers" unit. (The plumbers were directed to block leaks to the press.)

Republicans and Democrats on the House Judiciary Committee engaged in some skirmishing over which witnesses to call before the committee. They also disagreed over various committee procedures. But with evidence pointing to presidential wrongdoing, increasing numbers of Republicans assailed Nixon's actions even though he was the leader of their party.

In early July, the House Judiciary Committee released transcripts of eight presidential conversations. The White House allegedly had not meant to share the transcripts with Congress. The new transcripts revealed that Nixon was more deeply implicated in the Watergate coverup than the White House had admitted. In one March 22, 1973, meeting about a pending hearing before the Senate Watergate Committee, Nixon appeared to want to stop witnesses from providing information about the scandal. He told top aides: "I want you all to stonewall it, let them plead the Fifth Amendment, coverup or anything else."

The committee also prepared transcripts of tapes that the White House had previously transcribed. The two versions of transcripts differed significantly. The committee version cast Nixon in a worse light. Both versions, for example, included a conversation between Nixon and White House counsel John W. Dean III on March 13, 1973. The men had discussed whether it was too late to "go the hang-out road"—that is, tell everything and hope for the best. In the White House version, Dean responded that it was too late. But the committee version had the president answering, "yes it is." In other words, Nixon wanted to suppress information about the Watergate scandal.

The committee's transcripts also indicated that the president favored making cash payments to the Watergate burglars to buy their silence. In addition, Nixon wanted to retaliate against his enemies. He was particularly angry at Edward Bennett Williams, an attorney for the Democratic National Committee and *The Washington Post*. In one conversation that the White House had failed to transcribe, the committee transcription quoted the president as saying, "I think we are going to fix that son-of-a-bitch. Believe me. We are going to. We've got to, because he's a bad man."

SUPREME COURT ARGUMENTS

On July 8, St. Clair and Watergate special prosecutor Leon Jaworski came before the Supreme Court. They argued over whether Jaworski had the right to order the president to turn over the tapes of 64 presidential conversations. The heart of the legal question for the high court was whether the president had to obey the law like any other citizen.

Jaworski said that the president did not have the authority to make the final decision about which documents are covered by executive privilege. The privilege gives the president the authority to keep certain documents private if their disclosure could harm the nation. "Now, the president may be right in how he reads the Constitution. But he may also be wrong," Jaworski contended. "And if he is wrong, who is there to tell him so? And if there is no one, then the president is of course free to pursue his course of erroneous interpretations. What then becomes of our constitutional form of government?"

St. Clair, however, responded that the law must be applied more carefully to an incumbent president. He also said that executive privilege applied even to presidential conversations relating to a criminal conspiracy. "We should not destroy the privilege in anticipation of a later finding of criminality," he told the court.

The justices were expected to issue their historic ruling within weeks.

WATERGATE COMMITTEE REPORT

The Senate Watergate Committee, 18 months after it began the most intensive congressional investigation into alleged presidential corruption in American history, issued its final report in July. The 2,217-page document provided details of White House corruption, even though most of the conclusions had already been leaked to the press. The findings, adopted unanimously by the seven-member committee, did not assess whether Nixon was involved in the Watergate coverup. On that question, the committee deferred to the House Judiciary Committee. But the report stated that the scandal "reflects an alarming indifference displayed by some in high places to concepts of morality and public responsibility and trust. Indeed, the conduct of many Watergate participants seems grounded on the belief that the ends justified the means, that the laws could be flaunted to maintain the present administration in office."

The Senate committee also released a 350-page report that examined allegations of financial corruption. The report charged that Nixon campaign funds were used improperly. For example, Charles G. Rebozo, Nixon's close friend, paid tens of thousands of dollars to upgrade the president's private estate in Key Biscayne, Fla. At least some of the money may have come from political contributions—even though such contributions are not supposed to be used for private purposes. The report also said that Nixon gave a platinum-and-diamond earring set to his wife, which was paid for with $4,562.33 in leftover campaign funds.

In addition, the report concluded that top administration officials, including Nixon, misused the Internal Revenue Service (IRS). The White House put pressure on the IRS to find something wrong with the tax returns of Lawrence F. O'Brien, the former Democratic national chairman. But the IRS gave unusually favorable treatment to Rebozo when it investigated his tax problems.

Republican senator Howard H. Baker Jr. of Tennessee, the vice chairman of the Senate Watergate Committee, issued an additional report on the role of the CIA in the Watergate scandal. The report indicated that the CIA might have known in advance of plans for the break-in at the offices of Daniel Ellsberg's psychiatrist. (For more about the break-in, see page 44.) The agency also may have known about the break-in of the Democratic National Committee's Watergate headquarters. The report charged that the CIA destroyed records that might have shed light on its involvement with the White House on Watergate.

Even before the release of the Watergate committee's report, some Republican senators were scathing in their assessment of Nixon's actions. Sen. Lowell P. Weicker of Connecticut, the junior Republican on the Senate Judiciary Committee, issued a particularly stinging statement. He said that "every major substantive part of the Constitution was violated, abused and undermined during the Watergate period." Among the constitutional violations that Weicker cited, based on the Senate Watergate Committee investigation:

- Use of private investigators by the White House to investigate the private lives of politicians and public figures
- Attempts to conceal the break-in of the office of Daniel Ellsberg's psychiatrist
- Warrantless wiretaps of government officials and reporters
- Use of campaign funds to pay the Watergate burglars so that they would not disclose information about the break-in

ANALYZING THE EVIDENCE

The House Judiciary Committee wrapped up its closed-door hearings in mid-July. Some of the most damaging testimony came from the president's former personal attorney, Herbert W. Kalmbach. He was serving a prison term after pleading guilty to violating campaign fund-raising laws while working for the president. Kalmbach told the committee about the exchange of promises of ambassadorships for campaign contributions. He also reaffirmed that the dairy industry pledged campaign support just before the administration increased milk price supports.

St. Clair presented his final argument to the committee on July 18. He maintained that the president had neither participated in nor approved of the Watergate coverup. He also defended domestic surveillance activities as necessary for national security. He denied a connection between campaign contributions and administration decisions regarding milk price supports and the handling of an antitrust case against the International Telephone and Telegraph Corporation.

The committee then moved into a critical phase of analyzing the evidence. There appeared to be little doubt that it would recommend impeachment. The committee's special counsel, John M. Doar, reportedly told committee members in a private meeting that "reasonable men acting reasonably would find the president guilty" of abusing the powers of his office.

The committee also released thousands of pages of evidence about alleged Nixon administration misdeeds. For example, former White House aide John D. Ehrlichman allegedly urged the IRS to audit supporters of the 1972

Democratic presidential nominee, George McGovern. The administration used wiretaps against newsmen and government employees, and it weighed illegal efforts to monitor subversive groups. The committee also disclosed a conversation between Nixon and his top aides about the political risks of an investigation into the Watergate break-in. The conversation took place just two weeks after the June 17, 1972, break-in. This appeared to contradict Nixon's claim that he had no knowledge of a Watergate coverup before March 1973.

By late July, a number of House Judiciary Committee Republicans were joining Democrats in indicating their support for some articles of impeachment. Formal committee debate began on July 24. The members all spoke publicly about their views on the evidence. Seven of the committee's 17 Republicans indicated that they would vote for impeachment. With virtually all committee Democrats supporting at least certain articles of impeachment, the committee appeared certain to recommend impeachment. Even though White House spokesman Ronald L. Ziegler had referred to the committee as "a kangaroo court," the members insisted that their inquiry had been fair and nonpartisan.

Members also negotiated carefully over the wording of the impeachment articles. They debated over how specific to make the charges against Nixon. They also considered, but ultimately rejected, a proposal to delay impeachment proceedings while they reviewed additional White House tapes.

SUPREME COURT RULING

Nixon suffered a potentially fatal blow on July 24. The Supreme Court, in a unanimous ruling, decisively rejected his efforts to withhold evidence from the Watergate special prosecutor. The Court agreed with the order of U.S. District Court judge John J. Sirica directing Nixon to deliver the tapes of 64 White House conversations to Jaworski. Sirica would listen to the tapes privately, excise the portions that were not useful as evidence, and turn over the rest to Jaworski. The ruling was particularly significant in that three of the eight justices who participated in it had been appointed by Nixon. But that did not lead them to rule in his favor.

The justices agreed that a president has the right to preserve the confidentiality of some conversations. But that right cannot justify the withholding of evidence needed in a criminal trial. If Nixon were allowed to keep evidence secret, the result "would cut deeply into the guarantee of due process of law and gravely impair the basic function of the courts. . . . Without access to specific facts, a criminal prosecution may be totally frustrated."

Hours later, Nixon issued a statement. He said he was disappointed in the decision, but he would comply with it completely. "I respect and accept the court's decision," he said. He also said he hoped that the special circumstances of the case would not set a precedent that future administrations would have to share private conversations.

Nixon's statement marked an important moment in American history. Earlier in the Watergate scandal, he had

indicated he might not comply with a Supreme Court decision on turning over the tapes. If Nixon had refused to obey the Supreme Court, it would have deepened the already grave constitutional crisis of Watergate. It would have raised questions about whether a president had to accept the rulings of the high court.

Impeachment proceedings against President Nixon, which had moved at glacial speed for almost six months, picked up an apparently irreversible momentum during the week ending July 27 and headed for a late-August decision in the House of Representatives.

In the House Judiciary Committee, enough of the 17-member Republican minority joined the Democratic majority by July 26 to forge bipartisan support for charges that the President had obstructed justice and abused his powers. The committee, authorized by the full House to begin its inquiry Feb. 6, moved slowly and deliberately until public hearings beginning July 24 brought the impeachment issue into sharp focus—polarizing support and opposition.

Thus, nine months after the national uproar sparked by the firing of Watergate special prosecutor Archibald Cox, the House was readying itself for the first debate on the impeachment of a president since 1868.

And in the Senate, whose leaders had earlier been reticent to discuss any contingency plans for proceedings should impeachment move to the trial stage, Assistant Majority Leader Robert C. Byrd (D W.Va.) July 25 notified his colleagues to expect a six-day work week, if a trial occurred.

Accelerating Pace

For six months, the special staff assembled for the inquiry had gathered and organized mountains of information related to the charges against the President. For two months, from May 9 to July 17, the committee had met to receive that information and to hear witnesses. Out of the public eye, with members bound by rules of confidentiality, the progress of the impeachment inquiry was imperceptible.

But the pace accelerated in mid-July—within and outside the committee itself. On July 12, John D. Ehrlichman, Nixon's former chief domestic adviser, was convicted of conspiracy to burglarize the office of Daniel Ellsberg's psychiatrist. A week later, special inquiry counsel John M. Doar abandoned his posture of neutrality

and recommended that the committee send a resolution of impeachment to the House. White House Press Secretary Ronald L. Ziegler responded by describing the impeachment inquiry as "a kangaroo court."

A serious crack in the ranks of Republican members of the House was opened July 23 when Lawrence J. Hogan (R Md.) announced that he would vote for impeachment, charging that the President had "lied repeatedly" to the American people about the Watergate break-in and coverup. Hogan, a member of the Judiciary Committee, was joined later in the week by several other Republicans on the committee who indicated their willingness to support certain articles of impeachment.

And on July 24, a unanimous Supreme Court dealt a damaging blow to Nixon's claims of executive privilege as a basis for refusing to comply with subpoenas for information—including those from the committee.

Outcome Clear

Within hours of the opening of formal committee debate July 24, the outcome was clear. As each member spoke publicly to his colleagues and the nation for the first time in the proceeding, expressing his feelings and his views on the charges and the evidence, seven of the committee's 17 Republican members indicated concern sufficient to justify a vote for impeachment.

On the second day of debate, July 25, all three of the committee's more conservative southern Democrats—Walter Flowers of Alabama, James R. Mann of South Carolina and Ray Thornton of Arkansas—expressed their willingness to support certain articles of impeachment.

By their carefully worded statements, the committee members thoroughly refuted all charges that their inquiry had been unfair or purely the result of partisan motivation. "Common sense would be revolted if we engaged in this process for petty reasons," said Barbara C. Jordan (D Texas). "Congress has a lot to do. . . . Today we are not being petty. We are trying to be big."

Each member took part of his allotted 15 minutes to praise the work of Chairman Peter W. Rodino Jr. (D N.J.)

and, in most cases, of the committee's inquiry staff, which one Republican, Hamilton Fish Jr. (N.Y.), described as probably "the finest law firm in the United States."

A key factor mentioned by many of the previously uncommitted members who indicated that they were leaning toward a vote for impeachment was the effect on the nation and its government of a vote not to impeach the President. "What if we fail to impeach?" asked Flowers. "Do we ingrain forever in the very fabric of our Constitution a standard of conduct in our highest office that in the least is deplorable and at worst is impeachable?"

Court Ruling

By limiting the use of executive privilege as a defense to a demand for evidence, the Supreme Court undercut the President's position of refusing to comply with impeachment inquiry subpoenas. The committee July 26 refused to delay their deliberations to determine if they might, as a result of the ruling, receive additional evidence from the White House.

But several members in their general statements took note of the impact of the decision on a claim of privilege in order to withhold information. Others, such as Jordan, criticized Nixon for refusing to say, until late the afternoon of the ruling, that he would comply. "Yesterday the American people waited with great anxiety for eight hours, not knowing whether their President would obey an order of the Supreme Court," she said.

Under pressure from Federal Judge John J. Sirica, Special White House counsel James D. St. Clair agreed July 26 to turn over to him 20 of the 64 subpoenaed conversations by July 30 and to report to him on the status of the other 44 conversations by Aug. 2. The White House said there would be "no problem" with the timetable.

Amending the Articles

The opening of committee debate on the articles of impeachment July 26 was delayed while a bipartisan group of committee members worked with Rodino and staff members to hammer out a new version of the article charging Nixon with obstruction of justice.

As had been the case earlier in the week, liberal and moderate members of the committee operated in traditional legislative fashion to draft a measure acceptable to the broadest possible number of committee members. The articles of impeachment proposed July 24 by Harold D. Donohue (D Mass.) were the product of such a process.

Paul S. Sarbanes (D Md.), a member of the committee and the House for only four years, was the Democrat chosen to propose that the newly drafted article concerning the charges of obstruction of justice be substituted for the first of the original proposed articles. Sarbanes, the son of Greek immigrants and a Rhodes Scholar, was highly respected by his fellow committee members, despite his junior status, for his intelligence and his articulate and persuasive manner of arguing his point of view.

The substitute he proposed, he said, simply tightened the language of the earlier proposal. It did not change the charge against the President or the specifics of the alleged efforts to cover up the Watergate break-in.

Sarbanes Text

Following is the text of the Sarbanes substitute article:

Article I

In his conduct of the office of President of the United States, Richard M. Nixon, in violation of his constitutional oath faithfully to execute the office of President of the United States and, to the best of his ability, preserve, protect, and defend the Constitution of the United States, and in violation of his constitutional duty to take care that the laws be faithfully executed, has prevented, obstructed, and impeded the administration of justice, in that:

On June 17, 1972, and prior thereto, agents of the Committee for the Re-election of the President committed illegal entry of the headquarters of the Democratic National Committee in Washington, District of Columbia, for the purpose of securing political intelligence. Subsequent thereto, Richard M. Nixon, using the powers of his high office, made it his policy, and in furtherance of such policy did act directly and personally and through his close subordinates and agents, to delay, impede, and obstruct the investigation of such illegal entry; to cover up, conceal and protect those responsible; and to conceal the existence and scope of other unlawful covert activities.

The means used to implement this policy have included one or more of the following:

(1) making false or misleading statements to lawfully authorized investigative officers and employees of the United States;

(2) withholding relevant and material evidence or information from lawfully authorized investigative officers and employees of the United States;

(3) approving, condoning, acquiescing in, and counseling witnesses with respect to the giving of false or mis-

leading statements to lawfully authorized investigative officers and employees of the United States and false or misleading testimony in [duly] instituted judicial and congressional proceedings;

(4) interfering or endeavoring to interfere with the conduct of investigations by the Department of Justice of the United States, the Federal Bureau of Investigation, and the Office of Watergate Special Prosecution Force;

(5) approving, condoning, and acquiescing in the surreptitious payment of substantial sums of money for the purpose of obtaining the silence or influencing the testimony of witnesses, potential witnesses or individuals who participated in such illegal entry and other illegal activities;

(6) endeavoring to misuse the Central Intelligence Agency, an agency of the United States;

(7) disseminating information received from officers of the Department of Justice of the United States to subjects of investigations conducted by lawfully authorized investigative officers and employees of the United States, for the purpose of aiding and assisting such subjects in their attempts to avoid criminal liability;

(8) making false or misleading public statements for the purpose of deceiving the people of the United States into believing that a thorough and complete investigation had been conducted with respect to allegations of misconduct on the part of personnel of the executive branch of the United States and personnel of the Committee for the Re-election of the President, and that there was no involvement of the President, and that there was no involvement of such personnel in such misconduct; or

(9) endeavoring to cause prospective defendants, and individuals duly tried and convicted, to expect favored treatment and consideration in return for their silence or false testimony, or rewarding individuals for their silence or false testimony.

In all of this, Richard M. Nixon has acted in a manner contrary to his trust as President and subversive of constitutional government, to the great prejudice of the cause of law and justice and to the manifest injury of the people of the United States.

Wherefore Richard M. Nixon, by such conduct, warrants impeachment and trial, and removal from office.

A Move to Delay

Before Sarbanes introduced his proposed substitute article, Robert McClory (R Ill.), the second-ranking Republican member, moved that the committee delay its action on the articles of impeachment so that Nixon might have time to give to the committee the 64 taped conversations which he was now under Supreme Court order to give the Watergate special prosecutor.

McClory's motion gave the President until noon July 27 to give the committee "his unequivocal assurance" that he would turn over the tapes. If he complied, debate on the proposed articles would be postponed for 10 days.

The Illinois Republican admitted that he had a "strong feeling there is no intention for [the President] to provide the materials to the committee." But, McClory said, he wanted to put the committee's request on the record. "These [tapes] contain highly relevant information valuable to us," he said. "For us to conclude the proceedings without [having the information] would be inconsistent with our role here."

Rodino opposed the motion. "The May 22 letter from the President said he would decline to submit any more material to the committee," he said. "There's no question whatsoever . . . that the President has no intention of complying. We have been fair, we have been patient." He called it an "idle, futile gesture" for the committee "to delay a vote knowing full well that we have the President's full response as categorical and decisive as it will be."

The motion was rejected, 11–27. One Democrat, James R. Mann (D S.C.), joined 10 Republicans to support the motion. Twenty Democrats and seven Republicans opposed it.

Opposition Arguments

Sarbanes' substitute article of impeachment ran into opposition from Edward Hutchinson (R Mich.), the ranking Republican member of the committee, and Charles E. Wiggins (R Calif.). The article was vague and did not include any specific charges that the President could respond to, said Hutchinson.

"It does not set forth with specific detail the alleged incidents," he said. "You leave the respondent [the President] trying to find out specifically what he's charged with, what he has to answer to."

Sarbanes said he had no objection to including in the committee report on the articles "back-up information" for the allegations in the article. "I don't want the details included in the article. If we did that, it would take 18 volumes," he said.

Wiggins and Charles W. Sandman Jr. (R N.J.), impeachment opponents, pressed Sarbanes to tell them when the coverup policy was "declared." Sarbanes said the committee members had "varying factual matters from which they can draw conclusions when the policy was established." Some of the evidence indicated that it started immediately after the Watergate break-in, while other evidence showed it began in March and April of 1973, he said. "The language in this article covers this broad time period," said Sarbanes.

Disagreement over Specifics

The debate over the need for specifically worded articles of impeachment consumed the afternoon session. Sarbanes and other Democrats argued that specific wording was not needed because:

- St. Clair had taken part in all the evidentiary proceedings and was aware of all the charges against Nixon.
- Relevant details would be included in the committee report.
- St. Clair would have the opportunity, before a Senate trial, to seek further particulars.

Sandman, Wiggins and other Republican opponents of impeachment argued that the President, like any citizen, was entitled to know precisely what the charges against him were in order to prepare a defense.

Underlying this disagreement was a basic clash of strategies. Republican defenders of the President, aware that specific charges facilitate the task of a defense counsel and that no figurative "murder weapon" had been found in the volumes of evidence, sought to have the charges spelled out. Democratic advocates of impeachment pointed out that it was a pattern of conduct, not any one fact, which they viewed as the grounds for impeachment, and thus they sought approval for broader articles.

"We'd have to have articles that run into volumes and volumes," said Sarbanes. There is here an "extensive pattern of conduct to be spelled out in the report."

What we want, argued Sandman, is "simple facts."

"One of the problems" responded Sarbanes "is that there is a course of conduct and not a summary of events" under scrutiny.

"What is so wrong about a simple sentence saying what happened?" queried Sandman.

"I'm concerned that the President is entitled to know what facts will be adduced against him," said M. Caldwell Butler (R Va.), questioning associate inquiry counsel Albert E. Jenner Jr., an expert on matters of evidence.

In pretrial proceedings, replied Jenner, a defendant is entitled to ask of the trial judge and to receive, without the use of subpoenas, any and all material on which the charges against him are based.

The reason that charges must be couched in specific language, argued David W. Dennis (R Ind.), is to tell a man what he is charged with and to limit proof to those particular charges. "Just because you're a congressional committee doesn't mean you can tear up the Constitution," he added heatedly.

"What bothers me the most are these loose statements that the President is going to trial without knowing what the charges are," said Mann. "Every bit of the evidence before the committee has gone to the President's counsel. . . . The evidence will be available tomorrow or the next day. He'll have all the evidence we have. He's got some we don't have."

"Three-fourths of all the charges leveled against the President are not included in the articles, and the President deserves to know what we left out," said Sandman.

Continuing the argument, Rodino pointed out: "We do know that the House of Representatives has indeed impeached without articles of impeachment. . . . This discussion and this issue of requiring specificity . . . seems to me to be begging of a question that has long been settled. . . . The House of Representatives is not the trial body, but the body recommending articles of impeachment even if in the broadest sense."

"Somewhere down the line," said Hutchinson, "the House of Representatives has got to draft articles of impeachment before it goes to the Senate. We should take the responsibility. . . ."

"I did not state we should not perfect the articles," rejoined Rodino. "In impeachment proceedings there is no requirement that the articles be specifically set out."

"We can go to the floor with as broad and nebulous a resolution as we desire," said Lawrence J. Hogan (R Md.), earlier the first Republican member of the committee to state that he would vote for impeachment.

"In fairness, we ought to expose the totality of the evidence," argued Wiggins. "We're talking about what happens in the Senate. . . . Wouldn't it be a damning indictment of this committee if after all this time and all this money we couldn't state the case with some specificity?"

Into the Evening

Continuing the debate into the evening session, Jordan observed that "it is apparently difficult for the committee to translate its views of the Constitution into impeachment provisions. Some of the arguments offered earlier are phantom arguments, bottomless arguments.

"If we have not offered the President due process in these proceedings, what is due process? This committee suffered the counsel of the President to sit in these proceedings every day. The committee was under no compulsion to do that. . . . All the President's witnesses were called. The President's counsel was allowed to cross-examine the witnesses. . . . This is due process tripled, due process quadrupled."

Flowers asked Sarbanes if he was prepared to itemize the arguments in support of the nine areas of offenses set out in his arguments. Sarbanes responded that he was.

William S. Cohen (R Maine) asked Doar if he felt that the article, as proposed by Sarbanes, was sufficiently specific to put the President on notice of the charges. Doar responded that he felt the second section of the Sarbanes proposal, which he described as the "operative" one, did put the President on notice.

"Does the Sarbanes substitute violate due process?" asked Fish.

"It does not," responded Jenner. "It satisfies the Constitution in whole. It puts the President on notice of specific charges." Jenner also warned that indictments could result in "strangling" the prosecution on the evidence.

"I see no difficulty in proceeding with an article" backed up by a committee report, noted Thornton.

Bringing up what he described as the first of nine amendments, one to strike each subparagraph of the Sarbanes amendment, Sandman stated that the proposed article was "not a legitimate article of impeachment," that it was not sufficiently specific.

"A simple parking ticket has to be specific," he argued. "The House of Representatives is entitled to know specifically what you're going to prove. Let's itemize this thing now."

Objecting to the extended argument, John Conyers Jr. (D Mich.) said: "We've examined counsel, we've established the fact and we've made it clear there are two views here. It's time to start voting."

Charles B. Rangel (D N.Y.) suggested that Sandman's motion was "just to take time." Rodino chastised the members. "Parliamentary delay only shows the people that we're afraid to meet the issue," he said. Attempting to limit the discussion of the motion, Rodino offered to give two minutes to each of the 20 members who indicated they wished to speak on the Sandman amendment. But some members objected, and therefore each of the 20 members was allowed to speak for five minutes.

Protesting what he saw as an illustration of "the distance we are in danger of departing from the law and the Constitution," Dennis described impeachment proceedings as "at least quasi-criminal" in nature and requiring—as a sort of indictment—"a plain, concise and simple statement of the facts charged."

Other Committee Actions

Earlier in the week, the committee members had agreed to release virtually all the evidence and testimony the committee had received in executive session after July 2—the day on which it began hearing the testimony of witnesses. This agreement was reached July 22, after the committee had voted 20–18 to adopt an amendment by Wiggins, excluding from this material to be released the White House "political matters" memos from Gordon C. Strachan to H. R. Haldeman, which had not been cited as evidence of impeachable offenses.

Wiggins argued that of the 21 memos supplied to the committee by the White House, only six or seven had been cited as evidence and that they were the only ones that should be released. Edwards, Drinan and Thornton voted with all the committee Republicans for the Wiggins amendment.

The committee began releasing this information July 24 with Book I of the witnesses' testimony, including that of Alexander Butterfield, Paul O'Brien and Fred C. LaRue. Book II, containing the testimony of William O. Bittman, John N. Mitchell and John W. Dean III, was released July 25, followed July 26 by Book III, with the testimony of the last witnesses, Henry E. Petersen, Charles W. Colson and Herbert W. Kalmbach.

On July 23, the committee agreed by a vote of 21–16 to a procedure under which it would vote on each article at the conclusion of debate on that article, instead of voting on all articles at once.

The Committee Debate

The general committee debate which preceded consideration of the articles of impeachment gave the American public a first and dramatic look at the 38 committee members as they expressed a wide range of opinions and emotions. The nationally televised debates July 24 and 25 clearly revealed a crucial splintering of Republican Party ranks with more than a half dozen Republicans joining what appeared to be solid Democratic support for impeachment of the President.

"Make no mistake about it. This is a turning point—whatever we decide," said Chairman Peter W. Rodino Jr. (D N.J.), opening the long-awaited committee debate on impeachment on the evening of July 24. The high-ceilinged hearing room was filled with members of Congress, the committee staff and the press. The kleig lights were blazing and the television cameras were whirring when Rodino formally opened the session at 7:45 p.m. with six firm raps of his gavel.

July 24 Debate

On the opening night, 11 committee members had the opportunity to speak—six Democrats and five Republicans. All of the Democrats either stated or implied that they would vote for impeachment. Three of the Republicans indicated their opposition to impeachment, but two indicated that they might be persuaded to vote for impeachment.

Rodino. "We are ready to debate resolutions whether or not the Committee on the Judiciary should recommend that the House of Representatives adopt articles calling for the impeachment of Richard M. Nixon," said Rodino. "Our judgment is not concerned with an individual but with a system of constitutional government.

"For more than two years there have been serious allegations, by people of good faith and sound intelligence, that the President, Richard M. Nixon, has committed grave and systematic violations of the Constitution," he said. "We have deliberated. We have been patient. We have been fair. Now the American people, the House of Representatives and the Constitution and the whole history of our republic demand that we make up our minds."

Edward Hutchinson (R Mich.). The ranking Republican made clear the strict standard he set for impeachment. "In determining in my own mind," he said, "I would have to decide whether . . . the offense charged is of sufficient gravity to warrant removal of the President from office because of it. . . . Some offenses may be charged for which there is convincing evidence; and still such offenses may not, in the judgment of a member, be so serious as to justify impeachment and the removal of a President of the United States from office."

Later, seconded by several other Republicans on the committee, Hutchinson suggested that the committee delay its deliberations until it obtained the tapes which the Supreme Court had ordered Nixon to provide to the Watergate special prosecutor.

Harold D. Donohue (D Mass.). Setting the framework for committee debate, Donohue introduced the proposed resolution and articles of impeachment at 8:08 p.m. "Resolved, that Richard M. Nixon, President of the United States, is impeached for high crimes and misdemeanors, and that the following articles of impeachment be exhibited to the Senate," he read slowly and deliberately. The first article accused the President of

obstructing justice in the Watergate coverup. The second listed 10 alleged abuses of presidential power, including Nixon's defiance of the Judiciary Committee's subpoenas.

"The awesome constitutional duty of each member of this committee is to make an impartial determination as to whether or not the evidence before us warrants a reasonable judgment that Richard M. Nixon, as President, has seriously, gravely, purposefully and persistently abused and misused the power intrusted in him by the people of these United States," said Donohue.

Robert McClory (R Ill.). The second-ranking Republican on the committee said he found the evidence related to the Watergate coverup "less than convincing . . .[based on] circumstantial evidence, innuendo and wishful thinking." But, he continued, he was disturbed by the President's refusal to comply with committee subpoenas and by the allegations of abuse of presidential power.

"We may ask, 'Is the office of the presidency being operated in the manner contemplated by the Constitution when, under the guise of national security, dissatisfaction with the head of the FBI, or personal animosity against enemies, we experience burglaries, wiretaps, bugging, unlawfully provided shredding and concealment of evidence, misuse of the CIA, FBI, IRS and a host of other misdeeds?'

"The question remains," he concluded, "whether these acts and omissions of Richard Nixon as President are to be approved or denounced. If the President is to be called to account for such acts and omissions, impeachment is the appropriate and constitutionally designated vehicle for bringing these specific charges against him."

Jack Brooks (D Texas). Brooks described the committee's task: to decide whether Nixon was involved in the "governmental corruption unparalleled in the history of the United States" which had been laid before the committee in its inquiry. "There is no political gain for anyone or any political party in this procedure. . . . If ever there was a time to put aside partisanship, it is now," he said.

Henry P. Smith III (R N.Y.). Smith expressed concern over the secret bombing of Cambodia ordered by Nixon, but said that on the other charges he had seen no "clear and convincing evidence" of the President's personal involvement in impeachable crimes.

Robert W. Kastenmeier (D Wis.). Saying he would vote for impeachment, Kastenmeier described the evidence as "a case of history in the abuse of presidential power . . . a pattern of presidential disregard for truth and for law."

Charles W. Sandman Jr. (R N.J.). Challenging those who advocated impeachment, Sandman said: "Find me clear and direct evidence involving the President of the United States in an impeachable offense and I will vote for impeachment." He called all the evidence presented up to that time circumstantial and unconvincing.

Don Edwards (D Calif.). Edwards said he would vote for impeachment. "I have concluded . . . that President Nixon has consciously and intentionally engaged in serious misdeeds; that he has corrupted and subverted our political and governmental processes to the extent that he should be impeached," he said.

Tom Railsback (R Ill.). In comments highly critical of the President, Railsback recited, step by step, the allegations of Nixon's involvement in the Watergate coverup. "If there's anything that's going to affect adversely our democracy, our freedom . . . it's misuse of a sensitive agency like the IRS, the FBI or the CIA. . . . I wish the President could do something to absolve himself. I am just very, very concerned."

William L. Hungate (D Mo.). The last speaker of the evening debate, Hungate said flatly that he found the President guilty of impeachable offenses. "On this committee we are all lawyers . . . and to become lawyers we took the same oath to uphold the Constitution which Richard M. Nixon took," he said. "We, as congressmen, to become congressmen, took the same oath of office to uphold the Constitution which Richard M. Nixon took. If we are to be faithful to our oaths, we must find him faithless to his."

July 25 Debate

On the second day of general debate, 27 committee members—15 Democrats and 12 Republicans—presented their views. As expected, all the Democrats indicated they would vote for impeachment. Five of the Republicans also appeared to lean toward impeachment.

In resuming the debate on the morning of July 25, the committee heard first from Charles E. Wiggins (R Calif.), the man often described as the President's chief defender on the committee, a description which he said made him wince.

Wiggins. Wiggins warned that "if we were to decide this upon any other basis than the law, we would be doing greater violence to the Constitution than any alleged to be done by Richard Nixon." The 38 books of material presented to the committee by its staff, Wiggins said, contained only a small amount of hard, non-circumstantial, admissible evidence. The evidence on which impeachment should be based, he argued, should be "clear and convincing . . . at least not ambiguous, at least not confused and jumbled."

John Conyers Jr. (D Mich.). Endorsing impeachment, Conyers said that it was necessary to impeach Nixon "to restore to our government the proper balance of constitutional power and to serve notice on all future presidents that such abuse of power will never again be tolerated."

David W. Dennis (R Ind.). "The question . . . is whether or not proof exists, convincing proof of adequate weight and evidentiary competence, to establish that the President of the United States has been guilty of high crimes and misdemeanors within the meaning of the Constitution," stated Dennis, who said that of the various charges, only those related to obstruction of justice presented the committee with "really serious problems."

Joshua Eilberg (D Pa.). "What we are faced with is a gross disregard for the Constitution and the very safeguards in it which the framers hoped would prevent the President from becoming a king or dictator," said Eilberg, stating that he would vote for impeachment.

Hamilton Fish Jr. (R N.Y.). "I find myself deeply troubled over evidence of presidential complicity in thwarting justice and in the alleged abuse of power in that great office, particularly the use of the enormous power of the United States Government to invade and impinge upon the private rights of individuals," said Fish. "If the evidence is clear, then our constitutional duty is no less clear."

Jerome R. Waldie (D Calif.). "Has there been one shred of evidence exonerating or exculpating the President?" asked Waldie, one of the first members of Congress to advocate impeachment. Waldie found it "our obligation and our duty . . . to impeach this President," who he said had so jeopardized the "fragile" liberties of the American people.

Wiley Mayne (R Iowa). "Never before in history has any President been subjected to the intense investigation of personal and political life as Richard Nixon," said Mayne, stating that the draft articles of impeachment did not meet his standards for impeachment and that only the charges involving the Watergate coverup raised any real possibility that he might vote to impeach Nixon.

Walter Flowers (D Ala.). "What if we fail to impeach? Do we ingrain forever in the very fabric of our Constitution a standard of conduct in our highest office that in the least is deplorable and at worst is impeachable?" asked Flowers, still declining to announce how he would vote.

Lawrence J. Hogan (R Md.). "It is impossible for me to condone the long train of abuses to which he [Nixon] has subjected the presidency and the people of this country," Hogan said. "The Constitution and my oath of office demand that I 'bear true faith and allegiance' to the principles of law and justice upon which this nation was founded, and I cannot, in good conscience, turn away from evidence of evil that is so clear and compelling."

James R. Mann (D S.C.). "We have built our country on the Constitution," Mann said, "and that system has resulted in men putting that system above their own political careers. . . . How much I would like to have all the evidence. How much I would have liked to have heard the transcripts."

M. Caldwell Butler (R Va.). "Watergate is our [the Republican Party's] shame," Butler said. " . . . These things have happened in our house, and it is our responsibility to do what we can to clear it up. . . . There are frightening implications for the future of our country if we do not impeach the President of the United States, because we will, by this impeachment proceeding, be establishing a standard of conduct for the President of the United States which will for all time be a matter of public record. If we fail to impeach, we have condoned and left unpunished a course of conduct totally inconsistent with the reasonable expectations of the American people."

Paul S. Sarbanes (D Md.). "Underlying all the constitutional relationships we talk about is the necessity for standards of honesty, truth and integrity," Sarbanes said. "Our own system of free government cannot operate if those standards are not honored. . . . You must ask yourself whether a chief executive with men who flagrantly abused our constitutional processes should be called to account for their actions. . . . "

William S. Cohen (R Maine). "There are . . . three major allegations which are of great concern to me," Cohen said. "These include the failure to faithfully execute the laws of this country, engaging in a conspiracy to obstruct justice and the use and abuse of government agencies for political advantage and to harass and intimidate private citizens for expressing their political views and preferences. . . . I wondered many times to myself: How in the world did we ever get from the Federalist Papers to the edited transcripts? It has been said that what is at stake is the very soul of America. I agree."

George E. Danielson (D Calif.). "It has been argued that there is no question that within the totality of the long series of events into which we have been inquiring, many wrongs, many offenses have been committed . . . but that there is no evidence that President Richard Nixon had anything to do with those offenses," Danielson said. "I submit that in the case of Richard Nixon there is ample direct evidence to prove the connection."

Trent Lott (R Miss.). "There is not one iota of evidence that the President had any prior knowledge of the Watergate break-in," Lott said. "The President didn't participate in the Watergate coverup. . . . The contempt of Congress charge is so ludicrous that it deserves no comment."

John F. Seiberling (D Ohio). "The evidence in these proceedings is overwhelming," Seiberling said. "The pattern of conduct revealed of President Nixon and his associates is unmistakable. The President and his associates used the government to destroy anything he saw as a threat to his power. . . . What we do here is going to set the standard for future conduct of presidents. . . . We will permanently weaken the presidency and the entire constitutional system if we fail to impeach" President Nixon.

Harold V. Froehlich (R Wis.). "I am discouraged by the moral tone that shines through tape after tape and transcript after transcript, but that is not an impeachable offense," said Froehlich. "I refuse to support contempt of Congress as an article of impeachment. . . . The evidence that troubles me [involves] the obstruction of justice [in the Watergate coverup]. . . ."

Robert F. Drinan (D Mass.). "I have been troubled," Drinan said, "because the process of choosing articles of impeachment is not necessarily done in the order of their gravity but to some extent on their capacity to 'play in Peoria.' There has been no shortage of lawless acts on which to focus in this impeachment inquiry. But only history will be able to discover why the greatest deception and possibly the most impeachable offense of President Nixon may not become a charge against him. I speak of the concealment of the clandestine war in Cambodia."

Carlos J. Moorhead (R Calif.). "I can't jump over that moat" [and vote for impeachment]. "I could not vote for impeachment and give up my own conscience," he said.

Charles B. Rangel (D N.Y.). "May this nation never again have conversations in its White House that deal with burglary and robbery, obstruction of justice and bribery, defamation of character, buying witnesses and selling off jobs, misuse of campaign funds and abuse of governmental agencies, income tax fraud and illegal bombing of foreign countries, with covering up the truth instead of seeking to reveal it," said Rangel. "I uphold my oath of office and call for the impeachment of a man who has not."

Joseph J. Maraziti (R N.J.). "We should settle for no less than hard evidence that the President has committed an impeachable offense," Maraziti said. "We have accumulated a mass of information . . . and I must say that in many areas there is a lack of conclusiveness, a lack of certainty and a lack of the kind of evidence we ought to have if we seek to remove the chief of state of this government."

Barbara C. Jordan (D Texas). "If the impeachment clause of the Constitution will not reach the offenses here, then perhaps that 18th-century Constitution should be abandoned to a 20th-century paper shredder," said Jordan.

Delbert L. Latta (R Ohio). "If the committee decides to recommend impeachment based on direct evidence of presidential involvement in wrongdoing, the case is not here," Latta said. "It is that simple."

Ray Thornton (D Ark.). "I must say," said Thornton, "that while I will reserve my final judgment until the vote, I can now say that on the basis of all the evidence which is now before us, I have reached the firm conviction that President Richard M. Nixon has violated his oath of office by abuse of power and obstruction of justice and that these offenses constitute high crimes and misdemeanors under the Constitution requiring trial on these charges before the Senate of the United States. To find otherwise would be to repeal the right of this body to act as a check."

Elizabeth Holtzman (D N.Y.). "The thousands of pages before this committee bear witness to a systematic arrogation of power; to a thorough-going abuse of the President's oath of office . . . a seamless web of misconduct," Holtzman said. "To preserve the rule of law and our Constitution which the people of this country and all of us hold dear, Richard Nixon must be impeached and removed from office."

Wayne Owens (D Utah). "I believe that the impeachment and removal of this President . . . would be to the public benefit of my country," Owens stated. "If we set standards of impeachment which are too narrow, if we fail to impeach now, with this evidence before us, we are saying to future presidents: 'You are not required to obey the law.' And we would . . . render impotent the impeachment power which the Constitution vested in Congress as the last resort to prevent serious abuses of power by any president."

Edward Mezvinsky (D Iowa). "Don't you think that when a man whose income is in the hundreds of thousands of dollars looks at his tax return and sees he's only paying the government $793 that he has an obligation to scrutinize his return and make certain that every deduction is proper? Especially if he's President of the United States?" asked Mezvinsky. "I believe that this tax matter falls into the pattern of abuse of office because it is evident that the President entertained an expectation for and took advantage of favorable treatment by the IRS. . . ."

Concluding the period of general debate at 10:45 p.m., Hutchinson stated that he remained "unconvinced by the articles . . . by a review of the impeachment process itself." Rodino, on the other hand, stated publicly for the first time that he believed the President had been judged and found wanting and that therefore he would advocate adoption of the articles of impeachment.

The Court's Ruling

Nixon's fate was sealed on July 24 with one of the most momentous decisions in the history of the U.S. Supreme Court. The justices ruled unanimously that the president had to turn over the tapes sought by the Watergate special prosecutor.

This historic ruling imposed a clear limit on the president's considerable powers. The high court agreed that a president has the right to keep some documents secret by claiming executive privilege. But the justices ruled that a president must also bow to the judicial process and release documents needed for a criminal investigation. In other words, a president, just like the rest of us, must cooperate with a prosecutor.

The decision put an end to Nixon's yearlong battle to keep the White House tapes secret. The tapes, as it turned out, would contain conclusive evidence of his attempts to suppress the investigation into the Watergate coverup. Just over two weeks after the court's decision, Nixon would resign.

The intervention of the Supreme Court in Watergate is one of the most important events in all of U.S. constitutional history. At the time of the decision, Congress and the special prosecutor were deadlocked with the White House over the question of whether Nixon had to cooperate with the Watergate investigation. It was not clear if any entity in the country could hold Nixon accountable. By unanimously issuing a strongly worded decision, the justices forced Nixon to answer to our nation's legal processes. The ruling affirmed that the United States is governed by laws that must be respected by even the most powerful individuals.

What made the ruling all the more significant was that four of the eight justices who signed it had been appointed to the Supreme Court by Nixon himself. Instead of siding with Nixon out of loyalty, they based their decision on their view of constitutional principles. At other times, however, justices have been accused of following their own political biases. In 2000, for example, the Supreme Court splintered over the question of how to handle that year's disputed presidential election between Democrat Al Gore and Republican George W. Bush. With conservative justices generally siding with Bush and liberal justices generally siding with Gore, the court ordered an end to vote recounts in Florida. The decision effectively handed the election to Bush. But the decision drew criticism in many quarters, partly because the justices were perceived as being influenced by their political preferences.

It was a central irony of Watergate that the Supreme Court to which Nixon had carefully appointed four men sympathetic to the arguments of prosecutors resoundingly rejected his claim of absolute privilege to withhold evidence from the Watergate special prosecutor.

The President's general need to preserve the confidentiality of his conversations was not strong enough to justify Nixon's withholding of evidence relevant to a criminal trial, the unanimous court held July 24. Were he to do so, it "would cut deeply into the guarantee of due process of law and gravely impair the basic function of the courts. . . . Without access to specific facts, a criminal prosecution may be totally frustrated."

Without dissent and without the participation of Justice William H. Rehnquist, one of Nixon's appointees, the court affirmed the order of Federal Judge John J. Sirica directing Nixon to turn over to him the tapes of 64 White House conversations subpoenaed by Jaworski for use as evidence in the Watergate coverup trial. Sirica would listen to the tapes privately, excise the portions that were not useful as evidence and turn over to Jaworski those that were potentially relevant and admissible as evidence.

Jurisdiction and Justiciability

Dealing first with several threshold questions, the court found that it could review the Sirica order even though Nixon had not officially refused to comply and had been held in contempt. "Here . . . the traditional contempt avenue to immediate appeal is peculiarly inappropriate due to the unique setting in which the question arises. To require a President of the United States to place himself in the posture of disobeying an order of the court merely to trigger the procedural mechanism for review of the ruling would be unseemly and present an unnecessary occasion for constitutional confrontation between two branches of the government."

Rejecting St. Clair's contention that this was a dispute between two parts of the executive branch and therefore was not a matter for the courts to decide, the court held that the special prosecutor had been delegated "unique authority and tenure" including the "explicit power to contest the invocation of executive privilege in the process of seeking evidence deemed relevant to the performance of his specially delegated duties."

The Claim of Privilege

Reaffirming its 1803 decision, *Marbury v. Madison*, establishing the power of the courts to review the actions of the other two branches, Chief Justice Warren E. Burger wrote that "notwithstanding the deference each branch must accord the others, the 'judicial power of the United States' vested in the federal courts by Article III, section 1 of the Constitution can no more be shared with the Executive Branch than the Chief Executive, for example, can share with the Judiciary the veto power, or the Congress share with the Judiciary the power to override a presidential veto. Any other conclusion would be contrary to the basic concept of separation of powers and the checks and balances. . . . We therefore reaffirm that it is 'emphatically the province and the duty' of this court 'to say what the law is' with respect to the claim of privilege presented in this case." No mention was made of the pending impeachment inquiry or St. Clair's argument that the court's decision would interfere in that process.

"Neither the doctrine of separation of powers, nor the need for confidentiality of high-level communications, without more, can sustain an absolute, unqualified, presidential privilege of immunity from judicial process under all circumstances. The President's need for complete candor and objectivity from advisers calls for great deference from the courts. However when the privilege depends solely on the broad undifferentiated claim of public interest in the confidentiality of such conversations, a confrontation with other values arises. Absent a claim of need to protect military, diplomatic or sensitive national security secrets, we find it difficult to accept the argument that even the very important interest in confidentiality . . . is significantly diminished by production of such material for *in camera* inspection. . . .

"To read the Article II powers of the President as providing an absolute privilege as against a subpoena essential to enforcement of criminal statutes on no more than a generalized claim of the public interest in confidentiality of nonmilitary and nondiplomatic discussions would upset the constitutional balance of 'a workable government' and gravely impair the role of the courts under Article III [of the Constitution]."

There is a limited executive privilege with a constitutional base, wrote Burger: "A President and those who assist him must be free to explore alternatives in the process of shaping policies and making decisions and to do so in a way many would be unwilling to express except privately. These are the considerations justifying a presumptive privilege for presidential communications. . . fundamental to the operation of government and inextricably rooted in the separation of powers." To the extent that confidentiality relates to the President's ability to discharge his presidential powers effectively, that privilege has a constitutional basis, he wrote.

"But," he continued, "this presumptive privilege must be considered in light of our historic commitment to the rule of law." The rights to a fair trial and to due process are guaranteed by the Constitution, he pointed out, and "it is the manifest duty of the court to vindicate those guarantees and to accomplish that it is essential that all relevant and admissible evidence be produced."

"We cannot conclude that advisers will be moved to temper the candor of their remarks by the infrequent occasions of disclosure because of the possibility that such conversations will be called for in the context of a criminal prosecution," the court held. "The President's broad interest in confidentiality of communications will not be vitiated by disclosure of a limited number of conversations preliminarily shown to have some bearing on the pending criminal cases.

"We conclude that when the ground for asserting privilege as to subpoenaed materials sought for use in a criminal trial is based only on the generalized interest in confidentiality, it cannot prevail over the fundamental demands of due process of law in the fair administration of criminal justice. The generalized assertion of privilege must yield to the demonstrated specific need for evidence in a pending criminal trial."

NIXON'S REACTION TO DECISION

Following [is] President Nixon's reaction to the Supreme Court tapes decision. Nixon's statement was made through his counsel, James D. St. Clair, July 24 at San Clemente, Calif.:

I have reviewed the decision of the Supreme Court with the President. He's given me this statement, which he's asked me to read to you. And this is the President's statement as he gave it to me:

"My challenge in the courts to the subpoena of the special prosecutor was based on the belief that it was unconstitutionally issued, and on my strong desire to protect the principle of presidential confidentiality in a system of separation of powers.

"While I am, of course, disappointed in the result, I respect and accept the court's decision, and I have instructed Mr. St. Clair to take whatever measures are necessary to comply with that decision in all respects. For the future it will be essential that the special circumstances of this case not be permitted to cloud the right of Presidents to maintain the basic confidentiality without which this office cannot function. I was gratified, therefore, to note that the court reaffirmed both the validity and the importance of the principle of executive privilege, the principle I had sought to maintain. By complying fully with the court's ruling in this case, I hope and trust that I will contribute to strengthening rather than weakening this principle for the future, so that this will prove to be not the precedent that destroyed the principle but the action that preserved it."

That concludes the President's statement. As we all know, the President has always been a firm believer in the rule of law, and he intends his decision to comply fully with the court's ruling as an action in furtherance of that belief. Therefore, in accordance with his instructions, the time-consuming process of reviewing the tapes subject to the subpoena, and the preparation of the index and analysis required by Judge Sirica's order, will begin forthwith.

Thank you all very much.

Excerpts from Supreme Court Ruling on Nixon Tapes

Following are excerpts from the opinion issued by the Supreme Court July 24 upholding a lower court decision ordering President Nixon to comply with the Watergate special prosecutor's subpoena for presidential tape recordings and other documents:

MR. CHIEF JUSTICE BURGER delivered the opinion of the Court.

These cases present for review the denial of a motion, filed on behalf of the President of the United States, in the case of United States v. Mitchell et al. (D.C. Crim. No. 74-110), to quash a third-party subpoena duces tecum issued by the United States District Court for the District of Columbia, pursuant to Fed. Rule Crim. Proc. 17 (c). The subpoena directed the President to produce certain tape recordings and documents relating to his conversations with aides and advisors. The court rejected the President's claims of absolute executive privilege, of lack of jurisdiction, and of failure to satisfy the requirements of Rule 17 (c). The President appealed to the Court of Appeals. We granted the United States' petition for certiorari before judgment, and also the President's responsive cross-petition for certiorari before judgment, because of the public importance of the issues presented and the need for their prompt resolution. —U.S.—, —(1974).

On March 1, 1974, a grand jury of the United States District Court for the District of Columbia returned an indictment charging seven named individuals with various offenses, including conspiracy to defraud the United States and to obstruct justice. Although he was not designated as such in the indictment, the grand jury named the President, among others, as an unindicted co-conspirator. On April 18, 1974, upon motion of the Special Prosecutor, see n. 8, infra, a subpoena duces tecum was issued pursuant to Rule 17 (c) to the President by the United States District Court and made returnable on May 2, 1974. This subpoena required the production, in advance of the September 9 trial date, of certain tapes, memoranda, papers, transcripts, or other writings relating to certain precisely identified meetings between the President and others. The Special Prosecutor was able to fix the time, place and persons present at these discussions because the White House daily logs and appointment records had been delivered to him. On April 30, the President publicly released edited transcripts of 43 conversations; portions of 20 conversations subject to subpoena in the present case were included. On May 1, 1974, the President's counsel filed a "special appearance" and a motion to quash the subpoena, under Rule 17(c). This motion was accompanied by a formal claim of privilege. At a subsequent hearing, further motions to expunge the grand jury's action naming the President as an unindicted co-conspirator and for protective orders against the disclosure of that information were filed or raised orally by counsel for the President.

On May 20, 1974, the District Court denied the motion to quash and the motions to expunge and for protective orders. —F. Supp.—(1974). It further ordered "the President or any subordinate officer, official or employee with custody or control of the documents or objects subpoenaed" id., at—, to deliver to the District Court, on or before May 31, 1974, the originals of all subpoenaed items, as well as an index and analysis of those items, together with tape copies of those portions of the subpoenaed recordings for which transcripts had been released to the public by the President on April 30. The District Court rejected jurisdictional challenges based on a contention that the dispute was non-justiciable because it was between the Special Prosecutor and the Chief Executive and hence "intra-executive" in character; it also rejected the contention that the judiciary was without

authority to review an assertion of executive privilege by the President. The court's rejection of the first challenge was based on the authority and powers vested in the Special Prosecutor by the regulation promulgated by the Attorney General; the court concluded that a justiciable controversy was presented. The second challenge was held to be foreclosed by the decision in Nixon v. Sirica,— U.S. App. D.C.—,487 F. 2d 700 (1973).

The District Court held that the judiciary, not the President, was the final arbiter of a claim of executive privilege. The court concluded that, under the circumstances of this case, the presumptive privilege was overcome by the Special Prosecutor's prima facie "demonstration of need sufficiently compelling to warrant judicial examination in chambers. . . ."—F. Supp., at—. The court held, finally, that the Special Prosecutor had satisfied the requirements of Rule 17 (c). . . .

On May 24, 1974, the President filed a timely notice of appeal from the District Court order, and the certified record from the District Court was docketed in the United States Court of Appeals for the District of Columbia Circuit. On the same day, the President also filed a petition for writ of mandamus in the Court of Appeals seeking review of the District Court order.

Later on May 24, the Special Prosecutor also filed, in this Court, a petition for a writ of certiorari before judgment. On May 31, the petition was granted with an expedited briefing schedule.—U.S.—(1974). On June 6, the President filed, under seal, a cross-petition for writ of certiorari before judgment. This cross-petition was granted June 15, 1974,—U.S.—(1974), and the case was set for argument on July 8, 1974.

I

Jurisdiction

The threshold question presented is whether the May 20, 1974, order of the District Court was an appealable order and whether this case was properly "in," 28 U.S.C. 1254, the United States Court of Appeals when the petition for certiorari was filed in this Court. Court of Appeals jurisdiction under 28 U.S.C. 1291 encompasses only "final decisions of the district courts. . . ."

The finality requirement of 28 U.S.C. 1291 embodies a strong congressional policy against piecemeal reviews, and against obstructing or impeding an ongoing judicial proceeding by interlocutory appeals. See, e.g., Cobbledick v. United States, 309 U.S. 323, 324–326 (1940). This requirement ordinarily promotes judicial efficiency and hastens the ultimate termination of litigation. . . .

The requirement of submitting to contempt, however, is not without exception and in some instances the purposes underlying the finality rule require a different result. . . .

Here too the traditional contempt avenue to immediate appeal is peculiarly inappropriate due to the unique setting in which the question arises. To require a President of the United States to place himself in the posture of disobeying an order of a court merely to trigger the procedural mechanism for review of the ruling would be unseemly, and present an unnecessary occasion for constitutional confrontation between two branches of the Government. Similarly, a federal judge should not be placed in the posture of issuing a citation to a President simply in order to invoke review. . . .

II
Justiciability

In the District Court, the President's counsel argued that the court lacked jurisdiction to issue the subpoena because the matter was an intra-branch dispute between a subordinate and superior officer of the Executive Branch and hence not subject to judicial resolution. That argument has been renewed in this Court with emphasis on the contention that the dispute does not present a "case" or "controversy" which can be adjudicated in the federal courts. The President's counsel argues that the federal courts should not intrude into areas committed to the other branches of Government. He views the present dispute as essentially a "jurisdictional" dispute within the Executive Branch which he analogizes to a dispute between two congressional committees. Since the Executive Branch has exclusive authority and absolute discretion to decide whether to prosecute a case, Confiscation Cases, 7 Wall. 454 (1869), United States v. Cox, 342 F. 2d 167, 171 (CA5), cert. denied, 381 U.S. 935 (1965), it is contended that a President's decision is final in determining what evidence is to be used in a given criminal case. Although his counsel concedes the President has delegated certain specific powers to the Special Prosecutor, he has not "waived nor delegated to the Special Prosecutor the President's duty to claim privileges as to all materials . . . which fall within the President's inherent authority to refuse to disclose to any executive officer." Brief for the President 47. The Special Prosecutor's demand for the items therefore presents, in the view of the President's counsel, a political question under Baker v. Carr, 369 U.S. 186 (1962), since it involves a "textually demonstrable" grant of power under Art. II.

The mere assertion of a claim of an "intra-branch dispute," without more, has never operated to defeat federal jurisdiction; justiciability does not depend on such a surface inquiry. In United States v. ICC, 337 U.S. 426 (1949), the Court observed, "courts must look behind names that symbolize the parties to determine whether a justiciable case or controversy is presented." Id., at 430. . . .

Our starting point is the nature of the proceeding for which the evidence is sought—here a pending criminal prosecution. It is a judicial proceeding in a federal court alleging violation of federal laws and is brought in the name of the United States as sovereign. Berger v. United States, 295 U.S. 78, 88 (1935). Under the authority of Art. II, 2, Congress has vested in the Attorney General the power to conduct the criminal litigation of the United States Government. 28 U.S.C. 516. It has also vested in him the power to appoint subordinate officers to assist him in the discharge of his duties. 28 U.S.C. 509, 510, 515, 533. Acting pursuant to those statutes, the Attorney General has delegated the authority to represent the United States in these particular matters to a Special Prosecutor with unique authority and tenure. The regulation gives the Special Prosecutor explicit power to contest the invocation of executive privilege in the process of seeking evidence deemed relevant to the performance of these specially delegated duties. 38 Fed. Reg. 30739. . . .

So long as this regulation remains in force the Executive Branch is bound by it, and indeed the United States as the sovereign composed of the three branches is bound to respect and to enforce it. Moreover, the delegation of authority to the Special Prosecutor in this case is not an ordinary delegation by the Attorney General to a subordinate officer; with the authorization of the President, the Acting Attorney General provided in the regulation that the Special Prosecutor was not to be removed without the "consensus" of eight designated leaders of Congress. Note 8, supra.

The demands of and the resistance to the subpoena present an obvious controversy in the ordinary sense, but that alone is not sufficient to meet constitutional standards. In the constitutional sense, controversy means more than disagreement and conflict; rather it means the kind of controversy courts traditionally resolve. Here at issue is the production or nonproduction of specified evidence deemed by the Special Prosecutor to be relevant and admissible in a pending criminal case. It is sought by one official of the Government within the scope of his express authority; it is resisted by the Chief Executive on the ground of his duty to preserve the confidentiality of the communications of the President. Whatever the correct answer on the merits, these issues are "of a type which are traditionally justiciable. . . ."

In light of the uniqueness of the setting in which the conflict arises, the fact that both parties are officers of the Executive Branch cannot be viewed as a barrier to justiciability. It would be inconsistent with the applicable law and regulation, and the unique facts of this case to conclude other than that the Special Prosecutor has standing to bring this action and that a justiciable controversy is presented for decision.

III
Rule 17 (c)

The subpoena duces tecum is challenged on the ground that the Special Prosecutor failed to satisfy the requirements of Fed. Rule Crim. Proc. 17 (c), which governs the issuance of subpoenas duces tecum in federal criminal proceedings. If we sustained this challenge, there would be no occasion to reach the claim of privilege asserted with respect to the subpoenaed material. . . .

Against this background, the Special Prosecutor, in order to carry his burden, must clear three hurdles: (1) relevancy; (2) admissibility; (3) specificity. . . .

With respect to many of the tapes, the Special Prosecutor offered the sworn testimony or statements of one or more of the participants in the conversations as to what was said at the time. As for the remainder of the tapes, the identity of the participants and the time and place of the conversations, taken in their total context, permit a rational inference that at least part of the conversations relate to the offenses charged in the indictment. . . .

We also conclude there was a sufficient preliminary showing that each of the subpoenaed tapes contains evidence admissible with respect to the offenses charged in the indictment. The most cogent objection to the admissibility of the taped conversations here at issue is that they are a collection of out-of-court statements by declarants who will not be subject to the cross-examination and that the statements are therefore inadmissible hearsay. Here, however, most of the tapes apparently contain conversations to which one or more of the defendants named in the indictment were party. . . .

Here, however, there are other valid potential evidentiary uses for the same material and the analysis and possible transcription of the tapes may take a significant period of time. Accordingly, we cannot say that the District Court erred in authorizing the issuance of the subpoena duces tecum. . . .

In a case such as this, however, where a subpoena is directed to a President of the United States, appellate review, in deference to a coordinate branch of government, should be particularly meticulous to ensure that the standards of Rule 17 (c) have been correctly applied. United States v. Burr, 25 Fed. Cas. 30, 34 (No. 14,692d) (1807). From our examination of the materials submitted by the Special Prosecutor to the District Court in sup-

port of his motion for the subpoena, we are persuaded that the District Court's denial of the President's motion to quash the subpoena was consistent with Rule 17 (c). We also conclude that the Special Prosecutor has made a sufficient showing to justify a subpoena for production before trial. . . .

IV
The Claim of Privilege
A.

Having determined that the requirements of Rule 17(c) were satisfied, we turn to the claim that the subpoena should be quashed because it demands "confidential conversations between a President and his close advisors that it would be inconsistent with the public interest to produce." App. 48a. The first contention is a broad claim that the separation of powers doctrine precludes judicial review of a President's claim of privilege. The second contention is that if he does not prevail on the claim of absolute privilege, the court should hold as a matter of constitutional law that the privilege prevails over the subpoena duces tecum.

In the performance of assigned constitutional duties each branch of the Government must initially interpret the Constitution and the interpretation of its powers by any branch is due great respect from the others. The President's counsel, as we have noted, reads the Constitution as providing an absolute privilege of confidentiality for all presidential communications. Many decisions of this Court, however, have unequivocally reaffirmed the holding of Marbury v. Madison, 1 Cranch 137 (1803), that "it is emphatically the province and duty of the judicial department to say what the law is." Id., at 177.

No holding of the Court has defined the scope of judicial power specifically relating to the enforcement of a subpoena for confidential presidential communications for use in a criminal prosecution, but other exercises of powers by the Executive Branch and the Legislative Branch have been found invalid as in conflict with the Constitution. Powell v. McCormack, supra; Youngstown, supra. In a series of cases, the Court interpreted the explicit immunity conferred by express provisions of the Constitution on Members of the House and Senate by the Speech or Debate Clause, U.S. Const. Art. I, 6. Doe v. McMillan, 412 U.S. 306 (1973); Gravel v. United States, 408 U.S. 606 (1973); United States v. Brewster, 408 U.S. 501 (1972); United States v. Johnson, 383 U.S. 169 (1966). Since this Court has consistently exercised the power to construe and delineate claims arising under express powers, it must follow that the Court has authority to interpret claims with respect to powers alleged to derive from enumerated powers. . . . Notwithstanding the deference each branch must accord the others, the "judicial power of the United States" vested in the federal courts by Art. III, 1 of the Constitution can no more be shared with the Executive Branch than the Chief Executive, for example, can share with the Judiciary the veto power, or the Congress share with the Judiciary the power to override a presidential veto. Any other conclusion would be contrary to the basic concept of separation of powers and the checks and balances that flow from the scheme of a tripartite government. The Federalist, No. 47, p. 313 (C.F. Mittel ed. 1938). We therefore reaffirm that it is "emphatically the province and the duty" of this Court "to say what the law is" with respect to the claim of privilege presented in this case. Marbury v. Madison, supra, at 177.

B

In support of his claim of absolute privilege, the President's counsel urges two grounds one of which is common to all governments and one of which is peculiar to our system of separation of powers. The first ground is the valid need for protection of communications between high government officials and those who advise and assist them in the performance of their manifold duties; the importance of this confidentiality is too plain to require further discussion. Human experience teaches that those who expect public dissemination of their remarks may well temper candor with a concern for appearances and for their own interests to the detriment of the decision-making process. Whatever the nature of the privilege of confidentiality of presidential communications in the exercise of Art. II powers the privilege can be said to derive from the supremacy of each branch within its own assigned area of constitutional duties. Certain powers and privileges flow from the nature of enumerated powers; the protection of the confidentiality of presidential communications has similar constitutional underpinnings.

The second ground asserted by the President's counsel in support of the claim of absolute privilege rests on the doctrine of separation of powers. Here it is argued that the independence of the Executive Branch within its own sphere, Humphrey's Executor v. United States, 295 U.S. 602, 629–630; Kilbourn v. Thompson, 103 U.S. 168, 190–191 (1880), insulates a president from a judicial subpoena in an ongoing criminal prosecution, and thereby protects confidential presidential communications.

However, neither the doctrine of separation of powers, nor the need for confidentiality of high level communications, without more, can sustain an absolute, unqualified presidential privilege of immunity from judicial process under all circumstances. The President's need for complete candor and objectivity from advisers calls for great deference from the courts. However, when the privilege depends solely on the broad, undifferentiated claim of public interest in the confidentiality of such conversations, a confrontation with other values arises. Absent a claim of need to protect military, diplomatic or sensitive national security secrets, we find it difficult to accept the argument that even the very important interest in confidentiality of presidential communications is significantly diminished by production of such material for in camera inspection with all the protection that a district court will be obliged to provide.

The impediment that an absolute unqualified privilege would place in the way of the primary constitutional duty of the Judicial Branch to do justice in criminal prosecutions would plainly conflict with the function of the courts under Art. III. In designing the structure of our Government and dividing and allocating the sovereign power among three coequal branches, the Framers of the Constitution sought to provide a comprehensive system, but the separate powers were not intended to operate with absolute independence. . . . To read the Art. II powers of the President as providing an absolute privilege as against a subpoena essential to enforcement of criminal statutes on no more than a generalized claim of the public interest in confidentiality and nondiplomatic discussions would upset the constitutional balance of "a workable government" and gravely impair the role of the courts under Art. III.

C

Since we conclude that the legitimate needs of the judicial process may outweigh presidential privilege, it is necessary to resolve those competing interests in a manner that preserves the essential functions of each branch. The right and indeed the duty to resolve that question does not free the judiciary from according high respect to the representations made on behalf of the President. United States v. Burr, 25 Fed. Cas. 187, 190, 191–192 (No. 14,694) (1807).

The expectation of a President to the confidentiality of his conversations and correspondence, like the claim of confidentiality of judicial deliberations, for example, has all the values to which we accord deference for the privacy of all citizens and added to those values the necessity for protection of the public interest in candid, objective, and even blunt or harsh opinions in presidential decision-making. A President and those who assist him must be free to explore alternatives in the process of shaping policies and making decisions and to do so in a way many would be unwilling to express except privately. These are the considerations justifying a presumptive privilege for presidential communications. The privilege is fundamental to the operation of government and inextricably rooted in the separation of powers under the Constitution. In Nixon v. Sirica,—U.S. App. D.C.—, 487 F. 2d 700 (1973), the Court of Appeals held that such presidential communications are "presumptively privileged," id., at 717, and this position is accepted by both parties in the present litigation. We agree with Mr. Chief Justice Marshall's observation, therefore, that "in no case of this kind would a court be required to proceed against the President as against an ordinary individual." United States Burr, 25 Fed. Cas. 187, 191 (No. 14,694) (CCD Va. 1807).

But this presumptive privilege must be considered in light of our historic commitment to the rule of law. This is nowhere more profoundly manifest than in our view that "the twofold aim [of criminal justice] is that guilt shall not escape or innocence suffer." Berger v. United States, 295 U.S. 78, 88 (1935). We have elected to employ an adversary system of criminal justice in which the parties contest all issues before a court of law. The need to develop all relevant facts in the adversary system is both fundamental and comprehensive. The ends of criminal justice would be defeated if judgments were to be founded on a partial or speculative presentation of the facts. The very integrity of the judicial system and public confidence in the system depend on full disclosure of all the facts, within the framework of the rules of evidence. To ensure that justice is done, it is imperative to the function of courts that compulsory process be available for the production of evidence needed either by the prosecution or by the defense.

Only recently the Court restated the ancient proposition of law, albeit in the context of a grand jury inquiry rather than a trial,

> "that the public . . . has a right to every man's evidence" except for those persons protected by a constitutional, common law, or statutory privilege, United States v. Bryan, 339 U.S., at 331 (1949); Blackmer v. United States, 284 U.S. 421, 438; Branzburg v. United States, 408 U.S. 665, 688 (1973).

The privileges referred to by the Court are designed to protect weighty and legitimate competing interests. Thus the Fifth Amendment to the Constitution provides that no man "shall be compelled in any criminal case to be a witness against himself." And, generally, an attorney or a priest may not be required to disclose what has been revealed in professional confidence. These and other interests are recognized in law by privileges against

forced disclosure, established in the Constitution, by statute, or at common law. Whatever their origins, these exceptions to the demand for every man's evidence are not lightly created nor expansively construed, for they are in derogation of the search for truth.

In this case the President challenges a subpoena served on him as a third party requiring the production of materials for use in a criminal prosecution on the claim that he has a privilege against disclosure of confidential communications. He does not place his claim of privilege on the ground they are military or diplomatic secrets. As to these areas of Art. II duties the courts have traditionally shown the utmost deference to presidential responsibilities. In C. & S. Air Lines v. Waterman Steamship Corp., 333 U.S. 103, 111 (1948), dealing with presidential authority involving foreign policy considerations, the Court said:

> The President, both as Commander-in-Chief and as the Nation's organ for foreign affairs, has available intelligence services whose reports are not and ought not to be published to the world. It would be intolerable that courts, without the relevant information, should review and perhaps nullify actions of the Executive taken on information properly held secret. Id., at 111.

In United States v. Reynolds, 345 U.S. 1 (1952), dealing with a claimant's demand for evidence in a damage case against the Government the Court said:

> It may be possible to satisfy the court, from all the circumstances of the case, that there is a reasonable danger that compulsion of the evidence will expose military matters which, in the interest of national security, should not be divulged. When this is the case, the occasion for the privilege is appropriate, and the court should not jeopardize the security which the privilege is meant to protect by insisting upon an examination of the evidence, even by the judge alone, in chambers.

No case of the Court, however, has extended this high degree of deference to a President's generalized interest in confidentiality. Nowhere in the Constitution[,] as we have noted earlier, is there any explicit reference to a privilege of confidentiality, yet to the extent this interest relates to the effective discharge of a President's powers, it is constitutionally based.

The right to the production of all evidence at a criminal trial similarly has constitutional dimensions. The Sixth Amendment explicitly confers upon every defendant in a criminal trial the right "to be confronted with the witnesses against him" and "to have compulsory process for obtaining witnesses in his favor." Moreover, the Fifth Amendment also guarantees that no person shall be deprived of liberty without due process of law. It is the manifest duty of the courts to vindicate those guarantees and to accomplish that it is essential that all relevant and admissible evidence be produced.

In this case we must weigh the importance of the general privilege of confidentiality of presidential communications in performance of his responsibilities against the inroads of such a privilege on the fair administration of criminal justice. The interest in preserving confidentiality is weighty indeed and entitled to great respect. However[,] we cannot conclude that advisers will be moved to temper the candor of their remarks by the infrequent occasions of disclosure because of the possibility that such conversations will be called for in the context of a criminal prosecution.

On the other hand, the allowance of the privilege to withhold evidence that is demonstrably relevant in a criminal trial would cut deeply into the guarantee of due process of law and gravely impair the basic function of the courts. A President's acknowledged need for confidentiality in the communications of his office is general in nature, whereas the constitutional need for production of relevant evidence in a criminal proceeding is specific and central to the fair adjudication of a particular criminal case in the administration of justice. Without access to specific facts a criminal prosecution may be totally frustrated. The President's broad interest in confidentiality of communications will not be vitiated by disclosure of a limited number of conversations preliminarily shown to have some bearing on the pending criminal cases.

We conclude that when the ground for asserting privilege as to subpoenaed materials sought for use in a criminal trial is based only on the generalized interest in confidentiality, it cannot prevail over the fundamental demands of due process of law in the fair administration of criminal justice. The generalized assertion of privilege must yield to the demonstrated, specific need for evidence in a pending criminal trial.

D

We have earlier determined that the District Court did not err in authorizing the issuance of the subpoena. If a president concludes that compliance with a subpoena would be injurious to the public interest he may properly, as was done here, invoke a claim of privilege on the return of the subpoena. Upon receiving a claim of privilege from the Chief Executive, it became the further duty of the District Court to treat the subpoenaed mate-

rial as presumptively privileged and to require the Special Prosecutor to demonstrate that the presidential material was "essential to the justice of the [pending criminal] case," United States v. Burr, supra, at 192. Here the District Court treated the material as presumptively privileged, proceeded to find that the Special Prosecutor had made a sufficient showing to rebut the presumption and ordered an in camera examination of the subpoenaed material. On the basis of our examination of the record we are unable to conclude that the District Court erred in ordering the inspection. Accordingly we affirm the order of the District Court that subpoenaed materials be transmitted to that court. We now turn to the important question of the District Court's responsibilities in conducting the in camera examination of presidential materials or communications delivered under the compulsion of the subpoena duces tecum.

E

Enforcement of the subpoena duces tecum was stayed pending this Court's resolution of the issues raised by the petitions for certiorari. Those issues now having been disposed of, the matter of implementation will rest with the District Court. "[T]he guard, furnished to [the President] to protect him from being harassed by vexatious and unnecessary subpoenas, is to be looked for in the conduct of the [district] court after the subpoenas have been issued; not in any circumstances which is to precede their being issued." United States v. Burr, supra, at 34. Statements that meet the test of admissibility and relevance must be isolated; all other material must be excised. At this stage the District Court is not limited to representations of the Special Prosecutor as to the evidence sought by the subpoena; the material will be available to the District Court. It is elementary that in camera inspection of evidence is always a procedure calling for scrupulous protection against any release or publication of material not found by the court, at that stage, probably admissible in evidence and relevant to the issues of the trial for which it is sought. That being true of an ordinary situation, it is obvious that the District Court has a very heavy responsibility to see to it that presidential conversations, which are either not relevant or not admissible, are accorded that high degree of respect due the President of the United States. Mr. Chief Justice Marshall sitting as a trial judge in the Burr case, supra, was extraordinarily careful to point out that:

> [I]n no case of this kind would a Court be required to proceed against the President as against an ordinary individual. United States v. Burr, 25 Fed. Cases 187, 191 (No. 14,694).

Marshall's statement cannot be read to mean in any sense that a President is above the law, but relates to the singularly unique role under Art. II of a President's communications and activities related to the performance of duties under that Article. Moreover, a President's communications and activities encompass a vastly wider range of sensitive material than would be true of any "ordinary individual." It is therefore necessary in the public interest to afford presidential confidentiality the greatest protection consistent with the fair administration of justice. The need for confidentiality even as to idle conversations with associates in which casual reference might be made concerning political leaders within the country or foreign statesmen is too obvious to call for further treatment. We have no doubt that the District Judge will at all times accord to presidential records that high degree of deference suggested in United States v. Burr, supra, and will discharge his responsibility to see to it that until released to the Special Prosecutor no in camera material is revealed to anyone. This burden applies with even greater force to excised material; once the decision is made to excise, the material is restored to its privileged status and should be returned under seal to its lawful custodian.

Since this matter came before the Court during the pendency of a criminal prosecution, and on representations that time is of the essence, the mandate shall issue forthwith.

Affirmed.

Points to Ponder

- In the Watergate case, the Supreme Court had to balance two competing rights—the right of the president to protect private documents and the right of the criminal justice system to gain access to evidence. Did the Court come up with a solution that sufficiently protected executive privilege? Did it give federal courts too much power to review executive actions?

- The Court issued a unanimous decision on Watergate. But on many controversial cases in recent years, the justices have disagreed with each other, sometimes even issuing a ruling by just a 5–4 margin. Why do you think the Constitution is so difficult to interpret that even Supreme Court justices may disagree with each other? If the Court rules on a momentous issue by a 5–4 margin, should that ruling be given as much weight as if the justices had been unanimous? Is it realistic to expect all the justices to agree on a controversial issue, given how divided our political leaders are?

IMPEACHMENT:
3 Articles Sent to House Floor

At the end of July, the House Judiciary Committee made the historic decision to approve three articles of impeachment. President Nixon, according to the committee, had violated his oath of office. He had obstructed justice in the Watergate coverup, abused his presidential powers, and acted in contempt of Congress. The committee voted for the articles of impeachment by wide margins: 27–11 for obstruction of justice, 28–10 for abuse of presidential powers, and 21–17 for contempt of Congress. However, it decisively rejected two other articles of impeachment.

The committee's bipartisan votes for impeachment signaled that the full House would probably move ahead with a majority vote for impeachment. In the Senate, where a two-thirds vote was required to remove the president, Nixon's prospects looked increasingly grim. Moreover, the administration continued to suffer from widening scandals. On July 28, Nixon's former treasury secretary was indicted for accepting bribes and other crimes in connection with an increase in milk price supports.

With impeachment looking more and more likely, only few Republicans rose to defend the president. The Senate Rules Committee began looking into how to conduct a trial in the Senate that would follow impeachment. White House aides signaled their growing pessimism about the situation.

For many Judiciary Committee members, both Democrats and Republicans, the decision to vote on impeachment was a difficult one. "Americans revere their president," said James R. Mann, a committee Democrat whose South Carolina district had overwhelmingly voted for Nixon in 1972. But Mann, along with all of the other committee Democrats and nearly half of its Republicans, nevertheless supported at least two articles of impeachment. On the other side, 10 Republican members of the committee opposed any article of impeachment. They vowed to defend Nixon on the House floor, where debate was expected to begin in late August.

Much of the committee's work in the days leading up to the votes was spent on refining the impeachment articles. A group of southern Democrats and moderate Republicans, known as the "fragile coalition," played an especially important role. The suspense was particularly noticeable leading up to the vote on the first article of impeachment: obstruction of justice. The charge meant that Nixon had

tried to block the criminal investigation into the Watergate break-in. Committee members debated the wording of that article. They agreed to a version that charged that Nixon "engaged personally and through his subordinates and agents in a course of conduct or plan designed to delay, impede and obstruct" the Watergate break-in.

Some Republicans tried to remove several sections from the first article. These sections charged that Nixon had made false statements to investigative officers, advised witnesses to give false testimony, misused the CIA, and engaged in other misdeeds. The committee overwhelmingly rejected such changes. Instead, members agreed to minor wording revisions, such as changing "illegal entry" to "unlawful entry."

When it came time to vote on the first article, several members were clearly anguished. Hamilton Fish Jr., a New York Republican whose constituents had supported the president's re-election bid, said he reached his decision "with deep reluctance only after I have been persuaded that the evidence for such a vote is clear."

All the committee's Democrats, joined by six Republicans, approved the obstruction of justice article. The committee then took up the second article, charging that Nixon had abused his powers to violate, or threaten to violate, the constitutional rights of individual citizens. Many committee members viewed this as a more serious offense than obstruction of justice. They believed that Nixon had used government agencies to spy on or to harass his political opponents. The second article also charged Nixon with failing to take action against close aides who had engaged in illegal activities and with interfering with the FBI and other agencies.

Charles E. Wiggins, a California Republican who doggedly defended the president, opposed the second article. He claimed that none of the misdeeds rose to the level of an impeachable offense. He proposed several changes to weaken the language of the impeachment article. But a majority of committee members opposed his suggestions, and the committee approved the second article by a lopsided margin.

Committee members then took up the third article. It accused the president of contempt of Congress, which is a crime. Specifically, it stated that the president had failed "without lawful cause or excuse" to obey four committee subpoenas for tapes and documents needed for its investigation. Robert McClory, an Illinois Republican who proposed the article, said the president's response to subpoenas "has been that he should be the sole arbiter of what he should and what he should not turn over. . . . If he's to be the sole arbiter, then how in the world can we conduct a thorough and complete and fair investigation?"

The committee agreed to narrow the language of the contempt of Congress article. The revised article focused on Nixon's failure to produce certain materials and removed a broad explanation of the reason for the subpoenas. Otherwise, some committee members feared, it might appear as though the House was overreaching in its efforts to obtain presidential documents. Even with the narrower language, almost all the committee Republicans opposed impeaching Nixon for contempt of Congress. They argued that the committee should have gone to court to force

Nixon to comply with the subpoenas instead of impeaching him for his lack of cooperation. As a result, the vote was far closer on the contempt of Congress article than on the other two articles.

The committee rejected two other articles. One charged Nixon with tax fraud. The committee rejected this article by a 26–12 vote. The other charged Nixon with illegally bombing Cambodia. This article also was rejected by a 26–12 vote.

Bowing to the Supreme Court's unanimous ruling, the White House turned over tapes of 30 private conversations to U.S. District Court judge John J. Sirica. These tapes were among the 64 that had been subpoenaed by Watergate special prosecutor Leon Jaworski. However, the White House raised new claims of executive privilege. It said that 10 of the conversations should not have to be made public and were unrelated to Watergate. In addition, at least one of the tapes had a gap of more than five minutes.

"Americans revere their President . . . and rightly they should," said James R. Mann (D S.C.) in his soft southern accent July 29. "But if there is no accountability, another President will feel free to do as he chooses. And the next time, there may be no watchman in the night." Then Mann, whose district overwhelmingly supported Richard Nixon's election in 1972, cast a vote recommending the impeachment of the President.

In dramatic public sessions ending July 30, the House Judiciary Committee approved three articles of impeachment, recommending to the House that Richard Nixon be impeached and removed as President because he had violated his oath of office by obstruction of justice in the Watergate coverup (Article I), by abuse of his presidential powers in a variety of ways (Article II), and by contempt of Congress (Article III) in refusing to comply with the committee's subpoenas.

But not everyone agreed, as the arguments and votes of at least 10 committee Republicans showed. Nixon's defenders were led by Charles E. Wiggins (R Calif.), who vowed to carry the fight to the House floor. Debate there was to begin Aug. 19.

The paradox of pro-impeachment votes like Mann's was but one of the remarkable events of the week ending Aug. 3. For the first time in more than a century, the formal process of repudiation of a President—elected less than two years earlier with more than 60 per cent of the popular vote—had begun. (*See texts of articles, pp. 268.*)

The agonizing and the arguing, eloquence and the evidence of 38 men and women—conveyed to the public at large through the medium of television—had a substantial and still unmeasured impact upon the American public.

As if to reassure their audience, members of the committee time and again emphasized that they were acting as representatives of their constituents. Walter Flowers (D Ala.) told his colleagues in his opening statement: "We here in this room are the representatives of the people of the United States . . . and we have an awesome task to do that no one else can do for us." Later, announcing his intention to support the first article of impeachment, he assured his pro-Nixon constituents and friends that "the only way that I could vote for impeachment would be on the realization . . . that . . . my friends would do the same thing if they were in my place on this unhappy day and confronted with all of the facts that I have."

When the crucial vote came—on approval of Article I charging the President with obstruction of justice—all three southern conservative Democrats—Mann, Flowers and Ray Thornton (D Ark.)—voted for impeachment, joined by what came to be described as the "fragile coalition"—six Republicans—William S. Cohen (R Maine), Tom Railsback (R Ill.), Hamilton Fish Jr. (R N.Y.), Lawrence J. Hogan (R Md.), M. Caldwell Butler (R Va.) and Harold V. Froehlich(R Wis.). On the second article these six Republicans were joined in support of impeachment by Robert McClory (R Ill.).

The impact of the votes of these 10 members of the committee upon their undecided or wavering colleagues—and the White House—was immediate and drastic. Few members of the House would state publicly that they opposed impeachment; the large majority of Republicans, including House Minority Leader John J. Rhodes (R Ariz.), described themselves as undecided. The Senate directed its Rules Committee to begin studying the rules guiding the conduct of a Senate impeachment trial.

And the White House, in a complete reversal of its earlier strategy of delay, suggested that the House might swiftly impeach the President by voice vote, speeding the process to the trial stage. Adverse reaction from members of Congress quickly sank the suggestion, but the fact that it was ever voiced by White House aides was seen as a measure of the pessimism within the circles closest to the President.

New shocks to the Nixon administration came from other directions during the week. On July 29, former Treasury Secretary John B. Connally was indicted for conspiracy to obstruct justice, perjury and accepting bribes from milk producers who sought an increase, later granted, in milk price supports. On July 31, John D. Ehrlichman, former chief domestic adviser to the President, was sentenced to serve a minimum of 20 months in prison for his role in the burglary, by the White House "plumbers" unit, of the office of Daniel Ellsberg's psychiatrist.

A Test of Strength

The strength of the forces urging more specifically worded articles came to a test at 11:30 Friday night, July 26. By an 11–27 vote, the committee firmly rejected the motion by Charles W. Sandman Jr. (R N.J.) to strike out the first subsection of the article proposed by Paul S. Sarbanes (D Md.)—that section which charged that the President had made false statements to investigative officers: Six Republicans—Henry P. Smith III (R N.Y.), Railsback, Fish, Hogan, Butler and Cohen—joined the solid ranks of Democrats to defeat the Sandman motion. The committee then recessed until noon July 27. (*See Vote 2, p. 265.*)

DEAN SENTENCING

Former White House counsel John Wesley Dean III was sentenced Aug. 2 to serve one to four years in prison.

"I realize the wrongs I've done . . . but to say I'm sorry is really not enough," said Dean,

standing before Federal Judge John J. Sirica, who sentenced him. Dean's attorneys had asked Sirica to delay the sentencing until he could examine the White House tapes which were being turned over to him as a result of the Supreme Court decision July 24 rejecting Nixon's claim of executive privilege to withhold the tapes. The attorneys said that the evidence which the tapes might contain might suggest that Dean deserved only a light sentence.

Dean, the key witness at the Senate Watergate hearings in the summer of 1973, left his White House post April 30, 1973. It was his testimony which first pointed directly to President Nixon as personally involved in the Watergate coverup. He had pleaded guilty Oct. 19, 1973, to charges of conspiring to obstruct justice and to defraud the United States. Sentencing had been deferred.

Sirica gave Dean until Sept. 3 to put his affairs in order and said he would recommend that Dean serve his sentence in the minimum security prison at Lompoc, Calif. Dean could have received a maximum penalty of five years in prison and a $10,000 fine.

A Switch of Strategy

When the weary committee members met again July 27—Saturday—Sandman and his fellow advocates of specificity were well aware that their arguments would not convince the majority of the committee to reword any of the articles. "The argument was exhausted yesterday," he said, withdrawing similar amendments he had intended to propose, aimed at striking out each of the other subsections of Sarbanes' proposed Article I. "There is no way that the outcome of this vote will be changed by debate."

"We are bowing . . . to the obvious," said Delbert L. Latta (R Ohio), one of those who had backed Sandman's efforts. "We don't have the votes. . . . We are not deserting our position, which is a valid one," he said, indicating that he would argue that position on the House floor, when it became the forum for the impeachment charges.

The committee then adopted several amendments to Sarbanes' article which:

* Changed the phrase "illegal entry" to "unlawful entry," and which charged the President with

causing the making of false statements to the American people as well as with making such statements. The committee adopted these, proposed by Hogan, by voice vote.

- Added congressional committees to the list of investigators obstructed by Nixon. The committee adopted this amendment, proposed by George E. Danielson (D Calif.), by a 24–14 vote. Flowers opposed the amendment. All the other Democrats, joined by Robert McClory (R Ill.), Smith, Charles E. Wiggins (R Calif.) and David W. Dennis (R Ind.), voted for it. *(See Vote 3, p. 265.)*

- Reworded the basic charge in the article to state that Nixon "engaged personally and through his subordinates and agents in a course of conduct or plan designed to delay, impede and obstruct" the Watergate break-in investigation—instead of making it his policy to do so. The committee agreed to this amendment, proposed by Railsback by voice vote; Wiggins later commented that he felt that this change made the article more difficult to prove than it would have been with the original wording.

Getting the Facts on Record

In a shift of strategy designed to lay out a litany of facts backing up each of the charges within the Sarbanes substitute, Flowers adopted Sandman's proposals to strike the various subsections of that article. "Are we capable of proving satisfactorily . . . in a clear and convincing manner the allegations?" he asked, calling up an amendment to strike the second subsection.

Assuring his colleagues and the audience that he was not trying to delay a vote, Flowers explained that he was using the device of the amendments "to elicit from members of the panel or staff specifics of what charges, what information, what evidence do we have that would come" within this subsection. Flowers then yielded time to Cohen, who agreed that "fundamental fairness requires that we articulate the operative facts upon which the House tends to rely." Cohen proceeded to do just that for the second subsection, which charged the President with withholding evidence from investigators.

Sandman, amazed by the persistence of Flowers in what he had decided was a lost cause, exclaimed: "If you were to stand on your head and do the fanciest of tricks, you would have 12 votes, no more. . . . There is no point in the continuation of this kind of argument. . . . You're going to have a far better forum on another day. . . . So please, let's not bore the American public."

Special counsel John M. Doar assured committee members that the staff was preparing a bill of particulars supporting each of the charges in the article. The committee then by voice vote rejected Flowers' amendment and recessed for two hours at mid-afternoon.

When the session reconvened, Flowers resumed, calling up an amendment to strike out the third subsection of the proposed Sarbanes substitute article—which charged the President with condoning and advising witnesses to testify falsely and give false statements to investigators. Debate, at Flowers' request, was limited to 20 minutes on this and all similar amendments he proposed that day.

Butler opposed this motion, outlining the specifics backing up the charge; Wiggins argued for the motion and against the evidence. Shortly after five o'clock, the vote came and the amendment was rejected 12–25, with Railsback, Fish, Hogan, Butler and Cohen opposing it with all the other Democrats except Flowers, who voted "present." *(See Vote 4, p. 265.)*

For the next hour and a half, the pattern continued. Flowers called up amendments to strike the fourth, seventh, eighth and ninth subsections of the article. The evidence in support of the fifth and sixth subsections—which dealt with hush money and misuse of the CIA—had already been adequately aired, he said. In each case, he immediately yielded time to another member who outlined the evidence in support of the particular charge, putting on record before all those watching the facts which had convinced a majority of the members to back that charge.

Hogan, a former FBI agent, outlined the specifics of the charge that Nixon had interfered with the investigations of the FBI, the Justice Department, the special prosecutor and congressional committees. Wiggins and Trent Lott (R Miss.) challenged the evidence as insufficient to prove presidential involvement in such obstruction. The amendment was rejected by a vote of 11–26; again Flowers voted "present." McClory joined the five Republicans who had opposed the previous amendment in opposing this one with the Democrats. *(See Vote 5, p. 265.)*

Charles B. Rangel (D N.Y.), Railsback and William L. Hungate (D Mo.) set out the evidence backing up the charge that Nixon gave information he received from Assistant Attorney General Henry E. Petersen about the grand jury investigation to persons implicated in that investigation, chiefly H. R. Haldeman and John D. Ehrlichman. Dennis and Wiley Mayne (R Iowa) supported the motion to strike that section, attacking the evidence and citing Petersen's testimony to the committee that he did not feel the President had done anything wrong.

Sandman expressed curiosity about Flowers' "present" vote. Flowers responded that the "caliber of debate is so outstanding on both sides . . . that it leaves me undecided." And he proceeded to vote "present" as the committee, 11–26, rejected his amendment to strike the seventh subsection. The break-down of the vote was identical to the one immediately preceding. (*See Vote 6, p. 265.*)

Wayne Owens (D Utah) and Jerome R. Waldie (D Calif.) set out the evidence for the charge that Nixon had made false and misleading statements to the nation concerning the investigation of the Watergate and related allegations. Lott, Dennis and Carlos J. Moorhead (R Calif.) criticized the evidence as insufficient to prove the charge. The committee rejected the amendment, 12–25, with Flowers casting another "present," and McClory slipping back into the ranks of the Republicans supporting the deletion of that section. (*See Vote 7, p. 266.*)

Hungate and Hogan set out the facts supporting the charge that Nixon tried to buy the silence or false testimony of witnesses by promises of favored treatment. McClory and Joseph J. Maraziti (R N.J.) argued that the section should be deleted because the evidence on which it was based was at best contradictory.

Calling the debate "a fruitless waste of time," Sandman urged Flowers to drop his efforts. "Two hundred million people know what you are up to," he said; "you aren't kidding anybody."

"Vote your conscience on this one, because you certainly haven't on the other eight," he urged. Flowers said he was convinced and would support this amendment. At 6:50 p.m. the last amendment was rejected, 15–23. Only Hogan, Cohen and Butler joined the other Democrats in opposing the amendment. (*See Vote 8, p. 266.*)

Obstruction of Justice

The facts were all on the record.

Before the crucial vote on the substitute Article I proposed by Sarbanes, Flowers and Fish—both until that moment publicly uncommitted on the article—asked for time to explain the vote they were about to cast, a vote which ran against the feelings of many of their constituents, their friends and, in some cases, their families.

Pale and weary, Flowers spoke first:

"I know for certain that I have nothing to gain politically or otherwise from what I must do here, but after weeks of searching through the facts and agonizing over the constitutional requirements it is clear to me what I must do. . . .

"There are many people in my district who will disagree with my vote here. Some will say that it hurts them deeply for me to vote for impeachment. I can assure them that I probably have enough pain for them and me. I have close personal friends who strongly support President Nixon. To several of these . . . I say that the only way I could vote for impeachment would be on the realization to me anyway that they, my friends, would do the same thing if they were in my place on this unhappy day and confronted with all of the same facts that I have. . . . I hope not one of us ever has to look into another matter of impeachment again."

Then Fish, whose father, a former member of Congress, was one of the leaders of the national anti-impeachment lobby, spoke somberly:

"I intend to vote in favor of this, the first article of impeachment. This comes after long deliberation, but it comes because an analysis of the evidence in this proceeding has led me to this inescapable conclusion. . . . My decision . . . is reached at all with deep reluctance only after I have been persuaded that the evidence for such a vote is clear."

Then the roll-call began. Some cast their votes in strong voices, most came more softly, some were almost inaudible.

Down the roster of Democrats from Harold D. Donohue (D Mass.) to Mezvinsky came a solid line of "ayes" as Flowers, Thornton and Mann, the three southern conservatives on that side of the committee, joined with their colleagues in support of the article.

Then came the first resounding "no-oo", cast by Edward Hutchinson (R Mich.), the committee's ranking Republican, followed by negative votes from McClory, Smith and Sandman. The first critical break in the Republican ranks came with Railsback's "aye"— the 21st vote to favor impeachment. More damaging defections from presidential support came with the "ayes" of Fish, Hogan, Butler, Cohen and—a less expected vote—Harold V. Froehlich (R Wis.). Chairman Rodino, the last to vote, added his "aye," making the vote 27–11, approving the Sarbanes substitute for the obstruction of justice article proposed July 24 by Donohue. (*See Vote 9, p. 266.*)

Quickly, the committee moved to the final vote, approving Article I as amended by the adoption of the Sarbanes substitute by the same vote of 27–11. Then Rodino announced that the article would be reported to the House stating that "Richard M. Nixon has prevented, obstructed and impeded the administration of justice . . . has acted in a manner contrary to his trust as President and subversive of constitutional government, to the great prejudice of the cause of law and justice and to the manifest injury of the people of the United States . . . [and] warrants impeachment and trial and removal from office." (*See Vote 10, p. 266.*)

Abuse of Presidential Powers

From obstruction of justice, the committee on Monday, July 29, moved on to another proposed article, charging the President with abuse of his powers in such a manner that violated, or threatened to violate, the constitutional rights of individual citizens.

"Article II is our reaffirmation of the Bill of Rights," said Don Edwards (D Calif.), noting that each section charged Nixon with actions which threatened to violate some right guaranteed to citizens by the first 10 amendments to the Constitution. Member after member stated that they found this article and the charges it contained more serious than Article I.

Debate was spirited and intense, but fatigue and the inevitable air of anticlimax that followed the momentous Saturday vote approving Article I began to show as the day wore on. There was no doubt that the article would be approved; the precise margin was the only question.

Hungate Substitute

As a substitute for two earlier drafts of an abuse-of-powers article—one proposed by Harold D. Donohue (D Mass.) July 24 and the other drafted by McClory—Hungate proposed a compromise version. The Hungate substitute had been drawn up July 28 at a caucus of committee Democrats, in consultation with several Republican members, including McClory. The Hungate proposal dropped the charge—contained in the Donohue proposal—that the President had abused his powers and was in contempt of Congress for refusing to comply with Judiciary Committee subpoenas. The compromise version charged that the President had used his powers in violation of his oath "faithfully to execute the office of President . . . and in disregard of his constitutional duty to take care that the laws be faithfully executed." The conduct cited to substantiate this charge included:

- Attempting to obtain confidential Internal Revenue Service (IRS) information and to cause audits or other discriminatory tax investigations of certain citizens.
- Directing improper electronic surveillance by the FBI, the Secret Service and other personnel and concealing the records of that surveillance.

- Authorizing and allowing the creation and work of the White House "plumbers" unit.
- Failing to act when he knew of illegal actions by his close aides and subordinates.
- Interfering with the FBI, the Justice Department, the office of the special prosecutor and the CIA in their lawful operations.

Point of Order

Immediately after the clerk finished reading the Hungate substitute, Wiggins, one of the President's most persistent defenders on the committee, raised a point of order. He claimed that "Article II fails to state an impeachable offense under the Constitution."

Wiggins questioned "whether an abuse of power falls within the meaning of the phrase 'high crimes and misdemeanors'" in the Constitution's impeachment clause. "My problem is this: Just what is abusive conduct?" he asked. "That is an empty phrase. . . . It must reflect our subjective view of impropriety."

THE TAPES

With new claims of executive privilege and revelation of at least one more gap in the tape of a presidential conversation, the tapes of 30 White House conversations were turned over to Federal Judge John J. Sirica July 30 and Aug. 2.

The tapes were among the 64 subpoenaed April 18 at the request of special Watergate prosecutor Leon Jaworski for use as evidence in the Watergate coverup trial set to begin Sept. 9. Sirica May 20 rejected a White House motion to quash the subpoena and ordered them turned over to him for a private examination of them to determine whether or not they should be passed on to Jaworski.

The White House had lost the battle before the Supreme Court which unanimously upheld Sirica's order July 24.

As special White House counsel James D. St. Clair delivered the first 20 tapes to Sirica July 30, it was disclosed that:

- The President had raised claims of executive privilege, asking that portions of 10 of the conversations be withheld from Jaworski as covered by privilege and unrelated to the Watergate coverup.

- Portions of each of the 20 tapes turned over July 30 had been released in transcript form by the White House April 30.
- There was a gap of more than five minutes in at least one of these tapes—one of a 45-minute meeting between Nixon and aides H. R. Haldeman and John D. Ehrlichman on April 17, 1973, less than two weeks before they resigned. St. Clair explained that during the meeting the tape reel apparently ran out and was not immediately replaced.

Among the 10 tapes turned over to Sirica Aug. 2 were several to which Nixon listened early in May before deciding against a proposal on the exchange of tapes which Jaworski and St. Clair had tentatively worked out. Those Nixon heard included two telephone conversations between Nixon and former special counsel Charles W. Colson on June 20, 1972; three meetings of Nixon and Haldeman on June 23, 1972; six meetings of Nixon and these aides and Ehrlichman in February and March 1973; and two telephone conversations between Nixon and Haldeman on June 4, 1973, after Nixon had reviewed some of the tapes.

Also in the group of tapes subpoenaed was that of a March 22, 1973, conversation between Nixon and Haldeman, a portion of which St. Clair produced for the House Judiciary Committee in transcript form July 18.

Adoption of the article, he warned, would transform the American political system. "Adoption of such an article would imbed in our constitutional history for the first time . . . the principle that a president may be impeached because of the view of Congress that he has abused his powers although he may have acted in violation of no law," said Wiggins. "We are in effect saying that a president may be impeached in the future if a Congress expresses no confidence in his conduct."

Danielson countered that the second article "is certainly the most important article this committee may pass out. The offenses charged in this article are truly a high crime and misdemeanor. The offenses charged are uniquely presidential offenses. No one else can commit them. . . . Only the president can violate the oath of the office of president. . . . Only the president can harm the presidency."

Rodino rejected Wiggins' point of order.

Explaining his substitute, Hungate said it dealt with "repetitive conduct" outlined in the five subsections. "If only one violation had occurred," he said, "I doubt if we should be here."

McClory said the proposed article "gets to the crux of our responsibility here. . . . There's nothing mysterious about it . . . there's nothing evil or malignant about it. It directs its attention directly to this responsibility that is . . . reposed in the President."

THE 'FRAGILE COALITION' THAT DECIDED FINAL VOTES

Even before the House Judiciary Committee cast its first vote on impeachment, it appeared likely to approve at least one of the impeachment articles. Yet members spent a total of six days debating and revising the articles. Why did they spend so much time if impeachment was almost certain to pass?

There were two primary reasons for the extended debate. One was that impeachment opponents wanted to make it as difficult as possible for the Senate to convict Nixon and thereby remove him from office. Their goal was to narrow the impeachment charges and make them harder to prove in a Senate trial. For example, Wiggins proposed an amendment to a section of the second article regarding the administration's misuse of the IRS. His amendment would have required proof that the president had specific knowledge of the abuse or that he oversaw the misconduct of his aides.

Wiggins and his allies argued that the article otherwise would be unfair to the president. That is because impeachment could be "based on the actions of his subordinates, not based on his [the President's] instructions," said Dennis, another impeachment opponent. But Wiggins's wording would have also made it difficult to prove the president's guilt. Most of the committee members opposed Wiggins. They argued that the president, after setting down general policy, is responsible for the actions of his aides. The committee easily rejected Wiggins's amendments, as well as other proposals that would have undermined the case against the president.

The other reason for the extended debate had to do with influencing the number of members voting for impeachment. Both sides wanted to *amass as many votes as possible. The advocates of impeachment needed decisive, bipartisan support in order to build up momentum for a Senate trial, where a two-thirds vote was needed to convict the president. Conversely, impeachment opponents wanted the committee vote to be as narrow as possible. A close vote would send a message to the president that most Republicans, and possibly even some conservative Democrats, stood by Nixon.*

Both sides tried to win over seven members in the political middle. These seven, known as the "fragile coalition," consisted of southern Democrats and moderate Republicans. They moderated some of the language in the impeachment articles. By coming together to vote for two of the articles, they ensured that impeachment had strong, bipartisan backing.

In the end, the decision of the House Judiciary Committee to impeach Richard M. Nixon for "high crimes and misdemeanors" rested with seven men. These men, the "swing" votes on the 38-member panel, shaped the eventually adopted articles of impeachment and gave legitimacy and bipartisan tone to the move to remove the President from office. They backed the two articles on obstruction of justice and abuse of power, split on the third article charging contempt of Congress and opposed the last two proposed articles which dealt with the secret bombing of Cambodia and tax evasion.

As the committee completed its examination of the evidence July 22, it was divided into the proponents of impeachment, the opponents of impeachment and those who were undecided. The balance depended on three Democrats and seven Republicans. Without the votes of some Republicans and some southern Democrats, it was unlikely that articles, if voted by the House, would be upheld by the Senate.

On July 22, two days before the committee began its televised debate, the "fragile coalition" emerged that helped to draft the articles and to develop the strategy of the pro-impeachment forces. Its formation had been slow and tentative, as committee members for six months groped their way through the mass of evidence.

'FRAGILE COALITION'

The "fragile coalition" included Tom Railsback (R Ill.), Hamilton Fish Jr. (R N.Y.), William S. Cohen (R Maine), M. Caldwell Butler (R Va.), James R. Mann (D S.C.), Walter Flowers (D Ala.) and Ray Thornton (D Ark.). They met in Railsback's office at his invitation at 8 o'clock on the morning of July 23, the day before debate began—all moderate men of cautious temperament, predominantly junior members ranging in age from 33 to 53.

Despite the imminence of debate on impeachment, for the pro-impeachment group at least, "there was an almost total absence of preparation in terms of articles, the ability of members to understand the facts in a comprehensive way, and strategy," said one aide to a committee member.

"If this group had met and disbanded or decided against impeaching Nixon, Nixon would never have been impeached," said another staff member.

Initially, the existence of the group was extremely confidential. "The southern Democrats were very sensitive that this would telegraph where they were going to go," commented an aide.

THE LEADERS

Railsback emerged as the leader of the Republicans and by all accounts, Mann, the deliberate South Carolinian, emerged as the key member of the group. "He gave the group its intellect," acknowledged one Republican staff aide. But he also played a broader role. "He could cross the aisle," said one Democratic aide, referring to Mann's ability to bring the middle core of Republicans and Democrats together and to serve as a link between them and the larger pro-impeachment faction on the committee. "Few others of the committee could" mediate in this way, the aide continued. "I think he could do it because he's very conservative, comes from the South, and could gain the confidence of this growing middle group."

"There's a certain trustworthiness in Mann," said one Republican aide, "that he would keep confidences, give you the straight story, that he was a man of moderation."

THE STRATEGY

The impeachment articles introduced by Rep. Harold D. Donohue (D Mass.) July 24 just after debate opened had been hastily drawn up and, said an aide, "were introduced just to introduce something." They reflected the influence of the Railsback-Mann group, though, for they were far more moderate than the proposed articles drafted by John M. Doar, impeachment staff counsel.

By then, the Railsback-Mann group was working on its own articles, concentrating first on obstruction of justice. According to one aide, "after a couple of sessions on the philosophical level, they got down to drafting. On Wednesday (July 24), they met from 10 a.m. to 6 p.m. and drafted a large part of what became known as the Sarbanes substitute (the eventually approved Article I)."

"There were constant phone calls to the Democratic drafting committee. Mann was the liaison here." The Democratic drafting committee members were Paul S. Sarbanes (D Md.), Don Edwards (D Calif.), John Conyers Jr. (D Mich.) and Jack Brooks (D Texas).

By the time the committee adopted the Sarbanes substitute July 27, the "swing" group had already picked up the support of two more conservative Republicans—Lawrence J. Hogan (R Md.) and Harold V. Froehlich (R Wis.). Froehlich had been told of the Railsback meetings early in the week but had not joined them. "He had made up his mind," recalled one aide, "but he had a hard time finding a way to justify it."

After Article I was adopted, the Railsback-Mann group played a less active part in drafting Articles II and III, according to Democratic and Republican sources. But they had established the bipartisan coalition providing a solid margin for impeachment in that most difficult part of the debate—the first vote for impeachment.

Committee Chairman Peter W. Rodino Jr. (D N.J.) did not at first get involved with the pro-impeachment groups. "He wanted to let the middle group emerge and . . . take over the leadership," said one staff member.

But as debate began, he became a part of the coalition, and was closely involved in the drafting of the Sarbanes substitute and in planning the strategy.

OTHER ROLES

Two other committee members played prominent parts in the adoption of the first two articles: Sarbanes and William L. Hungate (D Mo.).

According to Republican and Democratic aides, Rodino picked them as floor leaders for the articles because they were border state Democrats not identified with any group on the committee.

His support, he added, was based on the clause of the Constitution that required the President to take care that the laws be faithfully executed. "The President is bound by his solemn oath of office to see that the laws are faithfully executed. . . . There is clear violation of the President's responsibility when he permits multiple acts of wrongdoing by large numbers of those who surround him. . . . While this article may seem less dramatic . . . than the Watergate break-in and coverup [Article I]," he said, "it is[,] nevertheless, positive and responsible."

Hutchinson objected to the article: "Is it really fair?" he asked. "Does it depict the whole truth to examine the entire record of this administration . . . and to cull from that huge mass of official actions this relative handful of specific allegations and derive from them the proposition that the President's conduct has been repeatedly unlawful?"

Misuse of IRS

In an attempt to narrow the charges, hence making them more difficult to prove, Wiggins proposed an amendment to the first subsection concerning misuse of the IRS. The amendment required proof that the president knew of or directed the misconduct of his aides. The IRS charge included the President's alleged attempt to have tax records of his administration's "enemies" audited and to have Lawrence F. O'Brien, former chairman of the Democratic National Committee, sent to jail on tax charges.

Backing the amendment, Dennis said it was needed to prevent impeachment "based on the actions of his subordinates, not based on his [the President's] instructions."

Opponents of the amendment argued that it would lower the standard of presidential responsibility. "This amendment would unduly . . . restrict the proof the managers must make before the Senate," said Danielson. "The language . . . would require . . . knowledge of prior actions. If the President sets down general policy and his aides misuse the President's power, then the President is responsible."

Hogan, Butler and Cohen opposed the amendment; the latter two worried that it would exclude from punishment the President's "ratification" of aides' actions—approval after the fact.

Opponents of the amendment picked up the support of Wiley Mayne (R Iowa), an impeachment critic. Calling the President's misuse of the IRS "absolutely indefensible," Mayne said, "I certainly do not want to do anything to dilute or limit in any way whatever responsibility the President may have had for the very outrageous attempt to use the Internal Revenue Service for political purposes. . . . Nothing in this record . . . is more disappointing or more cause for concern" than the attempt to "prostitute" the IRS, he said.

Wiggins' first amendment was defeated, 9–28. Seven Republicans, including Mayne, joined the committee's 21 Democrats to reject it. (*See Vote 11, p. 266.*)

Watergate Coverup

Wiggins then introduced an amendment to narrow the charge in the fourth subsection that the President failed to "take care that the laws were faithfully executed" to only his failure to act to stop the Watergate burglary coverup. The provision included the words "and other matters" to include other illegal activities such as the break-in at the office of Dr. Lewis J. Fielding, illegal wiretapping and illegal campaign financing.

"This pushes beyond all reason . . . the apparent desire on the part of the majority to not specify with particularity the conduct they condemn," Wiggins charged.

Waldie, an impeachment backer, supported the amendment. "In this instance," he said, "we have strayed . . . far into generalities." Deletion, he said, "would do no violence to our standards of fairness."

Opponents claimed that the facts backed up the charge. Hogan called the "argument of specificity" raised by Wiggins "a red herring."

Before the amendment was voted on, the panel adopted by a voice vote an amendment by McClory to tighten the section. The Hungate substitute used the Watergate coverup as its only example, referring to other illegal actions as "other matters." McClory's amendment changed that language to other "unlawful activities."

Wiggins' amendment was then defeated, 14–24. Two Democrats, Waldie and Flowers, and one Republican, Railsback—who were consistent voters for

impeachment—voted with impeachment opponents in support of the amendment. (*See Vote 12, p. 266.*)

Misuse of FBI

Wiggins introduced a third amendment, to delete the charge in the second subsection that the President misused the FBI and Secret Service by having them conduct illegal wiretapping and concealing the records of the illegal taps.

Wiggins, Dennis, Carlos J. Moorhead (R Calif.) and Joseph J. Maraziti (R N.J.) claimed the taps from 1969 through 1971 were legal and were necessitated by considerations of national security. They cited the leak of the Pentagon Papers, *The New York Times* leaks on the secret bombing of Cambodia, and the strategic arms limitation talks and the Vietnam war as the reason for the wiretaps.

Opponents, however, rebutted the national security rationale. "These taps were clearly political," said Edwards, who charged that the taps were used to gather political intelligence. "The mere assertion of national security is not enough," said Joshua Eilberg (D Pa.). "The Nixon White House made the secret police a reality in the United States."

The Wiggins amendment was defeated, 10–28. Seven Republicans, including McClory and Froehlich, joined 21 Democrats in opposing it. (*See Vote 13, p. 266.*)

By voice vote the committee then adopted an amendment by Cohen to clarify the illegal activities referred to in the fourth subsection—the "take care" section. Cohen's amendment added, as examples of such activities, those related to the confirmation of Richard G. Kleindienst as attorney general, the break-in at the office of Daniel Ellsberg's psychiatrist and the campaign financing practices of the Committee to Re-Elect the President.

'Plumbers' Amendment

Wiggins then proposed his fourth amendment of the day, which would delete the third subsection of the Hungate substitute, which charged the President with creating and allowing the activities of the White House "plumbers," financed partially with campaign funds and involved in illegal use of the CIA.

Opposing the amendment, Fish called the "plumbers" unit "a public relations effort. . . . National security . . . was not the issue."

When the committee resumed its debate after dinner July 29, Mayne argued that national security concerns led to the creation of the unit, asking, "Is it a high crime and misdemeanor to be less than letter perfect in the performance of one's office?" Wiggins argued that the President was legitimately concerned about the leaks, and that he felt in good faith that the situation required decisive action. This was not a proper ground for impeachment, Wiggins emphasized.

Waldie responded that he viewed this as one of the most serious offenses with which Nixon was charged. Cohen responded that the totality of the evidence showed a pattern of conduct which threatened to "shred" constitutional rights. By a voice vote, the amendment was rejected.

Brooks' Motion

To air the charges concerning Nixon's attempts to misuse the IRS, Jack Brooks (D Texas) offered an amendment to strike out the first subsection of Hungate's substitute article, which dealt with these charges. In the 40 minutes of debate, the President's defenders—chiefly Latta, Sandman and Dennis—argued that there was, on the one hand, no evidence of presidential involvement in such efforts, except for the Sept. 15, 1972, taped conversation with John W. Dean III. On the other hand, they argued, there had in fact been no misuse of IRS powers. It was "just talk," said Dennis, conceding that it was not talk he would condone, but there was no evidence of action.

"If this President, with whom you may agree politically, can get by with the abuses described in this article, then so may succeeding chief executives with whom you do not agree," warned Flowers.

Sandman charged that the majority was impeaching the President of the United States "for a thought, not a deed."

But Fish advised his colleagues that "those who look for a smoking pistol [in the evidence] are not going to find it, because the room's too full of smoke." Brooks then withdrew his motion, having accomplished his purpose of airing the facts behind the charge.

General Debate

There being no more amendments, the committee then moved into general debate on the Hungate substitute. "If the proof were here, this article would be more important than Article I," said Dennis. "But here you just don't have the evidence."

McClory announced that he would vote for the second article, finding that there was clear and convincing evidence to back each charge.

"Isn't it amazing," asked Cohen, how so many committee members "have overlooked the attempted wrongful acts" with which Article II charged the President? Those attempted actions, he said, raised for him the specter of an American "Gulag Archipelago."

"I suppose it was inevitable," said Waldie, "that a time would come when this concentration of power [in the presidency] would be checked. . . . That duty has fallen first to this committee."

Sandman, saying that he believed each American president to have been a good man and a great man, refused to support the article. "I would like to believe, in the absence of extremely good proof, that the President did what he did for good reasons," that whatever he did, he did in the best interest of the country, he said.

"Did President Nixon—a recognized, sophisticated, astute public official . . . a stickler for detail . . . know of these operations being directed by trusted and loyal members of his staff?" asked Donohue. "I believe he did."

Flowers signaled his vote for the article. "If this President fails to take care that the laws are faithfully executed . . .then this President has abused his public trust and deserves to be impeached," he said.

Mann also indicated his support for the article. "It isn't the presidency that is in jeopardy from us," he said, "but if there be no accountability, another president may do as he pleases."

"Stop and think," admonished Sarbanes, "what it means if the agencies of the government are not administered in an even-handed manner . . . not to serve the people but to maintain themselves in power. . . . We came perilously close to losing our basic freedoms; we are taking a long step forward in restoring" them.

At 11:16 p.m., the roll-call began. Again the Democrats stood solidly united in favor of impeachment, joined by seven Republicans—the six who had voted for the first article and McClory. The vote was 28–10 to adopt the Hungate substitute. A moment later, the amended Article II was approved by an identical vote. (*See Votes 14, 15, p. 266.*)

Contempt of Congress

On July 30, the sixth and final day of its impeachment debate, the House Judiciary Committee turned to consider a third article, one charging President Nixon with contempt of Congress for defying committee subpoenas seeking materials needed for the impeachment inquiry.

The charge had originally been included in the second article but was dropped from the Hungate substitute adopted July 29. Instead, it was offered as a separate article July 30 by McClory, its leading proponent. It accused the President of failing "without lawful cause or excuse" to obey four committee subpoenas—April 11, 1974, May 15, 1974, May 30, 1974, and June 24, 1974—for 147 tapes and documents needed for its investigation.

"The subpoenaed papers and things were deemed necessary by the committee to its inquiry . . . to determine whether sufficient grounds exist to impeach Richard M. Nixon, President of the United States," the article stated. "In refusing to produce these papers and things, he [Nixon] has acted in derogation of the power of impeachment, vested solely in the House of Representatives by the Constitution of the United States."

McClory said his proposed article concerned the House's "basic and very fundamental" right to conduct an impeachment proceeding, and to obtain access to all the evidence to carry out this responsibility.

"The President's position" in response to committee subpoenas, McClory charged, "has been that he should be the sole arbiter of what he should and what he should not turn over. . . . If he's to be the sole arbiter, then how in the world can we conduct a thorough and complete and fair investigation? We just couldn't."

The Illinois Republican warned the committee that House action on the President's refusal to obey the panel's subpoenas would guide future Congresses as well as establishing the standard by which future Presidents could gauge what information they were required to provide the House in future impeachment inquiries.

"We are now faced . . . with whether the President is contemptuous of Congress," said McClory.

Thornton's Proposal

Thornton proposed an amendment to McClory's proposed article, narrowing the contempt charge to Nixon's failure to produce materials subpoenaed as direct evidence on questions of fact demonstrated by other evidence to be substantial grounds for impeachment. His amendment struck out the original broad explanation of the reason for the subpoenas and replaced it with the statement that the committee felt the subpoenas necessary to resolve "fundamental factual questions relating to presidential direction, knowledge or approval of actions demonstrated by other evidence to be substantial grounds for impeachment."

Thornton said his amendment was needed to "prevent a distortion of the balance of power between the executive and legislative branch. . . . If we do nothing, we may indeed limit the authority of the legislative branch to make an proper inquiry," he warned. But if the House's subpoena authority in impeachment inquiries was

expanded too far, "we might distort the balance of power" among the three branches.

John F. Seiberling (D Ohio) said the amendment made "clear that we're not establishing the broad power to receive presidential documents. We're limiting it to an impeachment inquiry."

Danielson called the amendment a sensible restraint. "The question we have here is . . . critical to the separation and allocation of powers under the Constitution," he said.

Opposition came from impeachment opponents joined by some proponents of impeachment who did not want their subpoena power in impeachment cases restricted or who felt that the Supreme Court should settle the subpoena question.

Froehlich called the contempt of Congress question "a classic case in separation of powers. . . . We have two great branches of government involved in a stalemate both arguing the Constitution. . . . The committee. . . should have gone to court and asked the court to say what the law is," he said.

Wiggins accused backers of the contempt article of inconsistency. "If logic and common sense have any place in this proceedings, you impeach him on the evidence or on not providing the evidence," he said. Impeachment supporters "want to have their cake and eat it too," he said, by impeaching the President for not providing evidence needed for the investigation while saying that they had sufficient evidence to impeach him for other offenses.

Owens argued against the amendment, warning that it would dilute the power of the House in the impeachment process which, he said, must remain unfettered. "The power to compel evidence in an impeachment inquiry must be considered absolute."

The Thornton amendment was adopted 24 to 14. Three Democrats—Conyers, Flowers and Owens—joined 11 Republicans, including Railsback, Hogan and Froehlich—to oppose it. Four Republicans who had supported other articles of impeachment—McClory, Fish, Butler and Cohen—backed the amendment.

Debate on Article

The debate on the amended McClory article was sharp and contained not-so-subtle warnings that the committee's bipartisan impeachment coalition would split apart if impeachment articles beyond the first two were pushed.

Supporters of the article claimed its passage was essential to establish the precedent that future Presidents were required to honor House subpoenas in impeachment inquiries.

"The historical precedent we're setting here is so great," Hogan said. "If we don't pass this article today, the whole impeachment process becomes meaningless."

Robert W. Kastenmeier (D Wis.) said the President's refusal to obey the committee's subpoenas was "a high crime in the classic sense which the framers intended when they used that phrase in the Constitution."

Edwards said that the committee would "diminish or destroy this only safety valve in our Constitution," if it did not approve the article. "And for this power to have any meaning at all, any vitality at all, we simply must be able to get this evidence."

Opponents argued that the dispute over access to evidence should have been handled by the courts.

"Here we have a constitutional confrontation between two coequal branches of government," said Smith. "The third coequal branch [the courts] should be the arbiter." Smith also argued the President was not required to submit evidence against himself. "We have a long tradition in this country that the accused shall not be compelled to present evidence against himself," he said.

Railsback, who had voted for the first two articles, split with his Illinois colleague and warned that the third article would have a negative influence on House Republicans. The committee should have gone to court to arbitrate this dispute, he said.

Turning to impeachment supporters on the Democratic side, Railsback warned emotionally, "watch what happens to your fragile coalition" if articles charging contempt of Congress, tax fraud, misuse of government money for the President's personal purposes and the secret bombing of Cambodia are pursued.

"This doesn't stand on its own as an impeachable offense," said Flowers, opposing the article.

Hutchinson, who had voted against the issuance of each of the committee's subpoenas, opposed the article. The separation of powers meant, he said, that the President could not order the House of Representatives to do anything and the House could not order the President to do anything. He said that the Supreme Court ruling of the week before—in the case of *U.S. v. Nixon*—had changed his previous feeling that a claim of executive privilege must fall before an impeachment inquiry. Now, he said, he felt that the court had indicated that there was a place for executive privilege, even in such proceedings.

"The committee should not take this long step toward further diminishing the power of the President," Latta warned.

On the contrary, responded McClory, if the committee did not approve this article, the power of the House to impeach a President would be "sterile indeed."

Then, by the narrowest margin on any article, the committee voted, 21–17, to approve Article III. Flowers and Mann voted with most Republicans against the article; McClory and Hogan voted for it with the remaining Democrats. *(See Vote 17, p. 266.)*

Judiciary Committee Votes

1. Delay Proceedings. McClory (R Ill.) motion to delay committee deliberations on the articles of impeachment for 10 days if President Nixon agreed by noon July 27 to make available to the committee the tapes of the 64 presidential conversations which he had been ordered by the Supreme Court to turn over to Federal Judge John J. Sirica. Motion defeated 11–27: R 10–7; D 1–20. July 26, 1974.

2. False Statements. Sandman (R N.J.) amendment striking out the first subsection of the proposed Sarbanes article of impeachment charging the President with making false and misleading statements to investigators. Amendment rejected 11–27: R 11–6; D 0–21. July 26, 1974.

3. Congressional Committees. Danielson (D Calif.) amendment adding congressional committees to the list of investigators in the fourth subsection of the proposed Sarbanes article with which Nixon was alleged to have interfered. Amendment adopted 24–14: R 4–13; D 20–1. July 27, 1974.

4. Counseling Witnesses. Flowers (D Ala.) amendment striking out the third subsection of the proposed Sarbanes article charging the President with approving and counseling persons to give false and misleading statements to investigators. Amendment rejected 12–25: R 12–5; D 0–20. Flowers voted "present." July 27, 1974.

5. Investigations. Flowers (D Ala.) amendment striking out the fourth subsection of the proposed Sarbanes article charging the President with interfering with investigations by the Justice Department, the FBI, the Watergate special prosecution force and congressional committees. Amendment rejected 11–26: R 11–6; D 0–20. Flowers voted "present." July 27, 1974.

6. Information. Flowers (D Ala.) amendment striking out the seventh subsection of the proposed Sarbanes article charging the President with conveying information from the Justice Department about investigations to the targets of those investigations. Amendment rejected 11–26: R 11–6; D 0–20. Flowers voted "present." July 27, 1974.

7. Misleading the People. Flowers (D Ala.) amendment striking out the eighth subsection of the proposed Sarbanes article charging the President with making false and misleading statements to deceive the American people about the kind of investigation which had been conducted into the Watergate charges. Amendment rejected 12–25: R 12–5; D 0–20. Flowers voted "present." July 27, 1974.

8. Promises to Witnesses. Flowers (D Ala.) amendment striking out the ninth subsection of the proposed Sarbanes article charging the President with causing prospective defendants and persons already convicted to expect favored treatment in return for their silence or false testimony. Amendment rejected 15–23: R 14–3; D 1–20. July 27, 1974.

9. Sarbanes Article. Approval of Sarbanes (D Md.) proposed substitute article of impeachment for the article proposed by Donohue (D Mass.), charging the President with obstruction of justice and finding that he should be impeached. Approved 27–11: R 6–11; D 21–0. July 27, 1974.

10. Obstruction of Justice. Approval of article of impeachment, as amended by adoption of the Sarbanes substitute, charging the President with obstruction of justice and finding that he should be impeached. Approved 27–11: R 6–11; D 21–0. July 27, 1974.

11. Personal Involvement. Wiggins (R Calif.) amendment striking the phrase "acting personally and through his subordinates and agents" that referred to the President and replacing it with "personally and through his subordinates and agents acting with his knowledge or pursuant to his instructions" in the first subsection of the proposed Hungate article charging the President with attempting illegally to obtain confidential income tax information from the Internal Revenue Service. Amendment rejected 9–28: R 9–7; D 0–21. July 29, 1974.

12. Presidential Duty. Wiggins (R Calif.) amendment narrowing the charge in the fourth subsection of the proposed Hungate article to the President's failure to stop the Watergate coverup. Other unlawful activities were

not to be covered. Amendment rejected 14–24: R 12–5; D 2–19. July 29, 1974.

13. Illegal Wiretaps. Wiggins (R Calif.) amendment striking the second subsection of the proposed Hungate article charging the President with misusing the FBI and Secret Service by having them conduct illegal wiretapping and then concealing the records of the illegal wiretaps. Amendment rejected 10–28: R 10–7; D 0–21. July 29, 1974.

14. Abuse of Powers. Hungate (D Mo.) amendment in the nature of a substitute for Article II as proposed by Donohue (D Mass.) charging the President with abusing his powers and finding that he should be impeached. Adopted 28–10: R 7–10; D 21–0. July 29, 1974.

15. Abuse of Powers. Approval of Article II as amended by adoption of the Hungate substitute, charging the President with abuse of powers and finding that he should be impeached. Approved 28–10: R 7–10; D 21–0. July 29, 1974.

16. Contempt of Congress. Thornton (D Ark.) amendment to the McClory article narrowing the contempt of Congress charge against the President to cover only his failure to produce materials subpoenaed by the House Judiciary Committee and dealing with offenses established by other evidence. Amendment adopted 24–14: R 6–11; D 18–3. July 30, 1974.

17. Contempt of Congress. Approval of McClory (R Ill.) Article III charging the President with willful disobedience of the committee's subpoenas without lawful cause or excuse, thereby usurping judgment necessary to the House's exercise of the sole power of impeachment. Approved 21–17: R 2–15; D 19–2. July 30, 1974.

18. Secret Cambodia Bombing. Conyers (D Mich.) article charging the President with authorizing and ratifying the concealment from Congress of the facts concerning the bombing of Cambodia in derogation of Congress' constitutional power to declare war. Rejected 12–26: R 0–17; D 12–9. July 30, 1974.

19. Tax Evasion. Mezvinsky (D Iowa) article charging the President with knowingly and fraudulently evading portions of his federal income taxes from 1969 through 1972 and violating his oath of office by receiving unconstitutional emoluments. Rejected 12–26: R 0–17; D 12–9. July 30, 1974.

HOUSE JUDICIARY COMMITTEE IMPEACHMENT VOTES

DEMOCRATS	1	2	3	4	5	6	7	8	9	10	11	12	13	14	15	16	17	18	19
Rodino (N.J.)	N	N	Y	N	N	N	N	N	Y	Y	N	N	N	Y	Y	Y	Y	N	Y
Donohue (Mass.)	N	N	Y	N	N	N	N	N	Y	Y	N	N	N	Y	Y	Y	Y	N	N
Brooks (Texas)	N	N	Y	N	N	N	N	N	Y	Y	N	N	N	Y	Y	Y	Y	N	Y
Kastenmeier (Wis.)	N	N	Y	N	N	N	N	N	Y	Y	N	N	N	Y	Y	Y	Y	Y	Y
Edwards (Calif.)	N	N	Y	N	N	N	N	N	Y	Y	N	N	N	Y	Y	Y	Y	Y	Y
Hungate (Mo.)	N	N	Y	N	N	N	N	N	Y	Y	N	N	N	Y	Y	Y	Y	Y	N
Conyers (Mich.)	N	N	Y	N	N	N	N	N	Y	Y	N	N	N	Y	Y	N	Y	Y	Y
Eilberg (Pa.)	N	N	Y	N	N	N	N	N	Y	Y	N	N	N	Y	Y	Y	Y	N	Y
Waldie (Calif.)	N	N	Y	N	N	N	N	N	Y	Y	N	Y	N	Y	Y	Y	Y	Y	N
Flowers (Ala.)	N	N	N	P	P	P	P	Y	Y	Y	N	Y	N	Y	Y	N	N	N	N
Mann (S.C.)	Y	N	Y	N	N	N	N	N	Y	Y	N	N	N	Y	Y	Y	N	N	N
Sarbanes (Md.)	N	N	Y	N	N	N	N	N	Y	Y	N	N	N	Y	Y	Y	Y	N	N
Seiberling (Ohio)	N	N	Y	N	N	N	N	N	Y	Y	N	N	N	Y	Y	Y	Y	N	Y
Danielson (Calif.)	N	N	Y	N	N	N	N	N	Y	Y	N	N	N	Y	Y	Y	Y	N	Y
Drinan (Mass.)	N	N	Y	N	N	N	N	N	Y	Y	N	N	N	Y	Y	Y	Y	Y	N
Rangel (N.Y.)	N	N	Y	N	N	N	N	N	Y	Y	N	N	N	Y	Y	Y	Y	Y	Y
Jordan (Texas)	N	N	Y	N	N	N	N	N	Y	Y	N	N	N	Y	Y	Y	Y	Y	Y
Thornton (Ark.)	N	N	Y	N	N	N	N	N	Y	Y	N	N	N	Y	Y	Y	Y	Y	N
Holtzman (N.Y.)	N	N	Y	N	N	N	N	N	Y	Y	N	N	N	Y	Y	Y	Y	Y	Y
Owens (Utah)	N	N	Y	N	N	N	N	N	Y	Y	N	N	N	Y	Y	N	Y	Y	N
Mezvinsky (Iowa)	N	N	Y	N	N	N	N	N	Y	Y	N	N	N	Y	Y	Y	Y	Y	Y

REPUBLICANS	1	2	3	4	5	6	7	8	9	10	11	12	13	14	15	16	17	18	19
Hutchinson (Mich.)	Y	Y	N	Y	Y	Y	Y	Y	N	N	Y	Y	Y	N	N	Y	N	N	N
McClory (Ill.)	Y	Y	Y	Y	N	N	Y	Y	N	N	N	N	Y	Y	Y	Y	Y	N	N
Smith (N.Y.)	Y	N	Y	Y	Y	Y	Y	Y	N	N	Y	Y	Y	N	N	N	N	N	N
Sandman (N.J.)	N	Y	N	Y	Y	Y	Y	Y	N	N	Y	Y	Y	N	N	N	N	N	N
Railsback (Ill.)	N	N	N	N	N	N	N	Y	Y	Y	N	Y	N	N	Y	N	N	N	N
Wiggins (Calif.)	N	Y	Y	Y	Y	Y	Y	Y	N	N	Y	Y	Y	N	N	N	N	N	N
Dennis (Ind.)	Y	Y	Y	Y	Y	Y	Y	Y	N	N	Y	Y	Y	N	N	N	N	N	N
Fish (N.Y.)	N	N	N	N	N	N	N	Y	Y	Y	N	N	Y	N	Y	Y	Y	N	N
Mayne (Iowa)	N	Y	N	Y	Y	Y	Y	Y	N	N	N	Y	N	N	N	N	N	N	N
Hogan (Md.)	Y	N	N	N	N	N	N	Y	Y	N	N	N	Y	Y	Y	Y	N	N	N
Butler (Va.)	Y	N	N	N	N	N	N	N	Y	Y	N	N	N	Y	Y	Y	Y	N	N
Cohen (Maine)	N	N	N	N	N	N	N	Y	Y	N	N	N	Y	Y	Y	Y	N	N	N
Lott (Miss.)	N	Y	N	Y	Y	Y	Y	Y	N	N	AB	Y	Y	N	N	Y	N	N	N
Froehlich (Wis.)	Y	Y	N	Y	Y	Y	Y	Y	Y	Y	Y	Y	Y	N	N	N	N	N	N
Moorhead (Calif.)	Y	Y	N	Y	Y	Y	Y	Y	N	N	Y	Y	Y	N	N	N	N	N	N
Maraziti (N.J.)	Y	Y	N	Y	Y	Y	Y	Y	N	N	Y	Y	N	N	N	N	N	N	N
Latta (Ohio)	Y	Y	N	Y	Y	Y	Y	Y	N	N	Y	Y	N	N	N	N	N	N	N

11–27	11–27	24–14	12–25	11–26	11–26	12–25	15–23	27–11	27–11	9–28	14–24	10–28	28–10	28–10	24–14	21–17	12–26	12–26
			1P	1P	1P	1P												

Texts of Articles

Obstruction of Justice Text

Following is the text of the obstruction of justice article approved by the committee:

Article I

In his conduct of the office of President of the United States, Richard M. Nixon, in violation of his constitutional oath faithfully to execute the office of President of the United States and, to the best of his ability, preserve, protect, and defend the Constitution of the United States, and in violation of his constitutional duty to take care that the laws be faithfully executed, has prevented, obstructed, and impeded the administration of justice, in that:

On June 17, 1972, and prior thereto, agents of the Committee for the Re-election of the President committed unlawful entry of the headquarters of the Democratic National Committee in Washington, District of Columbia, for the purpose of securing political intelligence. Subsequent thereto, Richard M. Nixon, using the powers of his high office, engaged personally and through his close subordinates and agents, in a course of conduct or plan designed to delay, impede, and obstruct the investigation of such unlawful entry; to cover up, conceal and protect those responsible; and to conceal the existence and scope of other unlawful covert activities.

The means used to implement this course of conduct or plan included one or more of the following:

(1) making false or misleading statements to lawfully authorized investigative officers and employees of the United States;

(2) withholding relevant and material evidence or information from lawfully authorized investigative officers and employees of the United States;

(3) approving, condoning, acquiescing in, and counseling witnesses with respect to the giving of false or misleading statements to lawfully authorized investigative officers and employees of the United States and false or misleading testimony in duly instituted judicial and congressional proceedings;

(4) interfering or endeavoring to interfere with the conduct of investigations by the Department of Justice of the United States, the Federal Bureau of Investigation, the Office of Watergate Special Prosecution Force, and Congressional Committees;

(5) approving, condoning, and acquiescing in, the surreptitious payment of substantial sums of money for the purpose of obtaining the silence or influencing the testimony of witnesses, potential witnesses or individuals who participated in such unlawful entry and other illegal activities;

(6) endeavoring to misuse the Central Intelligence Agency, an agency of the United States;

(7) disseminating information received from officers of the Department of Justice of the United States to subjects of investigations conducted by lawfully authorized investigative officers and employees of the United States, for the purpose of aiding and assisting such subjects in their attempts to avoid criminal liability;

(8) making or causing to be made false or misleading public statements for the purpose of deceiving the people of the United States into believing that a thorough and complete investigation had been conducted with respect to allegations of misconduct on the part of personnel of the executive branch of the United States and personnel of the Committee for the Re-election of the President, and that there was no involvement of such personnel in such misconduct; or

(9) endeavoring to cause prospective defendants, and individuals duly tried and convicted, to expect favored treatment and consideration in return for their silence or false testimony, or rewarding individuals for their silence or false testimony.

In all of this, Richard M. Nixon has acted in a manner contrary to his trust as President and subversive of constitutional government, to the great prejudice of the cause of law and justice and to the manifest injury of the people of the United States.

Wherefore Richard M. Nixon, by such conduct, warrants impeachment and trial, and removal from office.

—Adopted July 27, 1974,
by a 27–11 vote

Abuse of Power Text

Following is the text of the abuse of power article approved by the committee:

Article II

Using the powers of the office of President of the United States, Richard M. Nixon, in violation of his constitutional oath faithfully to execute the office of President of the United States and, to the best of his ability, preserve, protect, and defend the Constitution of the United States, and in disregard of his constitutional duty to take care that the laws be faithfully executed, has repeatedly engaged in conduct violating the constitutional rights of citizens, impairing the due and proper administration of justice and the conduct of lawful inquiries, or contravening the laws governing agencies of the executive branch and the purposes of these agencies.

This conduct has included one or more of the following:

(1) He has, acting personally and through his subordinates and agents, endeavored to obtain from the Internal Revenue Service, in violation of the constitutional rights of citizens, confidential information contained in income tax returns for purposes not authorized by law, and to cause, in violation of the constitutional rights of citizens, income tax audits or other income tax investigations to be initiated or conducted in a discriminatory manner.

(2) He misused the Federal Bureau of Investigation, the Secret Service, and other executive personnel, in violation or disregard of the constitutional rights of citizens, by directing or authorizing such agencies or personnel to conduct or continue electronic surveillance or other investigations for purposes unrelated to national security, the enforcement of laws, or any other lawful function of his office; he did direct, authorize, or permit the use of information obtained thereby for purposes unrelated to national security, the enforcement of laws, or any other lawful function of his office; and he did direct the concealment of certain records made by the Federal Bureau of Investigation of electronic surveillance.

(3) He has, acting personally and through his subordinates and agents, in violation or disregard of the constitutional rights of citizens, authorized and permitted to be maintained a secret investigative unit within the office of the President, financed in part with money derived from campaign contributions, which unlawfully utilized the resources of the Central Intelligence Agency, engaged in covert and unlawful activities, and attempted to prejudice the constitutional right of an accused to a fair trial.

(4) He has failed to take care that the laws were faithfully executed by failing to act when he knew or had reason to know that his close subordinates endeavored to impede and frustrate lawful inquiries by duly constituted executive, judicial, and legislative entities concerning the unlawful entry into the headquarters of the Democratic National Committee, and the cover-up thereof, and concerning other unlawful activities including those relating to the confirmation of Richard Kleindienst as Attorney General of the United States, the electronic surveillance of private citizens, the break-in into the offices of Dr. Lewis Fielding and the campaign financing practices of the Committee to Re-elect the President.

(5) In disregard of the rule of law, he knowingly misused the executive branch, including the Federal Bureau

of Investigation, the Criminal Division, and the Office of Watergate Special Prosecution Force, of the Department of Justice, and the Central Intelligence Agency, in violation of his duty to take care that the laws be faithfully executed.

In all of this, Richard M. Nixon has acted in a manner contrary to his trust as President and subversive of constitutional government, to the great prejudice of the cause of law and justice and to the manifest injury of the people of the United States.

Wherefore Richard M. Nixon, by such conduct, warrants impeachment and trial, and removal from office.

—Adopted July 29, 1974,
by a 28–10 vote

Contempt of Congress Text

Following is the text of the contempt of Congress article approved by the committee:

Article III

In his conduct of the office of President of the United States, Richard M. Nixon, contrary to his oath faithfully to execute the office of President of the United States and, to the best of his ability, preserve, protect, and defend the Constitution of the United States, and in violation of his constitutional duty to take care that the laws be faithfully executed, has failed without lawful cause or excuse to produce papers and things as directed by duly authorized subpoenas issued by the Committee on the Judiciary of the House of Representatives on April 11, 1974, May 15, 1974, May 30,1974, and June 24, 1974, and willfully disobeyed such subpoenas. The subpoenaed papers and things were deemed necessary by the Committee in order to resolve by direct evidence fundamental, factual questions relating to Presidential direction, knowledge, or approval of actions demonstrated by other evidence to be substantial grounds for impeachment of the President. In refusing to produce these papers and things Richard M. Nixon, substituting his judgement as to what materials were necessary for the inquiry, interposed the powers of the Presidency against the lawful subpoenas of the House of Representatives, thereby assuming to himself functions and judgments necessary to the exercise of the sole power of impeachment vested by the Constitution in the House of Representatives.

In all of this, Richard M. Nixon has acted in a manner contrary to his trust as President and subversive of constitutional government, to the great prejudice of the cause of law and justice, and to the manifest injury of the people of the United States.

Wherefore, Richard M. Nixon, by such conduct, warrants impeachment and trial, and removal from office.

—Adopted July 30, 1974,
by a 21–17 vote

TEXTS OF ARTICLES NOT APPROVED

INCOME TAXES

In his conduct of the office of President of the United States, Richard M. Nixon, in violation of his constitutional oath faithfully to execute the office of the President of the United States, and, to the best of his ability, preserve, protect and defend the Constitution of the United States and in violation of his constitutional duty to take care that the laws be faithfully executed, did receive emoluments from the United States in excess of the compensation provided by law pursuant to Article II, Section 1, Clause 7 of the Constitution, and did willfully attempt to evade the payment of a portion of Federal income taxes due and owing by him for the years 1969, 1970, 1971, and 1972, in that:

(1) He, during the period for which he has been elected President, unlawfully received compensation in the form of government expenditures at and on his privately-owned properties located in or near San Clemente, California, and Key Biscayne, Florida.

(2) He knowingly and fraudulently failed to report certain income and claimed deductions in the years 1969, 1970, 1971, and 1972 on his Federal income tax returns which were not authorized by law, including deductions for a gift of papers to the United States valued at approximately $576,000.

In all of this, Richard M. Nixon has acted in a manner contrary to his trust as President and subversive of constitutional government, to the great prejudice of the cause of law and justice and to the manifest injury of the people of the United States.

Wherefore Richard M. Nixon, by such conduct, warrants impeachment and trial, and removal from office.

—Rejected July 30, 1974,
by a 12–26 vote

CAMBODIA BOMBING

In his conduct of the office of President of the United States, Richard M. Nixon, in violation of his constitutional oath faithfully to execute the office of President of the United States and, to the best of his ability, preserve, protect, and defend the Constitution of the United States, and in disregard of his constitutional duty to take care that the laws be faithfully executed, on and subsequent to March 17, 1969, authorized, ordered, and ratified the concealment from the Congress of the facts and the submission to the Congress of false and misleading statements concerning the existence, scope and nature of American bombing operations in Cambodia in derogation of the power of the Congress to declare war, to make appropriations and to raise and support armies, and by such conduct warrants impeachment and trial and removal from office.

—Rejected July 30, 1974,
by a 12–26 vote

Points to Ponder

- After reviewing the Judiciary Committee articles of impeachment, how would you have voted on them? Were Nixon's actions serious enough to warrant impeachment?

- If you were president, what would you do next if you wanted to hold on to your office? How could you persuade members of the House to vote against impeachment, or members of the Senate to vote against conviction?

- Impeaching a president ensures that the nation's top executive is held accountable, but it also removes from office a politician who was elected by the people. With this in mind, do you think the House of Representatives should impeach a president whenever it has evidence of misdeeds? Or should it reserve impeachment only for the most serious transgressions?

THE TRANSITION:
Nixon Resigns, Ford Takes Over

President Nixon resigned on Aug. 9, 1974. His fate was sealed a few days earlier, with the release of tapes of White House conversations that clearly showed he had participated in the coverup of the Watergate scandal. Those tapes cost him most of his remaining support in Congress. His only options were to resign or to face almost certain impeachment by the House and conviction by the Senate.

No other president has resigned. (President Clinton, in 1998, heard some scattered calls to resign when he was facing impeachment by the House. But Clinton retained the support of most Democrats and faced little risk of conviction in the Senate.) Many in Congress hailed Nixon's decision because it spared the country a wrenching debate over forcing him from office. Vice President Gerald R. Ford assumed the presidency and assured an anxious nation that he would focus on important issues, such as inflation.

THE LAST DAYS

After the House Judiciary Committee recommended impeachment, the full House of Representatives was expected to bring up the issue in late August. Nixon's outnumbered supporters planned to argue that there was not enough evidence for impeachment. They also weighed a strategy of presenting an alternative to impeachment. This could consist of a House resolution censuring Nixon for his actions. Nixon's supporters faced difficult odds. Most House members appeared to favor impeachment, as did a solid majority of the public. The Senate's reaction was more difficult to predict. There, a two-thirds vote would be needed to convict the president and remove him from office.

But on Aug. 5, the political landscape changed abruptly. The White House, bowing to a Supreme Court decision, released transcripts of conversations between Nixon and his former chief of staff, H. R. Haldeman. The conversations had taken place just days after the Watergate break-in. The transcripts showed clearly that Nixon wanted to use the CIA to suppress an investigation into the break-in.

In their conversations, Haldeman told Nixon that the FBI had determined that the president's re-election committee had paid money to the Watergate burglars. He briefed the president on a plan to have top CIA officials tell

the FBI to steer clear of investigating certain aspects of Watergate. Nixon approved the plan. He instructed Haldeman that the CIA should tell the FBI, "Don't go any farther into this case." He said that the FBI should be told that its investigation could reopen problems from the Bay of Pigs. (This was an aborted attempt by the United States to overthrow Cuba president Fidel Castro in 1961. Although there was no direct connection between the Bay of Pigs and Watergate, several of the burglars were Cuban-American.)

At one point in the transcript, Nixon told Haldeman to tell the CIA, "The president just feels that ah, without going into the details—don't, don't lie to them to the extent to say there is no involvement, but just say this is a comedy of errors, without getting into it, the president believes that it is going to open the whole Bay of Pigs thing up again. And, ah, because these people are plugging for (unintelligible) and that they should call the FBI in and (unintelligible) don't go any further into this case period!" Slightly later in the conversation, Nixon asked Haldeman, "Well, can you get it done?" Haldeman said, "I think so."

In a final attempt to salvage his presidency, Nixon released a written statement with the tapes. He acknowledged that the transcripts contradicted his previous denials about being involved in Watergate. However, he maintained that the full record of his actions did not show that he tried to stop an FBI investigation. On the contrary, he said he talked with FBI Director L. Patrick Gray III a few weeks after the conversation with Haldeman. He urged Gray to "press ahead vigorously" with the investigation into Watergate. "Whatever mistakes I made in the handling of Watergate, the basic truth remains that when all the facts were brought to my attention I insisted on a full investigation and prosecution of those guilty," Nixon said. "I am firmly convinced that the record, in its entirety, does not justify the extreme step of impeachment and removal of a president."

Unfortunately for Nixon, few lawmakers agreed. The release of the Aug. 5 transcripts shattered most of his remaining support in Congress. The 10 Republicans on the House Judiciary Committee who had opposed impeachment all said the transcripts had changed their minds. One of Nixon's most eloquent supporters, Republican Charles E. Wiggins of California, now believed Nixon should resign or be impeached. "I am now possessed of information which establishes beyond a reasonable doubt that on June 23, 1972, the president personally agreed to certain actions, the purpose and intent of which were to interfere with the FBI investigation of the Watergate break-in," he said. One of the top Republicans in the House commented on the transcripts, "It looks like a smoking gun to me."

Congressional leaders warned that Nixon could count on no more than a dozen or so supporters in each chamber of Congress. On the evening of Aug. 7, Nixon decided to resign. The following evening, he told the nation in a televised speech that he had decided to step down. His resignation would be effective the next day. He did not admit guilt. Instead, he said, "I regret deeply any injuries that may have been done in the course of the events that led to this decision. I would say only that if some of my judgments were wrong, and some were wrong, they were made in what I believed at the time to be the best interest of the nation."

His reason for resigning, he said, was his loss of support in Congress. He said:

Throughout the long and difficult period of Watergate, I have felt it was my duty to persevere, to make every possible effort to complete the term of office to which you elected me.

In the past few days, however, it has become evident to me that I no longer have a strong enough political base in the Congress to justify continuing that effort. As long as there was a base, I felt strongly that it was necessary to see the constitutional process through to its conclusion, that to do otherwise would be unfaithful to the spirit of that deliberately difficult process, and a dangerously destabilizing precedent for the future.

President Gerald Ford announces his pardon of Richard Nixon from the Oval Office. September 8, 1974.

But with the disappearance of that base, I now believe that the constitutional purpose has been served, and there is no longer a need for the process to be prolonged.

Later in the speech, he added, "To continue to fight through the months ahead for my personal vindication would almost totally absorb the time and attention of both the president and the Congress in a period when our entire focus should be on the great issues of peace abroad and prosperity without inflation at home."

Nixon sent his letter of resignation to Secretary of State Henry Kissinger the next day. Minutes later, Ford was sworn in as the nation's 38th president.

THE NEW PRESIDENT

Ford said he would try to move the nation forward. "Our long national nightmare is over," he said. "Our Constitution works. Our great republic is a government of laws and not of men."

Members of Congress hailed Nixon's decision to resign. They also welcomed the ascension of Ford, who had served in the House for years before becoming vice president. But an important question remained: would Nixon be prosecuted for his offenses? It was estimated that he could face 30 to 60 years in prison for the crimes he was charged with in the articles of impeachment.

Some in Congress floated the idea of granting Nixon immunity, which would have meant that he could not be prosecuted for crimes connected with Watergate. They said that Nixon had already paid a high price for his transgressions. The time had come for reconciliation, not prosecution of an ex-president, they said. But others said that Nixon should not be treated differently than anyone else. "How can we tell our young people that they ought to respect the law if a man who commits a most heinous crime is granted immunity?" asked Robert C. Byrd of West Virginia, one of the top Democrats in the Senate.

Politicians also discussed whether Ford should grant a pardon to Nixon, thereby sparing him from prosecution. But Ford had addressed the issue of a pardon in 1973 when the Senate was considering approving his nomination to be vice president. A senator asked Ford whether, if a president resigned, his successor would have the power to prevent a criminal investigation. At that time, Ford had said, "I do not think the public would stand for it . . . and whether he has the technical authority or not, I cannot give you a categorical answer."

Instead of taking action, elected leaders seemed content to wait for the decision of Watergate special prosecutor Leon Jaworski or the grand jury on whether to issue a criminal indictment against Nixon.

Meanwhile, the House of Representatives on Aug. 20 took the formal action of accepting the Judiciary Committee's report that had recommended Nixon's impeachment. Even though Nixon no longer faced impeachment, this meant that the House put a stamp of approval on the committee's inquiry and final report. The vote was 412–3, with only a trio of Nixon's defenders voting no.

It was over at last. President Gerald R. Ford began binding the wounds inflicted by more than two years of Watergate scandals which, near the end, had left the nation divided and numb.

"Our long national nightmare is over. Our Constitution works. Our great republic is a government of laws and not of men," Ford assured those gathered to observe his inauguration shortly after noon on Aug. 9 in the East Room of the White House.

Signaling his priorities, Ford had announced earlier that Secretary of State Henry A. Kissinger would stay on in the Ford administration. Immediately after his inaugural remarks, Ford met with congressional leaders of both parties. Later in the day he met with economic advisers, telling them that control of inflation was his "high and first priority."

Ford's swift and unprecedented ascent from House Minority Leader to President was made possible by the two greatest scandals of American history. He was chosen by President Nixon as vice president after Spiro T. Agnew resigned that post in October 1973, pleading "no contest" to tax evasion charges based on his acceptance of bribes. Ford was sworn in as Vice President Dec. 6, 1973.

Nixon Resignation

Nine months later Ford became President with Nixon's resignation—a resignation which came the day after Republican congressional leaders informed Nixon that his only alternative was certain impeachment in the House and likely conviction in the Senate.

In a televised resignation speech at nine o'clock on the evening of Aug. 8, Nixon said that he was resigning because, "It has become evident to me that I no longer have a strong enough political base in the Congress to justify continuing that effort" to stay in office.

Nixon made no mention of impeachment in his speech, but the erosion of support for him—which eventually brought about his departure from office—was the direct result of the charges lodged against him by the House Judiciary Committee. The committee late in July recommended his impeachment for obstruction of justice, abuse of his powers and contempt of Congress.

Debate in the House on impeachment was scheduled to begin Aug. 19. His supporters in the House were girding themselves to argue that the evidence was not sufficient to justify impeachment.

Final Blow

Their effort was shattered Aug. 5 by Nixon's release of three transcripts of conversations with former White House chief of staff H. R. Haldeman on June 23, 1972, six days after the Watergate break-in. Nixon acknowledged in an accompanying statement that he had withheld the contents of the tapes from his staff and his attorneys despite the fact that they contradicted his previous declarations of non-involvement and lack of knowledge of the Watergate coverup.

The transcripts showed clearly Nixon's participation in the coverup, approving the invocation of CIA involvement as a means of obstructing the FBI investigation of the Watergate break-in.

With a few exceptions, members of Congress who had supported the President were left with no choice but to call for his departure from office, by resignation or by impeachment. Rep. Charles E. Wiggins (R Calif.), Nixon's most eloquent defender in the House, announced shortly after release of the transcripts that he would support impeachment. Within hours, every other member of the House Judiciary Committee who had opposed impeachment had shifted his vote to support the obstruction of justice charge.

Even before their release, Assistant Senate Minority Leader Robert P. Griffin (R Mich.) had called for Nixon's resignation. Afterwards, Barber B. Conable Jr. (R N.Y.), third-ranking Republican in the House, commented, "It looks like a smoking gun to me." He said he would vote for impeachment. House Republican leader John J. Rhodes (R Ariz.) also joined the pro-impeachment forces Aug. 6.

On Aug. 7, Rhodes and other of Nixon's own party leaders told Nixon he could muster no more than 10 or 15 votes in each chamber against impeachment.

The decision, made Wednesday evening, Aug. 7, was an agonizing one. The emotion which was controlled as Nixon gave his resignation speech broke forth as he met with 50 of his closest congressional friends an hour before.

One Republican representative present told Congressional Quarterly that after Nixon explained to them the reasons he would later relate to the nation for his decision, "he quit talking and was struggling against breaking down. . . . He finally choked . . . and said, 'I guess what I'm trying to say is that I hope I haven't let you down.' "

"There wasn't a dry eye in the house," commented the participant. "In fact, many of the members were crying openly. . . ."

After an emotional farewell to his cabinet members and staff on the morning of Aug. 9, Nixon with his family left the White House for San Clemente, no longer the western White House.

Nixon's letter of resignation reached Secretary of State Kissinger shortly after 11:30 a.m. Aug. 9. No effective time was specified in the letter, making it effective upon receipt. Ford automatically became the nation's 38th President at that time, minutes before he was sworn in by Chief Justice Warren E. Burger.

By choosing to become the first President in history to resign his office, Nixon avoided impeachment and conviction, also a historic first. The House Judiciary Committee report, in support of its recommendation of impeachment, was still being prepared, and it was expected that it would be filed with the House. But the impeachment proceedings themselves would go no further.

The question of the President's possible indictment on some of the charges lodged against him by the committee was left open.

Members of Congress had discussed the possibility of passing a bill granting the President immunity from prosecution after his resignation, but at week's end the prospects for such a move were dimmed by a variety of questions about the propriety and the validity of such a measure.

Reaction of Relief

The reaction to the President's resignation and Ford's move to the Oval Office was one of overwhelming relief. Rhodes called it "an act of supreme statesmanship."

Rep. Lawrence J. Hogan (R Md.), whose decision to support impeachment had been one of the elements in

the momentum toward impeachment, described the President's action as "an admirable and patriotic act which merits the praise and respect of all Americans."

Congressional leaders hailed Ford, noting that he was "one of ours"—a man who had served in Congress for years with many of them. Ford's move and Nixon's departure were also expected to alter drastically the political equation in the upcoming elections, removing the issue of Watergate which had so unified Democrats and haunted Republicans.

The Final Week

Release of the damning June 23 transcripts and the accompanying statement came a week after the House Judiciary Committee had recommended Nixon's impeachment for obstruction of justice, abuse of his powers and contempt of Congress.

During the week, the public optimism of the White House had been slowly deflated by the recognition that impeachment was likely—and conviction by the Senate a live possibility. "You would have to put the President in the role of the underdog," said Deputy White House Press Secretary Gerald L. Warren Aug. 2, describing the battle to come in the House as "an uphill struggle." The President did not plan to resign, he said.

"The situation has eroded," said Ford Aug. 3, maintaining his belief that the President had not committed any impeachable offenses.

Sparking rumors of an impending announcement, the President summoned Alexander M. Haig Jr., Ronald L. Ziegler, James D. St. Clair and two speechwriters to Camp David on Sunday, Aug. 4.

On Monday, Griffin stated to reporters: "I think we've arrived at the point where both the national interest and his own interests would be best served by his [Nixon's] resigning."

'Act of Omission'

Then, in late afternoon Aug. 5, the announcement came: the President was releasing the transcripts of three recorded conversations on June 23, 1972, with H. R. Haldeman, then his chief of staff. The tapes of these conversations had been turned over to Judge John J. Sirica Aug. 2.

Accompanying the transcripts was the President's statement taking full responsibility and stating deep regret for "this . . . serious act of omission." He made plain that neither his staff nor St. Clair had known of the contents of the conversations, leading to reports that Nixon had released the transcripts and made his statement only after St. Clair learned of their contents and threatened to resign. St. Clair had not heard the tapes until directed by Sirica the previous week to do so.

Reaction to this disclosure was immediate. "The most devastating thing that can be said of it," said Speaker Carl Albert (D Okla.) "is that it speaks for itself."

Nixon should resign, said Robert McClory (R Ill.), the most senior Republican on the House Judiciary Committee to support impeachment. Any delay was now "only a question of his personal stubbornness, personal stonewalling," he said.

Majority Leader Thomas P. O'Neill Jr. (D Mass.) said he felt no more than 75 members would oppose impeachment.

That evening, Ford announced that he would cease to repeat his still-held belief in the President's innocence. He had not been informed before the President's statement of its contents.

As statements from members of Congress in favor of Nixon's departure from office—by resignation or impeachment—flooded Capitol Hill Aug. 6, Nixon called a sudden cabinet meeting. Queried afterward, cabinet members insisted that Nixon said he would not resign but would "fight on" to stay in office. Treasury Secretary William E. Simon said, "The President sincerely believes he has not committed an impeachable offense."

Rhodes Statement

Tuesday afternoon, Minority Leader Rhodes made his announcement: he would vote for impeachment based on Article I, obstruction of justice, and perhaps—based on the new evidence—for Article II, abuse of powers.

Conable and John B. Anderson (R Ill.), the third and fourth ranking Republican House leaders, also expressed their support for impeachment. All three expressed doubts about the suggestion that the President be granted immunity, by Congress, from prosecution after he left office.

And Sen. Robert Dole (R Kan.), who served as national party chairman during the 1972 campaign, said Aug. 6 that if the President had 40 votes the previous week in the Senate against conviction, he had no more than 20 left, far short of the 34 needed to survive a trial.

But Sen. Carl T. Curtis (R Neb.) continued to defend the President, warning against panic. The United States would become like a "banana republic," he said, if it ousted Nixon, placing Ford and Ford's choice for vice president—neither of whom had been elected to their offices—in the nation's highest posts.

The Decision

Rumors that the President would resign reached a crescendo Wednesday, Aug. 7. *The Providence Journal-Bulletin*, which late in 1973 had broken the story of Nixon's minimal income tax payments during his first term in the White House, reported that Nixon had made an "irrevocable" decision to resign. No longer denying such reports, Warren simply stated, "I cannot confirm that."

Senate Minority Leader Hugh Scott (R Pa.) said that the President's Aug. 5 statement had removed any presumption that he was innocent of the charges against him.

Shortly after five o'clock, President Nixon met with Sen. Barry Goldwater (R Ariz.), Scott and Rhodes. Afterwards, Goldwater said: "There has been no decision made. We made no suggestions. We were merely there to offer what we see as the condition on both floors."

Scott added: "We have told him that the situation is very gloomy on Capitol Hill." Just how gloomy was shown by later reports that the Republican leaders had told Nixon he could not expect more than 10 votes in the House and 15 in the Senate against his impeachment and conviction.

But there were still some vocal supporters in Congress. Sen. William Lloyd Scott (R Va.) said that he continued to support the President. "There's no doubt he won't resign," Scott added. And Rep. Earl F. Landgrebe (R. Ind.) told reporters: "Don't confuse me with the facts. I've got a closed mind. I will not vote for impeachment."

Just after noon on Thursday, Aug. 8, it was announced that the President would meet with congressional leaders in the early evening and would address the nation at nine o'clock. Rhodes said then that the President would resign. "I feel relief . . . sorrow . . . gratitude, but also optimism," he said.

Defection of Defenders

Even before the release of the additional transcripts, Republican support for Nixon was shaky.

On Aug. 2 Representatives Paul Findley (R Ill.) and Delbert L. Latta (R Ohio) introduced a resolution censuring Nixon for moral insensitivity, negligence and maladministration. They hoped to provide a vehicle through which Congress could express its strong disapproval of Nixon's actions without going so far as to impeach him.

Revealing the impact of the televised proceedings of the House Judiciary Committee and its recommendations, public opinion in early August swung heavily in favor of impeachment and—less heavily—in favor of conviction. A Harris poll completed Aug. 2 and taken after the committee had acted showed that the percentage of persons questioned who favored impeachment by the House had risen to 66 per cent from 53 per cent, that the percentage favoring conviction by the Senate had risen to 56 per cent from 47 per cent.

One clear measure of the damage done to the President's case by his admission Aug. 5 came with the shift—from opposition to support of impeachment—of every one of his 10 Republican supporters on the House Judiciary Committee. Their defense of him—and their criticism of the case presented by impeachment advocates—had been based on the lack of direct, specific, hard evidence.

One of those supporters, Charles W. Sandman Jr. (R N.J.), said after the new transcripts were released: "These conversations contain specific, clear and convincing evidence constituting the criminal charge of obstruction of justice, leaving me no recourse but to support impeachment on Article I," charging the President with obstructing justice.

"I've always felt that in order to impeach a President you had to have direct evidence," added Latta, "and here the President was furnishing the direct evidence himself." Findley abandoned his censure effort and said he would support impeachment.

Most dramatic of the announcements came from Charles E. Wiggins (R Calif.), the silver-haired Republican who had patiently and articulately defended the President—and argued that the evidence was insufficient to justify impeachment.

"The facts . . . known to me have now changed," said Wiggins, shortly after the President's statement. "I am now possessed of information which establishes beyond a reasonable doubt that on June 23, 1972, the President personally agreed to certain actions, the purpose and intent of which were to interfere with the FBI investigation of the Watergate break-in. . . .

"After considerable reflection, I have reached the painful conclusion that the President of the United States should resign. . . .

If the President did not resign, Wiggins concluded, halting and obviously emotional, "I am prepared to conclude that the magnificent career of public service of Richard Nixon must be terminated involuntarily and [I] shall support those portions of Article I . . . which are sustained by the evidence."

"It is clear to me the evidence is there to support Article I," said Edward Hutchinson (R Mich.), the ranking Republican on the committee.

"I hope he will resign, but if not I have no alternative but to vote for Article I," said Trent Lott (R Miss.). David W. Dennis (R Ind.), Henry P. Smith III (R N.Y.), Carlos J. Moorhead (R Calif.), Wiley Mayne (R Iowa) and

Joseph J. Maraziti (R N.J.) also indicated that they would support impeachment if the President did not resign.

As a result the lengthy schedule of debate originally planned for impeachment was telescoped: if opposition was minimal, the reason for extended debate had disappeared. Albert and other House leaders said Aug. 6 that they expected the House to conclude action on impeachment within the week of Aug. 19, instead of consuming two weeks, as initially planned.

Text of Aug. 5 Statement

Following is the text of President Nixon's Aug. 5 statement issued with the release of the transcripts of three June 23, 1972, White House tape recordings:

I have today instructed my attorneys to make available to the House Judiciary Committee, and I am making public, the transcripts of three conversations with H. R. Haldeman on June 23, 1972. I have also turned over the tapes of these conversations to Judge Sirica, as part of the process of my compliance with the Supreme Court ruling.

On April 29, in announcing my decision to make public the original set of White House transcripts, I stated that "as far as what the President personally knew and did with regard to Watergate and the cover-up is concerned, these materials—together with those already made available—will tell it all."

Shortly after that, in May, I made a preliminary review of some of the 64 taped conversations subpoenaed by the special prosecutor.

Among the conversations I listened to at that time were two of those of June 23. Although I recognized that these presented potential problems, I did not inform my staff or my counsel of it, or those arguing my case, nor did I amend my submission to the Judiciary Committee in order to include and reflect it. At the time, I did not realize the extent of the implications which these conversations might now appear to have. As a result, those arguing my case, as well as those passing judgment on the case, did so with information that was incomplete and in some respects erroneous. This was a serious act of omission for which I take full responsibility and which I deeply regret.

Since the Supreme Court's decision twelve days ago, I have ordered my counsel to analyze the 64 tapes, and I have listened to a number of them myself. This process has made it clear that portions of the tapes of these June 23 conversations are at variance with certain of my previous statements. Therefore, I have ordered the transcripts made available immediately to the Judiciary Committee so that they can be reflected in the Committee's report, and included in the record to be considered by the House and Senate.

In a formal written statement on May 22 of last year, I said that shortly after the Watergate break-in I became concerned about the possibility that the FBI investigation might lead to the exposure either of unrelated covert activities of the CIA, or of sensitive national security matters that the so-called "plumbers" unit at the White House had been working on, because of the CIA and plumbers connections of some of those involved. I said that I therefore gave instructions that the FBI should be alerted to coordinate with the CIA, and to ensure that the investigation not expose these sensitive national security matters.

That statement was based on my recollection at the time—some eleven months later—plus documentary materials and relevant public testimony of those involved.

The June 23 tapes clearly show, however, that at the time I gave those instructions I also discussed the political aspects of the situation, and that I was aware of the advantages this course of action would have with respect to limiting possible public exposure of involvement by persons connected with the re-election committee.

My review of the additional tapes has, so far, shown no other major inconsistencies with what I have previously submitted. While I have no way at this stage of being certain that there will not be others, I have no reason to believe that there will be. In any case, the tapes in their entirety are now in the process of being furnished to Judge Sirica. He has begun what may be a rather lengthy process of reviewing the tapes, passing on specific claims of executive privilege on portions of them, and forwarding to the special prosecutor those tapes or those portions that are relevant to the Watergate investigation.

It is highly unlikely that this review will be completed in time for the House debate. It appears at this stage, however, that a House vote of impeachment is, as a practical matter, virtually a foregone conclusion, and that the issue will therefore go to trial in the Senate. In order to ensure that no other significant relevant materials are withheld, I shall voluntarily furnish to the Senate everything from these tapes that Judge Sirica rules should go to the special prosecutor.

I recognize that this additional material I am now furnishing may further damage my case, especially because attention will be drawn separately to it rather than to the evidence in its entirety. In considering its implications, therefore, I urge that two points be borne in mind.

The first of these points is to remember what actually happened as a result of the instructions I gave on June 23. Acting Director Gray of the FBI did coordinate with Director Helms and Deputy Director Walters of the CIA. The CIA did undertake an extensive check to see whether any of its covert activities would be compromised by a full FBI investigation of Watergate. Deputy Director Walters then reported back to Mr. Gray that they would not be compromised. On July 6, when I called Mr. Gray, and when he expressed concern about improper attempts to limit his investigation, as the record shows, I told him to press ahead vigorously with his investigation—which he did.

The second point I would urge is that the evidence be looked at in its entirety, and the events be looked at in perspective. Whatever mistakes I made in the handling of Watergate, the basic truth remains that when all the facts were brought to my attention I insisted on a full investigation and prosecution of those guilty. I am firmly convinced that the record, in its entirety, does not justify the extreme step of impeachment and removal of a President. I trust that as the Constitutional process goes forward, this perspective will prevail.

Resignation Statement Text

Following is the text of President Nixon's Aug. 8 televised address in which he announced his resignation from office.

Good evening.

This is the 37th time I have spoken to you from this office, where so many decisions have been made that shaped the history of this Nation. Each time I have done so to discuss with you some matter that I believe affected the national interest.

In all the decisions I have made in my public life, I have always tried to do what was best for the Nation. Throughout the long and difficult period of Watergate, I have felt it was my duty to persevere, to make every possible effort to complete the term of office to which you elected me.

In the past few days, however, it has become evident to me that I no longer have a strong enough political base in the Congress to justify continuing that effort. As long as there was a base, I felt strongly that it was necessary to see the constitutional process through to its conclusion, that to do otherwise would be unfaithful to the spirit of that deliberately difficult process, and a dangerously destabilizing precedent for the future.

But with the disappearance of that base, I now believe that the constitutional purpose has been served, and there is no longer a need for the process to be prolonged.

I would have preferred to carry through to the finish whatever the personal agony it would have involved, and my family unanimously urged me to do so. But the interests of the Nation must always come before any personal considerations.

From the discussions I have had with Congressional and other leaders, I have concluded that because of the Watergate matter I might not have the support of the Congress that I would consider necessary to back the very difficult decisions and carry out the duties of this office in the way the interests of the Nation would require.

I have never been a quitter. To leave office before my term is completed is abhorrent to every instinct in my body. But as President, I must put the interest of America first. America needs a full-time President and a full-time Congress, particularly at this time with the problems we face at home and abroad.

To continue to fight through the months ahead for my personal vindication would almost totally absorb the time and attention of both the President and the Congress in a period when our entire focus should be on the great issues of peace abroad and prosperity without inflation at home.

Resign at Noon

Therefore, I shall resign the Presidency effective at noon tomorrow. Vice President Ford will be sworn in as President at that hour in this office.

As I recall the high hopes for America with which we began this second term, I feel a great sadness that I will not be here in this office working on your behalf to achieve those hopes in the next 2 1/2 years. But in turning over direction of the Government to Vice President Ford, I know, as I told the Nation when I nominated him for that office ten months ago, that the leadership of America will be in good hands.

In passing this office to the Vice President, I also do so with the profound sense of the weight of responsibility that will fall on his shoulders tomorrow and, therefore, of the understanding, the patience, the cooperation he will need from all Americans.

As he assumes that responsibility, he will deserve the help and the support of all of us. As we look to the future, the first essential is to begin healing the wounds of this Nation; to put the bitterness and the divisions of the recent past behind us and to rediscover those shared ideals that lie at the heart of our strength and unity as a great and as a free people.

By taking this action, I hope that I will have hastened the start of that process of healing which is so desperately needed in America.

I regret deeply any injuries that may have been done in the course of the events that led to this decision. I would say only that if some of my judgments were wrong, and some were wrong, they were made in what I believed at the time to be the best interest of the Nation.

To those who have stood with me during these past difficult months, to my family, my friends, to many others who joined in supporting my cause because they believed it was right, I will be eternally grateful for your support.

And to those who have not felt able to give me your support, let me say I leave with no bitterness toward those who have opposed me, because all of us, in the final analysis, have been concerned with the good of the country however our judgments might differ.

So, let us all now join together in affirming that common commitment and in helping our new President succeed for the benefit of all Americans.

I shall leave this office with regret at not completing my term, but with gratitude for the privilege of serving as your President for the past 5 1/2 years. These years have been a momentous time in the history of our Nation and the world. They have been a time of achievement in which we can all be proud, achievements that represent the shared efforts of the Administration, the Congress and the people.

Challenges Ahead

But the challenges ahead are equally great and they, too, will require the support and the efforts of the Congress and the people working in cooperation with the new Administration.

We have ended America's longest war, but in the work of securing a lasting peace in the world, the goals ahead are even more far-reaching and more difficult. We must complete a structure of peace so that it will be said of this generation, our generation, of Americans, by the people of all nations, not only that we ended one war, but that we prevented future wars.

We have unlocked the doors that for a quarter of a century stood between the United States and the People's Republic of China.

We must now ensure that the one quarter of the world's people who live in the People's Republic of China will be and remain not our enemies but our friends.

In the Middle East, 100 million people in the Arab countries, many of whom have considered us their enemy for nearly 20 years, now look on us as their friends. We must continue to build on that friendship so that peace can settle at last over the Middle East and so that the cradle of civilization will not become its grave.

Together with the Soviet Union we have made the crucial breakthroughs that have begun the process of limiting nuclear arms. But we must set as our goal not just limiting, but reducing and finally destroying these terrible weapons so that they cannot destroy civilization and so that the threat of nuclear war will no longer hang over the world and the people.

We have opened the new relation with the Soviet Union. We must continue to develop and expand that new relationship so that the two strongest nations of the world will live together in cooperation rather than confrontation.

Around the world, in Asia, in Africa, in Latin America, in the Middle East, there are millions of people who live in terrible poverty, even starvation. We must keep as our goal turning away from production for war and expanding production for peace so that people everywhere on this earth can at least look forward in their children's time, if not in our own time, to having the necessities for a decent life.

Here in America, we are fortunate that most of our people have not only the blessings of liberty, but also the means to live full and good and, by the world's standards, even abundant lives. We must press on, however, to a goal of not only more and better jobs, but of full opportunity for every American, and of what we are striving so hard right now to achieve, prosperity without inflation.

For more than a quarter of a century in public life I have shared in the turbulent history of this era. I have fought for what I believed in. I have tried to the best of my ability to discharge those duties and meet those responsibilities that were entrusted to me.

Sometimes I have succeeded and sometimes I have failed, but always I have taken heart from what Theodore Roosevelt once said about the man in the arena, "whose face is marred by dust and sweat and blood, who strives valiantly, who errs and comes short again and again because there is not effort without error and short-coming, but who does actually strive to do the deeds, who knows the great enthusiasms, the great devotions, who spends himself in a worthy cause, who at the best knows in the end the triumphs of high achievements and who at the worst, if he fails, at least fails while daring greatly."

Parting Pledge

I pledge to you tonight that as long as I have a breath of life in my body, I shall continue in that spirit. I shall continue to work for the great causes to which I have been dedicated throughout my years as a Congressman, a Senator, a Vice President and President; the cause of peace not just for America but among all nations, prosperity, justice and opportunity for all of our people.

There is one cause above all to which I have been devoted and to which I shall always be devoted for as long as I live.

When I first took the oath of office as President five and one-half years ago, I made this sacred commitment: "To consecrate my office, my energies and all the wisdom I can summon to the cause of peace among nations."

I have done my very best in all the days since to be true to that pledge. As a result of these efforts, I am confident that the world is a safer place today, not only for the people of America, but for the people of all nations, and that all of our children have a better chance than before of living in peace rather than dying in war.

This, more than anything, is what I hoped to achieve when I sought the Presidency. This, more than anything, is what I hope will be my legacy to you, to our country, as I leave the Presidency.

To have served in this office is to have felt a very personal sense of kinship with each and every American. In leaving it, I do so with this prayer: May God's grace be with you in all the days ahead.

Nixon's Farewell Text

Reprinted from *Congressional Quarterly Weekly Report,* August 17, 1974

Following is the text of former President Nixon's farewell remarks to the cabinet and White House staff Aug. 9, his last public comments as President.

Members of the Cabinet, Members of the White House staff, all of our friends here:

I think the record should show that this is one of those spontaneous things that we always arrange whenever the President comes in to speak, and it will be so reported in the press, and we don't mind because they have to call it as they see it.

But on our part, believe me, it is spontaneous.

You are here to say goodbye to us and we don't have a good word for it in English. The best is au revoir. We will see you again.

I just met with the members of the White House staff, you know, those who serve here in the White House day in and day out, and I asked them to do what I ask all of you to do to the extent that you can and, of course, are requested to do so: To serve our next President as you have served me and previous Presidents—because many of you have been here for many years—with devotion and dedication, because this office, great as it is, can only be as great as the men and women who work for and with the President.

This house, for example, I was thinking of it as we walked down this hall, and I was comparing it to some of the great houses of the world that I have been in. This isn't the biggest house. Many, and most, in even smaller countries are much bigger. This isn't the finest house. Many in Europe, particularly, and in China, Asia, have paintings of great, great value, things that we just don't have here, and probably will never have until we are 1000 years old, or older.

But this is the best house. It is the best house because it has something far more important than numbers of people who serve, far more important than numbers of rooms or how big it is, far more important than numbers of magnificent pieces of art.

This house has a great heart, and that heart comes from those who serve. I was rather sorry they didn't come down. We said goodbye to them upstairs. But they are really great. And I recall after so many times I have made speeches, and there have been some of them pretty tough, yet, when I always come back, or after a hard day—and my days usually have run rather long—I would always get a lift from them because I might be a little down, but they always smiled.

And so it is with you. I look around here and I see so many on this staff that, you know, I should have been by your offices and shaken hands, and I would love to have talked to you and found out how to run the world—everybody wants to tell the President what to do, and boy he needs to be told many times—but I just haven't had the time. But I want you to know that each and every one of you, I know, is indispensable to this Government.

Pride in Cabinet

I am proud of this Cabinet. I am proud of all the members who have served in our Cabinet. I am proud of our sub-Cabinet. I am proud of our White House staff. As I pointed out last night, sure we have done some things wrong in this Administration, and the top man always takes the responsibility, and I have never ducked it. But I want to say one thing: We can be proud of it—5 1/2 years—no man or no woman came into this Administration and left it with more of this world's goods than when he came in. No man or no woman ever profited at the public expense or the public till. That tells something about you.

Mistakes, yes. But for personal gain, never. You did what you believed in. Sometimes right, sometimes wrong. And I only wish that I were a wealthy man—at the present time I have got to find a way to pay my taxes (Laughter)—and if I were, I would like to recompense you for the sacrifices all of you have made to serve in Government.

But you are getting something in Government—and I want you to tell this to your children, and I hope the Nation's children will hear it, too—something in Government service that is far more important than money. It is a cause bigger than yourself. It is the cause of making this the greatest Nation in the world, the leader of the world, because without our leadership the world will know nothing but war, possibly starvation, or worse, in the years ahead. With our leadership it will know peace, it will know plenty.

We have been generous and we will be more generous in the future as we are able to. But most important, we must be strong here, strong in our hearts, strong in our souls, strong in our belief, and strong in our willingness to sacrifice, as you have been willing to sacrifice, in a pecuniary way, to serve in Government.

Rugged Life in Government

There is something else I would like for you to tell your young people. You know, people often come in and say, "What will I tell my kids?" They look at Government and say it is sort of a rugged life and they see the mistakes that are made. They get the impression that everybody is here for the purpose of feathering his nest. That is why I made this earlier point—not in this Administration, not one single man or woman.

And I say to them, "There are many careers. This country needs good farmers, good businessmen, good plumbers, good carpenters."

I remember my old man. I think that they would have called him sort of a little man, common man. He didn't consider himself that way. You know what he was? He was a streetcar motorman first, and then he was a farmer, and then he had a lemon ranch. It was the poorest lemon ranch in California, I can assure you. He sold it before they found oil on it. (Laughter)

And then he was a grocer. But he was a great man because he did his job and every job counts up to the hilt, regardless of what happens.

Nobody will ever write a book, probably, about my mother. Well, I guess all of you would say this about your mother—my mother was a saint. And I think of here, two boys dying of tuberculosis, nursing four others in order that she could take care of my older brother for three years in Arizona, and seeing each of them die, and when they died, it was like one of her own.

Yes, she will have no books written about her. But she was a saint.

Now, however, we look to the future. I had a little quote in the speech last night from T. R. As you know, I kind of like to read books. I am not educated, but I do read books, (Laughter) and the T. R. quote was a pretty good one.

Here is another one I found as I was reading, my last night in the White House, and this quote is about a young man. He was a young lawyer in New York. He had married a beautiful girl and they had a lovely daughter, and then suddenly she died, and this is what he wrote. This was in his diary.

He said: "She was beautiful in face and form and lovelier still in spirit. As a flower she grew and as a fair young flower she died. Her life had been always in the sunshine. There had never come to her a single great sorrow. None ever knew her who did not love and revere her for her bright and sunny temper and her saintly unselfishness. Fair, pure and joyous as a maiden, loving, tender and happy as a young wife. When she had just become a mother, when her life seemed to be just begun and when the years seemed so bright before her, then by a strange and terrible fate death came to her. And when my heart's dearest died, the light went from my life forever."

That was T. R. in his 20's. He thought the light had gone from his life forever—but he went on. And he not only became President, but as an ex-President, he served his country always in the arena, tempestuous, strong, sometimes wrong, sometimes right, but he was a man.

Example for All

And as I leave, let me say that is an example I think all of us should remember. We think sometimes when things happen that don't go the right way; we think that when you don't pass the bar exam the first time—I happened to, but I was just lucky; I mean my writing was so poor the bar examiner said, "We have just got to let the guy through." (Laughter) We think that when someone dear to us dies, we think that when we lose an election, we think that when we suffer a defeat, that all is ended. We think, as T. R. said, that the light had left his life forever.

Not true. It is only a beginning always. The young must know it; the old must know it. It must always sustain us because the greatness comes not when things go always good for you, but the greatness comes when you are really tested, when you take some knocks, some disappointments, when sadness comes, because only if you have been in the deepest valley can you ever know how magnificent it is to be on the highest mountain.

And so I say to you on this occasion, as we leave, we leave proud of the people who have stood by us and worked for us and served this country.

We want you to be proud of what you have done. We want you to continue to serve in Government, if that is your wish. Always give your best, never get discouraged, never be petty; always remember others may hate you,

but those who hate you don't win unless you hate them, and then you destroy yourself.

And so, we leave with high hopes, in good spirit and with deep humility, and with very much gratefulness in our hearts. And I can only say to each and every one of you, we come from many faiths, we pray perhaps to different gods, but really the same God in a sense, but I want to say to each and every one of you, not only will we always remember you, not only will we always be grateful to you, but always you will be in our hearts and you will be in our prayers.

Thank you very much.

Ford Becomes Ninth Vice President To Fill Vacant Post

When Ford became president, he lacked any electoral mandate. Eight vice presidents had previously moved up to the highest office because of a presidential vacancy. But they had campaigned successfully as their presidents' running mates. Ford, however, became vice president only because he was nominated by Nixon and confirmed by Congress. He was tapped to replace the previous vice president, Spiro Agnew, who had resigned.

But Ford did have one advantage over the past vice presidents who had assumed the presidency. In the other cases, the vice presidents generally had little time to prepare. The presidents they succeeded typically died suddenly of natural causes or were assassinated. In contrast, the slow demise of Nixon's presidency meant that Ford knew he faced a strong chance of becoming the nation's chief executive.

In fact, Ford later said that Nixon's chief of staff, Alexander M. Haig Jr., warned him on Aug. 1 that he should prepare himself to be president. Haig told him about the contents of a tape of a June 23, 1972, conversation that showed Nixon was involved in the Watergate coverup. The tape's impact on Nixon's presidency would be "devastating, even catastrophic" Haig said. Ford recalled being "shocked and stunned." But he also readied himself for the challenge to come.

Gerald R. Ford was the ninth vice president to step up to the presidency because of a vacancy in the nation's highest office. He was the first to succeed to the office because of a presidential resignation.

In the past, unscheduled transitions in the presidency have been, with few exceptions, sudden. Assassination of President John F. Kennedy in 1963, and the deaths of

Presidents Franklin D. Roosevelt in 1945 and Warren G. Harding in 1923, all stunned the nation. So did the deaths of Presidents William Henry Harrison in 1841, Zachary Taylor in 1850 and Abraham Lincoln in 1865.

Only in the case of Presidents William McKinley and James A. Garfield was there a warning that the end was coming. McKinley lived six days after being shot at Buffalo, N.Y., in September 1901, and Garfield survived two months and 17 days following wounds inflicted on him in a Washington, D.C., railroad terminal in July 1881.

But the transition to the Ford presidency was unique in American history. President Nixon's resignation was the result of a long period of increasing pressure. By early August, according to the Gallup Poll, 64 per cent of Americans favored impeachment of the President and 55 per cent favored his removal from office. And Republicans as well as Democrats in Congress were calling for his removal.

VICE PRESIDENTIAL SUCCESSIONS

President	Date of Vacancy	New President
William Henry Harrison	April 4, 1841	John Tyler
Zachary Taylor	July 9, 1850	Millard Fillmore
Abraham Lincoln	April 15, 1865	Andrew Johnson
James A. Garfield	Sept. 19, 1881	Chester Alan Arthur
William McKinley	Sept. 14, 1901	Theodore Roosevelt
Warren G. Harding	Aug. 2, 1923	Calvin Coolidge
Franklin D. Roosevelt	April 12, 1945	Harry S Truman
John F. Kennedy	Nov. 22, 1963	Lyndon B. Johnson
Richard M. Nixon	Aug. 9, 1974	Gerald R. Ford

Points to Ponder

- Does reading President Nixon's Aug. 5 statement affect your opinion about his honesty and integrity during the Watergate scandal? Why or why not? If you had been a firm supporter of the president and a member of his party, would this statement make you rethink that position? Would you be influenced by the declining public confidence in his credibility?

- How should we rate Nixon's tenure in office? On one hand, Nixon was a respected leader on domestic and foreign policy issues. On the other hand, he became embroiled in the worst political scandal in U.S. history. Does that make him a good president, or a bad president, or something in between?

- Do you think Nixon was concerned about his legacy after leaving the White House? If you were in his position, what would you have done to rebuild your esteem in the eyes of the American people? Or would you have been so humiliated by being forced to resign that you would have just stayed out of the public eye?

PART IV: THE PARDON AND COVERUP TRIAL

INTRODUCTION: The Aftermath:
Pardon for Nixon, Convictions at the Coverup Trial

Jan. 9, 1975, was Richard Nixon's 62nd birthday. Physically weak from the phlebitis condition that had nearly cost him his life and still depressed by the collapse of his presidency, he spent the day as usual in seclusion at his estate in San Clemente, California.

A few days earlier, on Jan. 1, three of Nixon's closest advisers during his first term in the White House had been found guilty of conspiracy in the Watergate coverup. In addition, his former treasury secretary, John B. Connally, was awaiting trial on charges of accepting bribes.

Nixon was losing the last vestiges of power. On Feb. 9, the six-month transition period provided by law for ex-presidents to put their affairs in order would end. Soon most of the staff and services to which Nixon had become accustomed would be gone.

But Nixon himself was a free man, with no expectation of ever being charged and tried for alleged federal crimes.

The new president, Gerald R. Ford, had granted Nixon a full pardon on Sept. 8, 1974. Ford's sudden announcement—the most unpopular decision of his young presidency—put an abrupt end to a growing public debate over whether Nixon should be prosecuted.

THE PARDON DEBATE

Before the pardon, some observers had argued that Nixon should not be prosecuted because he already had paid a high enough price in suffering and humiliation. But others asserted that if "equal justice under law" were to be more than an empty slogan, the former president should be brought to trial. The American Bar Association, for example, described the prosecution of Nixon's former colleagues as "unfair and unequal treatment" if the president was to remain free.

Others questioned why Nixon should be pardoned when he had refused to grant amnesty to draft resisters and deserters while he was chief executive. But this argument lost its force when Ford gave high priority to limited amnesty as one of his administration's first orders of business.

Ford himself had weighed in on the issue during his vice presidential confirmation hearings in 1973. At that time, he was asked if a new president could halt or prevent an investigation of a former president's affairs. "I don't think the public would stand for it," Ford had replied.

Between Nixon's resignation and the pardon, some members of Congress considered taking action to protect Nixon. They floated the idea of passing a law that would grant Nixon immunity from prosecution. Another possibility would be to pass a sense-of-Congress resolution—which would not be legally binding—opposing prosecution. "The man has been punished and, for God's sake, enough is enough," said Senate Republican leader Hugh Scott of Pennsylvania.

Vice president–designate Nelson A. Rockefeller signaled a shift in the administration's position on Aug. 23, 1974, when he said he thought Nixon should not be prosecuted. Ford himself left his options open on Aug. 28, at his first full-scale news conference after becoming president. Rockefeller's opinion, he said in a clue to his future action, "coincides with the general view and the point of view of the American people. I subscribe to that point of view."

PARDON AND REACTION

Ford issued the pardon on a Sunday morning. In his announcement of the pardon, he called the Nixon downfall "an American tragedy in which we have all played a part."

Ford said that only he as President had "the constitutional power to firmly shut and seal this book." He said he was more concerned with the future of the country than with Nixon personally, but he accepted the argument that Nixon and his family had suffered enough.

"After years of bitter controversy and divisive national debate, I have been advised and I am compelled to conclude that many months and perhaps more years will have to pass before Richard Nixon could obtain a fair trial by jury in any jurisdiction of the United States under governing decisions of the Supreme Court," he said.

"I deeply believe in equal justice for all Americans, whatever their station or former station. The law, whether human or divine, is no respecter of persons but the law is a respecter of reality. The facts as I see them are that a former President of the United States, instead of enjoying equal treatment with any other citizen accused of violating the law, would be cruelly and excessively penalized either in preserving the presumption of his innocence or in obtaining a speedy determination of his guilt in order to repay a legal debt to society."

The nation's reaction was immediate. Ford's critics questioned his timing, since Nixon had not yet been formally charged with a crime. They also worried about the effect of the pardon on the judicial process. Sam J. Ervin Jr. of North Carolina, chairman of the Senate select committee that had investigated the scandal in 1973, spoke for many of his colleagues when he took issue with Ford's decision. "President Ford ought to have allowed the legal processes to take their course, and not issued any pardon to former President Nixon until he has been indicted, tried and convicted," Ervin said. Ervin and other critics, however, did not question Ford's authority to grant the pardon.

Nixon, responding from San Clemente, admitted no complicity in the scandal. But he acknowledged that he had made mistakes in his handling of Watergate. In a statement issued shortly after the pardon, he said: "Looking back on what is still in my mind a complex and confusing maze of events, decisions, pressures and personalities, one thing I can see clearly now is that I was wrong in not acting more decisively and more forthrightly in dealing with Watergate, particularly when it reached the stage of judicial proceedings and grew from a political scandal into a national tragedy."

Soon after, it was reported that Ford was considering a blanket pardon for nearly 50 other persons involved in Watergate-related litigation. But the report was greeted with such violent disapproval that the idea died quickly. It would, said assistant Senate majority leader Robert C. Byrd of West Virginia, "complete the coverup of the coverup."

HOUSE COMMITTEE HEARINGS

After the pardon, the public learned details about the events leading up to Ford's announcement. Consultations over the pardon had begun Aug. 30 between lawyers for the White House and for Nixon. In addition, Watergate special prosecutor Leon Jaworski had informed Ford of other legal matters under consideration that might have involved the former president. Such matters were numerous and could, if they had led to conviction, have resulted in years of imprisonment and thousands of dollars in fines for Nixon.

Later in September, the House Judiciary Subcommittee on Criminal Justice began an inquiry into Ford's decision to pardon Nixon. The subcommittee chairman, Democrat William L. Hungate of Missouri, had written Ford Sept. 17 asking several questions. Ford had answered Sept. 20 that he already had explained the pardon in his public statement. "I am satisfied that it was the right course to follow in accord with my own conscience and conviction," he wrote Hungate. "I hope that the subcommittee will agree that we should now all try, without undue recrimination about the past, to heal the wounds that divide Americans."

The subcommittee found Ford's response inadequate. Ford then made a historic appearance on Capitol Hill on Oct. 17 to testify before Hungate's subcommittee. "I want to assure you," he said, "there was no deal, period, under no circumstances."

THE COVERUP TRIAL

Further complicating the debate over the pardon, former top aides to the president faced a conspiracy trial for their alleged parts in the Watergate coverup. Why, their lawyers wanted to know, should they not be pardoned too? But their pleas for dismissal of the charges were not accepted, and the trial finally started Oct. 1, 1974, in the courtroom of U.S. District Court judge John J. Sirica.

There were five defendants: H. R. Haldeman, Nixon's former chief of staff; John D. Ehrlichman, the former White House domestic affairs adviser; John N. Mitchell, the former attorney general and election campaign director; Robert C. Mardian, former assistant attorney general and deputy campaign director, and Kenneth W. Parkinson, a former lawyer for the Nixon re-election committee. A sixth defendant, former Haldeman assistant Gordon C. Strachan, was granted a separate trial.

The trial lasted three months. Many of the witnesses had appeared before the Senate Watergate Committee. This time their testimony was supported by tapes and transcripts of presidential conversations. The judge and jury spent days listening to tapes on headphones.

Evidence pointed more directly than ever at Nixon. One of the most dramatic revelations of the trial was the disclosure that Nixon had offered Ehrlichman and Haldeman, before they resigned in April 1973, $200,000 to $300,000 in cash from a secret fund to defend themselves.

Ehrlichman accused his former boss of lying to him. Ehrlichman's lawyers attempted to subpoena the former president to come to Washington to testify.

Nixon never came, because his health prevented it. During the trial, he was hospitalized twice because of his phlebitis. The second time, after surgery to remove a blood clot from his leg, he went into shock and nearly died. Three court-appointed physicians examined Nixon in late November and said that he would not be able to testify until February 1975 at the earliest.

The trial, climaxing the work of Watergate special prosecutors that had begun in May 1973, ended Jan. 1, 1975. Haldeman, Ehrlichman, Mitchell, and Mardian were found guilty. Parkinson was acquitted.

A PARDON FOR NIXON AND WATERGATE IS BACK

President Gerald R. Ford announced in September that he would pardon former President Richard Nixon. He hoped to spare Nixon a criminal trial and also end the "American tragedy" of Watergate. But his decision sparked heated debate. Some critics questioned whether it was right to pardon the ex-president when few citizens who had committed serious crimes could expect such special treatment. They also said that Ford should have waited to see if Nixon would be tried and convicted before issuing a pardon. But others said that Nixon had suffered enough. Watergate special prosecutor Leon Jaworski weighed in with a mild statement, saying he respected the president's right to issue the pardon.

FORD'S DECISION

Ford asked his staff at the end of August to study the question of pardoning Nixon. He was frustrated by the media's continuing focus on Watergate, and he wanted to move the nation forward. He believed that months or even years could pass before Nixon was put on trial. He also may have been concerned by reports of Nixon's poor health and deep depression after leaving office. One of Ford's aides, Benton Becker, warned him that the former president might not survive to the end of the year.

On the morning of Sunday, Sept. 8, Ford announced his momentous decision. He pardoned Nixon "for all offenses . . . which he . . . has committed or may have committed" as president. The White House counsel said that the granting of the pardon implied Nixon's guilt, since there was no other reason to issue a pardon.

Nixon issued a statement accepting the pardon. He did not admit guilt. However, he did concede that he had handled the Watergate scandal poorly. He said, "Looking back on what is still in my mind a complex and confusing maze of events, decisions, pressures and personalities, one thing I can see clearly now is that I was wrong in not acting more decisively and more forthrightly in dealing with Watergate, particularly when it reached the stage of judicial proceedings and grew from a political scandal into a national tragedy."

Ford faced a barrage of criticism for his decision. Critics argued that he should have allowed the judicial process to take its course before stepping in. Sam J. Ervin Jr., who had chaired the Senate Watergate Committee, called the pardon "expedient, incompatible with good government and bad precedent for the future." Critics also questioned whether the country could trust Ford because the new president had said as recently as Aug. 28 that he believed he should wait for a judicial verdict before considering a pardon. Some questioned whether Ford and Nixon had agreed to some sort of deal in which Nixon would resign in exchange for being pardoned. The White House, however, strenuously denied such a bargain had been made. In October, Ford even appeared personally before the House Judiciary Committee to answer questions about the pardon and to deny that any secret deal had been struck. (It was extremely unusual, and possibly even unprecedented, for a sitting president to testify before Congress.)

The pardon was controversial for an additional reason. It sought to give Nixon control of the White House tapes and other presidential documents. Beginning in 1979, Nixon would have the authority to destroy the tapes, which contained critical evidence of his involvement in Watergate. That provision of the pardon sparked especially heated opposition in Congress. Late in 1974, Congress passed a law giving the National Archives the authority to gradually release transcripts of Watergate-related tapes to the public. Those transcripts have provided many unseemly details about the Nixon presidency.

Many observers wondered how the pardon would affect the trials of other Watergate figures. The White House briefly floated the possibility of pardons for all the Watergate defendants. But it quickly retreated in the face of outrage from Democrats and Republicans alike on Capitol Hill.

Even limiting the pardon to Nixon sparked a dangerous political backlash for Ford and his fellow Republicans. While most Republicans praised the decision for tempering justice with mercy, Democrats in Congress, along with several Republicans, denounced it. Even one of Ford's first appointees, press secretary Jerald F. terHorst, raised objections. Voters made their feelings known in the November elections, electing huge Democratic majorities in Congress.

Ford himself, who had won generally favorable reviews in his first month in office, faced ongoing questions about his decision. His presidency suffered from repeated conflicts with the Democratic-controlled Congress. He never entirely recovered from the controversy over the pardon and, in a close election, he was turned out of office in 1976.

WATERGATE TRIAL

Although Nixon no longer faced criminal investigation, Watergate remained in the news during the fall of 1974. Three former top White House aides were put on trial on charges of criminal conspiracy, obstruction of justice, and lying in the Watergate coverup. The defendants were H. R. Haldeman, former White House chief of staff; John D. Ehrlichman, former White House chief domestic advisor; and John N. Mitchell, former attorney general and head of the Nixon re-election effort. Two other men also faced charges related to Watergate. They were Robert C. Mardian, a former assistant attorney general and Nixon re-election aide, and Kenneth W. Parkinson, a Washington lawyer hired by the Nixon re-election committee after the Watergate break-in.

During the trial, the prosecution played the much-discussed tapes of White House conversations. These tapes provided overwhelming evidence of Nixon's involvement in the Watergate coverup, along with the culpability of his former top aides. In fact, Nixon emerged as the chief Watergate coverup conspirator.

There was no longer any doubt about the meaning of Nixon's decisions, such as his order to pay off convicted Watergate burglar E. Howard Hunt Jr. to keep him quiet. One of the tapes, for example, included a conversation between Nixon and White House counsel John W. Dean III on March 21, 1973, about hush money for Hunt. Nixon asked, "Would you agree that that's a buy time thing, you better damn well get that done, but fast?" Nixon asked. When Dean responded that Hunt should be given some sort of "signal," the president said, "Yes."

The tapes also showed that Nixon and Haldeman had concocted a coverup plan on June 23, 1972—six days after the arrests of the Watergate burglars. The plan would aim to derail the FBI investigation of the break-in. On the tapes, Haldeman suggested that they could use the CIA to block the FBI's probe. "Good. Good deal," said Nixon.

When the coverup began unraveling in March 1973, Nixon worried about Dean giving critical evidence to prosecutors. The conversations showed an increasingly panicky president seeking reassurance from Haldeman and Ehrlichman. In particular, he worried about whether Dean had tried to record a conversation that included a discussion of hush money to Hunt. Nixon and Haldeman discussed ways that they could counter Dean's testimony.

The tapes also revealed that Nixon offered Haldeman and Ehrlichman $200,000 to $300,000 in cash to help defend themselves. He made the offer days before the two men resigned. In another revelation, the prosecution showed that the Watergate burglars had expected presidential pardons as well as hush money. The evidence was a memo by Hunt and his wife that warned that, "half measures will not be acceptable" if the Watergate defendants were expected to remain silent. The memo insisted on pardons for the defendants.

On Jan. 1, 1975, the jury returned guilty verdicts against Haldeman, Ehrlichman, Mitchell, and Mardian. Parkinson was acquitted. (Mardian's conviction would later be overturned on procedural grounds. Haldeman, Ehrlichman, and Mitchell went to prison.) An aide to Nixon said that the former president, while "deeply anguished by Watergate," would not comment on the convictions because of the advice of his attorney.

President Ford's Aug. 9 declaration that the nation's long Watergate nightmare was over became inoperative a month later as the nation and Congress reacted angrily to his pardon of former President Nixon.

With an act of mercy which raised more questions than it resolved, Ford, on Sunday morning, Sept. 8, granted Nixon a "full, free and absolute pardon . . . for all offenses against the United States which he . . . has committed or may have committed" during his years as president.

In a statement from his California home, Nixon accepted the pardon, saying that he would for the rest of his life bear the burden "that the way I tried to deal with Watergate was the wrong way."

Later, White House counsel Philip W. Buchen, who oversaw the negotiations with Nixon leading up to the pardon announcement, said that the granting of a pardon "can imply guilt—there is no other reason for granting a pardon." He said that he had so advised President Ford.

Transcript of Ford's Pardon of Nixon

Following is the text of President Ford's Sept. 8 statement pardoning former President Nixon:

Ladies and gentlemen, I have come to a decision which I felt I should tell you, and all of my fellow American citizens, as soon as I was certain in my own mind and in my own conscience that it was the right thing to do.

I have learned already in this office that the difficult decisions always come to this desk. I must admit that many of them do not look at all the same as the hypothetical questions that I have answered freely and perhaps too fast on previous occasions. My customary policy is to try and get all the facts and to consider the opinions of my countrymen and to take counsel with my most valued friends. But these seldom agree, and in the end the decision is mine.

To procrastinate, to agonize and to wait for a more favorable turn of events that may never come or more compelling external pressures that may as well be wrong as right, is itself a decision of sorts and a weak course for a President to follow.

I have promised to uphold the Constitution, to do what is right as God gives me to see the right, and to do the very best that I can for America. I have asked your help and your prayers not only when I became President, but many times since.

The Constitution is the supreme law of our land and it governs our actions as citizens. Only the laws of God, which govern our consciences, are superior to it. As we are a nation under God, so I am sworn to uphold our laws with the help of God. And I have sought such guidance and searched my own conscience with special diligence to determine the right thing for me to do with respect to my predecessor in this place, Richard Nixon, and his loyal wife and family.

Theirs is an American tragedy in which we all have played a part. It could go on and on and on or someone must write "The End" to it.

I have concluded that only I can do that. And if I can, I must.

There are no historic or legal precedents to which I can turn in this matter, none that precisely fit the circumstances of a private citizen who has resigned the presidency of the United States. But it is common knowledge that serious allegations and accusations hang like a sword over our former President's head, threatening his health, as he tries to reshape his life, a great part of which was spent in the service of this country and by the mandate of its people.

After years of bitter controversy and divisive national debate, I have been advised and I am compelled to conclude that many months and perhaps more years will have to pass before Richard Nixon could obtain a fair trial by jury in any jurisdiction of the United States under governing decisions of the Supreme Court.

I deeply believe in equal justice for all Americans, whatever their station or former station. The law, whether human or divine, is no respecter of persons but the law is a respecter of reality. The facts as I see them are that a former President of the United States, instead of enjoying equal treatment with any other citizen accused of violating the law, would be cruelly and excessively penalized either in preserving the presumption of his innocence or in obtaining a speedy determination of his guilt in order to repay a legal debt to society.

During this long period of delay and potential litigation, ugly passions would again be aroused, and our people would again be polarized in their opinions, and the credibility of our free institutions of government would again be challenged at home and abroad. In the end, the courts might well hold that Richard Nixon had been denied due process and the verdict of history would even more be inconclusive with respect to those charges arising out of the period of his presidency of which I am presently aware.

But it is not the ultimate fate of Richard Nixon that most concerns me—though surely it deeply troubles every decent and every compassionate person. My concern is the immediate future of this great country. In this I dare not depend upon my personal sympathy as a longtime friend of the former President nor my professional judgment as a lawyer. And I do not.

As President, my primary concern must always be the greatest good of all the people of the United States, whose servant I am.

As a man, my first consideration is to be true to my own convictions and my own conscience.

My conscience tells me clearly and certainly that I cannot prolong the bad dreams that continue to reopen a chapter that is closed. My conscience tells me that only I, as President, have the constitutional power to firmly shut and seal this book. My conscience says it is my duty, not merely to proclaim domestic tranquility, but to use every means that I have to ensure it.

I do believe that the buck stops here, that I cannot rely upon public opinion polls to tell me what is right. I do believe that right makes might, and that if I am wrong 10 angels swearing I was right would make no difference. I do believe with all my heart and mind and spirit that I, not as President, but as a humble servant of God, will receive justice without mercy if I fail to show mercy.

Finally, I feel that Richard Nixon and his loved ones have suffered enough, and will continue to suffer no matter what I do, no matter what we as a great and good nation can do together to make his goal of peace come true.

Now, therefore, I, Gerald R. Ford, President of the United States, pursuant to the pardon power conferred upon me by Article II, Section 2, of the Constitution, have granted and by these presents do grant a full, free, and absolute pardon unto Richard Nixon for all offenses against the United States which he, Richard Nixon, has committed or may have committed or taken part in during the period from January 20, 1969, through August 9, 1974.

In witness whereof, I have hereunto set my hand this 8th day of September in the year of our Lord Nineteen Hundred Seventy Four, and of the independence of the United States of America the 199th.

PARDON PROCLAMATION

Following is the text of the proclamation by which President Ford Sept. 8 pardoned former President Nixon:

Richard Nixon became the thirty-seventh President of the United States on January 20, 1969, and was re-elected in 1972 for a second term by the electors of forty-nine of the fifty states. His term in office continued until his resignation on August 9, 1974.

Pursuant to resolutions of the House of Representatives, its Committee on the Judiciary conducted an inquiry and investigation on the impeachment of the President extending over more than eight months. The hearings of the committee and its deliberations, which received wide national publicity over television, radio, and in printed media, resulted in votes adverse to Richard Nixon on recommended articles of impeachment.

As a result of certain acts or omissions occurring before his resignation from the office of President, Richard Nixon has become liable to possible indictment and trial for offenses against the United States. Whether or not he shall be so prosecuted depends on findings of the appropriate grand jury and on the discretion of the authorized prosecutor. Should an indictment ensue, the accused shall then be entitled to a fair trial by an impartial jury, as guaranteed to every individual by the Constitution.

It is believed that a trial of Richard Nixon, if it became necessary, could not fairly begin until a year or more has elapsed. In the meantime, the tranquility to which this nation has been restored by the events of recent weeks could be irreparably lost by the prospects of bringing to trial a former President of the United States. The prospects of such trial will cause prolonged and divisive debate over the propriety of exposing to further punishment and degradation a man who has already paid the unprecedented penalty of relinquishing the highest elective office in the United States.

Now, therefore, I, Gerald R. Ford, President of the United States, pursuant to the pardon power conferred upon me by Article II, Section 2, of the Constitution, have granted and by these presents do grant a full, free, and absolute pardon unto Richard Nixon for all offenses against the United States which he, Richard Nixon, has committed or may have committed or taken part in during the period from January 20, 1969, through August 9, 1974.

In witness whereof, I have hereunto set my hand this 8th day of September in the year of Our Lord Nineteen Hundred Seventy-Four, and of the independence of the United States of America the 199th.

TEXT OF NIXON'S STATEMENT

Following is the text of former President Nixon's Sept. 8 statement issued after President Ford announced a pardon for Nixon:

I have been informed that President Ford has granted me a full and absolute pardon for any charges which might be brought against me for actions taken during the time I was President of the United States.

In accepting this pardon, I hope that his compassionate act will contribute to lifting the burden of Watergate from our country.

Here in California, my perspective on Watergate is quite different than it was while I was embattled in the midst of the controversy, and while I was still subject to the unrelenting daily demands of the presidency itself.

Looking back on what is still in my mind a complex and confusing maze of events, decisions, pressures and personalities, one thing I can see clearly now is that I was wrong in not acting more decisively and more forthrightly in dealing with Watergate, particularly when it reached the stage of judicial proceedings and grew from a political scandal into a national tragedy.

No words can describe the depths of my regret and pain at the anguish my mistakes over Watergate have caused the nation and the presidency—a nation I so deeply love and an institution I so greatly respect.

I know many fair-minded people believe that my motivations and action in the Watergate affair were intentionally self-serving and illegal. I now understand how my own mistakes and misjudgments have contributed to that belief and seemed to support it. This burden is the heaviest one of all to bear.

That the way I tried to deal with Watergate was the wrong way is a burden I shall bear for every day of the life that is left to me.

The Pardon

A spokesman for Watergate special prosecutor Leon Jaworski said that Jaworski, who did not take part in the decision, accepted it as a constitutional exercise of the President's constitutional power "to grant reprieves and pardons for offenses against the United States, except in cases of impeachment."

With that exercise of his power, Ford ended the month-long honeymoon he had enjoyed with Congress and the American people, reopening the questions of Watergate for the upcoming elections and setting off a barrage of criticism of the new President.

Critics were further outraged by the White House announcement, soon after the pardon, that the expected decision by Ford on some form of amnesty for draft evaders and deserters from the Viet Nam war—set to come Sept. 10—would be postponed because of Ford's involvement in the negotiations leading up to Nixon's pardon. The White House later said that some decision on this matter would be reached by the end of September.

And the criticism mounted even higher Sept. 10 when acting White House Press Secretary John W. Hushen said that he was authorized to say that pardons for all the Watergate defendants were under consideration by Ford. The White House retreated the next day, saying Ford was not considering a blanket pardon but would consider individual requests for pardons on their merits, after the individuals involved were tried. A few hours after the White House announcement the Senate, by a vote of 55–24, Sept. 11 adopted a resolution (S Res 401) expressing the sense of the Senate that no future pardons should be granted to Watergate defendants until after they were tried, found guilty and had exhausted all appeals.

The same day, Federal Judge John J. Sirica rejected requests by three of the Watergate coverup defendants that the case against them be dismissed because Nixon's pardon created the impression that they were guilty. Sirica delayed the start of that trial one day, to Oct. 1.

A Question of Timing

Little question was raised of Ford's power to pardon Nixon, even before any indictment was filed. The questions—and the criticism—were aimed instead at his timing and the wisdom of his short-circuiting the judicial processes already at work.

"If warranted at all," said Sen. John L. McClellan (D Ark.) Sept. 9, "this pardon is premature."

"President Ford ought to have allowed the legal processes to take their course, and not issued any pardon to former President Nixon until he had been indicted, tried and convicted," said Sen. Sam J. Ervin Jr. (D N.C.).

Before announcing the pardon, it was later revealed, Ford had asked for and received from Jaworski's office a list of the matters under investigation other than the Watergate coverup possibly involving the former President. They included the question of his tax deductions for the disallowed gift of pre-presidential papers, obstruction of justice in the Pentagon Papers trial, the concealing of FBI wiretap records at the White House, certain wiretaps of White House aides, misuse of the Internal Revenue Service, the dairy industry campaign contribution pledge and the increase in milk price supports, the challenge to *The Washington Post* ownership of two television stations, false testimony to the Senate about the settlement of the International Telephone and Telegraph Corp. anti-trust case and the handling of certain campaign contributions.

Concerning all the items but the coverup, deputy special prosecutor Henry S. Ruth Jr. had stated to Jaworski in a memo that "none of these matters at the moment rises to the level of our ability to prove even a probable criminal violation by Mr. Nixon."

The Reasons

Ford's credibility, one of his strong points, was called into question by his action. Earlier—during his confirmation hearings in 1973 and in response to a question Aug. 28—he had indicated his intention to await the working of the judicial process before considering the exercise of the pardon power.

But, he said, in his Sept. 8 statement, certain difficult decisions "do not look at all the same as the hypothetical questions that I have answered freely and perhaps too fast on previous occasions."

Stating his desire to end the "American tragedy" of Nixon and Watergate, Ford said he would follow his conscience, not the public opinion polls. *Newsweek* magazine reported Sept. 8 that 58 per cent of the American people polled opposed giving Nixon any immunity from prosecution.

"Serious allegations and accusations hang like a sword over our former President's head and threaten his health as he tries to reshape his life, a great part of which was spent in the service of this country," Ford said, referring obliquely to continuing reports of Nixon's unstable mental and physical health in the weeks since his resignation. Through the week, reports mounted of Nixon's depression and ill health, the latter reportedly related to a recurrence of the phlebitis which had affected him earlier in the summer.

In light of the intense publicity of Watergate and impeachment, it would be months or years before Nixon could get a fair trial, said Ford. "[A] former President of the United States, instead of enjoying equal treatment with any other citizens accused of violating the law, would be cruelly and excessively penalized either in preserving the presumption of his innocence or in obtaining a speedy determination of his guilt."

For the nation's good and because Nixon and his family had suffered enough, Ford then signed the statement granting Nixon his pardon. (*See text, p. 289.*)

The White House then released an agreement between Nixon and the government under which he retained ownership of his papers and the White House tapes, which would be held in a government depository for at least three years.

The Negotiations

The talks and research which led up to Ford's Sunday-morning announcement were well-kept secrets.

Ford directed White House counsel Buchen Aug. 30 to research the question of pardon and to consult with Jaworski concerning the investigations possibly involving the former President. Only two days earlier, on Aug. 28, he had said that "until any legal process has been undertaken, I think it is unwise and untimely for me to make my commitment" on the question of pardoning Nixon.

Jaworski was asked for a list of the matters under investigation with regard to Nixon, which he provided, and for his estimate of the length of time which must elapse before Nixon could obtain a fair trial. He told Ford, through Buchen, that at least nine months would need to pass before such a trial could begin.

A week after Buchen began these consultations, negotiations between Washington and San Clemente began. Buchen chose Benton L. Becker, a young Washington lawyer, to represent the White House. Becker flew to San Clemente Thursday, Sept. 5, in an Air Force plane and began meeting with Nixon's attorney, Herbert J. Miller Jr.—also from Washington—and Nixon aide Ronald L. Ziegler. Later, Nixon joined the discussion.

Late Saturday afternoon, Sept. 7, Becker returned to Washington with an agreement to be signed by a government official concerning the disposition of Nixon's files and White House tapes—and with only the "general substance" of a statement which Nixon agreed to make in accepting the pardon. After a series of telephone calls between Becker and Ziegler later on Saturday, a compromise statement was agreed upon.

Nixon's Future

Some clouds remained on Nixon's legal horizon even after his pardon. It was still possible that he would be charged with state crimes, or named in additional federal civil suits. Furthermore, the bar associations of New York and California were reportedly investigating his behavior with an eye to possibly disbarring him from the practice of law. To forestall such further embarrassment, Nixon let it be known Sept. 9 that he would resign from the California bar and was considering a similar move in New York. Aides explained that he did not intend to practice law again.

But the letter of resignation he sent to the California bar was rejected by its board of governors Sept. 12, because he made no mention of the disbarment investigation underway.

By removing the possibility of prosecution for Watergate-related offenses, the pardon made it unlikely for Nixon successfully to claim that he could not testify because of the possibility that he would incriminate himself. The Fifth Amendment grants persons the privilege not to incriminate themselves by their own testimony.

Nixon had already been subpoenaed to give a deposition in a civil suit in North Carolina by persons who claim they were illegally denied access to a Billy Graham rally there which Nixon attended.

He was also subpoenaed by his former domestic adviser, John D. Ehrlichman, to appear as a witness for the defense in the Watergate coverup trial, set to begin Oct. 1 in Washington. The pardon would not protect Nixon from perjury charges.

A Bargain?

Nixon's pardon paralleled in some respects the bargain which led to the 1973 resignation of Vice President Spiro T. Agnew. In both cases, criminal charges appeared imminent against the nation's highest elected officials, who thereby resigned—but received no other actual criminal penalty.

Unlike Agnew, however, Nixon's resignation had not come as the result of a bargain. Buchen Sept. 10 steadfastly denied that there had been any bargain made, before Nixon resigned, between Ford and Nixon concerning a pardon. "I can assure you he [Ford] did not make a deal," Buchen said.

Also unlike Agnew, Nixon was not required to enter any plea to any criminal charge. Buchen denied all reports that the White House had tried to obtain from Nixon a statement admitting some degree of wrongdoing in connection with Watergate. And no bill of particulars had been released against Nixon, as against Agnew, unless the House Judiciary Committee's report on impeachment was considered in that category.

The Fall-Out

Two resignations quickly followed Ford's announcement. The first was that of his press secretary and long-time friend, Jerald F. terHorst.

The second, Sept. 9, was that of Philip A. Lacovara, counsel to Jaworski and a lifetime Republican. During the week Jaworski denied rumors that his own resignation was imminent.

By foreclosing the strong possibility—implied in Ford's Sept. 8 statement—that Nixon would have been indicted had he not been pardoned, the pardon created considerable consternation within the office of the special prosecutor and within the ranks of the grand jury which had earlier named Nixon an unindicted co-conspirator in the Watergate coverup.

Lacovara, who had assisted Jaworski in arguing the historic tapes case before the Supreme Court in July and who had come to that office from the office of the solicitor general in the Justice Department, said that he resigned as a result of Ford's decision to pardon Nixon.

The Watergate Defendants

The pardon for Nixon raised a complex of questions concerning all the other persons who had been charged, convicted, or imprisoned on Watergate-related charges—

chief among them the six defendants to go on trial Sept. 30 for obstructing justice in the Watergate coverup.

Evaluation of the impact of Nixon's pardon on the fate of the coverup defendants—John N. Mitchell, John D. Ehrlichman, H. R. Haldeman, Robert C. Mardian, Gordon C. Strachan and Kenneth W. Parkinson—was mixed. Mitchell's attorney, William Hundley, saw the pardon as a help to his client. "You can't give the top guy a pardon and bury the rest of them," he told *The New York Times* Sept. 8. "This ought to create an atmosphere of leniency toward those who worked for the president."

But on the other hand, another defense attorney worried: "The public is going to construe this as a pardon of a criminal. It's bound to have some effect on the men who were his assistants."

Others pointed out that the concern which Ford expressed about the impact of pretrial publicity on the chances for a fair trial might buttress the defendants' long-argued claim that they had no opportunity of obtaining an unbiased jury for their trial—and that the trial should be delayed.

A pardon for these defendants—along with the many other individuals charged with Watergate-related crimes—was suggested Sept. 9 by Frank J. Strickler, one of Haldeman's attorneys, as "a logical extension" of the pardon for Nixon.

A General Pardon

The fact that a pardon was under consideration for the defendants might provide a basis for them to move that the trial be delayed until that question was settled.

Explosions of disapproval were set off on Capitol Hill by the suggestion that Ford might be moving toward a general pardon for all persons charged with Watergate-related offenses. That would "complete the coverup of the coverup," said Assistant Senate Majority Leader Robert C Byrd (D W.Va.). Speaker of the House Carl Albert (D Okla.) described such a mass pardon as "an abuse of presidential power." And House Republican leader John J. Rhodes (R. Ariz.), who approved of Ford's pardoning Nixon, said that such a pardon for his aides was not called for because they "have not been forced to suffer the special consequences that a fallen president must bear."

The trial balloon was thoroughly deflated. The following day, Sept. 11, Rhodes and Senate Minority Leader Hugh Scott (R Pa.) met with Ford and then announced that Ford was not considering a blanket pardon, but was simply preparing to consider any requests he might receive from individuals seeking such clemency. Buchen said that this sort of study need not interfere with the start of the coverup trial.

The Pardon Power

The Constitution grants presidents the authority to issue pardons, thereby ending punishment for law-breakers. Presidents have used this power carefully, but there have been some high-profile, and occasionally controversial, pardons in U.S. history. These include Andrew Johnson's wholesale pardons to thousands of former Confederate officials and soldiers in 1968, Jimmy Carter's decision to grant amnesty to people who evaded the draft during the Vietnam War, and George H. W. Bush's pardons of six top officials in the Reagan administration who were associated with a major scandal.

Other well-known pardons include the decision by President Warren G. Harding in 1921 to pardon Eugene V. Debs, a leading socialist. Debs had been imprisoned for his anti-war activities during World War I. In 1989 Ronald Reagan pardoned George Steinbrenner, the owner of the New York Yankees. Steinbrenner had pleaded guilty to making illegal contributions to the 1972 Nixon re-election campaign.

In pardoning his predecessor, President Ford invoked a power that is clearly provided in the Constitution and is firmly rooted in legal tradition. The man he pardoned, former President Nixon, himself granted 863 pardons and 63 commutations of sentences during his 67 months of office. And Nixon's predecessors similarly exercised executive clemency regularly and often, for a variety of reasons. (*See pardons glossary box, below.*)

The power to pardon is provided for in Article II, Section 2 of the Constitution, a provision drawn from English law, where, William Blackstone observed in his *Commentaries*, the authority was available to a magistrate "to extend mercy wherever he thinks it is deserved."

PARDONS: A GLOSSARY

Amnesty: A general pardon. It is an act of oblivion for past acts, granted by a government to persons guilty of a crime, usually political—treason, sedition, rebellion. It is often conditioned upon the offenders' return to obedience and duty within a specified time. Derived from a Greek word meaning forgetfulness, an amnesty forgets the offense, while a pardon forgives the offender.

Amnesty may be granted by either the president, through his pardoning power, or Congress, by statute.

Clemency: Not a legal term, it is the disposition of a person to use his authority less rigorously than it permits. In court, defendants often seek clemency from a sentencing judge. The term "executive clemency" embraces the various forms of a pardon.

Commutation: In criminal law, the change of a punishment from a greater to a lesser penalty. Whereas a pardon releases from punishment, a commutation is merely a change of punishment and need not be accepted to be effective. Both derive from the pardoning power and are granted by the executive.

Pardon: An act of grace, proceeding from the executive's power to execute the laws, which exempts the person on whom it is bestowed from the punishment for a crime. In the eyes of the law, it reaches both the punishment for the offense and the guilt of the offender. It must be accepted by the offender to be effective, and it cannot be limited by Congress. A pardon may be absolute or conditional, full or partial, or general.

Reprieve: In criminal law, the withdrawing of any sentence for a period of time. A stay of a sentence already imposed, it is ordinarily an act of clemency designed to give a prisoner time to seek a lighter sentence, as in the stay of a death sentence.

But in this country, the Founding Fathers envisioned the use of the broad power for more practical reasons. Constitutional scholar Edward S. Corwin wrote in a 1957 study of presidential power that the framers intended the pardon power for use as an instrument of law enforcement. When the Constitutional Convention was considering limiting the power for use only after conviction, it was persuaded to reject that limitation because "pardon before conviction might be necessary in order to obtain the testimony of witnesses."

Supreme Court Rulings

Regardless of the intentions of those early lawmakers, however, the pardoning power in practice has been used more as an instrument of mercy than law enforcement. In one of the first pardon cases decided by the Supreme Court, Chief Justice John Marshall wrote that "a pardon is an act of grace, proceeding from the power entrusted with the execution of the laws, which exempts the individual, on whom it is bestowed, from the punishment the law inflicts for a crime he has committed." (*U.S. v. Wilson, 1833*)

The scope of the power was outlined in an 1867 high court decision involving a Confederate sympathizer, Augustus H. Garland, who was prevented by law from practicing law in federal courts because he could not swear he had always supported the Union. Garland argued that, since he had been given a full pardon by President Andrew Johnson, his civil right to practice federal law should be restored. The court agreed. (*Ex parte Garland, 1867*)

"When the pardon is full," Justice Stephen Field said in the majority opinion, "it releases the punishment and blots out of existence the guilt, so that in the eye of the law the offender is as innocent as if he had never committed the offense." Justice Field noted that a pardon can be issued before or after conviction. If granted prior to conviction—as in Nixon's case—"it prevents any of the penalties and disabilities consequent upon conviction from attaching. . . . It makes him, as it were, a new man." The court held that Congress could not, by passing a law, limit the president's pardoning power by imposing additional requirements upon pardoned persons seeking to exercise their civil rights again.

Despite the court's holding that a pardon "blots out the existence of guilt," later rulings held that a pardoned person tried for another crime may be treated as an habitual offender and thus receive a stiffer sentence than a first offender, and that a pardon protects an offender from criminal, but not civil, contempt of court.

A pardon may take several forms. An absolute or unconditional pardon forgives the offense without any condition. A conditional pardon may be limited in time or contingent upon some action, such as a requirement that the recipient leave the state. A full pardon absolves the person of all legal consequences, whereas a partial pardon relieves only a portion of the punishment. A general pardon, or amnesty, extends to all parties participating in an offense, usually political.

President Ford's pardon of Nixon was "full, free and absolute," a phrase that the pardoning attorney's office of the Department of Justice said is not part of its normal lexicon. A spokesman for the office said that the Ford pardon—his first—also differed from normal procedure in that a pardon is usually granted only after a three-year hiatus in which the recipient has demonstrated his rehabilitation.

Past Pardons

A pardon before conviction, while accepted in law, is also unusual. In a Sept. 8 press conference, White House counsel Philip W. Buchen cited 21 such instances in American history, many involving grants of amnesty to deserters or rebels. A spokesman for the pardoning attorney said that under the three administrations preceding President Ford's there had been three pre-conviction pardons—two by President Kennedy and one by President Johnson. Pardons are often granted to restore to a person civil rights lost upon conviction.

Of the pardons granted by President Nixon, the most publicized was his commutation of the prison sentence of former labor leader James R. Hoffa in 1971, after federal authorities had turned down three requests for parole. Exactly one year later, Nixon commuted the prison term of Angelo (Gyp) De Carlo, a convicted Mafia leader who was said to be dying of terminal cancer. Commutation authority derives from the pardoning power, and the pardoning attorney's spokesman said it is granted only in "extremely unusual" circumstances, generally to inmates who are sick, have been denied parole often, or have demonstrated "meritorious service" during their confinement.

Lawrence M. Traylor, the pardoning attorney, said that under normal circumstances, a pardon cannot be revoked. "A pardon has traditionally been analogized to a grant, a deed" since it involves both offer and acceptance, Traylor said. "Once the deed has been accepted, it's a complete transfer." However, he said, there has been at least one case in which a pardon was obtained fraudulently and later revoked.

Presidents in modern history have been liberal in their use of the pardoning power. According to the Justice Department, President Franklin Roosevelt granted 2,721 pardons in 141 months, President Truman granted 1,911 in 93 months, President Eisenhower granted 1,110 in 96 months, President Kennedy granted 471 in 34 months, and President Johnson granted 960 in 61 months.

The Political Impact

Judging by their reaction to Ford's pardon of Nixon, the "long national nightmare" of Watergate appeared to have become a recurring bad dream for many members of Congress.

Following Ford's unexpected Sunday morning statement, senators, representatives and others, in and out of government, began voicing diverse opinion on the Nixon pardon, once again reviving intense national debate on Watergate issues.

Reaction generally split along party lines, although a number of Republicans joined Democrats in criticizing Ford's decision. Sen. Edward W. Brooke (R Mass.), the first Republican senator to call publicly for Nixon's resignation, issued a statement Sept. 8, labeling Ford's "blanket pardon without Mr. Nixon's full confession of his involvement on the Watergate scandal, a serious mistake."

Democrats in Congress who attacked Ford's action questioned the fairness of the pardon to other Watergate figures, said it created a double standard of justice and claimed that it would be impossible for the nation ever to learn the full story of the Watergate affair.

Assistant Senate Majority Leader Robert C. Byrd (D W.Va.), said the pardon "demonstrates that someone is above the law" and revives "the lack of faith in government." Sen. Sam J. Ervin Jr. (D N.C.) called the pardon "expedient, incompatible with good government and bad precedent for the future."

But Senate Majority Leader Mike Mansfield (D Mont.), refusing to criticize Ford for his action, suggested that special Watergate prosecutor Jaworski proceed with his investigation of the Nixon role in Watergate. Jaworski has the "authority to investigate and prosecute offenses against the United States and that takes in everybody," Mansfield said.

Republicans in Congress who supported the pardon, argued that Ford had tempered justice with mercy. "No man is above the law. But the law is purposely flexible so as to accommodate varying degrees of reality and circumstance," House Republican leader John J. Rhodes (Ariz.) remarked. Sen. Robert Taft Jr. (Ohio) said that by granting the pardon President Ford "had taken another step in putting Watergate behind us."

But there were divisions in the Republican ranks. Rep. Wiley Mayne (Iowa), a member of the House Judiciary Committee said that his "first impression is that it [the pardon] is premature and might well have been deferred" until Jaworski indicated what action he would take against Nixon. Sen. Howard H. Baker Jr. (Tenn.) expressed the "possibility that this may reopen a caustic and divisive debate in the country." And Sen. Robert W. Packwood (Ore.) declared: "I don't think Ford should have done it. No man is literally above the law."

Election Impact

While controversy raged over the legal and ethical implications of Ford's decision, speculation surfaced on the impact the pardon would have on the campaigns of candidates seeking election to Congress in November.

The pardon "puts Watergate back on center stage," declared Rep. Richard F. Vander Veen (D Mich.), who campaigned on that issue earlier this year in a special election for Ford's former seat in the House. Vander Veen predicted that "the pardon will have a negative impact locally and in elections around the country in November. . . ."

Although some local political observers also noted that the fallout from the Ford announcement would hurt Republicans, who a month ago were relieved by the Nixon resignation, there was strong disagreement on this point—by both Republicans and Democrats at the national level.

At the Southern Governors Conference Sept. 9, Democratic National Chairman Robert S. Strauss said Democrats would be better served by focusing on economic issues rather than the pardon in their campaigns. Gov. Jimmy Carter (D Ga.), head of the party's 1974 campaign committee, predicted that the pardon would have "very little effect" on the November elections.

On the Republican side, Mary Louise Smith, the newly designated Republican National Committee chairman agreed: "I think the effects on the November elections will be minimal," she said.

Honeymoon Views

What impact Ford's decision would have on his honeymoon with Congress, as well as with the press and the public, drew differing views from congressional leaders. At one extreme, Sen. Byrd said the Ford action had "tarred him" by identifying his administration with the Watergate scandal.

While Warren G. Magnuson (D Wash.), who opposed the pardon, noted that honeymoons "do have an end," Mansfield and Rhodes were not so certain the pardon had marked a turning point in Ford's relationship with the Senate and House. "It may cause a little strain, but I don't think it will affect his relations with Congress," Mansfield said. "Will it knock out the honeymoon? Not necessarily," said Rhodes. "His store of goodwill is greater than that."

Impeachment Revival

In the wake of the Ford announcement, some House members called for a revival of impeachment proceedings against the former President, one of the few courses

available for countering certain consequences of the pardoning action. Mansfield expressed his disappointment that "the constitutional process of impeachment . . . was 'cut off at the pass' " when the House accepted rather than approved the findings of the House Judiciary Committee.

But House Judiciary Committee Chairman Peter W. Rodino Jr. (D N.J.) Sept. 10 restated his strong objection to resuming the proceedings. Rodino said the principal purpose of impeachment was removal from office and that the procedure should not be used to accomplish any other objective.

THE TAPES TO NIXON

The damning tapes which led to his resignation from the presidency, under threat of certain impeachment, belong to Richard Nixon—who may, after Sept. 1, 1979, have them destroyed. That was the result of an agreement between Nixon and General Services Administrator Arthur F. Sampson, made public by the White House Sept. 8.

The decision that Nixon should have his presidential papers and the White House tapes was in line with the practice followed with modern presidents and their papers. Due to the many legal demands concerning the materials and their possible use as evidence, some restrictions were placed on Nixon's treatment of them.

After a resolution of pending legal problems, chiefly related to the Sept. 30 trial of the men indicted for the Watergate coverup, the papers and tapes would be transferred to a government facility about 10 miles from San Clemente, Nixon's California residence. There Nixon would have control over access to the papers and tapes.

For three years, until Sept. 1, 1977, Nixon agreed that he would withdraw none of the original papers unless they were subpoenaed, although he could copy any of the papers he wished. For five years, until Sept. 1, 1979, the tapes would remain on deposit. Nixon agreed to make no copies of any tape without the agreement of the government.

On Sept. 1, 1979, the tapes would become government property. Sampson agreed that he, or his successor, would then destroy any tape which Nixon wished. Nixon would continue to have access to the tapes. Five years later, on Sept. 1, 1984, or earlier, should Nixon die before that date, all remaining tapes would be destroyed.

Such explicit authority for a former president to destroy records of his administration was unusual. Nixon indicated in the letter that he would order destruction if necessary "to guard against the . . . tapes being used to injure, embarrass or harass any persons and properly to safeguard the interests of the United States."

Nixon stipulated that any official receiving a subpoena for the tapes or papers should inform him in order that he might respond or raise any privilege or defense which he might have.

Nixon also asserted sole literary rights to the materials, fueling reports that he would use the tapes as well as the papers to write his memoirs.

The question of the tapes, unresolved for the month following Nixon's resignation, was a sticky one which had threatened to involve the Ford White House in Watergate-related legal battles over evidence.

On Aug. 14, the White House announced that all unsubpoenaed tapes belonged to Nixon and would be transferred to him. Later, it was revealed that the decision was reached by former Nixon lawyers J. Fred Buzhardt and James D. St. Clair. St. Clair resigned Aug. 14. The following day, Ford named Philip W. Buchen as White House counsel, succeeding Buzhardt. Ford then, through Buchen, ordered the Nixon tapes and papers held in White House custody.

TerHorst Resignation

One of President Ford's oldest friends—and one of his first appointees—resigned soon after Ford announced his pardon of former President Nixon. Jerald F. terHorst, who had served as White House press secretary for a month, resigned Sept. 8 because, he said, he could not in good conscience defend Ford's decision to pardon Nixon.

Friends said another reason was that ter-Horst felt he had been misled by White House officials about the decision and other matters as well and felt his credibility with reporters was damaged.

A few days before his resignation, ter-Horst had been asked about rumors that Ford was about to pardon Nixon. TerHorst reportedly questioned several of Ford's advisers, including White House counsel Philip W. Buchen, and on their word told the reporters the rumors were untrue.

On another occasion, about a week before the pardon, terHorst had been asked whether Alexander M. Haig Jr. planned to leave his job as White House chief of staff. TerHorst said he did not.

A day later, it became public knowledge that Haig was being considered for appointment to command NATO and United States forces in Europe, among other job possibilities.

TerHorst returned to his old employer, *The Detroit News*, where he had been Washington bureau chief, to write a three-times-a-week column.

TerHorst's deputy, John W. Hushen, was named acting press secretary. Hushen, who had come to the White House from his post as a Justice Department spokesman, had once been afraid he would lose his job at Justice because of his association there with former Attorneys General John N. Mitchell and Richard G. Kleindienst.

Points to Ponder

- What do you think of President Ford's decision to pardon former President Nixon? Should Nixon have been prosecuted for breaking the law, or do you think he had already been punished enough by being forced out of office?

- What risks did Ford take by issuing a pardon?

- Do you think Ford issued the pardon because he thought it was best for the nation, or did he act out of loyalty to Nixon?

EPILOGUE: LASTING EFFECTS OF WATERGATE

Watergate was the most serious political scandal in the nation's history. For the first time, a president was directly implicated in illegal activity and forced to resign. Top White House aides were found guilty of felonies and sentenced to prison. In many ways, the scandal had a lasting impact on the United States.

Watergate spurred discussion in political circles about how to prevent such an abuse of power from happening again. In the aftermath of the scandal, Congress passed a number of reforms. One of its most important acts was to help special prosecutors investigate allegations against high-ranking executive branch officials. Mindful that secret campaign contributions had paid for many Watergate abuses, lawmakers also tried to clean up the system of campaign funding.

In addition, the tenor of federal politics changed for a while. Richard Nixon's immediate successors in the Oval Office tended to shy away from broad assertions of executive authority. In the wake of Watergate, Congress emerged, in many respects, as the most powerful branch in government. Some critics even began referring to the legislative branch as the "imperial Congress" (as opposed to previous assertions of an "imperial presidency"), and they worried that it was taking too much authority into its hands.

But politics tends to move in cycles. Over time, the impact of Watergate tended to diminish, partly because the congressional reforms, although well intended, did not fully succeed in improving government. Moreover, the public grew less concerned with reining in a president's power. As other priorities emerged—such as winning the Cold War or competing successfully in the global economy—the presidency gradually regained much of its former stature. After the terrorist attacks of September 11, 2001, a president once again asserted extraordinarily broad powers in the name of national security, initially with widespread public support.

But the public, it appears, has never fully regained its trust in politicians. Reporters have grown increasingly aggressive, digging into misbehavior at all levels of government. Of Nixon's six presidential successors through 2006, three came under fire for serious scandals involving themselves or top aides, and one—Bill Clinton—was impeached.

SPECIAL PROSECUTOR POWERS

Nixon's decision to fire the first special Watergate prosecutor, Archibald Cox, raised deep concerns across the political spectrum. How could an investigator scrutinize a president's behavior, critics wondered, if the president had the authority to fire that person?

Congress tried to solve this problem by passing a law in 1978 called the Ethics in Government Act. It created a system in which the Justice Department could examine allegations against the president or other high-ranking executive branch officials. If the department found evidence of misconduct, it could then ask a panel of federal judges to appoint a special prosecutor, who would be very difficult to remove.

But what seemed like a good solution soon faced criticism. Two potential problems emerged. First, too many special prosecutors were being appointed. Second, a few of the prosecutors conducted elaborate investigations that lasted for years.

During the presidency of Jimmy Carter, two special prosecutors were appointed to look into allegations that high-ranking officials, including White House chief of staff Hamilton Jordan, had used illegal drugs. A third special prosecutor was appointed during the first year of Ronald Reagan's presidency to look into allegations that Reagan's labor secretary, Raymond Donovan, had ties to organized crime. In each of these cases, the special prosecutor concluded that there was insufficient evidence to prove a crime. Even though the evidence was weak, the officials who were investigated had to spend large amounts of money defending themselves, and their political careers were tarnished. As a result, critics wondered if the new law made it too easy to appoint a special prosecutor.

Congress amended the law in 1982 to make it less likely that an investigation would be launched if there was little evidence of wrongdoing. It also changed the term *special prosecutor* to *independent counsel*. Despite the new law, several independent counsels who launched investigations during the Reagan years ended their probes without finding clear evidence of criminal behavior. Then, in 1986, Lawrence E. Walsh was appointed independent counsel to investigate the most serious scandal since Watergate, the

Iran-contra affair. High-ranking administration officials were accused of selling arms to Iran and using funds received from the sales to aid Nicaraguan fighters known as contras. Walsh's investigation resulted in criminal charges against several top Reagan aides, including Defense Secretary Caspar W. Weinberger and two national security advisors. But Walsh also came under fire because his investigation lasted long after Reagan left office and cost tens of millions of dollars. And ultimately, President George H. W. Bush pardoned several key figures who were indicted, convicted, or pled guilty to crimes.

Even more controversial was a series of investigations launched during the Clinton years. Seven independent counsels were appointed to look into various allegations of misconduct by Clinton and his aides. One of the counsels, Kenneth W. Starr, investigated Clinton's involvement in Whitewater, a failed Arkansas land deal. Through that investigation, Starr eventually learned about Clinton's affair with a White House intern, Monica Lewinsky. Clinton provided misleading information about the affair while under oath, and Starr accused him of perjury. The House of Representatives impeached him, but Clinton was acquitted by the Senate.

By this time, lawmakers of both parties had grown concerned that independent counsels were abusing their power and conducting virtually limitless investigations into the executive branch. Congress accordingly let the law expire in 1999. The government returned to the previous system in which the Justice Department appoints a special prosecutor when serious allegations were raised against the executive branch. In retrospect, many experts said, the special prosecutor system had worked during Watergate. After all, although Nixon fired one special prosecutor, the resulting political storm forced his administration to appoint another who was equally aggressive.

The new system was first tested in 2003. After concerns were raised that George W. Bush's administration had illegally leaked the identity of Valerie Plame, a CIA official whose husband had publicly criticized the war in Iraq, the attorney general responded by appointing a special prosecutor, Patrick Fitzgerald. The ensuing investigation was widely seen as thorough (some Bush supporters even complained that it was overly zealous). It resulted in an indictment against I. Lewis "Scooter" Libby, the chief of staff to Vice President Dick Cheney.

CAMPAIGN FINANCE REFORM

Even before Watergate, Congress had taken some steps to reform the campaign finance system. It limited contributions to political candidates and required the contributions to be publicly disclosed. But the revelations about

secret campaign contributions to Nixon's re-election campaign spurred Congress to toughen campaign finance requirements. In 1974 lawmakers passed the Federal Election Campaign Act amendments, which set strict limits on contributions by donors and spending by campaigns. To reduce the influence of money on presidential campaigns, they created a system under which presidential candidates would receive funding from the government instead of from private donors. Congress also created a new agency, the Federal Election Commission, to enforce the rules.

But the new system quickly ran into problems. In 1976 the Supreme Court ruled that Congress could not limit spending by political campaigns. The justices said that restricting a candidate's ability to buy ads or take other actions to promote political views was a violation of the First Amendment right to free speech. In response, Congress amended the law. Outside organizations, such as political parties or groups known as political action committees, would be allowed to spend large amounts of money for activities such as encouraging voter turnout. The organizations could help a candidate as long as they did not run advertisements explicitly urging people to vote for that candidate.

The new law solved some problems but created new ones. Money that went to outside organizations did not have to be reported. Record amounts were spent on campaigns. Reformers worried that special interest groups were gaining disproportionate influence over politicians. In 1999 two representatives—Republican Chris Shays of Connecticut and Democrat Martin Meehan of Massachusetts—warned that the law had failed to clean up problems with campaign financing. "While the 1974 law worked well for a number of years, people have found more and better ways to get around the law," they concluded in a joint statement at a congressional hearing. "Today we have a political campaign system that is more loophole than law."

Congress again overhauled the campaign finance system in 2002. The new law loosened restrictions on direct contributions to candidates, which have to be publicly disclosed. At the same time, it clamped down on contributions to outside organizations that do not have to be disclosed. But lawmakers could not remove money altogether from the political system. This is partly because of legal constraints: under the Constitution, citizens have a basic right to spend money to promote political messages. There are also political obstacles to campaign finance reform. Congressional incumbents of both parties benefit from regulations that make it easier for them than for potential challengers to raise and spend money. Moreover, Democrats and Republicans tend to be wary of any change that might help one party while disadvantaging the other.

As a result, the new law has failed to limit the amount of money spent on campaigns. Instead, a new type of outside organization emerged from a loophole in the law. These organizations, known as Section 527s (after a section in the tax code), spent hundreds of millions of dollars trying to influence voters in the 2004 presidential campaign. Because they did not directly support a particular candidate, they avoided being regulated by the Federal Election Commission. As a result, more money than ever is being spent on political activities.

PRESIDENTIAL POWER

Another immediate impact of Watergate was a shift in the balance of power from the presidency to Congress. This was partly the result of public distrust of the White House. In addition, a large number of young and often aggressive Democrats won seats in Congress in the November 1974 elections, and they had no interest in deferring to the president.

President Gerald R. Ford, his popularity weakened after his pardon of Nixon, lost his share of battles with Congress. In just two years, Congress forced a dozen pieces of legislation into law by overriding Ford's vetoes. Only one other president in history—Andrew Johnson—had more of his vetoes overridden. Congress also effectively ended the Vietnam War by rejecting Ford's pleas to provide military aid to the South Vietnamese. And senators, disregarding the president's objections, released a stunning report that the CIA had tried to assassinate world leaders.

Ford and his successors—Jimmy Carter and Ronald Reagan—also backed away from broad claims of executive privilege, the right of a president to withhold documents that could harm the national interest. They did not want to ignite controversy so soon after Nixon appeared to abuse executive privilege by refusing to turn over documents about Watergate.

If Watergate was a fateful event that weakened the presidency, it took another fateful event to strengthen it. The attempted assassination of Reagan in 1981 had the unexpected effect of bolstering Reagan's power. Both the public and Congress responded to the shooting by rallying behind the president. Congress soon passed a controversial package of tax cuts that Reagan had proposed. Reagan subsequently asserted considerable power and achieved many of his policy objectives, including laying the groundwork for victory in the Cold War against the Soviet Union.

Another tragic event, the terrorist attacks of September 11, 2001, wiped away much of the lingering legacy of Watergate. President George W. Bush, at a time of national emergency, assumed extraordinary powers. He asserted that his administration could detain suspected terrorists, or "enemy combatants," indefinitely without charges. He also approved the use of wiretaps, in certain cases, without warrants from a judge. The Supreme Court has ruled some of Bush's tactics to be unconstitutional, and a number of lawmakers have expressed uneasiness. Generally, however, Congress has deferred to the president. As a result, Bush has emerged as one of the most powerful chief executives in history.

OTHER ISSUES

In other ways, Watergate has left a more lasting legacy. It is no longer considered extraordinary for a president to face impeachment. In almost 200 years of U.S. history before Watergate, only one president—Andrew Johnson in 1868—was impeached. Just a quarter-century after Nixon's resignation, however, the House impeached Clinton. In addition, there have been scattered rumblings of impeachment during George W. Bush's presidency, partly because of concerns that he misled the country into war with Iraq.

In another change since Watergate, the public appears to enjoy greater access to government documents. In 1974

Source: AP Images/Ben Margot

Joan Felt and her father, Mark Felt, who revealed in 2005 that he was the anonymous Watergate source known as "Deep Throat," who leaked secrets about the coverup to reporters Bob Woodward and Carl Bernstein.

Congress strengthened the Freedom of Information Act, which requires federal agencies to open their records. Although open-government advocates have complained that agencies should be more cooperative, citizens in general have more legal leverage to review government documents than they did before Watergate.

For their part, the media have remained assertive in their dealings with presidents and other politicians. Reporters played an important role, for example, in uncov-

Washington Post reporters Bob Woodward, right, and Carl Bernstein, whose reporting of the Watergate scandal won a Pulitzer Prize, sit in the newsroom of the Post in May 1973.

ering scandals or possible abuses of power in the administrations of Bill Clinton and George W. Bush. They produced deeply critical portraits of several powerful politicians, such as George H. W. Bush's vice president, Dan Quayle. In many cases, reporters used anonymous sources, a practice popularized by the *Washington Post*'s Bob Woodward and Carl Bernstein during Watergate. (The identity of Woodward and Bernstein's most important source, known mysteriously as "Deep Throat," was not revealed until 2005. Only then did Mark Felt, the former number-two official in the FBI, announce that he had been Deep Throat.)

The more the press has revealed about political misbehavior, however, the lower it has sunk in the public's esteem. A 2003 survey by the Pew Research Center for the People and the Press, for example, showed that about two-thirds of people believed the media to be biased. About a third went as far as to label the press "immoral," compared with just 13 percent who used that term in a poll in 1985. To some degree, this trend may be a natural byproduct of the media's aggressiveness: when the press criticizes a politician, the politician tends to respond with biting attacks on the press. (Nixon helped perfect such a strat-

egy.) But reporters also have caused some of their own problems. They have sometimes gotten facts wrong in high-profile stories, given too much credence to anonymous sources, or even, in a few cases, made up stories altogether. In a particularly infamous case, the *Washington Post* returned a Pulitzer Prize in 1981 that had been awarded for a gripping series of stories about an 8-year-old heroin addict. The stories, it turned out, had been entirely made up by the reporter, Janet Cooke.

A FLEXIBLE CONSTITUTION

It might seem that the lessons of Watergate should have a more lasting impact. If a president abuses his power, shouldn't Congress be able to fix the system and prevent such abuses from happening again?

But government tends to move in cycles. Sometimes Americans prefer Congress or the courts to take the lead on an issue; sometimes they prefer the president to be in front. Sometimes corruption may appear to be such a big problem that prosecutors should be given enormous power; at other times the priority may be to allow high-ranking officials to do their jobs without the distraction of ongoing investigations.

The Constitution permits such cycles, enabling power to move among the executive, legislative, and judicial branches of government, as well as between the states and Washington. In the immediate aftermath of the Watergate scandal, the presidency was weakened because of public mistrust. But thanks to the Constitution, presidents were able to regain power at critical moments, such as following the 2001 terrorist attacks. One of the greatest strengths of the Constitution is its flexibility.

The aftermath of Watergate has highlighted the weaknesses of the U.S. system of government. For example, there may not be any perfect way to prevent money from influencing the political process because the right to free speech allows citizens to assert the right to buy political ads, erect billboards, or take other actions to promote their side of a particular issue. But freedom of speech also means that every citizen, whether rich or poor, has a voice—which ensures that money, while influential, cannot entirely drown out the political dialogue.

It also appears that there is no perfect way to investigate the executive branch. Critics have worried that special prosecutors were too weak during Watergate because Nixon had the right to fire them, and too strong subsequently because they could mount investigations for years without oversight. Nevertheless, the system for holding the executive branch accountable appears to work, at least most of the time. This is largely because elected officials have to be responsive to the public in order to stay in office.

Watergate and its aftermath revealed a system of government that works but has flaws. Nixon abused his office and won re-election after breaking the law. But he resigned in disgrace when Congress and the legal system forced him to turn over incriminating documents. After the scandal, lawmakers and public pressure resulted in various reforms to the system. Some of the changes have been more successful than others. Even when the reforms have fallen short, however, governmental checks and balances have helped to limit abuses of power. In the end, the biggest scandal in U.S. history failed to derail the country's system of government.

APPENDIX

WHITE HOUSE EDITED TRANSCRIPTS OF PRESIDENTIAL CONVERSATIONS

This appendix contains some of the most significant transcripts of conversations between President Nixon and his top aides in the Oval Office of the White House. These transcripts show that Nixon and several of his top aides tried to prevent investigators from learning the truth about the Watergate break-in. By interfering with a criminal investigation, they violated federal law.

The first of these transcripts is known as the "smoking gun" conversation. It took place between Nixon and White House chief of staff H. R. Haldeman on June 23, 1972—just a week after the break-in at the Watergate offices of the Democratic National Committee. The two men discussed how to stop the FBI from investigating the break-in. Their tactics would have illegally obstructed a criminal investigation.

The second transcript is of a conversation between Nixon, Haldeman, and Counsel to the President John W. Dean on Sept. 15, 1972. That transcript provides details about why the break-in occurred and who the key partici-

pants in Watergate were. At their meeting, the three men also discussed the coverup.

The third transcript has become known as the "cancer on the presidency" conversation. On March 21, 1973, Dean warned Nixon that the administration's attempts to contain the crisis were failing. He likened the coverup to a cancerous growth. He also warned the president that some of the Watergate participants, including E. Howard Hunt Jr., were asking for "hush money"—a large payment in exchange for not giving testimony. When Dean told Nixon that the cost of buying the men's silence could be a million dollars, the president said he knew where he could get the funds. In this conversation, Dean also detailed the history of the coverup and the involvement of Nixon's re-election committee in 1972.

Just a few days after the March 21 meeting, Dean decided to provide evidence to the Watergate special prosecutor, and he became a key witness against top White House officials.

Transcript of Conversations between President Nixon and H. R. Haldeman, June 23, 1972

This is a transcript of what has become known as the "smoking gun" tape. It clearly incriminated Nixon and Haldeman in the Watergate coverup. The transcript is of conversations between the two men that took place just a week after the Watergate break-in. In it, they discussed ways to prevent the FBI from investigating.

In these conversations, the president approved a plan suggested by Haldeman to have top officials of the CIA tell the FBI to stay out of certain investigations of the Watergate break-in. About two hours after getting the president's approval, Haldeman

met with CIA director Richard C. Helms and Gen. Vernon A. Walters, the deputy director. Walters later testified that he was "ordered" by Haldeman to inform L. Patrick Gray III, then acting FBI director, that unspecified CIA activities in Mexico might be uncovered if the bureau pursued its investigation there.

The participants are identified by the following letters: **P.** *for the president and* **H.** *for Haldeman.*

H. Now, on the investigation, you know the Democratic break-in thing, we're back in the problem area because the FBI is not under control, because Gray doesn't exactly know how to control it and they have—their investigation is now leading into some productive areas—because they've been able to trace the money—not through the money itself—but through the bank sources—the banker. And, and it goes in some directions we don't want it to go. Ah, also there have been some things—like an informant came in off the street to the FBI in Miami who was a photographer or has a friend who is a photographer who developed some films through this guy Barker and the films had pictures of Democratic National Committee letterhead documents and things. So it's things like that that are filtering in. Mitchell came up with yesterday, and John Dean analyzed very carefully last night and concludes, concurs now with Mitchell's recommendation that the only way to solve this, and we're set up beautifully to do it, ah, in that and that—the only network that paid any attention to it last night was NBC—they did a massive story on the Cuban thing.

P. That's right.

H. That the way to handle this now is for us to have Walters call Pat Gray and just say, "Stay [the] hell out of this—this is ah, business here we don't want you go to any further on it." That's not an unusual development, and ah, that would take care of it.

P. What about Pat Gray—you mean Pat Gray doesn't want to?

H. Pat does want to. He doesn't know how to, and he doesn't have, he doesn't have any basis for doing it. Given this, he will then have the basis. He'll call Mark Felt in [W. Mark Felt, FBI deputy associate director in 1972], and the two of them—and Mark Felt wants to cooperate because he's ambitious—

P. Yeah.

H. He'll call him in and say, "We've got the signal from across the river to put the hold on this." And that will fit rather well because the FBI agents who are working the case, at this point, feel that's what it is.

P. This is CIA? They've traced the money? Who'd they trace it to?

H. Well they've traced it to a name, but they haven't gotten to the guy yet.

P. Would it be somebody here?

H. Ken Dahlberg.

P. Who the hell is Ken Dahlberg?

H. He gave $25,000 in Minnesota and, ah, the check went directly to this guy Barker.

P. It isn't from the Committee, though, from Stans?

H. Yeah. It is. It's directly traceable and there's some more through some Texas people that went to the Mexican bank which can also be traced to the Mexican bank—they'll get their names today.

H. —And (pause)

P. Well, I mean, there's no way—I'm just thinking if they don't cooperate, what do they say? That they were approached by the Cubans. That's what Dahlberg has to say, the Texans too, that they—

H. Well, if they will. But then we're relying on more and more people all the time. That's the problem and they'll stop if we could take this other route.

P. All right.

H. And you seem to think the thing to do is get them to stop?

P. Right, fine.

H. They say the only way to do that is from White House instructions. And it's got to be to Helms and to—ah, what's his name. . . . ? Walters.

P. Walters.

H. And the proposal would be that Ehrlichman and I call them in, and say, ah—

P. All right, fine. How do you call him in—I mean you just—well, we protected Helms from one hell of a lot of things.

H. That's what Ehrlichman says.

P. Of course, this Hunt, that will uncover a lot of things. You open that scab there's a hell of a lot of things and we just feel that it would be very detrimental to have this thing go any further. This involves these Cubans, Hunt, and a lot of hanky-panky that we have nothing to do with ourselves. Well what the hell, did Mitchell know about this?

H. I think so. I don't think he knew the details, but I think he knew.

P. He didn't know how it was going to be handled though—with Dahlberg and the Texans and so forth? Well who was the asshole that did? Is it Liddy? Is that the fellow? He must be a little nuts!

H. He is.

P. I mean he just isn't well screwed on is he? Is that the problem?

H. No, but he was under pressure, apparently, to get more information, and as he got more pressure, he pushed the people harder to move harder—

P. Pressure from Mitchell?

H. Apparently.

P. Oh, Mitchell, Mitchell was at the point (unintelligible).

H. Yeah.

P. All right, fine, I understand it all. We won't second-guess Mitchell and the rest. Thank God it wasn't Colson.

H. The FBI interviewed Colson yesterday. They determined that would be a good thing to do. To have him take an interrogation, which he did, and that—the FBI guys working the case concluded that there were one or two possibilities—one, that this was a White House—they don't think that there is anything at the Election Committee—they think it was either a White House operation and they had some obscure reasons for it—non-political, or it was a—Cuban and the CIA. And after their interrogation of Colson yesterday, they concluded it was not the White House, but are now convinced it is a CIA thing, so the CIA turnoff would—

P. Well, not sure of their analysis, I'm not going to get that involved. I'm (unintelligible).

H. No, sir, we don't want you to.

P. You call them in.

H. Good deal.

P. Play it tough. That's the way they play it and that's the way we are going to play it.

H. O.K.

P. When I saw that news summary, I questioned whether it's a bunch of crap, but I thought, er, well it's good to have them off us awhile, because when they start bugging us, which they have, our little boys will not know how to handle it. I hope they will though.

H. You never know.

P. Good.

Return to Strategy

Other matters are discussed. Then the conversation returns to the break-in coverup strategy.

P.   When you get in—when you get in (unintelligible) people, say, "Look the problem is that this will open the whole, the whole Bay of Pigs thing, and the president just feels that ah, without going into the details—don't, don't lie to them to the extent to say there is no involvement, but just say this is a comedy of errors, without getting into it, the President believes that it is going to open the whole Bay of Pigs thing up again. And, ah, because these people are plugging for (unintelligible) and that they should call the FBI in and (unintelligible) don't go any further into this case period!

P.   (inaudible) our cause—

H.   Get more done for our cause by the opposition than by us.

P.   Well, can you get it done?

H.   I think so.

Second Meeting

P.   O.K., just postpone (scratching noises) (unintelligible). Just say (unintelligible) very bad to have this fellow Hunt, ah, he knows too damned much, if he was involved—you happen to know that? If it gets out that this is all involved, the Cuba thing it would be a fiasco. It would make the CIA look bad, it's going to make Hunt look bad, and it is likely to blow the whole Bay of Pigs thing which we think would be very unfortunate—both for CIA, and for the country, at this time, and for American foreign policy. Just tell him to lay off. Don't you?

H.   Yep. That's the basis to do it on. Just leave it at that.

P.   I don't know if he'll get any ideas for doing it because our concern political (unintelligible). Helms is not one to (unintelligible)—I would just say, lookit, because of the Hunt involvement, whole cover basically this.

H.   Yep. Good move.

P.   Well, they've got some pretty good ideas on this Meany thing. Shultz did a good paper. I read it all (voices fade).

Third Meeting

H.   No problem

P.   (unintelligible)

H.   Well, it was kind of interest[ing]. Walters made the point and I didn't mention Hunt, I just said that the thing was leading into directions that were going to create potential problems because they were exploring leads that led back into areas that would be harmful to the CIA and harmful to the government (unintelligible) didn't have anything to do (unintelligible). (Telephone)

P.   Chuck? I wonder if you would give John Connally a call he's on his trip—I don't want him to read it in the paper before Monday about this quota thing and say—look, we're going to do this, but that I checked, I asked you about the situation (unintelligible) had an understanding it was only temporary and ah (unintelligible) O.K.? I just don't want him to read it in the papers. Good. Fine.

H.   (unintelligible) I think Helms did to (unintelligible) said, I've had no—

P.   God (unintelligible).

H.   Gray called and said, yesterday, and said that he thought—

P.   Who did? Gray?

H.   Gray called Helms and said I think we've run right into the middle of a CIA covert operation.

P.   Gray said that?

H.   Yeah. And (unintelligible) said nothing we've done at this point and ah (unintelligible) says well it sure looks to me like it is (unintelligible) and ah, that was the end of that conversation (unintelligible) the problem is it tracks back to the Bay of Pigs and it tracks back to some other the leads run out to people who had no involvement in this, except by contacts and connection, but it gets to areas that are liable to be raised? The whole problem (unintelligible) Hunt. So at that point he kind of got the picture. He said, he said we'll be very happy to be helpful (unintelligible) handle anything you want. I would like to know the reason for being helpful, and I made it clear to him he wasn't going to get explicit (unintelligible) generality, and he said fine. And Walters (unintelligible). Walters is going to make a call to Gray. That's the way we put it and that's the way it was left.

Money

P.   How does that work though, how, they've got to (unintelligible) somebody from the Miami bank.

H.   (unintelligible). The point John makes—the Bureau is going on on this because they don't know what they are uncovering (unintelligible) continue to pursue it. They don't need to because they already have their case as far as the charges against these men (unintelligible) and ah, as they pursue it (unintelligible) exactly, but we didn't in any way say we (unintelligible). One thing Helms did raise. He said, Gray—he asked Gray why they thought they had run into a CIA thing and Gray said because of the characters involved and the amount of money involved, a lot of dough. (unintelligible) and ah, (unintelligible).

P.   (unintelligible)

H.   Well, I think they will.

P.   If it runs (unintelligible) what the hell who knows (unintelligible) contributed CIA.

H.   Ya, it's money CIA gets money (unintelligible) I mean their money moves in a lot of different ways, too.

P.   Ya. How are (unintelligible)—a lot of good—

H.   (unintelligible)

P.   Well you remember what the SOB did on my book? When I brought out the fact, you know—

H.   Ya.

P. That he knew all about Dulles? (expletive deleted) Dulles knew. Dulles told me. I know, I mean (unintelligible) had the telephone call. Remember, I had a call put in—Dulles just blandly said and knew why.

H. Ya.

P. Now, what the hell! Who told him to do it? The president? (unintelligible)

H. Dulles was no more Kennedy's man than (unintelligible) was your man (unintelligible).

P. (unintelligible) covert operation—do anything else (unintelligible).

Transcript of Meeting with President Nixon, H. R. Haldeman, and John Dean, Sept. 15, 1972

In this meeting of Nixon, Haldeman, and Dean, the three men discussed how Dean should contain the investigation into the Watergate burglary. Dean summarized some of his actions, and Nixon and Haldeman gave him advice on several issues. Nixon and Haldeman also downplayed the importance of the bugging of the Democratic National Committee.

On the same day, a federal grand jury indicted G. Gordon Liddy, E. Howard Hunt Jr., and five other men in connection with the Watergate break-in. Dean testified before the Senate Watergate Committee in June 1973 that this was the first conversation he had with Nixon about Watergate, that the president congratulated him about doing "a good job," and that he left the meeting "with the impression that the president was well aware of what had been going on regarding the success of keeping the White House out of the Watergate scandal. . . ."

The transcript, among those supplied to the House Judiciary Committee April 30, 1974, was edited by the White House to delete expletives, personal characterizations, and irrelevancies.

*The participants are identified by the following letters: **P.** for the president, **D.** for Dean, and **H.** for Haldeman.*

This opens just as Dean comes in the door.

P. Hi, how are you? You had quite a day today didn't you. You got Watergate on the way didn't you?

D. We tried.

H. How did it all end up?

D. Ah, I think we can say well at this point. The press is playing it just as we expect.

H. Whitewash?

D. No, not yet—the story right now—

P. It is a big story.

H. Five indicted plus the WH former guy and all that.

D. Plus two White House fellows.

H. That is good that takes the edge off whitewash really that was the thing [Nixon campaign manager John N.] Mitchell kept saying that to people in the country Liddy and Hunt [G. Gordon Liddy and E. Howard Hunt Jr., Watergate conspirators] were big men. Maybe that is good.

P. How did MacGregor [Clark MacGregor, who succeeded Mitchell as campaign manager] handle himself?

D. I think very well he had a good statement which said that the Grand Jury had met and that it was now time to realize that some apologies may be due.

H. Fat chance.

D. Get the damn (inaudible).

H. We can't do that.

P. Just remember, all the trouble we're taking, we'll have a chance to get back one day. How are you doing on your other investigations?

H. What has happened on the bug?

P. What bug?

D. The second bug there was a bug found in the telephone of one of the men at the DNC [Democratic National Committee].

P. You don't think it was left over from the other time?

D. Absolutely not, the Bureau has checked and re-checked the whole place after that night. The man had specifically checked and re-checked the telephone and it was not there.

P. What the hell do you think was involved?

D. I think DNC was planted.

P. You think they did it?

D. Uh huh

P. (expletive deleted)—do they really want to believe that we planted that?

H. Did they get anything on the finger prints?

D. No, nothing at all—either on the telephone or on the bug. The FBI has unleashed a full investigation over at the DNC starting with [Democratic chairman Lawrence F.] O'Brien right now.

H. Laughter. Using the same crew—

D. The same crew—the Washington Field Office.

P. What kind of questions are they asking him?

D. Anything they can think of because O'Brien is charging them with failing to find all the bugs.

H. Good, that will make them mad.

D. So [acting FBI director L. Patrick] Gray is pissed and his people are pissed off. So maybe they will move in because their reputation is on the line. I think that is a good development.

"A Good Development"

P. I think that is a good development because it makes it look so (expletive deleted) funny. Am I wrong?

D. No, no sir. It looks silly. If we can find that the DNC planted that, the whole story will reverse.

P. But how could they possible find it, though?

D. Well, they are trying to ascertain who made the bug. It is a custom made product. If they can get back to the man who manufactured it and who he sold it to and how it came down through the chain.

P. Boy, You never know when those guys get after it—they can really find it.

D. The resources that have been put against this whole investigation to date are really incredible. It is truly a larger investigation than was conducted against the after inquiry of the JFK assassination.

P. Oh.

D. Good statistics supporting the finding.

H. Isn't that ridiculous—this silly thing.

P. Yes. (expletive deleted) [Sen. Barry] Goldwater [R Ariz.] put it in context when he said "(expletive deleted) everybody bugs everybody else. You know that."

D. That was priceless.

P. It happens to be totally true. We were bugged in '68 on the plane and in '62 even running for Governor— (expletive deleted) thing you ever saw.

D. It is a shame that evidence to the fact that that happened in '68 was never around. I understand that only the former director had that information.

H. No, that is not true.

D. There was evidence of it?

H. There are others who have information.

P. How do you know? Does De Loache [Cartha D. De Loach, a former assistant FBI director] know?

D. DeLoache?

H. I have some stuff too—on the bombing incident and too in the bombing halt stay.

P. The difficulty with using it, of course, is it reflects on [former President Lyndon B.] Johnson. If it weren't for that, I would use it. Is there any way we could use it without using his name—saying that the DNC did it? No—the FBI did the bugging.

D. That is the problem—would it reflect on Johnson or [former Vice President Hubert H.] Humphrey?

H. Johnson. Humphrey didn't do it.

P. Oh, hell no.

H. He was bugging Humphrey, too.

P. (expletive deleted)

P. Well, on the other hand. I want you to ask [former Treasury Secretary John B.] Connally. What crazy things we do. That this might help with the bombing. I don't think he will talk to Johnson—and also it would reflect on the Bureau. They hate to admit that.

H. It is a rough one on them with all this stuff that they don't do congressmen, etc.

P. It isn't worth it—the hell with it. What is the situation on the little red box? Have they found the box yet?

D. Gray has never had access to the box. He is now going to pursue the box. I spoke to him just about thirty minutes ago. Pat said, "I don't know about the box. Don't know where it is now. We never had an opportunity before when it was first released in the press that there was a box to go in but we have decided now we have grounds to go in and find it."

H. The latest public story was that she handed it over to Edward Bennett Williams [a Washington lawyer].

D. That is right.

H. The Bureau ought to go into Edward Bennett Williams and start questioning him and have him tied up for a couple of days.

P. Yeah, I hope they do. The Bureau better get over pretty quick and get that little red box. We want it cleared up. We want to get to the bottom of it. If any body is guilty over here we want to know.

H. It will probably be in the news!

D. You might be interested in some of the allocations we got. The Stans [Maurice H. Stans, finance director of the Nixon campaign] libel action was assigned to Judge Richey [Judge Charles R. Richey of the U.S. District Court for the District of Columbia].

P. (expletive deleted)

D. Well now that is good and bad. Judge Richey is not known to be one of the (inaudible) on the bench, that is considered by me. He is fairly candid in dealing with people about the question. He has made several entrees off the bench—one to [Attorney General Richard G.] Kleindienst and one to Roemer McPhee [H. Roemer McPhee, a Republican Party lawyer] to keep Roemer abreast of what his thinking is. He told Roemer he thought Maury ought to file a libel action.

P. Did he?

H. Can he deal with this concurrently with the court case?

D. Yeah. The fact that the civil case drew to a halt—that the depositions were halted he is freed.

H. It was just put off for a few days, wasn't it?

D. It did more than that—he had been talking to [Earl J.] Silbert, one of the assistant U.S. attorneys down here. Silbert said, "We are going to have a hell of a time drawing these indictments because these civil depositions will be coming out and the Grand Jury has one out on this civil case but it is nothing typical."
(Someone asked the President if he wanted Mitchell's call—he said, "Yeah.")

D. Based on that when Silbert had told Richey this and with a casual encounter—in fact it was just in the hall, so Richey stopped the civil case so Silbert can get the indictment down.
(Telephone call from John Mitchell:)
Hello.

P. (comments only from here on until end of call:)
Well are you still alive.
I was just sitting here with John Dean and he tells me you were going to be sued or something. Good, Good. Yeah. Good. Sure. Well I tell you just don't let this keep you or your colleagues from concentrating on the big game. This thing is just one of those side issues and a month later everybody looks back and wonders what all the shooting was about. OK, John. Good night. Get a good night's sleep. And don't bug anybody without asking me? OK? Yeah. Thank you.

D. Three months ago I would have had trouble predicting there would be a day when this would be forgotten, but I think I can say that 54 days from now nothing is going to come crashing down to our surprise.

P. That what?

D. Nothing is going to come crashing down to our surprise.

"Way You Have Handled All This . . . Skillful"

P.   Oh well, this is a can of worms as you know a lot of this stuff that went on. And the people who worked this way are awfully embarrassed. But the way you have handled all this seems to me has been very skillful putting your fingers in the leaks that have sprung here and sprung there. The Grand Jury is dismissed now?

D.   That is correct. They have completed and they have let them go so there will be no continued investigation prompted by the Grand Jury's inquiry. The GAO [General Accounting Office] report referred over to Justice is on a shelf right now because they have hundreds of violations—they have violations of [Sen. George] McGovern [D S.D.], of [Senator] Humphrey [D Minn.], violations of [Sen. Henry M.] Jackson [D Wash.], and several hundred congressional violations. They don't want to start prosecuting one any more than they prosecute the other.

P.   They definitely will not prosecute us unless they prosecute the others.

D.   Well, we are talking about technical violations referred over also.

P.   What about watching the McGovern contributors and all that sort of thing?

D.   We have (inaudible) eye out on that. His I understand is not in full compliance.

P.   He asked?

D.   No.

P.   Well, not yet. His 300 committees—have they all reported yet?

D.   We have a couple delinquent state committees.

P.   It said in the paper that McGovern had 300 committees reported.

D.   No, they have not. There are a lot of things he has never done—as he has never disclosed the fact that he has some 300 committees. *The Wall Street Journal* piece that picked it up and carried that story brought out his committees.

P.   Can we say anything publicly about it?

D.   Purpose there hasn't been a tax sham—it is hard to comprehend why he set up that many committees. He doesn't have that many large contributors, but they may have to disburse through a great number of smaller committees.

H.   Unless someone is stealing $900,000.

D.   That's right.

P.   It could be. That could be possible.

H.   He may be getting $900,000 from somebody. He may have two or three angels.

P.   I don't think he is getting a hell of a lot of small money. I don't believe (expletive deleted). Have you had the P.O. checked yet?

H.   That is John's area. I don't know.

P.   Well, let's have it checked.

D.   Well as I see it, the only problems we may have are the human problems and I will keep a close watch on that.

P.   Union?

D.   Human.

H.   Human frailties.

D.   People get annoyed—some finger pointing—false accusations—any internal dissension of any nature.

P.   You mean on this case?

D.   On this case. There is some bitterness between the Finance Committee and the Political Committee—they feel they are taking all the heat and all the people upstairs are bad people—not being recognized.

"This Is a War"

P.   We are all in it together. This is a war. We take a few shots and it will be over. We will give them a few shots and it will be over. Don't worry. I wouldn't want to be on the other side right now. Would you?

D.   Along that line, one of the things I've tried to do, I have begun to keep notes on a lot of people who are emerging as less than our friends because this will be over some day and we shouldn't forget the way some of them have treated us.

P.   I want the most comprehensive notes on all those who tried to do us in. They didn't have to do it. If we had had a very close election and they were playing the other side I would understand this. No—they were doing this quite deliberately and they are asking for it and they are going to get it. We have not used the power in this first four years as you know. We have never used it. We have not used the Bureau and we have not used the Justice Department but things are going to change now. And they are either going to do it right or go.

D.   What an exciting prospect.

P.   Thanks. It has to be done. We have been (expletive deleted) fools for us to come into this election campaign and not do anything with regard to the Democratic senators who are running, et cetera. And who the hell are they after? They are after us. It is absolutely ridiculous. It is not going to be that way any more.

Transcript of Meeting between President Nixon and John Dean, March 21, 1973

This transcript, of a meeting between Nixon and Dean on March 21, 1973, has become known as the "cancer on the presidency" tape. Dean warned that the coverup was no longer working effectively, and it could bring down the administration. He compared the break-in and ensuing coverup to a "cancer" that was destroying the presidency. Dean also warned Nixon that members of the White House "plumbers" unit, especially E. Howard Hunt Jr., were asking for money in order not to provide damaging testimony. He provided a detailed account of the entire coverup process.

The participants in the conversation are identified by the following letters: **P.** *for the president and* **D.** *for Dean.*

P. Well, sit down, sit down.

D. Good morning.

P. Well what is the Dean summary of the day about?

D. John caught me on the way out and asked me about why [Acting FBI Director L. Patrick] Gray was holding back on information, if that was under instructions from us. And it was and it wasn't. It was instructions proposed by the attorney general, consistent with your press conference statement that no further raw data was to be turned over to the full committee. And that was the extent of it. And then Gray, himself, who reached the conclusion that no more information should be turned over, that he had turned over enough. So this again is Pat Gray making decisions on his own on how to handle his hearings. He has been totally (unintelligible) to take any guidance, any instruction. We don't know what he is going to do. He is not going to talk about it. He won't review it, and I don't think he does it to harm you in any way, sir.

P. No, he is just quite stubborn and also he isn't very smart. You know—

D. He is bullheaded.

P. He is smart in his own way but he's got that typical (expletive deleted) this is right and I am going to do it.

D. That's why he thinks he is going to be confirmed. He is being his own man. He is being forthright and honest. He feels he has turned over too much and so it is conscious decision that he is harming the Bureau by doing this and so he is not going to.

P. We have to get the boys off the line that this is because the White House told him to do this and everything. And also, as I told [presidential assistant John D.] Ehrlichman, I don't see why our little boys can't make something out of the fact that (expletive deleted) this is the only responsible position that could possibly be made. The FBI cannot turn over raw files. Has anybody made that point? I have tried to several times.

D. Sam Ervin [chairman of the Senate Watergate Committee] has made that point himself. In fact, in reading the transcript of Gray's hearings, Ervin tried to hold Gray back from doing what he was doing at the time he did it. I thought it was very unwise. I don't think that anyone is criticizing your position on it.

P. Let's ma[k]e a point that raw files, I mean that point should be made that we are standing for the rights of innocent individuals. The American Civil Liberties Union is against it. We are against it. [Former FBI Director J. Edgar] Hoover had the tradition, and it will continue to be the tradition. All files are confidential. See if we can't get someone inspired to put that out. Let them see what is in one.

D. (expletive deleted) You—

P. Any further word on [Hoover's former assistant, William C.] Sullivan? Is he still—

D. Yes, he is going to be over to see me today, this morning someplace, sometime.

P. As soon as you get that, I will be available to talk to you this afternoon. I will be busy until about one o'clock. Anytime you are through I would like to see what it is he has. We've got something but I would like to see what it is.

D. The reason that I thought we ought to talk this morning is because in our conversations, I have the impression that you don't know everything I know and it makes it very difficult for you to make judgments that only you can make on some of these things and I thought that—

P. In other words, I have to know why you feel that we shouldn't unravel something?

D. Let me give you my over-all first.

P. In other words, your judgment as to where it stands, and where we will go.

"A Cancer . . . That Is Growing"

D. I think that there is no doubt about the seriousness of the problem we've got. We have a cancer within, close to the presidency, that is growing. It is growing daily. It's compounded, growing geometrically now, because it compounds itself. That will be clear if I, you know, explain some of the details of why it is. Basically, it is because (1) we are being blackmailed; (2) people are going to start perjuring themselves very quickly that have not had to perjure themselves to protect other people in the line. And there is no assurance—

P. That that won't bust?

D. That that won't bust. So let me give you the sort of basic facts, talking first about the Watergate; and then about [political saboteur Donald H.] Segretti; and then about some of the peripheral items that have come up. First of all on the Watergate: how did it all start, where did it start? O.K.! It started with an instruction to me from Bob Haldeman to see if we couldn't set up a perfectly legitimate campaign intelligence operation over at the Re-Election Committee. Not being in this business, I turned to somebody who had been in this business, [Treasury aide John J.] Jack Caulfield. I don't remember whether you remember Jack or not. He was your original bodyguard before they had the candidate protection, an old city policeman.

P. Yes, I know him.

D. Jack worked for John and then was transferred to my office. I said Jack came up with a plan that, you know— a normal infiltration, buying information from secretaries and all that sort of thing. He did, he put together a plan. It was kicked around. I went to Ehrlichman with it. I went to Mitchell with it, and the consensus was that Caulfield was not the man to do this. In retrospect, that might have been a bad call because he is an incredibly cautious person and wouldn't have put the situation where it is today. After rejecting that, they said we still need something so I was told to look around for someone who could go over to 1701 [1701 Pennsylvania Ave, NW, Nixon re-election committee headquarters] and do this. That is when I came up with Gordon Liddy. They needed a lawyer. Gordon had an intelligence background from his FBI service. I was aware of the fact that he had done some extremely sensitive things for the White House while he had been at the White House and he had apparently done them well. Going out into Ellsberg's [Daniel Ellsberg released the Pentagon Papers] doctor's office—

P.   Oh, yeah.

D.   And things like this. He worked with leaks. He tracked these things down. So the report that I got from [White House aide Egil] Krogh was that he was a hell of a good man and not only that a good lawyer and could set up a proper operation. So we talked to Liddy. He was interested in doing it. I took Liddy over to meet [campaign director John N.] Mitchell. Mitchell thought highly of him because Mitchell was partly involved in his coming to the White House to work for Krogh. Liddy had been at Treasury before that. Then Liddy was told to put together his plan, you know, how he would run an intelligence operation. This was after he was hired over there at the Committee. [Nixon campaign aide Jeb Stuart] Magruder called me in January and said I would like to have you come over and see Liddy's plan.

P.   January of '72?

D.   January of '72.

D.   "You come over to Mitchell's office and sit in a meeting where Liddy is going to lay his plan out." I said I don't really know if I am the man, but if you want me there I will be happy to. So I came over and Liddy laid out a million dollar plan that was the most incredible thing I have ever laid my eyes on: all in codes, and involved black bag operations, kidnapping, providing prostitutes to weaken the opposition, bugging, mugging teams. It was just an incredible thing.

P.   Tell me this: Did Mitchell go along—?

D.   No, no, not at all, Mitchell just sat there puffing and laughing. I could tell from—after Liddy left the office I said that is the most incredible thing I have ever seen. He said I agree. And so Liddy was told to go back to the drawing board and come up with something realistic. So there was a second meeting. They asked me to come over to that. I came into the tail end of the meeting. I wasn't there for the first part. I don't know how long the meeting lasted. At this point, they were discussing again bugging, kidnapping and the like. At this point I said right in front of everybody, very clearly, I said, "These are not the sort of things (1) that are ever to be discussed in the office of the Attorney General of the United States—that was where he still was—and I am personally incensed." And I am trying to get Mitchell off the hook. He is a nice person and doesn't like to have to say no when he is talking with people he is going to have to work with.

P.   That's right.

D.   So I let it be known. I said "You all pack that stuff up and get it the hell out of here. You just can't talk this way in this office and you should re-examine your whole thinking."

P.   Who all was present?

D.   It was Magruder, Mitchell, Liddy and myself. I came back right after the meeting and told Bob, "Bob, we have a growing disaster on our hands if they are thinking this way," and I said, "The White House has got to stay out of this and I, frankly, am not going to be involved in it." He said, "I agree John." I thought at that point that the thing was turned off. That is the last I heard of it and I thought it was turned off because it was an absurd proposal.

P.   Yeah.

D.   Liddy—I did have dealings with him afterwards and we never talked about it. Now that would be hard to believe for some people, but we never did. That is the fact of the matter.

P.   Well, you were talking with him about other things.

D.   We had so many other things.

P.   He had some legal problems too. But you were his adviser, and I understand you had conversations about the campaign laws, etc. Haldeman told me that you were handling all of that for us. Go ahead.

D.   Now. So Liddy went back after that and was over at 1701, the Committee, and this is where I come into having put the pieces together after the fact as to what I can put together about what happened. Liddy sat over there and tried to come up with another plan that he could sell. (1) They were talking to him, telling him that he was putting too much money in it. I don't think they were discounting the illegal points. Jeb is not a lawyer. He did not know whether this is the way the game was played and what it was all about. They came up, apparently, with another plan, but they couldn't get it approved by anybody over there. So Liddy and Hunt apparently came to see [White House counsel Charles W.] Chuck Colson, and Chuck Colson picked up the telephone and called Magruder and said, "You all either fish- or cut bait. This is absurd to have these guys over there and not using them. If you are not going to use them, I may use them." Things of this nature.

P.   When was this?

D.   This was apparently in February of '72.

P.   Did Colson know what they were talking about?

D.   I can only assume, because of his close relationship with Hunt, that he had a damn good idea what they were talking about, a damn good idea. He would probably deny it today and probably get away with denying it. But I still—unless Hunt [Watergate conspirator E. Howard Hunt Jr.] blows on him—

P.   But then Hunt isn't enough. It takes two doesn't it?

D.   Probably. Probably. But Liddy was there also and if Liddy were to blow—

"Criminal Liability in White House"

P.   Then you have a problem—I was saying as to the criminal liability in the White House.

D.   I will go back over that, and take out any of the soft spots.

P.   Colson, you think was the person who pushed?

D. I think he helped to get the thing off the dime. Now something else occurred though—

P. Did Colson—had he talked to anybody here?

D. No. I think this was—

P. Did he talk with Haldeman?

D. No, I don't think so. But here is the next thing that comes in the chain. I think Bob was assuming, that they had something that was proper over there, some intelligence gathering operation that Liddy was operating. And through [Haldeman assistant Gordon C.] Strachan, who was his tickler, he started pushing them to get some information and they—Magruder—took that as a signal to probably go to Mitchell and to say, "They are pushing us like crazy for this from the White House." And so Mitchell probably puffed on his pipe and said, "Go ahead," and never really reflected on what it was all about. So they had some plan that obviously had, I gather, different targets they were going to go after. They were going to infiltrate, and bug, and do all this sort of thing to a lot of these targets. This is knowledge I have after the fact. Apparently after they had initially broken in and bugged the DNC [Democratic National Committee] they were getting information. The information was coming over here to Strachan and some of it was given to Haldeman, there is no doubt about it.

P. Did he know where it was coming from?

D. I don't really know if he would.

P. Not necessarily?

D. Not necessarily. Strachan knew it. There is no doubt about it, and whether Strachan—I have never come to press these people on these points because it hurts them to give up that next inch, so I had to piece things together. Strachan was aware of receiving information, reporting to Bob. At one point Bob even gave instructions to change their capabilities from [Sen. Edmund S.] Muskie to [Sen. George] McGovern, and passed this back through Strachan to Magruder and apparently to Liddy. And Liddy was starting to make arrangements to go in and bug the McGovern operation.

P. They had never bugged Muskie, though, did they?

D. No, they hadn't, but they had infiltrated it by a secretary.

P. By a secretary?

D. By a secretary and a chauffeur. There is nothing illegal about that. So the information was coming over here and then I, finally, after—. The next point in time that I became aware of anything was on June 17th when I got the word that there had been this break in at the DNC and somebody from our Committee had been caught in the DNC. And I said, "Oh, (expletive deleted)." You know, eventually putting the pieces together—

P. You knew what it was.

D. I knew who it was. So I called Liddy on Monday morning and said, "First, Gordon, I want to know whether anybody in the White House was involved in this." And he said, "No, they weren't." I said, "Well I want to know how in (expletive deleted) name this happened." He said, "Well, I was pushed without mercy by Magruder to get in there and to get more information." That the information was not satisfactory. That Magruder said, "The White House is not happy with what we are getting."

P. The White House?

D. The White House. Yeah!

P. Who do you think was pushing him?

D. Well, I think it was probably Strachan thinking that Bob wanted things, because I have seen that happen on other occasions where things have said to have been of very prime importance when they really weren't.

P. Why at that point in time I wonder? I am just trying to think. We had just finished the Moscow trip. The Democrats had just nominated McGovern. I mean, (expletive deleted), what in the hell were these people doing? I can see their doing it earlier. I can see the pressures, but I don't see why all the pressure was on them.

D. I don't know, other than the fact that they might have been looking for information about the conventions.

P. That's right.

D. Because, I understand that after the fact that there was a plan to bug [Democratic chairman Lawrence] Larry O'Brien's suite down in Florida. So Liddy told me that this is what had happened and this is why it had happened.

P. Where did he learn that there were plans to bug Larry O'Brien's suite?

D. From Magruder, long after the fact.

P. Magruder is (unintelligible)

D. Yeah. Magruder is totally knowledgeable on the whole thing.

P. Yeah.

D. Alright now, we have gone through the trial. I don't know if Mitchell has perjured himself in the Grand Jury or not.

P. Who?

D. Mitchell. I don't know how much knowledge he actually had. I know that Magruder has perjured himself in the Grand Jury. I know that Porter has perjured himself in the Grand Jury.

P. Who is [Herbert L.] Porter? (unintelligible)

D. He is one of Magruder's deputies. They set up this scenario which they ran by me. They said, "How about this?" I said, "I don't know. If this is what you are going to hang on, fine."

P. What did they say in the Grand Jury?

D. They said, as they said before the trial in the Grand Jury, that Liddy had come over as counsel and we knew he had these capacities to do legitimate intelligence. We had no idea what he was doing. He was given an authorization of $250,000 to collect information, because our surrogates were out on the road. They had no protection, and we had information that there were going to be demonstrations against them, and that we had to have a plan as to what liabilities they were going to be confronted with and Liddy was charged with doing this. We had no knowledge that he was going to bug the DNC.

P. The point is, that is not true?

D. That's right.

P. Magruder did know it was going to take place?

D. Magruder gave the instructions to be back in the DNC.

P. He did?

D. Yes.

P. You know that?

D. Yes.

P. I see. O.K.

"No One Over Here Knew That"

D. I honestly believe that no one over here knew that. I know that as God is my maker, I had no knowledge that they were going to do this.

P. Bob didn't either, or wouldn't have known that either. You are not the issue involved. Had Bob known, he would be.

D. Bob—I don't believe specifically knew that they were going in there.

P. I don't think so.

D. I don't think he did. I think he knew that there was a capacity to do this but he was not given the specific direction.

P. Did Strachan know?

D. I think Strachan did know.

P. (unintelligible) Going back into the DNC—Hunt, etc.—this is not understandable!

D. So—those people are in trouble as a result of the Grand Jury and the trial. Mitchell, of course, was never called during the trial. Now—

P. Mitchell has given a sworn statement, hasn't he?

D. Yes, Sir.

P. To the Jury?

D. To the Grand Jury.—

P. You mean the Goldberg arrangement?

D. We had an arrangement whereby he went down with several of them, because of the heat of this thing and the implications on the election, we made an arrangement where they could quietly go into the Department of Justice and have one of the assistant U.S. Attorneys take their testimony and then read it before the Grand Jury.

P. I thought Mitchell went.

D. That's right, Mitchell was actually called before the Grand Jury. The Grand Jury would not settle for less, because the jurors wanted him.

P. And he went?

D. And he went.

P. Good!

D. I don't know what he said. I have never seen a transcript of the Grand Jury. Now what has happened post June 17? I was under pretty clear instructions not to investigate this, but this could have been disastrous on the electorate if all hell had broken loose. I worked on a theory of containment—

P. Sure.

D. To try to hold it right where it was.

P. Right.

D. There is no doubt that I was totally aware of what the Bureau was doing at all times. I was totally aware of what the Grand Jury was doing. I knew what witnesses were going to be called. I knew what they were asked, and I had to.

P. Why did [Assistant Attorney General Henry E.] Petersen play the game so straight with us?

D. Because Petersen is a soldier. He kept me informed. He told me when we had problems, where we had problems and the like. He believes in you and he believes in this Administration. This Administration has made him. I

don't think he has done anything improper, but he did make sure that the investigation was narrowed down to the very, very fine criminal thing which was a break for us. There is no doubt about it.

P. Do you honestly feel that he did an adequate job?

D. They ran that investigation out to the fullest extent they could follow a lead and that was it.

P. But the way is, where I suppose he could be criticized for not doing an adequate job. Why didn't he call Haldeman? Why didn't he get a statement from Colson? Oh, they did get Colson!

D. That's right. But as based on their FBI interviews, there was no reason to follow up. There were no leads there. Colson said, "I have no knowledge of this" to the FBI. Strachan said, "I have no knowledge." They didn't ask Strachan any questions about Watergate. They asked him about Segretti. They said, "what is your connection with Liddy?" Strachan just said, "Well, I met him over there." They never really pressed him. Strachan appeared, as a result of some coaching, to be the dumbest paper pusher in the bowels of the White House.

P. I understand.

D. Alright. Now post June 17th: These guys immediately—It is very interesting. (Dean sort of chuckled) Liddy, for example, on the Friday before—I guess it was on the 15th, no, the 16th of June—had been in Henry Petersen's office with another member of my staff on campaign compliance problems. After the incident, he ran [Attorney General Richard G.] Kleindienst down at Burning Tree Country Club and told him "you've got to get my men out of jail." Kleindienst said, "You get the hell out of here, kid. Whatever you have to say, just say to somebody else. Don't bother me." But this has never come up. Liddy said if they all got counsel instantly and said we will ride this thing out. Alright, then they started making demands. "We have to have attorneys fees. We don't have any money ourselves, and you are asking us to take this through the election." Alright, so arrangements were made through Mitchell, initiating it. And I was present in discussions where these guys had to be taken care of. Their attorneys fees had to be done. [Nixon personal attorney Herbert W.] Kalmbach was brought in. Kalmbach raised some cash.

P. They put that under the cover of a Cuban Committee, I suppose?

D. Well, they had a Cuban Committee and they had some of it was given to Hunt's lawyer, who in turn passed it out. You know, when Hunt's wife was flying to Chicago with $10,000 she was actually, I understand after the fact, now, was going to pass that money to one of the Cubans—to meet him in Chicago and pass it to somebody there.

"Keep That Cover"

P. (unintelligible) but I would certain[ly] keep that cover for whatever it is worth.

D. That's the most troublesome post-thing because (1) Bob is involved in that; (2) John is involved in that; (3) I am involved in that; (4) Mitchell is involved in that. And that is an obstruction of justice.

P. In other words, the bad it does. You were taking care of witnesses. How did Bob get in it?

D. Well, they ran out of money over there. Bob had $350,000 in a safe over here that was really set aside for polling purposes. And there was no other source of money, so they came over and said you all have got to give us some money. I had to go to Bob and say, "Bob, they need some money over there." He said "What for." So I had to tell him what it was for because he wasn't just about to send money over there willy-nilly. And John was involved in those discussions. And then we decided there was no price too high to pay to let this thing blow up in front of the election.

P. I think we should be able to handle that issue pretty well. May be some lawsuits.

D. I think we can too. Here is what is happening right now. What sort of brings matters to the (unintelligible). One, this is going to be a continual blackmail operation by Hunt and Liddy and the Cubans. No doubt about it. And McCord [Watergate conspirator James W. McCord Jr.], who is another one involved. McCord has asked for nothing. McCord did ask to meet with somebody, with Jack Caulfield who is his old friend who had gotten him hired over there. And when Caulfield had him hired, he was a perfectly legitimate security man. And he wanted to talk about commutation, and things like that. And as you know Colson has talked indirectly to Hunt about commutation. All of these things are bad, in that they are problems, they are promises, they are commitments. They are the very sort of things that the Senate is going to be looking most for. I don't think they can find them, frankly.

P. Pretty hard.

D. Pretty hard. Damn hard. It's all cash.

P. Pretty hard I mean as far as the witnesses are concerned.

D. Alright, now, the blackmail is continuing. Hunt called one of lawyers from the Re-Election Committee on last Friday to leave it with him over the weekend. The guy came in to see me to give a message directly to me. From Hunt to me.

P. Is Hunt out on bail?

D. Pardon?

P. Is Hunt on bail?

D. Hunt is on bail. Correct. Hunt now is demanding another $72,000 for his own personal expenses; another $50,000 to pay attorneys fees; $120,000. Some (1) he wanted it as of the close of business yesterday. He said, "I am going to be sentenced on Friday, and I've got to get my financial affairs in order." I told this fellow O'Brien [Paul L. O'Brien, an attorney for the Nixon re-election committee]. "If you want money, you came to the wrong man, fellow. I am not involved in the money. I don't know a thing about it. I can't help you. You better scramble about elsewhere." O'Brien is a ball player. He carried tremendous water for us.

P. He isn't Hunt's lawyer?

D. No he is our lawyer at the Re-Election Committee.

P. I see.

D. So he is safe. There is no problem there. So it raises the whole question. Hunt has now made a direct threat against Ehrlichman. As a result of this, this is his blackmail. He says, "I will bring John Ehrlichman down to his knees and put him in jail. I have done enough seamy things for he and Krogh, they'll never survive it."

P. Was he talking about Ellsberg?

D. Ellsberg, and apparently some other things. I don't know the full extent of it.

P. I don't know about anything else.

D. I don't know either, and I hate to learn some of these things. So that is that situation. Now, where are at the soft points? How many people know about this? Well, let me go one step further in this whole thing. The Cubans that were used in the Watergate were also the same Cubans that Hunt and Liddy used for this Californian Ellsberg thing, for the break in out there. So they are aware of that. How high their knowledge is, is something else. Hunt and Liddy, of course, are totally aware of it, of the fact that it is right out of the White House.

P. I don't know what the hell we did that for!

D. I don't know either.

P. What in the (expletive deleted) caused this? (unintelligible)

D. Mr. President, there have been a couple of things around here that I have gotten wind of. At one time there was a desire to do a second story job on the Brookings Institute where they had the Pentagon papers. Now I flew to California because I was told that John had instructed it and he said, "I really hadn't. It is a misimpression, but for (expletive deleted), turn it off." So I did. I came back and turned it off. The risk is minimal and the [g]ain is fantastic. It is something with a (unintelligible) risk and no gain. It is just not worth it. But—who knows about all this now? You've got the Cubans' lawyer, a man by the name of [Henry R.] Rothblatt, who is a no good, publicity seeking (characterization deleted), to be very frank with you. He has had to be pruned down and tuned off. He was canned by his own people because they didn't trust him. He didn't want them to plead guilty. He wants to represent them before the Senate. So F. Lee Bailey, who was a partner of one of the men representing McCord, got in and cooled Rothblatt down. So that means that F. Lee Bailey has knowledge. Hunt's lawyer, a man by the name of [William O.] Bittmann, who is an excellent criminal lawyer from the Democratic era of Bobby Kennedy, he's got knowledge.

P. He's got some knowledge?

D. Well, all the direct knowledge that Hunt and Liddy have, as well as all the hearsay they have. You have these two lawyers over at the Re-election Committee who did an investigation to find out the facts. Slowly, they got the whole picture. They are solid.

P. But they know?

D. But they know. You've got, then an awful lot of the principals involved who know. Some people's wives know. Mrs.

Hunt was the savviest woman in the world. She had the whole picture together.

P. Did she?

D. Yes. Apparently, she was the pillar of strength in that family before the death.

P. Great sadness. As a matter of fact, there was a discussion with somebody about Hunt's problem on account of his wife and I said, of course commutation could be considered on the basis of his wife's death, and that is the only conversation I ever had in that light.

D. Right.

D. So that is it. That is the extent of the knowledge. So where are the soft spots on this? Well, first of all, there is the problem of the continued blackmail which will not only go on now, but it will go on while these people are in prison, and it will compound the obstruction of justice situation. It will cost money. It is dangerous. People around here are not pros at this sort of thing. This is the sort of thing Mafia people can do: washing money, getting clean money, and things like that. We just don't know about those things, because we are not criminals and not used to dealing in that business.

P. That's right.

D. It is a tough thing to know how to do.

P. Maybe it takes a gang to do that.

D. That's right. There is a real problem as to whether we could even do it. Plus there is a real problem in raising money. Mitchell has been working on raising some money. He is one of the ones with the most to lose. But there is no denying the fact that the White House, in Ehrlichman, Haldeman and Dean are involved in some of the early money decisions.

P. How much money do you need?

D. I would say these people are going to cost a million dollars over the next two years.

P. We could get that. On the money, if you need the money you could get that. You could get a million dollars. You could get it in cash. I know where it could be gotten. It is not easy, but it could be done. But the question is who the hell would handle it? Any ideas on that?

D. That's right. Well, I think that is something that Mitchell ought to be charged with.

P. I would think so too.

D. And get some pros to help him.

P. Let me say there shouldn't be a lot of people running around getting money—

D. Well he's got one person doing it who I am sure is—

P. Who is that?

D. He has Fred LaRue [Frederick C. LaRue, a Nixon campaign aide] doing it. Now Fred started out going out trying to solicit money from all kinds of people.

P. No!

D. I had learned about it, and I said, "(expletive deleted) It is just awful! Don't do it!" People are going to ask what the money is for. He has apparently talked to Tom Pappas [Thomas A. Pappas, a Nixon fund raiser].

P. I know.

D. And Pappas has agreed to come up with a sizeable amount, I gather.

P. What do you think? You don't need a million right away, but you need a million? Is that right?

D. That is right.

P. You need it in cash don't you? I am just thinking out loud here for a moment. Would you put that through the Cuban Committee:

D. No.

P. It is going to be checks, cash money, etc. How if that ever comes out, are you going to handle it? Is the Cuban Committee an obstruction of justice, if they want to help?

D. Well they have priests in it.

P. Would that give a little bit of a cover?

D. That would give some for the Cubans and possibly Hunt. Then you've got Liddy. McCord is not accepting any money. So he is not a bought man right now.

P. OK. Go ahead.

D. Let me continue a little bit right here now. When I say this is a growing cancer, I say it for reasons like this. Bud Krogh, in his testimony before the Grand Jury, was forced to perjure himself. He is haunted by it. Bud said, "I have not had a pleasant day on my job." He said, "I told my wife all about this. The curtain may ring down one of these days, and I may have to face the music, which I am perfectly willing to do."

P. What did he perjure himself on, John?

D. Did he know the Cubans. He did.

P. He said he didn't?

D. That is right. They didn't press him hard.

P. He might be able to—I am just trying to think. Perjury is an awful hard rap to prove. If he could just say that I—well, go ahead.

D. Well, so that is one perjury. Mitchell and Magruder are potential perjurers. There is always the possibility of any one of these individuals blowing. Hunt. Liddy. Liddy is in jail right now, serving his time and having a good time right now, I think Liddy in his own bizarre way the strongest of all of them. So there is that possibility.

P. Your major guy to keep under control is Hunt?

D. That is right.

P. I think. Does he know a lot?

D. He knows so much. He could sink Chuck Colson. Apparently he is quite distressed with Colson. He thinks Colson has abandoned him. Colson was to meet with him when he was out there after, you know, he had left the White House. He met with him through his lawyer. Hunt raised the question he wanted money. Colson's lawyer told him Colson wasn't doing anything with money. Hunt took offense with that immediately, and felt Colson had abandoned him.

P. Just looking at the immediate problem, don't you think you have to handle Hunt's financial situation damn soon?

D. I think that is—I talked with Mitchell about that last night and—

P. It seems to me we have to keep the cap on the bottle that much, or we don't have any options.

D. That's right.

P. Either that or it all blows right now?

D. That's the question.

P. We have Hunt, Krogh. Well go ahead with the other ones.

D. Now we've got Kalmbach. Kalmbach received, at the close of the '68 campaign in January of 1969, he got a million $700,000 to be custodian for. That came down from New York, and was placed in safe deposit boxes here. Some other people were on the boxes. And ultimately, the money was taken out to California. Alright, there is knowledge of the fact that he did start with a million seven. Several people know this. Now since 1969, he has spent a good deal of this money and accounting for it is going to be very difficult for Herb. For example, he has spent close to $500,000 on private polling. That opens up a whole new thing. It is not illegal, but more of the same thing.

INDEX